Advanced Autonomous Systems and Artificial Intelligence Stage

Advanced Autonomous Systems and Artificial Intelligence Stage

Guest Editors

Florian Ion Tiberiu Petrescu
Liviu Marian Ungureanu

MDPI

Basel • Beijing • Wuhan • Barcelona • Belgrade • Novi Sad • Cluj • Manchester

Guest Editors

Florian Ion Tiberiu Petrescu
Theory of Mechanisms and
Robots Department
National University of
Science and Technology
Polytechnic Bucharest
Bucharest
Romania

Liviu Marian Ungureanu
Theory of Mechanisms and
Robots Department
National University of
Science and Technology
Polytechnic Bucharest
Bucharest
Romania

Editorial Office
MDPI AG
Grosspeteranlage 5
4052 Basel, Switzerland

This is a reprint of the Special Issue, published open access by the journal *Technologies* (ISSN 2227-7080), freely accessible at: https://www.mdpi.com/journal/technologies/special_issues/834K7R6T49.

For citation purposes, cite each article independently as indicated on the article page online and as indicated below:

Lastname, A.A.; Lastname, B.B. Article Title. *Journal Name* **Year**, *Volume Number*, Page Range.

ISBN 978-3-7258-6590-1 (Hbk)
ISBN 978-3-7258-6591-8 (PDF)
https://doi.org/10.3390/books978-3-7258-6591-8

Contents

Preface . . . . **vii**

Liviu Marian Ungureanu and Iulian-Sorin Munteanu
Advanced Autonomous Systems and the Artificial Intelligence Stage
Reprinted from: *Technologies* **2026**, *14*, 9, https://doi.org/10.3390/technologies14010009 . . . . . **1**

Lucas McLeland, Brian Erickson, Brendan Ruchlin, Eryn Daman, James Mejia, Benjamin Ho, et al.
Center of Mass Auto-Location in Space
Reprinted from: *Technologies* **2025**, *13*, 246, https://doi.org/10.3390/technologies13060246 . . . . **6**

Antonio Santo, Enrique Heredia, Carlos Viegas, David Valiente and Arturo Gil
Ground Segmentation for LiDAR Point Clouds in Structured and Unstructured Environments Using a Hybrid Neural–Geometric Approach
Reprinted from: *Technologies* **2025**, *13*, 162, https://doi.org/10.3390/technologies13040162 . . . . **30**

Marius Cristian Luculescu, Luciana Cristea and Attila Laszlo Boer
Artificial Vision System for Autonomous Mobile Platform Used in Intelligent and Flexible Indoor Environment Inspection
Reprinted from: *Technologies* **2025**, *13*, 161, https://doi.org/10.3390/technologies13040161 . . . . **53**

Timothy Sands
Autonomous Real-Time Mass Center Location and Inertia Identification for Grappling Space Robotics
Reprinted from: *Technologies* **2025**, *13*, 148, https://doi.org/10.3390/technologies13040148 . . . . **86**

Roland Szabo
Implementing Computer Vision in Android Apps and Presenting the Background Technology with Mathematical Demonstrations
Reprinted from: *Technologies* **2025**, *13*, 27, https://doi.org/10.3390/technologies13010027 . . . . **120**

Băjenaru Valentina-Daniela, Istrițeanu Simona-Elena and Paul-Nicolae Ancuța
Advanced Autonomous System for Monitoring Soil Parameters
Reprinted from: *Technologies* **2025**, *13*, 38, https://doi.org/10.3390/technologies13010038 . . . . **150**

Romy Sauvayre, Jessica S. M. Gable, Adam Aalah, Melvin Fernandes Novo, Maxime Dehondt and Cédric Chauvière
The Impact of Autonomous Vehicle Accidents on Public Sentiment: A Decadal Analysis of Twitter Discourse Using roBERTa
Reprinted from: *Technologies* **2024**, *12*, 270, https://doi.org/10.3390/technologies12120270 . . . . **167**

Bianca Ghinoiu, Victor Vlădăreanu, Ana-Maria Travediu, Luige Vlădăreanu, Abigail Pop, Yongfei Feng and Andreea Zamfirescu
EEG-Based Mobile Robot Control Using Deep Learning and ROS Integration
Reprinted from: *Technologies* **2024**, *12*, 261, https://doi.org/10.3390/technologies12120261 . . . . **178**

José Luis Pérez-Gudiño , Marco Antonio Gómez-Guzmán, Chayanne García-Valdez, Roberto Valentín Carrillo-Serrano,Gerardo Israel Pérez-Soto and Juvenal Rodríguez-Reséndiz
The Low-Cost Mechanism of a DefinedPath Guide Slot-Based Passive Solar Tracker Intended for Developing Countries
Reprinted from: *Technologies* **2024**, *12*, 250, https://doi.org/10.3390/technologies12120250 . . . . **197**

Dragoș-Ioan Săcăleanu, Mihai-Gabriel Matache, Ștefan-George Roșu, Bogdan-Cristian Florea, Irina-Petra Manciu and Lucian-Andrei Perișoară
IoT-Enhanced Decision Support System for Real-Time Greenhouse Microclimate Monitoring and Control
Reprinted from: *Technologies* **2024**, *12*, 230, https://doi.org/10.3390/technologies12110230 . . . . **218**

Ioannis Polymeropoulos, Stavros Bezyrgiannidis, Eleni Vrochidou and George A. Papakostas
Enhancing Solar Plant Efficiency: A Review of Vision-Based Monitoring and Fault Detection Techniques
Reprinted from: *Technologies* **2024**, *12*, 175, https://doi.org/10.3390/technologies12100175 . . . . **243**

Tareq Alhmiedat, Laila A. AlBishi, Fady Alnajjar, Mohammed Alotaibi, Ashraf M. Marei and Rakan Shalayl
Improving Diabetes Education and Metabolic Control in Children Using Social Robots: A Randomized Trial
Reprinted from: *Technologies* **2024**, *12*, 209, https://doi.org/10.3390/technologies12110209 . . . . **288**

Fernando J. Pantusin, Christian P. Carvajal, Jessica S. Ortiz and Víctor H. Andaluz
Virtual Teleoperation System for Mobile Manipulator Robots Focused on Object Transport and Manipulation
Reprinted from: *Technologies* **2024**, *12*, 146, https://doi.org/10.3390/technologies12090146 . . . . **307**

Albandari Alotaibi, Hanan Alatawi, Aseel Binnouh, Lamaa Duwayriat, Tareq Alhmiedat and Osama Moh'd Alia
Deep Learning-Based Vision Systems for Robot Semantic Navigation: An Experimental Study
Reprinted from: *Technologies* **2024**, *12*, 157, https://doi.org/10.3390/technologies12090157 . . . . **329**

Gabriel Popa, Mihail Andrei, Emil Tudor, Ionuț Vasile and George Ilie
Fast Detection of the Stick–Slip Phenomenon Associated with Wheel-to-Rail Sliding Using Acceleration Sensors: An Experimental Study
Reprinted from: *Technologies* **2024**, *12*, 134, https://doi.org/10.3390/technologies12080134 . . . . **348**

Preface

The Advanced Autonomous Systems and Artificial Intelligence Stage Reprint presents a selection of fifteen research papers that reflect the rapid evolution of intelligent and autonomous technologies. The field has experienced significant growth in recent years, driven by the need for systems that can operate with higher levels of autonomy, perceive complex environments, support human users, and make reliable decisions under uncertainty. This Reprint was assembled to document these advances and to offer readers a coherent view of the current research landscape. The scope of this Reprint is intentionally broad, covering topics from robotic perception, navigation, and control to human–machine interaction, explainable artificial intelligence, and smart infrastructures. The contributions highlight both theoretical developments and practical implementations, demonstrating how researchers are integrating classical modeling techniques with modern learning-based strategies. The aim is to provide a resource that not only summarizes the state of the art but also inspires new ideas and collaborations across disciplines. As these technologies mature, questions of safety, transparency, and societal acceptance become central. The selected papers address these challenges while also exploring new opportunities for innovation in areas such as energy efficiency, assistive robotics, teleoperation, and environmental monitoring. This Reprint is addressed to researchers, graduate students, engineers, and professionals engaged in robotics, artificial intelligence, mechanical design, systems engineering, and related fields. We express our sincere appreciation to the authors for their contributions and to the reviewers for their valuable feedback. Their work has made this Reprint a meaningful reflection of the progress and aspirations of the scientific community.

We dedicate this Special Issue to the memory of Florian Ion Tiberiu Petrescu, who passed away during the preparation of this volume. His contributions to the field and to this scientific initiative remain deeply appreciated.

Florian Ion Tiberiu Petrescu and Liviu Marian Ungureanu
Guest Editors

technologies

MDPI

Editorial

Advanced Autonomous Systems and the Artificial Intelligence Stage

Liviu Marian Ungureanu [1] and Iulian-Sorin Munteanu [2,*]

[1] Theory of Mechanisms and Robots Department, 060042 Bucharest, Romania; liviu.ungureanu@upb.ro
[2] Theory of Mechanisms and Robots Department, National University of Science and Technology POLITEHNICA Bucharest, 060042 Bucharest, Romania
* Correspondence: iulian.munteanu0306@upb.ro

Abstract

This Editorial presents an integrative overview of the Special Issue "Advanced Autonomous Systems and Artificial Intelligence Stage", which assembles fifteen peer-reviewed articles dedicated to the recent evolution of AI-enabled and autonomous systems. The contributions span a broad spectrum of domains, including renewable energy and power systems, intelligent transportation, agricultural robotics, clinical and assistive technologies, mobile robotic platforms, and space robotics. Across these diverse applications, the collection highlights core research themes such as robust perception and navigation, semantic and multi modal sensing, resource-efficient embedded inference, human–machine interaction, sustainable infrastructures, and validation frameworks for safety-critical systems. Several articles demonstrate how physical modeling, hybrid control architectures, deep learning, and data-driven methods can be combined to enhance operational robustness, reliability, and autonomy in real-world environments. Other works address challenges related to fall detection, predictive maintenance, teleoperation safety, and the deployment of intelligent systems in large-scale or mission-critical contexts. Overall, this Special Issue offers a consolidated and rigorous academic synthesis of current advances in Autonomous Systems and Artificial Intelligence, providing researchers and practitioners with a valuable reference for understanding emerging trends, practical implementations, and future research directions.

Keywords: artificial intelligence; autonomous systems; robotics; human–machine interaction; intelligent control

1. Introduction

Over the past decade, automation and autonomy have shifted from the realm of "promising technologies" to that of critical infrastructure across industrial production, transportation, energy, agriculture, healthcare, and space applications. The integration of advanced mechanical and mechatronic systems with Artificial Intelligence (AI) defines a new development stage in which autonomous systems become not only more performant, but also safer, more adaptable, and increasingly user-centric [1,2].

In particular, the rapid evolution of AI in safety-critical domains such as medicine and healthcare has highlighted both the potential and the challenges associated with algorithmic decision-making, explainability, and trust [1–3]. At the same time, advances in sensing, smart materials, and embedded systems further strengthen the technological foundation for autonomous platforms operating in complex environments [4–7].

The Special Issue "Advanced Autonomous Systems and Artificial Intelligence Stage" gathers 15 contributions that capture this multidimensional evolution, illustrating how AI [8–11] and autonomy [9,12] intersect in real-world systems, from robotics and space applications to agriculture, renewable energy, assistive technologies, and human–machine interaction.

2. Advanced Autonomy in Robotics and Space Applications

A central focus of this Special Issue is autonomous robotics for hard-to-access environments, with a particular emphasis on space applications. Several contributions address real-time autonomous methods for center-of-mass localization and inertia identification in robotic platforms, in both single-spacecraft scenarios and grappling operations involving large structures. These works are closely aligned with the broader international effort to achieve robust and verifiable AI-enabled decision-making in safety-critical systems [1,10,11].

In parallel, other papers examine mobile robotics for terrestrial monitoring and indoor inspection, including advanced soil parameter monitoring systems and intelligent indoor inspection platforms. They demonstrate how robust perception, data fusion, and intelligent control can be tailored for planetary-like terrains, precision agriculture, or industrial environments, drawing on the same methodological foundations that underpin modern AI applications in sensing and monitoring [7,9].

3. Perception, Computer Vision, and Semantic Navigation

A second major pillar of this Special Issue is advanced perception, achieved through the integration of computer vision and LiDAR in autonomous architectures. The contributions include the following:

- Neural–geometric methods for ground segmentation in LiDAR point clouds, designed to support safe navigation in structured and unstructured environments.
- Deep-learning-based semantic navigation for mobile robots, where object detection and scene understanding are essential for reliable mapping and path planning.
- Mobile implementations of computer vision in Android applications, including real-time image processing scenarios, thereby connecting high-performance perception algorithms with widely available computational platforms.
- These works resonate with broader trends in AI and machine learning, where real-time, resource-constrained inference is increasingly deployed on embedded and wearable devices [7–9]. For example, recent advances in real-time sign-language recognition [8] and wearable fall-detection systems [9] highlight how vision and sensor-based AI can be deployed in everyday environments, extending beyond traditional laboratory settings. The contributions in this Special Issue thus reinforce the importance of perception as a core enabler of autonomy in both mobile and stationary systems.

4. Human–Machine Interaction, BCI, and Social Robotics

A defining feature of the current stage in autonomous systems is user centrality. It is not sufficient for systems to be accurate and fast; they must also be interpretable, intuitive, and aligned with human needs [2,3]. Two main directions in the Special Issue illustrate this shift:

1. Brain–Computer Interfaces (BCIs) based on EEG signals and deep learning for the control of mobile robots. These systems combine advanced neural architectures with real-time control frameworks, reflecting a broader movement toward human-in-the-loop AI and assistive robotics [1,7].

https://doi.org/10.3390/technologies14010009

2. Social robots in pediatric diabetes education, where robot-assisted interventions are assessed in terms of knowledge acquisition and metabolic control in children. This area is closely connected to the more general landscape of AI in healthcare, where issues of explainability, safety, and clinical integration are widely discussed [1–3,10,11].

Together, these studies underscore the transition from purely performance-driven autonomy to empathetic, human-centered autonomy, with tangible clinical and assistive benefits.

5. Precision Agriculture, Renewable Energy, and Smart Infrastructure

Intelligent autonomy is also a key enabler in agriculture, energy, and infrastructure, domains that are central to sustainable development. The Special Issue includes the following:

- An IoT-enhanced decision support system for real-time greenhouse microclimate monitoring and control, which leverages wireless sensor networks and cloud-based analytics for precision agriculture.
- A low-cost passive solar tracker with a guide-slot mechanism, optimized for developing countries and designed to maximize energy capture with minimal actuation.
- A comprehensive review of vision-based monitoring and fault detection techniques for solar plants, highlighting the role of computer vision and AI in predictive maintenance and fault diagnosis.

These contributions are situated within a broader technological context where advanced materials, micro- and nano-engineered structures, and additive manufacturing technologies (such as electrospun fibers and 3D printing) are increasingly integrated into smart energy and environmental systems [4–6,12]. The convergence of AI, advanced sensing, and novel materials paves the way for more efficient, resilient, and adaptive infrastructures.

6. Safety, Reliability, and Social Perception

A mature autonomous system must be safe, reliable, explainable, and socially accepted. This Special Issue includes contributions that explicitly address these dimensions. For instance, one study focuses on the fast detection of the stick–slip phenomenon in wheel–rail interactions using acceleration sensors, enabling early intervention in critical traction scenarios. This type of work reflects the importance of high-fidelity sensing and robust signal processing in safety-critical transport systems [7,9].

Another contribution offers a decadal analysis of public discourse on autonomous vehicle accidents, using a transformer-based language model (roBERTa) to examine sentiment and perception on social media. This aligns with the growing literature on the societal and ethical implications of AI, where public trust, transparency, and accountability are key themes [2,3,10,11].

In this context, explainable AI (XAI) and interpretable models are not simply desirable features, but necessary conditions for responsible deployment in domains such as healthcare, mobility, and public safety [2,3,10,11].

7. Teleoperation, Virtual Reality, and Human–Robot Collaboration

In parallel with fully autonomous systems, teleoperation and human–robot collaboration remain indispensable for scenarios where full autonomy is either infeasible or undesirable. This Special Issue features:

- A virtual teleoperation framework for mobile manipulator robots, developed in Unity, which integrates kinematic and dynamic models to enable realistic simulation and control in virtual environments. Such frameworks support safe experimentation, training, and validation before real-world deployment.

https://doi.org/10.3390/technologies14010009

- An application integrating advanced information capture and AI-assisted transfer modules for robotic control during dental implant surgery, illustrating how virtual planning, 3D modeling, and intelligent guidance can enhance precision and safety in medical procedures.

These developments are consonant with broader trends in AI-enabled medical imaging and synthetic data generation [11], as well as with the integration of sensing and actuation in wearable and ambient devices [7,9]. They highlight how human–robot collaboration and extended reality (XR) technologies can bridge the gap between autonomous decision-making and clinical or industrial practice.

8. Conclusions and Perspectives

The Special Issue "Advanced Autonomous Systems and Artificial Intelligence Stage" brings together 15 articles that collectively offer a coherent picture of how autonomy and AI intersect in contemporary engineering and science. Across diverse domains, three core trends emerge:

1. Integration of physical models and AI, where domain knowledge in mechanics, mechatronics, and materials is combined with modern machine learning and deep learning approaches [1–3,5–7,12].
2. Human-centered interaction, illustrated by BCI-controlled robots, social robots in healthcare, and systems explicitly designed around user needs and human factors [1–3,7–10].
3. Sustainability, safety, and societal acceptance, underlined by contributions on renewable energy, precision agriculture, transport safety, and social perceptions of autonomous vehicles [2–4,8–11].

Taken together, these contributions confirm that advanced autonomous systems and AI are no longer confined to laboratory prototypes, but are increasingly embedded in real-world, safety-critical, and socially impactful applications.

Acknowledgments: We express our heartfelt gratitude to our dear colleague, researcher, and academic, Florian Ion Petrescu, whose unwavering dedication, professional integrity, and passion for scientific excellence shaped this Special Issue from its earliest stages. His passing, which occurred before the printed Reprint was completed, leaves a profound sense of loss within our community. This publication stands not only as a scholarly contribution but also as a tribute to his memory and to the remarkable legacy he leaves behind.

Conflicts of Interest: The authors declare no conflict of interest.

References

1. Nagendran, M.; Chen, Y.; Lovejoy, C.A.; Gordon, A.C.; Komorowski, M.; Harvey, H.; Topol, E.J.; Ioannidis, J.P.A.; Collins, G.S.; Maruthappu, M. Artificial Intelligence versus Clinicians: Systematic Review of Design, Reporting Standards, and Claims of Deep Learning Studies. *BMJ* **2020**, *368*, m689. [CrossRef] [PubMed]
2. Antoniadi, A.M.; Du, Y.; Guendouz, Y.; Wei, L.; Mazo, C.; Becker, B.A.; Mooney, C. Current Challenges and Future Opportunities for XAI in Machine Learning-Based Clinical Decision Support Systems: A Systematic Review. *Appl. Sci.* **2021**, *11*, 5088. [CrossRef]
3. Tjoa, E.; Guan, C. A Survey on Explainable Artificial Intelligence (XAI): Toward Medical XAI. *IEEE Trans. Neural Netw. Learn. Syst.* **2021**, *32*, 4793–4813. [CrossRef] [PubMed]
4. Luraghi, A.; Peri, F.; Moroni, L.; Bianchini, P.; Cencetti, M.; Giannitelli, S.M. Electrospinning for Drug Delivery Applications: A Review. *J. Control Release* **2021**, *334*, 463–484. [CrossRef] [PubMed]
5. Yang, D.L.; Faraz, F.; Wang, J.X.; Radacsi, N. Combination of 3D Printing and Electrospinning Techniques for Biofabrication. *Adv. Mater. Technol.* **2022**, *7*, 2101309. [CrossRef] [PubMed]
6. Wu, S.; Dong, T.; Li, Y.; Sun, M.; Qi, Y.; Liu, J.; Kuss, M.A.; Chen, S.; Duan, B. State-of-the-art Review of Advanced Electrospun Nanofiber Yarn-Based Textiles for Biomedical Applications. *Appl. Mater. Today* **2022**, *27*, 101473. [CrossRef] [PubMed]

https://doi.org/10.3390/technologies14010009

7. Kolosov, D.; Penkov, D.; Sokolova, A.; Müller, H.; De Luca, V. Contactless Camera-Based Heart Rate and Respiratory Rate Monitoring Using AI on Hardware. *Sensors* **2023**, *23*, 4550. [CrossRef]
8. García-Gil, G.; López-Nores, M.; García-Duque, J.; Blanco-Fernández, Y. Real-Time Machine Learning for Accurate Mexican Sign Language Identification: A Distal Phalanges Approach. *Technologies* **2024**, *12*, 152. [CrossRef]
9. Villa, M.; Casilari, E. Wearable Fall Detectors Based on Low Power Transmission Systems: A Systematic Review. *Technologies* **2024**, *12*, 166. [CrossRef]
10. Petersson, L.; Durand, A.-C.; Hansagi, H.; Wolf, A.; Simonsson, U.; Ekelund, U. Challenges to Implementing Artificial Intelligence in Healthcare: A Qualitative Study of Stakeholder Perspectives. *BMC Health Serv. Res.* **2022**, *22*, 850. [CrossRef] [PubMed]
11. Müller-Franzes, G.; Niehues, J.M.; Khader, F.; Arasteh, S.T.; Haarburger, C.; Kuhl, C.; Wang, T.; Han, T.; Nolte, T.; Nebelung, S.; et al. A multimodal comparison of latent denoising diffusion probabilistic models and generative adversarial networks for medical image synthesis. *Sci. Rep.* **2023**, *13*, 12098. [CrossRef] [PubMed]
12. Li, L.; Wang, Y.; Guo, R.; Li, H.; Chen, S. Electrospun Fibers Control Drug Delivery for Tissue Regeneration and Cancer Therapy. *Adv. Fiber Mater.* **2022**, *4*, 1375–1413. [CrossRef]

https://doi.org/10.3390/technologies14010009

technologies

MDPI

Article

Center of Mass Auto-Location in Space †

Lucas McLeland [1], Brian Erickson [1], Brendan Ruchlin [1], Eryn Daman [1], James Mejia [1], Benjamin Ho [1], Joshua Lewis [1], Bryan Mann [1], Connor Paw [1], James Ross [1], Christopher Reis [1], Scott Walter [1], Stefanie Coward [1], Thomas Post [1], Andrew Freeborn [1] and Timothy Sands [2,3,4,*]

1 Department of Astronautical Sciences, U.S. Air Force Test Pilot School, Edwards AFB, CA 93524, USA
2 Sibley School of Mechanical and Aerospace Engineering, Cornell University, Ithaca, NY 14853, USA
3 Department of Mechanical Engineering (CVN), Columbia University, New York, NY 10027, USA
4 Department of Mechanical Engineering (SCPD), Stanford University, Stanford, CA 94305, USA
* Correspondence: tas297@cornell.edu
† Approved for public release; Distribution is unlimited 412TW-PA-25150.

Abstract: Maintaining a spacecraft's center of mass at the origin of a body-fixed coordinate system is often key to precision trajectory tracking. Typically, the inertia matrix is estimated and verified with preliminary ground testing. This article presents groundbreaking preliminary results and significant findings from on-orbit space experiments validating recently proposed methods as part of a larger study over multiple years. Time-varying estimates of inertia moments and products are used to reveal time-varying estimates of the location of spacecraft center of mass using geosynchronous orbiting test satellites proposing a novel two-norm optimal projection learning method. Using the parallel axis theorem, the location of the mass center is parameterized using the cross products of inertia, and that information is extracted from spaceflight maneuver data validating modeling and simulation. Mass inertia properties are discerned, and the mass center is experimentally revealed to be over thirty centimeters away from the assumed locations in two of the three axes. Rotation about one axis is found to be very well balanced, with the center of gravity lying on that axis. Two-to-three orders of magnitude corrections to inertia identification are experimentally demonstrated. Combined-axis three-dimensional maneuvers are found to obscure identification compared with single-axis maneuvering as predicted by the sequel analytic study. Mass center location migrates 36–95% and subsequent validating experiments duplicate the results to within 0.1%.

Keywords: autonomous navigation; center of gravity; inertia tensor; experimental validation; space test; on-orbit experiments

1. Introduction

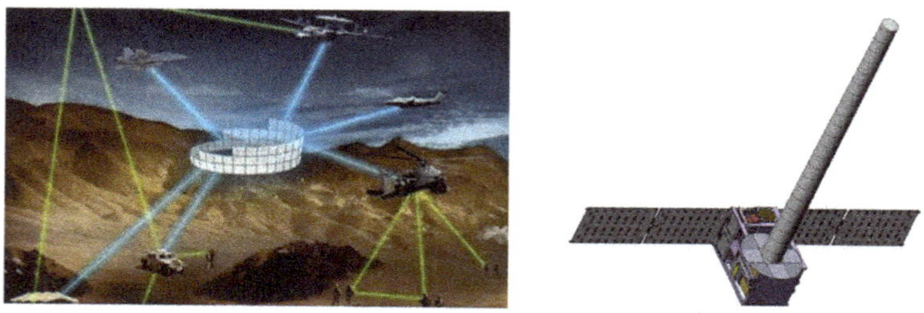

(a) (b)

Figure 1. Communication links in and from space. (**a**) The Space Development Agency (SDA) received approval from the International Telecommunication Union (ITU) for experimental use of Link 16 from space using radios flown on the Tranche 0 Transport satellites. Image credit: SDA [1], used in accordance with image use policy; [2] (**b**) Air Force Research Laboratory (AFRL) XVI satellite, host of Link 16 payload [3].

https://doi.org/10.3390/technologies13060246

Earth-orbiting spacecraft (e.g., Figure 1) often waste fuel due to correcting trajectory tracking errors due to mass imbalance, shortening their mission lifecycles. Amelioration holds promise of substantial savings. In the remainder of this section of this article, the current state of the research field is reviewed, and key publications are cited. Controversial and diverging hypotheses are introduced. Finally, the main aim of this work is briefly mentioned, and the principal conclusions are highlighted after foremostly introducing the general problem statement.

Problem Statement: Generally, inertia *moments* are estimated on the ground, while some recent attempts have been made to estimate them on an orbit. The estimation of inertia *products* is relatively rare, despite the ability to parameterize the location of the mass center using the parallel axis theorem. This study elaborates a novel process for determining the time-varying location of the mass center on orbit by using the parallel axis theorem to parameterize the problem and then estimating the time-varying inertia properties leads to the auto-location of the spacecraft's center of mass.

Research objectives: (1) Using only attitude empirical angle knowledge, find mass imbalanced inertia components and (2) convert mass imbalance to center of gravity coordinates, and then calculate that location.

Key contributions: Seminal proposal of a novel mass center auto-location method is introduced, realizing improvements over the comparative state-of-the-art benchmark. Rapid convergence is validated in spaceflight experiments.

1.1. Review of the Literature

One mission context for the center of mass auto-location is grappling space robotics (e.g., Figure 2), and the U.S. Naval Academy provides a worthy benchmark launched into space in December 2018. Two 3D-printed manipulator arms are attached to the RSAT–P (USNA–19) cubesat on the NASA ELaNa XIX space mission.

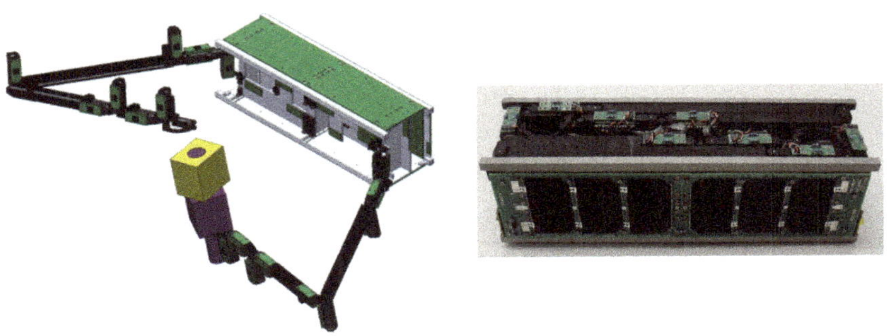

(**a**) (**b**)

Figure 2. U.S. Naval cubesat grappling space robot (images credit: U.S. Navy), launched in 2018 [4]. Used in accordance with published image use policy [2]. (**a**) Computer-aided drawing depicting two robotic arms with cameras on each end effector and at the cube satellite's mid-body; (**b**) actual hardware with robot arms stowed.

Such robotic space missions necessitate autonomous knowledge of mass properties in situ, and many approaches have appeared in the recent literature. A very recent proposal includes using an extended Kalman filter combined with a Rauch–Tung–Striebel smoother was used to estimate the offset, where the chi-square test was used to eliminate outliers, where a slightly improved performance was achieved detecting gravitational waves [5]. Laser range finders are one ubiquitous system used to locate the center of mass on orbit. Center of mass values used for Ajisai geodetic satellites using satellite laser ranging relied on [6], the work of Otsubo and Appleby. These values have been superseded by the relatively new work described in [7], which revealed that a major contributor to the error budget in satellite laser ranging (SLR) for reference frame realization has been a limited accuracy of the CoM corrections The new values [7] can result in a roughly twenty millimeter change for big targets compared with earlier modeling [6], where the study also concluded that standard center of mass corrections yield inaccurate on-orbit solutions. The latest corrections are presented in [8]. The concept of corrections is depicted in Figure 3.

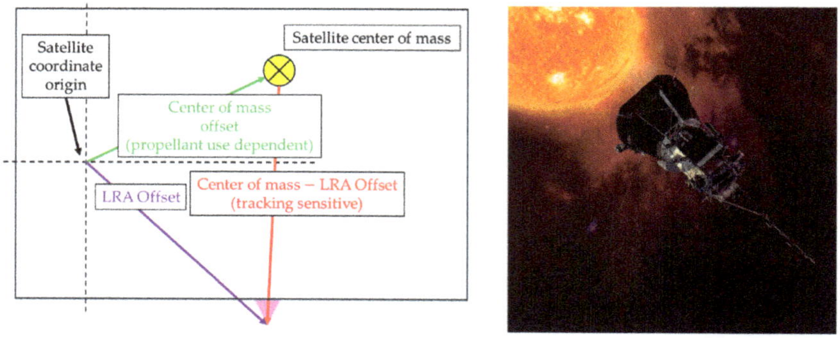

(a) (b)

Figure 3. (**a**) Center of mass correction concept from [7,8] for satellites with laser retroreflector arrays (LRA). (**b**) U.S. Navy GEOSAT spacecraft [9]. Image credit: NASA. Used in accordance with image use policy [10].

The center of mass correction using laser ranging data was also employed by the CHAMP satellite [11], the Etalon-1 and -2 satellites [12], Galileo-101 and -102 satellites [13], and U.S. Navy GEOSAT spacecraft [14].

Correction may be accomplished using a set of three internal shifting masses (ISMs) that can be displaced and a mass estimation method based in the recursive least squares algorithm claiming "...a convergence of an acceptable value of the position of the center of mass of the satellite in approximately 120 s, while the relative error is less than 5%" [15]. The method proposed in this manuscript is similar to the method proposed in [15], but merely topically. The latter technique uses recursive least squares to estimate the location, while the presently proposed method uses a novel 2-norm optimal estimator to produce values for inertia moments and products (useful within themselves) and then the inertia products (only) are used to directly calculate the mass center location by accepting parameterization using the parallel axis theorem. The latter method (from reference [15]) yields initial rapid convergence, then divergence before stabilizing with a finite, but noticeable offset. In 2021, optimization of mass center location was proposed using linear means, incrementally adding environmental disturbances as constraints and then optimizing component mass locations [16].

More recently, inflight estimation of the position of the center of gravity was elaborated using arrays of accelerometers [17]. Integer programming models were proposed for accurate center of gravity control in [18]. An integrated estimation approach sequentially combined a Huber-extended Kálmán filter and extended Kálmán filter to estimate the center of gravity location. The Huber version of the filter is used first to find the estimated distance between a vehicle's front axle and the center of gravity, while the extended filter locates the center of gravity with a claimed performance of a two percent estimation error within two seconds [19]. Similar to the comments in the preceding paragraph's comparison of the methods in reference [15], the methods proposed in [19] are similar topically, but quite different than the methods presently proposed. The methods in reference [19] propose using

Kalman filtering methods for state estimation (particularly velocity), then Huang modeling to estimate the mass center, while the presently proposed methods use a novel two-norm optimal estimator for the inertia components (moments and products), then uses the products to directly calculate the mass center location by accepting parameterization using the parallel axis theorem. Meanwhile, [20] integrated observers for real-time estimation of the height of the mass center. Reference [21] proposed combining an adaptive Kálmán filter and extended Kálmán filter to estimate mass center location and particularly focused on persistence of excitation. H∞ methods (used in control theory to synthesize controllers to achieve stabilization with guaranteed performance) and the extended Kálmán filter joint estimation method was used to determine the mass center position in [22]. Adaptive online estimation was proposed in [23] for height location only of the mass center.

Feedback linearizing control was used in [24] to account for time-varying mass center location during spacecraft orbital refueling.

The historical approaches described generally fall into two categories: accelerometer sensing to utilize first principles for estimation or alternatively filtering approaches. Meanwhile, some novel approaches have been recently suggested.

1.2. State-of-the-Art Benchmarks

The following list highlights the current developing state-of-the art deterministic artificial intelligence ("deterministic AI systems operate under the principle that every set of particular conditions will always lead to the same outcome" [25]):

1. Mass center coordinate estimation based on an overall brightness average determined from a three-dimensional vision system [26].
2. Reference [27] presents an exact analytic method for calculating the volume, mass, center of gravity, and inertia properties of wing segments and rotors of constant density, emphasizing analysis requiring the analytical solution of several volume integrals (necessarily a quite lengthy process). The goal of this present study is akin to this state-of-the-art benchmark, while avoiding such complications.
3. Reference [28] combines multiple accelerometers and gyroscopes into an inertial measurement unit mounted on the pitch and yaw axes, where the roll axis houses the gyroscope used to determine the spin axis.
4. References [29,30] proposed a novel approach to use any attitude maneuver to analytically find the location of the mass center necessitating nonlinear enhanced Luenberger observers to estimate the constituent variables, permitting angle data alone to yield mass center location estimates.

1.3. Novelties Presented

1. This present manuscript presents results validating the declared state-of-the-art benchmark with tests on orbit using experimental satellites depicted in Figure 1.
2. A seminal method is proposed and tested, and results are presented relative to the comparative benchmark.
3. An additional novelty stems from the seminal introduction of a two-norm optimal projection learning method.

2. Materials and Methods

The methods adopted for this study accept a commonplace practice (displayed in Equation (1)) of analysis followed by the verification of analysis with modeling, simulation, and experimental validation using on-orbit space tests.

$$\boxed{Predict} \rightarrow \boxed{Test} \rightarrow \boxed{Validation} \tag{1}$$

Analysis begins by defining the inertia matrix and components, while the mass center location is parameterized using the parallel axis theorem. Next, three estimation techniques are introduced as follows: a classical approach, nonlinear adaptive estimation (chosen as the comparative benchmark for this study), and two-norm optimal projection learning. The equations introduced in Section 2 are simulated in MATLAB®/SIMULINK®, R2022b and the simulation is briefly introduced, focusing on the overall simulation topology and the systems used to estimate the mass center location.

Periodically, short tables are presented to define proximal variables, acronyms, and such (e.g., Tables 1–5 and Table A1) with a large summary table provided in Appendix B.

2.1. Inertia Matrix

Inertia matrices are ubiquitously diagonalized by transformation to the refence frame defined by the eigenvectors' basis, eliminating the commonplace utility of off-diagonal inertia products. Accordingly, a very common derivation of all the terms of inertia matrices is presented next, especially due to the high importance of off-diagonal inertia products (remaining expressed in the body-fixed reference frame). The rigid body moments of inertia are defined in Equation (2) and expressed for the continuums of mass distributions in Equation (3). The vector identity in Equation (3) is used to modify Equation (3) into Equation (4), which simplifies to Equation (7)'s expression of the angular momentum vector. Defining the moment of inertia components in Equation (8) permits redefining the angular momentum terms, as displayed in Equation (9) formulated in matrix–vector form in Equation (10).

Table 1. Table of proximal variables and nomenclature [1].

Variable/Acronym	Definition	Variable/Acronym	Definition
H_{cm}	Centroidal angular momentum	A, B, C	Dummy variables
$\boldsymbol{r}_{dm,i}$	Radius vector to differential mass, i	$\boldsymbol{r}_i$	Radius vector to point i
m_i	Differential mass, i	dm	Differential mass
ω	Angular velocity vector	$\boldsymbol{v}_{dm,i}$	Velocity vector of differential mass, i

[1] Such tables are offered throughout the manuscript to aid readability.

$$H_{cm} = \sum_{i=1}^{n} \boldsymbol{r}_{dm,i} \times \underbrace{m_i(\boldsymbol{\omega} \times \boldsymbol{r}_{dm,i})}_{linear\ momentum} \tag{2}$$

$$H_{cm} = \int_M \boldsymbol{r}_{dm,i} \times \underbrace{\boldsymbol{v}_{dm,i} dm}_{P=mv} = \int_M \boldsymbol{r}_{dm,i} \times (\boldsymbol{\omega} \times \boldsymbol{r}_{dm,i}) dm \tag{3}$$

$$\text{Use vector identity}: \ A \times B \times C = (A \cdot C)B - (A \cdot B)C \tag{4}$$

$$H_{cm} = \int_M (\boldsymbol{r}_i \cdot \boldsymbol{r}_i)\boldsymbol{\omega} - (\boldsymbol{r}_i \cdot \boldsymbol{\omega})\boldsymbol{r}_i dm \tag{5}$$

$$(\boldsymbol{r}_i \cdot \boldsymbol{\omega}) \neq 0 \text{ unless planar body with 2D motion in its own plane} \tag{6}$$

$$H_{cm} = \begin{pmatrix} \omega_x \int\limits_M (x^2+y^2+z^2)dm - \int\limits_M (\omega_x x + \omega_y y + \omega_z z)xdm \end{pmatrix}\hat{x}_B + \begin{pmatrix} \omega_y \int\limits_M (x^2+y^2+z^2)dm - \int\limits_M (\omega_x x + \omega_y y + \omega_z z)ydm \end{pmatrix}\hat{y}_B + \begin{pmatrix} \omega_z \int\limits_M (x^2+y^2+z^2)dm - \int\limits_M (\omega_x x + \omega_y y + \omega_z z)zdm \end{pmatrix}\hat{z}_B \quad (7)$$

$$\begin{aligned} J_{xx} &\equiv \int\limits_M (y^2+z^2)dm, & J_{xy} = J_{yx} &\equiv \int\limits_M xydm \\ J_{yy} &\equiv \int\limits_M (x^2+z^2)dm, & J_{yz} = J_{zy} &\equiv \int\limits_M yzdm \\ J_{zz} &\equiv \int\limits_M (x^2+y^2)dm, & J_{xz} = J_{zx} &\equiv \int\limits_M xzdm \end{aligned} \quad (8)$$

$$\begin{aligned} H_{cm} = &(J_{xx}\omega_x - J_{xy}\omega_y - J_{xz}\omega_z)\hat{x}_B \\ &+\left(-J_{yx}\omega_x + J_{yy}\omega_y - J_{yz}\omega_z\right)\hat{y}_B \\ &+(-J_{zx}\omega_x - J_{zy}\omega_y + J_{zz}\omega_z)\hat{z}_B \end{aligned} \quad (9)$$

$$\{H_{cm}\} = \underbrace{\begin{bmatrix} J_{xx} & -J_{xy} & -J_{xz} \\ -J_{yx} & J_{yy} & -J_{yz} \\ -J_{zx} & -J_{zy} & J_{zz} \end{bmatrix}}_{[J]} \underbrace{\begin{Bmatrix} \omega_x \\ \omega_y \\ \omega_z \end{Bmatrix}}_{\{\omega\}} \quad (10)$$

Table 2. Table of proximal variables and nomenclature [1].

Variable/Acronym	Definition	Variable/Acronym	Definition
$\{\omega\} \equiv \{\omega_x \quad \omega_y \quad \omega_z\}^T$	Angular velocity [radians/second]	J_{xx}, J_{yy}, J_{zz}	Moments of inertia
$\hat{x}_B, \hat{y}_B, \hat{z}_B$	Unit vectors	$J_{xy}, J_{yx}, J_{yz}, J_{zy}, J_{xz}, J_{zx}$	Products of inertia
x, y, z	Positional coordinates	$[J]$	Moment of inertia matrix

[1] Such tables are offered throughout the manuscript to aid readability.

The derivation embodied in Equations (2)–(10) reveals time-varying mass distribution, where $\boldsymbol{r}_{dm,i} = \boldsymbol{r}(t)_{dm,i}$; $m_i = m_i(t)$; $\boldsymbol{\omega} = \boldsymbol{\omega}(\boldsymbol{t})$; and, similarly, the coordinates of differential masses: $x = x(t); y = y(t); z = z(t)$. Utilizing the time-varying nature necessitates some parameterization of the location of the mass center and some method of discerning the time-varying values of the inertia matrix. Next, in Section 2.2, the center of mass location is parameterized by assuming that the actual location is potentially (likely) unknown and not at the center of the body coordinate system. The parallel axis theorem is used to solve the three-dimensional coordinates of the mass center location. Afterwards, Section 2.3 introduces one option for inertia matrix component estimation.

2.2. Center of Mass Location Estimation

By not diagonalizing the inertia matrix, off-balance rotation manifests in non-zero inertia products. Assuming the center of mass resides at some point other than the origin of the body-fixed axes, the parallel axis theorem (depicted in Figure 4) may be used to parameterize the location. Using such parameterization, the problem of estimating the location of the center of mass devolves into a commonplace problem of estimating the components of the inertia matrix, e.g., [30].

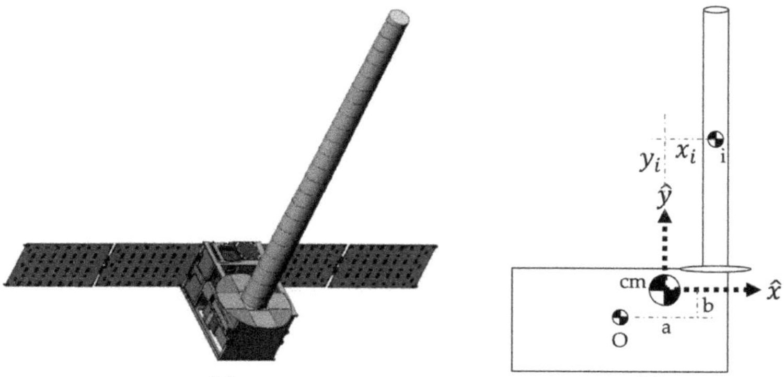

(**a**) (**b**)

Figure 4. (**a**) Air Force Research Laboratory (AFRL) XVI satellite, host of Link 16 payload. [3] (**b**) Schematic of center of mass offset from spacecraft body axes centered at origin, O, corresponding to the parallel axis theorem.

Theorem 1. *Parallel axis theorem. The moment of inertia J_O about some point other than the center of mass is the sum of the moment of inertia J_{cm} about the center of mass and the moment of inertia relative to the fixed distance between axes in the rigid body represented by the product of the total mass and the square of the distance (see Equation (11)).*

$$J_O = J_{cm} + MR_O^2 \tag{11}$$

The following proof mirrors [31], since the version most closely illuminates the use of the parallel axis theorem in this manuscript to reveal the three-dimensional location of the center of mass.

Proof. Consider a rigid system of particles of mass $M = \sum_i m_i$, rotating about a fixed axis O along axis y. Place the origin of the coordinate system at the center-of-mass (cm) of our system of particles. The general point i has coordinates (x_i, y_i), the x coordinate of O is a, and the y coordinate of O is b. Since the center of mass is at $(0, 0)$, by the definition of the center-of-mass (the unique point at any given time where the weighted relative position of the distributed mass sums to zero), Equation (12) results as follows:

Box 1. Key relationship between mass center location and inertia cross products.

$$x_{cm} = \sqrt{\frac{J_{xy}J_{xz}}{mJ_{yz}}} \quad y_{cm} = \sqrt{\frac{J_{xy}J_{yz}}{mJ_{xz}}}, \quad z_{cm} = \sqrt{\frac{J_{xz}J_{yz}}{mJ_{xy}}} \tag{12}$$

□

By definition, $J_O = \sum_i m_i r_{iO}^2$, where r_{iO} is measured from O, not from the mass center. Thus, $r_{iO}^2 = (x_i - a)^2 + (y_i - b)^2$, leading to Equation (13). But, since $x_{cm} = \sum_i \frac{m_i x_i}{M} = 0$ and similarly for y, the cross terms in Equation (13) go to zero once the sum over i is finished, leading to Equation (14). Since $\left(x_i^2 + y_i^2\right) = r_i^2$, where r_i is now measured from the mass center, and $\left(a^2 + b^2\right) = R_O^2$ is just R_O^2, where R_O is the distance from O to the mass center, Equations (13)–(15) result, whose terms are conveniently defined in Table 3.

$$J_O = \sum_i m_i\left[(x_i - a)^2 + (y_i - b)^2\right] = \sum_i m_i\left[x_i^2 - 2ax_i + a^2 + y_i^2 - 2by_i^2 + b^2\right] \tag{13}$$

$$J_O = \sum_i m_i\left(x_i{}^2 + y_i{}^2\right) - \sum_i m_i\left(a^2 + b^2\right) \tag{14}$$

$$J_y = J_{cm} + MR_y^2 \tag{15}$$

Table 3. Table of proximal variables and nomenclature [1].

Variable/Acronym	Definition	Variable/Acronym	Definition
$J_y = J_O$	Inertia moment about a fixed axis O along y	y	Robot arm base parallel axis
J_{cm}	Inertia moment about mass center	$\hat{y}$	Body center parallel axis
M	Total system mass	r_{iO}	Radius from parallel axis (not mass center)
R_O	Distance from O to the mass center	r_i	Radius vector to the mass center
R_y	Distance to axis y	m_i	Differential mass element
O	Fixed axis along axis y	(x_i, y_i)	Center of mass coordinates
a	x coordinate of O	b	y coordinate of O

[1] Such tables are offered throughout the manuscript to aid readability.

Having articulated the equations used to locate the mass center, the original problem has reduced to a different problem of inertia component identification. Next, in Section 2.3, the new problem solution is introduced by three disparate methods. The classical approach would necessitate estimating only the inertia moments (not products). The benchmark and proposed approaches estimate both moments and products, where only the products are used to analytically calculate the mass center location using Equation (12).

2.3. *Inertia Matrix Component Estimation*

One classical approach uses linearized double-integrator versions of the governing differential equations, while the benchmark for this study uses the full, coupled, and nonlinear equations with a simplified linear estimation. Meanwhile, the approach proposed also uses the full, coupled, and nonlinear equations with two-norm optimal projection learning.

2.3.1. Classical Approach

One ubiquitous classical approach displayed in Equation (16) is to treat the nonlinear coupled set of differential equations as if they were a simple uncoupled linear set of so-called double integrator equations. One necessary assumption is to treat the body axes as if they were equivalent to the eigen axes, diagonalizing the inertia matrix by transforming it to coordinates of a disparate reference frame of measurement (the frame spanned by the eigen axes).

$$\tau = [J]\{\dot{\omega}\} \to \begin{Bmatrix} \tau_x \\ \tau_y \\ \tau_z \end{Bmatrix} = \begin{bmatrix} J_x & 0 & 0 \\ 0 & J_y & 0 \\ 0 & 0 & J_z \end{bmatrix} \begin{Bmatrix} \dot{\omega}_x \\ \dot{\omega}_y \\ \dot{\omega}_z \end{Bmatrix} = \begin{Bmatrix} J_x\dot{\omega}_x \\ J_y\dot{\omega}_y \\ J_z\dot{\omega}_z \end{Bmatrix} \to \begin{Bmatrix} \tau_x \\ \tau_y \\ \tau_z \end{Bmatrix} = \begin{Bmatrix} J_x\dot{\omega}_x \\ J_y\dot{\omega}_y \\ J_z\dot{\omega}_z \end{Bmatrix} \tag{16}$$

The approach is simple: divide the known torque components by the component angular velocity to reveal the principal moment (not product) of inertia for each of the three axes.

2.3.2. Comparative Benchmark Approach (Nonlinear Adaptive Estimation)

The comparative benchmark approach for this study parameterizes the nonlinear coupled set of differential equations into a system matrix, $\mathbf{\Phi}$, with the inertia matrix components used to form the regression vector, β, where this parameterization is adopted in the proposed approach described in Section 2.3.3. The rate of change of the regression vector is defined in negative feedback with a combined measure of trajectory tracking error, $\mathbf{s}$, using a positive constant, $\mathbf{\Gamma}$, as the adaption gain displayed in Equations (17) and (18).

$$\dot{\hat{\beta}} = -\mathbf{\Gamma}^{-1}\mathbf{\Phi}^T\mathbf{s} \tag{17}$$

$$\mathbf{s} = \ddot{\theta} + \lambda\dot{\theta} \tag{18}$$

2.3.3. Proposed Approach (Two-Norm Optimal Projection Learning)

Identical regression parameterization (displayed in Equation (20)) is maintained in the proposed approach, where the feedback-based gain adaption is replaced with projection learning based on two-norm optimal least squares, as indicated in Equation (21), where terms are conveniently defined in Table 4.

$$\tau = [J]\{\dot{\omega}\} + \{\omega\} \times [J]\{\omega\} \tag{19}$$

$$\tau = \underbrace{\begin{bmatrix} \dot{\omega}_x & \dot{\omega}_y - \omega_x\omega_z & \dot{\omega}_z - \omega_x\omega_y & -\omega_y\omega_z & 0 & \omega_y\omega_z \\ \omega_x\omega_z & \dot{\omega}_x + \omega_y\omega_z & 0 & \dot{\omega}_y & \dot{\omega}_z - \omega_x\omega_y & -\omega_x\omega_z \\ -\omega_x\omega_y & 0 & \dot{\omega}_x - \omega_y\omega_z & \omega_x\omega_y & \dot{\omega}_y + \omega_x\omega_z & \dot{\omega}_z \end{bmatrix}_d}_{[\Phi]_d} \underbrace{\begin{Bmatrix} \hat{J}_{xx} \\ \hat{J}_{xy} \\ \hat{J}_{xz} \\ \hat{J}_{yy} \\ \hat{J}_{yz} \\ \hat{J}_{zz} \end{Bmatrix}}_{\hat{\beta}} \tag{20}$$

$$\hat{\beta} = \left\{ \hat{J}_{xx} \;\; \hat{J}_{xy} \;\; \hat{J}_{xz} \;\; \hat{J}_{yy} \;\; \hat{J}_{yz} \;\; \hat{J}_{zz} \right\}^T = [\Phi]_d\left([\Phi]_d{}^T[\Phi]_d\right)^{-1}[\Phi]_d\tau \tag{21}$$

Table 4. Table of proximal variables and nomenclature [1].

Variable/Acronym	Definition	Variable/Acronym	Definition
$[\omega_x]_d$	Desire angular velocity about $\hat{x}$	$[\dot{\omega}_x]_d$	Desire angular acceleration about $\hat{x}$
$[\omega_y]_d$	Desire angular velocity about $\hat{y}$	$[\dot{\omega}_y]_d$	Desire angular acceleration about $\hat{y}$
$[\omega_z]_d$	Desire angular velocity about $\hat{z}$	$[\dot{\omega}_z]_d$	Desire angular acceleration about $\hat{z}$
$[\Phi] = \Phi$	Regression matrix of sensor data	$[\Phi]_d = \Phi_d$	Regression matrix of desired states
β	Unknown predicted variables	$\hat{\beta}$	Estimated variables
τ	Total control torque signal	τ_{ff}	Feedforward control signal
$\hat{J}_{xx}$	Estimated moment of inertia about $\hat{x}$	$\hat{J}_{xy} = \hat{J}_{yx}$	Estimated $\hat{x}\hat{y}$ inertia product
$\hat{J}_{yy}$	Estimated moment of inertia about $\hat{y}$	$\hat{J}_{xz} = \hat{J}_{zx}$	Estimated $\hat{x}\hat{z}$ inertia product
$\hat{J}_{zz}$	Estimated moment of inertia about $\hat{z}$	$\hat{J}_{yz} = \hat{J}_{zy}$	Estimated $\hat{y}\hat{z}$ inertia product

[1] Such tables are offered throughout the manuscript to aid readability.

$$\boxed{Analysis} \rightarrow \boxed{Simulation\ verification} \rightarrow \boxed{Experimental\ validation} \tag{22}$$

As reminded by Equation (22), following the analysis, modeling and simulation preface experimental validating spaceflight tests. Figure 5 contains a top level topology of spacecraft guidance and control, where this study focuses exclusively on the rotational mechanics subsystems. This topology is provided by the very simulation used to verify the analysis. Within the subsystem labeled "Controllers", novel subsystems are created to estimate and to learn the inertia components (displayed in Figure 6), while the mass center location is simulated in the attitude control system displayed in Figure 7, where nomenclature is conveniently defined in Table 5.

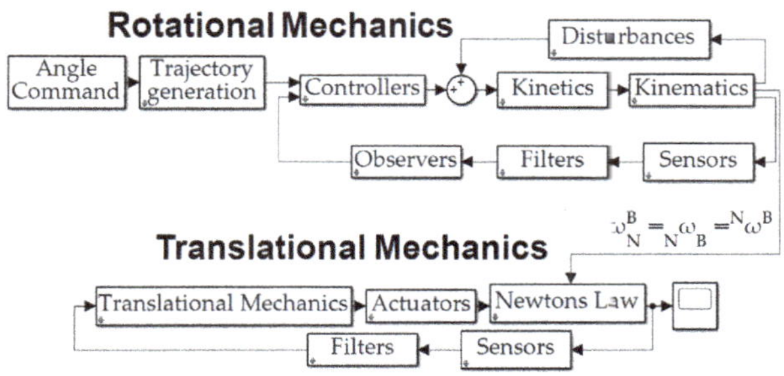

Figure 5. Top level topology of spacecraft guidance and control. More detailed elaboration of modeling and simulation may be found in [29,30].

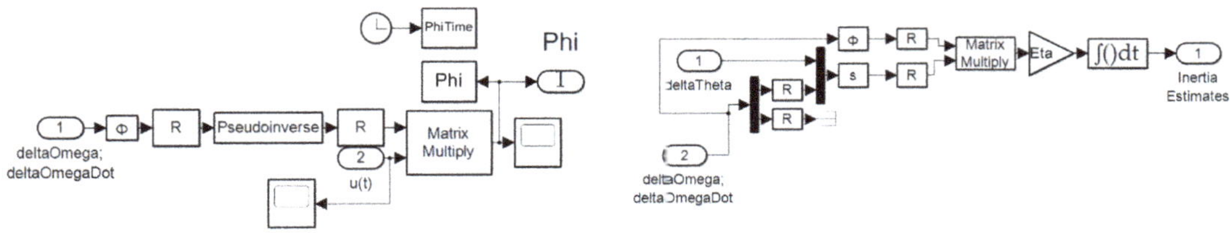

(**a**) (**b**)

Figure 6. Inertia matrix component identification schemes. (**a**) Learning feedback inertia matrix estimator elaborated in Equation (21) [32]; (**b**) nonlinear adaptive inertia estimation scheme in accordance with Equation (17).

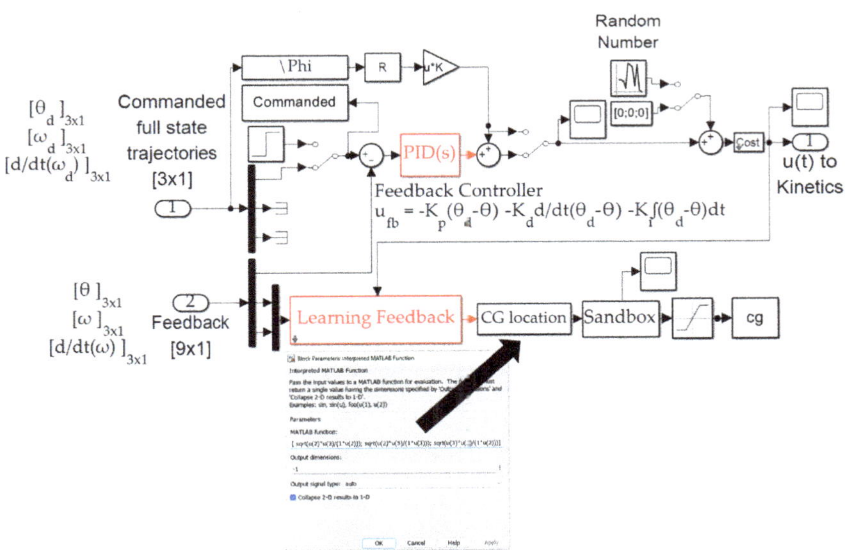

Figure 7. Attitude determination and control system simulated in MATLAB®/SIMULINK®.

Table 5. Table of proximal variables and nomenclature [1].

Variable/Acronym	Definition	Variable/Acronym	Definition
$[\theta_d]$	Desired angular state vector	$[\theta]$	Angular state vector
$[\omega_d]$	Desired angular velocity vector	$[\omega]$	Angular velocity vector
$\left[\frac{d}{dt}(\omega_d)\right]$	Desired angular acceleration vector	$\left[\frac{d}{dt}(\omega)\right]$	Angular acceleration vector
u_{fb}	Feedback control	K_i	Integral gain
K_p	Proportional gain	K_d	Derivative gain

[1] Such tables are offered throughout the manuscript to aid readability.

2.4. Implementation Procedure

Substantial modeling and simulations are performed and presented in references [29,30], where a very brief summary of key findings is presented in Section 3. The review of modeling and simulation results serves as a preface to the spaceflight experiments.

3. Results

This section presents the on-orbit experimental results after reviewing the key findings from modeling and simulation. The computational models that analyzed the data are depicted in Appendix A. Section 3.1 includes the key modeling and simulation results, while Section 3.2 includes the key results from spaceflight experiments, including mass inertia identification and center of mass auto-location. Figure 8 displays the spacecraft mounted in a rideshare stack on the launch vehicle and the 2023 launch to space.

(**a**) (**b**)

Figure 8. Source of known torques $\left\{\tau_x \quad \tau_y \quad \tau_z\right\}^T$ in Equation (16); onboard set of three reaction wheels. (**a**) XVI (depicted in Figures 1 and 3) spacecraft stacked in a rideshare mission [32]; credit: SpaceX. (**b**) XVI in the Transporter-8 rideshare mission launched on board a Falcon 9 on 12 June 2023 [33]. Image credit: SpaceX webcast.

3.1. Key Results from Modeling and Simulation

Estimated products of inertia are fed to Equation (12) to determine the location of the center of gravity (i.e., center of mass), where the inertia products may alternatively be estimated by nonlinear adaptive estimation (Equation (17)) or by two-norm optimal projection learning (Equation (21)), respectively, in Sections 3.1.1 and 3.1.2. To aid repeatability,

SIMULINK® systems and subsystems, and MATLAB® line code used in the SIMULINK® callbacks are provided in this Appendix A.

3.1.1. Center of Gravity Auto-Location by Nonlinear Adaption

Auto-location adaption is apparent twice in Figure 9 in response to the single axis rotational slew maneuver. The estimated location migrates roughly 0.15, 0.1 $\pm$0.02, and 0.225 m, respectively, in the $\hat{x}$, $\hat{y}$, and $\hat{z}$ directions, and then migration completely stops when the excitation of the maneuver ends. In particular, notice the location does not converge to an identifiable place during the maneuver, and the results may be deemed as unsuccessful.

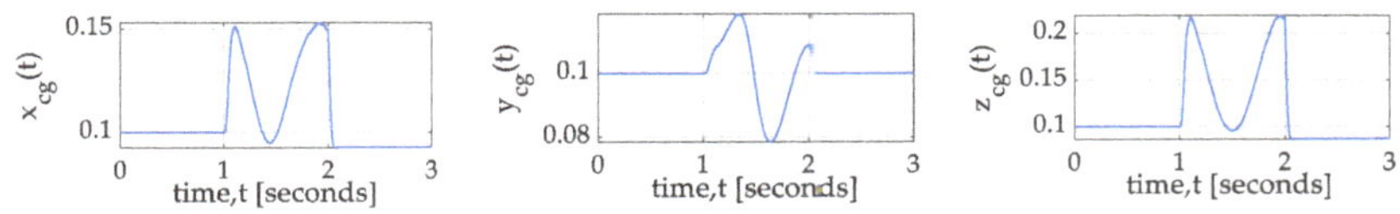

(**a**) (**b**) (**c**)

Figure 9. Center of gravity auto-location using nonlinear adaption: for a single thirty-degree yaw maneuver with coupled motion in roll and pitch, where the command has white noise added to aid persistent excitation (**a**) x coordinate [meters]; (**b**) y coordinate [meters]; (**c**) z coordinate [meters].

3.1.2. Center of Gravity Auto-Location by Nonlinear Projection-Based Regression Learning

Auto-location adaption is apparent only once in Figure 10 in response to the single axis rotational slew maneuver. The estimated location converges to roughly 0.2529 m aft ($\hat{x}$), 0.4927 m less in $\hat{y}$, and 0.225 m up in $\hat{z}$. Since the simulated mass center location is known, in particular, notice that the location converges to an identifiable place very quickly after maneuver initiation, and the results may be deemed successful.

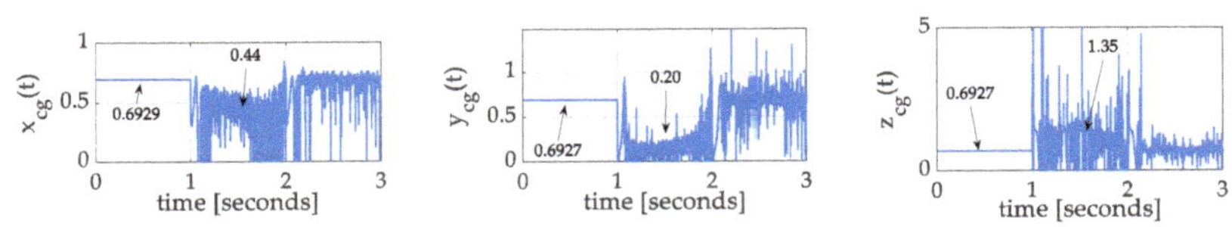

(**a**) (**b**) (**c**)

Figure 10. Center of gravity auto-location using projection regression-based learning. The location rapidly converges to an approximate place during maneuvering and then convergence ends when the maneuver is complete, lacking persistent excitation. (**a**) x coordinate [meters]; (**b**) y coordinate [meters]; (**c**) z coordinate [meters].

3.2. Key Results from Spaceflight Experiments Flown on 20 December 2024

Much like the recent validation of inertia identification in space studied by Nocerino, et al. [34], the methods presented here are similarly validating with spaceflight experiments flown in December of 2024. Key results are first presented with rate data from the onboard sensors during the spaceflight test. Next, wheel torques and quaternion (relative to an earth centered inertial coordinate system) data provided by the satellite operators are presented together with attitude angles produced by mathematical analysis of rate data, assuming a 3–2–1 rotation sequence. Such a sequence expresses the rotation angle as a yaw rotation about the inertial $\hat{z}$ axis followed by a pitch rotation about an intermediate $\hat{y}$ axis (between the inertial and body frames), and then, finally, a roll rotation about the body $\hat{x}$ axis.

Figure 11a presents the angular rates and quaternions, while Figure 12 provides different displays of Euler angles.

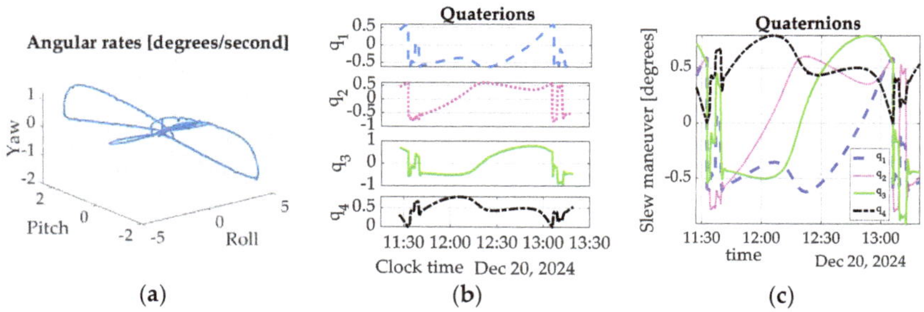

Figure 11. Angular rates, quaternions, and Euler angles in degrees versus time in seconds: (**a**) three separate plots for roll, pitch, and yaw torques; (**b**) quaternions versus time (**c**), quaternions versus time, Euler angles versus time.

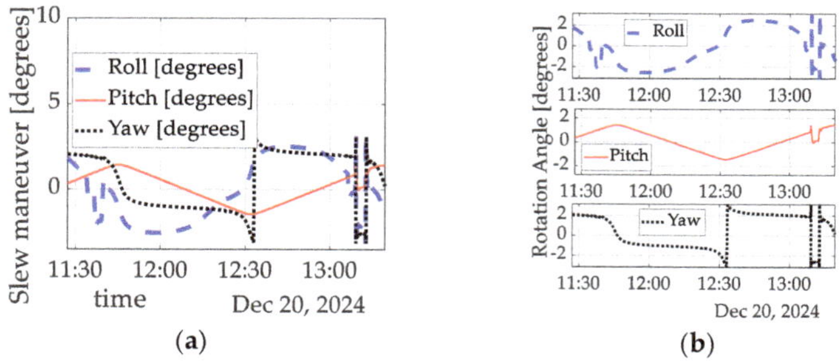

Figure 12. Euler angles in degrees versus time in seconds: (**a**) Euler angles versus time; (**b**) three separate plots for roll, pitch, and yaw angles.

3.3. Inertia Auto-Identification

Figure 13 displays the roll, pitch, and yaw angle estimation errors achieved by the nonlinear enhanced Luenberger observers. The observers are chosen to leverage their rapid field-tunable nature. Notice the limited estimation accuracy achieved by the rapid field tuning of observer gains that might potentially limit the eventual convergence of the auto-location algorithm, which is elaborated in Section 3.4. Impacts on intermediate quantities (estimated mass moments and products of inertia) are seemingly only mildly affected, as displayed in Figure 14.

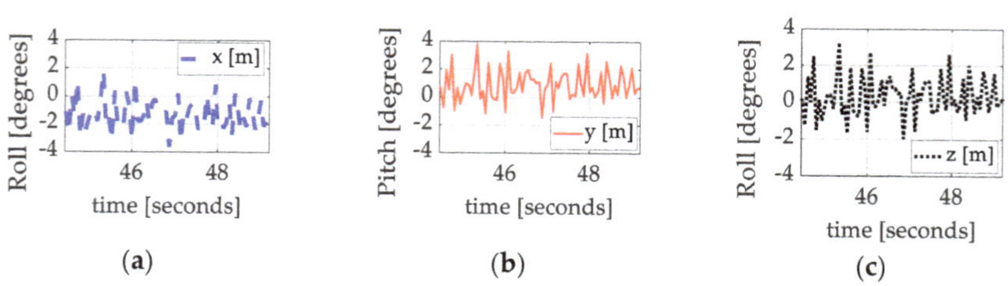

Figure 13. Luenberger state estimation errors (**a**) *roll* angle; (**b**) *pitch* angle; (**c**) *z* angle.

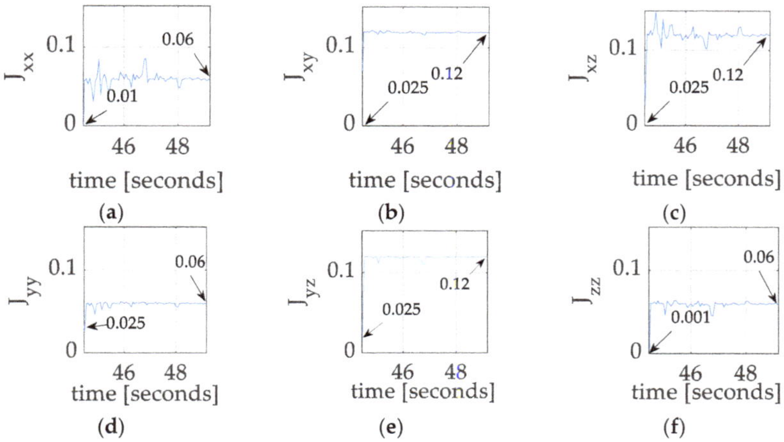

Figure 14. Nonlinear adaption time-varying mass moment of inertia values for space experiment flown 20 December 2024. (**a**) J_{xx}; (**b**) J_{xy}; (**c**) J_{xz}; (**d**) J_{yy}; (**e**) J_{yz}; (**f**) J_{zz}.

3.4. Center of Mass Location Auto-Location

Inertia estimation by nonlinear adaption and by nonlinear projection-based regression learning is calculated using Equation (17) and Equation (21), respectively. Using those estimates, the location of the center of mass is found by Equation (12). The location using nonlinear adaption is displayed in Figure 15, while the location using nonlinear projection-based regression learning is displayed in Figure 16.

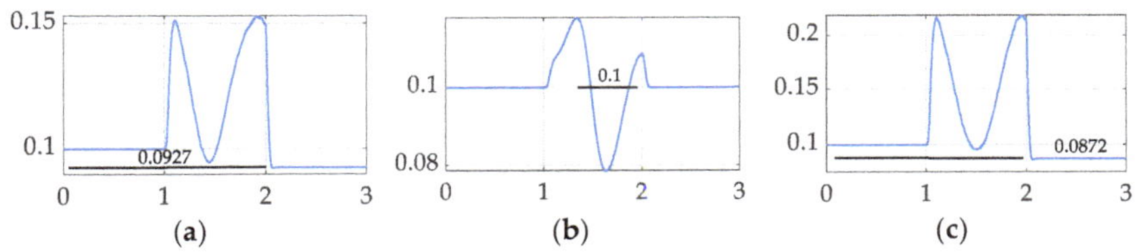

Figure 15. Nonlinear adaption time-varying location of the center of mass for space experiment flown 20 December 2024. (**a**) x coordinate; (**b**) y coordinate; (**c**) z coordinate.

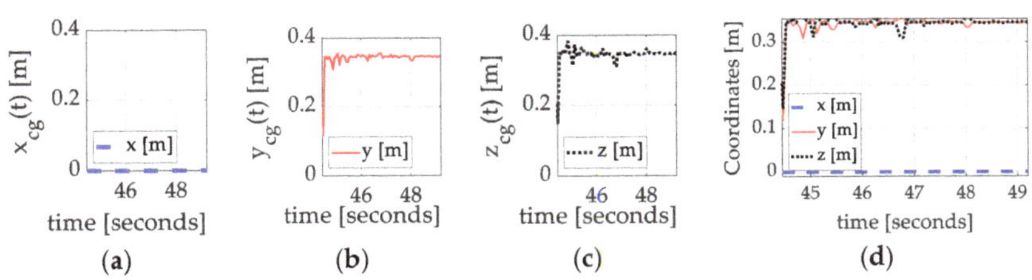

Figure 16. Projection regression-based learning time-varying location of the center of mass for space experiment flown 20 December 2024. (**a**) x coordinate; (**b**) y coordinate converges to 34.80 cm; (**c**) z coordinate converges to 34.39 cm; (**d**) combined three-axis display of initial space test experiment.

As a reminder of the results of modeling and simulation from [29,30], Figure 15 illustrates the relative ineffectiveness of nonlinear adaption to auto-locate the center of gravity. The algorithm indeed quickly diverges from the initially estimated location; however, it does not consistently converge to a new (presumably correct) location. Instead, it oscillates inconsistently, which is a ubiquitous feature of nonlinear adaption, where parameters are adjusted based on the M.I.T. rule [35].

Figure 16 displays the results of space experiments flown 20 December 2024 using projection regression-based learning time-varying location of the center of mass. According to Figure 16a, the mass about the $\hat{x}$ axis is seemingly well balanced. Meanwhile, the mass about the $\hat{y}$ axis is quite off-balance according to Figure 16b, and the learned location converges to 34.80 cm. Similarly, the mass about the $\hat{z}$ axis is quite off-balance according to Figure 16c, and the learned location converges to 34.39 cm. Two subsequent validating experiments are executed, and the converged values of mass center location are essentially identical to the initial experimental results.

4. Discussion

The study results confirmed the roll axis was probably well aligned, while the other two axes had erroneous mass and inertia distribution assumptions. The rapidly convergent mass center coordinates oscillated slightly before final convergence. The use of nonlinear enhanced Luenberger observers should be the source of such slight oscillations. The observers are classical control forms that ubiquitously induce oscillatory settling. The oscillations were most pronounced in the output of the observers (state estimates), relatively ameliorated in the subsequent inertia estimation, and even further ameliorated in the location estimates. The convergent inertia estimation indicates potential efficacy responding to grappling objects of unknown mass and inertia properties and possible mass gain and loss due to collisions in space.

The original problem statement described how inertia moments were proposed to be estimated in space during maneuvering operations rather than on the ground, while the estimation of inertia products would be performed using the introduced parameterization of the location of the mass center using the parallel axis theorem. Estimation of the time-varying inertia properties thereby leads to the auto-location of the spacecraft's center of mass. The original research objectives were illustrated by using only empirical attitude angle knowledge to find imbalanced inertia components and then convert that mass imbalance to center of gravity coordinates. Auto-location of the center of gravity was seminally illustrated with estimation convergence improvements over the comparative state-of-the-art benchmark. Improvements achieved included great convergence that was also faster, i.e., from millimeter convergence over hundreds of days to hundreds of millimeters in minutes achieved in this study. Unexpectedly, relatively poor motion state estimation was used to nonetheless produce rapid accurate estimation of the location of the mass center.

Future Research Directions

Recommended future research is conveniently tabularized below, with sub-tabularized rationale, purpose served, and expected outcomes:

1. Enhance Luenberger observer tuning for improved accuracy.
    a. Rationale: Figure 13 reveals poor state estimation errors that nonetheless led to precise estimation of inertia components and mass center location. Very recent attempts to repeat these experiments produced similar results, but subsequent experiments on a different spacecraft (seeking generalizability) did not produce good inertia estimation or mass center location estimation. Since all other aspects of the proposed method are analytic, the remaining potential cause of the loss of estimation performance is the relatively poor state estimation.
    b. Purpose served: continue to seek generalizable application to any spacecraft.
    c. Expected outcomes: improved inertia estimation should lead to robust gravity center estimation.
2. Empirical validation of these initial results.

   a. Rationale: experimental validation of analytic and simulation results necessitate repeatability and generalizability.
   b. Purpose served: expand the applicability of the proposed methods.
   c. Expected outcomes: increased inertia estimation accuracy should improve the inputs to (12), directly leading to robust mass center location estimation.

3. Grapple with objects of unknown mass.
   a. Rationale: space robotic grappling requires rapid inertia identification and mass center location to update guidance and control systems.
   b. Purpose served: improves stability and accuracy.
   c. Expected outcomes: substantially improves robustness and accuracy.
4. Recover from collision damage with significant mass losses and/or gains.
   a. Rationale: spacecraft that have experienced such collisions need autonomous methods to rapidly update system models to recommence operations.
   b. Purpose served: autonomously recovers from substantial damage.
   c. Expected outcomes: Equation (20) retains utility for control with updated mass center and inertia components.
5. Application of these methods to flexible spacecraft.
   a. Rationale: flexible spacecraft modeling can be more realistic and typically follows rigid body treatments to ascertain whether the higher order modeling is necessary.
   b. Purpose served: potentially increases modeling accuracy.
   c. Expected outcomes: potential increase in grappling ability.
6. Sensitivity analysis how angular velocity cross terms affect the conditioning of the regression matrix.
   a. Rationale: to justify using the higher order model, including the transport theorem cross products, rather than the ubiquitous so-called double integrator model.
   b. Purpose served: potentially ability to use simplified models without increasing model accuracy.
   c. Expected outcomes: potential decrease in computational burden.

Author Contributions: Conceptualization, T.S.; methodology, T.S.; software, E.D., B.E., B.H., J.L., B.M., L.M., J.M., C.P., B.R., J.M. and T.S.; validation, E.D., B.E., B.H., J.L., B.M., L.M., J.M., C.P., B.R., J.M. and T.S.; formal analysis, E.D., B.E., B.H., J.L., B.M., L.M., J.M., C.P., B.R., J.M. and T.S.; investigation, E.D., B.E., B.H., J.L., B.M., L.M., J.M., C.P., B.R., J.M., S.W., J.R., S.C. and T.S.; resources, S.W., J.R. and S.C.; data curation, E.D., B.E., B.H., J.L., B.M., L.M., J.M., C.P., B.R., J.M. and T.S.; writing—original draft preparation, T.S., C.R., S.W. and T.P.; writing—review and editing, T.S. and A.F.; visualization, T.S.; supervision, T.S. and A.F.; project administration, S.W., J.R., S.C. and T.S. All authors have read and agreed to the published version of the manuscript.

Funding: This research received no external funding.

Institutional Review Board Statement: Not applicable for studies not involving humans or animals.

Informed Consent Statement: Not applicable for studies not involving humans.

Data Availability Statement: Data supporting reported results can be obtained by contacting the corresponding author.

Acknowledgments: The deterministic artificial intelligence methods used in Section 2.3.3 were inspired by theoretical proposals from the U.S. Air Force Institute of Technology (for nonlinear chaotic circuits), the U.S. Naval Postgraduate School (for rotational mechanics), and Cornell University (for chaotic Lorenz systems, amongst others).

Conflicts of Interest: The authors declare no conflicts of interest.

Appendix A

To aid repeatability, SIMULINK® systems and subsystems, and MATLAB® line code used in the SIMULINK® callbacks are provided in this appendix. Figure A1 displays the highest level topology, where "Spaceflight Data" is the input of rotation angles and optional actual applied torques. The "CG location" subsystem implements Equation (12). Figure A2 displays the nonlinear enhanced Luenberger observer, where the nonlinear label indicates inclusion of the cross products to create the estimated torque. Figure A3 displays the SIMULINK® system used to convert estimates of angular velocities and accelerations into estimates of inertia values (both inertia moments and products). Figure A4 displays an optional torque estimator constructed in SIMULINK® in case actual torque values are not available. Estimated angular velocities and accelerations are combined in accordance with Euler's moment equations to produce applied torque estimates.

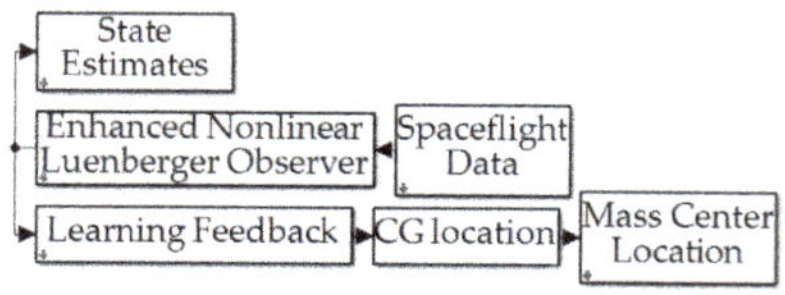

Figure A1. Top level system topology constructed in SIMULINK®.

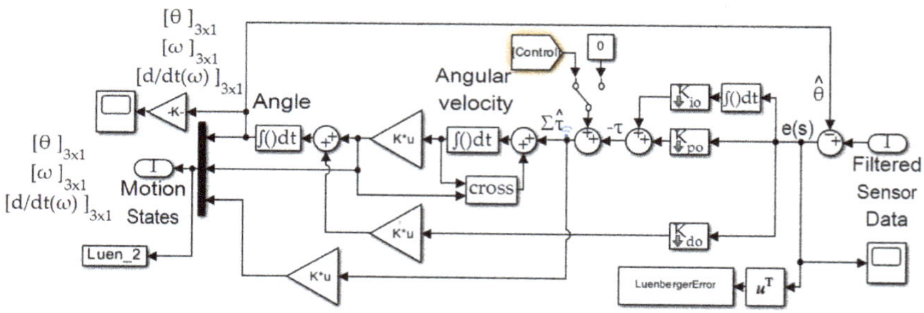

Figure A2. Nonlinear enhanced Luenberger observer system built in SIMULINK®. The estimator accepts as input angle-only data from spaceflight experiments and output estimates of angles, angular rates, angular accelerations, and torques. The three gains are tuned seeking "unity gain", where the ratio of input angles and output estimated angles is unity. Observer gains K_{po}, K_{do}, K_{io} are manually tuned using so-called classical controls rules: proportional gain K_{po} is increased to generate estimate movement towards the true values; derivative gain K_{do} is increased to decrease estimate overshoot; and integral gain K_{io} is increased very slightly to yield zero steady-state errors (when converged).

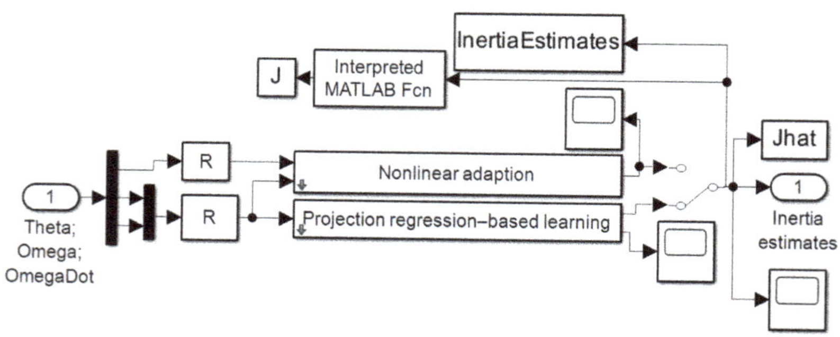

Figure A3. SIMULINK® system used to convert input estimates of angular velocities and accelerations into output estimates of inertia values (both inertia moments and products).

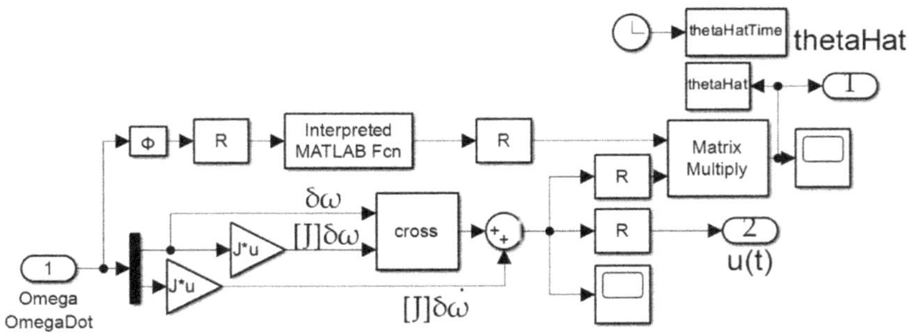

Figure A4. Optional torque estimator constructed in SIMULINK® in case actual torque values are not available. Estimated angular velocities and accelerations are combined in accordance with Euler's moment equations to produce applied torque estimates.

Appendix A.1. Simulink Start Function Callbacks

```
clear all; close all; clc;
Data = readtable('Quaternions'); %%% Open angular rate table and separate data into new
chacter vectors %%%
Torques = readtable('CommandedWheelTorque');
mass = 1; %SV mass in kg
stoptime = max(size(Data));
timestep = 1%1/stoptime;
Time = Data(:,1); time = table2array(Time); [Hour,Minute,Second] = hms(time); [Year,Month,
Day] = ymd(time);
q1 = Data(:,2); q1 = table2array(q1);
q2 = Data(:,3); q2 = table2array(q2);
q3 = Data(:,4); q3 = table2array(q3);
q4 = Data(:,5); q4 = table2array(q4);
Quaternion = [q1 q2 q3 q4]; dcm = quat2dcm(Quaternion); eulerAngles = quat2eul
(Quaternion,'ZYX');
roll = eulerAngles(:,1); pitch = eulerAngles(:,2); yaw = eulerAngles(:,3);
torque1 = Torques(:,2); torque1 = table2array(torque1);
torque2 = Torques(:,3); torque2 = table2array(torque2);
torque3 = Torques(:,4); torque3 = table2array(torque3);
tau1 = regexp(torque1,'\d+(\.)?(\d+)?','match'); out = strjoin([tau1{:}],'');
tau2 = regexp(torque2,'\d+(\.)?(\d+)?','match'); out = strjoin([tau2{:}],'');
tau3 = regexp(torque3,'\d+(\.)?(\d+)?','match'); out = strjoin([tau3{:}],'');
lambda = 10; Eta = 1;
J = 0.1.*ones(3);
Ko = [0.01; 0.1; 0.001];
Ko = [0.01; 0.1; 0.001];
Kpo = Ko(1); Kdo = Ko(2); Kio = Ko(3);
%figure(1);
%subplot(3,1,1); plot(time,torque1,'--','linewidth',3); grid; %axis([0 5863 -0.75 0.75]);
%       set(gca,'FontName','Palatino Linotype','FontSize',24,'xtick',[]); set(text,'Color','k');
%       ylabel('\tau_x','FontName','Palatino Linotype','FontSize',24);
%       title('Quaterions','FontName','Palatino Linotype','FontSize',24);
% subplot(3,1,2); plot(time,torque1,'m:','linewidth',3); grid; %axis([0 5863 -1 0.75]);
%       set(gca,'FontName','Palatino Linotype','FontSize',24,'xtick',[]); set(text,'Color','k');
%       ylabel('\tau_y','FontName','Palatino Linotype','FontSize',24);
```

```
% subplot(3,1,3); plot(time,torque1,'g','linewidth',3); grid; %axis([0 5863 -1 1]);
%      set(gca,'FontName','Palatino Linotype','FontSize',24,'xtick',[]); set(text,'Color','k');
%      ylabel('\tau_z','FontName','Palatino Linotype','FontSize',24);
%      xlabel('Clock time','FontName','Palatino Linotype','FontSize',24);
figure(2);
 subplot(4,1,1); plot(time,q1,'--','linewidth',3); grid; %axis([0 5863 -0.75 0.75]);
     set(gca,'FontName','Palatino Linotype','FontSize',24,'xtick',[]); set(text,'Color','k');
     ylabel('q_1','FontName','Palatino Linotype','FontSize',24);
     title('Quaterions','FontName','Palatino Linotype','FontSize',24);
 subplot(4,1,2); plot(time,q2,'m:','linewidth',3); grid; %axis([0 5863 -1 0.75]);
     set(gca,'FontName','Palatino Linotype','FontSize',24,'xtick',[]); set(text,'Color','k');
     ylabel('q_2','FontName','Palatino Linotype','FontSize',24);
 subplot(4,1,3); plot(time,q3,'g','linewidth',3); grid; %axis([0 5863 -1 1]);
     set(gca,'FontName','Palatino Linotype','FontSize',24,'xtick',[]); set(text,'Color','k');
     ylabel('q_3','FontName','Palatino Linotype','FontSize',24);
 subplot(4,1,4); plot(time,q4,'k-.','linewidth',3); grid; %axis([0 5863 0 0.7]);
     set(gca,'FontName','Palatino Linotype','FontSize',24); set(text,'Color','k');
     ylabel('q_4','FontName','Palatino Linotype','FontSize',24);
     xlabel('Clock time','FontName','Palatino Linotype','FontSize',24);
figure(3);
plot(time,q1,'--b','LineWidth',4); axis tight; hold on;
plot(time,q2,'m:','LineWidth',2); axis tight;
plot(time,q3,'g','LineWidth',3); axis tight;
plot(time,q4,'k-.','LineWidth',3); axis tight;
xlabel('time','FontName','Palatino Linotype','FontSize',24);
ylabel('Slew maneuver [degrees]','FontName','Palatino Linotype','FontSize',24);
title('Quaternions','FontName','Palatino Linotype','FontSize',24)
set(gca,'FontName','Palatino Linotype','FontSize',24); set(text,'Color','k');
legend('q_1','q_2','q_3','q_4', 'location',' North')
hold off; grid;
 figure(4);
 plot3(roll, pitch, yaw,'linewidth',3); grid;
 xlabel('Roll','FontName','Palatino Linotype','FontSize',24);
 ylabel('Pitch','FontName','Palatino Linotype','FontSize',24);
 zlabel('Yaw','FontName','Palatino Linotype','FontSize',24);
 title('Euler Angles [degrees]','FontName','Palatino Linotype','FontSize',24);
 set(gca,'FontName','Palatino Linotype','FontSize',24); set(text,'Color','k');
 figure(5);
 plot(time,eulerAngles(:,1),'--b','LineWidth',4); axis tight; hold on;
 plot(time,eulerAngles(:,2),'r','LineWidth',2); axis tight;
 plot(time,eulerAngles(:,3),':k','LineWidth',3); axis tight;
 xlabel('time','FontName','Palatino Linotype','FontSize',24);
 ylabel('Slew maneuver [degrees]','FontName','Palatino Linotype','FontSize',24);
 title('Slew Maneuver','FontName','Palatino Linotype','FontSize',24)
 set(gca,'FontName','Palatino Linotype','FontSize',24); set(text,'Color','k');
 legend('Roll [degrees]','Pitch [degrees]','Yaw [degrees]','location',' North')
 hold off; grid;
 figure(6);
 subplot(3,1,1); plot(time,eulerAngles(:,1),'--b','LineWidth',4); axis tight;
    title('Slew Maneuver','FontName','Palatino Linotype','FontSize',24)
```

```
legend('Roll','location','SouthWest'); grid;
set(gca,'FontName','Palatino Linotype','FontSize',24); set(text,'Color','k');
subplot(3,1,2); plot(time,eulerAngles(:,2),'r','LineWidth',2); axis tight;
ylabel('Angle [degrees]','FontName','Palatino Linotype','FontSize',24);
legend('Pitch','location','SouthWest'); grid;
set(gca,'FontName','Palatino Linotype','FontSize',24); set(text,'Color','k');
subplot(3,1,3); plot(time,eulerAngles(:,3),':k','LineWidth',3); axis tight;
legend('Yaw','location','SouthWest'); grid;
xlabel('time','FontName','Palatino Linotype','FontSize',24);
set(gca,'FontName','Palatino Linotype','FontSize',24); set(text,'Color','k');
xlabel('time','FontName','Palatino Linotype','FontSize',24);
set(gca,'FontName','Palatino Linotype','FontSize',24); set(text,'Color','k');
```

Appendix A.2. Simulink Stop Function Callbacks

```
InertiaEstimates = squeeze(InertiaEstimates); InertiaEstimates = InertiaEstimates';
Jhat = squeeze(Jhat); Jhat = Jhat';
StateEstimates = squeeze(StateEstimates); StateEstimates = StateEstimates';
Luen_2 = squeeze(Luen_2); Luen_2 = Luen_2';
figure(7);
thetaHat = squeeze(thetaHat);thetaHat = thetaHat';
    set(gca,'FontName','Palatino Linotype','FontSize',24); set(text,'Color','k');
subplot(2,3,1); plot(tout./15,thetaHat(:,1)); grid;
    set(gca,'FontName','Palatino Linotype','FontSize',24); set(text,'Color','k');
    xlabel('time [seconds]','FontName','Palatino Linotype','FontSize',24);
    ylabel('J_x_x','FontName','Palatino Linotype','FontSize',24);
    %axis([44.45 49.2 0 0.152]);
subplot(2,3,2); plot(tout./15,thetaHat(:,2)); grid;
    set(gca,'FontName','Palatino Linotype','FontSize',24); set(text,'Color','k');
    xlabel('time [seconds]','FontName','Palatino Linotype','FontSize',24);
    ylabel('J_x_y','FontName','Palatino Linotype','FontSize',24);
    %axis([44.45 49.2 0 0.152]);
subplot(2,3,3); plot(tout./15,thetaHat(:,3)); grid;
    set(gca,'FontName','Palatino Linotype','FontSize',24); set(text,'Color','k');
    xlabel('time [seconds]','FontName','Palatino Linotype','FontSize',24);
    ylabel('J_x_z','FontName','Palatino Linotype','FontSize',24);
    %axis([44.45 49.2 0 0.152]);
subplot(2,3,4); plot(tout./15,thetaHat(:,4)); grid;
    set(gca,'FontName','Palatino Linotype','FontSize',24); set(text,'Color','k');
    xlabel('time [seconds]','FontName','Palatino Linotype','FontSize',24);
    ylabel('J_y_y','FontName','Palatino Linotype','FontSize',24);
    %axis([44.45 49.2 0 0.152]);
subplot(2,3,5); plot(tout./15,thetaHat(:,5)); grid;
    set(gca,'FontName','Palatino Linotype','FontSize',24); set(text,'Color','k');
    xlabel('time [seconds]','FontName','Palatino Linotype','FontSize',24);
    ylabel('J_y_z','FontName','Palatino Linotype','FontSize',24);
    %axis([44.45 49.2 0 0.152]);
subplot(2,3,6); plot(tout./15,thetaHat(:,6)); grid;
    set(gca,'FontName','Palatino Linotype','FontSize',24); set(text,'Color','k');
    xlabel('time [seconds]','FontName','Palatino Linotype','FontSize',24);
    ylabel('J_z_z','FontName','Palatino Linotype','FontSize',24);
```

```
    %axis([44.45 49.2 0 0.152]);
figure(8);
plot(tout./15,cg(:,1),'--b','LineWidth',4); axis tight; hold on;
plot(tout./15,cg(:,2),'r','LineWidth',2); axis tight;
plot(tout./15,cg(:,3),':k','LineWidth',3); axis tight;
xlabel('time [seconds]','FontName','Palatino Linotype','FontSize',24);
ylabel('Coordinates [m]','FontName','Palatino Linotype','FontSize',24);
%axis([44.45 49.2 0 0.355]);
title('Center of mass location','FontName','Palatino Linotype','FontSize',24)
set(gca,'FontName','Palatino Linotype','FontSize',24); set(text,'Color','k');
legend('x [m]','y [m]','z [m]','location','SouthWest')
hold off; grid;
figure(9);
title('Center of mass location','FontName','Palatino Linotype','FontSize',24);
subplot(3,1,1); plot(tout./15,cg(:,1),'--b','LineWidth',4); axis tight; hold on;
    title('CG location','FontName','Palatino Linotype','FontSize',24)
    ylabel('x_c_g(t) [m]','FontName','Palatino Linotype','FontSize',24);
    legend('x [m]','location','SouthWest'); grid;
    xlabel('time [seconds]','FontName','Palatino Linotype','FontSize',24);
    set(gca,'FontName','Palatino Linotype','FontSize',24); set(text,'Color','k');
    %axis([44.45 49.2 0 0.4]);
subplot(3,1,2); plot(tout./15,cg(:,2),'r','LineWidth',4); axis tight;
    ylabel('y_c_g(t) [m]','FontName','Palatino Linotype','FontSize',24);
    legend('y [m]','location','SouthWest'); grid;
    xlabel('time [seconds]','FontName','Palatino Linotype','FontSize',24);
    set(gca,'FontName','Palatino Linotype','FontSize',24); set(text,'Color','k');
    %axis([44.45 49.2 0 0.4]);
subplot(3,1,3); plot(tout./15,cg(:,3),':k','LineWidth',4); axis tight;
    legend('z [m]','location','SouthWest'); grid;
    ylabel('z_c_g(t) [m]','FontName','Palatino Linotype','FontSize',24);
    xlabel('time [seconds]','FontName','Palatino Linotype','FontSize',24);
    set(gca,'FontName','Palatino Linotype','FontSize',24); set(text,'Color','k');
    %axis([44.45 49.2 0 0.4]);
    hold off;
figure(10);
subplot(3,1,1); plot(tout./15,LuenbergerError(:,1),'--b','LineWidth',4); axis tight; hold on;
    ylabel('Roll [degrees]','FontName','Palatino Linotype','FontSize',24);
    legend('x [m]','location','SouthWest'); grid;
    set(gca,'FontName','Palatino Linotype','FontSize',24); set(text,'Color','k');
    title('Luenberger Estimator Errors','FontName','Palatino Linotype','FontSize',24)
    xlabel('time [seconds]','FontName','Palatino Linotype','FontSize',24);
    %axis([44.45 49.2 -4 4]);
subplot(3,1,2); plot(tout./15,LuenbergerError(:,2),'r','LineWidth',2); axis tight;
    ylabel('Pitch [degrees]','FontName','Palatino Linotype','FontSize',24);
    legend('y [m]','location','SouthWest'); grid;
    set(gca,'FontName','Palatino Linotype','FontSize',24); set(text,'Color','k');
    xlabel('time [seconds]','FontName','Palatino Linotype','FontSize',24);
    %axis([44.45 49.2 -4 4]);
subplot(3,1,3); plot(tout./15,LuenbergerError(:,3),':k','LineWidth',3); axis tight;
    ylabel('Roll [degrees]','FontName','Palatino Linotype','FontSize',24);
```

```
legend('z [m]','location','SouthWest'); grid;
xlabel('time','FontName','Palatino Linotype','FontSize',24);
set(gca,'FontName','Palatino Linotype','FontSize',24); set(text,'Color','k');
xlabel('time [seconds]','FontName','Palatino Linotype','FontSize',24);
%axis([44.45 49.2 -4 4]);
hold off;
```

Appendix B

This appendix contains a summary table of variables and nomenclature used throughout the manuscript. While proximal tables are provided throughout the manuscript, inclusion of one large summary table is provided for the convenience of the readership.

Table A1. Table of proximal variables and nomenclature [1].

Variable/Acronym	Definition
H_{cm}	Centroidal angular momentum
$r_{dm,i}$	Radius vector to differential mass, i
m_i	Differential mass, i
ω	Angular velocity vector
$\{\omega\} \equiv \{\omega_x \quad \omega_y \quad \omega_z\}^T$	Angular velocity [radians/second]
$\hat{x}_B, \hat{y}_B, \hat{z}_B$	Unit vectors
x, y, z	Positional coordinates
$J_y = J_O$	Inertia moment about a fixed axis O along y
J_{cm}	Inertia moment about the mass center
M	Total system mass
R_O	Distance from O to the mass center
R_y	Distance to axis y
O	Fixed axis along axis y
A, B, C	Dummy variables
r_i	Radius vector to point i
dm	Differential mass
$v_{dm,i}$	Velocity vector of differential mass, i
J_{xx}, J_{yy}, J_{zz}	Moments of inertia
$J_{xy}, J_{yx}, J_{yz}, J_{zy}, J_{xz}, J_{zx}$	Products of inertia
$[J]$	Moment of inertia matrix
y	Robot arm base parallel axis
$\hat{y}$	Body center parallel axis
r_{iO}	Radius from parallel axis (not mass center)
r_i	Radius vector to the mass center
m_i	Differential mass element
(x_i, y_i)	Center of mass coordinates
a	x coordinate of O
b	y coordinate of O
$[\theta_d]$	Desired angular state vector
$[\omega_d]$	Desired angular velocity vector
$\left[\frac{d}{dt}(\omega_d)\right]$	Desired angular acceleration vector
u_{fb}	Feedback control
K_p	Proportional gain
$[\theta]$	Angular state vector
$[\omega]$	Angular velocity vector
$\left[\frac{d}{dt}(\omega)\right]$	Angular acceleration vector
K_i	Integral gain
K_d	Derivative gain

[1] Such tables are offered throughout the manuscript to aid readability.

References

1. SDA Gets OK to Begin Limited Testing of Data Satellites Link 16 Nodes. Available online: https://www.sda.mil/sda-gets-ok-to-begin-limited-testing-of-data-satellites-link-16-nodes/ (accessed on 16 December 2024).
2. Department of Defense Photographs and Imagery, Unless Otherwise Noted, Are in the Public Domain. Use of Department of Defense Imagery. Available online: https://www.defense.gov/Contact/Help-Center/Article/Article/2762906/use-of-department-of-defense-imagery/ (accessed on 16 December 2024).
3. Nanosats Database: XVI Satellite. Available online: https://www.nanosats.eu/sat/xvi (accessed on 16 December 2024).
4. Available online: https://www.usna.edu/Users/aero/kang/Research.php#panel3RSatPRoboticArmSatellitePrototype (accessed on 4 February 2025).
5. Wei, X.; Huang, L.; Shen, T.; Cai, Z. Calibration of the in-orbit center-of-mass of TaiJi-1. *arXiv* **2024**, arXiv:2307.01724v2. [CrossRef]
6. Otsubo, T.; Appleby, G. System-dependent center-of-mass correction for spherical geodetic satellites. *J. Geophys. Res.* **2003**, *108*, 2201. [CrossRef]
7. Rodríguez, J.; Appleby, G.; Otsubo, T. Upgraded modelling for the determination of centre of mass corrections of geodetic SLR satellites: Impact on key parameters of the terrestrial reference frame. *J. Geod.* **2019**, *93*, 2553–2568. [CrossRef]
8. Rodríguez, J. *Centre of Mass Corrections Updates for Geodetic Spherical Satellites: Changes in the Latest Releases in Preparation for the Computation of ITRF2020 Products*; Technical Report IT-CDT 2022-11; Yebes Observatory: Yebes, Spain, 22 November 2022.
9. Geosat: U.S. Navy GEOdetic SATellite. Available online: https://science.nasa.gov/mission/geosat/ (accessed on 16 December 2024).
10. NASA Images and Media Usage Guidelines. Available online: https://www.nasa.gov/nasa-brand-center/images-and-media/ (accessed on 16 December 2024).
11. Neubert, R. The Retro-Reflector for the CHAMP Satellite: Final Design and Realization. In Proceedings of the 11th International Laser Ranging Workshop, Deggendorf, Germany, 21–25 September 1988.
12. International Laser Ranging Service: Etalon-1 and -2: Array Offset Information. Available online: https://ilrs.gsfc.nasa.gov/missions/satellite_missions/current_missions/eta1_com.html (accessed on 16 December 2024).
13. International Laser Ranging Service: Galileo: Array Offset Information. Available online: https://ilrs.gsfc.nasa.gov/missions/satellite_missions/current_missions/ga01_com.html (accessed on 16 December 2024).
14. Lemoine, F.; Rowlands, D.; Lillibridge, J.; Smith, W.; Zelensky, N.; Beckley, B.; Chinn, D.; Scharroo, R. Evaluation of the GEOSAT and GEOSAT Follow-On Precise Orbit Ephemeris. In Proceedings of the 2007 Ocean Surface Topography Science Team Meeting, Hobart, Australia, 12–15 March 2007. Available online: https://www.aviso.altimetry.fr/fileadmin/documents/OSTST/2007/lemoine_gfo_pod.pdf (accessed on 16 December 2024).
15. Hernández-Arias, H.; Prado-Molina, J. On-Orbit Center Of Mass Relocation System For a 3U Cubesat. *Int. J. Sci. Technol. Res.* **2018**, *7*, 44–51.
16. Alharam, A.; Albalooshi, A.; Sleptchenko, A. Linear cubesat center of gravity optimization. In Proceedings of the AerospaceEurop Confrence 2021, Warsaw, Poland, 23–26 November 2021.
17. Al-Rawashdeh, Y.M.; Elshafei, M.; Al-Malki, M.F. In-Flight Estimation of Center of Gravity Position Using All-Accelerometers. *Sensors* **2014**, *14*, 17567–17585. [CrossRef] [PubMed]
18. Zhao, X.; Xiao, W. Uncertainty Analysis of Aircraft Center of Gravity Deviation and Passenger Seat Allocation Optimization. *Mathematics* **2024**, *12*, 1591. [CrossRef]
19. Wu, F.; Sun, C.; Li, H.; Zheng, S. Real-Time Center of Gravity Estimation for Intelligent Connected Vehicle Based on HEKF-EKF. *Electronics* **2023**, *12*, 386. [CrossRef]
20. Park, G.; Choi, S.B. An Integrated Observer for Real-Time Estimation of Vehicle Center of Gravity Height. *IEEE Trans. Intell. Transp. Syst.* **2021**, *22*, 5660–5671. [CrossRef]
21. Huang, X.; Wang, J. Real-Time Estimation of Center of Gravity Position for Lightweight Vehicles Using Combined AKF–EKF Method. *IEEE Trans. Veh. Technol.* **2014**, *63*, 4221–4231. [CrossRef]
22. Lin, C.; Gong, X.; Xiong, R.; Cheng, X. A novel H∞ and EKF joint estimation method for determining the center of gravity position of electric vehicles. *Appl. Energy* **2017**, *194*, 609–616. [CrossRef]
23. Fu, Z.; Hu, Q.; Li, B. Adaptive online estimation of centre of gravity height for commercial vehicles. *Int. J. Heavy Veh. Syst.* **2021**, *28*, 206–225. [CrossRef]
24. Han, X.; Li, Z.; Li, H.; Huang, L.; Pang, Y. Variable mass control and parameter identification of spacecraft orbit refueling process. *Math. Prob. Eng.* **2022**, *17*, 9660218. [CrossRef]
25. Gaine Technology. Probabilistic and Deterministic Results in AI Systems. 31 July 2023. Available online: https://www.gaine.com/blog/probabilistic-and-deterministic-results-in-ai-systems (accessed on 11 March 2024).
26. Holubek, R.; Vagaš, M. Center of Gravity Coordinates Estimation Based on an Overall Brightness Average Determined from the 3D Vision System. *Appl. Sci.* **2022**, *12*, 286. [CrossRef]

27. Moulton, B.C.; Hunsaker, D.F. Analytic Solutions for Volume, Mass, Center of Gravity, and Inertia of Wing Segments and Rotors of Constant Density. *Aerospace* **2024**, *11*, 492. [CrossRef]
28. Liu, F.; Su, Z.; Zhao, H.; Li, Q.; Li, C. Attitude Measurement for High-Spinning Projectile with a Hollow MEMS IMU Consisting of Multiple Accelerometers and Gyros. *Sensors* **2019**, *19*, 1799. [CrossRef] [PubMed]
29. Sands, T.; Kim, J.J.; Agrawal, B.N. Spacecraft fine tracking pointing using adaptive control. In Proceedings of the 58th International Astronautical Congress, Hyderabad, India, 24–28 September 2007.
30. Sands, T. Autonomous Real–Time Mass Center Location and Inertia Identification for Grappling Space Robotics. *Technologies* **2025**, *13*, 148. [CrossRef]
31. Adams, G. Arizona State University Physics Department Proof of the Parallel Axis Theorem. Available online: https://www.public.asu.edu/~gbadams/sum00/parallelaxisT.pdf (accessed on 16 December 2024).
32. SatCatalog. Available online: https://www.satcatalog.com/component/rwp050/ (accessed on 16 December 2024).
33. Foust, J. SpaceX Launches Eighth Dedicated Smallsat Rideshare Mission. Available online: https://spacenews.com/spacex-launches-eighth-dedicated-smallsat-rideshare-mission/ (accessed on 11 March 2025).
34. Alessia Nocerino, A.; Opromolla, R.; Fasano, G.; Grassi, M.; Balaguer, P.; John, S.; Cho, H.; Bevilacqua, R. Experimental validation of inertia parameters and attitude estimation of uncooperative space targets using solid state LIDAR. *Acta Astronaut.* **2023**, *210*, 428–436. [CrossRef]
35. Gupta, D.; Kumar, A.; Giri, V. Effect of adaptation gain and reference model in MIT and Lyapunov rule–based model reference adaptive control for first- and second-order systems. *Trans. Inst. Meas. Control* **2024**, *46*, 1635–1654. [CrossRef]

technologies

MDPI

Article

Ground Segmentation for LiDAR Point Clouds in Structured and Unstructured Environments Using a Hybrid Neural–Geometric Approach

Antonio Santo [1,*], Enrique Heredia [1], Carlos Viegas [2], David Valiente [1,*] and Arturo Gil [1,*]

[1] University Institute for Engineering Research, Miguel Hernández University, 03202 Elche, Alicante, Spain; e.heredia@umh.es

[2] Department of Mechanical Engineering, Association for the Development of Industrial Aerodynamics (ADAI), University of Coimbra, Rua Luís Reis Santos, Pólo II, 3030-788 Coimbra, Portugal; carlos.viegas@uc.pt

* Correspondence: a.santo@umh.es (A.S.); dvaliente@umh.es (D.V.); arturo.gil@umh.es (A.G.)

Abstract: Ground segmentation in LiDAR point clouds is a foundational capability for autonomous systems, enabling safe navigation in applications ranging from urban self-driving vehicles to planetary exploration rovers. Reliably distinguishing traversable surfaces in geometrically irregular or sensor-sparse environments remains a critical challenge. This paper introduces a hybrid framework that synergizes multi-resolution polar discretization with sparse convolutional neural networks (SCNNs) to address these challenges. The method hierarchically partitions point clouds into adaptive sectors, leveraging PCA-derived geometric features and dynamic variance thresholds for robust terrain modeling, while a SCNN resolves ambiguities in data-sparse regions. Evaluated in structured (SemanticKITTI) and unstructured (Rellis-3D) environments, two different versions of the proposed method are studied, including a purely geometric method and a hybrid approach that exploits deep learning techniques. A comparison of the proposed method with its purely geometric version is made for the purpose of highlighting the strengths of each approach. The hybrid approach achieves state-of-the-art performance, attaining an F1-score of 95.4% in urban environments, surpassing the purely geometric (91.4%) and learning-based baselines. Conversely, in unstructured terrains, the geometric variant demonstrates superior metric balance (80.8% F1) compared to the hybrid method (75.8% F1), highlighting context-dependent trade-offs between precision and recall. The framework's generalization is further validated on custom datasets (UMH-Gardens, Coimbra-Liv), showcasing robustness to sensor variations and environmental complexity. The code and datasets are openly available to facilitate reproducibility.

Keywords: ground segmentation; LiDAR point clouds; annotation procedure; autonomous navigation; traversability estimation

1. Introduction

In an increasingly complex technological landscape, marked by substantial advances in the field of artificial intelligence (AI) algorithms, the attainment of fully autonomous navigation has emerged as a key challenge. This capability is regarded as a critical enabling technology across a range of domains, including robotics and environmental monitoring. In these domains, the interpretation of terrain through point cloud analysis serves as the foundational element for the development of safe and adaptive navigation systems [1].

Historically, the analysis of ground planes was approached through terrain analysis algorithms based on heuristic methods. These pioneering techniques relied on geometric computations to model ground conditions [2–4]. However, such early frameworks exhibited critical limitations, including limited adaptability to dynamic environments, insufficient robustness under contextual variations, and an over-reliance on predefined rule-based thresholds.

The exponential progress in computational power, sensor technology and AI algorithms has revolutionized ground detection techniques. In this technological transition, LiDAR-based sensing systems have become a fundamental component, offering distinct advantages, including precise measurements, long-range detection capabilities, and resistance to ambient light variations and electromagnetic interference. These developments have given rise to a variety of methodologies for ground plane detection through spatial environmental representations, including two-dimensional occupancy maps [5], digital elevation models (DEMs) [6], and voxel-based 3D occupancy frameworks [7–9]. Ground segmentation in point clouds, however, transcends these conventional approaches, serving as a critical enabler for advanced applications such as road boundary extraction [10,11], target tracking [12], and object detection [13,14].

The complexity of ground segmentation, a task requiring the precise separation of traversable terrain from obstacles in dense and heterogeneous point clouds, coupled with the significant challenges of generating and annotating large-scale datasets for robust algorithm evaluation, forms the core motivation for this research. Current methods struggle to adapt to dynamic environments where sensor noise and geometric irregularities degrade performance, particularly in unstructured terrains. Furthermore, the manual annotation of LiDAR data is still very time-consuming.

The present study proposes a novel LiDAR point cloud ground segmentation method that combines the following two complementary approaches: an advanced geometric analysis and AI techniques. The core innovation lies in a multi-resolution cylindrical space discretization framework, explicitly designed to mitigate the usual sparsity of LiDAR point clouds. This spatial partitioning strategy enables robust terrain characterization, effectively addressing the limitations of conventional segmentation methods that struggle with heterogeneous point distributions. As a complementary methodological component, we introduce a sparse neural network based on TE-NeXt (Traversability Estimation ConvNeXt) [15] that operates in regions where low point density hinders reliable geometric segmentation. This hybrid architecture leverages geometric features for structural coherence while employing learned feature representations to resolve ambiguities in data-sparse zones, thereby achieving comprehensive traversable-terrain separation across diverse environmental conditions.

The integration of geometric analysis and AI techniques introduces a novel paradigm to address the inherent challenges of 3D point cloud traversable terrain segmentation, achieving superior performance in both structured and unstructured environments. In summary, the main contributions of this paper are as follows:

- A novel pipeline that maximizes geometric feature extraction while compensating for information-scarce regions through TE-NeXt [15], enabling robust terrain modeling in sparse point clouds.
- Rigorous benchmarking on structured (SemanticKITTI) and unstructured (Rellis-3D) environments, preserving raw point cloud integrity by evaluating all scene elements without algorithmic modifications or data preprocessing.

- Introduction of novel LiDAR domain adaptation datasets to validate model generalization across sensor configurations and environmental conditions, addressing critical gaps in cross-sensor generalization for ground segmentation.

The remaining sections of the paper are structured as follows: Section 2 outlines the prevailing methodologies employed for addressing ground segmentation. Section 3 presents the proposed method in detail. Then, Section 4 presents the databases on which the performance of the method has been evaluated. The subsequent section (Section 5) provides a comparison of the results of the proposed method with the state of the art. In addition, a qualitative evaluation is provided with data collected by the authors in two very different contexts to validate the adaptation and applicability in real-world environments. Finally, Section 6 presents the conclusions drawn from the study.

2. Related Work

This section introduces the most representative techniques in the context of ground segmentation and traversability analysis. The state of the art has been divided into different parts as follows: Section 2.1 describes probabilistic models for ground segmentation, Section 2.2 provides a detailed exposition of methods based on geometric heuristics, Section 2.3 offers a comprehensive introduction to methods employing visual data, and ultimately, Section 2.4 offers a state-of-the-art overview of methods based on AI techniques.

2.1. Probabilistic Ground Segmentation Models

Probabilistic methods represent a sophisticated approach to terrain analysis, providing a robust framework for dealing with uncertainty in spatial measurements captured by sensors. Thus, Markov Random Fields (MRFs) [16] are considered as one of the main probabilistic methods for the task of ground segmentation. Zhang et al. [17] developed a multi-label MRF in polar coordinates, incorporating local smoothness constraints and slope thresholds to filter obstacles. On the other hand, Huang et al. [18] employed an MRF that operates on local features such as height and gradients between adjacent points.

Among the predominant probabilistic approaches for ground segmentation, Gaussian Process Regression (GPR) [19] is distinguished by its unique approach to deriving probabilistic estimations through continuous surface modeling, compared to discrete grid-based methods. Chen et al. [20] introduced sparse covariance functions to GPR-based pipelines, improving computational efficiency while preserving discriminative power for the identification of ground points in sparse and noisy point clouds.

Following the probabilistic methodology, Del Pino et al. [21] used a probabilistic graph-based model to represent and analyze the ground geometry. It applies stochastic estimation techniques to iteratively update the ground plane parameters (height and slope).

2.2. Geometric-Based Ground Segmentation Methods

In the context of ground segmentation for LiDAR point clouds, geometric approaches have emerged as the predominant strategy, primarily due to their real-time processing capabilities. These methods excel in transforming complex 3D spatial data into computationally efficient 2.5D representations, thereby facilitating precise terrain surface identification in dynamic and unstructured environments. However, a critical limitation of this approach is the frequent occurrence of under-segmentation artifacts, where points from distinct objects are erroneously merged into a single segment. Recent studies have sought to address these challenges through various innovative techniques. Proposals such as [22] developed an elevation map employing euclidean clustering principles and an adaptive multi-plane extraction method based on Random Sample Consensus (RANSAC) [23]. Similarly, Steinke et al. [24] proposed a 2D elevation map representation coupled with a point height variance analysis approach to classify cells as terrain. Expanding on the concept of data representation, Oh et al. [25] introduced a graph-based approach known as Tri-Grid Field (TGF) to model terrain geometry, facilitating the analysis of local convexity and concavity to determine environmental traversability.

Another prevalent form of representation of the three-dimensional environment is the Digital Terrain Model (DTM). Studies such as Refs. [26,27] aim to create such models by applying morphological filters to airborne LiDAR data for ground segmentation. Morphological operations are employed to filter objects based on their size and height relative to the terrain, thereby preserving steep features. The DTMs represent the bare-earth surface by excluding non-ground features such as buildings and vegetation while preserving key terrain characteristics like slopes, ridges, and cliffs. Morphological filters, while effective in simple terrain, face challenges in complex environments (urban, mountainous, and forested) due to their parameter sensitivity, computational limitations, and difficulty in preserving topographic detail.

However, the challenges of processing raw and unorganized point clouds have driven the development of methods that directly operate on 3D spatial data without prior structuring. Himmelsbach et al. [28], LineFit, pioneered a uniform angular sector discretization framework to mitigate radial sparsity in LiDAR point clouds, particularly at increasing sensor distances. This approach implements an adaptive linear adjustment to estimate straight-line equations per radial bin, with ground points determined through a multi-criteria filter. Conversely, Zermas et al. [29] proposed the technique named Ground Plane Fitting (GPF), dividing point clouds into three parts along the x-axis, implementing a deterministic plane estimation algorithm that utilizes adaptive seed selection with low spatial variance for ground plane estimation based on Principal Component Analysis (PCA). This approach avoids stochastic methods such as RANSAC [23], bypassing the time-consuming computation of iterations and introducing robustness to point density.

Recent advances in the field have addressed the sensitivity to point density variations through the implementation of non-uniform polar discretization strategies. Lim et al. [30], Patchwork, introduced the Concentric Zone Model (CZM), partitioning the spatial domain into annular subregions. In line with the methodology of Zermas et al. [29], the authors of this work implemented a Regional Ground Plane Fitting (R-GPF) that estimates partial planes in each bin by principal component analysis, with adaptive selection of initial seeds to avoid local minima. Building on this work, Lee et al. [31], Patchwork++, incorporated Temporal Terrain Reversal (TGR) to mitigate partial under-segmentation issues by leveraging information from previous frames.

Further advancements in the area include the work of Deng et al. [32] and Dong et al. [33], who proposed voxel neighborhood continuity analysis. These approaches utilize contextual relationships between adjacent voxels to enhance segmentation robustness in complex terrains with abrupt elevation changes. Deng et al. [32], RT-GS, determined ground continuity between adjacent grids by comparing the normal vectors and average heights of ground planes, while Dong et al. [33] employed spatial relationships between sectors to address areas with insufficient information for confident plane extraction.

2.3. Visual-Based Ground Segmentation Methods

Visual ground segmentation methods have emerged as a computationally efficient paradigm for terrain identification in complex urban environments. These approaches exploit the structured nature of LiDAR data by projecting 3D point clouds onto 2D representations, enabling the application of image processing techniques while preserving spatial relationships. Early work by Moosmann et al. [34] introduced a local convexity criterion operating directly on spherical range images, enabling ground–object separation in non-flat environments without compromising 3D geometric representation.

This foundational work inspired subsequent advances in range-image processing, such as Bogoslavskyi et al. [35]. The authors developed a slope-based segmentation method which transformed raw LiDAR scans into slope images through pairwise row-pixel analysis, followed by Savitsky–Golay smoothing and ground labeling.

Contemporary techniques such as the Jumping Convolution Process (JCP) [36] or DipG-Seg [37] demonstrate this progression through hierarchical refinement frameworks. These approaches combine non-linear filtering with majority-vote kernel convolutions based on convolution to improve segmentation accuracy. Despite these advancements, fundamental limitations persist in purely image-based segmentation. The widespread reliance on independent slope features, calculated from isolated vertical pixel pairs, proves to be inadequate for complex terrains. This constraint arises from the limited receptive field of slope operators, which cannot capture contextual relationships across adjacent regions.

2.4. Learning-Based Ground Segmentation Methods

Machine learning has emerged as a principal paradigm for addressing ground segmentation challenges. Recent techniques, such as PSVM [38] and PSVM-2 [39], take advantage of Support Vector Machine (SVM) classifiers to analyze geometric descriptors derived from raw LiDAR point clouds. These include surface normals, local curvature metrics, and contextual terrain features. A key innovation in these approaches is their multi-resolution pyramidal framework, which hierarchically fuses spatial information across varying scales to enhance segmentation robustness in heterogeneous environments.

However, these methods rapidly transitioned toward visual data as the primary input, largely driven by the remarkable performance of convolutional neural networks (CNNs) in image classification tasks. This shift was the key factor that led to the development of specialized network architectures such as GA-Nav [40], DeconvNet [41], or the bilateral architecture proposed in [42]. All of these frameworks exclusively utilize visual inputs for pixel-wise terrain classification, aiming to identify traversable paths by distinguishing navigable ground surfaces from obstacles in complex environments.

From a two-dimensional perspective to a three-dimensional domain, CNNs become impractical when handling sparse 3D point clouds, where data sparsity stems from the irregular spatial distribution of non-zero measurements. The direct application of conventional 2D convolution kernels to these irregular 3D structures results in computational demands that scale cubically with data density. Thus, two possible approaches emerge.

The first alternative integrates geometric priors with learned representations to balance adaptability and computational efficiency. GndNet [43] exemplifies this approach by employing an encoder–decoder architecture that relies on PointNet and a Pillar Feature Encoding network to estimate terrain elevation in grids. SectorGS-Net [44] focuses on sector-wise feature encoding, enabling more adaptive and context-aware ground segmentation in complex outdoor environments. Recent hybrid frameworks, such as those proposed by Atas et al. [45], combine geometric features with robot dynamics (orientation and movement) through a fully connected neural network.

The second approach is based on the notion of sparse convolution, a concept derived from signal processing. Conventional 2D convolution systematically scans all grid positions; in contrast, sparse convolution dynamically focuses computational resources on occupied voxels via hash-based memory management. By eliminating redundant computations in empty spaces, SCNNs achieve significant gains in both computational efficiency and memory utilization, enabling real-time performance in autonomous systems that rely on LiDAR-based terrain analysis. Studies such as [46,47] use SCNNs to predict per-voxel traversability from geometric features (height, density, and structural context).

In light of the significant advancements witnessed in recent years, an alternative approach involves the utilization of Large Language Models (LLMs) to facilitate 3D segmentation through textual instructions. Researchers have proposed approaches based on contrastive learning, which aims to align a textual description with geometric points belonging to a specific class. This alignment can be achieved through the fusion of 3D embeddings [48] or by directly processing point clouds [49,50].

3. Methodology

The method proposed in this article primarily falls within the geometric approaches category, with a secondary emphasis on machine learning paradigms through the use of a sparse neural network to overcome the sensitivity of geometric approaches to sparse data as point clouds. Specifically, our approach lies at the intersection of non-uniform polar discretization methods (such as those proposed by Lim et al. [30] and Lee et al. [31]) and approaches that utilize neighborhood analysis to enhance robustness in complex terrains (Deng et al. [32] and Dong et al. [33]). The main limitations this method aims to overcome are as follows: (i) robustness to the incremental dispersion of data inherent to LiDAR technology and (ii) independence from parameter selection or decision thresholds that determine the performance of geometric methods, limiting their adaptability to diverse environment. By addressing these aspects, the proposed method offers a more versatile and robust solution for ground segmentation in diverse environments, bridging the gap between purely geometric and learning-based approaches.

3.1. Problem Statement

Given a LiDAR point cloud $\mathcal{P} = \{\mathbf{p}_i\}_{i=1}^{N}$, where $\mathbf{p}_i = (x_i, y_i, z_i) \in \mathbb{R}^3$, we define the ground segmentation task as a binary segmentation problem, wherein each point of the cloud is assigned a label $\mathbf{l}_i \in \{0,1\}$ obstacle and traversable ground, respectively. Therefore, the datasets under consideration have been reduced to two labels. Points within the traversability category are defined as follows: road, parking, sidewalk, other ground, and lane marking in structured environments (SemanticKITTI) and terrain, grass, dirt, and mud in unstructured environments (Rellis-3D). Conversely, the obstacle category includes all other classes represented in the datasets under review, such as building, bicycle, car, person, and so forth.

This section introduces a novel methodology for traversable ground segmentation in 3D point cloud data, combining an iterative multi-resolution polar mapping framework with TE-NeXt [15] to address the challenges of terrain feature extraction across diverse environmental conditions, as illustrated in Figure 1. The method begins by discretizing the spatial domain into coarse-resolution polar sectors by means of CZM. This initial discretization establishes the core representation of the environment, allowing the efficient extrapolation of geometric knowledge from historically traversed regions across the entire discretized space.

Following this initialization, sector classification is iteratively refined using geometric criteria designed to minimize the dependence on point density. Thus, at each level of resolution, for each sector and its adjacencies, the plane coefficients are estimated after a selection of seeds suitable for carrying out Principal Component Analysis (PCA), mitigating the density-dependent limitations in traditional methods like RANSAC. In order to address the limitations of the geometric approach, as will be discussed in Section 5, TE-NeXt [15] is introduced. This network is based on an encoder–decoder architecture adapted to the three-dimensional domain and follows the development philosophy presented in ConvNeXt [51].

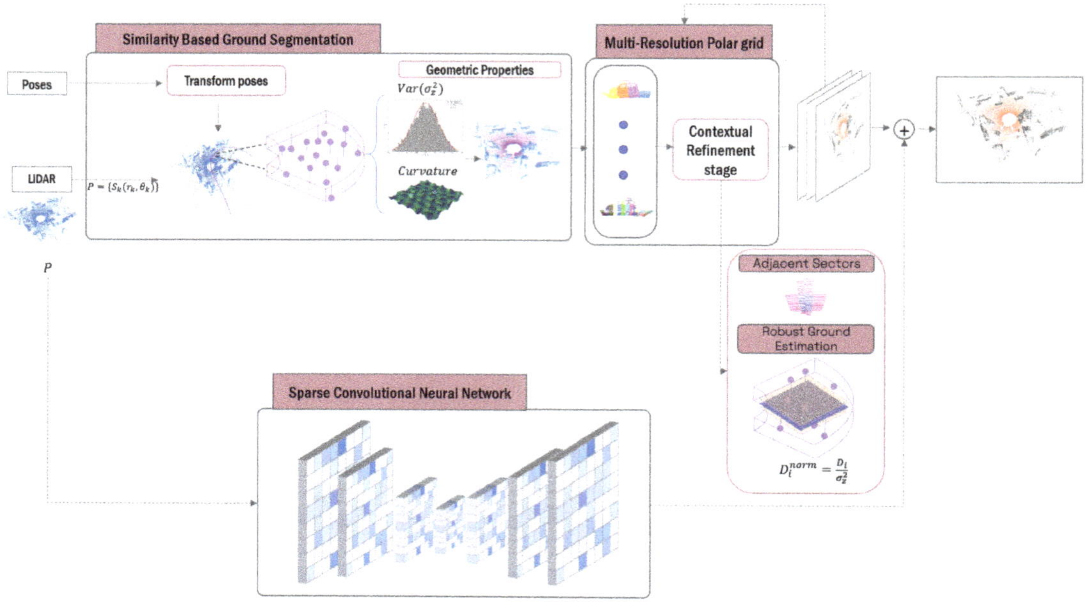

Figure 1. Multi-stage traversable ground segmentation framework overview. This figure illustrates the processes involved in the segmentation of traversable ground. Given an input point cloud, prior knowledge is employed to identify analogous sectors. Thereafter, the discretization and calculation of ground detection planes are performed iteratively through various resolutions.

3.2. Similarity-Based Ground Segmentation

The representation of continuous domains through finite elements constitutes the main strategy in 3D data processing. In the context of point cloud-based ground segmentation, single-plane surface detection reveals limitations when applied to complex terrains. Therefore, the procedure of dividing the three-dimensional space into zones of variable geometry allows for the extraction of local features, the modeling of surface variability, and the mitigation of point-cloud scattering effects. Thus, the proposed approach implements the polar discretization designed in [30], partitioning the 3D space, $\mathcal{P}$, into sectors $\{\mathcal{S}_k(r_k, \theta_k)\}$ with adaptive radial resolution.

Existing methodologies in the literature, as discussed in Section 2, rely on the aforementioned discretization and human-defined thresholds to classify individual points as traversable ground or obstacles. These approaches aim to achieve optimal segmentation by manually tuning geometric or statistical criteria, such as slope limits or elevation variances. In contrast, modern machine learning (ML) paradigms, particularly self-supervised methods, exploit learnt patterns from historical data to automate decision-making. The proposed method extends this concept by incorporating spatio-temporal context, ensuring that the initial ground plane estimation is based on both historical and future positional experiences. This strategy is tested in widely used datasets in the field, which provide spatio-temporal pose associations for each point cloud. The decision to utilize positional data is grounded in the fact that the proposed method is specifically tailored for intelligent mobile systems. Positional information allows the incorporation of terrain features from previously traversed areas, which serve as key discriminative factors for identifying traversable ground. In the absence of such positional data, the method can still be implemented; however, it would lack of the similarity-based component for detecting traversable ground.

Figure 2 illustrates a concentric zone model applied to 3D point clouds. The space is divided into polar segments with varying resolutions based on the radial distance from the sensor. Specifically, the model partitions the space into distinct zones, which are further subdivided into X concentric rings. Each ring corresponds to an annular region defined by two radii, r_i and r_{1+1}. Additionally, each ring is segmented into angular sectors determined by azimuthal θ and polar ϕ angles in spherical coordinates. Furthermore, the coordinates which define the prior geometric knowledge from regions previously traversed by the robotic platform are represented as white points in Figure 2. This knowledge contributes to the identification of traversable terrain properties by means of historical navigation data. Coordinate transformations are facilitated by the global reference frames associated with each point cloud, which are obtained through classical algorithms such as the Iterative Closest Point (ICP) or visual odometry. Specifically, positions, ${}^{L}t_j$, are projected into the current sensor frame, L, via Equation (1). This equation represents the homogeneous transformations applied to positional data measured in a global reference system, G, to a local system, L. The matrix $\left({}^{G}T_{\mathrm{L}}\right)^{-1}$ is the homogeneous transformation matrix that allows the transformation of coordinates from the global system to the local system. The coordinates of the positions, j, expressed in the global system G are denoted as ${}^{G}t_j$.

$$ {}^{L}t_j = \left({}^{G}T_{\mathrm{L}}\right)^{-1} \cdot {}^{G}t_j \tag{1} $$

Once the Cartesian coordinates are projected into the local polar grid, an adaptive threshold is computed based on two sector-wise geometric properties derived from PCA. First, the height variance, represented as σ_z^2 in Equation (2), quantifies elevation consistency within each K sector, where $\bar{z} = \frac{1}{|N|}\sum_{i=1}^{N} z_i$ represents the mean height of the N points in the sector. Second, the surface curvature, $\mathcal{C}$, is derived from the eigenvalues, Equation (3), where lower curvature values indicate planar regions characteristic of ground surfaces.

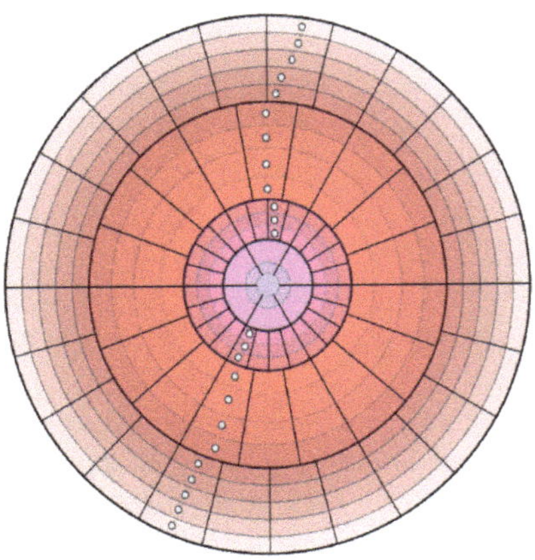

Figure 2. Projection of Cartesian coordinates at the coarsest polar resolution level (Level 0).

$$ \sigma_z^2 = \frac{1}{N-1}\sum_{i=1}^{N}(z_i - \bar{z})^2 \tag{2} $$

$$ \mathcal{C} = \frac{\lambda_3}{\lambda_1 + \lambda_2 + \lambda_3} \tag{3} $$

To establish dynamic thresholds, the method aggregates these metrics across K sectors, computing the global mean μ and standard deviation σ of both geometric properties extracted. Thus, a sector S_k is classified as traversable if it satisfies the dual thresholding criterion shown in Equation (4), where α and β are tunable parameters controlling the classification confidence. Algorithm 1 delineates the implementation of the aforementioned methodology.

$$\mu_{\sigma_z} - \beta\sigma_{\sigma_z} \leq \sigma^2_{z,k} \leq \mu_{\sigma_z} + \beta\sigma_{\sigma_z} \quad \text{and} \quad \mu_C - \alpha\sigma_C \leq C_k \leq \mu_C + \alpha\sigma_C \tag{4}$$

Algorithm 1 Ground Segmentation via similarity search

Input: Point cloud $\mathcal{P} = \{\mathbf{p}_i \in \mathbb{R}^3\}$, poses $\mathcal{T}$
Output: Labeled ground points $\mathcal{L} = \{l_i \in \{0,1\}\}$
Step 1: Pose Projection
Project past/future poses to current coordinate system: ${}^{L}t_j \leftarrow \left({}^{G}T_{\mathrm{L}}\right)^{-1} \cdot {}^{G}t_j$
Step 2: Cylindrical Discretization
Partition $\mathcal{P}$ into sectors $\{\mathcal{S}_k(r_k, \theta_k)\}$ with adaptive radial resolution
Step 3: Geometric Feature Extraction
for each sector $\mathcal{S}_k$ **do**
  Compute eigenvalues $\lambda_1 \geq \lambda_2 \geq \lambda_3$ via PCA
  Curvature: $\mathcal{C}_k \leftarrow \frac{\lambda_3}{\lambda_1+\lambda_2+\lambda_3}$
  Height variance: $\sigma^2_{z,k} \leftarrow \frac{1}{N}\sum_{i\in\mathcal{N}}(z_i - \bar{z}_k)^2$
end for
Compute global statistics:
$\mu_\mathcal{C} \leftarrow \mathrm{mean}(\{\mathcal{C}_k\}), \sigma_\mathcal{C} \leftarrow \mathrm{std}(\{\mathcal{C}_k\})$
$\mu_{\sigma_z} \leftarrow \mathrm{mean}(\{\sigma^2_{z,k}\}), \sigma_{\sigma_z} \leftarrow \mathrm{std}(\{\sigma^2_{z,k}\})$
Step 4: Sector Classification
for each sector $\mathcal{S}_k$ **do**
  if $\mathcal{C}_k \leq \mu_\mathcal{C} + 2\sigma_\mathcal{C}$ **and** $\sigma^2_{z,k} \leq \mu_{\sigma_z} + 2\sigma_{\sigma_z}$ **then**
    Label all $\mathbf{p}_i \in \mathcal{S}_k$ as $l_i = 1$
  end if
end for

3.3. Multi-Resolution Polar Grid

Following the initial classification of sectors based on the geometric criteria outlined previously, the method addresses residual cases where traversable ground points remain misclassified due to the following two primary challenges:

1. Vertical structures (e.g., walls, vegetation) introduce non-planar artifacts that skew the local curvature and height variance metrics (Equations (2) and (3)).
2. Sparse data ambiguities are present in sectors with minimal point density (e.g., distant regions). There is an absence of sufficient data for reliable PCA-based feature extraction (Equation (3)).

To address these challenges, we propose a hierarchical multi-resolution polar discretization framework comprising N distinct resolution levels. To illustrate the disparities among various resolutions, refer to Figure 3. The n_0 level of discretization, as illustrated in Figure 3a, demonstrates a uniform resolution, signifying a coarser discretization, with individual cells encompassing larger spatial domains equidistant from the sensor origin. Conversely, the finest granularity is achieved at Level n_1, as demonstrated in Figure 3b, where high-resolution cells enable the precise localization of terrain features. The framework's adaptive granularity allows the progressive refinement of geometric feature isolation, critical for robust ground plane detection.

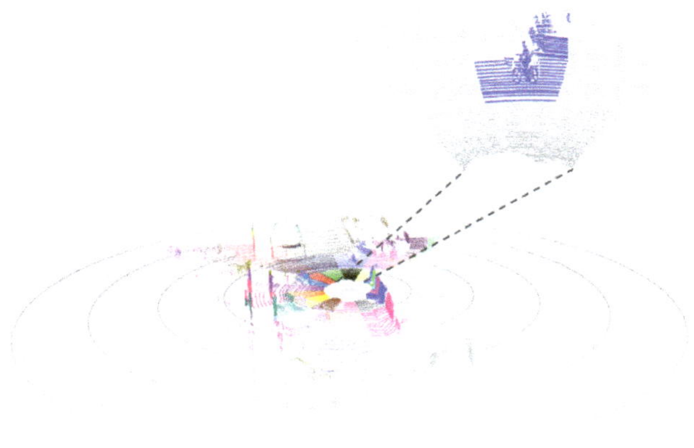

(a)

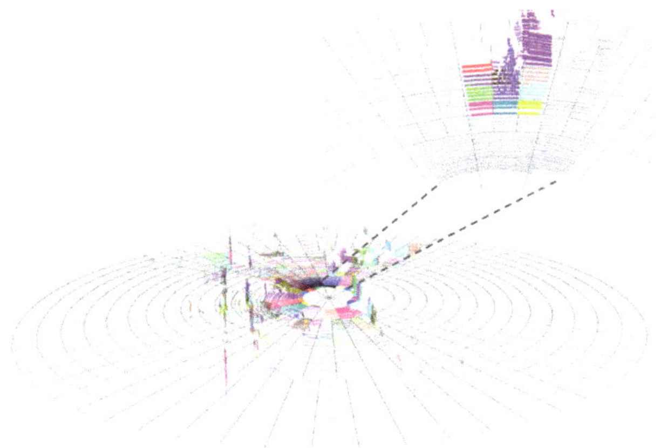

(b)

Figure 3. Multi-resolution polar grid overview. (**a**) Uniform resolution grid. (**b**) Variable resolution grid.

Contextual Refinement Stage

For each resolution level, sectors classified as obstacles by the similarity-based module undergo a neighborhood-centric geometric analysis. This analysis selectively incorporates neighboring sectors that share the same spatial discretization, ensuring alignment within the same area. Consequently, the algorithm aggregates geometric data from the R-adjacent sectors for every unclassified circular sector. Given the possibility of encountering geometries that distort the geometrical study, this work follows the philosophy of [31]. The pipeline implements a three-stage filtering process as follows:

- Height-based point prioritization : It addresses geometric distortions caused by vertical structures (e.g., vegetation and walls) by selectively retaining low-elevation points as candidates for traversable ground plane estimation.

- Robust plane estimation: The retained points serve as seeds for traversable ground plane estimation via PCA. The optimal plane $\mathbf{n} \cdot \mathbf{p} + d = 0$, where $\mathbf{n}$ is the normal vector and d the planar offset.
- Geometric consistency validation: Given that the point-plane distance, $\mathcal{D}_i = \frac{|\mathbf{n} \cdot \mathbf{p}_i + d|}{\|\mathbf{n}\|}$, is a relative quantity contingent on the plane's orientation and offset (normal vector n and d, respectively) and the dynamic threshold, derived from seed point elevations, $\tau_{\text{dist}} = \mu_z + k\sigma_z$, is an absolute measure, where μ_z is the mean elevation, σ_z is the standard deviation of elevation seeds and k is a statistical confidence parameter; the direct comparison of D_i and τ_{dist} is dimensionally inconsistent, as they encode distinct physical and statistical phenomena. To establish a valid decision framework, we normalize the distance by the standard deviation σ_z. This normalization converts geometric deviations into unitless multiples of the standard deviation, where k determines how many standard deviations away from the mean, μ_z, the threshold should be set. This allows for controlling the sensitivity of the threshold to outliers or deviations, Equation (5). By expressing deviations in terms of statistical significance, this approach bridges geometric and empirical criteria, ensuring cross-domain compatibility and interpretable validation.

$$\mathcal{D}_i^{\text{norm}} = \frac{|\mathbf{n} \cdot \mathbf{p}_i + d|}{\|\mathbf{n}\| \cdot \sigma_z} \leq k \tag{5}$$

The process is described in detail in Algorithm 2.

Algorithm 2 Ground segmentation via multi-resolution polar discretization

Input: Point cloud $\mathcal{P}$, number of polar discretizations N
Output: Labeled ground points $\mathcal{L} = \{l_i \in \{0,1\}\}$

for $n = 1$ to N **do**
  Perform polar discretization at resolution level n to divide $\mathcal{P}$ into sectors $\mathcal{S}_n$
  for each sector $s \in \mathcal{S}_n$ **do**
    Identify neighboring sectors: $s_{\text{up}}, s_{\text{down}}, s_{\text{left}}, s_{\text{right}}$
    Collect points from s and its neighbors: $\mathcal{P}_s = s \cup s_{\text{up}} \cup s_{\text{down}} \cup s_{\text{left}} \cup s_{\text{right}}$
    Height-based Point Prioritization $\mathcal{S}_{\text{seed}} \leftarrow \{\mathbf{p}_j \in \mathcal{P}_s\}$
    Robust Plane Estimation $(\mathbf{n}, d) \leftarrow \text{PCA}(\mathcal{S}_{\text{seed}})$
    Geometric consistency Validation $\tau_d = \mu_z + k\sigma_z$ of $\mathcal{S}_{\text{seed}}$
    for each point $p \in \mathcal{P}_s$ **do**
      $d_i^{\text{norm}} \leftarrow \frac{|\mathbf{n}^\top \mathbf{p}_i + d|}{\|\mathbf{n}\| \cdot \sigma_z}$
      if $d_i^{\text{norm}} \leq k$ **then**
        $l_i = 1$
      else
        $l_i = 0$
      end if
    end for
  end for
end for

3.4. Sparse Convolutional Neural Network

As previously stated in Section 2.4, sparse convolutional neural networks are becoming the most predominant approach to process point clouds in recent years. Thus, given any point cloud, B, a sparse vector $\mathbf{S}$ is defined according to Equation (6), as a set of coordinates, $\vec{p}_j$, describing the cloud after applying a part-integer function and a scaling factor, v, that determines the degree of discretization of the space. Furthermore, the sparse vectors enable the storage of feature vectors, $\vec{f}_j$, associated with all the discretized spaces represented.

The calculation of these values is derived from the weighting of the feature vectors, $\mathbf{f}_i$, of each point that is encompassed in a discretized space, $\mathcal{V}_j$. The processing of the input data is carried out using the Minkowski Engine library (https://github.com/NVIDIA/MinkowskiEngine, accessed on 3 April 2025) [52].

$$\bar{p}_j = floor(\vec{p}_i) = floor\left(\frac{x_i}{v}, \frac{y_i}{v}, \frac{z_i}{v}\right) \tag{6}$$

$$\bar{\mathbf{f}}_j = \frac{1}{|\mathcal{V}_j|} \sum_{i \in \mathcal{V}_j} \mathbf{f}_i \tag{7}$$

Figure 4 illustrates TE-NeXt architecture [15], which is the sparse network employed through the proposed method. TE-NeXt is a dedicated convolutional neural network, specifically designed for the 3D semantic segmentation of point clouds, with a particular emphasis on the estimation of traversability. TE-NeXt builds upon the U-Net style architecture [53], replacing the standard residual blocks, introduced by classical ResNet networks [54], with a proprietary block inspired by ConvNeXt [51] design principles. This block demonstrates greater abstraction than classical ResNet blocks since it allows the employment of large 3D kernel sizes to model long-range dependencies combined with linear convolutions that reduce computational cost, allow cross-channel mixing and adjust dimensions for skip connections.

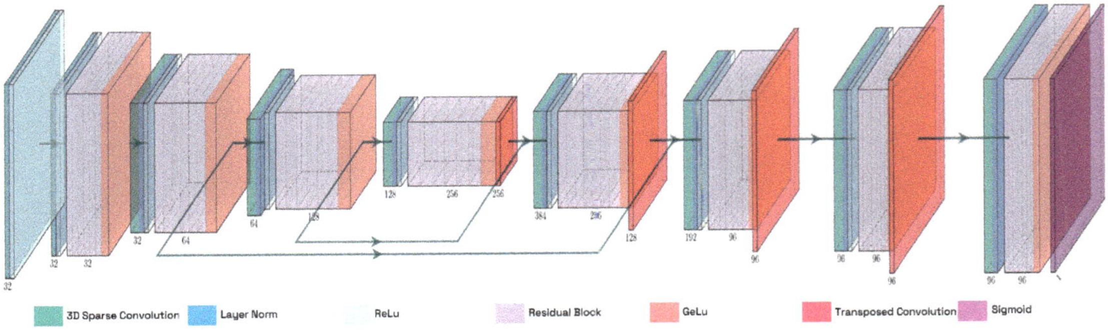

Figure 4. Detailed illustration of the TE-NeXt architecture. A LiDAR point cloud is subjected to the extraction of descriptors at varying resolutions on the left-hand side of the image. Once the information has been encoded, the initial dimensions are recovered in order to obtain a label for each given point.

4. Datasets and Experimental Setup

In order to perform a quantitative evaluation of the performance of the proposed method, a comparison is made against two publicly available and widely recognized datasets in autonomous navigation research, as follows:

- SemanticKITTI [55]: It represents a comprehensive large-scale dataset for LiDAR-based semantic scene understanding, extending the KITTI Vision Odometry Benchmark [56]. This benchmark offers dense per-point semantic annotations across the full 360° field of view captured by the Velodyne HDL-64E LiDAR sensor, with over 43,000 LiDAR scans from 22 sequences. The sequences cover a variety of highly structured environments including city streets, residential areas, highways, and countryside roads.
- Rellis-3D [57]: It is a multimodal dataset explicitly designed for off-road robotic perception and autonomous navigation, serving as a critical counterpart to urban-centric autonomous driving benchmarks. The dataset comprises 13,556 annotated LiDAR

scans organized into five sequences, acquired using an Ouster OS1-64 sensor. Each sequence captures unstructured natural terrains—including vegetated slopes, gravel paths, and muddy surfaces—under varying illumination and weather conditions.

The evaluation framework is presented in Table 1, in which the previously mentioned datasets can be observed. In addition to these datasets, an alternative method of validation has been developed. Two datasets have been captured in real and very different contexts in order to validate the generalization of the algorithm. The experiments are based on structured and unstructured environments, in the cities of Elche (Spain) and Coimbra (Portugal), respectively. More specifically, the datasets have been collected as follows:

- UMH-Gardens: The study focuses on two sequences situated within the university campus of the Miguel Hernández University of Elche, utilizing the HUSKY A-200 robotic platform. This platform is equipped with an Ouster OS1-128 LiDAR and a georeferenced system with real-time kinematic (RTK) technology, ensuring centimetric precision in measurement. The trajectories followed to capture these sequences are shown in Figure 5a,b.
- Coimbra-Liv: This dataset has been captured using a combustion vehicle with the aim of covering a large area of forest in the surroundings of the city of Coimbra. The vehicle was equipped with a LiDAR Livox HAP sensor, which stands out because of its high angular resolution, though at the expense of a reduced horizontal field of view. Furthermore, the vehicle was also equipped with an enclosed multi-dual-frequency RTK GNSS receiver, which has been designed for use in outdoor environments and is capable of providing centimeter-accurate positioning. The trajectories followed in these experiments are illustrated in Figure 5c,d.

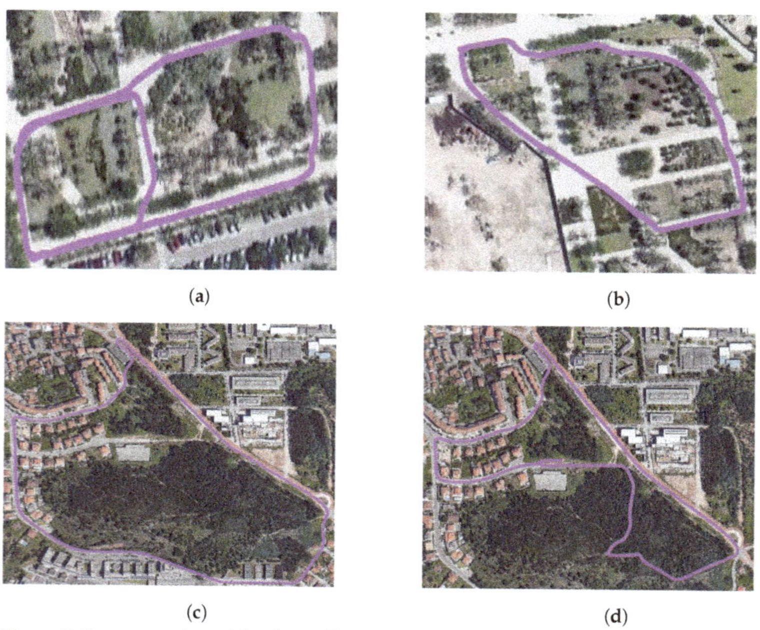

Figure 5. Representation of the data collected. (**a**,**b**) Traversed environments within the University of Elche campus. (**c**,**d**) Environments captured within the city of Coimbra. The trajectories followed are colored in purple ■.

Table 1. Summary of the datasets employed in the evaluation.

Dataset	Sem.KITTI	Rellis-3D	UMH-Gardens	Coimbra-Liv
Environment	Urban/Highway (Structured)	Off-road (Unstructured)	Urban (Structured)	Urban (Structured)/Off-road Unstructured)
LiDAR Sensor	Velodyne HDL-64E	Ouster OS1-64	Ouster OS1-64	Livox HAP
Vertical Fov	26.9° (−24.8° to +2.0°)	45° (−22.5° to +22.5°)	45° (−22.5° to +22.5°)	25° (−12.5° to +12.5°)
Vertical Angular Resolution	0.42°	0.35°	0.35°	0.23°
Horizontal Fov	360°	360°	360°	120°
Horizontal Angular Resolution	0.09°	0.18°	0.18°	0.18°
Annotated Classes	✓	✓	X	X

5. Results and Discussion

The evaluation is conducted across two distinct environmental contexts to rigorously assess generalization. First, structured urban environments are analyzed, ensuring equitable comparison with state-of-the-art methods. These settings are characterized by geometric regularity (e.g., flat roads and vertical curbs), which facilitates direct performance comparison with existing geometric and learning-based approaches. Secondly, unstructured natural terrains are evaluated in order to quantify robustness in geometrically inconsistent scenarios.

As a complement to the quantitative benchmarks, this article presents qualitative results for the custom-captured UMH-Gardens and Coimbra-Liv datasets introduced in Figure 5. These proprietary datasets, acquired in mixed urban–natural environments, provide a realistic case study for validating the efficacy of the proposed method under real-world conditions.

5.1. Evaluation Metrics

The proposed method and other competitive state-of-the-art methods are evaluated on the following three widely used metrics: precision, recall, and the F1-score. In this context, precision measures the proportion of correctly classified ground points (true positives, TP) relative to all points predicted as ground, $Precision = \frac{TP}{TP+FP}$. It evaluates the model's ability to avoid false positives (FP), which is particularly critical in safety-critical applications like autonomous navigation, where misclassifying obstacles as ground can lead to dangerous outcomes. Recall measures the proportion of correctly classified ground points relative to all actual ground points in the dataset, $Recall = \frac{TP}{TP+FN}$. It reflects the model's ability to identify all ground points, minimizing the false negatives (FN) and ensuring that critical terrain features are not missed. The F1-score is the harmonic mean of precision and recall, $F_1score = 2 \cdot \frac{Precision \cdot Recall}{Precision+Recall}$, providing a single metric that balances these two aspects. It is particularly useful when there is an imbalance between FP and FN, as it penalizes extreme values in either metric.

5.2. Quantitative Evaluation

5.2.1. Results in Structured Environments

Structured environments are defined as urban areas that are generally created under human supervision and therefore stand out for their regular geometries. Table 2 presents the results of the traversable ground segmentation methods evaluated on the SemanticKITTI dataset [55]. The proposed method is implemented in the following two distinct versions:

- Pure geometric version: Relies exclusively on geometric heuristics derived from multi-resolution polar discretization and adaptive thresholding.
- Hybrid geometric-SCNN version: Combines geometric heuristics with TE-NexT [15] to address regions where geometric distortions prevent reliable heuristic-based classification.

The pure geometric version achieves the highest precision (95.1%) among all methods, demonstrating its ability to minimize false positives by strictly adhering to geometric rules. However, this is achieved at the cost of a low recall (88.0%), which leads to false negatives in complex regions, such as sloped surfaces or areas with sparse point distributions. In contrast, the hybrid version successfully mitigates this trade-off by exploiting the SCNN to refine ambiguous regions where heuristic-based methods obtain low precision. This approach significantly improves recall (96.3%) while maintaining high precision (94.5%), resulting in an F1-score of 95.4%. While Patchwork++ achieves the highest recall (99.3%), its lower precision (73.23%) leads to a reduced F1-score compared to the proposed hybrid method.

Table 2. Traversable ground estimation performance of methods in urban environments (SemanticKITTI).

Method	Precision (%)	Recall (%)	F1-Score (%)
RANSAC	67.0	88.7	76.3
LineFit [28]	87.8	71.9	78.0
GPF [29]	74.5	95.5	82.5
Patchwork [30]	72.7	98.1	89.6
Patchwork++ [31]	73.2	**99.3**	83.3
RT-GS [32]	77.3	98.5	85.7
PSVM [38]	89.4	89.0	89.2
PSVM-2 [39]	92.6	90.8	91.7
Ours (only geometric)	**95.1**	88.0	91.4
Ours (geometric-SCNN)	94.5	96.3	**95.4**

Note: Bold values indicate the best performance for each metric.

To address the demands of real-world applications, Table 3 presents a detailed comparison of the performance of both variants of the method (pure geometric and hybrid geometric-SCNN), together with the best performing state-of-the-art method, P-SVM2, on all SemanticKITTI sequences. We conduct a comprehensive scene migration experiment designed to evaluate the method's robustness across diverse structured environments with limited training data. The hybrid variant is exclusively trained on the SemanticKITTI sequence 08. Following our previous analysis, the experimental results reveal distinct performance characteristics between the pure geometric and hybrid variants. The geometric method achieves superior precision scores, demonstrating its effectiveness in minimizing false positives through strict geometric constraints. However, this conservative classification strategy has been shown to have a significant impact on the system's recall performance, as it frequently misclassifies legitimate traversable ground points in complex or ambiguous regions as obstacles. The hybrid geometric-SCNN approach, conversely, exhibits more balanced performance metrics. While its precision does not exceed that of the pure geometric variant, it achieves substantially higher recall rates, since it learns from features to decide ambiguous cases. This balanced trade-off is reflected on its superior F1-score, indicating greater overall segmentation reliability.

5.2.2. Results in Unstructured Environments

Following the same methodology described in the previous section, Table 4 presents the performance of the proposed method in unstructured environments, such as natural terrains. To the best of our knowledge, there exist no results previously published on the traversable ground segmentation on unstructured datasets such as the Rellis-3D or any other similar dataset. Consequently, given the scarcity of robust approaches specifically designed for these challenging scenarios, the comparison is more limited. The table includes results from the two variants of the proposed method (previously explained), as well as those from a sparse convolutional neural network (TE-NeXt) and classical approaches such as RANSAC.

Table 3. Generalization comparison of the proposed method on the SemanticKITTI database (structured environments).

	Precision (%)			Recall (%)			F1 (%)		
Num.	**P-SVM2**	**Ours (Geometric)**	**Ours (Hybrid)**	**P-SVM2**	**Ours (Geometric)**	**Ours (Hybrid)**	**P-SVM2**	**Ours (Geometric)**	**Ours (Hybrid)**
00	91.4	96.0	**96.1**	91.6	89.8	**97.0**	91.3	92.9	**96.2**
01	86.6	93.3	**93.5**	84.4	88.7	**94.6**	88.8	90.7	**93.2**
02	92.1	**96.3**	95.6	93.5	84.8	**96.5**	90.7	90.0	**95.6**
03	**91.3**	83.6	78.0	**91.6**	90.0	91.0	**91.0**	85.9	86.3
04	87.4	94.6	**95.3**	85.6	90.3	**98.0**	89.3	92.2	**95.4**
05	91.4	94.6	**94.7**	90.5	87.9	**96.7**	91.4	91.0	**94.8**
06	89.0	**97.8**	97.6	88.4	90.7	**98.0**	89.6	94.0	**97.6**
07	91.4	96.0	**96.4**	91.8	92.0	**97.7**	91.1	93.9	**96.6**
09	90.4	**95.4**	94.1	90.4	85.0	**95.2**	90.5	90.0	**94.2**
10	91.0	**94.0**	91.6	91.1	81.0	**98.1**	91.0	86.0	**92.0**
Full	92.6	**95.1**	94.5	90.8	88.0	**96.3**	91.7	91.4	**95.4**

Note: Bold values indicate the best performance in each metric across the SemanticKITTI sequences.

As observed in structured environments, the purely geometric variant of the proposed method demonstrates the highest precision, achieving a value of 78.6%. This result is expected due to the restrictive nature of geometric constrains when classifying traversable ground points. On the contrary, both versions that incorporate neural networks report significantly lower precision values, indicating that their predictions generate a considerable number of false positives. In unstructured environments, this limitation can be particularly critical for safety-demanding applications, where false positives may lead to the misclassification of obstacles as traversable terrain.

Similarly to the findings observed in structured environments (Section 5.2.1), the recall metrics of learning-based methods demonstrate a higher efficacy, with values approaching 91%, which signifies the inference of fewer false negatives. In terms of metric stability, the geometric approach demonstrates the most balanced performance, achieving an F1-score of 80.77%, reflecting its robustness and reliability across diverse sequences. The hybrid method closely follows, with an F1-score of 75.8%, while TE-NeXt achieves a score of 76.8%. These results highlight the importance of balancing precision and recall in safety-demanding applications like autonomous navigation in unstructured terrains.

Table 4. Traversable ground estimation performance of methods in natural environments (Rellis-3D).

Method	Precision (%)	Recall (%)	F1-Score (%)
RANSAC	54.2	86.3	66.5
TE-NeXt [15]	66.2	**91.0**	76.8
Ours (only geometric)	**78.6**	83.1	**80.8**
Ours (geometric-SCNN)	64.8	90.8	75.8

Note: Bold values indicate the best performance in each metric.

Table 5 presents the performance of the proposed methods across individual test sequences in the Rellis-3D dataset, excluding sequence 04, which was used for training the neural network in the comparison. The results provide a detailed breakdown of precision, recall, and F1-score for each sequence, offering insights into the behavior of both geometric and learning-based approaches under varying terrain conditions.

The geometric approach consistently achieves the highest precision across all test sequences, with values ranging from 72.0% to 93.6%, and an overall precision of 78.6%. This result highlights its restrictive nature when classifying traversable points, as it minimizes false positives by confidently rejecting obstacles points. However, this conservative characteristic comes at the cost of recall, where the geometric method lags behind other approaches. The trade-off between precision and recall is evident in learning-based methods, which tend to classify more points as traversable, including false positives. This bias reduces false negatives but increases false positives, leading to lower precision scores (e.g., TE-NeXt achieves 66.2% overall precision). Unlike in structured environments, the hybrid approach does not generate the best overall results (F1-score), mainly due to the absence of well-defined geometries that allow the neural networks to establish discriminative patterns between the inferred classes.

Table 5. Generalization comparison of the proposed method on the Rellis-3D database (unstructured environment).

	Precision (%)			Recall (%)			F1 (%)		
Num.	TE-NeXt	Ours (Geometric)	Ours (Hybrid)	TE-NeXt	Ours (Geometric)	Ours (Hybrid)	TE-NeXt	Ours (Geometric)	Ours (Hybrid)
00	67.6	**72.0**	65.3	84.4	75.0	**88.0**	71.3	70.5	**71.5**
01	50.0	**61.4**	49.1	95.3	**96.3**	83.0	62.2	**68.3**	61.9
02	61.0	**84.0**	59.7	94.0	82.0	**96.3**	71.0	**80.5**	70.4
03	90.2	**93.6**	89.2	87.6	79.5	**90.8**	88.6	85.6	**89.7**
Full	66.2	**78.6**	64.8	**91.0**	83.1	90.8	76.8	**80.8**	75.8

Note: Bold values indicate the best performance in each metric across the RELLIS-3D sequences.

5.3. Qualitative Evaluation

As illustrated in Figure 6, the output point clouds generated by the two variants introduced in the previous section, the geometric version and the hybrid version, are based on samples collected from the two trajectories that define the UMH-Gardens experiment. Specifically, Figure 6a,c corresponds to the results of the purely geometric approach, while Figure 6b,d shows the output of the hybrid method described in Figure 1.

In these figures, one can observe the previously mentioned facts from Section 5.2.1, in which the results were discussed. In structured environments, the geometric version generates numerous false negatives, highlighted in green circles throughout Figure 6a,c, due to the lack of flexibility of the geometric heuristics. Conversely, the hybrid version employs a neural network in these areas that has been geometrically discarded as ground and re-evaluates them, Figure 6b,d. Additionally, it is observed that despite employing polar discretization that offers advantages over dispersion, in distant areas, minor distortions result in the misclassification of ground points.

(a) (b)

Figure 6. *Cont.*

(c) (d)

Figure 6. Results of the UMH-Gardens experiment. (**a**) Point cloud labeled using the pure geometric method from the UMH-Gardens dataset on the trajectory shown in Figure 5a. (**b**) Point cloud labeled using the hybrid method from the UMH-Gardens dataset on the trajectory shown in Figure 5a. (**c**) Point cloud labeled using the pure geometric method from the Coimbra-Liv dataset on the trajectory shown in Figure 5b. (**d**) Point cloud labeled using the hybrid method from the Coimbra-Liv dataset on the trajectory shown in Figure 5b. The points classified as ground are represented in ■, and the points classified as non-ground are represented in ■.

Figure 7 illustrates the results obtained from the Coimbra-Liv experiment, which was designed to evaluate performance in semi-structured and unstructured environments. Figure 7a,b emphasizes the errors previously discussed in Section 5.2.2. Specifically, the geometric variant exhibits a tendency to generate false negatives (low recall) in regions that should be classified as traversable ground, highlighting its restrictive nature.

Conversely, the hybrid variant addresses this issue by introducing a bias toward traversable ground classification (reducing false negatives but increasing false positives). This effect is evident at the boundaries of the car geometry in Figure 7b, where the points are incorrectly classified as traversable ground. Consequently, the learning-based approach achieves lower precision due to an increase in false positives.

The same behavior is observed in Figure 7c,d, where the highlighted regions indicate areas where the hybrid method generates false positives. These results highlight the trade-off between precision and recall in hybrid approaches, especially in complex environments.

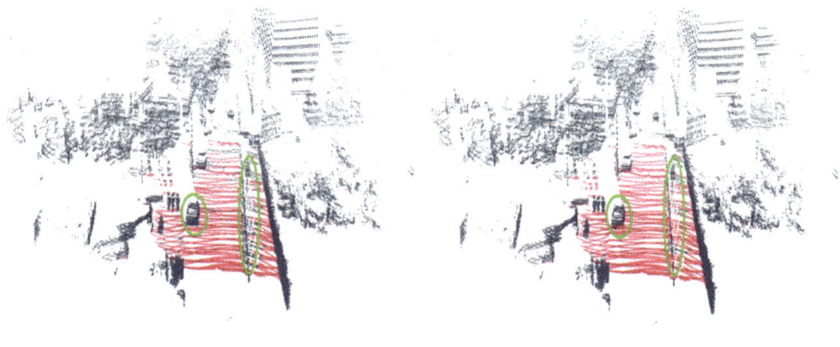

(a) (b)

Figure 7. *Cont.*

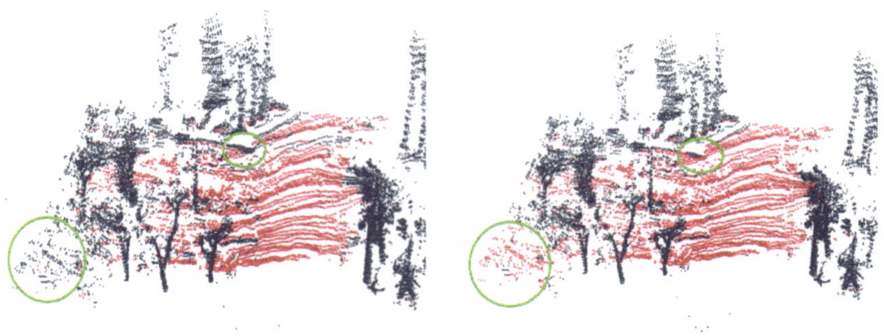

(c) (d)

Figure 7. Results of the Coimbra-Liv experiments. (**a**) Point cloud segmented using the geometric method on the trajectory shown in Figure 5c. (**b**) Point cloud segmented using the hybrid method on the trajectory shown in Figure 5c. (**c**) Point cloud segmented using the geometric method on the trajectory shown in Figure 5d. (**d**) Point cloud segmented using the hybrid method on the trajectory shown in Figure 5d. The points classified as ground are represented in ■, and the points classified as non-ground are represented in ■.

6. Conclusions

This paper has presented a hybrid traversable ground segmentation method for point clouds, combining geometric heuristics with deep learning techniques. Inspired by self-supervised learning methodologies, the proposed approach incorporates a similarity search module based on prior knowledge to perform an initial classification. Subsequently, multi-resolution polar discretizations are employed to apply geometric heuristics to refine the segmentation process. Finally, the incorporation of a sparse convolutional neural network technique is intended to enhance the flexibility of the final outcome, particularly with regard to points classified as ground. This approach is motivated by the observation that the geometric study imposes significant restrictions on the segmentation process.

The experiments focus on two versions of the proposed method as follows: the purely geometric variant and the hybrid variant. The findings highlight that both approaches exhibit distinct advantages and limitations depending on the environment in which they operate. In structured environments, the hybrid version achieves an F1-score of 95.4%, outperforming the geometric variant, which achieves 91.2%. This improvement is attributed to the restrictive nature of geometric heuristics when applied to point cloud data, where measurements are often distorted due to light reflection or sensor noise, leading to a high number of false negatives.

Conversely, in natural environments where geometries are diffused and clearly separating traversable ground points is a non-trivial task, the geometric variant demonstrates better metric balance, achieving an F1-score of 80.8% compared to 75.8% for the hybrid method. The flexibility that benefits the hybrid approach in structured settings becomes a disadvantage in natural terrains, as its less restrictive classification criteria lead to reduced performance under such conditions. Nonetheless, the hybrid approach confers higher reliability in terms of recall, which benefits non-critical approaches that require a higher spatial resolution at the cost of precision.

Future work will include the addition of visual information through a LiDAR-camera system, which will allow visual features to be introduced into the sparse tensors. Possibly with the aim of mitigating the main problem of supervised learning—the annotation process—we will investigate the usage of a hybrid method that allows the continuous estimation of traversability.

Author Contributions: Conceptualization, A.S.; methodology, A.S.; software, A.S. and E.H.; validation, A.S., D.V., and A.G.; formal analysis, A.S.; investigation, A.S.; resources, A.S.; data curation, A.S.; writing—original draft preparation, A.S.; writing—review and editing, D.V, A.G., and C.V.; visualization, A.S.; supervision, D.V. and A.G.; project administration, D.V. and A.G.; funding acquisition, D.V., A.G., and C.V. All authors have read and agreed to the published version of the manuscript.

Funding: MICIU/AEI/10.130-39/501100011033: TED2021-130901B-I00; European Union NextGenerationEU/PRTR: TED2021-130901B-I00; MICIU/AEI/10.13039/501100011033: PID2023-149575OB-I00; FEDER, UE: PID2023-149575OB-I00; Fundação para a Ciência e a Tecnologia: UIDB/50022/2020.

Institutional Review Board Statement: Not applicable.

Informed Consent Statement: Not applicable.

Data Availability Statement: The original data presented in the study are openly available: https://github.com/ARVCUMH/hybrid_geometric_neural_traversability.git (accessed on 3 April 2025).

Acknowledgments: This research work is part of the project TED2021-130901B-I00, funded by MICIU/AEI/10.13039/501100011033 and by the European Union NextGenerationEU/PRTR. It is also part of the project PID2023-149575OB-I00, funded by MICIU/AEI/10.13039/501100011033 and by FEDER, UE. Finally, national funds sponsored this research through FCT—Fundação para a Ciência e a Tecnologia—under project base funding (reference: UIDB/50022/2020), DOI: 54499/UIDB/50022/2020.

Conflicts of Interest: The authors declare no conflicts of interest.

References

1. Kabir, M.M.; Jim, J.R.; Istenes, Z. Terrain detection and segmentation for autonomous vehicle navigation: A state-of-the-art systematic review. *Inf. Fusion* **2025**, *113*, 102644. [CrossRef]
2. Koenig, S.; Likhachev, M. Fast replanning for navigation in unknown terrain. *IEEE Trans. Robot.* **2005**, *21*, 354–363. [CrossRef]
3. Borenstein, J.; Koren, Y. Real-time obstacle avoidance for fast mobile robots. *IEEE Trans. Syst. Man. Cybern.* **1989**, *19*, 1179–1187. [CrossRef]
4. Almeida, C.M.D.; Monteiro, A.M.V.; Câmara, G.; Soares-Filho, B.S.; Cerqueira, G.C.; Pennachin, C.L.; Batty, M. GIS and remote sensing as tools for the simulation of urban land-use change. *Int. J. Remote Sens.* **2005**, *26*, 759–774. [CrossRef]
5. Moravec, H.; Elfes, A. High resolution maps from wide angle sonar. In Proceedings of the 1985 IEEE International Conference on Robotics and Automation, St. Louis, MO, USA, 25–28 March 1985; Volume 2, pp. 116–121.
6. Langer, D.; Rosenblatt, J.; Hebert, M. A behavior-based system for off-road navigation. *IEEE Trans. Robot. Autom.* **1994**, *10*, 776–783. [CrossRef]

7. Hornung, A.; Wurm, K.M.; Bennewitz, M.; Stachniss, C.; Burgard, W. OctoMap: An efficient probabilistic 3D mapping framework based on octrees. *Auton. Robot.* **2013**, *34*, 189–206. [CrossRef]
8. Oleynikova, H.; Taylor, Z.; Fehr, M.; Siegwart, R.; Nieto, J. Voxblox: Incremental 3D euclidean signed distance fields for on-board mav planning. In Proceedings of the 2017 IEEE/RSJ International Conference on Intelligent Robots and Systems (IROS), Vancouver, BC, Canada, 24–28 September 2017; pp. 1366–1373.
9. Han, L.; Gao, F.; Zhou, B.; Shen, S. Fiesta: Fast incremental euclidean distance fields for online motion planning of aerial robots. In Proceedings of the 2019 IEEE/RSJ International Conference on Intelligent Robots and Systems (IROS), Macau, China, 4–8 November 2019; pp. 4423–4430.
10. Sun, P.; Zhao, X.; Xu, Z.; Wang, R.; Min, H. A 3D LiDAR data-based dedicated road boundary detection algorithm for autonomous vehicles. *IEEE Access* **2019**, *7*, 29623–29638. [CrossRef]
11. Wang, G.; Wu, J.; He, R.; Yang, S. A point cloud-based robust road curb detection and tracking method. *IEEE Access* **2019**, *7*, 24611–24625. [CrossRef]
12. Adnan, M.; Slavic, G.; Martin Gomez, D.; Marcenaro, L.; Regazzoni, C. Systematic and comprehensive review of clustering and multi-target tracking techniques for LiDAR point clouds in autonomous driving applications. *Sensors* **2023**, *23*, 6119. [CrossRef]
13. Fan, L.; Xiong, X.; Wang, F.; Wang, N.; Zhang, Z. Rangedet: In defense of range view for LiDAR-based 3D object detection. In Proceedings of the IEEE/CVF International Conference on Computer Vision, Montreal, BC, Canada, 11–17 October 2021; pp. 2918–2927.
14. Wu, J.; Xu, H.; Tian, Y.; Pi, R.; Yue, R. Vehicle detection under adverse weather from roadside LiDAR data. *Sensors* **2020**, *20*, 3433. [CrossRef]
15. Santo, A.; Cabrera, J.J.; Valiente, D.; Viegas, C.; Gil, A. TE-NeXt: A LiDAR-Based 3D Sparse Convolutional Network for Traversability Estimation. *arXiv* **2024**, arXiv:2406.01395.
16. Cross, G.R.; Jain, A.K. Markov random field texture models. *IEEE Trans. Pattern Anal. Mach. Intell.* **1983**, *1*, 25–39. [CrossRef] [PubMed]
17. Zhang, M.; Morris, D.D.; Fu, R. Ground segmentation based on loopy belief propagation for sparse 3D point clouds. In Proceedings of the 2015 International Conference on 3D Vision, Lyon, France, 19–22 October 2015; pp. 615–622.
18. Huang, W.; Liang, H.; Lin, L.; Wang, Z.; Wang, S.; Yu, B.; Niu, R. A fast point cloud ground segmentation approach based on coarse-to-fine Markov random field. *IEEE Trans. Intell. Transp. Syst.* **2021**, *23*, 7841–7854. [CrossRef]
19. Vasudevan, S.; Ramos, F.; Nettleton, E.; Durrant-Whyte, H. Gaussian process modeling of large-scale terrain. *J. Field Robot.* **2009**, *26*, 812–840. [CrossRef]
20. Chen, T.; Dai, B.; Liu, D.; Song, J. Sparse Gaussian process regression based ground segmentation for autonomous land vehicles. In Proceedings of the 27th Chinese Control and Decision Conference (2015 CCDC), Qingdao, China, 23–25 May 2015; pp. 3993–3998.
21. del Pino, I.; Santamaria-Navarro, A.; Zulueta, A.G.; Torres, F.; Andrade-Cetto, J. Probabilistic graph-based real-time ground segmentation for urban robotics. *IEEE Trans. Intell. Veh.* **2024**, *9*, 4989–5002. [CrossRef]
22. Liu, H.; Song, R.; Zhang, X.; Liu, H. Point cloud segmentation based on Euclidean clustering and multi-plane extraction in rugged field. *Meas. Sci. Technol.* **2021**, *32*, 095106. [CrossRef]
23. Fischler Furthermore, M. Random sample consensus: A paradigm for model fitting with applications to image analysis and automated cartography. *Commun. ACM* **1981**, *24*, 381–395. [CrossRef]
24. Steinke, N.; Goehring, D.; Rojas, R. Groundgrid: LiDAR point cloud ground segmentation and terrain estimation. *IEEE Robot. Autom. Lett.* **2023**, *9*, 420–426. [CrossRef]
25. Oh, M.; Jung, E.; Lim, H.; Song, W.; Hu, S.; Lee, E.M.; Park, J.; Kim, J.; Lee, J.; Myung, H. TRAVEL: Traversable ground and above-ground object segmentation using graph representation of 3D LiDAR scans. *IEEE Robot. Autom. Lett.* **2022**, *7*, 7255–7262. [CrossRef]
26. Hui, Z.; Jin, S.; Xia, Y.; Nie, Y.; Xie, X.; Li, N. A mean shift segmentation morphological filter for airborne LiDAR DTM extraction under forest canopy. *Opt. Laser Technol.* **2021**, *136*, 106728. [CrossRef]
27. Song, H.; Jung, J. An object-based ground filtering of airborne LiDAR data for large-area dtm generation. *Remote Sens.* **2023**, *15*, 4105. [CrossRef]
28. Himmelsbach, M.; Hundelshausen, F.V.; Wuensche, H.J. Fast segmentation of 3D point clouds for ground vehicles. In Proceedings of the 2010 IEEE Intelligent Vehicles Symposium, La Jolla, CA, USA, 21–24 June 2010; pp. 560–565.
29. Zermas, D.; Izzat, I.; Papanikolopoulos, N. Fast segmentation of 3D point clouds: A paradigm on LiDAR data for autonomous vehicle applications. In Proceedings of the 2017 IEEE International Conference on Robotics and Automation (ICRA), Singapore, 29 May–3 June 2017; pp. 5067–5073.

30. Lim, H.; Oh, M.; Myung, H. Patchwork: Concentric zone-based region-wise ground segmentation with ground likelihood estimation using a 3D LiDAR sensor. *IEEE Robot. Autom. Lett.* **2021**, *6*, 6458–6465. [CrossRef]
31. Lee, S.; Lim, H.; Myung, H. Patchwork++: Fast and robust ground segmentation solving partial under-segmentation using 3D point cloud. In Proceedings of the 2022 IEEE/RSJ International Conference on Intelligent Robots and Systems (IROS), Kyoto, Japan, 23–27 October 2022; pp. 13276–13283.
32. Deng, W.; Chen, X.; Jiang, J. A Staged Real-Time Ground Segmentation Algorithm of 3D LiDAR Point Cloud. *Electronics* **2024**, *13*, 841. [CrossRef]
33. Dong, L.; Liu, D.; Dong, Y.; Park, B.; Wan, Z. An efficient ground segmentation approach for LiDAR point cloud utilizing adjacent grids. *Mach. Vis. Appl.* **2024**, *35*, 108. [CrossRef]
34. Moosmann, F.; Pink, O.; Stiller, C. Segmentation of 3D LiDAR data in non-flat urban environments using a local convexity criterion. In Proceedings of the 2009 IEEE Intelligent Vehicles Symposium, Xi'an, China, 3–5 June 2009; pp. 215–220.
35. Bogoslavskyi, I.; Stachniss, C. Fast range image-based segmentation of sparse 3D laser scans for online operation. In Proceedings of the RSJ International Conference on Intelligent Robots and Systems (IROS), Daejeon, Republic of Korea, 9–14 October 2016; pp. 163–169.
36. Shen, Z.; Liang, H.; Lin, L.; Wang, Z.; Huang, W.; Yu, J. Fast ground segmentation for 3D LiDAR point cloud based on jump-convolution-process. *Remote Sens.* **2021**, *13*, 3239. [CrossRef]
37. Wen, H.; Liu, S.; Liu, Y.; Liu, C. Dipg-seg: Fast and accurate double image-based pixel-wise ground segmentation. *IEEE Trans. Intell. Transp. Syst.* **2023**, *25*, 5189–5200. [CrossRef]
38. Fusaro, D.; Olivastri, E.; Donadi, I.; Evangelista, D.; Menegatti, E., Pretto, A. Pyramidal 3D feature fusion on polar grids for fast and robust traversability analysis on CPU. *Robot. Auton. Syst.* **2023**, *170*, 104524. [CrossRef]

39. Li, W.; Fusaro, D.; Olivastri, E.; Mosco, S.; Bellotto, N.; Pretto, A. P-SVM2: Enhancing LiDAR-based Traversability Analysis with Augmented Point Cloud Descriptor for Autonomous Mobile Systems. In Proceedings of the 2024 IEEE International Conference on Cybernetics and Intelligent Systems (CIS) and IEEE International Conference on Robotics, Automation and Mechatronics (RAM), Hangzhou, China, 8–11 August 2024; pp. 352–359.
40. Guan, T.; Kothandaraman, D.; Chandra, R.; Sathyamoorthy, A.J.; Weerakoon, K.; Manocha, D. Ga-nav: Efficient terrain segmentation for robot navigation in unstructured outdoor environments. *IEEE Robot. Autom. Lett.* **2022**, *7*, 8138–8145. [CrossRef]
41. Sharma, S.; Ball, J.E.; Tang, B.; Carruth, D.W.; Doude, M.; Islam, M.A. Semantic segmentation with transfer learning for off-road autonomous driving. *Sensors* **2019**, *19*, 2577. [CrossRef]
42. Urrea, C.; Vélez, M. Enhancing Autonomous Visual Perception in Challenging Environments: Bilateral Models with Vision Transformer and Multilayer Perceptron for Traversable Area Detection. *Technologies* **2024**, *12*, 201. [CrossRef]
43. Paigwar, A.; Erkent, Ö.; Sierra-Gonzalez, D.; Laugier, C. GndNet: Fast ground plane estimation and point cloud segmentation for autonomous vehicles. In Proceedings of the 2020 IEEE/RSJ International Conference on Intelligent Robots and Systems (IROS), Las Vegas, NV, USA, 25–29 October 2020; pp. 2150–2156.
44. He, D.; Abid, F.; Kim, Y.M.; Kim, J.H. SectorGSnet: Sector learning for efficient ground segmentation of outdoor LiDAR point clouds. *IEEE Access* **2022**, *10*, 11938–11946. [CrossRef]
45. Atas, F.; Cielniak, G.; Grimstad, L. From Simulation to Field: Learning Terrain Traversability for Real-World Deployment. *arXiv* **2025**, arXiv:2501.06904.
46. Frey, J.; Hoeller, D.; Khattak, S.; Hutter, M. Locomotion policy guided traversability learning using volumetric representations of complex environments. In Proceedings of the 2022 IEEE/RSJ International Conference on Intelligent Robots and Systems (IROS), Kyoto, Japan, 23–27 October 2022; pp. 5722–5729.
47. Ruetz, F.A.; Lawrance, N.; Hernández, E.; Borges, P.V.; Peynot, T. ForestTrav: 3D LiDAR-only forest traversability estimation for autonomous ground vehicles. *IEEE Access* **2024**, *12*, 37192–37206. [CrossRef]
48. Zhu, C.; Wang, T.; Zhang, W.; Pang, J.; Liu, X. Llava-3D: A simple yet effective pathway to empowering lmms with 3D-awareness. *arXiv* **2024**, arXiv:2409.18125.
49. He, S.; Ding, H.; Jiang, X.; Wen, B. Segpoint: Segment any point cloud via large language model. In Proceedings of the European Conference on Computer Vision, Milan, Italy, 29 September–4 October 2024; Springer: Berlin/Heidelberg, Germany, 2024; pp. 349–367.
50. Huang, K.C.; Li, X.; Qi, L.; Yan, S.; Yang, M.H. Reason3D: Searching and reasoning 3D segmentation via large language model. In Proceedings of the International Conference on 3D Vision 2025, Singapore, 25–28 March 2025.
51. Liu, Z.; Mao, H.; Wu, C.Y.; Feichtenhofer, C.; Darrell, T.; Xie, S. A convnet for the 2020s. In Proceedings of the IEEE/CVF Conference on Computer Vision and Pattern Recognition, New Orleans, LA, USA, 18–24 June 2022; pp. 11976–11986.
52. Choy, C.; Gwak, J.; Savarese, S. 4d spatio-temporal convnets: Minkowski convolutional neural networks. In Proceedings of the IEEE/CVF Conference on Computer Vision and Pattern Recognition, Long Beach, CA, USA, 15–20 June 2019; pp. 3075–3084.
53. Ronneberger, O.; Fischer, P.; Brox, T. U-net: Convolutional networks for biomedical image segmentation. In Proceedings of the Medical Image Computing and Computer-Assisted Intervention–MICCAI 2015: 18th International Conference, Munich, Germany, 5–9 October 2015; proceedings, part III 18; Springer: Berlin/Heidelberg, Germany, 2015; pp. 234–241.
54. He, K.; Zhang, X.; Ren, S.; Sun, J. Deep residual learning for image recognition. In Proceedings of the IEEE Conference on Computer Vision and Pattern Recognition, Las Vegas, NV, USA, 27–30 June 2016; pp. 770–778.
55. Behley, J.; Garbade, M.; Milioto, A.; Quenzel, J.; Behnke, S.; Stachniss, C.; Gall, J. Semantickitti: A dataset for semantic scene understanding of LiDAR sequences. In Proceedings of the IEEE/CVF International Conference on Computer Vision, Seoul, Republic of Korea, 27 October–2 November 2019; pp. 9297–9307.
56. Geiger, A.; Lenz, P.; Urtasun, R. Are we ready for autonomous driving? the kitti vision benchmark suite. In Proceedings of the 2012 IEEE Conference on Computer Vision and Pattern Recognition, Providence, RI, USA, 16–21 June 2012; pp. 3354–3361.
57. Jiang, P.; Osteen, P.; Wigness, M.; Saripalli, S. Rellis-3D dataset: Data, benchmarks and analysis. In Proceedings of the 2021 IEEE International Conference on Robotics and Automation (ICRA), Xi'an, China, 30 May–5 June 2021; pp. 1110–1116.

technologies

MDPI

Article

Artificial Vision System for Autonomous Mobile Platform Used in Intelligent and Flexible Indoor Environment Inspection

Marius Cristian Luculescu *, Luciana Cristea * and Attila Laszlo Boer *

Product Design, Mechatronics and Environment Department, Faculty of Product Design and Environment, Transilvania University of Brasov, 500036 Brasov, Romania

* Correspondence: lucmar@unitbv.ro (M.C.L.); lcristea@unitbv.ro (L.C.); boera@unitbv.ro (A.L.B.)

Abstract: The widespread availability of artificial intelligence (AI) tools has facilitated the development of complex, high-performance applications across a broad range of domains. Among these, processes related to the surveillance and assisted verification of indoor environments have garnered significant interest. This paper presents the implementation, testing, and validation of an autonomous mobile platform designed for the intelligent and flexible inspection of such spaces. The artificial vision system, the main component on which the study focuses, was built using a Raspberry Pi 5 development module supplemented by a Raspberry Pi AI Kit to enable hardware acceleration for image recognition tasks using AI techniques. Some of the most recognized neural network models were evaluated in line with the application's specific requirements. Utilizing transfer learning techniques, these models were further developed and trained with additional image datasets tailored to the inspection tasks. The performance of these networks was then tested and validated on new images, facilitating the selection of the model with the best results. The platform's flexibility was ensured by mounting the artificial vision system on a mobile structure capable of autonomously navigating indoor environments and identifying inspection points, markers, and required objects. The platform could generate reports, make decisions based on the detected conditions, and be easily reconfigured for alternative inspection tasks. Finally, the intelligent and flexible inspection system was tested and validated for its deep learning-based vision system performance.

Keywords: DL—deep learning; CNN—Convolutional Neural Network; YOLO—You Only Look Once; autonomous; navigation; mobile robot; intelligent; inspection

1. Introduction

1.1. Automated Indoor Inspection

Automated indoor inspection can revolutionize how buildings and other controlled environments are managed and monitored without direct human intervention. In recent years, due to the implications and effects of this activity, this subject has become an increasingly important and complex concern through an approach based on the study and conception of the use of robots [1–4] and autonomous systems to analyze, monitor, and evaluate the conditions in an indoor environment [1,5], as well as detect anomalies, identify problems, and assess compliance with specific standards.

The success of indoor inspection depends on technological progress, addressing the challenges of navigation, detection, and autonomy, and the responsible integration of these solutions into society [3].

The most commonly implemented technologies for autonomous spatial monitoring include the mapping and analysis of spaces with the help of stereo cameras and LiDAR sensors [4,6], the detection and classification of elements using specialized algorithms for object recognition such as Convolutional Neural Networks (CNNs), the automatic collection of motion-related data [2–4,7] and environmental features, machine learning for predictions, anomaly detection, and automatic decision making based on artificial intelligence (AI) algorithms, the automatic inspection of spaces with autonomous mobile systems, and the detailed evaluation and analysis of spaces with reconstruction by 3D scanning systems [4,8].

The applications of such technologies vary from inspecting commercial and industrial spaces to smart houses, hospitals, and critical spaces such as laboratories or hazardous material warehouses [7].

1.2. Autonomous Indoor Inspection Systems

A high level of utility characterizes autonomous indoor inspection systems without human control. The first aspect considers the reduction in risks for humans. In hazardous environments, for example, spaces with toxic gases and inaccessible or unstable areas, mobile robots can replace humans, reducing the risk of accidents.

Autonomous systems can work continuously, reducing the time required for inspections with a human operator, but above all, eliminating the stress and monotony of repetitive activities and ensuring precise checks with a constant accuracy over time, which demonstrates the increased efficiency of these technologies [9].

The use of these systems can lead to increased accessibility to hard-to-use spaces. In the long term, operational costs are reduced compared to inspections performed with human operators.

An important aspect concerns the assurance of legal, compliance, and constancy requirements, elements that are respected in a reliable and documented way in the case of autonomous solutions.

Autonomous inspection is important not only from the perspective of safety and efficiency, but also for monitoring and optimizing energy consumption, the early detection of problems, and monitoring structural integrity, as well as for integration into IoT systems by creating intelligent ecosystems that can automatically manage conditions from the inside based on data collected by robots.

While autonomous inspection has immense potential, some significant challenges need to be addressed, as follows:

(a) Navigation and localization technologies that involve navigation in complex [2,10], unstructured, or dynamic environments and localization and mapping systems (SLAM—Simultaneous Localization and Mapping) that must be sufficiently accurate in low-light conditions or congested spaces [4];
(b) The detection and recognition of abnormal objects or conditions using advanced computer vision methods [1,2,4,11];
(c) Energy autonomy, i.e., practical solutions for energy management for the prolonged operation of robots;
(d) Interaction with the environment that considers adaptation to unpredictable obstacles and the ability to navigate safely among people, respecting ethical and legal norms [2,3,11,12];
(e) Data privacy and security must address issues related to people's privacy in indoor spaces and protection against cyber-attacks [4].

In this context, the development of autonomous mobile systems equipped with artificial vision to ensure analysis and monitoring following the specifics of the application and to ensure an increased efficiency is of particular importance for solving complex problems regarding the inspection and autonomous monitoring of indoor spaces and the accuracy, legal, compliance, and constancy requirements imposed.

In the work of Sanchez-Cubillo, J et al. [1], the suitability of such an autonomous system with computer vision is described in three inspection cases by introducing an AI algorithm capable of detecting, classifying, and following the characteristics of the environment. This study highlights the increased performance of autonomous inspection systems equipped with artificial intelligence.

Important studies have focused on the development of object detection based on AI techniques and its implementation on mobile platforms equipped with artificial vision systems. Compared to autonomous indoor inspection systems equipped with artificial vision, the great challenge is the analysis and high-precision processing of acquired image streams and the recognition of objects, people, and border situations.

Recent concerns aim to improve object detection and recognition performance by integrating artificial intelligence with artificial vision systems implemented in various applications. Bai, C. et al. [11] review the object detection of AI algorithms based on improvement methods such as multiscale, attention mechanism, and supervision. The study analyzes algorithms such as YOLO, SSD, and Transformer and states that the YOLO series algorithms are suitable for real-time object detection due to their fast speed and high accuracy, but with a poor performance for small objects. Algorithms in the SSD series provide a good performance in detecting small objects, but the detection accuracy is reduced [7].

In Song, Q. et al.'s [12] study, an improved multiscale parallel YOLO algorithm named YOLO-MSP is tested on pedestrian recognition. The proposed algorithm assures an increased accuracy and speed in pedestrian detection.

Halder et al. [4] review the usage of robots in inspecting and monitoring buildings and infrastructure. The report highlights that the research in this field is structured in the following eight directions: autonomous navigation, motion control systems, sensing, knowledge extraction, safety, multi-robot, human–robot collaboration, and data transmission [4].

Based on this study's results, there is a need to concentrate current research on solving the problems related to the realization of autonomous integrated mobile systems to inspect indoor spaces. This aspect involves solving problems related to autonomous navigation, optimal image selection and capture, and increasing the performance of the object recognition system, as well as decision making and data transmission [4].

The key contribution of this research includes integrating one of the latest advancements in edge computing for embedded artificial vision applications (Raspberry Pi AI Kit, launched in 2024) into an autonomous mobile inspection platform. To the best of our knowledge, this is the first embedded artificial vision system utilizing the Raspberry Pi AI Kit for an autonomous mobile inspection platform mentioned in a journal paper. A literature search in international databases such as Clarivate and Scopus found no published studies related to this AI accelerator. Other significant contributions include the design of a flexible system architecture enabling seamless adaptation to various mobile inspection platforms and implementing a specialized YOLO training methodology to improve detection accuracy and enhance generalization capabilities. All these contributions are outlined in the conclusions section.

In this context, the main objective of the research presented in this work was developing and implementing an autonomous mobile platform for intelligent and flexible indoor environment inspection to validate the concept and evaluate the performance of the artificial visual system.

2. Materials and Methods

The following specific objectives were established to achieve the main objective:

(a) **The development and implementation of a mobile platform (hardware)** capable of remote control and autonomous navigation based on sensor data;
(b) **The development and integration of a computer vision system (hardware)** to enhance the perception capabilities of the mobile platform;
(c) **The design and implementation of an object detection module (software)** utilizing artificial intelligence techniques;
(d) **The deployment of the object detection module** on the mobile platform, creating an artificial vision system;
(e) **The development and implementation of an autonomous navigation algorithm** leveraging object detection for enhanced mobility and decision making;
(f) **The development of a software module for managing the inspection process** in indoor environments, ensuring flexible missions and efficient data collection;
(g) **The comprehensive testing and validation of the artificial vision system** to assess its accuracy and operational efficiency under real-world conditions.

A detailed flowchart of the research is presented in Figure 1.

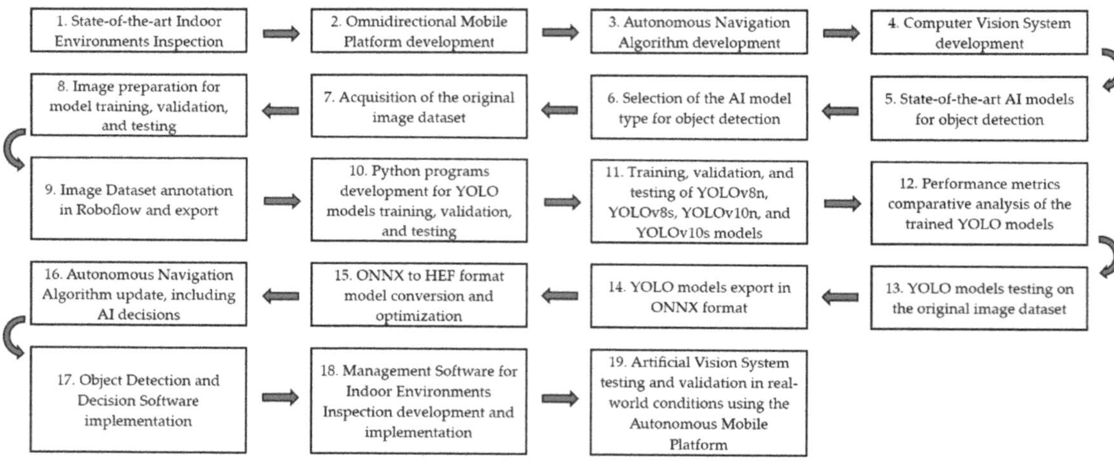

Figure 1. The research flowchart.

The steps covering the introduction and addressing all the specified objectives are detailed in the following sections of the paper.

2.1. Description of the Inspection Process

The inspection process is designed to verify the presence of specific objects within indoor environments and detect potentially undesirable situations, such as open windows or doors. To facilitate object presence verification, designated observation points are defined and marked. These locations are hereinafter referred to as Inspection Points (IPs).

At each IP, the autonomous mobile platform must stop and utilize the artificial vision system to determine whether the objects associated with that location are present or absent. Additionally, if the system detects open windows or doors during its movement, it immediately reports the event to the central server, triggering an alert.

The inspection process follows a structured sequence of steps, as follows: **system initialization**—the system starts from a predefined START point based on an inspection mission; **autonomous navigation**—the platform moves autonomously, leveraging sensor-based obstacle avoidance while simultaneously scanning its surroundings to identify IP markers; **IP detection and approach**—once an IP marker is identified, the system orients itself towards the designated location; **positioning at the IP**—the platform stops precisely at the identified IP; **object detection and verification**—the artificial vision system scans the area to identify and confirm the presence of predefined objects, and the inspection results are then transmitted to the central system; and **continuation of navigation**—the platform proceeds either to the next IP or towards the predefined STOP point.

Upon reaching the STOP point, the system may initiate a new inspection mission or return to its initial location. The START and STOP points are marked similarly to the IPs, ensuring a structured and efficient inspection workflow.

2.2. *Structure of the Inspection System*

Figure 2 presents the system's structure, comprising hardware and software components.

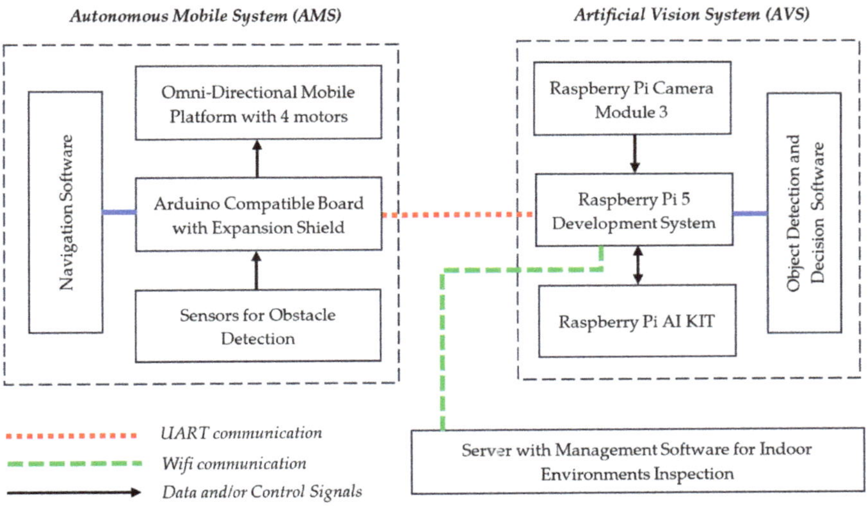

Figure 2. The structure of the autonomous mobile platform for intelligent and flexible indoor environment inspection.

This structure is further detailed in the following subsections, focusing on the materials used in the study and the methods applied to implement, test, and validate the platform.

2.3. *Hardware Subsystem*

The hardware subsystem comprises the following three main components: an omnidirectional mobile platform, a motion control subsystem, and a computer vision subsystem.

The development process starts with acquiring a Tscinbuny ESP32 Robot for Arduino Uno Starter Kit [13], which serves as the basis for the inspection platform to ensure a reliable mobility within indoor environments.

Figure 3 presents a comparative view of the initial mobile platform and the enhanced version resulting from system modifications.

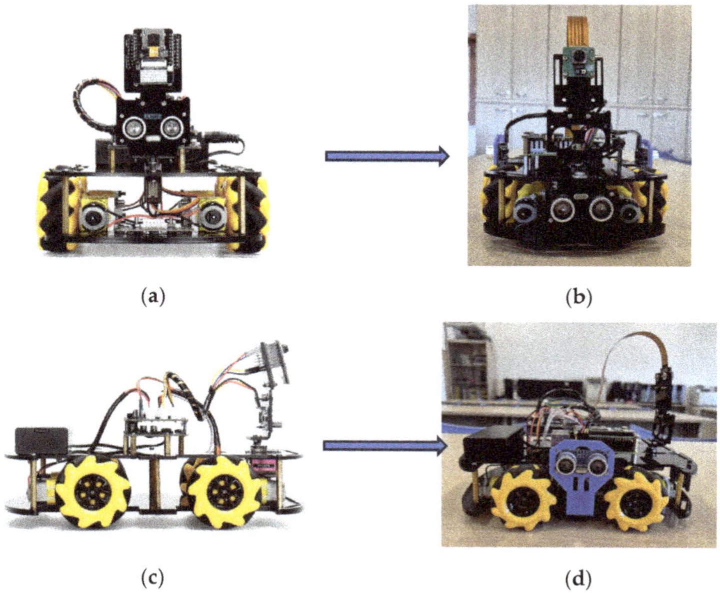

Figure 3. The autonomous mobile platform used for indoor environment inspection. (**a**) Tscinbuny ESP32 Robot for Arduino Uno—front view [13]; (**b**) modified platform—front view; (**c**) Tscinbuny ESP32 Robot for Arduino Uno—lateral view [13]; and (**d**) modified platform—lateral view.

2.3.1. Initial Structure of the Mobile Platform

The Tscinbuny Omni-Directional Mobile Platform contains a chassis equipped with the following components: four gear motors enabling Four-Wheel Drive (4WD); four Mecanum wheels facilitating omnidirectional movement; a tracking module featuring three line-following sensors positioned at the front of the robot; a servo motor that actuates the support for an ultrasonic sensor with a detection range of 2–400 cm; an ESP32 CAM module; and the Motion Control Subsystem (MSC). The system is powered by a module consisting of two 18,650 batteries, and video streaming is facilitated via the ESP32 CAM's Wi-Fi interface.

The MCS is implemented using an Arduino-compatible development board mounted with an Expansion Shield (ES). The ES incorporates drivers and connectors for each of the four DC motors and connectors for the sensors and the servo.

2.3.2. Modified Structure of the Mobile Platform

Several modifications and improvements are implemented to create a mobile platform capable of remote control and autonomous movement based on sensors for wall tracking or obstacle avoidance.

Remote control is facilitated through a connection to a web server hosted on the ESP32 CAM, with command transmission occurring via the Wi-Fi communication interface. The received commands are sent to the MCS through an asynchronous serial communication interface.

For obstacle avoidance and/or wall tracking, two additional ultrasonic sensors are installed on the lateral sides of the platform, and the position of the existing front-facing ultrasonic sensor is adjusted. The required distance to be maintained from walls or obstacles can be configured through the graphical interface of the inspection process management system.

2.3.3. Artificial Vision System

The ESP32 CAM module is replaced with a more powerful subsystem based on a Raspberry Pi 5 development board with 8 GB of RAM [14], paired with a Raspberry Pi Camera Module 3 [15] featuring a Sony IMX708 sensor, to develop and implement a computer vision system (hardware) for the mobile platform.

The camera offers a resolution of 11.9 Mpx (4608 × 2592 px) and a 75° field of view. The camera is mounted on a support that can be oriented with the help of a servo motor. The platform scans the environment during movement to identify markers for inspection points, START, or STOP. The scanning involves positioning the camera successively at −90°, −5°, 0°, +45°, and +90° relative to the direction of motion, capturing images from each position, and processing them to identify the markers.

The computer vision subsystem evolves into an artificial vision system when the Raspberry Pi 5 runs AI applications. Given the requirement for real-time object detection, the integration of a supplemental AI accelerator must be considered. A study evaluated the available AI accelerators for embedded systems on the market. Three models with the best performance are presented in Table 1.

Table 1. Comparison between AI accelerators [16].

Feature	Coral USB Accelerator	Coral M.2 Accelerator with Dual Edge TPU	Raspberry Pi AI Kit
Release Year	2020	2021	2024
Form Factor	USB 3.0 Type-C	M.2-2230-D3-E	M.2 2242
AI Chip	Edge TPU	Dual Edge TPU	Hailo-8L
Performance	4 TOPS	8 TOPS	13 TOPS
Connectivity	USB 3.0 Type-C	Two PCIe Gen2 × 1 interfaces	PCIe 3.0 (Single Lane, 8 Gbps)
Compatibility	Linux, macOS, Windows	Debian-based Linux, Windows 10	Raspberry Pi 5
AI Applications	AI NVR systems, home automation, vision projects	Industrial AI, edge AI development, traffic systems	Computer vision, object detection, smart home automation
Price	USD 59.99	USD 39.99	USD 70

Due to the 13 tera-operations per second (TOPS) neural network inference accelerator based on the Hailo-8L chip and the use of the Raspberry Pi 5 development board, the **Raspberry PI AI Kit** is selected for the artificial vision system [17].

2.4. Software Subsystem

The software subsystem consists of the following three components: the Platform Autonomous Navigation Software implemented on the MCS; the Object Detection and Decision Software (ODDS) implemented on the Raspberry Pi 5 development board; and the Management Software for Indoor Environments Inspection implemented on the server.

2.4.1. Platform Autonomous Navigation Software

Depending on the characteristics of the inspection environment, the platform can be programmed to navigate along a wall at a specified distance or to move freely. In both cases, obstacles are detected using ultrasonic sensors and avoided. Additionally, the camera of the artificial vision system is controlled to scan for markers corresponding to IPs. The software is loaded onto an Arduino-compatible development board, which sends commands to the four motors. Through various combinations of commands applied to the motors, the omnidirectional platform can move in the following directions: forward, backward, left, right, top left, top right, bottom left, bottom right, clockwise rotation, and counterclockwise rotation. Navigation is also influenced by the commands received from the Object Detection and Decision Software.

2.4.2. Object Detection and Decision Software

This program runs on the Raspberry Pi 5 and utilizes the Raspberry Pi AI Kit accelerator for real-time object detection and classification.

During the mobile platform's movement, the MCS commands the servo to position the camera mount, then sends a command via the UART (Universal Asynchronous Receiver-Transmitter) interface to the AVS to capture an image.

The ODDS receives the command, captures the image, and analyzes it using the AI module. If an IP marker is detected in the image, the ODDS calculates its position relative to the center of the image and sends a command via the UART to the MCS to direct the mobile platform towards the IP marker. If no IP marker is found, the ODDS sends a "Detection process finished" message to the MCS, prompting the camera to rotate to the next position.

When the mobile platform is positioned in front of the IP marker, with the camera oriented towards it, the MCS commands the platform to rotate 180° around its center. This action ensures that the platform's rear faces the marker, and the camera is directed towards the inspection area, allowing image capture for the inspection process. The ODDS then verifies if the required objects are in the inspection area and reports the results to the Management Software for Indoor Environments Inspection implemented on the server. Subsequently, the ODDS sends a command to the MCS to continue the inspection process and locate the next IP marker.

A detailed discussion of the motion and obstacle avoidance algorithms and the positioning at the IPs, including the challenges encountered, tests performed, the algorithm's performance in complex indoor environments with dynamic obstacles, such as moving people or objects, and the results, is presented in a separate paper focused on autonomous navigation.

2.4.3. AI Models Used for Object Detection

This subsection focuses on the object detection problem utilizing AI techniques [18–20]. While various solutions exist [18], the most promising results are typically achieved using Convolutional Neural Networks (CNNs) [5,21]. The object detection problem involves object recognition and the localization of objects within an image [22]. These models can be categorized based on their approach to generating region proposals, as follows: two-stage and one-stage detectors [23].

Two-stage detectors first generate potential regions of interest (ROIs), which represent possible object locations, and in the second step, they classify and refine the bounding boxes of these proposals to achieve more precise localization. In contrast, **one-stage detectors** predict object classes and bounding boxes in a single pass through the network.

Table 2 presents a comparison between these two categories based on their different features and the recommended applications and devices for deploying these models.

Table 2. Comparison between two-stage and one-stage models for object detection.

Feature	One-Stage (OS)	Two-Stage (TS)
Accuracy (mAP)	Good, but lower than TS	Higher than OS
Speed (FPS)	Fast–Very fast	Very slow–Medium
Computational Cost	Low–Medium	Medium–High
Complexity	Medium	High
Recommended devices	Edge, Embedded	With GPU
Recommended applications	Real-time apps, autonomous driving, video surveillance, robotics	High-precision object detection, medical imaging

The most important features are as follows: *Accuracy*, expressed by Mean Average Precision (mAP), a common metric for object detection (a higher mAP indicates a better accuracy); *Speed*, expressed by frames per second (FPS), indicating how many images the model can process per second (a higher FPS means faster processing); *Computational cost*, referring to the amount of processing power (CPU/GPU) (a higher cost generally means more demand on hardware); and *Complexity*, which describes the difficulty of implementing and training the model.

A detailed analysis of the two categories highlights the most important object detection models, summarized in Table 3 [5,8,11,19,21,24–26].

Table 3. Two-stage and one-stage model features for object detection.

Model Type	Algorithm	Accuracy (mAP)	Speed (FPS)	Computational Cost	Complexity
Two-stage	R-CNN	High	Very slow	High	Complex
	Fast R-CNN	High	Faster	Moderate	Moderate
	Faster R-CNN	Very high	Moderate	Moderate	More complex than Fast R-CNN
	Cascade R-CNN	Highest	Slower	High	Most complex
One-stage	YOLO	High	Very fast	Low	Relatively simple
	SSD	Moderate	Fast	Moderate	Moderate
	RetinaNet	High	Moderate	Moderate	Moderate
	EfficientDet	High	High	Moderate	Moderate

2.4.4. AI Model Analysis and Selection

The decision for model selection is based on the considerations outlined above, as well as specific constraints such as the real-time processing requirements, hardware compatibility, limitations, and particularities of the inspection process.

Since our platform is mobile, the artificial vision system must be implemented on an embedded system. Therefore, regarding the real-time processing requirements, a model with a low computational cost is crucial. This is why a one-stage detector has to be selected. Comparing the existing solutions, YOLO seems to be optimized for GPU, SSD has a moderate resource consumption and can run efficiently even on embedded devices with limited capabilities, and RetinaNet requires a powerful GPU, making it less suitable for real-time applications with limited resources.

As shown in Tables 2–4, the YOLO, SSD, and RetinaNet models analyzed exhibit significant differences in FPS across different hardware platforms. Depending on the version and hardware used, YOLO achieves between 30 and 161 FPS. SSD provides an intermediate performance, ranging between 20 and 60 FPS. RetinaNet achieves the lowest FPS, between 5 and 30 FPS.

In the analysis of object recognition models, the criteria Accuracy, expressed by Mean Average Precision (mAP), and Complexity, which describes the difficulty of implementing and training the model, are also considered.

Regarding accuracy, YOLO has a high accuracy, as can be observed in Table 4, depending on the version and dataset used. The latest versions (YOLOv8, YOLOv9, and YOLOv10) offer significant improvements over previous ones, maintaining a speed over 100 FPS. SSD has a moderate accuracy, with an mAP between 30% and 45%, performing worse than YOLO and RetinaNet. RetinaNet is the most accurate of the three.

Analyzing these models based on the difficulty of implementing and training the model, YOLO, despite requiring a powerful GPU for training, is relatively easy to implement due to extensive documentation and the availability of pre-trained models. SSD is the simplest to train and implement, with an architecture that is easier to optimize for resource-limited devices. RetinaNet is the most complex to train and implement, being more challenging than YOLO or SSD.

Regarding applicability in indoor environments, YOLO is a high-speed object detection model that is well-adapted to variable lighting conditions and can be optimized for edge computing. However, it has limitations in detecting very small or overlapping objects. SSD detects objects of various sizes well, but may struggle with small and overlapping objects, and RetinaNet provides the highest accuracy for small objects and improved detection in complex environments. However, it is too slow for autonomous mobile platforms and requires powerful hardware.

Choosing the appropriate model involves a trade-off between speed, accuracy, and the available hardware resources.

Given its high accuracy and fast processing speed requirements, the YOLO (You Only Look Once) model is selected, as it is one of the highest-performing models in terms of these features. YOLO's reduced complexity and low computational cost align with the system's needs.

The ODDS runs on the Raspberry Pi 5 platform, which is paired with the Raspberry Pi AI Kit—a new AI accelerator solution based on the Hailo-8L chip. The Hailo-8L chip can only execute HEF (Hailo Executable Format) binary files, and YOLO is one of the models that can be compiled and converted into HEF.

It is important to note that YOLO is not a single model, but a family of open-source models developed by various authors. Since the release of YOLOv1 in 2015, 11 versions have been released, up to YOLOv11 by the end of 2024, along with 8 variants [6,27–29]. Table 4 provides an overview of these versions based on the official GitHub repositories for each YOLO release and some references.

Table 4. YOLO family models [1,11,27,28,30,31].

Model	Release Year	Accuracy (mAP) %	Speed (FPS)	Model Size (MB)	Parameters (Million)	Key Features and Improvements
YOLOv1	2015	63.4	45	193	62	Introduced real-time object detection with a single neural network
YOLOv2	2016	76.8	40	193	67	Improved accuracy with batch normalization, high-resolution classifier, and anchor boxes
YOLOv3	2018	78.6	30	236	62	Added feature pyramid networks for better detection at different scales

Table 4. *Cont.*

Model	Release Year	Accuracy (mAP) %	Speed (FPS)	Model Size (MB)	Parameters (Million)	Key Features and Improvements
YOLOv4	2020	82	62	244	64	Incorporated CSPDarknet53, PANet, Mish activation, and Mosaic data augmentation
YOLOv5	2020	88	140	27	7.5	Focused on ease of use, smaller model sizes, and faster inference
YOLOv6	2022	52	123	17	15.9	Optimized for industrial applications and improved training strategies
YOLOv7	2022	56.8	161	72	36.9	Introduced extended efficient layer aggregation networks
YOLOv8	2023	53.9	111	68	43.7	Featured a new backbone and neck architecture and improved benchmark performance
YOLOv9	2024	54	112	69	44	Further optimized architecture and enhanced feature extraction
YOLOv10	2024	55	115	70	45	Better handling of small objects and refined training procedures
YOLOv11	2024	57	120	72	46	Enhanced feature extraction and optimized for efficiency and speed

The input image size for YOLO models can vary depending on the specific model and implementation, with common resolutions including 416 × 416, 640 × 640, and 1280 × 1280.

Some YOLO models have multiple variants—nano (n), small (s), medium (m), large (l), and extra-large (x)—each differing in size and complexity, which directly impacts speed, accuracy, and resource requirements [32].

For our system, the following two YOLO models developed by Ultralytics are considered for evaluation: YOLOv8, a state-of-the-art model for object detection, classification, and instance segmentation [6,28], and YOLOv11, the latest model in the series, which supports multiple tasks, including image classification, object detection, semantic segmentation, instance segmentation, keypoint detection, and Oriented Bounding Box (OBB) [29].

A conversion from ONNX (Open Neural Network Exchange) format to HEF (Hailo Executable Format) is necessary to deploy a trained YOLO model on the Raspberry Pi AI Kit [33]. Unfortunately, during our testing, the YOLOv11 model could not be directly converted into HEF format. As a result, we opt to replace it with YOLOv10.

The ODDS uses a YOLO model for object detection and classification. When an IP marker is detected with a confidence score exceeding a predefined threshold, its position in the image is calculated relative to the camera's center. The system determines the necessary adjustments by correlating this position with the camera's orientation angle relative to the platform's direction of movement. Then, it sends a command to the Motion Control Subsystem (MCS) to ensure that the platform moves directly toward the detected IP marker.

2.4.5. Dataset Used for Training, Validation, and Testing

The initial training, validation, and testing of the pre-trained YOLO models were conducted using a dataset consisting of 1033 images in .jpg format, containing objects categorized into nine classes. These were **IP markers** (four classes): *Inspection_1*, *Inspection_2*, *Inspection_3*, and *Inspection_4*; **Final position marker** (one class): *Stop_Sign* (indicating the end of the inspection process); **Target object for presence verification** (one class): *Fire_Extinguisher*; and **Structural elements for anomaly detection** (three classes): *Door_Open_DI3* (open door detection), *Window_Open_DI3* (open window detection in room areas), and *Window_Open_Hall* (open window detection in hallways). These high-resolution images were captured using the camera of a Samsung S24+ smartphone under varying lighting conditions and from multiple angles, including the presence of shadows and other surrounding objects, in order to ensure a certain level of dataset diversity.

From the initial 1033 images, smaller regions containing the objects of interest were cropped and used for training, validating, and testing the models. This preprocessing step aimed to enhance detection accuracy by focusing on relevant features. However, the final evaluation was conducted on the original, uncropped images to ensure the model's ability to generalize to unconstrained environments and to assess the model's real-world performance in detecting objects within full-scene contexts.

Figure 4 provides sample cropped images representing each class.

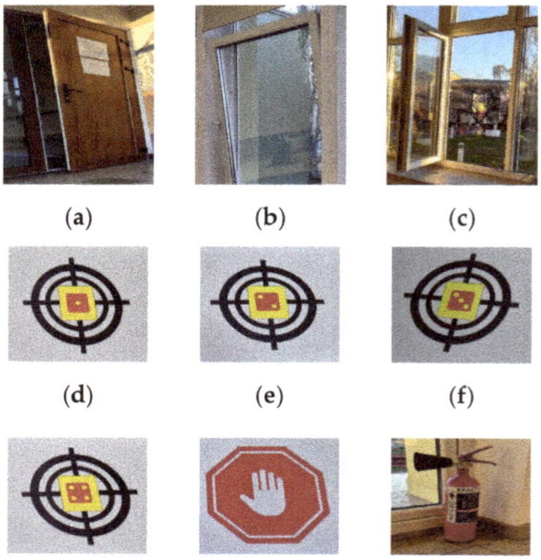

(a) (b) (c) (d) (e) (f) (g) (h) (i)

Figure 4. Image samples for the dataset classes. (**a**) Door_Open_DI3; (**b**) Window_Open_DI3; (**c**) Window_Open_Hall; (**d**) Inspection_1; (**e**) Inspection_2; (**f**) Inspection_3; (**g**) Inspection_4; (**h**) Stop_Sign; and (**i**) Fire_extinguisher.

Transfer learning was applied to train the model using pre-trained nano and small versions of YOLOv8 and YOLOv10. These models were imported and fine-tuned on the dataset using custom Python 3.12 scripts.

Image annotation was performed using Roboflow. Each uploaded image was manually annotated by drawing a bounding box around the target object and assigning it to one of the nine predefined classes. Once all 1033 images were labelled, the dataset was finalized.

The images were split automatically by Roboflow into the following three subsets: **training subset**—70% of the images (725 images); **validation subset**—20% of the images (208 images); and **testing subset**—10% of the images (100 images). Table 5 presents a detailed overview of the dataset structure.

Table 5. Dataset structure: number of images for model training, validation, and testing.

Class Number	Class Name	Training Count	Validation Count	Testing Count	Total Count
0	Door_Open_DI3	81	23	11	115
1	Fire_extinguisher	56	16	8	80
2	Inspection_1	56	16	8	80
3	Inspection_2	56	16	8	80
4	Inspection_3	57	16	7	80
5	Inspection_4	56	16	8	80
6	Stop_Sign	56	16	8	80
7	Window_Open_DI3	140	40	20	200
8	Window_Open_Hall	167	49	22	238
	TOTAL images	725	208	100	1033

After creating the dataset, it was exported in the YOLOv8-specific format, which included three folders (*train*, *valid*, and *test*) and a *data.yaml* configuration file.

Each folder contained an images subfolder with the dataset images and a labels subfolder with corresponding annotation files.

A label text file was generated for each image, containing the assigned class number and the normalized bounding box coordinates. All images were resized to 640 × 640 pixels using Roboflow to ensure compatibility with YOLOv8.

This dataset and custom Python scripts were used for training, validation, and testing. The results are presented in the following section.

2.4.6. Management Software for Indoor Environments Inspection

The entire inspection process is managed by a dedicated software module running on a server connected to the same network as the inspection area. This module provides the following functionalities: **Mission Planning**—users can create an inspection mission, define the inspection path, and specify Inspection Points (IPs) along with the objects that need to be verified at each location; **Navigation Mode Selection**—the system allows the user to choose whether the mobile platform navigates autonomously, following walls, or moves freely to locate IPs; **Automated Alerts**—if enabled, the system can receive alerts from the mobile platform when open doors or windows are detected, correlating these notifications with the last identified IP; and **Manual Control and Video Streaming**—the software includes an option for manual operation of the mobile platform and provides real-time video streaming from the onboard camera.

3. Results

This section details the evaluation methodology for model performance, the results obtained during the training process of YOLOv8 and YOLOv10, and their performance on the following two datasets: a test set of 100 cropped images and the entire dataset of 1,033 uncropped images.

All training and validation experiments were conducted on a laptop. The models were trained using the following two approaches: **fixed training** with 200 epochs and **adaptive training**, where the number of epochs was dynamically adjusted based on performance plateau detection to prevent overfitting.

After training, the models were exported in ONNX format and converted into HEF for deployment on the Raspberry Pi AI Kit to enable real-time object detection in the inspection process. Finally, the results obtained during the testing and validation of the artificial vision system are presented.

3.1. Model Performance Evaluation

In the context of YOLO-based object detection, model predictions involve the following two critical aspects: **object detection**, which determines the bounding box location, and **classification**, which assigns the correct class label to the detected object.

Object localization accuracy is evaluated using **Intersection over Union** (*IoU*), a key metric that measures how well the predicted bounding box overlaps with the ground truth bounding box. *IoU* is defined as follows:

$$IoU = \frac{Area\ of\ Overlap}{Area\ of\ Union} \tag{1}$$

where the *Area of Overlap* is the shared area between the predicted box and the ground truth box, while the *Area of Union* is the total area covered by both boxes combined (including the overlap). *IoU* values range from zero to one, with higher values indicating a better localization accuracy.

The classification performance of YOLO models is evaluated using the ***prediction score***, which measures the confidence level of the model in assigning an object to a specific class. It is defined as follows:

$$Prediction\ score = OC \times CP = (PO \times IoU) \times CP \tag{2}$$

where *OC* is the *object confidence* that measures the probability that an object exists within the predicted bounding box, *CP* is the *class probability* computed by the model to indicate the likelihood that the detected object belongs to a specific class, and *PO* is the probability computed by the model that the bounding box contains an object.

For each detected object, a prediction score is computed across all possible classes, and the highest score determines the assigned class label.

During training, the YOLO model is optimized to maximize the score for correct predictions and minimize it for incorrect predictions. Confidence is used in the loss function, which penalizes incorrect bounding boxes and class predictions.

When the model is evaluated, thresholds are set for IoU (typically IoU = 0.5) and for the prediction score so that the object can be classified in a specific class (typically conf = 0.25 for YOLO models). Based on these thresholds, YOLO model predictions are classified as follows:

- **True Positive** (TP) if the model correctly detects an object (IoU $\geq$ threshold) and classifies it into the correct category;
- **False Positive** (FP) if a bounding box is predicted but it does not sufficiently overlap with a ground truth box (IoU < threshold), or the class prediction is incorrect;
- **False Negative** (FN) if an object is present in the ground truth box, but the model fails to detect it, or the predicted bounding box is of the wrong class;
- **True Negative** (TN) if the model correctly identifies an image region as not containing any object of interest.

In object detection, true negatives (TNs) are generally not considered the same way as in classification problems, since YOLO models focus on detecting objects rather than confirming their absence. Consequently, TN is typically not computed for bounding boxes.

The performance of an object detection model is commonly evaluated using the following metrics: precision, recall, accuracy, F1-score, average precision, and mean average precision computed with the formulas presented below.

Precision measures the proportion of correct detections among all predicted detections, as follows:

$$Precision = \frac{TP}{TP + FP} \tag{3}$$

A high precision score indicates that most detected objects are correctly classified, minimizing false positives.

Recall quantifies the proportion of actual objects in the dataset that were successfully detected, as follows:

$$Recall = \frac{TP}{TP + FN} \tag{4}$$

A high recall score indicates that the model successfully detects most objects, minimizing false negatives.

Accuracy represents the proportion of correct predictions (both *TP* and *TN*) relative to all predictions, as follows:

$$Accuracy = \frac{TP + TN}{TP + TN + FP + FN} \times 100\% \tag{5}$$

F1-Score is the harmonic mean of precision and recall, and it is used when both precision and recall are equally important.

$$F1 - Score = 2 \times \frac{Precision \times Recall}{Precision + Recall} \tag{6}$$

The **average precision** (*AP*) quantifies the area under the precision–recall curve generated by varying the confidence threshold. For a single class, *AP* is computed with the following formula:

$$AP = \int_0^1 P(R)dR \tag{7}$$

where *P(R)* is the precision at each recall value.

Mean average precision (*mAP*) extends the *AP* by averaging it across all object classes in a dataset, providing a single value for the evaluation of the overall performance of an object detection model.

$$mAP = \frac{1}{N}\sum_{I=1}^{N} AP_i \tag{8}$$

where *N* is the number of classes and *APi* is the average precision for the i-th class.

The following two variants of mAP are commonly used for model performance evaluation: mAP@0.5 (Mean Average Precision at IoU = 0.5) and mAP@0.5:0.95 (Mean Average Precision across IoU thresholds ranging from 0.5 to 0.95 in steps of 0.05). While mAP@0.5 can easily achieve high scores because it allows for detections with only a moderate overlap, mAP@0.5:0.95 provides a more robust assessment of model performance by considering varying levels of overlap strictness.

3.2. Training, Validation, and Testing of YOLO Models

The training, validation, and testing of YOLO models were performed using Python programs running on a DELL Precision 3551 laptop, manufactured by DELL Technologies, and sourced from Brasov, Romania, equipped with an Intel® Core™ i7-10750H processor, 32 GB RAM, 1TB SSD, and an Nvidia Quadro P620 GPU with 4GB graphics memory.

Four pre-trained YOLO models were imported and trained using the 725-image dataset, with validation performed on an additional 208 images. The key characteristics of each imported model are summarized in Table 6.

The parameters of each YOLO model refer to learnable weights and biases that the model adjusts during training. Gradients are the partial derivatives of the loss function with respect to the parameters. Some parameters may not require gradient updates due to architectural constraints. Computational complexity represents the number of floating-point operations (FLOPs) required to process a single input image.

Table 6. Imported YOLO models' characteristics.

MODEL Type	Number of Layers	Number of Parameters	Number of Gradients	Computational Complexity
YOLOv8n	225	3,012,603	3,012,587	8.2 GFLOPs
YOLOv8s	225	11,139,083	11,139,067	28.7 GFLOPs
YOLOv10n	385	2,710,550	2,710,534	8.4 GFLOPs
YOLOv10s	402	8,073,318	8,073,302	24.8 GFLOPs

The following parameters were configured for training the YOLO models [34]: number of epochs = 200; batch size = 16; patience=100 (default setting); device = 0 (GPU used for processing instead of CPU); optimizer = SGD (Stochastic Gradient Descent); and initial learning rate lr0 = 0.01. Further discussions of these parameters and their influences on model performance are presented in the next section.

A confusion matrix was utilized to assess the training effectiveness of each model. This matrix compared the model's predictions to the actual ground truth labels, providing insights into the errors made by the model and identifying areas where it performed well.

A program for model testing was written in Python to compute and display for each following class: the total number of tested images; TP—true positive; FP—false positive; FN—false negative; precision; recall; F1-score; and accuracy for certain values of thresholds (Table 7).

Table 7. Results obtained with YOLOv8n, YOLOv8s, YOLOv10n, and YOLOv10s models tested on the VALIDATION dataset with a 0.25 confidence threshold.

Class Name	Total Images	TP	FP	FN	Precision	Recall	F1-Score	Accuracy
Door_Open_DI3	23	23	0	0	1.00	1.00	1.00	100.00%
Fire_extinguisher	16	16	0	0	1.00	1.00	1.00	100.00%
Inspection_1	16	16	0	0	1.00	1.00	1.00	100.00%
Inspection_2	16	16	0	0	1.00	1.00	1.00	100.00%
Inspection_3	16	16	0	0	1.00	1.00	1.00	100.00%
Inspection_4	16	16	0	0	1.00	1.00	1.00	100.00%
Stop_Sign	16	16	0	0	1.00	1.00	1.00	100.00%
Window_Open_DI3	40	40	0	0	1.00	1.00	1.00	100.00%
Window_Open_Hall	49	49	0	0	1.00	1.00	1.00	100.00%
TOTAL	208	208	0	0				100.00%

The program also generated a confusion matrix to analyze model performance across different classes further. As observed in Table 7, all four YOLO models correctly detected and classified all objects in the dataset.

A comparative analysis of model performance metrics for all four models (YOLOv8n, YOLOv8s, YOLOv10n, and YOLOv10s) after 200 training epochs is presented in Figure 5.

A comparison of the loss function trends for the models after 200 training epochs is illustrated in Figure 6.

The next step involved evaluating these models on the 100-image test dataset. The tests were conducted using a confidence threshold of 0.25 and an IoU threshold of 0.7, which are the default values for Ultralytics YOLO [35]. Figure 7 presents the confusion matrices, raw and normalized.

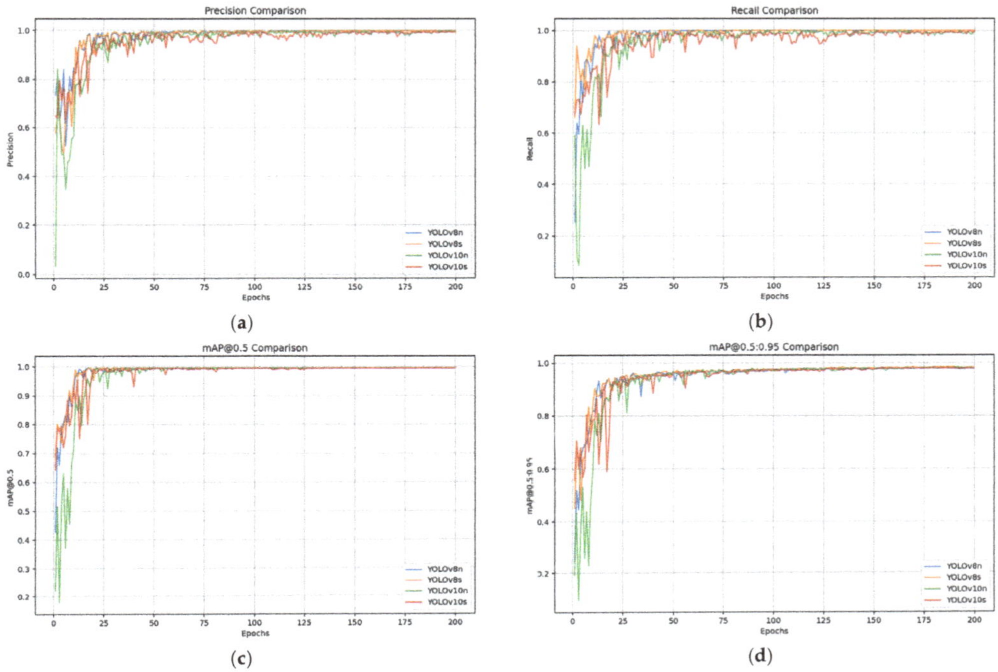

Figure 5. Metrics comparison for models YOLOv8n, YOLOv8s, YOLOv10n, and YOLOv10s. (**a**) Precision; (**b**) recall; (**c**) mAP@0.5; and (**d**) mAP@0.5:0.95.

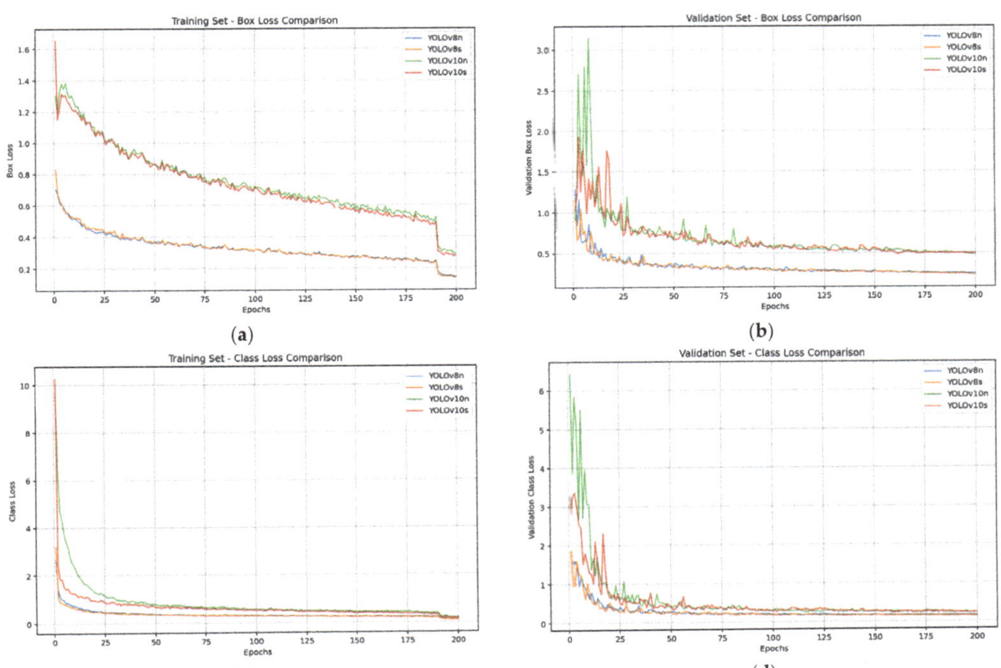

Figure 6. *Cont.*

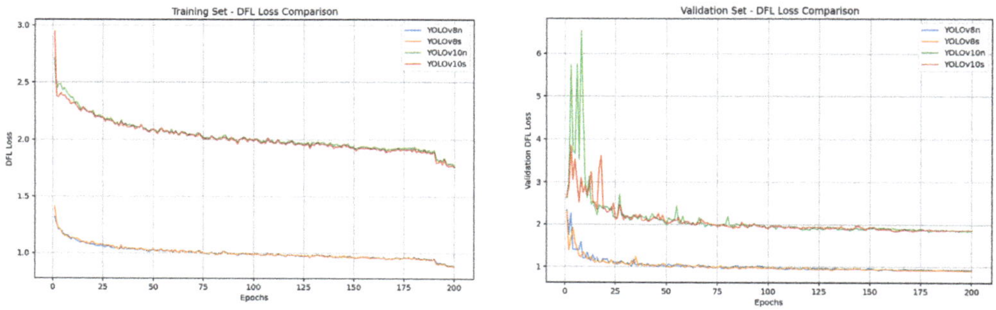

(e) (f)

Figure 6. Loss functions comparison for models YOLOv8n, YOLOv8s, YOLOv10n, and YOLOv10s. (**a**) Training set—box loss; (**b**) validation set—Box loss; (**c**) training set—class loss; (**d**) validation set—class loss; (**e**) training set—DFL loss; and (**f**) validation set—DFL loss.

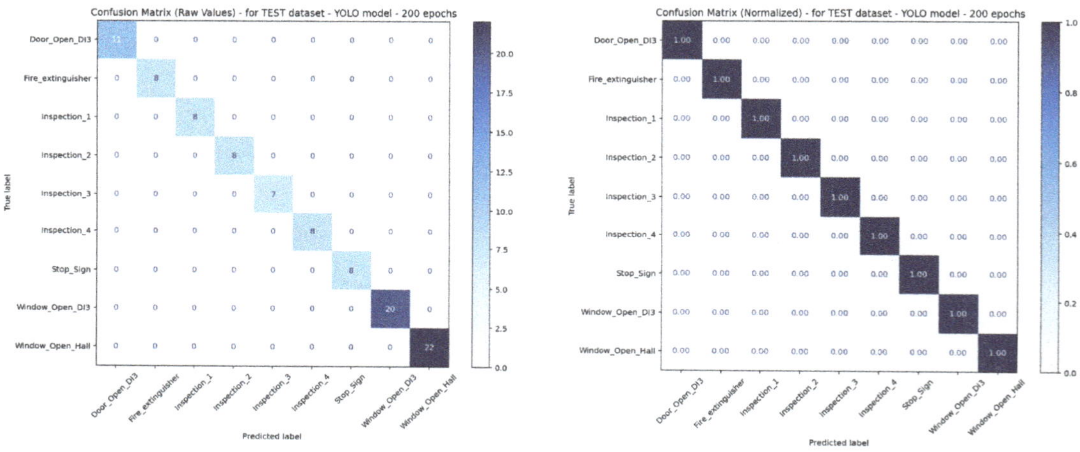

(a) (b)

Figure 7. The confusion matrices for the TEST dataset obtained with models YOLOv8n, YOLOv8s, YOLOv10n, and YOLOv10s. (**a**) Confusion matrix—raw values and (**b**) confusion matrix normalized.

With all four YOLO models trained for 200 epochs, detection and classification were perfect across all objects, as measured by precision, recall, F1-score, and accuracy.

As previously mentioned in Section 2.4.5, the dataset of 1033 images was split into 70% (725 images) for training, 20% (208 images) for validation, and 10% (100 images) for testing. Each image contained a single object, which was cropped from a larger image and manually annotated (Figure 8).

Table 8 presents the performance metrics for training, validation, and testing on the cropped images dataset, including the mAP@0.5 and mAP@0.5:0.95 for each YOLO model trained for 200 epochs.

All four trained YOLO models were tested on the entire set of 1033 original images (not cropped) to assess real-world performance. The corresponding confusion matrices are shown in Figure 9, which provides insights into how the models classified the objects in these images.

(**a**) (**b**) (**c**)

Figure 8. Image sample used for the training dataset. (**a**) Initial image; (**b**) cropped image containing the object that must be detected; and (**c**) annotated cropped image used in the training dataset.

Table 8. The metrics computed for each YOLO model trained with 200 epochs on cropped images dataset.

Model Type	Total Images	TP	FP	FN	Precision	Recall	F1-Score	Accuracy	mAP@0.5	mAP@0.5:0.95
YOLOv8n	725	725	0	0	1.000	1.000	1.000	100.000%	0.9989	0.9868
	208	208	0	0	1.000	1.000	1.000	100.000%	1.0000	0.9783
	100	100	0	0	1.000	1.000	1.000	100.000%	1.0000	0.9850
TOTAL	**1033**	**1033**	**0**	**0**	**1.000**	**1.000**	**1.000**	**100.000%**	**0.9989**	**0.9843**
YOLOv8s	725	725	0	0	1.000	1.000	1.000	100.000%	0.9989	0.9874
	208	208	0	0	1.000	1.000	1.000	100.000%	1.0000	0.9783
	100	100	0	0	1.000	1.000	1.000	100.000%	1.0000	0.9830
TOTAL	**1033**	**1033**	**0**	**0**	**1.000**	**1.000**	**1.000**	**100.000%**	**0.9989**	**0.9846**
YOLOv10n	725	721	0	4	1.000	0.996	0.998	99.638%	0.9934	0.9812
	208	208	0	0	1.000	1.000	1.000	100.000%	1.0000	0.9805
	100	100	0	0	1.000	1.000	1.000	100.000%	1.0000	0.9854
TOTAL	**1033**	**1029**	**0**	**4**	**1.000**	**0.997**	**0.999**	**99.746%**	**0.9955**	**0.9810**
YOLOv10s	725	724	0	1	1.000	0.998	0.999	99.802%	0.9967	0.9815
	208	208	0	0	1.000	1.000	1.000	100.000%	1.0000	0.9789
	100	100	0	0	1.000	1.000	1.000	100.000%	1.0000	0.9815
TOTAL	**1033**	**1032**	**0**	**1**	**1.000**	**0.999**	**0.999**	**99.861%**	**0.9967**	**0.9797**

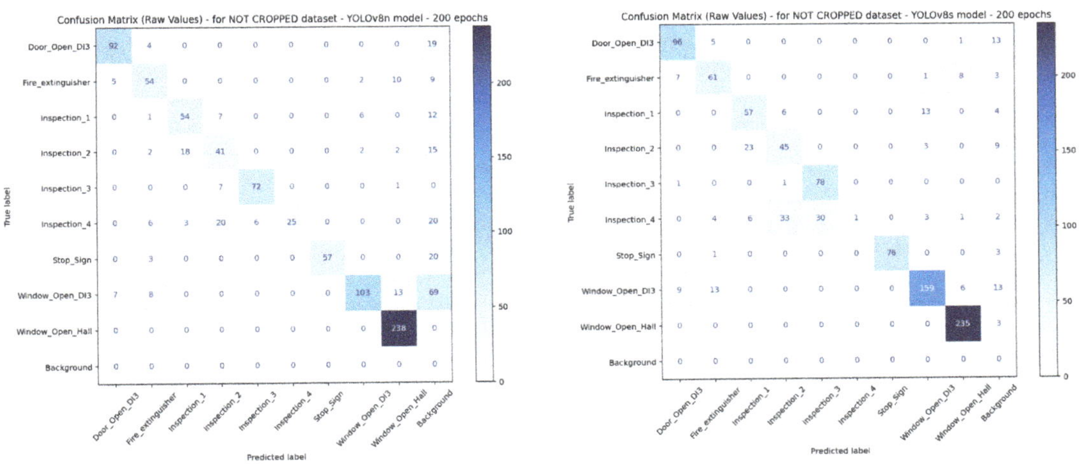

(**a**) (**b**)

Figure 9. *Cont.*

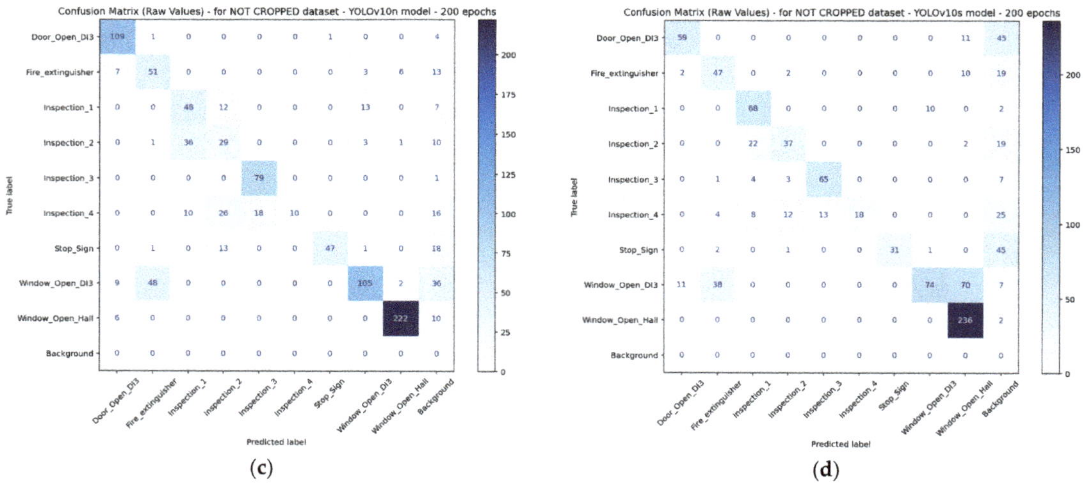

Figure 9. Confusion matrices obtained on the 1033 NOT CROPPED images dataset. (**a**) Model YOLOv8n; (**b**) model YOLOv8s; (**c**) model YOLOv10n; and (**d**) model YOLOv10s.

The computed metrics are summarized in Figure 10, where the tables were generated using Python-based evaluation scripts.

Upon analyzing their performances on the training, validation, and testing datasets (Table 8), the models exhibited an exceptional accuracy, raising concerns regarding overfitting. Overfitting in YOLO models occurs when the model learns the training data too precisely, capturing noise and specific details that reduce its generalization performance on new, unseen data. This overfitting leads to a high accuracy for the training set but a poorer performance for real-world images.

The *Patience* parameter was considered to mitigate overfitting. This parameter prevents excessive training by stopping the process when the validation performance plateaus.

Patience refers to the number of epochs to wait without improvement in validation metrics before stopping the training early [34]. In the 200-epoch training experiments, the *Patience* parameter was set to its default value of 100 epochs.

All four models were retrained with the *Patience* parameter set to 10 epochs to investigate the potential onset of overfitting before 200 epochs. Under these conditions, the training process automatically stopped at 50 epochs for the YOLOv8n and YOLOv10s models and 58 epochs for the YOLOv8s and YOLOv10n models, respectively.

All performance metrics were recomputed with these newly trained models, and the results are summarized in Table 9.

No significant differences were observed when comparing Table 9 with Table 8, suggesting that stopping early did not degrade performance. Consequently, the new models with fewer epochs were tested on the full dataset of 1033 original images to assess their generalization performance. The metrics can be observed in Table 10.

YOLOv8n model - trained with 200 epochs

Class	Total Images	TP	FP	FN	Precision	Recall	F1-Score	Accuracy
Door_Open_DI3	115	92	4	19	0.958	0.829	0.889	80.000%
Fire_extinguisher	80	54	17	9	0.761	0.857	0.806	67.500%
Inspection_1	80	54	14	12	0.794	0.818	0.806	67.500%
Inspection_2	80	41	24	15	0.631	0.732	0.678	51.250%
Inspection_3	80	72	8	0	0.900	1.000	0.947	90.000%
Inspection_4	80	25	35	20	0.417	0.556	0.476	31.250%
Stop_Sign	80	57	3	20	0.950	0.740	0.832	71.250%
Window_Open_DI3	200	103	28	69	0.786	0.599	0.680	51.500%
Window_Open_Hall	238	238	0	0	1.000	1.000	1.000	100.000%
Total	1033	736	133	164	0.800	0.792	0.790	67.806%

(a)

YOLOv8s model - trained with 200 epochs

Class	Total Images	TP	FP	FN	Precision	Recall	F1-Score	Accuracy
Door_Open_DI3	115	96	6	13	0.941	0.881	0.910	83.478%
Fire_extinguisher	80	61	16	3	0.792	0.953	0.865	76.250%
Inspection_1	80	57	19	4	0.750	0.934	0.832	71.250%
Inspection_2	80	45	26	9	0.634	0.833	0.720	56.250%
Inspection_3	80	78	2	0	0.975	1.000	0.987	97.500%
Inspection_4	80	1	77	2	0.013	0.333	0.025	1.250%
Stop_Sign	80	76	1	3	0.987	0.962	0.974	95.000%
Window_Open_DI3	200	159	28	13	0.850	0.924	0.886	79.500%
Window_Open_Hall	238	235	0	3	1.000	0.987	0.994	98.739%
Total	1033	808	175	50	0.771	0.868	0.799	73.246%

(b)

YOLOv10n model - trained with 200 epochs

Class	Total Images	TP	FP	FN	Precision	Recall	F1-Score	Accuracy
Door_Open_DI3	115	109	2	4	0.982	0.965	0.973	94.783%
Fire_extinguisher	80	51	16	13	0.761	0.797	0.779	63.750%
Inspection_1	80	48	25	7	0.658	0.873	0.750	60.000%
Inspection_2	80	29	41	10	0.414	0.744	0.532	36.250%
Inspection_3	80	79	0	1	1.000	0.988	0.994	98.750%
Inspection_4	80	10	54	16	0.156	0.385	0.222	12.500%
Stop_Sign	80	47	15	18	0.758	0.723	0.740	58.750%
Window_Open_DI3	200	105	59	35	0.640	0.745	0.689	52.500%
Window_Open_Hall	238	222	6	10	0.974	0.957	0.965	93.277%
Total	1033	700	218	115	0.705	0.797	0.738	63.396%

(c)

YOLOv10s model - trained with 200 epochs

Class	Total Images	TP	FP	FN	Precision	Recall	F1-Score	Accuracy
Door_Open_DI3	115	59	11	45	0.843	0.567	0.678	51.304%
Fire_extinguisher	80	47	14	19	0.770	0.712	0.740	58.750%
Inspection_1	80	68	10	2	0.872	0.971	0.919	85.000%
Inspection_2	80	37	24	19	0.607	0.661	0.632	46.250%
Inspection_3	80	65	8	7	0.890	0.903	0.897	81.250%
Inspection_4	80	18	37	25	0.327	0.419	0.367	22.500%
Stop_Sign	80	31	4	45	0.886	0.408	0.559	38.750%
Window_Open_DI3	200	74	119	7	0.383	0.914	0.540	37.000%
Window_Open_Hall	238	236	0	2	1.000	0.992	0.996	99.160%
Total	1033	635	227	171	0.731	0.727	0.703	57.774%

(d)

Figure 10. Metrics obtained on the 1,033 NOT CROPPED images dataset. (**a**) Model YOLOv8n; (**b**) model YOLOv8s; (**c**) model YOLOv10n; and (**d**) model YOLOv10s.

Table 9. The metrics computed for each YOLO model trained with a limited number of epochs on cropped images dataset.

Model Type	Total Images	TP	FP	FN	Precision	Recall	F1-Score	Accuracy	mAP@0.5	mAP@0.5:0.95
YOLOv8n 50 epochs	725	725	0	0	1.000	1.000	1.000	100.000%	0.9989	0.9588
	208	208	0	0	1.000	1.000	1.000	100.000%	1.0000	0.9496
	100	100	0	0	1.000	1.000	1.000	100.000%	1.0000	0.9644
TOTAL	**1033**	**1033**	**0**	**0**	**1.000**	**1.000**	**1.000**	**100.000%**	**0.9989**	**0.9561**
YOLOv8s 58 epochs	725	718	7	0	0.988	1.000	0.994	98.611%	0.9945	0.9645
	208	207	1	0	0.993	1.000	0.997	99.306%	1.0000	0.9590
	100	97	3	0	0.967	1.000	0.980	95.833%	0.9817	0.9519
TOTAL	**1033**	**1022**	**11**	**0**	**0.987**	**1.000**	**0.993**	**98.472%**	**0.9934**	**0.9610**
YOLOv10n 58 epochs	725	721	0	4	1.000	0.996	0.998	99.580%	0.9928	0.9564
	208	207	1	0	0.993	1.000	0.997	99.306%	0.9919	0.9386
	100	99	0	1	1.000	0.995	0.997	99.495%	0.9945	0.9583
TOTAL	**1033**	**1027**	**1**	**5**	**0.999**	**0.997**	**0.998**	**99.519%**	**0.9929**	**0.9520**
YOLOv10s 50 epochs	725	712	1	12	0.998	0.978	0.988	97.622%	0.9706	0.9356
	208	205	0	3	1.000	0.983	0.991	98.333%	0.9817	0.9451
	100	99	0	1	1.000	0.984	0.991	98.413%	0.9835	0.9503
TOTAL	**1033**	**1016**	**1**	**16**	**0.999**	**0.980**	**0.989**	**97.848%**	**0.9740**	**0.9374**

Table 10. New metrics obtained on the 1033 NOT CROPPED images dataset.

Model Type	Total Images	TP	FP	FN	Precision	Recall	F1-Score	Accuracy
YOLOv8n—50 epochs	1033	800	169	064	0.782	0.898	0.822	72.827%
YOLOv8s—58 epochs	1033	691	253	89	0.701	0.811	0.738	63.432%
YOLOv10n—58 epochs	1033	595	236	202	0.691	0.661	0.649	52.266%
YOLOv10s—50 epochs	1033	664	172	197	0.744	0.727	0.723	59.478%

3.3. Exporting YOLO Models to ONNX and Converting to HEF

The ultimate goal of training the YOLO models is their deployment on an autonomous mobile platform for the intelligent and flexible inspection of indoor environments. To achieve this, Ultralytics provides functionalities for exporting trained models into various formats, allowing them to be deployed across different devices and platforms [36]. The models are optimized for size and speed performance during the export process.

After comparing the results in Table 10 with those in Figure 9, no signs of overfitting were detected; therefore, the models trained for 200 epochs were selected for further use. These models were first exported in ONNX format and then converted into HEF to run on the Raspberry Pi AI Kit [37]. The conversion process from ONNX to HEF involves complex stages, including node remapping, optimization, calibration, and compilation, which adapt the model architecture and operations to Hailo's hardware. The following two different optimization strategies were employed: one using the 208-image validation dataset and another using COCO TRAIN2017, which contains 118,287 images, to evaluate whether the larger dataset could enhance performance compared to our dataset.

As a result, eight distinct HEF files were generated and deployed on the Raspberry Pi AI Kit for further testing and evaluation

3.4. Testing and Validation of the Artificial Vision System in Real-World Conditions Using the Autonomous Mobile Platform

For the final testing and validation phase, a real-world an inspection mission using the autonomous mobile platform was designed. The objects targeted for detection belonged to the following five classes: two inspection points located by IP markers (*Inspection_1* and *Inspection_3*); one object that must exist in the inspected area (*Fire_Extinguisher*); one class for open door identification (*Door_Open_DI3*); and one class for open window detection in hall areas (*Window_Open_Hall*).

The images captured by the Raspberry Pi Camera of the artificial vision system during the inspection mission were stored to ensure a consistent comparison across models. From these, a subset of 260 images was selected for analysis, including images with challenging conditions such as shadows, partial views of the objects of interest, and images with no objects. These images were randomly renamed.

The initial analysis computed standard performance metrics—precision, recall, F1-score, and accuracy—for the following eight models: four models optimized during the ONNX-to-HEF conversion using the initial 208-image validation dataset (denoted as YOLOv8n_VAL_SET, YOLOv8s_VAL_SET, YOLOv10n_VAL_SET, and YOLOv10s_VAL_SET) and four models optimized using the COCO TRAIN2017 dataset (denoted as YOLOv8n_COCO_SET, YOLOv8s_COCO_SET, YOLOv10n_COCO_SET, and YOLOv10s_COCO_SET).

Object detection on the Raspberry Pi AI Kit was performed using the *deepview-validator* Python script (version 3.2.2-post14), which has been updated for HEF support [38]. For each image, prediction scores were computed and bounding boxes were drawn, with each bounding box annotated with the predicted class name and the corresponding score (Figure 11).

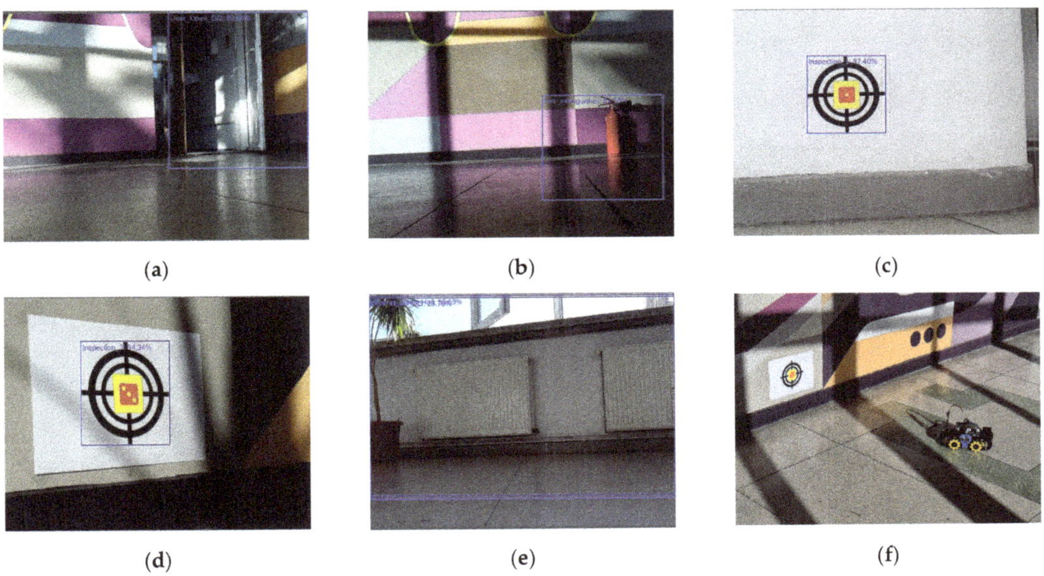

(a) (b) (c) (d) (e) (f)

Figure 11. Image samples from the inspection mission. (**a**) Door_Open_DI3; (**b**) Fire_extinguisher; (**c**) Inspection_1; (**d**) Inspection_3; (**e**) Window_Open_Hall; and (**f**) autonomous mobile platform approaching the *Inspection_3* IP marker during the mission.

The prediction scores were stored in .txt files, where each row contained the image file number alongside scores for the nine possible object classes that the model could classify. These data were imported into Excel for processing, where the true positives (TPs), false positives (FPs), and false negatives (FNs) were computed. Subsequently, the following key performance metrics were computed: precision, recall, F1-score, and accuracy.

Figure 12 presents a comparative analysis of accuracy across the YOLO models.

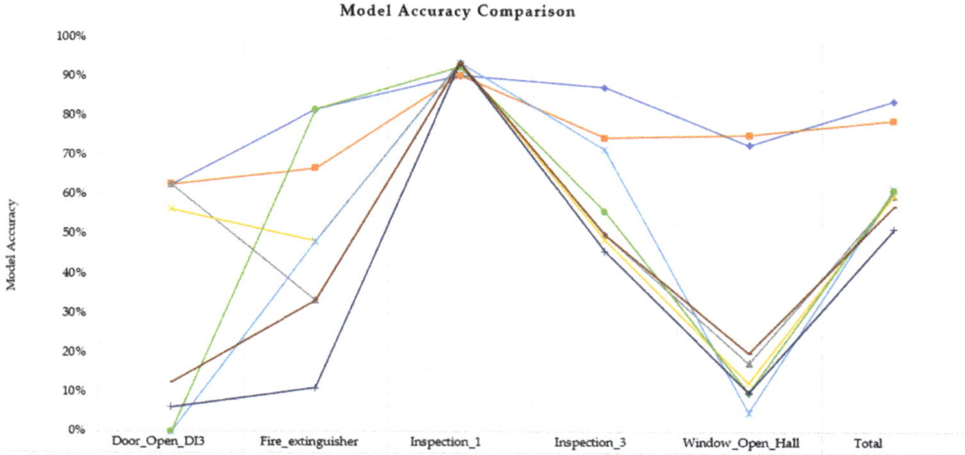

	Door_Open_DI3	Fire_extinguisher	Inspection_1	Inspection_3	Window_Open_Hall	Total
YOLOv8n - VAL	62.500%	81.481%	90.110%	87.143%	72.500%	83.607%
YOLOv8n - COCO	62.500%	66.667%	90.110%	74.286%	75.000%	78.689%
YOLOv8s - VAL	62.500%	33.333%	93.407%	50.000%	17.500%	59.836%
YOLOv8s - COCO	56.250%	48.148%	93.407%	48.571%	12.500%	59.836%
YOLOv10n - VAL	0.000%	48.148%	93.407%	71.429%	5.000%	61.475%
YOLOv10n - COCO	0.000%	81.481%	92.308%	55.714%	10.000%	61.066%
YOLOv10s - VAL	6.250%	11.111%	93.407%	45.714%	10.000%	51.230%
YOLOv10s - COCO	12.500%	33.333%	93.407%	50.000%	20.000%	56.967%

Class name

Figure 12. Model accuracy comparison.

The results indicate that the YOLOv8n model optimized using the 208-image validation dataset during the HEF conversion achieved the highest accuracy, reaching 83.607%. The following section provides a more detailed discussion regarding class performance and model comparisons.

Object detection systems are critical to modern indoor inspection protocols, particularly in applications requiring high precision, such as energy efficiency monitoring, security, and compliance. However, these systems are susceptible to object detection and recognition errors.

These errors typically manifest in the following two forms: false negatives (FNs), where an object is present but not detected, and false positives (FPs), where an object is incorrectly identified in an image. FN and FP detections directly affect such systems' reliability, introducing operational inefficiencies and potential risks.

For an autonomous mobile platform designed for intelligent and flexible indoor environment inspection, FN and FP detections pose several challenges depending on the category of objects being identified. These categories include IP markers, final position markers, target objects for presence verification, and structural elements for anomaly detection.

The accurate detection of IP markers is crucial for ensuring the correct and complete execution of the inspection process. FN errors (failure to identify an IP) disrupt the inspection sequence by omitting IPs, making it impossible to verify specific areas. Conversely, FP errors (the misidentification of an IP marker or recognition of an incorrect marker) can lead to erroneous or incomplete inspections, resulting in additional time and energy consumption. Given these implications, achieving a high detection accuracy for IP markers is essential. The test results presented in Figure 11 highlight a superior performance for these classes compared to others. This improvement can be attributed to the consistent visual characteristics of IP markers, which exhibit minimal variability.

Regarding target objects for presence verification, minimizing FP and FN responses is fundamental to maintaining the reliability of object detection systems in automated indoor inspection applications. While FP detections primarily lead to inefficiencies and unnecessary interventions, FN detections can have more serious consequences, impacting safety, security, and compliance. Addressing these challenges requires the continuous refinement of detection algorithms and implementation of adaptive learning techniques to enhance model accuracy across diverse indoor environments. Factors commonly encountered in real-world scenarios, such as variations in lighting conditions, object occlusions, and clutter levels, must be carefully considered. These conditions should be adequately represented in the training, validation, and testing datasets to ensure robustness.

Concerning structural elements for anomaly detection, FN errors, such as failing to detect an open window or door, can have significant consequences. Undetected openings in secured spaces may lead to unauthorized access or environmental contamination, compromising safety and product integrity. Furthermore, failing to detect such anomalies can result in substantial energy losses as heating or cooling systems continue to operate under the assumption of a sealed environment. Meanwhile, FP detections may trigger false alarms, leading to unnecessary human interventions and operational inefficiencies.

The second analysis focused on the computational performance of the models, considering the number of images that the models could process per second, called FPS—frames per second (higher values are better)—and latency, representing the time (in milliseconds) it took the models to process a single image (lower values are better).

If image processing for object detection and recognition was performed on the server instead of the embedded system, the system's performance in terms of FPS and latency would also be influenced by additional factors, such as network latency (due to communication with the server), battery power, and potential interference from other electronic devices.

This study performed the object detection and recognition process entirely on an embedded system consisting of a Raspberry Pi 5 and the Raspberry Pi AI Kit accelerator. Performance metrics were evaluated by comparing object detection executed on the Raspberry Pi 5 CPU versus detection utilizing the Raspberry Pi AI Kit with the Hailo-8L accelerator. This analysis emphasizes the advantages of employing the Raspberry Pi AI Kit accelerator, introduced in 2024, in contrast to running the YOLO model solely on the Raspberry Pi 5 CPU.

The following two model formats were compared to analyze speed: ONNX (executed on Raspberry Pi CPU) vs. HEF (executed on Raspberry Pi AI Kit with Hailo-8L accelerator). The tests were performed on Raspberry Pi 5 Model B Rev 1.0. For the ONNX format, a custom Python script based on the OpenCV and Ultralytics libraries was used, and for HEF, the *hailortcli* command line utility was used (version 4.18.0) [39,40].

Plots for FPS and latency are presented in Figure 13.

Based on the above data, we conclude that the Raspberry Pi AI Kit significantly enhanced processing speed (FPS) performance and latency reduction. Notably, the maximum FPS speedup factor achieved was approximately 15× compared to execution on the Raspberry Pi CPU.

Considering all the evaluated metrics, the YOLOv8n model was selected as the optimal choice for deployment on the autonomous mobile platform, and the artificial vision system was validated.

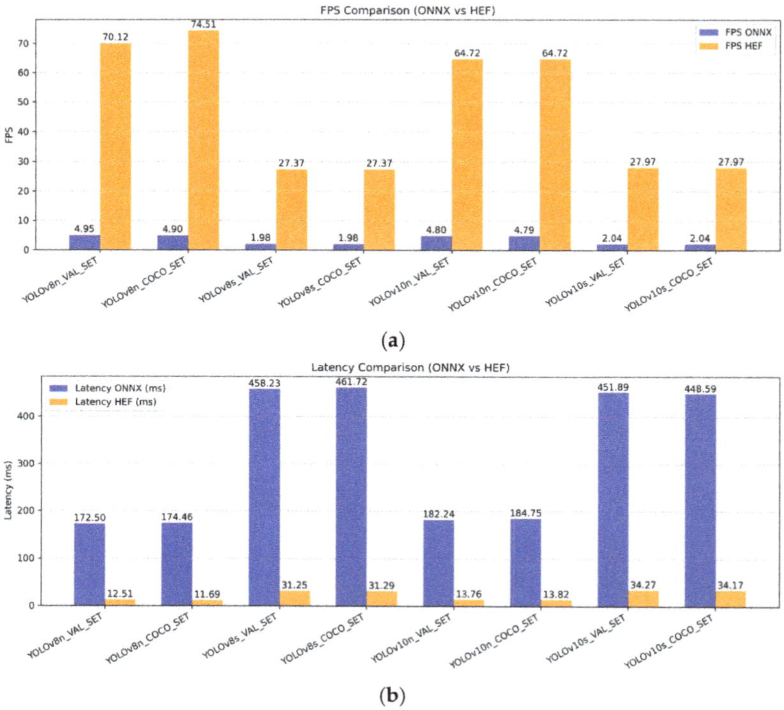

Figure 13. Object detection speed comparison ONNX vs HEF. (**a**) Frames per second (FPS) and (**b**) latency.

4. Discussion

4.1. AI Model Selection

The first challenge was selecting an appropriate object detection and classification model for the artificial vision system.

The choice of the Convolutional Neural Network model was based on a comprehensive analysis of the most high-performance solutions currently available, considering the specific requirements of the inspection application. These requirements included the following: a low computational cost, as the model would be deployed on an embedded system; a high processing speed, ensuring real-time object detection and classification; a high accuracy, to reliably identify objects in various conditions; and ease of training and implementation to facilitate model adaptation and optimization.

Given these constraints, a one-stage detection model was preferred, leading to the selection of the YOLO family. Several versions of YOLO were considered. Initially, YOLOv11, the latest version, was evaluated alongside YOLOv8, a state-of-the-art model, to compare their performances in the inspection task. However, at the time of the study, YOLOv11 lacked support for direct conversion to HEF, which was necessary for deployment on the Raspberry Pi AI Kit. Consequently, YOLOv10 was chosen for further analysis instead.

Due to hardware constraints on the available DELL Precision 3551 laptop, the experiments were conducted using only the nano (n) and small (s) variants of YOLO models. Larger versions, including medium (m), large (l), and extra-large (x), were excluded, as their size and complexity significantly impact training time, speed, accuracy, and resource requirements.

The training times for 200 epochs were recorded as follows: YOLOv8n took 9741.42 s (≈2 h, 42 min, 24 s); YOLOv8s took 22,450.20 s (≈6 h, 14 min, 10 s); YOLOv10n took 12,340.80 s (≈3 h, 25 min, 40 s); and YOLOv10s took 111,172.00 s (≈30 h, 52 min, 52 s).

4.2. Image Dataset Preparation

For the selection of images used for training, validation, and testing, smaller regions containing the target objects were cropped from larger images. This approach facilitated a more efficient and effective model training process, as evidenced by the test results on 100 newly introduced images that were not used during training or validation. However, a key objective was to evaluate model performance on the 1,033 original images. The results further confirm the effectiveness of the YOLO models [41,42].

4.3. Model Performance After Training and Validation

It is well established that Mean Average Precision (mAP) is the standard metric for evaluating object detection models such as YOLOv8 and YOLOv10. In this study, mAP was computed using the cropped image dataset, where annotations included ground truth bounding boxes and class labels. However, for the original (non-cropped) image set, mAP was not calculated, as this would require the comprehensive annotation of all objects within the images. Instead, alternative performance metrics were evaluated, including precision, recall, F1-score, and accuracy. It is also important to note that accuracy in object detection may be less informative due to class imbalances and the complexity of detecting multiple objects within an image. Therefore, as a future research direction, a more comprehensive analysis should be conducted using images containing multiple objects which are fully annotated to enable the calculation of mAP.

Object localization accuracy for IP markers is significantly more critical for managing the autonomous mobile system's orientation algorithm than the localization accuracy of objects that must be present within the inspected area. However, classification accuracy remains equally important in both cases.

As can be observed in Figure 4, the differences in the box loss and DFL (Distribution Focal Loss) trends between the nano and small model types are relatively minor. However, the small model achieves slightly better results, which aligns with its more advanced architecture. The nano model shows more fluctuations in its loss curve across epochs, likely due to its lower capacity and greater sensitivity to optimization noise. In contrast, the small model demonstrates a smoother and more stable convergence.

The differences in box loss and DFL loss trends are more pronounced between YOLOv8 and YOLOv10. These differences can be attributed to the two models' architectural modifications and training process variations. YOLOv10 has architectural changes compared to YOLOv8 regarding the backbone network, feature extraction, and loss function computation. These changes may introduce variations in how the models learn bounding box regression. YOLOv8n, for example, starts with a relatively low box loss value (0.70299 in epoch 1), decreases steadily, and reaches very low values in later epochs, with a final loss of 0.14613 at epoch 200. This trend indicates fast and stable convergence. YOLOv10n starts with a higher box loss (1.30431 in epoch 1), indicating that the initial predictions are worse than those of YOLOv8n. The box loss decreases slower in the early epochs but eventually catches up, achieving a final loss of 0.29594 at epoch 200. This case suggests slower convergence and a more complex loss function or learning process.

All four models demonstrate a good performance regarding precision, recall, mAP@0.5, and mAP@0.5:0.95 (Figure 5). Observing the saturation points, YOLOv8s and YOLOv10s reach peak performance earlier than their nano counterparts. YOLOv10n displays more fluctuations in its learning curve, suggesting a need for more refined hyperparameter tuning. The marginal differences between the models in their final epochs suggest that all models achieve strong generalization, with the choice between them being dependent on other factors such as computational efficiency and model size.

A comparative analysis of YOLOv8n, YOLOv8s, YOLOv10n, and YOLOv10s conducted on the original, uncropped images demonstrates that YOLOv8s provides the best balance of precision, recall, and F1-score (Figure 9), making it the preferred model for object detection tasks requiring a high sensitivity and accuracy. YOLOv8n also performs well in precision, while YOLOv10 models exhibit a relatively lower performance across all metrics. Also, a good performance is obtained by the YOLOv8n model trained with 50 epochs (Table 10).

4.4. Model Performance in Real-World Tests

We evaluated the accuracy of four YOLO models—YOLOv8n, YOLOv8s, YOLOv10n, and YOLOv10s—optimized on the following two distinct datasets: the VAL dataset (208 images used for validation) and the COCO Train2017.

YOLOv8n consistently demonstrated the highest accuracy across both datasets, achieving 83.607% on the VAL dataset and 78.689% on COCO. It showed a strong performance in all classes, especially *Inspection_1* and *Inspection_3*. **YOLOv10n** had a moderate performance with a 61.475% accuracy on VAL and 61.066% on COCO, but it struggled with some classes, particularly *Window_Open_Hall* and *Door_Open_DI3*. **YOLOv8s** and **YOLOv10s** showed a significant drop in accuracy on both datasets, with a 59.836% accuracy for YOLOv8s on both datasets and 51.230% on VAL and 56.967% on COCO for YOLOv10s. Both small models had difficulties in detecting more complex objects like *Fire_extinguisher* and *Window_Open_Hall*.

The observed results can be explained and confirmed by the key features and particularities of the YOLOv8 and YOLOv10 architectures.

YOLOv8 is known for having a better computational efficiency, focusing on improving small object detection, and a more refined architecture for general detection tasks. YOLOv8n, the lightest version, performs well due to its better backbone and efficient feature extraction, even though it is computationally more affordable. It achieves a relatively high accuracy, especially in classes like *Inspection_1* and *Inspection_3*, where clear object distinction helps the model to generalize well.

YOLOv10 introduces further optimizations focusing on a higher accuracy and robustness for complex tasks. However, its complexity and some trade-offs between performance and real-time speed may negatively affect the detection of small or occluded objects, as observed for models like YOLOv10n and YOLOv10s. YOLOv10n's architecture struggles with objects such as *Door_Open_DI3* and *Window_Open_Hall*.

Classes like *Inspection_1* and *Inspection_3* include relatively simple and easily distinguishable objects, which explains the strong performance observed across models.

Window_Open_Hall and *Door_Open_DI3* involve more complex objects, because various other items can appear behind glass windows or door frames, making their classification particularly challenging. The lower accuracy obtained for these classes can also be attributed to the fact that these objects are only partially visible in the images captured by the camera at the current height of the autonomous mobile platform. Repositioning the camera to capture the entire object within the image would improve the detection results. Therefore, future development will focus on either positioning the camera on a higher support to ensure that objects of interest are fully captured within the frame or introducing a scanning mode where the camera is oriented horizontally and vertically. However, the latter approach would complicate the platform's navigation algorithm.

In conclusion, YOLOv8n is the top performer, achieving the highest accuracy across both optimization datasets and demonstrating a strong performance across individual classes. As a result, this model has been selected for implementation on the autonomous mobile platform for intelligent and flexible indoor environment inspection.

It is well established that the Ultralytics YOLOv8 and YOLOv10 models are pre-trained on the COCO 2017 dataset, which comprises 118,287 images in its training set and 5000 images in its validation set, spanning 80 object classes. When applying transfer learning using these pre-trained models, the number of training images per class required for effective performance depends on several key factors, including object complexity and variability, background diversity, and the intended performance objectives, ranging from proof-of-concept validation to robust generalization across various real-world conditions.

As a general guideline, from 50 to 100 images per class may be sufficient for proof-of-concept implementations. However, to ensure strong generalization across diverse indoor environments, including varying lighting conditions, occlusions, and viewing angles, a substantially larger dataset between 500 and 2000 images per class is typically recommended.

In the present study, the dataset used for training consisted of 1033 images selected to validate the concept and evaluate the performance of different YOLO models. While the models demonstrated a high accuracy on this dataset, these results may not fully reflect their robustness in more complex and heterogeneous real-world inspection scenarios.

Future work will focus on expanding the training dataset by incorporating additional images collected during inspection missions. Furthermore, additional training sessions will be conducted to meet the performance requirements specific to the targeted indoor inspection processes.

5. Conclusions

This paper presents the implementation, testing, and validation of an autonomous mobile platform designed for the intelligent and flexible inspection of indoor environments.

The novelty of the research stems from the integration of a new type of AI accelerator into an embedded computer vision system, conferring the platform with the attribute of intelligent inspection based on an artificial vision system. The Raspberry Pi AI Kit, launched in 2024, based on the Hailo-8L chip, represents one of the latest advancements in edge computing for embedded artificial vision applications. This system runs a convolutional neural network model (YOLO) to enable real-time object detection and classification. Furthermore, the platform incorporates a decision-making algorithm to adjust its movement trajectory upon detecting predefined IP markers.

Another key contribution is the flexible system architecture, which allows for seamless adaptation to different mobile inspection platforms. The selection of the AI accelerator is driven by the necessity of implementing the artificial vision system on an embedded system capable of being integrated into an autonomous mobile platform. The system's flexibility is ensured by its high mobility, allowing the same equipment to be deployed across various locations while maintaining operational efficiency, enabling rapid, easily configurable, and customizable inspection processes tailored to the specific characteristics of different indoor environments.

Another significant aspect of this study concerns the training procedure employed for YOLO object detection models. Instead of training on full-frame images, smaller regions containing only objects of interest are extracted from the original images. These cropped images are used for training to enable the neural network to learn object-specific features more effectively. Following the training phase, the model is evaluated on the full original images to assess its ability to correctly detect and localize objects in complex environments.

This approach enhances the model's generalization capability, ensuring accurate detection across diverse scenarios.

The main advantages of this method include improved feature learning, while the model focuses exclusively on objects of interest without being influenced by background noise; reduced dataset requirements, considering that multiple training images can be generated from a single original image, minimizing the need for extensive labeled datasets; and a faster training process, because using smaller, relevant regions speeds up convergence and optimizes computational resources.

However, it is important to consider that background variations and lighting conditions can significantly impact real-world detection performance. These factors are present in the images used for the testing and validation phases to ensure a robust performance in real-world scenarios.

Images captured by the autonomous mobile platform during an inspection mission are stored to evaluate the YOLO models under real-world conditions. These images are used to test four YOLO models (YOLOv8n, YOLOv8s, YOLOv10n, and YOLOv10s), each with two optimized variants resulting from the conversion process to HEF, which can be run on the Hailo-8L AI accelerator.

The test results highlight YOLOv8n as the best-performing model, achieving an accuracy of 86.607% when optimized with the VAL dataset and 78.689% with the COCO TRAIN2017 dataset.

From a computational performance perspective, the significant contribution of the AI accelerator is evident, leading to an approximately 15-fold increase in FPS compared to running the model on the Raspberry Pi CPU.

Considering the results obtained, the hardware requirements, and the specificities of the inspection process, the YOLOv8n model is validated for implementation in the artificial vision system.

After the tests, it is determined that the system can be improved in the following areas: **the hardware structure of the platform**, including the repositioning of the camera at a higher height or adding the capability to orient it vertically; **the navigation algorithm**, as currently, the system does not return automatically to its initial starting location, but different variants for returning are being tested; route recording, navigation based on SLAM (Simultaneous Localization and Mapping), and navigation based on visual landmarks (arrow markers for the direction of movement of the system and the allocation of a marker for the START point); **enhancing the performance of the object detection and classification model** by *expanding the training set* with additional relevant images, *training the network using augmentation techniques*, which are crucial for improving the robustness and performance of YOLO models by introducing variability into the training data, thus helping the model generalize better to unseen data, and *testing various optimization algorithms* for training (SGD, Adam, AdamW, NAdam, RAdam, and RMSProp) [35]; and **optimizing the inspection platform for other scenarios**, such as those in industrial environments. All of these represent future research directions that the development team is considering.

The proposed solution advances current inspection practices through a flexible, modular architecture that allows for quick deployment in diverse indoor settings without major infrastructure changes. Its compact, embedded design enables local image processing, reducing latency and increasing reliability, even in low-connectivity environments.

Despite these advancements, several practical limitations must be acknowledged. The detection performance is influenced by real-world factors such as lighting variability, object occlusion, background clutter, and the physical constraints of the platform (e.g., camera angle and movement stability). Additionally, the training dataset used in this initial phase is relatively small and designed primarily for proof-of-concept validation. Expanding the dataset and refining the model are necessary for full operational deployment to ensure robust generalization in diverse inspection scenarios.

In conclusion, the proposed system provides a viable and scalable approach to indoor autonomous inspection. With continued dataset enrichment and algorithmic optimization, the platform holds significant potential for real-world applications in security, facility monitoring, energy efficiency assessment, and compliance verification.

Author Contributions: Conceptualization, M.C.L., L.C. and A.L.B.; methodology, M.C.L., L.C. and A.L.B.; software, M.C.L. and A.L.B.; validation, M.C.L., L.C. and A.L.B.; formal analysis, M.C.L., L.C. and A.L.B.; investigation, M.C.L., L.C. and A.L.B.; resources, M.C.L. and L.C.; data curation, M.C.L.; writing—original draft preparation, M.C.L. and L.C.; writing—review and editing, M.C.L. and L.C.; visualization, M.C.L.; supervision, L.C.; project administration, M.C.L. All authors have read and agreed to the published version of the manuscript.

Funding: This research received no external funding.

Institutional Review Board Statement: Not applicable.

Informed Consent Statement: Not applicable.

Data Availability Statement: The raw data supporting the conclusions of this article will be made available by the authors on request.

Conflicts of Interest: The authors declare no conflicts of interest.

References

1. Sanchez-Cubillo, J.; Del Ser, J.; Martin, J.L. Toward Fully Automated Inspection of Critical Assets Supported by Autonomous Mobile Robots, Vision Sensors, and Artificial Intelligence. *Sensors* **2024**, *24*, 3721. [CrossRef]
2. de M. Santos, R.C.C.; Silva, M.C.; Santos, R.L.; Klippel, E.; Oliveira, R.A.R. Towards Autonomous Mobile Inspection Robots Using Edge AI. In Proceedings of the 25th International Conference on Enterprise Information Systems (ICEIS 2023), Prague, Czech Republic, 24–26 April 2023; SCITEPRESS–Science and Technology Publications, Lda.: Setúbal, Portugal, 2023; Volume 1, pp. 555–562.
3. Pearson, E.; Szenher, P.; Huang, C.; Englot, B. Mobile Manipulation Platform for Autonomous Indoor Inspections in Low-Clearance Areas. In Proceedings of the ASME 2023 International Design Engineering Technical Conferences and Computers and Information in Engineering Conference IDETC/CIE2023, Boston, MA, USA, 20–23 August 2023.
4. Halder, S.; Afsari, K. Robots in Inspection and Monitoring of Buildings and Infrastructure: A Systematic Review. *Appl. Sci.* **2023**, *13*, 2304. [CrossRef]
5. Macaulay, M.O.; Shafiee, M. Machine learning techniques for robotic and autonomous inspection of mechanical systems and civil infrastructure. *Auton. Intell. Syst.* **2022**, *2*, 8. [CrossRef]
6. Dai, Y.; Kim, D.; Lee, K. An Advanced Approach to Object Detection and Tracking in Robotics and Autonomous Vehicles Using YOLOv8 and LiDAR Data Fusion. *Electronics* **2024**, *13*, 2250. [CrossRef]
7. Hütten, N.; Alves Gomes, M.; Hölken, F.; Andricevic, K.; Meyes, R.; Meisen, T. Deep Learning for Automated Visual Inspection in Manufacturing and Maintenance: A Survey of Open-Access Papers. *Appl. Syst. Innov.* **2024**, *7*, 11. [CrossRef]
8. Rane, N. YOLO and Faster R-CNN Object Detection for Smart Industry 4.0 and Industry 5.0: Applications, Challenges, and Opportunities. 25 October 2023. Available online: https://ssrn.com/abstract=4624206 (accessed on 17 January 2025). [CrossRef]
9. Toman, R.; Rogala, T.; Synaszko, P.; Katunin, A. Robotized Mobile Platform for Non-Destructive Inspection of Aircraft Structures. *Appl. Sci.* **2024**, *14*, 10148. [CrossRef]
10. Rea, P.; Ottaviano, E. Hybrid Inspection Robot for Indoor and Outdoor Surveys. *Actuators* **2023**, *12*, 108. [CrossRef]
11. Bai, C.; Bai, X.; Wu, K. A Review: Remote Sensing Image Object Detection Algorithm Based on Deep Learning. *Electronics* **2023**, *12*, 4902. [CrossRef]
12. Song, Q.; Zhou, Z.; Ji, S.; Cui, T.; Yao, B.; Liu, Z. A Multiscale Parallel Pedestrian Recognition Algorithm Based on YOLOv5. *Electronics* **2024**, *13*, 1989. [CrossRef]
13. TSCINBUNY. Available online: https://tscinbuny.com/products/tscinbuny-esp32-robot-for-arduino-uno-starter-kit-programmable-robot-educational-kit-4wd-60mm-omni-directional-wheel-chassis-with-wifi-app-obstacle-avoidance-line-tracking-smart-car-set (accessed on 17 January 2025).
14. Raspberry Pi 5. Available online: https://www.raspberrypi.com/products/raspberry-pi-5/ (accessed on 17 January 2025).

15. Raspberry Pi Camera Module 3. Available online: https://www.raspberrypi.com/products/camera-module-3/ (accessed on 17 January 2025).
16. Raspberry Pi AI Kit(Hailo-8L) vs. Coral USB Accelerator vs. Coral M.2 Accelerator with Dual Edge TPU. Available online: https://www.seeedstudio.com/blog/2024/07/16/raspberry-pi-ai-kit-vs-coral-usb-accelerator-vs-coral-m-2-accelerator-with-dual-edge-tpu/ (accessed on 17 January 2025).
17. Raspberry Pi AI Kit. Available online: https://www.raspberrypi.com/products/ai-kit/ (accessed on 17 January 2025).
18. Lin, L.; Guo, J.; Liu, L. Multi-scene application of intelligent inspection robot based on computer vision in power plant. *Sci. Rep.* **2024**, *14*, 10657. [CrossRef]
19. Serey, J.; Alfaro, M.; Fuertes, G.; Vargas, M.; Durán, C.; Ternero, R.; Rivera, R.; Sabattin, J. Pattern Recognition and Deep Learning Technologies, Enablers of Industry 4.0, and Their Role in Engineering Research. *Symmetry* **2023**, *15*, 535. [CrossRef]
20. Pavel, M.I.; Tan, S.Y.; Abdullah, A. Vision-Based Autonomous Vehicle Systems Based on Deep Learning: A Systematic Literature Review. *Appl. Sci.* **2022**, *12*, 6831. [CrossRef]
21. Li, Z.; Wang, Y.; Zhang, N.; Zhang, Y.; Zhao, Z.; Xu, D.; Ben, G.; Gao, Y. Deep Learning-Based Object Detection Techniques for Remote Sensing Images: A Survey. *Remote Sens.* **2022**, *14*, 2385. [CrossRef]
22. Trigka, M.; Dritsas, E. A Comprehensive Survey of Machine Learning Techniques and Models for Object Detection. *Sensors* **2025**, *25*, 214. [CrossRef]
23. Carranza-García, M.; Torres-Mateo, J.; Lara-Benítez, P.; García-Gutiérrez, J. On the Performance of One-Stage and Two-Stage Object Detectors in Autonomous Vehicles Using Camera Data. *Remote Sens.* **2021**, *13*, 89. [CrossRef]
24. Ramalingam, B.; Hayat, A.A.; Elara, M.R.; Gómez, B.F.; Yi, L.; Pathmakumar, T.; Rayguru, M.M.; Subramanian, S. Deep Learning Based Pavement Inspection Using Self-Reconfigurable Robot. *Sensors* **2021**, *21*, 2595. [CrossRef]
25. Alotaibi, A.; Alatawi, H.; Binnouh, A.; Duwayriat, L.; Alhmiedat, T.; Alia, O.M. Deep Learning-Based Vision Systems for Robot Semantic Navigation: An Experimental Study. *Technologies* **2024**, *12*, 157. [CrossRef]
26. Rane, L.N.; Choudhary, P.S.; Rane, J. YOLO and Faster R-CNN Object Detection in Architecture, Engineering and Construction (AEC): Applications, Challenges, and Future Prospects. *SSRN Electron. J.* **2023**. [CrossRef]
27. Zi, X.; Chaturvedi, K.; Braytee, A.; Li, J.; Prasad, M. Detecting Human Falls in Poor Lighting: Object Detection and Tracking Approach for Indoor Safety. *Electronics* **2023**, *12*, 1259. [CrossRef]
28. Wang, K.; Zhou, H.; Wu, H.; Yuan, G. RN-YOLO: A Small Target Detection Model for Aerial Remote-Sensing Images. *Electronics* **2024**, *13*, 2383. [CrossRef]
29. What is YOLO? The Ultimate Guide. 2025. Available online: https://blog.roboflow.com/guide-to-yolo-models (accessed on 17 January 2025).
30. Zhu, P.; Chen, B.; Liu, B.; Qi, Z.; Wang, S.; Wang, L. Object Detection for Hazardous Material Vehicles Based on Improved YOLOv5 Algorithm. *Electronics* **2023**, *12*, 1257. [CrossRef]
31. Terven, J.; Córdova-Esparza, D.-M.; Romero-González, J.-A. A Comprehensive Review of YOLO Architectures in Computer Vision: From YOLOv1 to YOLOv8 and YOLO-NAS. *Mach. Learn. Knowl. Extr.* **2023**, *5*, 1680–1716. [CrossRef]
32. Yunusov, N.; Bappy, S.; Abdusalomov, A.; Kim, W. Robust Forest Fire Detection Method for Surveillance Systems Based on You Only Look Once Version 8 and Transfer Learning Approaches. *Processes* **2024**, *12*, 1039. [CrossRef]
33. Raspberry Pi AI Kit: Custom Object Detection with Hailo8L. Available online: https://www.cytron.io/tutorial/raspberry-pi-ai-kit-custom-object-detection-with-h (accessed on 11 October 2024).
34. Model Training with Ultralytics YOLO. Available online: https://docs.ultralytics.com/modes/train/ (accessed on 17 January 2025).
35. Model Prediction with Ultralytics YOLO. Available online: https://docs.ultralytics.com/modes/predict/ (accessed on 17 January 2025).
36. Model Export with Ultralytics YOLO. Available online: https://docs.ultralytics.com/modes/export/ (accessed on 17 January 2025).
37. Raspberry Pi AI Kit: ONNX to HEF Conversion. Available online: https://www.cytron.io/tutorial/raspberry-pi-ai-kit-onnx-to-hef-conversion (accessed on 11 October 2024).
38. Deepview-Validator 3.3.1. Available online: https://pypi.org/project/deepview-validator/ (accessed on 4 February 2025).
39. Hailort. Available online: https://github.com/hailo-ai/hailort (accessed on 4 February 2025).
40. Hailo Application Code Examples. Available online: https://github.com/hailo-ai/Hailo-Application-Code-Examples (accessed on 4 February 2025).

41. Aktouf, L.; Shivanna, Y.; Dhimish, M. High-Precision Defect Detection in Solar Cells Using YOLOv10 Deep Learning Model. *Solar* **2024**, *4*, 639–659. [CrossRef]
42. Computer Vision Model Leaderboard. Available online: https://leaderboard.roboflow.com/ (accessed on 4 February 2025).

technologies

MDPI

Article

Autonomous Real-Time Mass Center Location and Inertia Identification for Grappling Space Robotics

Timothy Sands [1,2]

[1] Department of Mechanical Engineering (SCPD), Stanford University, Stanford, CA 94305, USA; dr.timsands@alumni.stanford.edu
[2] Sibley School of Mechanical and Aerospace Engineering, Cornell University, Ithaca, NY 14853, USA

Abstract: Grappling actions by space robots for the purposes of stabilizing, refueling, repair, and equipment replacement necessitate the autonomous abilities of a single grappling space robot to rapidly contend with large variations in total system inertia rapidly shifting a system's center of mass, as targets can be massive with possibly unknown or poorly known mass inertia properties. Grappling actions yield opportunities for a novel online calculation of the time-varying location of the combined system's center of mass. Two-norm optimal nonlinear, projection regression-based learning is implemented and juxtaposed to a comparative benchmark both qualitatively and quantitatively supported by a comparison of enhancements of Luenberger observers. Analysis precedes modeling and simulation to verify the design, and then, spaceflight experiments are proposed for the sequel to validate the simulation results. Time-varying mass locations are discerned, and the time-varying location of the mass center is revealed to be 36–95 percent different than initially assumed, and 58–317 percent corrections to inertia identification are demonstrated. Combined three-dimensional maneuvers obscures identification compared to single-axis maneuvering.

Keywords: spacecraft; space robotics satellite servicing; autonomous grapple; adaption; learning

1. Introduction

Autonomous robotic grappling (Figure 1) is the core requirement for on-orbit robotic servicing and assembly missions [1]. National Aeronautics and Space Administration (NASA) recently prototyped grappling arms for its Space Exploration Vehicle (SEV) [2].

(a) (b)

Figure 1. (**a**) NASA PickNik Robotics in-orbit robot addresses a common gap in deploying robotic arms into environments where full autonomy is still too difficult permitting a human operator to supervise and quickly intervene when the space robot gets stuck [3]. (**b**) Robotic Refueling Mission 3 (RRM3) technologies are developed to store and transfer super-cold cryogenic fluids [4]. Image credit: NASA [5]. See 'aside' note in Appendix A.

1.1. Review of the Literature

The long-term sustainability of space includes other robotic tasks like active debris removal [6], necessitating arms for grappling and various grasping and anchoring mechanisms [2]. (Figure 1) According to the Technical Committee for Space Robotics of the IEEE Robotics and Automation Society, priority areas for the technical committee include electromechanical design and control, and command and control (including teleoperated modes) [7]. The study in reference [8] emphasizes center of mass changes due to deployment of payloads or instruments, solar panels, gravity booms, magnetometers, antennas, cameras, solar sails, etc., and used recursive least squares to estimate the mass center's position. The study in [9] misaligns a thruster from the anticipated center of mass and uses the governing dynamic equations of motion to estimation the mass center location using multiple Kalman filters.

The determination of moments of inertia (but not inertia products) about two axes was proposed in 1948 for airplane components prior to flight, where the component would be suspended in a lab and subjected to standard pendulum experiments [10]. Similarly, the moments for the entire airplane were similarly treated in the study of [11]. Progress over the subsequent forty-six years added capabilities to use both angular acceleration methods and oscillation methods where the assumption is invoked that the suspension axis is assumed to be the axis of rotation [12]. Inertia cross-products were still not available. Twenty-nine years later, light detection and ranging was utilized to estimate inertia parameters within twenty percent, while location of the mass center was not performed [13,14]. Just this year, principal moments (not inertia cross products) of space tethers were estimated using unscented Kalman filters [15].

Mass center estimation was recently proposed using a force platform with inertial sensors for balance evaluation in quiet standing, and the results were compared to traditional methods using an optical motion capture system for truth values [16]. Three general classifications of methods were listed as follows, while this manuscript presents a novel alternative:

1. Integrate the horizontal acceleration of the center of mass [17];
2. Filter the center of pressure to estimate the center of mass [18];
3. Estimate the center of mass directly from the equations of motion of an inverted pendulum model.

Ref. [19] categorized the methods slightly differently as either sensors' networks or a single sensor while proposing using magneto-inertial measurement units. Calculation of the mass center was proposed [20–22] by electrostatic suspension of a proof mass in the satellite in an electrode cage, which is rigidly attached to the spacecraft. Accelerations of the proof mass were determined, and, then, relative accelerations between the spacecraft and proof mass were used to estimate the mass center. The procedure was used periodically to provide mass center location estimates. Follow-on experiments were presented in [23]. Arguably, this proof mass electrode cage may be considered state-of-the-art for spacecraft so equipped. The calculations involve estimations of angular velocities and quaternion fitting using regression (ASIDE: the methods proposed in this paper instead involve the estimation of all inertia components (moments and products) and use those estimates to deterministically calculate mass center location).

CFD methods were used in the study of [24] to investigate the aerodynamic performance of the free-fall wing, and the results indicate that wing fluttering and tumbling motions' tumbling frequencies are driven by changing locations of the moments of inertia around the tumbling axis. Furthermore, the changing position of the center of mass complicates the free-fall motion. The study in reference [25] used least squares, maximum likelihood, and Kalman filter estimators to estimate mass, center of mass, and moments of inertia of a multi-lift slung aircraft load. The study in reference [26] used image processing to locate centers of mass using Python-based programming (Community Edition).

Regression-based learning may function as a projection operator to enable data-driven learning of the operators in the Mori–Zwanzig formalism, where the authors of [27] proposed a principled method to extract the Markov and memory operators for any regression models. The research found that more expressive nonlinear regression models fill in the gap between the highly idealized and computationally efficient Mori's projection operator and the most optimal yet computationally infeasible Zwanzig's projection operator.

For certain applications, e.g., the on-orbit debris inspection of orbital natural objects, defunct satellites, and debris, etc., estimating the mass center requires mapping from a moving observer. Ref. [28] applies an observer to estimate internal angular orientation, angular velocity, and angular acceleration. Next, pose-graph mapping with visual odometry produces trajectories relative to a target-fixed frame.

Distinguished from these disparate approaches to autonomously estimate the mass center (while maintaining the usage of observers), this present study seeks to determine time-varying inertia identification and the proposed novel online calculation of time-varying locations of the combined system's center of mass using two norm optimal nonlinear, projection regression-based learning augmented with enhanced, nonlinear Luenberger observers in direct comparison to benchmark methods.

Box 1 provides pithy expressions of the manuscript's problem statements, research objectives, and key contributions to the technical field(s). One additional courtesy offered the readership is periodic tables of proximal variables and nomenclature intended to eliminate the necessity to flip back and forth between pages (e.g. Tables 1–6)

Box 1. Problem statements, research objectives, and key contributions

Problem statements: At all times, find a system's mass distribution and the location of the center of mass. How may the location be calculated given only timed, angular position data? To what degree of accuracy can metrics be discerned? Requiring how much computational burden? Requiring how much effort?

Research objectives: (1) Using only attitude angle data, discern mass inertia imbalance, (2) express that imbalance as an offset center of gravity, and then discern the location of the center of mass.

Key contributions: Center of gravity location estimation convergence is improved over the state-of-the-art comparative benchmark [21–23] from millimeter convergence over hundreds of days to hundreds of millimeters in minutes achieved in this study.

1.2. State-of-the-Art Benchmarks

The following list highlights the current state-of-the-art inertia moment and product determination as well as locating the mass center:

1. In 2022, Ref. [1] provided an overview survey of the algorithms and test and validation strategies for grappling the robotic free-flying spacecraft, de-emphasizing spacecraft docking and berthing. Core technologies identified includes orientation control (including distributed control systems) and the ability to adapt to unexpected loads. Those core technologies motivate the developments presented in this present study.
2. Nonlinear dynamics are highlighted as key, and, therefore, nonlinear approaches are adopted.
3. Despite insistence on nonlinear dynamics, linear time-invariant PID control laws are emphasized to be "straightforward to design and relatively easy to tune and provide performance sufficient to meet most operating requirements".
4. Since the dynamics are Hamiltonian, nonlinear adaptive control is also highlighted and adopted in this present study.

5. Trajectory planning is highlighted as well, and autonomous trajectory generation is adopted to permit nonlinear control proposals.
6. Air-bearing tables are highlighted to aid validation using laboratory experiments, and one such free-floating, highly flexible robotic gripper arm is described.

1.3. Novelties Presented

The following short list of novelties are combined sequentially to produce novel, autonomous, real-time space robotics:

1. Time-varying estimates of mass locations are found with classical adaptive methods compared to optimal learning leveraging nonlinear, projection regression-based methods. Estimates are supported in part by the novel use of nonlinear enhanced Luenberger observers.
2. Time-varying estimates of mass locations are used to find time-varying estimates of the location of the system center of mass. Estimates are supported in-part by the novel use of nonlinear enhanced Luenberger observers applying the fundamental relationships between products of inertia and mass center location.
3. The requirement to diagonalize the matrix of mass moments of inertia is eliminated.
4. The requirement to linearize the governing differential equations is eliminated.
5. The requirement to simplify governing equations (e.g., small angle assumption, etc.) is eliminated.
6. Analysis precedes modeling and simulation to verify the design, and then, spaceflight experiments are proposed for the sequel to validate the simulation results.

1.4. Conveniences of Presentation

Periodic tables of proximal variables and nomenclature definitions are provided to aid reading without necessitating flipping back and forth between pages seeking definitions of terms. Observers are presented topologically rather than using state space equations to aid remembrance and understanding. Lastly, simulations used to produce the data presented in this manuscript are used to produce the graphic topologies, and, furthermore, MATLAB®/SIMULINK® (R2023b) subsystems are included in the article Appendix, aiding repeatability by the readership.

2. Materials and Methods

Physics-based dynamics are foremost detailed in Section 2.1. Next, feedforward control using physics-based dynamic embodiment is presented in Section 2.2. followed by feedback instantiations: both the nonlinear adaption and projection regression-based learning of fully populated inertia matrix components. Nonlinear, enhanced Luenberger observers were introduced to support both feedback instantiations, and the observers were juxtaposed quantitatively to a comparative benchmark. Finally, location of the mass center was estimated using the estimated inertia components with the Final Value Theorem, which is briefly reviewed in the analysis of Section 2. As displayed in Figure 2, the canonical process is adopted of foremost analysis, followed by verification using modeling and simulation with experimental validation. Figure 3 displays the modeling and simulation topology.

$$\boxed{Analysis} \rightarrow \boxed{Simulation\ verification} \rightarrow \boxed{Experimental\ validation}$$

Figure 2. Process stages adopted in this study: analysis and hypothesis followed by the verification of analysis with modeling and simulation validated experimentally.

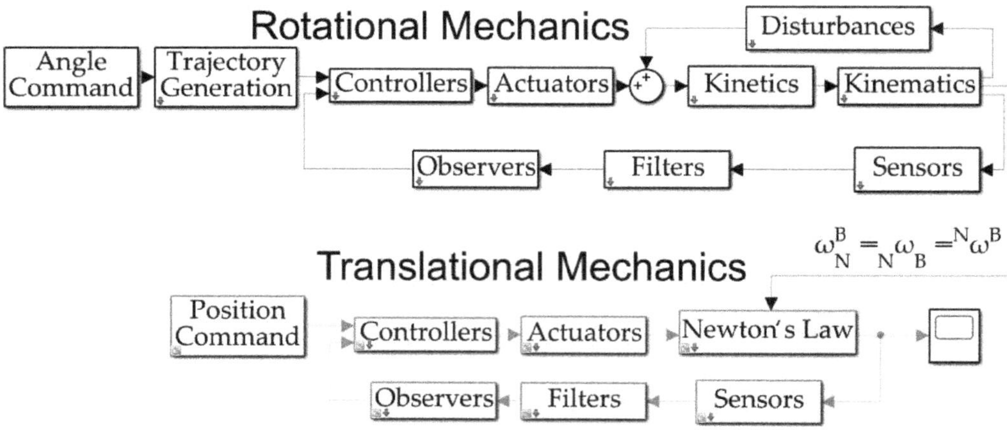

Figure 3. Space robot system topology represented by the MATLAB®/SIMULINK® simulation used to produce the quantitative results presented in this manuscript. The internal content of simulation subsystems is depicted in Appendix B. Notice that the translational subsystems of the six-degree-of-freedom motion simulation are deactivated, reducing the superfluous computational burden.

Foreshadowing the summarized methods, Here includes a pithy implementation procedure and lists the relevant sections and details that may be found.

Implementation procedure:

1	Use the physics-based governing dynamics to embody the control (Section 2.1).
a	Do not diagonalize the inertia matrix.
b	Do not linearize the governing equations of motion.
c	Do not use small-angle assumption to simplify the system equations.
d	Establish classical feedback control as a comparative benchmark.
2	Use nonlinear, enhanced Luenberger observers (Sections 2.4–2.6) to estimate all motion states and control.
3	Use projection-based nonlinear regression learning to learn the fully populated mass moments of inertia (masses and mass locations), including principal moments and off-diagonal products of inertia (Section 2.3).
4	Use off-diagonal products of inertia to estimate the location of the center of mass (Section 2.10).

2.1. Physics-Based Dynamics

The well-known Euler's moment equations (Equation (1)) govern rotations of objects of mass. The system of equations is nonlinear and coupled (especially for a fully populated inertia matrix $[J]$ with both moments and products of inertia), particularly noting the presence of the cross-product operation, which puts terms from the second and third equation into the first equation in the system. The equations were ubiquitously linearized and simplified by changing the basis of measurement to diagonalize the inertia matrix.

$$\tau = [J]\{\dot{\omega}\} + \{\omega\} \times [J]\{\omega\} \tag{1}$$

One motivation for linearization is to aid expression of the system of equations in a standard regression form (a matrix of 'knowns' multiplied by a vector of presumed 'unknowns'). Particularly stemming from a common practice to put the motion states into the vector of unknowns, often referred to as the "state vector", attempts to express Equation (1) into regression form can be seen in Equation (2).

$$\tau = \underbrace{\begin{bmatrix} J_{xx} & J_{xy} & J_{xz} & ? & ? & ? \\ J_{yx} & J_{yy} & J_{yz} & ? & ? & ? \\ J_{zx} & J_{zy} & J_{zz} & ? & ? & ? \end{bmatrix}}_{[\Phi?]} \underbrace{\begin{Bmatrix} \dot{\omega}_x \\ \dot{\omega}_y \\ \dot{\omega}_z \\ ? \\ ? \\ ? \end{Bmatrix}}_{\{\beta?\}} \tag{2}$$

Table 1. Table of proximal variables and nomenclature (1) [1].

Variable/Acronym	Definition	Variable/Acronym	Definition
$[J] = J$	Inertia matrix or tensor	J_{xx}	Moment of inertia about $\hat{x}$
$\{\dot{\omega}\} = \dot{\omega}$	Angular acceleration	$J_{xy} = J_{yx}$	$\hat{x}\hat{y}$ inertia product
$\{\omega\} = \omega$	Angular velocity	$J_{xz} = J_{zx}$	$\hat{x}\hat{z}$ inertia product
$\dot{\omega}_x$	Angular acceleration in the $\hat{x}$ direction	J_{yy}	Moment of inertia about $\hat{y}$
$\dot{\omega}_y$	Angular acceleration in the $\hat{y}$ direction	$J_{yz} = J_{zy}$	$\hat{y}\hat{z}$ inertia product
$\dot{\omega}_z$	Angular acceleration in the $\hat{z}$ direction	J_{zz}	Moment of inertia about $\hat{z}$
$[\Phi?] = \Phi?$	Regression matrix of knowns	$\{\beta?\} = \beta$	Unknown, predicted variables

[1] Such tables are offered throughout this manuscript to aid readability.

The inertia matrix $[J]$ is most often diagonalized using the eigenvalue coordinate transformation, or spectral decomposition. The transformation begins with relationships expressed in coordinates of the body fixed axes (where the inertia matrix is fully populated with moments and products). Transformation to a new basis vector set (i.e., the eigenvectors) leads to a diagonalized inertia matrix with only moments and no products, and the diagonalized matrix simplifies subsequent mathematics that are performed with the inertia matrix [29].

A common engineering practice is to simply assume the eigenvector basis is equivalent to the body frame basis vectors, where the engineer is comfortable accepting the accompanying error of such an assumption.

The inertia matrix will not be diagonalized in this present study, instead favoring increased accuracy. The inability of expressing Equation (2) in standard regression form must be re-addressed.

Noting the difficulties of Equation (2), omitting the common practice establishing the vector of unknowns, the mass moments and products may instead be used (Equation (3)). A more elaborate derivation from Equation (1) to Equation (3) is offered in Appendix A.

$$\tau = \underbrace{\begin{bmatrix} \dot{\omega}_x & \dot{\omega}_y - \omega_x\omega_z & \dot{\omega}_z - \omega_x\omega_y & -\omega_y\omega_z & 0 & \omega_y\omega_z \\ \omega_x\omega_z & \dot{\omega}_x + \omega_y\omega_z & 0 & \dot{\omega}_y & \dot{\omega}_z - \omega_x\omega_y & -\omega_x\omega_z \\ -\omega_x\omega_y & 0 & \dot{\omega}_x - \omega_y\omega_z & \omega_x\omega_y & \dot{\omega}_y + \omega_x\omega_z & \dot{\omega}_z \end{bmatrix}}_{[\Phi]} \underbrace{\begin{Bmatrix} J_{xx} \\ J_{xy} \\ J_{xz} \\ J_{yy} \\ J_{yz} \\ J_{zz} \end{Bmatrix}}_{\beta} \tag{3}$$

Equation (3) establishes the physics-based embodiment of the control with specific instantiations in both feedforward and feedback.

2.2. Feedforward Control Using Physics-Based Dynamic Embodiment

The feedforward instantiation of Equation (3) is presented in Equation (4), where the matrix of "knowns" necessitates having known angular velocities and angular accelerations. This necessity motivates the use of sinusoidal commanded trajectories, which will be shown to also aid estimation identifiability in Section 2.11.

$$\tau = \underbrace{\begin{bmatrix} \dot{\omega}_x & \dot{\omega}_y - \omega_x\omega_z & \dot{\omega}_z - \omega_x\omega_y & -\omega_y\omega_z & 0 & \omega_y\omega_z \\ \omega_x\omega_z & \dot{\omega}_x + \omega_y\omega_z & 0 & \dot{\omega}_y & \dot{\omega}_z - \omega_x\omega_y & -\omega_x\omega_z \\ -\omega_x\omega_y & 0 & \dot{\omega}_x - \omega_y\omega_z & \omega_x\omega_y & \dot{\omega}_y + \omega_x\omega_z & \dot{\omega}_z \end{bmatrix}_d}_{[\Phi]_d} \underbrace{\begin{Bmatrix} \hat{J}_{xx} \\ \hat{J}_{xy} \\ \hat{J}_{xz} \\ \hat{J}_{yy} \\ \hat{J}_{yz} \\ \hat{J}_{zz} \end{Bmatrix}}_{\hat{\beta}} \tag{4}$$

This embodiment may also be used in feedback, where actual trajectories are substituted for desired trajectories, and that instantiation is described later in Section 2.10, Combined Control.

Table 2. Table of proximal variables and nomenclature (2) [1].

Variable/Acronym	Definition	Variable/Acronym	Definition
$[\omega_x]_d$	Desire angular velocity about $\hat{x}$	$[\dot{\omega}_x]_d$	Desire angular acceleration about $\hat{x}$
$[\omega_y]_d$	Desire angular velocity about $\hat{y}$	$[\dot{\omega}_y]_d$	Desire angular acceleration about $\hat{y}$
$[\omega_z]_d$	Desire angular velocity about $\hat{z}$	$[\dot{\omega}_z]_d$	Desire angular acceleration about $\hat{z}$
$[\Phi] = \Phi$	Regression matrix of sensor data	$[\Phi]_d = \Phi_d$	Regression matrix of desired states
β	Unknown, predicted variables	$\hat{\beta}$	Estimated variables
τ	Total control signal	τ_{ff}	Feedforward control signal
$\hat{J}_{xx}$	Estimated moment of inertia about $\hat{x}$	$\hat{J}_{xy} = \hat{J}_{yx}$	Estimated $\hat{x}\hat{y}$ inertia product
$\hat{J}_{yy}$	Estimated moment of inertia about $\hat{y}$	$\hat{J}_{xz} = \hat{J}_{zx}$	Estimated $\hat{x}\hat{z}$ inertia product
$\hat{J}_{zz}$	Estimated moment of inertia about $\hat{z}$	$\hat{J}_{yz} = \hat{J}_{zy}$	Estimated $\hat{y}\hat{z}$ inertia product

[1] Such tables are offered throughout this manuscript to aid readability.

2.3. Regression-Based Projection for Learning

Feedback may be used to project trajectory tracking errors (Equation (5)) on the nonlinear, coupled system equations expressed in regression in Equation (4). The estimated torque is not likely provided by motion sensors (e.g., star trackers, sun sensors, limb lookers, etc.), so observers are investigated to provide the information (in addition to full state trajectories described later in Section 2.10.

$$\tau_{fb} = [\Phi]_d\left([\Phi]_d^{\,T}[\Phi]_d\right)^{-1}[\Phi]_d\delta\tau \tag{5}$$

$$\delta\tau = \tau_{ff} - \hat{\tau} \tag{6}$$

2.4. Luenberger Observers

Luenberger observers are sometimes referred to as state observers or simply observers and are well described in reference [30] for observable systems recently ubiquitously defined in so-called "state space" form or alternatively formulated in state-variable form. The discrete form of the estimator is often represented by the form presented in Equation (7) for discrete time index k, states designated x, the "hat" $\hat{}$ indicating an estimate, output y, where A_d is the discretized state matrix, and B_d is the discretized observer gain matrix, respectively.

$$\hat{x}(k+1) = A_d\hat{x}(k) + B_d u(k) + L_d[y(k) - \hat{y}(k)] \tag{7}$$

Rather than adopting the ubiquitous form of Equation (7), observers are presented in the sections below in topological form to highlight the enhancements to the observers.

2.5. Enhanced Luenberger Observers

Notice in Figure 4 the three channels on the right-hand side of the figure. The ubiquitous derivative channel is past forward (to the left of the graphic) of the next integrator compared to the integral and proportional channels. Since the signal to the left of an integrator (the integrator output) is the integral of the input signal, the input signal (to the right) is the derivative of the output signal, thus inducing derivative action on the input. This commonplace enhancement induces derivative action into the estimator without numerically differentiating noisy input signals.

Secondly, notice that the top-center topology in Figure 4 contains a manual switch with the control as a potential input. This enhancement is often applied to reduce or eliminate phase lag in the estimator.

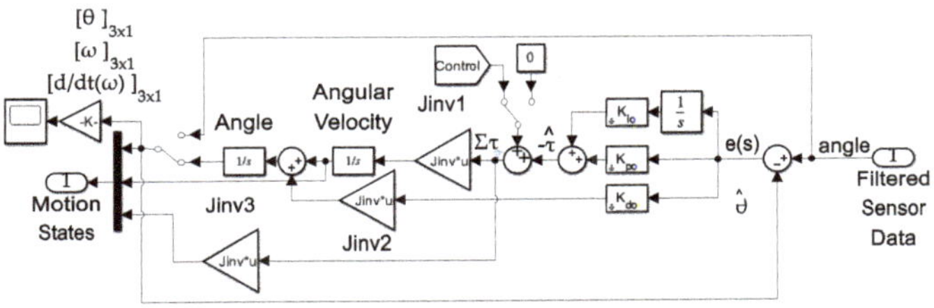

Figure 4. Luenberger and enhanced Luenberger observers built in MATLAB®/SIMULINK®.

Lastly, notice that the center channel or line passing down the middle of the estimator from right to left consists of a double integrator of states lacking the cross-products of motion stemming from the transport theorem of mechanical motion relating the time derivative of a Euclidean vector as evaluated in a non-rotating coordinate system to its time derivative in a rotating reference frame [31]. Adoption of enhancements accounting for transport theorem are presented below, including nonlinear enhancements accounting for the nonlinear coupling nature of the transport theorem terms (the cross-products in Equation (1)).

2.6. Nonlinear Enhanced Luenberger Observers

Notice Figure 5 contains predominantly the same content as Figure 4, the enhanced Luenberger observer. The new enhancements are depicted in the center of Figure 5 where the angular velocity signal is extracted, scaled by the mass moments of inertia, then used to create the cross-products which are added to the baseline double-integrator signal.

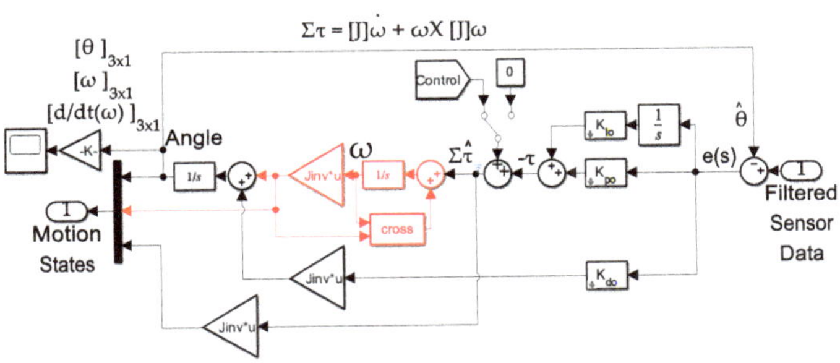

Figure 5. Nonlinear enhanced Luenberger observer built in MATLAB®/SIMULINK®.

2.7. Classical Feedback Adaption

Following initial parameterization in the inertial reference frame, classical feedback adaption was presented in the study of [32] in the body reference frame, greatly simplifying the algorithms, enhancing its usefulness as a contemporary replacement of the formerly ubiquitous M.I.T. Rule [33]. The subsystem is displayed in Figure A5 of Appendix B, codifying Equation (8).

2.8. Two-Norm Optimal Nonlinear, Projection Regression-Based Learning

An alternative to the classical feedback adaption approach is to project trajectory tracking errors onto the governing system equations parameterized into nonlinear regression form (without truncation, approximations, linearization, diagonalization, or other implications). The regression form is illustrated in the feedforward (τ_{ff}) portion of Equation (9)'s combined control, while the projection onto the system equations is displayed in the second term (τ_{fb}) using the two norm optimal pseudoinverse application of least squares. The subsystem is displayed in Figure A6 of Appendix B.

2.9. Combined Control

The feedforward control portion was identically the nonlinear, coupled governing equations of motion parameterized as a matrix $[\Phi]$ multiplied by a vector $\hat{\beta}$ where the matrix was built using desired (commanded) trajectories annotated by the subscribe "d", while, in feedback form, actual trajectories were used in accordance with Equation (5). The need for actual trajectories justifies the investigation of contemporary enhancements to Luenberger observers in Sections 2.4 and 2.5.

$$\tau = \underbrace{[\Phi]_d\{\hat{\beta}\}}_{\tau_{ff}}, \text{where } \hat{\beta} = \int \Gamma[\Phi]s(\delta\omega + \lambda\delta\dot{\omega})\mathrm{d}t \tag{8}$$

$$\tau = \underbrace{[\Phi]_d\{\hat{\beta}\}}_{\tau_{ff}} + \underbrace{[\Phi]_d\left([\Phi]_d{}^T[\Phi]_d\right)^{-1}[\Phi]_d\delta\tau}_{\tau_{fb}} \tag{9}$$

$$\delta\tau = Torque\ estimate \tag{10}$$

where *Torque estimate* is from Figures 4 and 5.

2.10. Estimating Location of the Center of Mass

Since the matrix of mass moments of inertia was not diagonalized, the cross-products of inertia (off-diagonal matrix terms) may be used to locate the center of mass using the parallel axis theorem. Figure 6 provides an illustrative example. Consider the desire to have a mass center located along the depicted central T_c axis. If the actual location is suspected to be at some other point, e.g., about the depicted y axis, the parallel axis theorem may be used to parameterize the problem.

Following a brief presentation of the parallel axis theorem with a small proof, the parameterization used to express three-dimensional locations (x, y, z coordinates) were revealed to be expressed strictly using the products of inertia. Thus, ubiquitous diagonalization of the inertia matrix by transforming basis vectors would eliminate the ability to use this formulation presented in Equation (12).

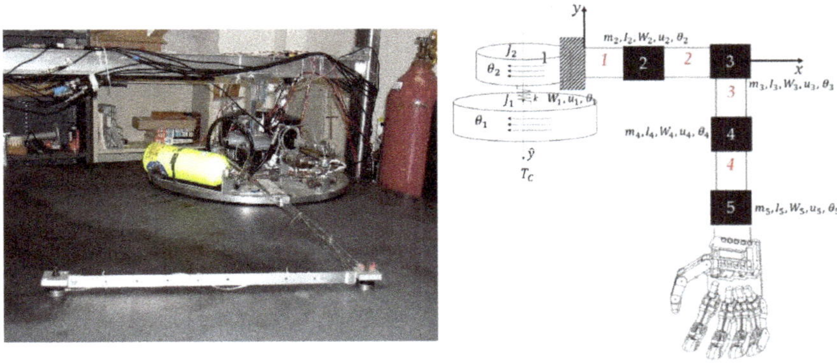

(a) (b)

Figure 6. Benchmark free-floating laboratory space gripper robot used in prequel studies [34]: (**a**) photo of laboratory hardware and (**b**) schematic used for prequel engineering analyses.

Table 3. Table of proximal variables and nomenclature (3) [1].

Variable/ Acronym	Definition	Variable/Acronym	Definition
$m_i \forall i = 2,\ldots,5$	Mass index	$[\Phi]_d$	Defined in Equation (4)
$I_i \forall i = 2,\ldots,5$	Moment of inertia index	$\{\hat{\beta}\}$	Defined in Equation (4)
$J_i \forall i = 1,\ldots,2$	Moments of inertia	Γ	Adaption gain
$u_i \forall i = 1,\ldots,5$	Translational displacements	λ	Positive constant reference trajectory gain
$\theta_i \forall i = 1,\ldots,5$	Rotational displacements	$[\Phi]$	Dynamic system matrix
T_C	Control torque	s	Combined error measure
τ_{ff}	Feedforward control	$\delta\omega$	Differential angular velocity
$\delta\tau$	Control difference	$\delta\dot{\omega}$	Differential angular acceleration
τ_{fb}	Feedback control	dt	Differential time

[1] Such tables are offered throughout this manuscript to aid readability.

Theorem: *Parallel axis theorem: The moment of inertia $J_y = J_O$about some point other than the center of mass is the sum of the moment of inertia J_{cm}about the center of mass and the moment of inertia relative to the fixed distance between axes (y and $\hat{y}$ in Figure 6) in the rigid body represented by the product of the total mass and the square of the distance (See Equation (11)).*

$$J_O = J_{cm} + MR_O^2 \tag{11}$$

The following proof mirrors the study of [35], since the version most closely illuminates the use of the parallel axis theorem in this manuscript to reveal the three-dimensional location of the center of mass. The nomenclature of the proof in the study of [35] was mapped to the nomenclature of the formerly investigated space robot [34].

Proof: Consider a rigid system of particles of mass $M = \sum_i m_i$, rotating about a fixed axis O along axis y. Place the origin of the coordinate system at the center of mass (cm) of our system of particles. The general point i has coordinates (x_i, y_i), the x coordinate of O is a, and the y coordinate of O is b. Since the center of mass is at $(0, 0)$, by the definition of the center of mass (the unique point at any given time where the weighted relative position of the distributed mass sums to zero), Equation (12) results.

$$x_{cm} = \sqrt{\frac{J_{xy}J_{xz}}{mJ_{xy}}}, \quad y_{cm} = \sqrt{\frac{J_{xy}J_{yz}}{mJ_{xz}}}, \quad z_{cm} = \sqrt{\frac{J_{xz}J_{yz}}{mJ_{xy}}} \tag{12}$$

By definition, $J_O = \sum_i m_i r_{iO}^2$, where r_{iO} is measured from O, not from the mass center. Thus, $r_{iO}^2 = (x_i - a)^2 + (y_i - b)^2$, leading to Equation (13). But, since $x_{cm} = \sum_i \frac{m_i x_i}{M} = 0$ and similarly for y, the cross terms in Equation (13) go to zero once the sum over i is achieved, leading to Equation (14). Since $(x_i{}^2 + y_i{}^2) = r_i{}^2$, where r_i is now measured from the mass center, and $(a^2 + b^2) = R_O{}^2$ is just $R_O{}^2$, where R_O is the distance from O to the mass center, Equation (15) results. □

$$J_O = \sum_i m_i \left[(x_i - a)^2 + (y_i - b)^2 \right] = \sum_i m_i \left[x_i^2 - 2ax_i + a^2 + y_i^2 - 2by_i^2 + b^2 \right] \tag{13}$$

$$J_O = \sum_i m_i \left(x_i{}^2 + y_i{}^2 \right) + \sum_i m_i \left(a^2 + b^2 \right) \tag{14}$$

$$J_y = J_{cm} + MR_y^2 \tag{15}$$

Table 4. Table of proximal variables and nomenclature (4) [1].

Variable/Acronym	Definition	Variable/ Acronym	Definition
$J_y = J_O$	Inertia moment about a fixed axis O along y	y	Robot arm base parallel axis
J_{cm}	Inertia moment about mass center	$\hat{y}$	Body center parallel axis
M	Total system mass	r_{iO}	Radius from parallel axis (not mass center)
R_O	Distance from O to the mass center	r_i	Radius vector to the mass center
R_y	Distance to axis y	m_i	Differential mass element
O	Fixed axis along axis y	(x_i, y_i)	Center of mass coordinates
a	x coordinate of O	b	y coordinate of O

[1] Such tables are offered throughout this manuscript to aid readability.

Equation (12) was extracted from the short proof of the parallel axis theorem, since it provides the time-varying location of the mass center giving known (or estimated) values of the products of inertia (which would not be available if the matrix had been previously diagonalized by transformation from the body axis basis to the eigenvector basis frame). Thus, the next necessary step of analysis is to elaborate the ability to estimate the inertia matrix, where moments and products together are used to embody the control, while the products of inertia alone are used to parameterize the location of the mass center.

2.11. Persistent Excitation of Estimation

Simple step commands do not provide sufficiently rich input signals to produce faithful estimates of system parameters and locations of the center of mass. More "rich" input signals were utilized to increase estimation confidence.

Definition 1: *Persistent excitation: Condition placed upon input commands to ensure that the signals provide sufficient information over time to accurately estimate system parameters (which eventually manifest as estimated locations of the system center of mass).*

A finite impulse response model of order n involves the inversion of the $n \times n$ matrix in Equation (16) where $\varphi(t)$ is defined in Equation (17) for control input signal u. Estimation will have a unique solution (i.e., the process is "identifiable") if and only if the matrix in Equation (16) is non-singular or invertible [36].

$$\frac{1}{N} \sum_{i=1}^{N} \varphi^T(t) \varphi(t) \tag{16}$$

$$\varphi(t) = \begin{bmatrix} u(t-1) & u(t-2) & \cdots & u(t-n) \end{bmatrix} \tag{17}$$

Table 5. Table of proximal variables and nomenclature (5) [1].

Variable/Acronym	Definition	Variable/Acronym	Definition
N	Covariance dimension	u	Control
n	Dimension of the control	$(t-i)\forall i = 1,\ldots,n$	Indexed time
φ	System equation	φ^T	Transposed system equation

[1] Such tables are offered throughout this manuscript to aid readability.

Impacts of persistent excitation on parameter convergence are described in the study of [37]. Modeling accuracy requires the convergence of estimated parameters necessitating persistent excitation. Increased precision and faster convergence stems from relatively stronger excitation. The closed-loop stability of nonlinear, adaptive (or learning) systems was increased by bounding parameter estimation, which was also aided by persistent excitation. A step command has one instance of excitation and accordingly only leads to the reliable estimation of one parameter. Meanwhile, a sinusoidal command has two instances of excitation (as the curve oscillatory reverses direction twice) leading to the reliable estimation of two parameters. Random signals (i.e., Gaussian) are very rich excitation, since values at any pair of times are identically distributed, statistically independent (and hence uncorrelated), and, accordingly, aid the reliable estimation of any number of parameters. Accordingly, white noise was added to command signals in this investigation.

Table 6. Persistent excitation of various input signals [1].

Input Signal	Order of Persistent Excitation
Step command	1
Sinusoidal commands	2
White noise commands	n

[1] Such tables are offered throughout this manuscript to aid readability.

Propositions for achieving exponentially convergent estimation when lacking persistent excitation is presented in the studies of [38,39]. In this research, the approach taken is to add small amplitude white noise to all input command signals, which are based on sinusoids as constructed in Figure A1 (sinusoids) and Figure A3 (additional white noise) in Appendix B. The recommended input command is displayed in Box 2.

Box 2. Input signal recommendation

Recommended input command: To maximize persistent excitation, autonomous sinusoidal trajectories are recommended with white noise added.

2.12. Generic Robotics On-Orbit Trainer (GROOT) and Long-Duration Propulsive EELV Secondary Payload Adapter (LDPE ESPA)

A generic, customizable simulation is the basic orbital and robotic simulation (BOARS), developed and maintained by NASA simulations and the graphics branch [40], including two orbital vehicles as depicted in Figure 7 in arbitrary orbits. A robotic dynamic manipulator developed in collaboration with the United States Space Force (USSF) and used at the U.S. Air Force Test Pilot School was attached to one of the vehicles called the Generic Robotics On-Orbit Trainer (GROOT) [41]. The software simulations that were developed and used to produce the results in Section 3 of this manuscript utilized configurations scaled from those currently in use for the GROOT.

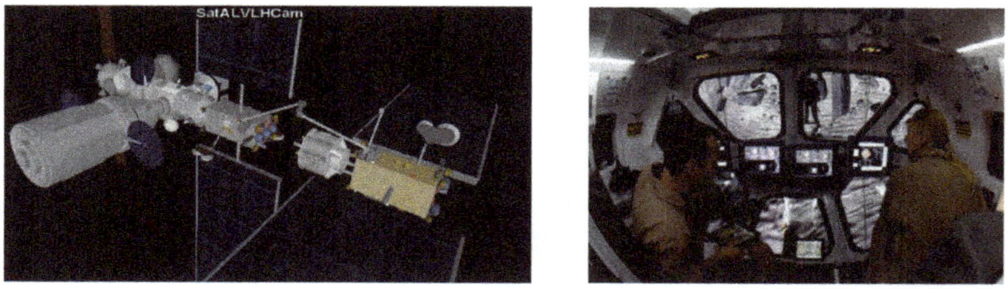

(a) **(b)**

Figure 7. (**a**) NASA basic orbital and robotic simulation (BOARS) [40] and (**b**) NASA exploration system simulations [41] for mission concept evaluation and operational insight to flight crew. Image credit: NASA, used in accordance with published image use policy [5].

2.13. Implementation Procedures

From Section 2, an implementation procedure immerges, summarized in Algorithm 1. The procedure was implemented using MATLAB®/SIMULINK® R2022b, where the subsystems are depicted in Appendix B to aid repeatability by the readership.

Algorithm 1 Pseudocode [1].

```
Input: Desired end state: final velocity and final acceleration
Output: Inertia matrix components and three-dimensional coordinates of the center of gravity
begin
Path planning using sinusoidal trajectories:
    DesiredVelocity = DesiredFinalVelocity * SineEquation
    DesiredAcceleration = DesiredFinalAcceleration * CosineEquation
Assemble feedforward control
    Parameterize Euler's moment equations into standard regression form
    Control_1 = DesiredStateMatrix * UnknownInertiaRegressionVector
OptionalFeedback = DesiredStateMatrixInverse * EstimatedTorque
EstimatedInertia = DesiredStateMatrixInverse * AppliedTorque
MassCenterCoordinates = Function(InertiaCrossProducts)
end
```

[1] Corresponding to Section 2.

Using the implementation procedure in Algorithm 1, simulations were created (as depicted in Appendix B), and the results are next presented in Section 3.

3. Results

This section presents the results of simulations of the proposed autonomous, online center of mass determination together with the nonlinear, coupled control and inertia identification and nonlinear, enhanced Luenberger observers.

3.1. Section Description

Section 3.2 describes the developed results incrementally beginning with the unperturbed system followed by the comparative benchmark. Introduced next is dynamic nonlinear feedforward augmented by (1) PID feedback and (2) inertia adaption. Next, dynamic, nonlinear feedforward with nonlinear, projection-based regression learning is applied. Estimation performance is compared next to evaluate Luenberger observer performance.

Section 3.3 performs the identification of mass moments and products. Identification is compared using nonlinear adaption versus nonlinear, projection-based learning. Section 3.4 extends the results of Section 3.3 to reveal the time-varying location of the center of mass again, comparing nonlinear adaption versus nonlinear, projection-based learning. While the baseline maneuver was a single thirty-degree yaw maneuver, compound maneuvers are evaluated next, before summary results are presented in Section 3.5.

3.2. *Incremental Development and Presentation of Results*

First, an unperturbed system is analyzed with classical feedback control. Next, a comparative benchmark for the study is analyzed, a highly perturbed system with classical feedback control. The perturbations include uniform variations to all values in the inertia matrix; random variations (white noise) added to the control to aid estimation; random noise added to sensor outputs; magnetic disturbance torques, aerodynamic disturbance torques, solar radiation pressure disturbance torques, and gravity gradient disturbance torques.

3.2.1. Unperturbed System

The unperturbed system is used to aid software troubleshooting and for investigating numeric precision. Numerical precision is studied using the quaternion normalization condition [42] displayed in Equation (18) as a figure of merit to iterate numerical integration solvers and evaluation step sizes. Solvers and step sizes were iterated until the error evaluating the quaternion normalization condition was always zero (or numeric zero), as displayed in Figure 8. Also displayed in Figure 8b is a display of the maneuver cost versus time, where the cost is calculated as one-half the time integral of the square of the control. Each case investigated is compared in part by the amount of control cost to perform the maneuver as one comparative figure of merit in addition to trajectory tracking error means and standard deviations.

$$\underline{q}(t) \equiv \begin{Bmatrix} q_1 & q_2 & q_3 & q_4 \end{Bmatrix}^T \rightarrow \left\| \underline{q} \right\| = 1 \tag{18}$$

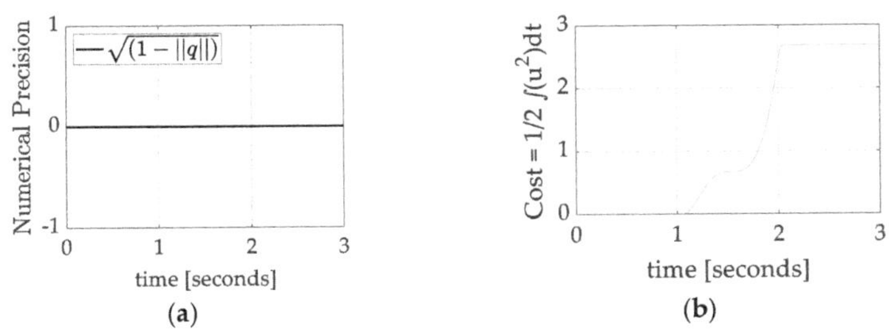

Figure 8. (**a**) Quaternion normalization condition from Equation (18) used to validate numerical precision of simulation results. (**b**) Quadratic cost of maneuver.

The initial case investigated is classical PID control of an unperturbed system without feedforward or inertia adaption or learning, and the case is presented in Figures 9 and 10 with quantitative data presented in Table 7.

Table 7. PID-controlled unperturbed system.

Cost=0.0083041	Roll [Degrees]	Pitch [Degrees]	Yaw [Degrees]
Mean	-8.7655×10^{-5}	0.00062823	0.0026512
Standard deviation [1]	0.00096123	0.00088184	0.0084459

[1] Mass moments uniformly perturbed 50%, control contains noise with variance 0.0001, and white sensor noise with 0.0334 degrees of deviation.

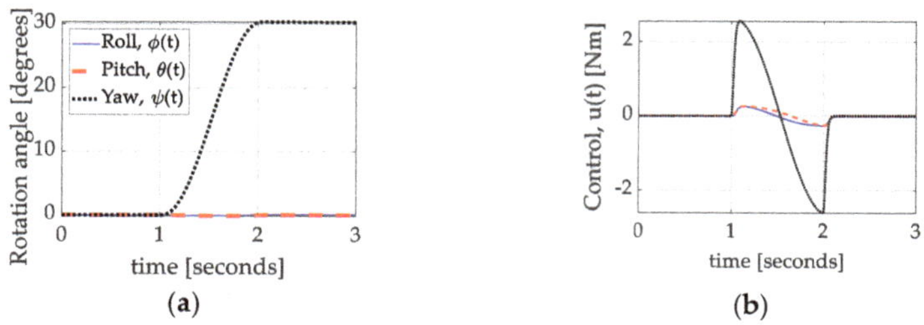

Figure 9. (**a**) Rotation during unperturbed system maneuver: Thirty-degree yaw with time in seconds on the abscissa and rotation angle in degrees on the ordinant with roll as the solid blue line, pitch as the dashed red line, and yaw as the dotted black line. The three-dimensional maneuver data with time in seconds on the abscissa, roll as the solid blue line, pitch as the dashed red line, and yaw as the dotted black line presented together in Figure 9a are elaborated separately in Figure 10. (**b**) The control utilized during the maneuver. Quantitative data corresponding to the qualitative display in Figures 9 and 10 are presented in Table 7.

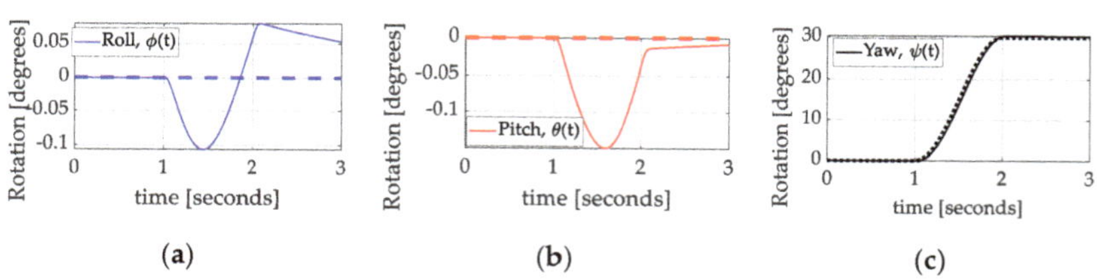

Figure 10. Commanded rotation versus actual rotation during unperturbed thirty-degree yaw with time in seconds on the abscissa and rotation angle in degrees on the ordinant: (**a**) roll; (**b**) pitch; and (**c**) yaw. Commanded rotation versus actual rotation during highly perturbed thirty-degree yaw with time in seconds on the abscissa and rotation angle in degrees on the ordinant: (**a**) roll; (**b**) pitch; and (**c**) yaw. Quantitative data corresponding to the qualitative display in Figure 11 are presented in Table 7.

3.2.2. Comparative Benchmark

The comparative benchmark case of classical PID control without feedforward or learning controlling a highly perturbed system with sensor noise is presented in Figures 12 and 13 with quantitative data presented in Table 8. Figure 12a simultaneously displays the roll, pitch, and yaw angles with respect to time. The commanded rotational maneuver is a thirty-degree yaw tracking a sinusoidal trajectory with no commanded roll or pitch, and the maneuver is performed with precision. The three axis controls are displayed in Figure 12b; notice the largest control corresponds to the yaw channel, while the relative smaller two channels of control counter the cross-coupled motion inherent with a fully populated inertia matrix. Figure 13 displays the same maneuver data as Figure 12a separated into three displays, one for each axis of motion: roll, pitch, and yaw. The three plots present qualitative information that matches the quantitative presentation of data in Table 8.

Table 8. PID-controlled highly perturbed system: uniformly varied inertia, sensors with white noise, and thirty-degree yaw maneuver tracking errors.

Cost=0.0083917	Roll [Degrees]	Pitch [Degrees]	Yaw [Degrees]
Mean	-8.5263×10^{-5}	0.0006306	0.0026536
Standard deviation [1]	0.00096242	0.00088425	0.0084479

[1] Mass moments uniformly perturbed 50%, control contains noise with variance 0.0001, and white sensor noise with 0.0334 degrees of deviation.

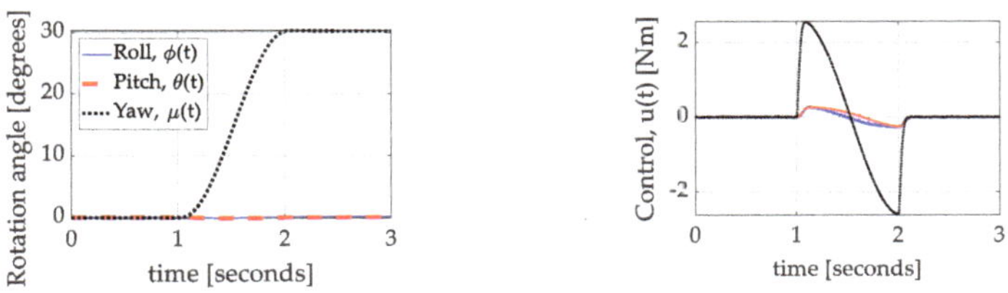

(**a**) (**b**)

Figure 11. PID control. (**a**) Rotation during unperturbed system maneuver: Thirty-degree yaw with time in seconds on the abscissa and rotation angle in degrees on the ordinant with roll as the solid blue line, pitch as the dashed red line, and yaw as the dotted black line. The three-dimensional maneuver data with time in seconds on the abscissa, roll as the solid blue line, pitch as the dashed red line, and yaw as the dotted black line presented together in Figure 11a are elaborated separately in Figure 12. (**b**) The control utilized during the maneuver. Quantitative data corresponding to the qualitative display in Figure 12 are presented in Table 8.

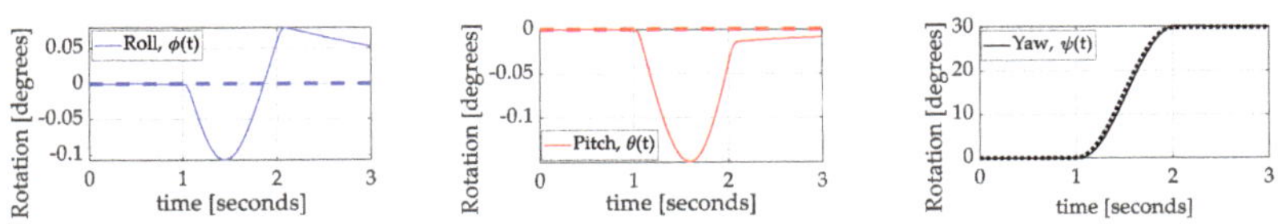

(**a**) (**b**) (**c**)

Figure 12. PID-controlled highly perturbed system: uniformly varied inertia, sensors with white noise. Commanded rotation versus actual rotation during highly perturbed thirty-degree yaw with time in seconds on the abscissa and rotation angle in degrees on the ordinant: (**a**) roll; (**b**) pitch; and (**c**) yaw. Commanded rotation versus actual rotation during highly perturbed thirty-degree yaw with time in seconds on the abscissa and rotation angle in degrees on the ordinant: (**a**) roll; (**b**) pitch; and (**c**) yaw. Quantitative data corresponding to the qualitative display in Figure 12 are presented in Table 8.

3.2.3. Dynamic Nonlinear Feedforward with PID Feedback and Inertia Adaption

Having foremost established an idealized performance controlling an unperturbed system, next, the controlled system was perturbed with some performance degradation. Next, this section displays the results (in Figures 13–17) of adding dynamic nonlinear feedforward and inertia adaption. Efforts were not made to optimize the adaption or the feedback gains, since tracking errors assist the estimation of the mass center location (the goal of this study). Estimation and tracking control is summarized in Box 3.

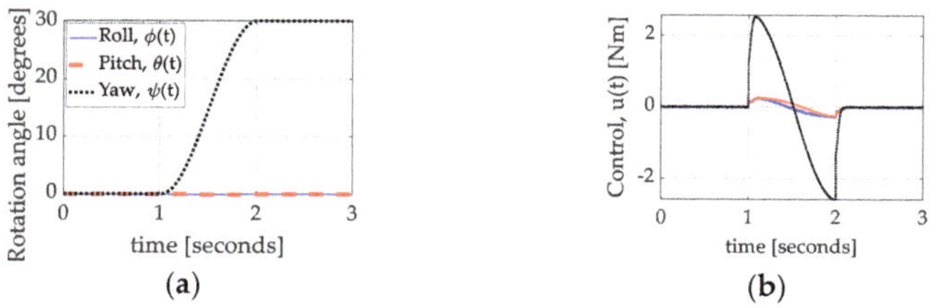

Figure 13. Dynamic nonlinear feedforward with PID feedback and inertia adaption with roll as the solid blue line, pitch as the dashed red line, and yaw as the dotted black line: (**a**) Rotation during highly perturbed (uniformly varied inertia, sensors with white noise) thirty-degree yaw with time in seconds on the abscissa and rotation angle in degrees on the ordinant. (**b**) control versus time. Quantitative data corresponding to the qualitative display in Figure 14 are presented in Table 9.

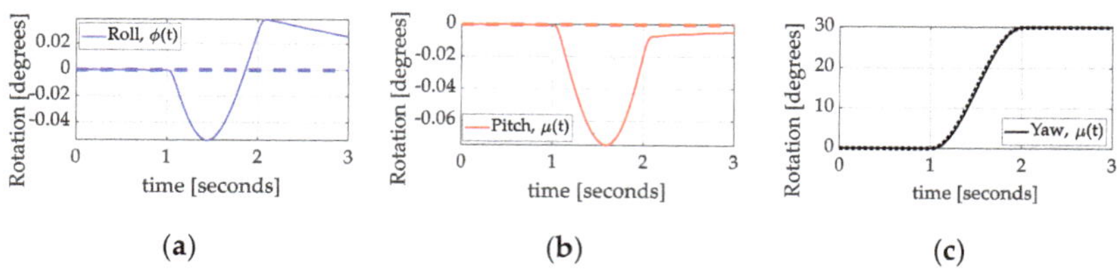

Figure 14. Dynamic nonlinear feedforward with PID feedback and inertia adaption. Commanded rotation versus actual rotation during highly perturbed thirty-degree yaw with time in seconds on the abscissa and rotation angle in degrees on the ordinant: (**a**) roll; (**b**) pitch; and (**c**) yaw. Commanded rotation versus actual rotation during highly perturbed thirty-degree yaw with time in seconds on the abscissa and rotation angle in degrees on the ordinant: (**a**) roll; (**b**) pitch; and (**c**) yaw. Quantitative data corresponding to the qualitative display Figure 15 are presented in Table 9.

Table 9. Dynamic nonlinear feedforward with PID feedback and inertia adaption. Highly perturbed (uniformly varied inertia, sensors with white noise) thirty-degree yaw maneuver tracking errors.

Cost=0.0075635	Roll [Degrees]	Pitch [Degrees]	Yaw [Degrees]
Mean	-2.7565×10^{-5}	0.0003158	0.0013581
Standard deviation [1]	0.00047434	0.00044734	0.0042131

[1] Mass moments uniformly perturbed 50%, control contains noise with variance 0.0001, and white sensor noise with 0.0334 degrees of deviation.

3.2.4. Dynamic Nonlinear Feedforward with PID Feedback and Nonlinear Projection-Based Regression Learning

Having, in the previous section, displayed the results of adding dynamic nonlinear feedforward and inertia adaption, this section replaces inertia adaption with nonlinear projection-based regression learning. As before, efforts were not made to optimize the adaption or the feedback gains since tracking errors assist the estimation of the mass center location (the goal of this study).

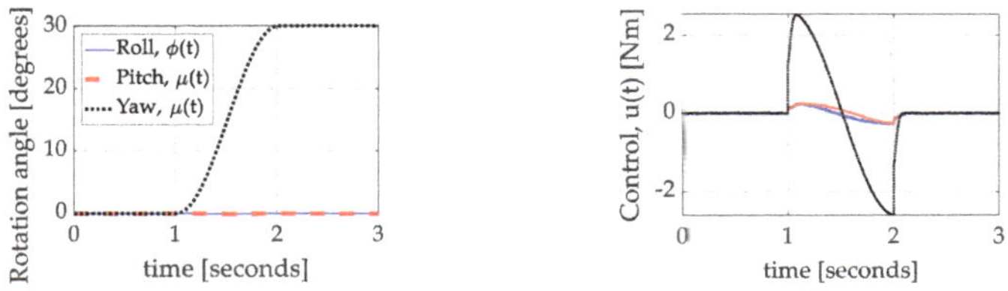

Figure 15. Dynamic nonlinear feedforward with PID feedback and nonlinear projection-based regression learningwith roll as the solid blue line, pitch as the dashed red line, and yaw as the dotted black line: (**a**) Rotation during highly perturbed (uniformly varied inertia, sensors with white noise) thirty-degree yaw with time in seconds on the abscissa and rotation angle in degrees on the ordinant. (**b**) control versus time. Quantitative data corresponding to the qualitative display in Figure 15 are presented in Table 10.

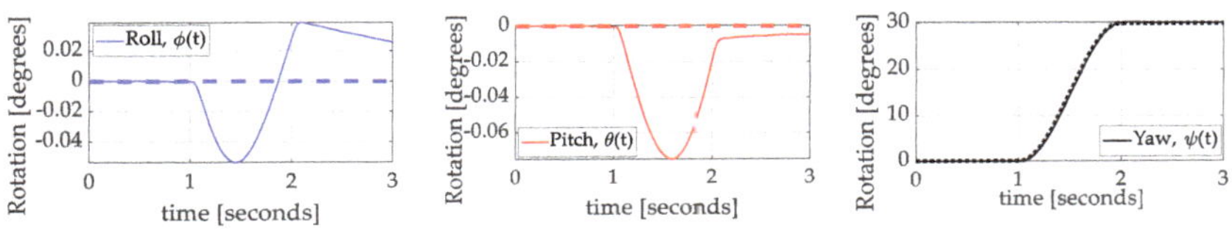

Figure 16. Dynamic nonlinear feedforward with PID feedback nonlinear projection-based regression learning. Commanded rotation versus actual rotation during highly perturbed thirty-degree yaw with time in seconds on the abscissa and rotation angle in degrees on the ordinant: (**a**) roll; (**b**) pitch; and (**c**) yaw. Commanded rotation versus actual rotation during highly perturbed thirty-degree yaw with time in seconds on the abscissa and rotation angle in degrees on the ordinant: (**a**) roll; (**b**) pitch; and (**c**) yaw. Quantitative data corresponding to the qualitative display in Figure 16 are presented in Table 10.

Table 10. Dynamic nonlinear feedforward with PID feedback and nonlinear feedforward nonlinear projection-based regression learning. Highly perturbed (uniformly varied inertia, sensors with white noise) thirty-degree yaw maneuver tracking errors.

Cost=0.0075635	Roll [Degrees]	Pitch [Degrees]	Yaw [Degrees]
Mean	-2.7565×10^{-5}	0.0003158	0.0013581
Standard deviation [1]	0.00047434	0.00044734	0.0042131

[1] Mass moments uniformly perturbed 50%, control contains noise with variance 0.0001, and white sensor noise with 0.0334 degrees of deviation.

Box 3. Identical tracking: adaption vs. nonlinear projection-based regression learning

Estimation vs. tracking control: Notice identical trajectory tracking results in Tables 9 and 10. Adaption and nonlinear projection-based regression learning methods are strictly used to estimate inertia components and mass center location and do not affect trajectory tracking performance.

3.2.5. Estimator Performance Comparison

With the backdrop of introducing tracking control options, the remaining topic of study is the performance of state estimation by disparate Luenberger observers. Those estimated states are used by both the inertia adaption scheme and the nonlinear projection-based regression learning. The goal of the comparison is merely to choose the Luenberger instantiations. The observer comparison is presented qualitatively in Figure 18 and quantitatively in Table 11. The nonlinear, enhanced observer was slightly superior in the maneuver axis but relatively substantially inferior in the non-maneuver axes. Observer performance is presented in Table 11 and summarized in Box 4.

Table 11. Observer estimation percent performance comparison. Highly perturbed (uniformly varied inertia, sensors with white noise) thirty-degree yaw maneuver tracking errors.

	Mean Roll [Degrees]	Mean Pitch [Degrees]	Mean Yaw [Degrees]
Benchmark Luenberger	−−	−−	−−
Nonlinear Luenberger [1]	77%	144.58%	−1.02%

[1] Mass moments uniformly perturbed 50%, control contains noise with variance 0.0001, and white sensor noise with 0.0334 degrees of deviation.

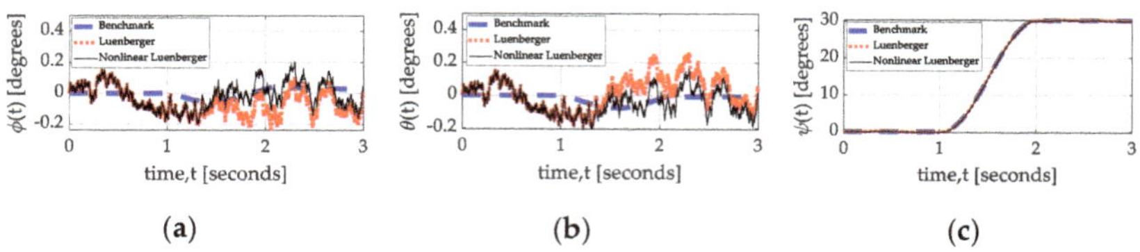

Figure 17. Estimated actual rotation during highly perturbed thirty-degree yaw with time in seconds on the abscissa and estimated rotation angle in degrees on the ordinant: (**a**) roll; (**b**) pitch; and (**c**) yaw. The actual rotation angle (dashed blue line), the rotation angle estimated by the enhanced Luenberger observer (dotted red line), and the rotation angle estimated by enhanced, nonlinear Luenberger observers: (**a**) roll; (**b**) pitch; and (**c**) yaw. Quantitative data corresponding to the qualitative display in Figure 17 are presented in Table 11.

Box 4. Observer recommendation

Observer recommendation: Simultaneous use of both Luenberger styles is recommended to leverage their relative strengths in the maneuver axis and non-maneuver axis.

3.3. *Identification of Mass Moments and Products*

The estimations from the Luenberger observers are used to estimate inertia moments and products using two disparate methods: the nonlinear adaption and nonlinear projection-based regression learning described, respectively, in Sections 3.3.1 and 3.3.2.

3.3.1. Identification of Mass Moments and Products by Nonlinear Adaption

Nonlinear adaption as proposed in the study of [43] and improved in the study of [32,44] were utilized to estimate the six inertia moments and products. The method was simulated in the study of [45] and experimentally validated in the study of [46].

A combined measure of error linearly combines angular acceleration and velocities using a constant gain. The gained, combined measure of error is multiplied by the system matrix with an adaption gain to establish the adaption rate, which is integrated to produce inertia component adaptions. The MATLAB®/SIMULINK® simulation subsystems are presented in Appendix B and the simulation results are displayed in Figure 18.

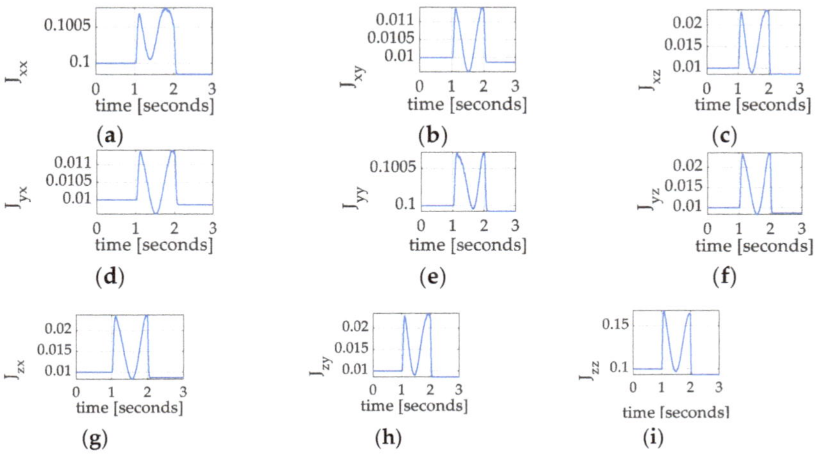

Figure 18. Nonlinear adaption derived inertia moments and products: Time-varying mass moments and products for a single, thirty-degree yaw maneuver with coupled motion in roll and pitch, where the command has white noise added to aid persistent excitation (**a**) J_{xx}; (**b**) J_{xy}; (**c**) J_{xz}; (**d**) J_{yx}; (**e**) J_{yy}; (**f**) J_{yz}; (**g**) J_{zx}; (**h**) J_{zy}; and (**i**) J_{zz}. Notice that the initial flat-line behavior during the initial quiescent period is followed by rapid location learning during the maneuver excitement, lastly followed by a slow, oscillatory settling following the maneuver during regulation. The moments and products of inertia seem to converge towards a certain value during the maneuver excitation but not during either period of regulation, lacking persistent excitation.

3.3.2. Identification of Mass Moments and Products by Nonlinear Projection-Based Regression Learning

Nonlinear projection-based regression learning was proposed just last year in the study of [47] to learn the six inertia moments and products. Referring to Figure 19, the method that was utilized included an analysis and simulation, while validating experimentation is proposed in this present manuscript.

$$\boxed{Analysis} \rightarrow \boxed{Simulation\ verification} \rightarrow \boxed{Experimental\ validation}$$

Figure 19. Process stages adopted in this study: analyze and hypothesize followed by verification of analysis with modeling and simulation validated experimentally.

Angle trajectory tracking error alone (not in a combine error measure as performed with nonlinear adaption) is projected on the system matrix used to embody the nonlinear feedforward control parameterized in regression form without linearization, diagonalization, or otherwise simplification. Figure 20 reveals the mass moments and products estimated by the learning algorithm, while the corresponding MATLAB®/SIMULINK® simulation subsystems are presented in Appendix B.

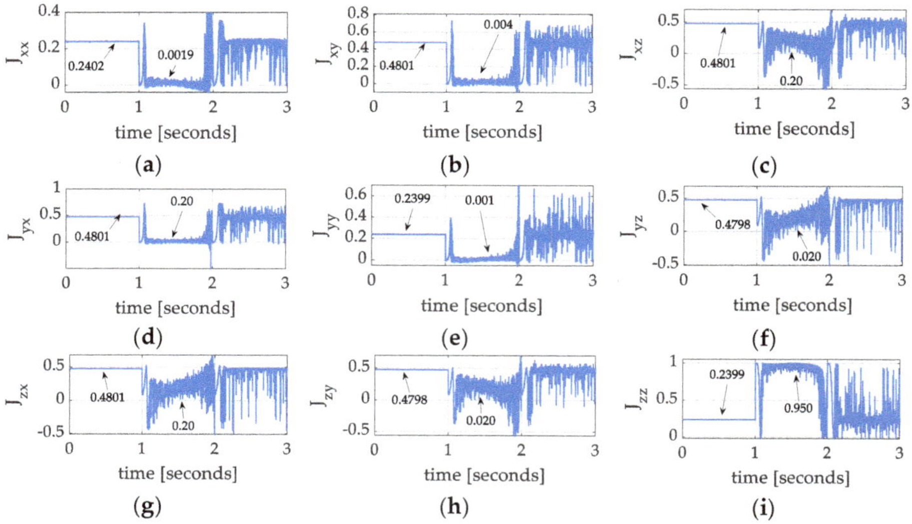

Figure 20. Projection regression-based learning inertia moments and products: Time-varying mass moments and products for a single, thirty-degree yaw maneuver with coupled motion in roll and pitch, where the command has white noise added to aid persistent excitation (**a**) J_{xx}; (**b**) J_{xy}; (**c**) J_{xz}; (**d**) J_{yx}; (**e**) J_{yy}; (**f**) J_{yz}; (**g**) J_{zx}; (**h**) J_{zy}; and (**i**) J_{zz}. Notice that the initial flat-line behavior during the initial quiescent period is followed by rapid location learning during the maneuver excitement, lastly followed by a slow, oscillatory settling following the maneuver during regulation. The moments and products of inertia seem to converge towards a certain value during the maneuver excitation but not during either period of regulation, lacking persistent excitation.

3.4. *Location of Mass Center*

Time-varying estimates of mass moments and products may be used with Equation (12) to directly calculate the location of the mass center (as a reminder that the inertia matrix must not be diagonalized). The estimates of inertia moments and products are produced with two disparate methods: nonlinear adaption and nonlinear projection-based regression learning, respectively, in Section 3.4.1. and Section 3.4.2.

3.4.1. Identification of Mass Center Coordinates by Nonlinear Adaption

Notice in Figure 21 that adaption occurs twice: at the beginning and the end of trajectory tracking. The roll channel depicted in subfigure (a) seems to indicate a proper mass center location roughly at 0.15 in the x direction. Meanwhile, the pitch channel adaption deviates from 0.1 ± 0.02 in the y direction, while the yaw channel location adaption displayed in subfigure (c) behaves similar to the roll channel, seemingly indicating a mass center location roughly 0.225 in the z direction. Lastly, notice, during the post-maneuver quiescent period, that the location estimate does not return to the initial estimate (at the beginning of the pre-maneuver quiescent period). As a reminder, the control signal contains a sinusoidal trajectory command (which is persistently exciting of order 2) with white noise added (which is persistently exciting of order n). Efficacy towards mass center location is presented in Box 5.

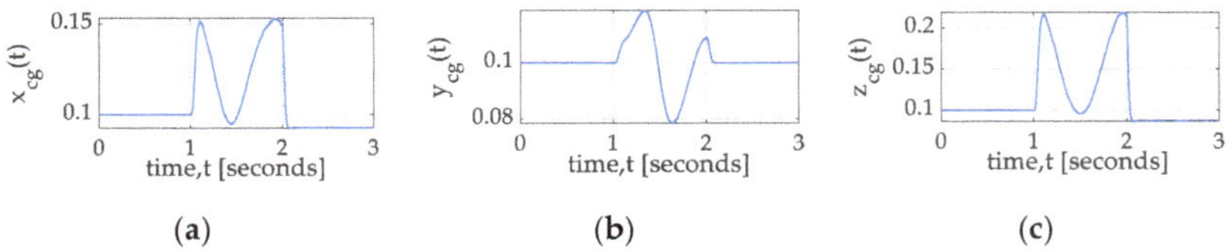

Figure 21. Nonlinear adaption time-varying location of the center of mass: For a single, thirty-degree yaw maneuver with coupled motion in roll and pitch, where the command has white noise added to aid persistent excitation (**a**) x coordinate; (**b**) y coordinate; and (**c**) z coordinate. Notice that the initial flat-line behavior during the initial quiescent period is followed by rapid location learning during the maneuver excitement, lastly followed by a slow, oscillatory settling following the maneuver during regulation. The location seems to approach the body axis origin in the x and y directions with slight movement away in the z direction.

3.4.2. Identification of Mass Center Coordinates by Nonlinear Projection-Based Regression Learning

Notice in Figure 22 that adjustment occurs many more times than twice. Especially focusing on the period between the beginning and the end of trajectory tracking, the roll channel depicted in subfigure (a) seems to indicate a proper mass center location roughly at 0.44 in the x direction. Meanwhile, the pitch channel adaption deviates from 0.20 in the y direction, while the yaw channel location adaption displayed in subfigure (c) seemingly indicates a mass center location roughly 1.35 in the z direction. Again, notice, during the post-maneuver quiescent period, that the location estimate does not return to the initial estimate (at the beginning of the pre-maneuver quiescent period). As a reminder, the control signal contains a sinusoidal trajectory command (which is persistently exciting of order 2) with white noise added (which is persistently exciting of order n).

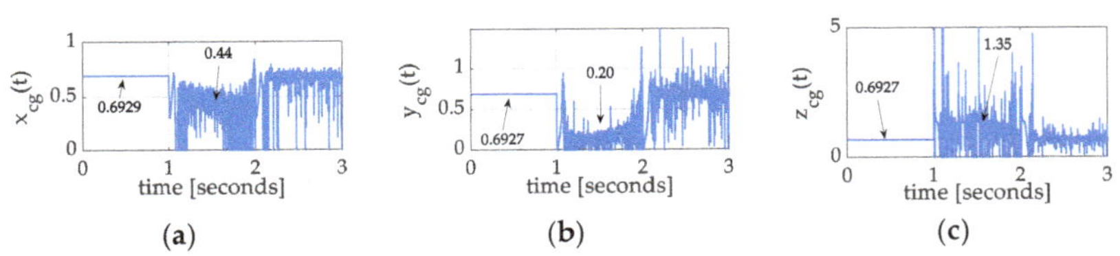

Figure 22. Projection regression-based learning time-varying location of the center of mass: Three-dimensional coordinate estimates (**a**) $\hat{x}$, (**b**) $\hat{y}$, and (**c**) $\hat{z}$; for a single, thirty-degree yaw maneuver with coupled motion in roll and pitch, where the command has white noise added to aid persistent excitation. Notice that the initial flat-line behavior during the initial quiescent period is followed by rapid location learning during the maneuver excitement. Furthermore, notice that the degree of convergence spans roughly 253, 493, and 657 mm in each axis, respectively, in mere seconds.

Box 5. Mass center recommendation

Locating the mass center: Compared to using nonlinear adaption, the use of nonlinear projection-based regression learning was more sensitive to identical cases of persistent excitation and accordingly produced better location of mass center.

3.4.3. Location of Center of Mass: Three-Dimensional Comparison

Both methods of inertia matrix components identification (adaption and learning) were implemented and compared in Figures 18–20. Immediately evident upon first glance is the fact that the adaptive approach converges relatively slowly compared to projection regression two-norm optimal learning. While developing the learning approach in Section 2 of this manuscript, the notion of having optimal estimates at every time step seemed attractive but clearly has drawbacks illustrated in Figures 22 and 23a compared to the nonlinear adaptive approach, whose results are displayed in Figures 21 and 23b. The two norm optimal pseudoinverse calculations in the learning approach seem to be highly excited by the presence of so many perturbations (indicating potentially poor applicability to deployed space robotic systems).

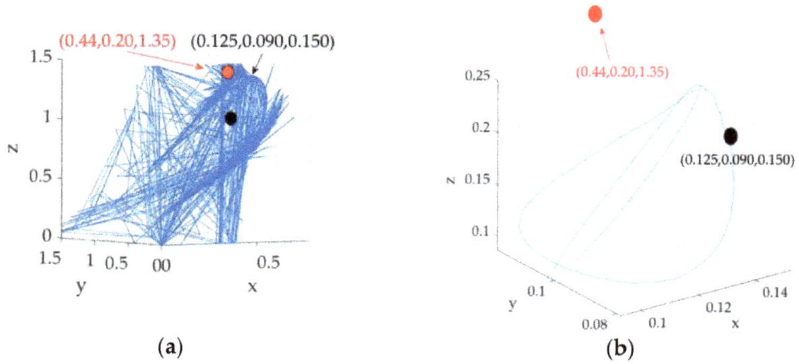

Figure 23. Comparison, time-varying location of the center of mass: (**a**) three-dimensional plot of learned cg location using projection regression-based learning; (**b**) three-dimensional plot of learned cg location using nonlinear adaption for inertia calculations. Both (**a**,**b**) use identical deterministic relationships to locate the center of mass using the products of inertia.

3.5. Compound Maneuvers

Compound maneuvers were investigated, and the results are summarized in Box 6 and displayed in Figures 24 and 25 and Table 12.

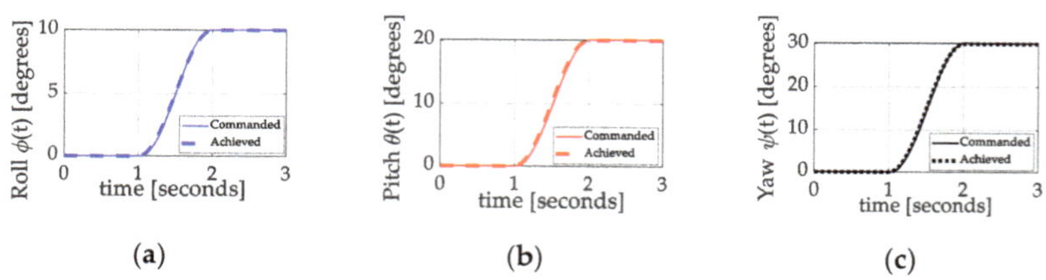

Figure 24. Compound maneuver trajectory tracking errors. Projection regression-based learning with nonlinear Luenberger observers: (**a**) roll; (**b**) pitch; and (**c**) yaw. Results presented in Figure 24 qualitatively are presented quantitatively in Table 12.

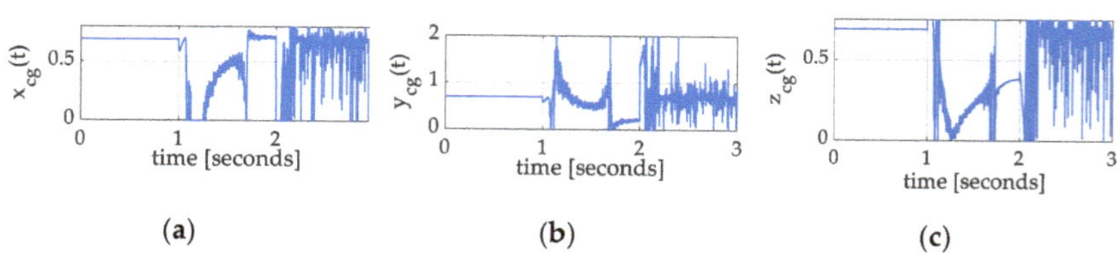

Figure 25. Compound maneuver estimated mass center location. Projection regression-based learning with nonlinear Luenberger observers: (**a**) $\hat{x}$-coordinate; (**b**) $\hat{y}$-coordinate; and (**c**) $\hat{z}$-coordinate.

Table 12. Compound maneuver trajectory tracking errors. Projection regression-based learning with nonlinear Luenberger observers.

	Roll [Degrees]	Pitch [Degrees]	Yaw [Degrees]
Error mean	0.00028129	-4.1077×10^{-5}	0.0027575
Error standard deviations [1]	0.0084356	0.0054244	0.011515

[1] Mass moments uniformly perturbed 50%, control contains noise with variance 0.0001, and white sensor noise with 0.0334 degrees of deviation.

Box 6. Compound maneuver recommendation

Single-axis versus compound-axis maneuvers: Compound maneuvers eliminated the learning convergence experienced with single-axis maneuvers. Single-axis maneuvers should be sequenced sequentially amongst all three axes.

3.6. Summary of Results

Results displayed in this manuscript are consolidated in this section and presented as percent performance difference relative to a comparative benchmark in Tables 12–16. Narrative results are subsequently discussed in Section 4 Discussion, aiming to highlight substantial results in plain verbiage (e.g., no use of "microradian", etc.) in favor of percent performance difference. Superlative results are highlighted in bold font to amplify information transmission when readers scan this manuscript.

Table 13. Attitude control trajectory tracking percent performance difference †.

Maneuver Case	Roll Errors		Pitch Errors		Yaw Errors	
	Mean	Deviation	Mean	Deviation	Mean	Deviation
Unperturbed PID unperturbed system *	3%	0%	0%	0%	899%	0%
Benchmark case **	--	--	--	--	--	--
Feedforward + feedback + adaption *** or learning ****	**−68%**	**−51%**	**−50%**	**−49%**	**−49%**	**−50%**

* Classical PID-controlled perturbed slew without feedforward or learning controlling the highly perturbed † system. ** Classical PID-controlled perturbed slew with feedforward but no adaption or learning controlling the highly perturbed † system. *** Classical PID-controlled perturbed slew with feedforward plus nonlinear inertia adaption controlling the highly perturbed † system. **** Classical PID-controlled perturbed slew with feedforward plus inertia learning controlling the highly perturbed † system. − Assumed mass moments uniformly perturbed 50%, control contains noise with variance 0.0001, and white sensor noise with 0.0334 degrees of deviation.

Table 14. Performance comparison of controlling highly perturbed system (uniformly varied inertia, sensors with white noise) [1] unless otherwise stated for a thirty-degree yaw maneuver.

Case	Cost
PID-controlled unperturbed system	−1%
Benchmark PID feedback	--
Nonlinear feedforward with inertia adaption and PID feedback	**−10%**
Nonlinear feedforward with regression-based inertia learning	**−10%**

[1] Mass moments uniformly perturbed 50%, control contains noise with variance 0.0001, and white sensor noise with 0.0334 degrees of deviation.

Table 15. Locating center of mass performance comparison ****, †.

Maneuver Case	x Coordinate	y Coordinate	z Coordinate
Nonlinear adaption	7%	0%	13%
Nonlinear projection-based regression learning	36%	71%	-95%

**** Classical PID-controlled perturbed slew with feedforward plus inertia learning controlling the highly perturbed† system. † Assumed mass moments uniformly perturbed 50%, control contains noise with variance 0.0001, and white sensor noise with 0.0334 degrees of deviation.

4. Discussion

Nonlinear adaptive methods for locating the mass center proved effective but less so than nonlinear projection-based regression learning. Using identical excitation, nonlinear adaptive methods were able to establish an average seven percent difference in coordinates of the mass center, while an average over seventy percent difference was achievable using nonlinear projection-based regression learning. Listed in Table 16, several recommendations are advised to repeat these results.

Table 16. Most significant recommendations.

1	Use the physics-based governing dynamics to embody the control (Section 2.1).
2	To maximize persistent excitation, autonomous sinusoidal trajectories are recommended with white noise added (Section 2.9).
3	Simultaneous use of both Luenberger styles is recommended to leverage their relative strengths in the maneuver axis and non-maneuver axis (Section 3.2).
4	Compared to using nonlinear adaption, the use of nonlinear projection-based regression learning was more sensitive to identical cases of persistent excitation and accordingly produced a better location of mass center (Section 3.4.2).
5	Compound maneuvers eliminated learning convergence experienced with single-axis maneuvers. Single-axis maneuvers should be sequenced sequentially amongst all three axes (Section 3.4.3).

Future Research Directions

While this prequel study introduces the first two steps of investigation (analysis and verification in simulations), validation with spaceflight experiments is planned for March 2025, after which a sequel will be published with the results of the spaceflight tests.

$$\boxed{Analysis} \rightarrow \boxed{Simulation\ verification} \rightarrow \boxed{Experimental\ validation} \tag{19}$$

5. Conclusions

Arguably, reference [22] presents the best recently proposed comparative benchmark, since that method was experimentally validated on the GRACE-C satellite. The method effectively generated convergent estimates of mass center coordinates, where the convergence spanned just greater than 0.3 mm over several hundred days. Meanwhile, convergence using the proposed methods (in simulations) spans roughly 200–600 mm, respectively, in each axis, and convergence occurs in mere seconds, assuming a single-axis slew maneuver. Multi-axis, compound slew maneuvers were completely ineffective using the proposed approach to estimate coordinates of the center of mass. Succinctly, the proposed methods seem to indicate advantages of speed and the quantity of coordinate convergence when compared to the state-of-the-art comparative benchmark. Spaceflight experiments planned for March 2025 will evaluate the efficacy of this proposed approach empirically.

Funding: This research received no external funding. The APC was funded by the corresponding author.

Data Availability Statement: Data supporting reported results can be obtained by contacting the corresponding author.

Conflicts of Interest: The author declares no conflicts of interest.

Appendix A

The nonlinear feedforward is developed step-by-step in this Appendix.

$$\tau = [J]\{\dot{\omega}\} + \{\omega\} \times [J]\{\omega\} \tag{A1}$$

$$\tau = \begin{bmatrix} J_{xx} & J_{xy} & J_{xz} \\ J_{yx} & J_{yy} & J_{yz} \\ J_{zx} & J_{zy} & J_{zz} \end{bmatrix} \begin{Bmatrix} \dot{\omega}_x \\ \dot{\omega}_y \\ \dot{\omega}_z \end{Bmatrix} + \begin{Bmatrix} \omega_x \\ \omega_y \\ \omega_z \end{Bmatrix} \times \begin{bmatrix} J_{xx} & J_{xy} & J_{xz} \\ J_{yx} & J_{yy} & J_{yz} \\ J_{zx} & J_{zy} & J_{zz} \end{bmatrix} \begin{Bmatrix} \omega_x \\ \omega_y \\ \omega_z \end{Bmatrix} \tag{A2}$$

$$\tau = \begin{bmatrix} J_{xx} & J_{xy} & J_{xz} \\ J_{yx} & J_{yy} & J_{yz} \\ J_{zx} & J_{zy} & J_{zz} \end{bmatrix} \begin{Bmatrix} \dot{\omega}_x \\ \dot{\omega}_y \\ \dot{\omega}_z \end{Bmatrix} + \begin{Bmatrix} \omega_x \\ \omega_y \\ \omega_z \end{Bmatrix} \times \begin{Bmatrix} J_{xx}\omega_x + J_{xy}\omega_y + J_{xz}\omega_z \\ J_{yx}\omega_x + J_{yy}\omega_y + J_{yz}\omega_z \\ J_{zx}\omega_x + J_{zy}\omega_y + J_{zz}\omega_z \end{Bmatrix} \tag{A3}$$

$$\tau = \begin{bmatrix} J_{xx}\dot{\omega}_x + J_{xy}\dot{\omega}_y - J_{xy}\omega_x\omega_z + J_{xz}\dot{\omega}_z - J_{xz}\omega_x\omega_y - J_{yy}\omega_y\omega_z + J_{zz}\omega_y\omega_z \\ J_{xx}\omega_x\omega_z + J_{xy}\dot{\omega}_x + J_{xy}\omega_y\omega_z + J_{yy}\dot{\omega}_y + J_{yz}\dot{\omega}_z - J_{yz}\omega_x\omega_y - J_{zz}\omega_x\omega_z \\ -J_{xx}\omega_x\omega_y + J_{xz}\dot{\omega}_x - J_{xz}\omega_y\omega_z + J_{yy}\omega_x\omega_y + J_{yz}\dot{\omega}_y + J_{yz}\omega_x\omega_z + J_{zz}\dot{\omega}_z \end{bmatrix} \tag{A4}$$

$$\tau = \underbrace{\begin{bmatrix} \dot{\omega}_x & \dot{\omega}_y - \omega_x\omega_z & \dot{\omega}_z - \omega_x\omega_y & -\omega_y\omega_z & 0 & \omega_y\omega_z \\ \omega_x\omega_z & \dot{\omega}_x + \omega_y\omega_z & 0 & \dot{\omega}_y & \dot{\omega}_z - \omega_x\omega_y & -\omega_x\omega_z \\ -\omega_x\omega_y & 0 & \dot{\omega}_x - \omega_y\omega_z & \omega_x\omega_y & \dot{\omega}_y + \omega_x\omega_z & \dot{\omega}_z \end{bmatrix}}_{[\Phi]} \underbrace{\begin{Bmatrix} J_{xx} \\ J_{xy} \\ J_{xz} \\ J_{yy} \\ J_{yz} \\ J_{zz} \end{Bmatrix}}_{\beta} \tag{A5}$$

Appendix B

This appendix displays all the simulation subsystems permitting repeatability by the readership using MATLAB®/SIMULINK®. Implementation steps are as follows:

1. Create a scheme of command. A sinusoidal scheme is depicted in Figure A1 and may be constructed by dragging and dropping the blocks depicted from the library to the simulation. The switching logic produces smooth sinusoids for angular displacement, velocity, and acceleration. The switch institutes to regulation at the final commanded value, smoothly exiting the sinusoidal curves, respectively. The syntax for the sinusoidal commands is displayed in Figure A2.
2. The attitude controllers are displayed in Figure A3, including both feedforward and feedback controllers. The project-based learning algorithm is also included. Additionally, notice that there is a manual switch away from the input sinusoidal trajectories and optionally towards a simple step command. Lastly, notice that artificially faked inertia values and random perturbations are included as switchable options as well.
3. Projection-based learning and/or nonlinear adaption feedback are displayed in Figures A4–A6.

The implementation steps elaborated so far in Appendix B yield an ability to produce endpoint commands, autonomous trajectory generation, and trajectory tracking abilities, where the outputs include the control torque (to be sent to the space robot). Additional outputs include time-varying inertia estimates and location of the center of mass. The control signal is routed to the actuator on the space robot.

4. The reaction wheel actuator is displayed in Figure A9, where the output torque from the actuator is routed to the governing equations of motion depicted in Figure A10 with expanded drilldown elaboration in Figures A11 and A12. The governing equations of motion produce angular velocities relative to the inertial reference frame but need to be expressed in the coordinates of a body frame of interest.
5. Figure A12 displays the high-level kinematic topology. Drill downs for quaternions are displayed in Figure A13 where the quaternions are used to construct a nine-element direction cosine matrix transformation between inertial and body coordinates.

The direction cosine matrix is used to extract Euler angles where a "3–2–1" rotation sequence is assumed, and that code is depicted in Figure A14.

6. While the true Euler angles cannot be known by the robot operators, sensors are simulated with additive noise and filters designed to counteract the noise in Figure A15.
7. The direction cosine matrix conveniently reveals the vector locations of the body axes and is used to calculate environmental disturbance torques.

The implementation steps elaborated so far in Appendix B now additionally include kinetics, kinematics, noisy sensors, and filters. Lastly, the simulation of environmental disturbances is elaborated.

8. The top-level topology of environmental disturbances is displayed in Figure A16 where each subsystem is individually displayed in Figure A17 for atmospheric, magnetic, solar radiation, and gravity gradient disturbances.

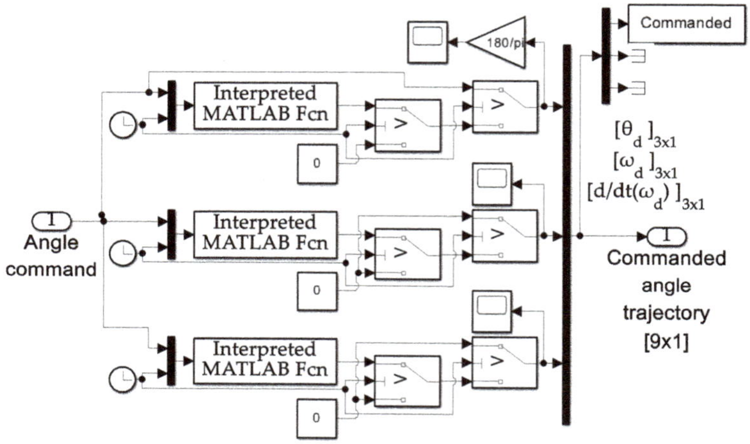

Figure A1. Internal content of trajectory generation subsystem depicted in Figure 3. Notice the sinusoidal attitude trajectories are formulated from the single input of angle commanded outside the space robot (presumably either autonomously by the demands of the translational motion subsystem or alternatively externally supplied by a human operator aiding the space robot's motion with remote-controls).

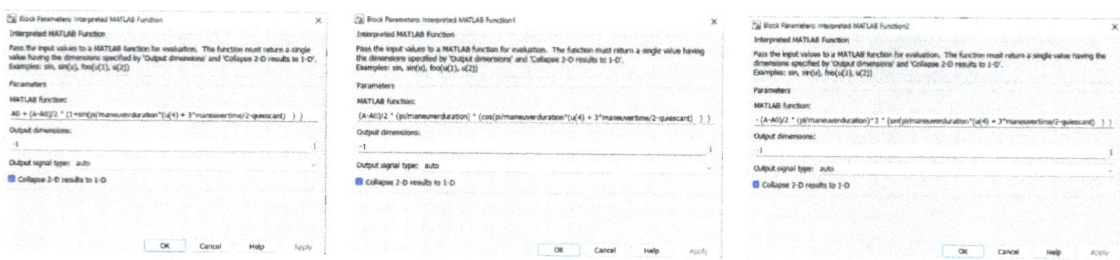

(a) (b) (c)

Figure A2. Pseudocode (labeled "Block Parameters") used in the three "Interpreted MATLAB Fcn" blocks in Figure A1 encoding the angle (**a**), angular rate (**b**), and angular acceleration (**c**) commands, respectively. Top-to-bottom subsystems in Figure A1 correspond to left-to-right block parameters in this figure. The pseudocode is provided to aid repeatability of the research results.

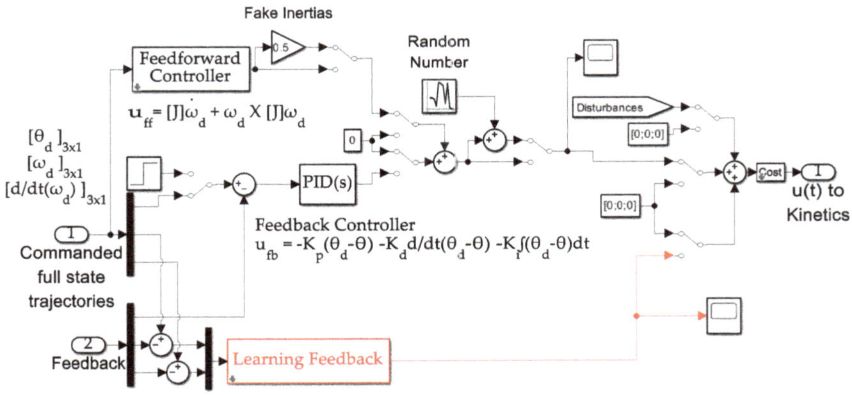

Figure A3. Internal content of "Controllers" subsystem depicted in Figure 3. Notice the use of manual switches permitting simulation iteration where all facets are held constant except the facet being investigated. Furthermore, notice the "fake inertia" gain block at the center-top of the figure permits simulation users to artificially make the feedforward command (based on the assumed values of the mass moments of inertia) artificially smaller or larger that assumed. Doing so permits simulation debugging, e.g., if the user artificially makes the mass moments to be assumed much larger, the learning feedback should produce the adaption of mass moments towards the values manually altered in the gain block.

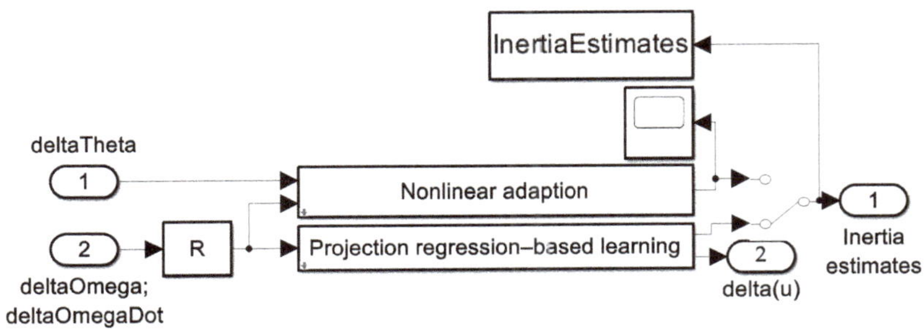

Figure A4. Internal content of "Learning Feedback" subsystem.

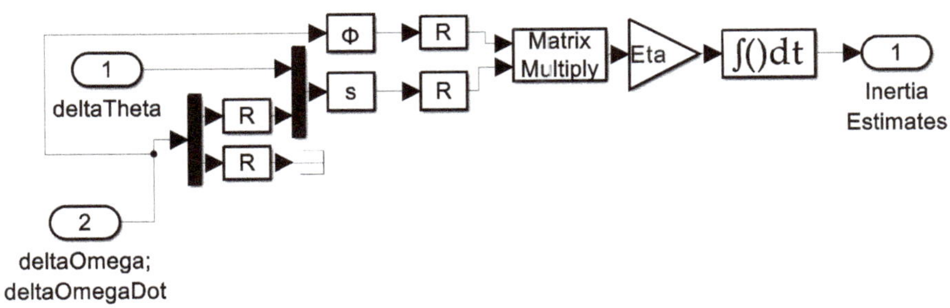

Figure A5. Internal content of "Nonlinear adaption" option in the "Learning Feedback" subsystem.

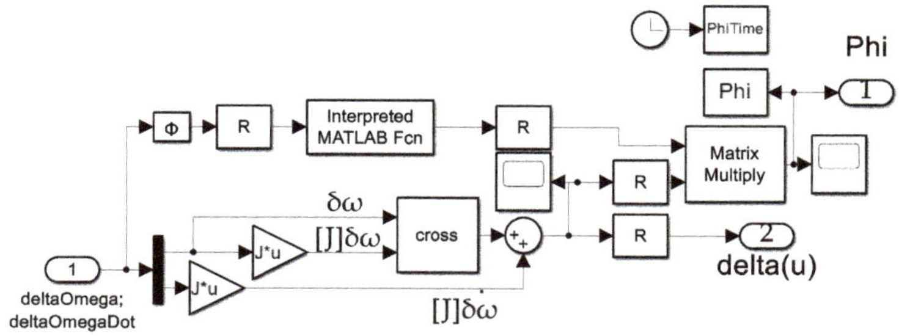

Figure A6. Internal content of "Projection regression-based learning" option in the "Learning Feedback" subsystem.

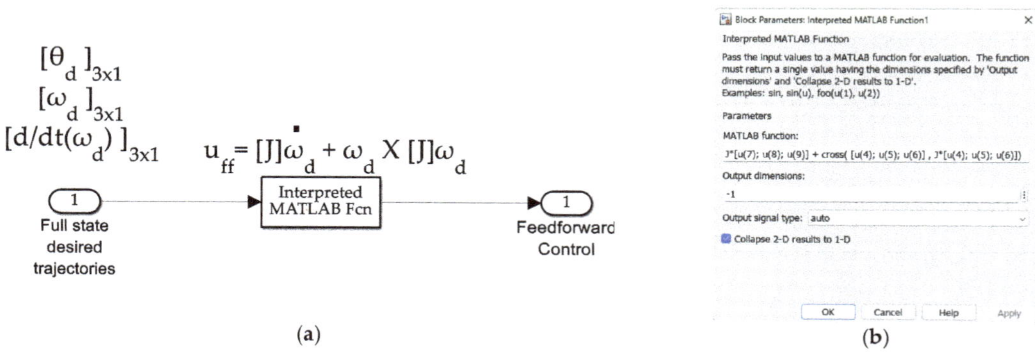

Figure A7. (**a**) Internal content of "Feedforward Control" subsystem in Figure A3. (**b**) Internal pseudocode of the "Interpreted MATLAB FCN" block in subfigure (**a**).

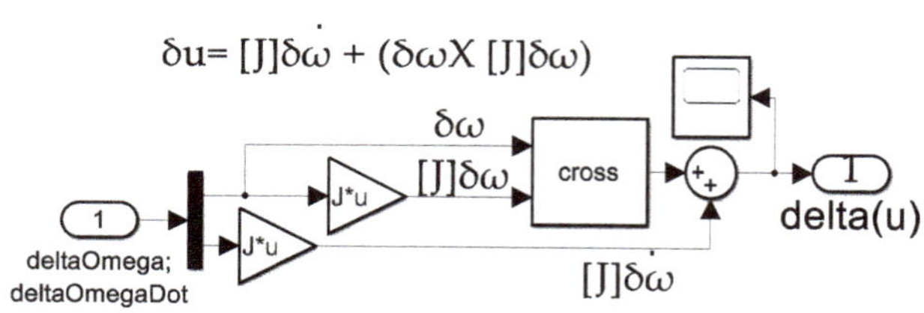

Figure A8. Internal content of "Learning Feedback" subsystem depicted in Figure A3.

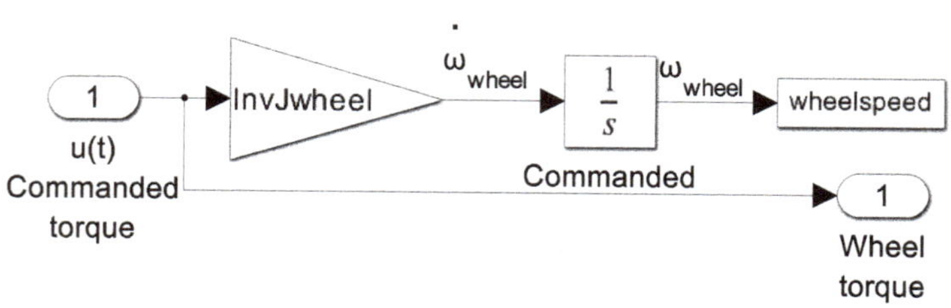

Figure A9. Internal content of "Actuators" subsystem depicted in Figure 3.

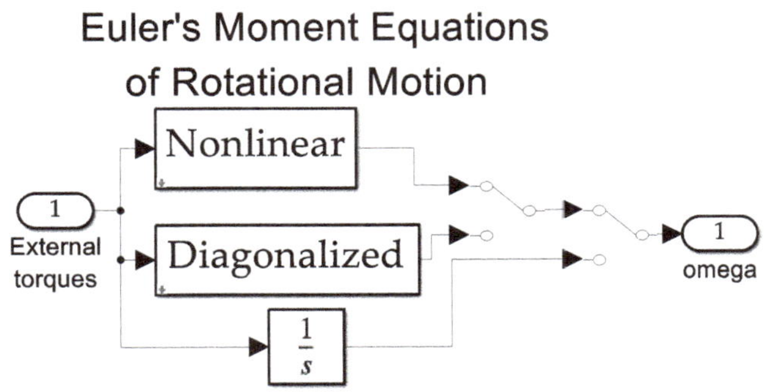

Figure A10. Internal content of "Kinetics" subsystem depicted in Figure 3. The upper two subsystems are elaborated in Figure A11, while the final (lowest) kinetic system is the simple integrator depicted on the bottom of this figure.

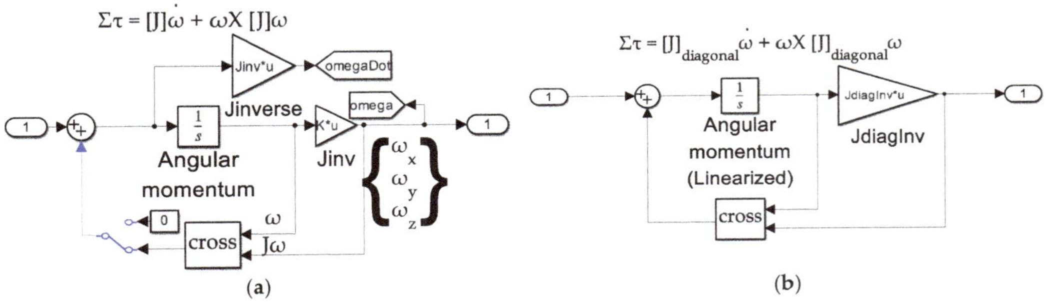

Figure A11. (**a**) Internal content of "Nonlinear" kinetics subsystem depicted in Figure A10. (**b**) Internal content of "Diagonalized" kinetics subsystem depicted in Figure A10.

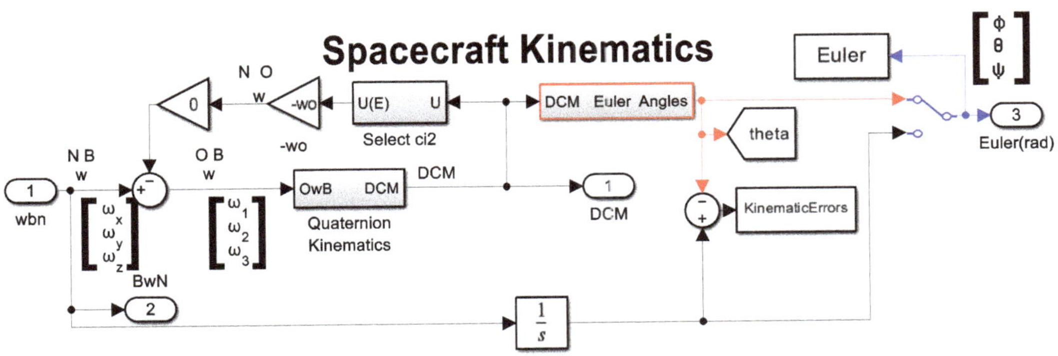

Figure A12. Internal content of "Kinematics" subsystem depicted in Figure 3.

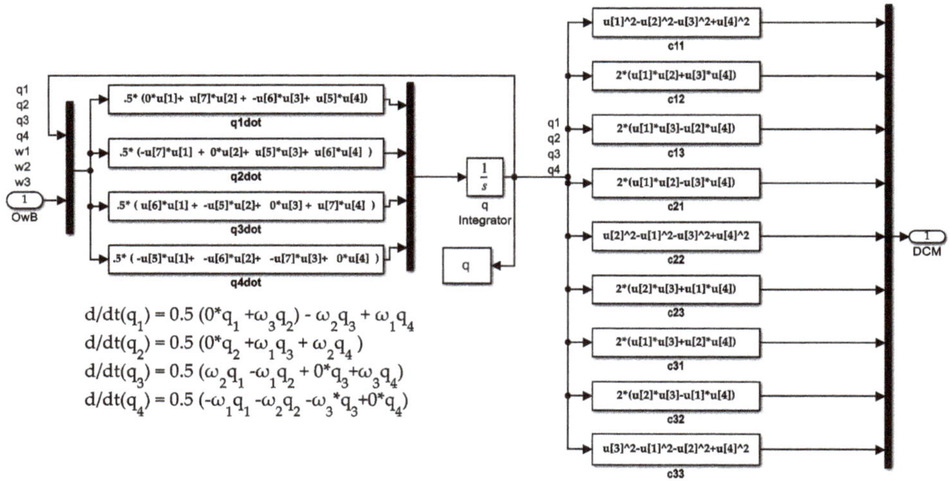

Figure A13. Internal content of "Quaternion Kinematics" subsystem depicted in Figure A12.

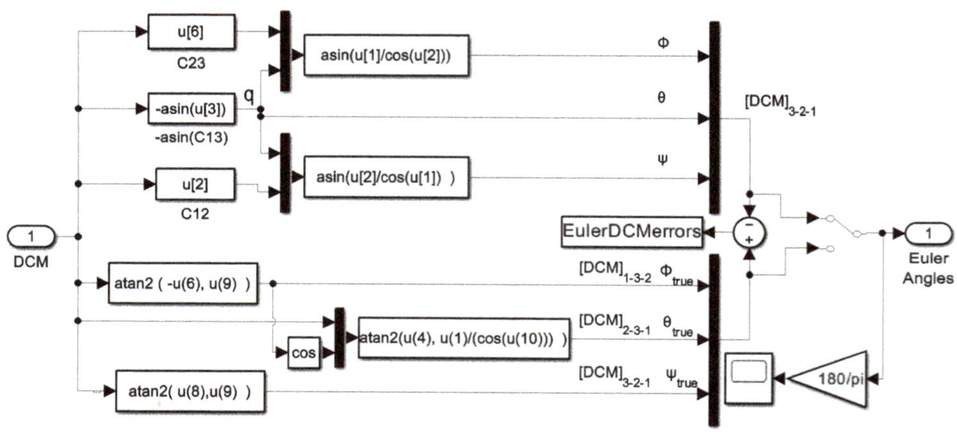

Figure A14. Internal content of "DCM Euler Angles" subsystem depicted in Figure A12.

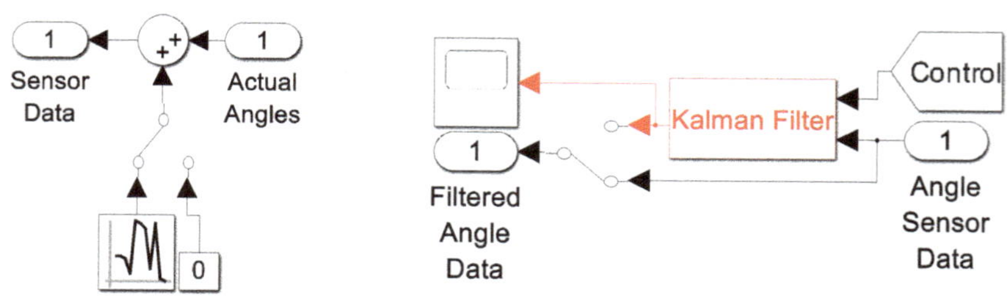

(**a**) (**b**)

Figure A15. Internal content of "Filters" subsystem and "Sensors" subsystems depicted in Figure 3 illustrated, respectively, in this figure's (**a**,**b**).

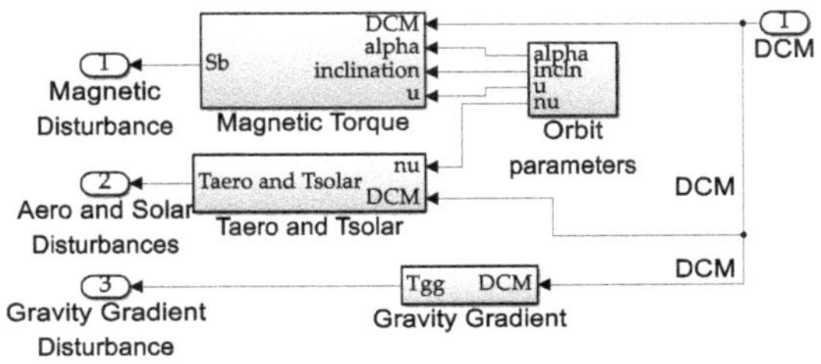

Figure A16. High-level topology of environmental disturbances.

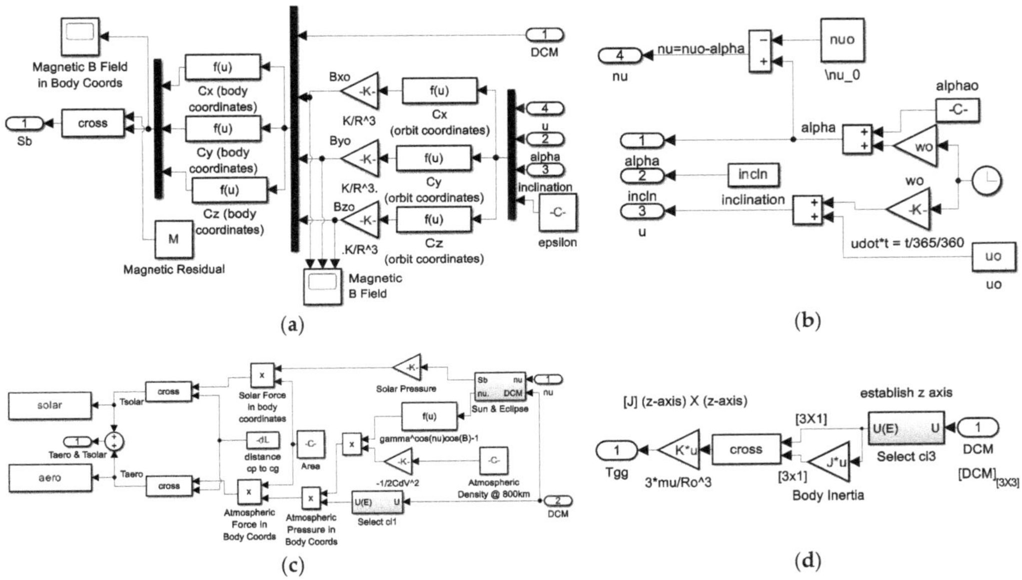

Figure A17. Internal content of "Space Environment Disturbances" depicted in Figure A16 illustrated, respectively, in this figure's (**a**–**d**): (**a**) subsystem labeled "Magnetic Torque" subsystem; (**b**) orbit parameters; (**c**) TAero and Tsolar; and (**d**) Gravity Gradient.

References

1. Henshaw, C.; Glassner, S.; Naasz, B.; Roberts, B. Grappling Spacecraft. *Annu. Rev. Control Robot. Auton. Syst.* **2022**, *5*, 137–159.
2. JPL Robotics. Available online: https://www-robotics.jpl.nasa.gov/what-we-do/research-tasks/prototype-grapple-arm-for-space-exploration-vehicle/ (accessed on 13 December 2024).
3. PickNik Awarded NASA SBIR Phase 2 for In-Orbit Robot Autonomy. Available online: https://www.aerospacemanufacturinganddesign.com/news/picnik-robotics-awarded-nasa-sbir-phase-2-robot-autonomy/ (accessed on 18 November 2024).
4. Robotic Refueling Mission 3 (RRM3). Available online: https://www.nasa.gov/nexis/robotic-refueling-mission-3/ (accessed on 18 November 2024).
5. NASA Images and Media Usage Guidelines. NASA Content—Images, Audio, Video, and Media Files Used in the Rendition of 3-Dimensional Models, such as Texture Maps and Polygon Data in Any Format—Generally Are Not Subject to Copyright in the United States. Available online: https://www.nasa.gov/nasa-brand-center/images-and-media/ (accessed on 18 November 2024).
6. Maclay, T.; Goff, J.; Sheehan, J.; Han, E. The development of commercially viable ADR services: Introduction of a small-satellite grappling interface. *J. Space Saf. Eng.* **2020**, *3*, 364–368.
7. IEEE Robotics & Automation Society, Technical Committee for Space Robotics. Available online: https://www.ieee-ras.org/space-robotics (accessed on 18 November 2024).
8. Hernández-Arias, H.; Prado-Molina, J. On-Orbit Center of Mass Relocation System for A 3U Cubesat. *Int. J. Sci. Tech. Res.* **2018**, *7*, 44–51.

9. Calaon, R.; Kiner, L.; Allard, C.; Schaub, H. Momentum management of a spacecraft equipped with a dual—Gimballed electric thruster. In Proceedings of the AAS Guidance and Control Conference, Breckenridge, CO, USA, 2–8 February 2023. Paper No. AAS-23-178.
10. Gracey, W. The experimental determination of the moments of inertia of airplanes by a simplified compound-pendulum method. Available online: https://ntrs.nasa.gov/citations/19930082299 (accessed on 25 March 2025).
11. Soule, H.; Miller, M. The experimental determination of the moments of inertia of airplanes. Available online: https://ntrs.nasa.gov/citations/19930091541 (accessed on 25 March 2025).
12. Genta, G.; Delpreta, C. Some considerations on the experimental determination of moments of inertia. *Meccanica* **1994**, *29*, 125–141.
13. Nocerino, A.; Opromolla, R.; Fasano, G.; Grassi, M.; Balaguer, P.; John, S.; Cho, H.; Bevilacqua, R. Experimental validation of inertia parameters and attitude estimation of uncooperative space targets using solid state LIDAR. *Acta Astronaut.* **2023**, *240*, 428–436.
14. Bourabah, D.; Field, L.; Botta, E. Estimation of uncooperative space debris inertial parameters after tether capture. *Acta Astronaut.* **2023**, *202*, 909–926. [CrossRef]
15. Field, L.; Bourabah, D.; Botta, E. Online Control and Moment of Inertia Estimation of Tethered Debris. In Proceedings of the AIAA SCITECH 2024 Forum, Orlando, FL, USA, 8–12 January 2024.
16. Sonobe, M.; Inoue, Y. Center of Mass Estimation Using a Force Platform and Inertial Sensors for Balance Evaluation in Quiet Standing. *Sensors* **2023**, *23*, 4933. [CrossRef]
17. Zatsiorsky, V.M.; King, D.L. An algorithm for determining gravity line location from posturographic recordings. *J. Biomech.* **1997**, *31*, 161–164.
18. Caron, O.; Faure, B.; Brenière, Y. Estimating the centre of gravity of the body on the basis of the centre of pressure in standing posture. *J. Biomech.* **1997**, *30*, 1169–1171.
19. Germanotta, M.; Mileti, I.; Conforti, I.; Del Prete, Z.; Aprile, I.; Palermo, E. Estimation of Human Center of Mass Position through the Inertial Sensors-Based Methods in Postural Tasks: An Accuracy Evaluation. *Sensors* **2021**, *21*, 601. [CrossRef]
20. Wang, F.; Bettadpur, S.; Save, H. Determination of the center–of–mass of gravity recovery and climate experimental satellites. *J. Spacecr. Rockets* **2010**, *47*, 371. [CrossRef]
21. Kornfeld, R.; Arnold, B.; Gross, M.; Dahya, N.; Klipstein, W.; Gath, P.; Bettadpur, S. GRACE-FO: The Gravity Recovery and Climate Experiment Follow-On Mission. *J. Spacecr. Rockets* **2019**, *56*, 931–951. [CrossRef]
22. Huang, Z.; Li, S.; Cai, L.; Fan, D.; Huang, L. Estimation of the Center of Mass of GRACE-Type Gravity Satellites. *Remote Sens.* **2022**, *14*, 4030. [CrossRef]
23. Pan, Z.; Xiao, Y. Data Quality Assessment of Gravity Recovery and Climate Experiment Follow-On Accelerometer. *Sensors* **2024**, *24*, 4286. [CrossRef]
24. Dou, Y.; Wang, K.; Zhou, Z.; Thomas, P.R.; Shao, Z.; Du, W. Investigation of the Free-Fall Dynamic Behavior of a Rectangular Wing with Variable Center of Mass Location and Variable Moment of Inertia. *Aerospace* **2023**, *10*, 458. [CrossRef]
25. Geng, J.; Langelaan, J.W. Estimation of Inertial Properties for a Multilift Slung Load. *J. Guid. Control Dyn.* **2021**, *2*, 220–237. [CrossRef]
26. Gahramanova, A. Locating Centers of Mass with Image Processing. *Undergrad. J. Math. Model* **2019**, *10*, 1. [CrossRef]
27. Lin, Y.T.; Tian, Y.; Perez, D.; Livescu, D. Regression-Based Projection for Learning Mori–Zwanzig Operators. *SIAM J. Appl. Dyn. Sys.* **2023**, *4*, 2890–2926. [CrossRef]
28. Setterfield, T.; Miller, D.; Leonard, J.; Saenz-Otero, A. Mapping and determining the center of mass of a rotating object using a moving observer. *Int. J. Robot. Res.* **2018**, *37*, 83–103. [CrossRef]
29. Diagonalize the Inertia Tensor. Available online: https://phys.libretexts.org/Bookshelves/Classical_Mechanics/Variational_Principles_in_Classical_Mechanics_(Cline)/13:_Rigid-body_Rotation/13.07:_Diagonalize_the_Inertia_Tensor (accessed on 26 November 2024).
30. Luenberger Observer. Available online: https://www.mathworks.com/help/sps/ref/luenbergerobserver.html (accessed on 19 November 2024).
31. Transport Theorem. Available online: https://en.wikipedia.org/wiki/Transport_theorem (accessed on 19 November 2024).
32. Fossen, T. Comments on 'Hamiltonian adaptive control of spacecraft'. *IEEE Trans. Autom. Control* **1993**, *38*, 671–672. [CrossRef]
33. Iven, M.; Mareels, B.; Anderson, R.; Bitmead, R.; Bodson, M.; Sastry, S. Revisiting the MIT rule for adaptive control. In *Adaptive Systems in Control and Signal Processing 1986*; IFAC Workshop Series; Pergamon Press Ltd.: Oxford, UK, 1987; pp. 161–166.
34. Kuck, E.; Sands, T. Space Robot Sensor Noise Amelioration Using Trajectory Shaping. *Sensors* **2024**, *24*, 666. [CrossRef] [PubMed]
35. Adams, G. Arizona State University Physics Department Proof of the Parallel Axis Theorem. Available online: https://www.public.asu.edu/~gbadams/sum00/parallelaxisT.pdf (accessed on 19 November 2024).
36. Zhu, Y. Identification Test Design and Data Pretreatment. In *Multivariable System Identification for Process Control*; Zhu, Y., Ed.; Elsevier Science: Maryland Heights, MO, USA, 2001; pp. 31–63.

37. Persistent Excitation Conditions and Their Implications. Section 8.1 of Study Guide on Adaptive and Self-Tuning Control. Available online: https://library.fiveable.me/adaptive-and-self-tuning-control/unit-8/robustness-issues-adaptive-control/study-guide/yLKsaWxBlamk2I48 (accessed on 22 November 2024).
38. Marino, R.; Tomei, P. On exponentially convergent parameter estimation with lack of persistency of excitation. *Syst. Control Lett.* **2022**, *159*, 105080.
39. Korotina, M.; Romero, J.; Aranovskiy, S.; Bobtsov, A.; Ortega, R. A new on-line exponential parameter estimator without persistent excitation. *Syst. Control Lett.* **2022**, *159*, 105079.
40. Software, Robotics, and Simulation Division. Available online: https://www.nasa.gov/software-robotics-and-simulation-division/ (accessed on 21 November 2024).
41. Dynamics Operations Training Systems. Available online: https://www.nasa.gov/general/generic-robotics-on-orbit-trainer/ (accessed on 21 November 2024).
42. Dai, Q.; Xiao, G.; Zhou, G.; Ye, Q.; Han, S. A novel Gaussian sum quaternion constrained cubature Kalman filter algorithm for GNSS/SINS integrated attitude determination and positioning system. *Front. Neurorobotics* **2024**, *18*, 1374531.
43. Slotine, J.; Di Benedetto, M. Hamiltonian adaptive control of spacecraft. *IEEE Trans. Autom. Control* **1990**, *35*, 848–852. [CrossRef]
44. Sands, T.; Kim, J.; Agrawal, B. Improved Hamiltonian Adaptive Control of spacecraft. In Proceedings of the IEEE Aerospace conference, Big Sky, MT, USA, 7–14 March 2009.
45. Sands, T.; Kim, J.; Agrawal, B. Spacecraft fine tracking pointing using adaptive control. In Proceedings of the 58th International Astronautical Congress, Hyderabad, India, 24–28 September 2007.
46. Sands, T.; Kim, J.; Agrawal, B. Spacecraft adaptive control evaluation. In Proceedings of the Infotech@Aerospace, Garden Grove, CA, USA, 19–21 June 2012.
47. Huang, B.; Sands, T. Novel learning for control of nonlinear spacecraft dynamics. *J. AppliedMath* **2023**, *1*, 42. [CrossRef]

technologies

MDPI

Article

Implementing Computer Vision in Android Apps and Presenting the Background Technology with Mathematical Demonstrations

Roland Szabo

Faculty of Electronics, Telecommunications and Information Technologies, Politehnica University Timisoara, Vasile Parvan Av., No. 2, 300223 Timisoara, Romania; roland.szabo@upt.ro; Tel.: +40-256-40-3351

Abstract: The aim of this paper is to create image-processing Android apps to launch on the Google Play Store. Three apps with different usages will be presented for different situations. The first app is a night-vision app on an Android phone that uses OpenCV. The second app is a tooth-brushing assistant application. The app is made for mobile phones and uses advanced image-processing techniques to detect when the tooth is brushed correctly or incorrectly. The main focus is on the direction of the toothbrush movement because this is one of the key aspects of correctly brushing teeth. The direction of movement of the brush is detected using movement vectors. The third app is a lane-detection app on the smartphone. Lane detection is carried out using OpenCV and TensorFlow libraries. The mobile app was implemented on the Android operating system. The app has a live video feed of the surroundings. When in the area of view, there will be a road with a lane. The system detects the lane and draws a green line over it.

Keywords: night vision; image motion analysis; lane detection; mobile applications; mobile computing

1. Introduction

This paper focuses on creating for the Google Play Store a total of three image processing applications. The three applications incorporate image-processing techniques using OpenCV, which was compiled in the Android applications in order to do different image-processing tasks.

1.1. Night-Vision App

The first app is a night vision app. The night vision app optimizes your night driving by adding a unique night mode to your car's navigation system. Modifies the brightness of the screen and adjusts the color temperature to minimize eye strain and enhance visibility on nocturnal drives. This application ensures a safe and comfortable trip, allowing drivers to concentrate on the road without unwanted interference.

1.2. Tooth-Brushing Assistant App Using Image-Processing Techniques

The second app is a tooth brushing app. The tooth brush app transforms dental care into an engaging and efficient process by instructing users on correct brushing techniques. Through detailed tutorials and interactive elements, the app simplifies the maintenance of oral health. It is ideal for people of any age seeking to achieve comprehensive dental hygiene in a pleasant and instructive manner.

https://doi.org/10.3390/technologies13010027

1.3. Lane and Car-Detection App Using Deep-Learning Algorithms with TensorFlow

The third app is a lane-detection app with deep learning algorithms. The lane-detection application enhances your driving experience by providing a virtual lane-assist feature. It utilizes real-time feedback to help drivers maintain their lane and prevent possible accidents. Developed to encourage safer driving practices, the lane-detection app is an essential tool for both daily drives and extended trips.

2. Related Works

2.1. Night-Vision App

Night vision in the automotive industry uses a thermal camera that can increase driver perception and distance of sight at night and in poor weather conditions, even in a situation where the headlights cannot increase visibility anymore [1]. These systems are installed as optional features in some expensive luxury cars [2]. The technology was first introduced in 2000 by Cadillac [3]. The technology is based on night-vision devices, which are enhanced optical devices that can improve image, thermo-imagery, and illumination [4].

This paper shows how to implement a night-vision feature on a mobile phone running Android OS [5]. With the help of mobile phone technology, many premium features of the automotive industry (navigation, GPS (Global Positioning System), HUD (Head-Up Display), night vision, and traffic-sign recognition) can be implemented for a low amount of money [6]. This affirmation is based on the fact that almost everyone has at least one mobile phone and that many people have an old, unused mobile phone that can be used for a certain embedded application [7].

By having a smartphone with many sensors and cameras, many insertion applications can be created, which can act as cheap versions of the premium features of premium vehicles [8]. Sometimes, the smartphone implementation can be used when the automotive implementation is not present in our car. Also, on mobile phones, for example, navigation apps can be better than on cars, which can have real-time traffic, danger, pit road, police location, or traffic-sign warnings. This is due to the fact that mobile phones have permanent active connectivity to the Internet, while cars do not, and there are a few people who buy a phone SIM (Subscriber Identity Module) card specially for the car to have an active connection to the Internet via 4G or 5G networks. This can only be possible when eSIM cards are built into cars in the manufacturing process.

To create a mobile phone application that can act as a vehicle night-vision system, the OpenCV library can be used. Even though mobile phones do not have thermal cameras, only if they are attached separately, using OpenCV can make an app that can mimic the night-vision feature for a luxury car. OpenCV has become advanced and has a good implementation for mobile platforms such as Android or iOS.

This paper presents the implementation of night-vision cameras for cars on Android using OpenCV.

The night system is implemented in expensive cars. If someone wants this feature on a cheaper car, it can be done with only a mobile phone and this app. No IR camera is needed. The entire night-vision system is made only with image-processing techniques using OpenCV. This is the novelty of the app. No other hardware is required, only a mobile phone. It works with any Android phone which has a rear camera. No special optics or lighting condition is needed because that is the goal of the app to make the surroundings visible in low lightning conditions. Other related published methods require an external IR camera, but the current method uses only the mobile phone's camera.

The night-vision application aims to improve visibility in low-light situations using smartphones. It uses image-processing techniques to modify brightness, contrast, and other settings to mimic night vision functions.

When comparing this application with ongoing scientific research in night vision technology, several significant differences become apparent.

The application uses digital image-processing methods on smartphone hardware, which is restricted by the quality of the camera sensor and does not have true infrared (IR) capabilities.

By contrast, contemporary night-vision technology often uses IR sensors, thermal imaging, or specialized low-light sensors. These technologies allow for the detection of heat signatures or light outside the visible spectrum, capabilities beyond what smartphone cameras can provide.

The application's effectiveness is fundamentally constrained by the smartphone's camera and ambient light conditions. It can increase visibility in low light, but it cannot function in complete darkness or in situations requiring thermal imaging.

Night-vision devices used in military, medical, or industrial fields offer far superior accuracy. These devices can work in near-total darkness and deliver precise images due to their advanced sensor technology.

This application is better suited for casual use cases, such as night photography or basic visibility improvement in low-light environments.

Night-vision technology is used in research and professional applications for critical tasks such as surveillance, wildlife monitoring, and medical diagnostics, where precision and reliability are essential.

Although the night vision application provides some functionality for casual users looking to enhance visibility in low light conditions, it is not good enough compared to the advanced capabilities of specialized night-vision devices used in scientific and professional settings.

Applications for night vision improve imaging in low-light environments utilizing sophisticated computer vision methods. Used in intelligent smart security robots on the Internet of Things, these applications incorporate event-based cameras alongside adaptive preprocessing to facilitate the identification and observation of obstacles in real time. Their primary aim is to increase visibility and decrease noise in dim conditions, making them perfect for surveillance and security tasks at night [9,10].

2.2. Tooth-Brushing Assistant App Using Image-Processing Techniques

We brush our teeth every morning, before going to bed, and after meals [11]. Have we ever wondered how we might not brush our teeth correctly? Not properly brushing teeth can sometimes be worse than not brushing teeth at all [12]. We must not think that brushing our teeth involves only teeth; we must also take care of our gums [13].

It is important to know the direction of tooth brushing movements, and it is also important to know the duration of tooth brushing [14].

If we do not brush our teeth in the correct direction, it is not OK. The teeth must be brushed with the up–down movement, not with the left-right movements, because if we brush them with left–right movements, we move all the bacteria from the teeth into the gum with the toothbrush [15]. If we brush the teeth with up–down movements, then we remove the bacteria from the teeth when we reach the edge of it. The direction of brushing is not the only thing that can affect the effect of cleaning. To correctly brush the teeth, it was empirically tested that a two-minute duration is enough for good tooth brushing. In fact, each half-arc should be brushed for 30 s. A half-arc is the left or right side of the upper teeth or lover teeth. In our mouth, we have four arcs, so brushing each half arc for 30 s will be a total of two minutes of tooth brushing.

It was found that quite a few adults brush their teeth correctly; we do not talk about children learning brushing techniques [16].

Today's mobile-phone-driven society can help solve these problems to have better oral hygiene and a better life [17].

Creating an app that helps brush your teeth can be a useful tool for adults and children [18].

The tooth-brushing app can be used mainly by kids to learn to brush their teeth or by dentists to show correct tooth brushing to patients. This app has the advantage that most tooth-brushing applications require you to buy a specific (electric) toothbrush that connects to the app via Bluetooth. This app works with any standard toothbrush and relies only on image processing, with OpenCV, to recognize the movement direction of tooth brushing. This is the novelty of the app.

The tooth-brushing app aims to help users improve their tooth brushing habits. It includes features such as timers, reminders, and educational content to encourage proper brushing techniques and oral care.

The app uses timers, reminders, and possibly gamification elements to motivate users to brush their teeth for the two minutes suggested twice daily. These features are designed to increase user engagement and adherence to good oral hygiene practices.

Research indicates that behavioral interventions, such as reminders and gamification, can effectively improve oral hygiene behaviors, particularly in children. Studies have shown that applications with interactive elements can increase motivation and consistency in brushing, leading to better overall oral health outcomes.

Although the app offers tools to support better brushing habits, its success largely depends on the adherence of the user and the precision of the brushing technique, which the app cannot directly monitor or correct.

Recent studies suggest that while apps like the toothbrushing app can be advantageous, they are most effective when paired with real-time feedback systems, such as smart toothbrushes that provide immediate feedback on brushing technique (pressure, coverage, duration). This integration has been shown to significantly improve oral hygiene by ensuring that users brush properly and thoroughly.

The app is likely to provide educational content to inform users about proper brushing techniques and the importance of oral hygiene.

Educational interventions delivered through mobile apps have been proven to increase knowledge about oral health, which is crucial for preventing dental problems. However, research also highlights the need for content customization to address individual user needs and preferences, which can further amplify the effectiveness of these apps.

The tooth-brushing app offers a useful tool to promote better brushing habits through reminders, timers, and educational content. However, its effectiveness could be improved by incorporating real-time feedback mechanisms and tailored educational content, as recommended by recent scientific research. Although the app serves as a helpful addition to oral hygiene practices, the incorporation of smart technology could markedly enhance its impact on users' oral health.

Tooth-brushing applications use computer-vision technology to improve dental hygiene by monitoring user movements and providing instant feedback. These applications utilize facial recognition and augmented reality (AR) overlays to ensure full brushing coverage. Using pose-estimation models, they guide users, thus improving dental care habits and making the process more engaging, especially for children [9,10].

2.3. *Lane- and Car-Detection App Using Deep-Learning Algorithms with TensorFlow*

In today's world, self-driving cars and lane-detection cars have started to emerge in our lives faster than we can imagine [19].

There is no need to talk about robots [20], which are only in the prototype state [21], but we can talk about robots that are present in our daily life and seem to be natural [22]. Robots like this are drones, robot vacuum cleaners, mops, window cleaners, and, of course, cars with some level of autonomous driving [23].

For autonomous driving, more sensors can be used [24], such as LiDARs or video cameras [25].

Video cameras can be a good approach [26] due to the existence of the vast OpenCV image-processing library [27].

One autonomous driving feature for cars is the detection of the lane [28]. For a car to be able to drive autonomously [29], having the lane-detection function installed is a good feature [30]. The lane-detection function can also help drivers keep the car on the road [31] when tired after a long drive [32].

Lane detection can be performed with image-processing techniques [33], but in addition to this, much more is needed, such as a trained neural network, to correctly detect the lane of the road and exclude false positives [34].

Lane detection and car detection are present in expensive cars. If a user wants this feature on a cheaper car, it can be done with only a mobile phone and this app. All lane detection and car detection are done with image processing, OpenCV, and the usage of a trained neural network using TensorFlow. This is the novelty of the app.

The lane-detection application is created to identify lanes, mainly using the smartphone camera to help drivers remain within their lanes. It probably employs image-processing algorithms to recognize and follow the road lane markings.

The application uses simple computer-vision techniques to detect lane lines from the video feed captured by the smartphone camera. This might involve edge-detection algorithms such as Canny edge detection [35], or the Hough transform [36] to identify straight or curved lines representing lane boundaries.

Modern lane-detection systems, particularly those utilized in advanced driver-assist systems (ADAS), use more advanced technologies. These include deep-learning models such as Convolutional Neural Networks (CNNs), trained on extensive datasets to accurately recognize and forecast lane positions under various conditions such as poor lighting or road obstacles. These models also incorporate data from multiple sensors (e.g., LiDAR [37], radar) to increase robustness.

The precision of lane detection depends on the quality of the smartphone camera and the environmental conditions (e.g., lighting, visibility of the road markings). Since it relies solely on the camera, its performance can be hindered by bad weather or if lane markings are worn or blocked.

Current research indicates that high-accuracy lane detection requires a combination of high-resolution cameras, sensor fusion, and advanced algorithms capable of handling different road conditions. Systems like Tesla's Autopilot [38] or Waymo's self-driving technology [39] use multiple sensors and redundancy to guarantee high reliability, which is crucial for safety in autonomous driving.

Considering that the application operates on a smartphone, it is probably constrained by the processing power of the device. Real-time lane detection might experience latency, especially on older devices or during complex image-processing tasks. The app can run on any standard Android phone. The minimal platform supported by OpenCV Java API is Android 2.2 (Froyo or API 8). Presently, almost all Android devices run a newer Android version than Android 2.2 Froyo. The latest Android version is Android 15, and all users are encouraged to run the latest Android version, if possible. The idea is that the better the phone hardware, the better will run the image processing on that mobile phone.

Cutting-edge lane-detection systems are intended for real-time processing with minimal delay. They employ dedicated hardware accelerators (such as GPUs or specialized AI chips) to ensure that lane detection and response times adhere to the strict requirements of high-speed driving.

This application might be appropriate for general driving assistance, providing an extra layer of safety by alerting drivers when they drift out of their lane.

Conversely, lane-detection systems in research and industry are essential components of fully autonomous vehicles, where they are integrated with other safety and navigation systems to deliver comprehensive driving solutions.

The lane-detection application offers a valuable tool for basic lane detection on a smartphone, suitable for casual driving assistance. However, compared to the sophisticated systems developed in scientific research and used in the automotive industry, it is not accurate, reliable, or capable of performing in real time. Advanced lane-detection systems use more intricate algorithms and sensor integration, delivering significantly better performance under a variety of driving conditions.

Applications for lane detection play an essential role in driving assistance systems. They use deep-learning methodologies, such as convolutional neural networks (CNNs), to identify road lanes in real time in diverse environmental scenarios. These applications improve navigation safety by offering precise lane tracking and supporting technologies for autonomous driving [9,10].

Table 1 shows a comparison of the state of the art in computer-vision mobile apps [9,10].

Table 1. Summary table comparison of the state of the art in computer-vision mobile apps [9,10].

App	Primary Application	Key Strategies	Advantages
Night Vision	Surveillance in low-light conditions	Adaptive preprocessing combined with event-based cameras	Enhanced clarity and diminished noise
Tooth Brushing	Observation of oral hygiene	Face identification, augmented reality, posture estimation	Improved brushing practices
Lane Detection	Assistance with driving	CNNs in deep learning	Real-time lane tracking with precision

3. Problem Formulation

3.1. Night-Vision App

Driving at night frequently requires managing the intense glare of screens and bright displays, which can cause eye strain and reduce driving concentration. Numerous navigation apps currently do not have adaptive night mode capabilities, which are necessary to provide a safer and more comfortable experience during night travel.

The project involved developing a night vision app for Android smartphones using OpenCV.

Smartphones do not come with thermal cameras unless they are added as external peripherals.

Due to the sophisticated image processing and filtering methods in OpenCV, it is feasible to achieve results similar to those produced by night-vision systems in high-end vehicles.

The outcome would be nearly identical, but the cost would be significantly lower, bordering on negligible.

3.2. Tooth-Brushing Assistant App Using Image-Processing Techniques

Several people fail to brush their teeth properly, resulting in inadequate oral hygiene and preventable dental issues such as cavities and periodontal disease. There is an absence of captivating and easy-to-use resources to instruct individuals on proper brushing methods and to make the experience more enjoyable.

The project involved developing a mobile app to assist individuals in brushing their teeth properly.

This involved identifying the toothbrush's motion direction and implementing a brushing timer.

To detect the brushing direction, image processing with OpenCV should be employed. Moreover, a brushing timer feature must be integrated. The timer aids users in knowing the remaining brushing time, ensuring they brush for at least two min.

3.3. Lane and Car-Detection App Using Deep-Learning Algorithms with TensorFlow

Unintentional lane changes and lane drifting are major factors in road accidents. Drivers frequently do not have access to real-time tools that offer prompt lane assistance and guidance, which can aid in maintaining safer driving practices and avoiding crashes.

The objective was to develop a lane-detection application. The decision to build the app for mobile phones was made to enhance its portability and simplicity of use in vehicles.

Android was selected as the operating system due to its status as the most extensively used mobile platform, featuring integrated image-processing libraries.

4. Problem Solving

4.1. Night-Vision App

An app was created that has a night-vision function using only OpenCV image-processing techniques.

This app can be used as a night-vision app for cars, but it can also be used as an app that is useful for searching for a lost object at night when light torches cannot help.

In automotive usage, it can be used to avoid collisions with pedestrians or animals.

The smartphone must be mounted on the windshield with a cell phone stand for vehicles. It must be ensured that the back camera of the smartphone faces the road ahead.

An old smartphone can be used with the night-vision app.

The application enjoys the benefit of showing just the street in night vision, with no different signs, which can sometimes be too much. Ideally, this application will help drivers avoid accidents with humans or animals crossing the road.

It is a good habit to use a car phone charger, as the screen of the smartphone is always on and can rapidly deplete the battery of the smartphone.

The night-vision app does not use near-infrared cameras used for ADAS in the automotive industry, but it can be quite effective when we do not have this premium feature in our car. The night-vision app is just an enhancement algorithm, but it can be used when someone does not have the night-vision feature in their car. The novelty lies in the fact that there is no such app as this in the Google Play Store.

Figure 1 shows the architecture diagram of the night-vision app.

Equations (1)–(4) were used to create the night-vision app.

Using x and y as spatial coordinates, let us represent the input image as $I(x, y)$.

The function Enhance($I(x, y)$) can be used to model the image-enhancement process, where the visibility of the input image is improved.

$$\text{Enhanced\_Image}(x, y) = \text{Enhance}(I(x, y)) \tag{1}$$

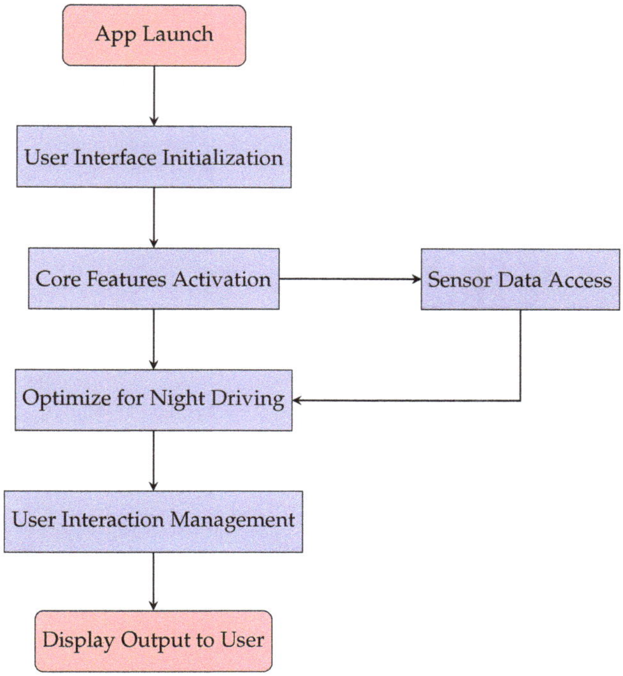

Figure 1. The architecture diagram of the night-vision app.

To see better at night, night vision (NV) frequently involves increasing low light levels. This amplification procedure is shown below.

$$\mathrm{NV}(I(x,y)) = k \cdot I(x,y) \tag{2}$$

where NV is the night-vision function and the constant k stands for the amplification factor.

Combining the effect of night vision with image enhancement:

$$\mathrm{Enhanced\_NV}(x,y) = \mathrm{Enhance}(\mathrm{NV}(I(x,y))) \tag{3}$$

This formula depicts the improved image after the night-vision effect was included.

Figure 2 shows the real image and the enhanced software image made with the mobile-phone app.

To further increase visibility, thresholding can be added to the improved image. We shall use T to represent the threshold value.

$$\mathrm{Thresholded\_Image}(x,y) = \begin{cases} \mathrm{Enhanced\_NV}(x,y), & \text{if } \mathrm{Enhanced\_NV}(x,y) > T \\ 0, & \text{otherwise} \end{cases} \tag{4}$$

To further improve visibility, the pixel values below a threshold T are set to zero using a thresholding procedure represented by this formula.

The following images were tested in really low visibility to see that the night-vision app works. Some of them might be blurry, but compared to the low-visibility conditions, they can be used to see some objects at night.

Figure 2. The image viewed by the mobile-phone app overlaid on the real image with poor visibility.

Figure 3 shows the actual screenshot from the mobile app while looking at a street at night.

Figure 3. A screenshot that was viewing the poor-visibility street at night from the previous figure.

Figure 4 shows the Android night-vision app.

The test was carried out under harsh conditions to test the app to the maximum. It was night and it was snowing, so there was close to no visibility, but the app can still see well at night and in poor weather conditions. It can be seen that at night, due to snowy weather, visibility is low, if not close to zero. In addition, the windshield shows a blurred image due to the moisture obtained by the melted snow that fell on the warm window.

Figure 4. A screenshot made with the mobile-phone app, which was viewing the street at night.

Even in these conditions, the software tries to make the images show well in these poor lighting and weather conditions. In the real image, only the first car that is the closest can be seen, but no buildings or other cars are seen in the background.

In the enhanced mobile-phone app, almost everything looks like daylight. Only a small noise is overlaid on the image viewed.

The software enhancement steps are the following: convert the image to grayscale, make a histogram equalization, and then make an adaptive gamma correction using a lookup table.

In case the weather is better and the only problem is that there are low lighting conditions, the app works even better, and everything can be seen more clearly.

The clarity of the viewed image can be seen, which was made at night when it was snowing. Not only the buildings in the background but also the people walking on the street can be seen.

It is clear how well the filtering was carried out. In some night-vision apps, when in the viewed image there is a light source, due to histogram equalization, the image will be overlaid by a white spot. In the current mobile-phone app, there is a light source, but the white spot is reduced to a minimum.

4.2. Tooth-Brushing Assistant App Using Image-Processing Techniques

The app was implemented for the Android operating system for mobile phones.

Android is the most widely distributed operating system for mobile phones.

The mobile-phone implementation is the most convenient because almost everyone owns a mobile phone, and users are excited to use mobile-phone apps for different tasks. Mobile phones make our lives easier.

Figure 5 shows the architecture diagram of the tooth-brushing app.

There is an advantage in using the mobile-phone environment because it has specially built OpenCV image-processing libraries for mobile operating systems (Android and iOS). The implementation of this paper will present an Android app built for Android. The only thing a mobile phone needs is a front camera, which is present in almost all modern phones. Mobile phones were chosen because tablets are also good for use while brushing teeth, but the application will also work quite well on tablets.

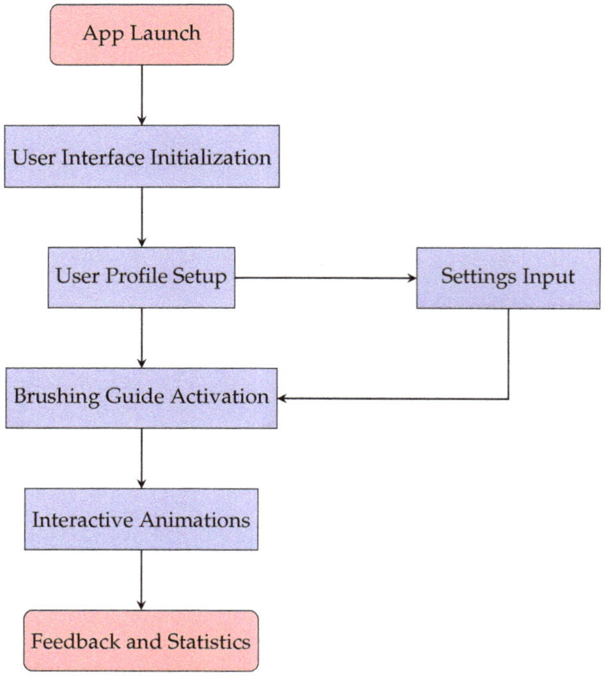

Figure 5. The architecture diagram of the tooth-brushing app.

To detect the direction of movement in brushing, two consecutive frames are used. The pixels in two consecutive frames are united.

To ease the system, not all pixels are united, but only certain ones. Initially, there is a grid. In addition, only pixels from the grid are united. The grid can be made with larger or smaller resolutions, but there is no need to unite all the pixels for movement detection. If there is no movement, the movement vector will be a dot; if there is movement, the movement vector will show the direction of the movement. After this, all it must be done is to detect if the direction is up–down or left–right. This can be detected easily by analyzing the coordinates of the points of moment vectors. After this, a decision can be made if the movement of the toothbrush is incorrect (left–right) or correct (up–down).

All that needs to be done is to overlay a timer on the image, allowing the user to know the duration of the brushing.

The pause of the stop buttons must be added to control the brushing timer.

The relative motion of the front camera does not influence the quality of detection of tooth brushing. The novelty lies in the fact that the app uses movement vectors to detect toothbrush movements and in the fact that there is no such app like this on the Google Play Store.

The following formulas were used for the toothbrush app.

The movement of a characteristic between consecutive frames is represented by the displacement vector represented in Equation (5).

$$\vec{v} = (dx, dy) \tag{5}$$

The horizontal and vertical displacements are denoted by dx and dy, respectively, in this instance.

The velocity vector shows how quickly a feature's position changes over time, represented in Equation (6).

$$\vec{v} = (\frac{dx}{dt}, \frac{dy}{dt}) \tag{6}$$

The horizontal and vertical components of the velocity are indicated, respectively, by $\frac{dx}{dt}$ and $\frac{dy}{dt}$.

The apparent motion of objects in an image due to the relative motion of the observer and the scene is represented by the optical flow represented in Equation 7.

$$\vec{F} = (u, v) \tag{7}$$

The horizontal and vertical components of optical flow are denoted by u and v, respectively, in this instance.

Motion estimate is a technique used to facilitate tasks such as object tracking and video reduction by estimating the movement of objects between frames represented in Equation (8).

$$\vec{M} = (dx, dy, dt) \tag{8}$$

In this case, the temporal displacement is represented by dt, and the spatial displacement is represented by dx and dy.

The motion of the entire image as a result of the scene or the motion of the camera is represented by global motion vectors represented in Equation (9).

$$\vec{G} = (tx, ty) \tag{9}$$

In this case, the translational motion in the horizontal and vertical directions is denoted by tx and ty, respectively.

Figure 6 shows the initial screen of the app It can be seen that the timer can count down from two minutes to allow the user to wash their teeth for two minutes. The play and stop buttons, which can start or stop the timer and detect the direction of tooth brushing, can also be seen. The information button is also available, which will show a small hint on how to use the app.

Figure 7 shows that the tooth-brushing app is started after pressing the play button. The timer starts to count down, and the direction detection is also started. The movement vectors of the app can be seen, which are drawn over the live image feed. The pixels of two consecutive frames are united with the movement vectors. If there is no movement, the vector will be shown as a dot, and if there is movement, then the direction of the movement will be shown as a line, with the movement vectors, by uniting the initial and current positions of the moving pixel. If the vector is vertical, then there is vertical movement (up–down) of the toothbrush, which is correct. If the vector is horizontal (left–right), then there is a horizontal movement of the toothbrush, which is incorrect. The standard tooth-brushing technique on many dentists' websites is with small up–down circular movements, not big left–right linear movements, and this is what the app tests with image processing. However, in the actual brushing process, such as the Bass brushing technique, horizontal brushing is required when cleaning the occlusal surfaces of teeth. The movement vectors are shown on the whole image, not only on the teeth. The movement vectors do not have to be drawn only on the teeth; they show the direction of the toothbrush movement, mainly left–right or up–down; the correct movement is up–down, and this is what the app recognizes. In the image, the pause and stop buttons can also be seen. The stop button will reset the timer to two minutes. The pause button will stop brushing your teeth, and the timer will not be reset. The pause button stops the detection of the movement of the toothbrush.

When the tooth brushing is paused, the movement vector is not drawn in the live video feed captured during tooth brushing.

Figure 8 shows the help screen of the tooth-brushing app. There is information on how to use the app and how to brush your teeth correctly. The teeth must be brushed with up–down movements, not left–right movements, for at least two minutes.

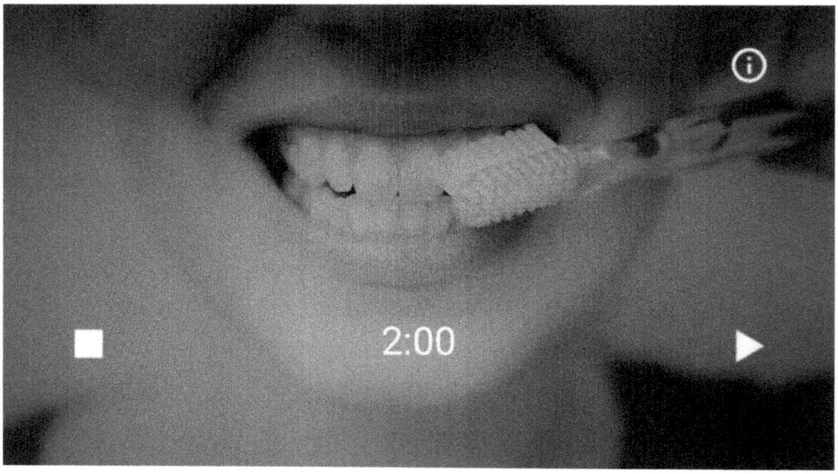

Figure 6. Initial screen of the tooth-brushing app.

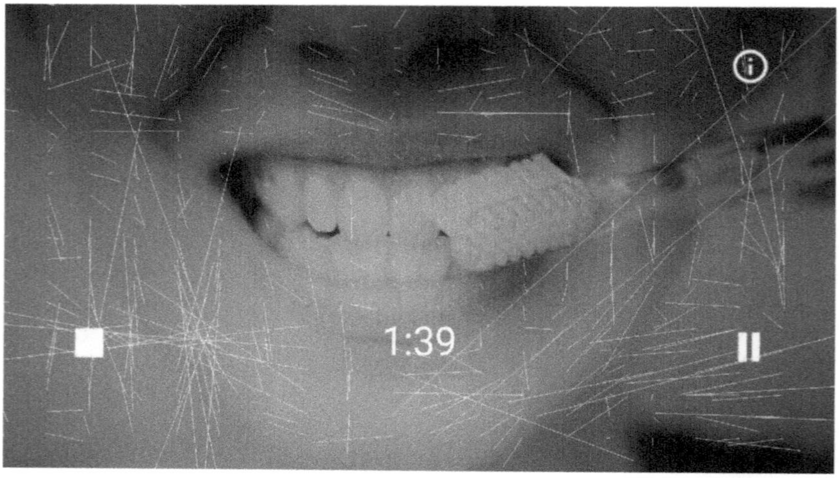

Figure 7. Tooth-brushing app with movement vectors.

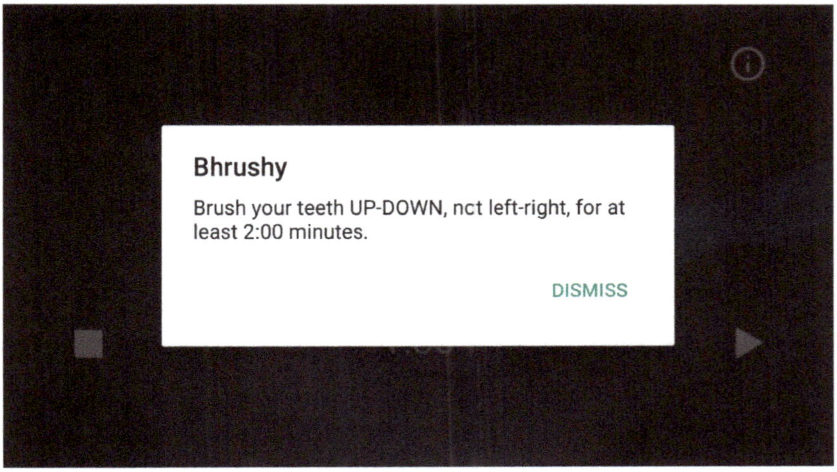

Figure 8. Help screen of the tooth-brushing app.

4.3. Lane and Car-Detection App Using Deep-Learning Algorithms with TensorFlow

The lane-detection app uses a TensorFlow database-trained neural network to recognize road lanes and cars. There is no such app on the Google Play Store.

The following formulas were used in order to implement lane detection.

The first relationship used is presented in Equation (10).

$$A_{cc} = \frac{\sum clip\ C_{clip}}{\sum clip\ S_{clip}} \tag{10}$$

where A_{cc} is the precision, in $clip\ C_{clip}$ are the number of estimated lane points that are properly cared for, and S_{clip} are the number of ground-truth points.

Figure 9 shows the architecture diagram of the lane-detection app.

The F_1 (Precision and Recall function) can also be computed as follows using Equation (11).

$$F_1 = \frac{2 \cdot \text{Precision} \cdot \text{Recall}}{\text{Precision} + \text{Recall}} \tag{11}$$

where precision is presented in Equation (12).

$$\text{Precision} = \frac{\text{TP}}{\text{TP} + \text{FP}} \tag{12}$$

The Recall is presented in Equation (13).

$$\text{Recall} = \frac{\text{TP}}{\text{TP} + \text{FN}} \tag{13}$$

where TP is the total points, FP is the false positives, and FN is the false negatives [40].

To detect lanes in photos using TensorFlow, a neural network model must first be trained to predict lanes. It will be given a mathematical illustration of a Convolutional Neural Network (CNN) architecture using TensorFlow for lane detection.

$$\mathbf{Z}^{[l]} = \text{Conv\_2D}(\mathbf{A}^{[l-1]}) \tag{14}$$

Equation (14) is the result of applying a convolutional layer l to the activation $\mathbf{A}^{[l-1]}$ of the previous layer. The input image is subjected to a convolutional filter through the Conv_2D operation.

$$\mathbf{A}^{[l]} = \text{ReLU}(\mathbf{Z}^{[l]}) \tag{15}$$

Equation (15) is the activation $\mathbf{A}^{[l]}$ of layer l, where the convolutional layer output $\mathbf{Z}^{[l]}$ is subjected element-wise to the rectified linear unit (ReLU) activation function.

$$\mathbf{A}^{[l]} = \text{MaxPooling\_2D}(\mathbf{Z}^{[l]}) \tag{16}$$

Equation (16) is the result of applying a max pooling layer to the output $\mathbf{Z}^{[l]}$ of the preceding layer, representing the output $\mathbf{A}^{[l]}$. Max pooling preserves significant characteristics while reducing the spatial dimensions of the feature maps.

$$\mathbf{Z}^{[l]} = \mathbf{W}^{[l]} \cdot \mathbf{A}^{[l-1]} + \mathbf{b}^{[l]} \tag{17}$$

Equation (17) is a representation of the output of the fully connected layer $\mathbf{Z}^{[l]}$, where $\mathbf{b}^{[l]}$ is the bias vector, $\mathbf{A}^{[l-1]}$ is the activation of the layer before it and $\mathbf{W}^{[l]}$ are the weights.

$$\hat{y} = \text{Softmax}(\mathbf{Z}^{[L]}) \tag{18}$$

Equation (18) addresses the result $\hat{y}$ of the last layer of the network, where the Softmax function is applied to the result $\mathbf{Z}^{[L]}$ of the last completely associated layer. The Softmax function yields a likelihood distribution over the classes (for example, the presence of lane markings).

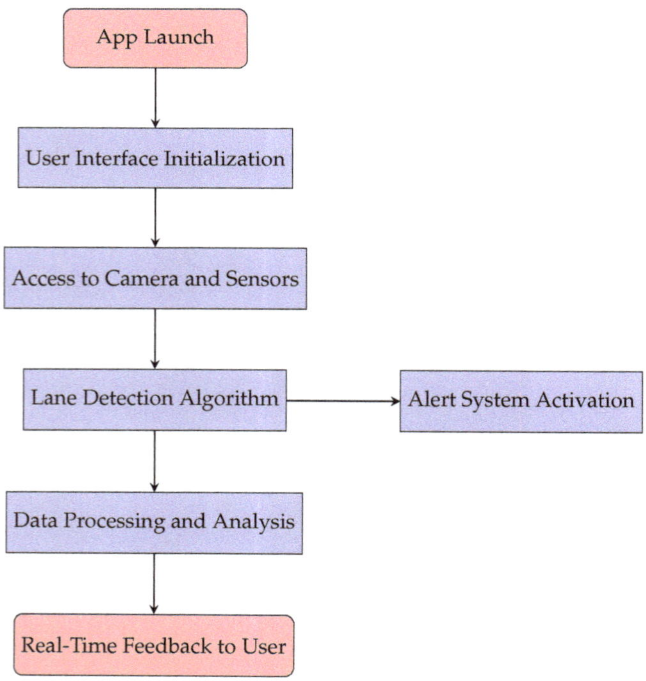

Figure 9. The architecture diagram of the lane-detection app.

These mathematical expressions offer a high-level summary of a common CNN architecture for lane detection based on TensorFlow. In practice, this involves defining the architecture, assembling the model, training it using annotated image data, and assessing its output.

Next, loss function and error plots used in training and testing the neural network will be presented.

Mean Squared Error (MSE) loss calculates the mean of the squared differences between the predicted values and the actual values as shown in Equation (19).

$$\mathcal{L}_{\text{MSE}} = \frac{1}{n}\sum_{i=1}^{n}(y_i - \hat{y}_i)^2 \tag{19}$$

where:

- n represents the total count of samples,
- y_i is the actual value,
- $\hat{y}_i$ denotes the predicted value.

The MSE loss plot is presented in Figure 10.

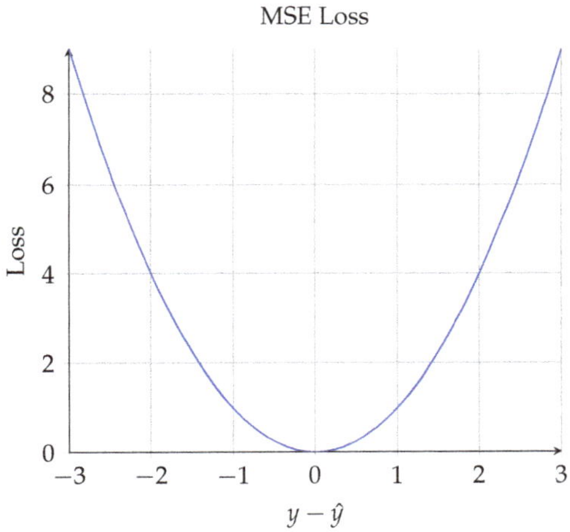

Figure 10. MSE loss.

Cross-Entropy Loss is frequently applied to classification problems. It quantifies the disparity between two probability distributions, the true labels, and the predicted probabilities.

The cross-entropy loss for binary classification is outlined in Equation (20).

$$\mathcal{L}_{\text{BCE}} = -\frac{1}{n}\sum_{i=1}^{n}[y_i \log(\hat{y}_i) + (1 - y_i)\log(1 - \hat{y}_i)] \tag{20}$$

where:

- n denotes the total sample count,
- y_i represents the binary true label,
- $\hat{y}_i$ is the estimated likelihood of belonging to the positive class.

The binary cross-entropy loss plot is presented in Figure 11.

In multi-class classification, the following section introduces the categorical cross-entropy loss as shown in Equation (21).

$$\mathcal{L}_{\text{CCE}} = -\frac{1}{n}\sum_{i=1}^{n}\sum_{j=1}^{k} y_{ij}\log(\hat{y}_{ij}) \tag{21}$$

where:

- n represents the total number of samples,

- k denotes the count of classes,
- y_{ij} is a binary indicator (0 or 1) indicating whether the class label j correctly classifies sample i,
- $\hat{y}_{ij}$ is the forecasted likelihood that sample i belongs to class j.

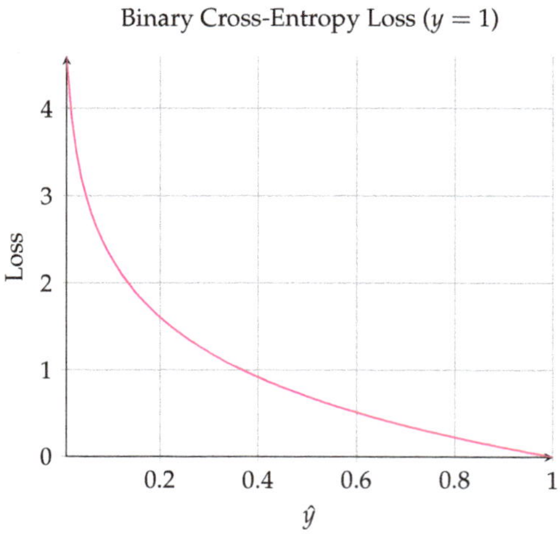

Figure 11. Binary cross-entropy loss.

The multi-class classification, the categorical cross-entropy loss plot, is presented in Figure 12.

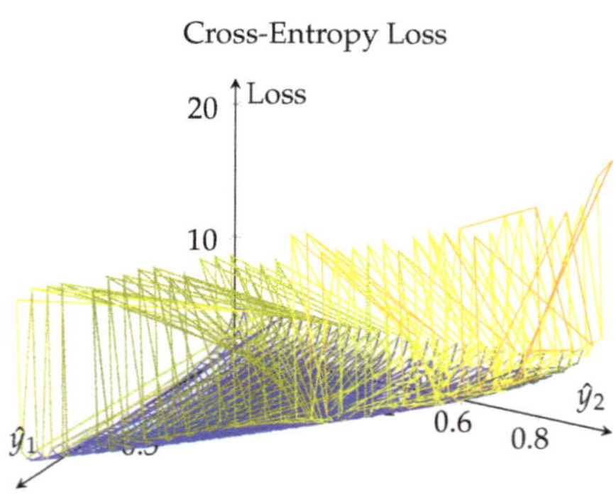

Figure 12. Multi-class classification cross-entropy loss.

Function: The cross-entropy loss for an actual label $y = [1, 0, 0]$ and predicted probabilities $\hat{y} = [\hat{y}_1, \hat{y}_2, \hat{y}_3]$ (where $\hat{y}_3 = 1 - \hat{y}_1 - \hat{y}_2$) is given by Equation (22).

$$\mathcal{L}_{\text{CE}} = -\log(\hat{y}_1) \tag{22}$$

Graph: We display the cross-entropy loss for $\hat{y}_1$ and $\hat{y}_2$, with $\hat{y}_3$ determined implicitly. The hinge loss plot is presented in Figure 13.

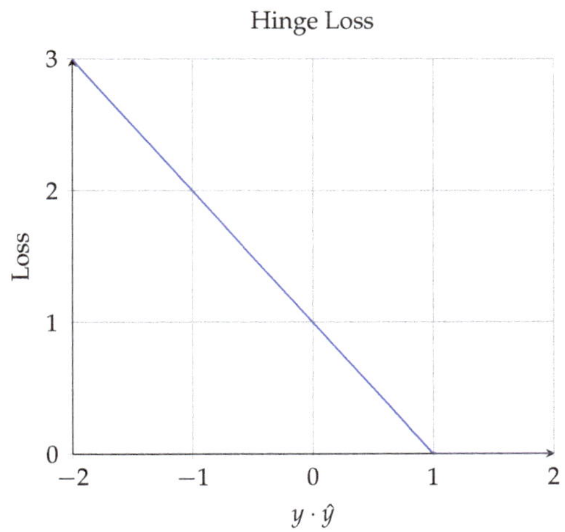

Figure 13. Hinge loss.

Function: The hinge loss is graphed as a function of $y \cdot \hat{y}$. The hinge loss becomes zero when $y \cdot \hat{y} \geq 1$ and grows linearly if it is less than that.

We visualize within the interval $-2 \leq y \cdot \hat{y} \leq 2$.

Hinge loss is commonly employed to train classifiers, such as support vector machines (SVMs), as shown in Equation (23).

$$\mathcal{L}_{\text{Hinge}} = \frac{1}{n} \sum_{i=1}^{n} \max(0, 1 - y_i \hat{y}_i) \tag{23}$$

where:

- n represents the total count of samples,
- y_i denotes the actual label, which can be either -1 or 1,
- $\hat{y}_i$ is the estimated label.

The Kullback–Leibler (KL) divergence quantifies the dissimilarity between a given probability distribution P and another reference probability distribution Q as shown in Equation (24).

$$\mathcal{L}_{\text{KL}} = \sum_{i=1}^{n} P(x_i) \log \frac{P(x_i)}{Q(x_i)} \tag{24}$$

where:

- $P(x_i)$ represents the actual probability distribution,
- $Q(x_i)$ is the estimated probability distribution.

The Kullback–Leibler (KL) divergence plot is presented in Figure 14.

Definition: The Kullback–Leibler (KL) divergence for two Bernoulli distributions with success probabilities p and q is expressed as shown in Equation (25).

$$D_{\text{KL}}(P \parallel Q) = p \log \frac{p}{q} + (1 - p) \log \frac{1 - p}{1 - q} \tag{25}$$

Constant p: For this plot, p is set to a constant value of 0.5.

Variable q: The value of q is adjusted from 0.01 to 0.99 to circumvent the undefined points at 0 and 1.

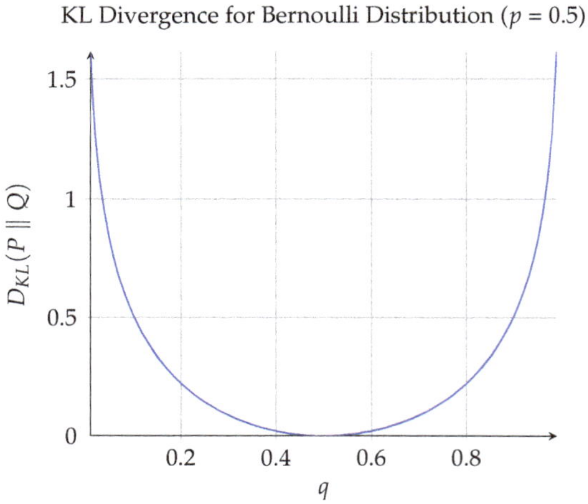

Figure 14. Kullback–Leibler (KL) divergence.

Mean Absolute Error (MAE) loss calculates the mean of the absolute deviations between forecasted and true values as shown in Equation (26).

$$\mathcal{L}_{\text{MAE}} = \frac{1}{n}\sum_{i=1}^{n} |y_i - \hat{y}_i| \tag{26}$$

where:

- n represents the count of samples,
- y_i represents the actual value,
- $\hat{y}_i$ is the value that is forecasted.

The MAE loss plot is presented in Figure 15.

Huber loss is more robust to outliers in data compared to Mean Squared Error (MSE). It merges the benefits of MSE and MAE by behaving quadratically for small errors and linearly for large errors, as shown in Equation (27).

$$\mathcal{L}_{\delta}(y, \hat{y}) = \begin{cases} \frac{1}{2}(y - \hat{y})^2 & \text{for } |y - \hat{y}| \leq \delta \\ \delta|y - \hat{y}| - \frac{1}{2}\delta^2 & \text{otherwise} \end{cases} \tag{27}$$

where:

- y represents the actual value,
- $\hat{y}$ denotes the value that is forecasted,
- δ is the cutoff point where the loss changes from quadratic to linear.

The Huber loss plot is presented in Figure 16.

Below, some performance metrics for the lane-detection app using TensorFlow are presented.

Figure 17 shows the Confusion Matrix of the algorithm used for detecting lanes.

Figure 18 shows validation dataset F1 score.

Figure 19 shows the number of training epochs and their associated accuracy levels.

Figure 20 shows the precision of the lane-detection system.

Figure 21 shows the evaluation of the model using the Dice score.

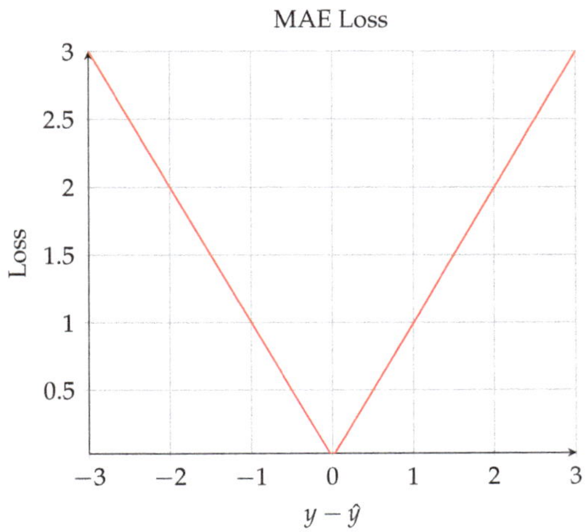

Figure 15. MAE loss.

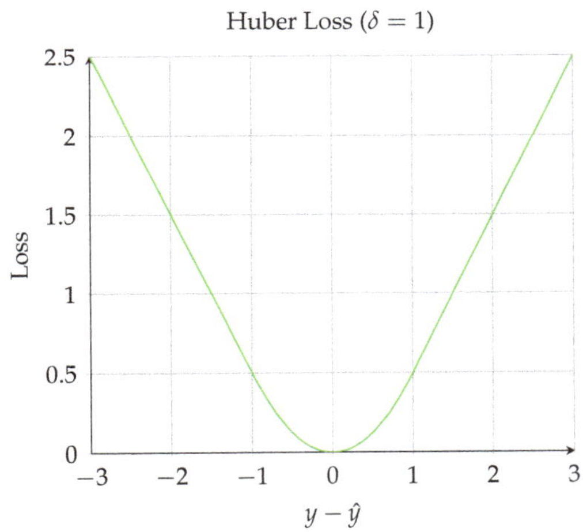

Figure 16. Huber loss.

Figure 22 shows a neural network simulation app, which is interesting for understanding how a neural network in TensorFlow is trained.

As seen in the neural network training app, the result was different every time the simulation was run, but the final result tended to be similar. Sometimes, it could not reach the desired result, but after a while, it would succeed. Sometimes, it was necessary to change some parameters in order to obtain the desired result, so the task when training the neural network is to configure the parameters in a way that the desired result will be reached the soonest as possible.

It was discovered that if the learning rate was set at a high value, then the system could reach the desired value many times faster, but there were many times when the system could not reach the desired value at all, so it is better to keep a medium learning rate, which could almost always reach the desired value, even if it takes a longer time.

It was also discovered that the ratio of training to test data did not influence the results too much. In this situation, there is not too much difference. Even if the feature numbers or the number of neurons were increased, there was not too much influence, but the system worked slower.

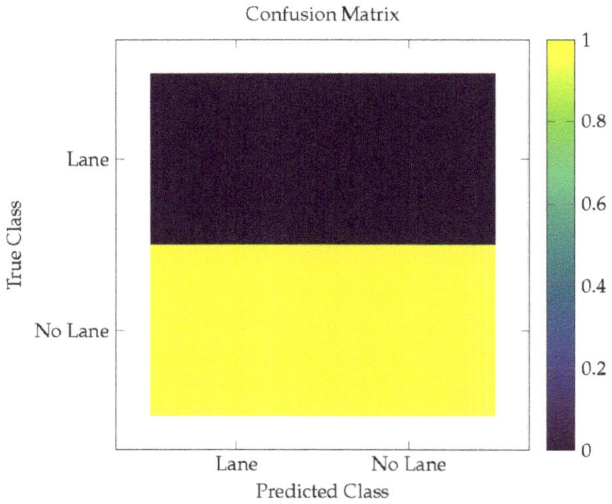

Figure 17. Confusion Matrix of the algorithm used for detecting lanes.

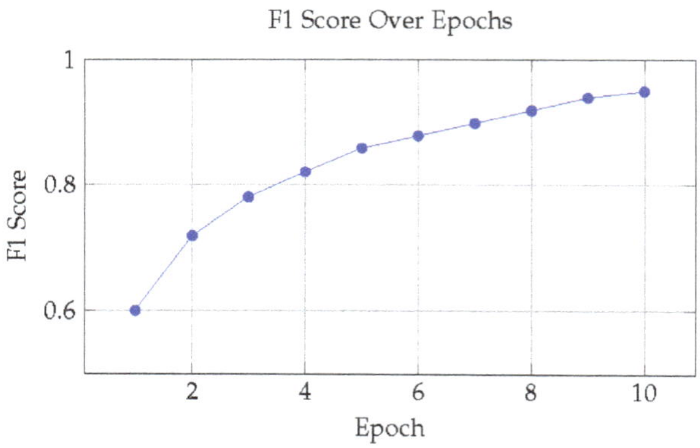

Figure 18. Validation dataset F1 score.

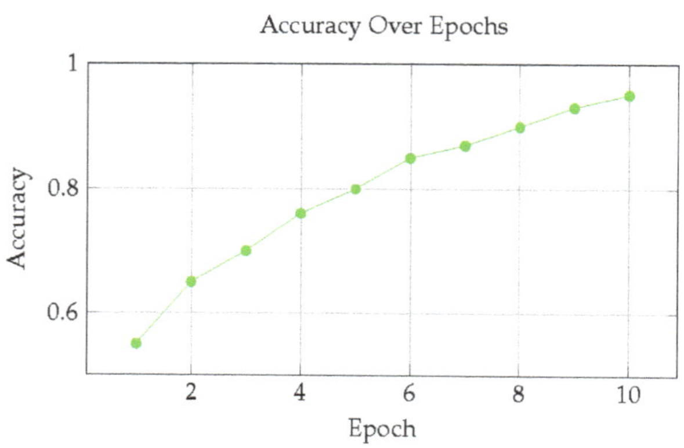

Figure 19. Number of training epochs and their associated accuracy levels.

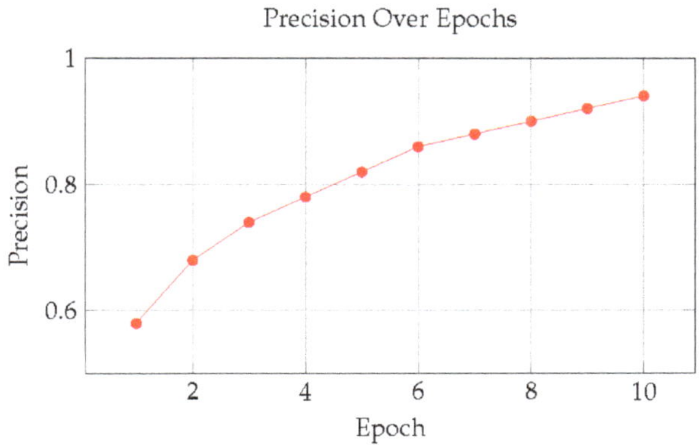

Figure 20. Precision of the lane-detection system.

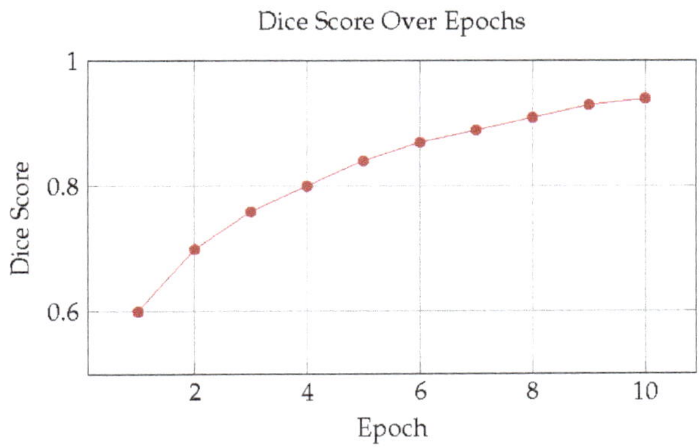

Figure 21. Evaluation of the model using the Dice score.

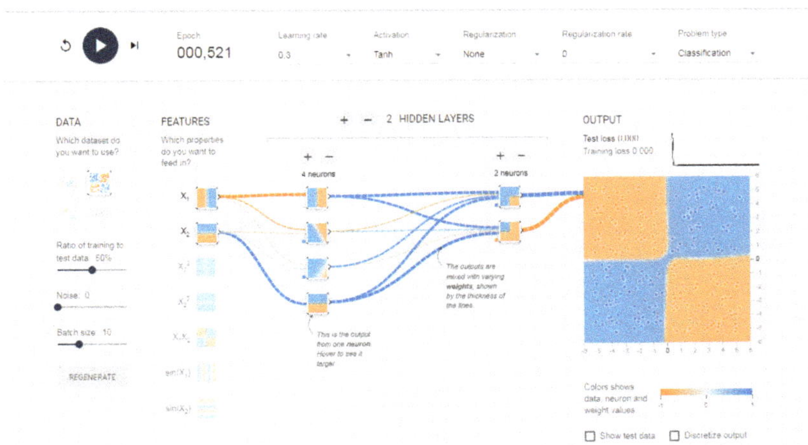

Figure 22. Trained neural network using TensorFlow [41].

It could also be seen that if the nose value was high, it was difficult for the system to obtain the desired values.

It was slow to show that if the batch size increased, the results were similar, but the time to obtain the desired results was longer.

It can be said that it is good to find the parameters to obtain the desired results almost at the same time.

Figure 23 shows that lane detection on curvy roads is carried out by the Android mobile-phone app.

Figure 24 shows the lane detection on a straight road made by the mobile-phone app on Android.

It can be seen that in both situations, the application works well, and the lane is detected. It can be seen that both mobile and side lanes on the road are detected.

These lines can guide a driver to stay on the road with the car, or it may even be possible to drive a self-driving car with this algorithm.

The software is configurable; the user can make changes, such as changing the color or the guidelines, which are overlaid in the live video feed. To do this, the user must click on the small gear button; this way, it will enable him to change the color of the guidelines, which detects the road lanes.

There can also be toggled whether one or both lanes are hidden and when only to have warnings for drivers to avoid being distracted by the app while driving.

The lane-detection app actually has two functionalities, which can be toggled using the gear button form the upper right corner. One functionality is the lane detection, and the other functionality is the car detection. The lane-detection app works better on empty country roads (Figures 23 and 24), while in congested traffic, the car-detection part of the app can be used, according to Figure 25.

The app can also be configured to detect cars on the road, also by tapping the gear icon (Figure 25).

The lane and car detection may seem opposite to each other, but both have some similarities. Both use image-recognition techniques using the OpenCV image-processing library on the Android operating system. Both use deep-learning algorithms, and the neural network is trained using TensorFlow.

The difference between the two parts of the app is that lane detection is used mainly in a low-traffic environment when we are going on an empty road, and we want to help keep the car on the road after a long drive when the driver is usually tired.

The car-detection part is used mainly in a high-traffic environment, when we want to detect other cars and obstacles, to avoid crashing into other cars, and also after a long drive when the driver is tired.

Both parts of the app can be used for a self-driving car app, where the self-driving car should avoid obstacles and keep the car on the road. If the app also includes traffic light and sign detection, it would be a complete self-driving car app.

Figure 23. Lane detection on a curved road made by the mobile-phone app.

Figure 24. Lane detection on a straight road made by the mobile-phone app.

Figure 25. Car detection made by the mobile-phone app.

4.4. Results

The apps were posted on the Google Play Store, and some real user reviews and ratings will be presented next.

The apps are quite new, and many of them have no ratings or reviews on Google Play, like the tooth-brushing app, which has no ratings or reviews.

The night-vision app has a few reviews. Below are quoted a few of them:

- "Best app for night time"
- "Program error"
- "Doesn't work"
- "Thank you for this AMAZING APP every other night-vision app was fake but thanks to you i can use it now, btw add colors"
- "Needs some light like how it gives a clear vision etc behind the tv"
- "ok close up but not good for distance"
- "Looked behind me TV really shows all. Needs some light but be sweet to check the engine etc."

The average rating for the night-vision app is 3.

The lane-detection app has no reviews, but the average rating is 3.429.

These ratings are not the best, but if we search for more famous apps made by Google LLC, like the Blogger app, which has a rating of 3.7, and the Google Classroom app, which has a rating of 2.5, than the ratings of the presented apps it is not so bad. Many times, mobile app users are ruthless when they make reviews.

5. Discussions

5.1. Night-Vision App

This article presented a night-vision app for vehicles. The app can be easily used in any car to avoid collisions with animals or pedestrians crossing the road. The app is actually an image enhancer that can be used at night when there is poor visibility or bad weather.

Many expensive cars already have these features installed. This phone app is an alternative to having this premium feature in the car, with almost zero investment, based on the fact that almost everyone owns at least one smartphone.

If the user owns more smartphones, one old smartphone can be placed in the car to be used as a night-vision camera only.

The night-vision app is a valuable tool crafted for drivers who travel at night, seeking a more optimized smartphone experience within their vehicles. It eases the accessibility of key features and lessens distractions during nighttime journeys.

The app features a user interface tailored to lower eye strain in dim lighting, utilizing dark themes and minimizing glare. By prioritizing simplicity, it cuts down on unnecessary on-screen items, enabling drivers to concentrate on driving. It works with most modern smartphones and promotes safe navigation and smartphone handling by offering straightforward options and decreasing the likelihood of distractions. It allows drivers to reach essential functions without juggling between multiple applications.

5.2. Tooth-Brushing Assistant App Using Image-Processing Techniques

As presented, a tooth-brushing app was created for the Android mobile-phone environment. The Android mobile-phone environment was chosen because it is the most widespread mobile-phone operating system.

The tooth-brushing app detected the correct tooth-brushing movements (up–down) using movement vectors, which were implemented using the OpenCV image-processing library.

The tooth-brushing app is a cutting-edge dental-hygiene application intended to enhance users' tooth-brushing behaviors. Suitable for all age groups, it assists users in adhering to correct methods and durations for superior oral care.

It features a detailed brushing guide accompanied by a timer to guarantee adequate coverage for all mouth regions. The app displays movement vectors to teach users effective brushing methods and dental-health approaches. It ensures proper tooth brushing, therefore decreasing the chances of cavities, gum issues, and plaque accumulation. Its appeal extends to both adults and children, promoting improved oral health habits for the entire family.

5.3. Lane- and Car-Detection App Using Deep-Learning Algorithms with TensorFlow

As presented, an app was created that could detect road lanes.

The uses OpenCV image-processing algorithm and TensorFlow are used to train the neural network for lane detection.

The app could configure the color of the overlaid line, which detects the road lane. The system can also be configured to hide one or both detected road lanes and to only issue warnings in the car that comes off the other side of the road. This way, the driver can focus on the road and not become distracted by the app.

The lane-detection application serves as a smart driving assistant aimed at enhancing road safety by assisting drivers in maintaining their lane position. It is particularly useful for extended journeys or when driving through unfamiliar areas, thus augmenting both ease and safety while driving.

Leveraging sophisticated algorithms, the app detects lane markings and offers real-time navigation assistance. It functions independently of continuous Internet connectivity, ensuring dependability even in remote locations. The risk of lane drifting, particularly due to fatigue or distractions, is significantly reduced. With dependable lane tracking, it boosts driver confidence when facing challenging conditions. Its user-friendly interface and uncomplicated functionality make it accessible to drivers of varying experience levels.

6. Conclusions

6.1. Night-Vision App

For the night-vision application, more image-enhancement functions were used from the OpenCV image-processing library. The innovation of this app is that it was made a night-vision app, even though the mobile phone does not have an infrared night-vision camera. The limitations are that it can obtain a better night-vision image with an external infrared night-vision camera than with a standard mobile-phone camera and image-processing techniques. The practical significance of the app is that it can be used quite well at night to see things in the dark.

The app was made only for the Android platform. Further enhancements could be to implement the app for the iOS platform, too. A good future study could be to implement the app for external thermal cameras, too. In this way, the warm bodies of humans and animals can be even better detected.

6.2. Tooth-Brushing Assistant App Using Image-Processing Techniques

For the tooth-brushing app, further enhancements can be made by adding a sensor to the toothbrush to detect the force the toothbrush applies to the teeth and gums. To protect the gums, it is not good to apply a large force to them during tooth brushing. When a strong force is applied to the gums, these can be harmed. The innovation of this app is that there are not many apps on the Google Play Store that actually can tell if a user brushes their teeth correctly just using image processing. Many apps connect to an external electric toothbrush via Bluetooth and check the direction of the tooth-brushing movement using an accelerometer. The innovation of this app is that it can work with any manual toothbrush. The limitations are that image processing can often present false negatives, usually when using toothpaste, which makes a lot of foam. The practical significance of the app is that it can be used quite well with any common toothbrush. There is no need to acquire an additional expensive electric toothbrush.

Another enhancement can be made to implement the app on the iOS operating system, too, to cover the other part of the mobile market.

6.3. Lane and Car-Detection App Using Deep-Learning Algorithms with TensorFlow

The lane-detection app can also be a starting point for autonomous cars. The innovation is that this app can detect lanes of cars with the usage of a mobile phone. There is no need to have this expensive feature that mostly premium cars have. The limitations are that the system uses only one camera from the mobile phone, so if it is accidentally covered, then the system cannot detect lanes or cars. The system is external, so it has no feedback to make the steering wheel vibrate when lanes are not followed or apply the brakes of the car to avoid an accident when using the car-detection algorithm. The practical significance of the app is that a cheap mobile phone can be used to achieve a premium feature.

Future enhancements can also be implemented to implement the app on the iOS operating system, i.e., to cover the rest of the mobile-phone users.

Another enhancement can also be adding traffic light and sign detection to build a complete self-driving car application.

Funding: This research was funded by MDPI (Multidisciplinary Digital Publishing Institute).

Institutional Review Board Statement: Not applicable.

Informed Consent Statement: Not applicable.

Data Availability Statement: All the images are available on request from the corresponding author.

Acknowledgments: The author would like to thank Politehnica University Timisoara, Romania for the given support.

Conflicts of Interest: The author declares no conflicts of interest.

Abbreviations

The following symbols and abbreviations are used in this manuscript:

GPS	Global Positioning System
HUD	Head-Up Display
SIM	Subscriber Identity Module
4G, 5G	fourth, fifth generation of broadband cellular network technology
eSIM	embedded-SIM (Subscriber Identity Module)
OpenCV	Open Computer-Vision Library
ADAS	advanced driver-assistance systems
CNNs	Convolutional Neural Networks
LiDAR	Light Detection And Ranging or Laser imaging, Detection, And Ranging
GPUs	Graphics Processing Units
iOS	iPhone Operating System
IR	Infra Red
IoT	Internet of Things
AR	Augmented Reality
x, y	spatial coordinates
$I(x, y)$	input image
NV	Night Vision
k	amplification factor constant
T	threshold value
$\vec{v}$	velocity vector
$\frac{dx}{dt}, \frac{dy}{dt}$	horizontal and vertical components of velocity
$\vec{F}$	optical flow
u, v	horizontal and vertical components of optical flow
$\vec{M}$	movement of objects
dx, dy	spatial displacement
dt	temporal displacement
$\vec{G}$	global motion
tx, ty	translational motion in the horizontal and vertical directions
A_{cc}	accuracy
C_{clip}	number of estimated lane points that are correctly managed
S_{clip}	number of truth ground points
F_1	Precision and Recall function
TP	Total Points
FP	False Positives
FN	False Negatives
$Z^{[l]}$	convolutional layer's output
Conv_2D	convolutional filter
$A^{[l-1]}$	activation of the preceding layer
$A^{[l]}$	activation of layer l
l	convolutional layer
ReLU	Rectified Linear Unit

$W^{[l]}$	weights
$b^{[l]}$	bias vector
$\hat{y}$	network's last layer
MSE	Mean Squared Error
n	total count of samples
y_i	actual value, binary true label, either -1 or 1
$\hat{y}_i$	predicted value, the estimated likelihood of belonging to the positive class
k	count of classes
y_{ij}	binary indicator (0 or 1) indicating whether the class label j correctly classifies sample i
$\hat{y}_{ij}$	forecasted likelihood that sample i belongs to class j
SVMs	support vector machines
KL	Kullback–Leibler
$P(x_i)$	actual probability distribution
$Q(x_i)$	estimated probability distribution
MAE	Mean Absolute Error
δ	cutoff point where the loss changes from quadratic to linear

References

1. Nowosielski, A.; Małecki, K.; Forczmański, P.; Smoliński, A.; Krzywicki, K. Embedded Night-Vision System for Pedestrian Detection. *IEEE Sens. J.* **2020**, *20*, 9293–9304. [CrossRef]
2. Purohit, M.; Chakraborty, A.; Kumar A.; Kaushik, B.K. Image Processing Framework for Performance Enhancement of Low-Light Image Sensors. *IEEE Sens. J.* **2021**, *21*, 8530–8542. [CrossRef]
3. Spivak, A.; Belenky, A.; Fish, A.; Yadid-Pecht, O. A Wide-Dynamic-Range CMOS Image Sensor with Gating for Night Vision Systems. *IEEE Trans. Circuits Syst. II Express Briefs* **2011**, *58*, 85–89. [CrossRef]
4. Liu, Z.; Blasch, E.; Xue, Z.; Zhao, J.; Laganiere, R.; Wu, W. Objective Assessment of Multiresolution Image Fusion Algorithms for Context Enhancement in Night Vision: A Comparative Study. *IEEE Trans. Pattern Anal. Mach. Intell.* **2012**, *34*, 94–109. [CrossRef] [PubMed]
5. Bhatnagar, G.; Wu, Q.M.J. A fractal dimension based framework for night vision fusion. *IEEE/CAA J. Autom. Sin.* **2019**, *6*, 220–227. [CrossRef]
6. Wang, Y.; Zhang, Y.; Guo, Q.; Zhao, M.; Jiang, Y. RNVE: A Real Nighttime Vision Enhancement Benchmark and Dual-Stream Fusion Network. *IEEE Signal Process. Lett.* **2024**, *31*, 131–135. [CrossRef]
7. Kim, J.; Jeon, M.-H.; Cho, Y.; Kim, A. Dark Synthetic Vision: Lightweight Active Vision to Navigate in the Dark. *IEEE Robot. Autom. Lett.* **2021**, *6*, 143–150. [CrossRef]
8. Warrant, E.; Oskarsson, M.; Malm, H. The Remarkable Visual Abilities of Nocturnal Insects: Neural Principles and Bioinspired Night-Vision Algorithms. *Proc. IEEE* **2014**, *102*, 1411–1426. [CrossRef]
9. Bandani, A.K.; Bollampally, A.; Sahithi, S.; Naik, R.; Kumar, N.; Goutham. Design of Spy Robot with Wireless Night Vision Camera Using Android. In Proceedings of the 2023 International Conference for Advancement in Technology (ICONAT), Goa, India, 24–26 January 2023; pp. 1–5.
10. Valentino, A.M.; Leonen, J.T. IoT-Based Smart Security Robot with Android App, Night Vision and Enhanced Threat Detection. In Proceedings of the 2023 IEEE 15th International Conference on Computational Intelligence and Communication Networks (CICN), Bangkok, Thailand, 22–23 December 2023; pp. 415–420.
11. Herath, B.; Dewmin, G.H.S.; Sukumaran, S.; Amarasinghe, Y.W.R.; De Silva, A.H.T.E.; Mitani, A.; Wijethunge, D.; Sampath, W.H.P. Design and Development of a Novel Oral Care Simulator for the Training of Nurses. *IEEE Trans. Biomed. Eng.* **2020**, *67*, 1314–1320. [CrossRef]
12. Lee, Y.-J.; Lee, P.-J.; Kim, K.-S.; Park, W.; Kim, K.-D.; Hwang, D.; Lee, J.-W. Toothbrushing Region Detection Using Three-Axis Accelerometer and Magnetic Sensor. *IEEE Trans. Biomed. Eng.* **2012**, *59*, 872–881.
13. Wang, M.-Y.; Yang, T.-H.; Huang, H.; Hsu, H.-Y.; Kuo, L.-C.; Su, F.-C.; Huang, C.-C. Evaluation of Hand Tendon Movement by Using High-Frequency Ultrasound Vector Doppler Imaging. *IEEE Trans. Biomed. Eng.* **2020**, *67*, 2945–2952. [CrossRef] [PubMed]
14. Xing, F.; Woo, J.; Gomez, A.D.; Pham, D.L.; Bayly, P.V.; Stone, M.; Prince, J.L. Phase Vector Incompressible Registration Algorithm for Motion Estimation From Tagged Magnetic Resonance Images. *IEEE Trans. Med. Imaging* **2017**, *36*, 2116–2128. [CrossRef] [PubMed]
15. Kruizinga, P.; Mastik, F.; Bosch, J.G.; de Jong, N.; van der Steen, A.F.W.; Van Soest, G. Measuring submicrometer displacement vectors using high-frame-rate ultrasound imaging. *IEEE Trans. Ultrason. Ferroelectr. Freq. Control.* **2015**, *62*, 1733–1744. [CrossRef] [PubMed]

16. Ouyang, Z.; Hu, J; Niu, J.; Qi, Z. An Asymmetrical Acoustic Field Detection System for Daily Tooth Brushing Monitoring. In Proceedings of the IEEE Global Communications Conference, Singapore, 4–8 December 2017; pp. 1–6.
17. Lutze, R. Practicality of Smartwatch Apps for Supporting Elderly People—A Comprehensive Survey. In Proceedings of the IEEE International Conference on Engineering, Technology and Innovation (ICE/ITMC), Stuttgart, Germany, 17–20 June 2018; pp. 1–7.
18. Demrozi, F.; Jereghi, M.; Pravadelli, G. Towards the automatic data annotation for human activity recognition based on wearables and BLE beacons. In Proceedings of the IEEE International Symposium on Inertial Sensors and Systems (INERTIAL), Kailua-Kona, HI, USA, 22–25 March 2021; pp. 1–4.
19. Jung, S.; Youn, J.; Sull, S. Efficient Lane Detection Based on Spatiotemporal Images. *IEEE Trans. Intell. Transp. Syst.* **2016**, *17*, 289–295. [CrossRef]
20. Wang, Y.; Jing, Z.; Ji, Z.; Wang, L.; Zhou, G.; Gao, Q.; Zhao, W.; Dai, S. Lane Detection Based on Two-Stage Noise Features Filtering and Clustering. *IEEE Sens. J.* **2022**, *22*, 15526–15536. [CrossRef]
21. Chen, S.; Huang, L.; Chen, H.; Bai, J. Multi-Lane Detection and Tracking Using Temporal-Spatial Model and Particle Filtering. *IEEE Trans. Intell. Transp. Syst.* **2022**, *23*, 2227–2245. [CrossRef]
22. Maghsoumi, H.; Masoumi, N.; Araabi, B.N. RoaDSaVe: A Robust Lane Detection Method Based on Validity Borrowing From Reliable Lines. *IEEE Sens. J.* **2023**, *23*, 14571–14582. [CrossRef]
23. Lu, P.; Cui, C.; Xu, S.; Peng, H.; Wang, F. SUPER: A Novel Lane Detection System. *IEEE Trans. Intell. Veh.* **2021**, *6*, 583–593. [CrossRef]
24. Mukhopadhyay, A.; Murthy, L.R.D.; Mukherjee, I.; Biswas, P. A Hybrid Lane Detection Model for Wild Road Conditions. *IEEE Trans. Artif. Intell.* **2023**, *4*, 1592–1601. [CrossRef]
25. Feng, Y.; Li, J. Robust Accurate Lane Detection and Tracking for Automated Rubber-Tired Gantries in a Container Terminal. *IEEE Trans. Intell. Transp. Syst.* **2023**, *24*, 11254–11264. [CrossRef]
26. Maghsoumi, H.; Masoumi, N.; Araabi, B.N. Lane Detection and Tracking Datasets: Efficient Investigation and New Measurement by a Novel "Dataset Scenario Detector" Application. *IEEE Trans. Instrum. Meas.* **2024**, *73*, 5007716. [CrossRef]
27. Luo, S.; Zhang, X.; Hu, J.; Xu, J. Multiple Lane Detection via Combining Complementary Structural Constraints. *IEEE Trans. Intell. Transp. Syst.* **2021**, *22*, 7597–7606. [CrossRef]
28. Zhang, J.; Deng, T.; Yan, F.; Liu, W. Lane Detection Model Based on Spatio-Temporal Network With Double Convolutional Gated Recurrent Units. *IEEE Trans. Intell. Transp. Syst.* **2022**, *23*, 6666–6678. [CrossRef]
29. Wang, H.; Liu, B. G-NET: Accurate Lane Detection Model for Autonomous Vehicle. *IEEE Syst. J.* **2023**, *17*, 2039–2048. [CrossRef]
30. Lee, C.; Moon, J.-H. Robust Lane Detection and Tracking for Real-Time Applications. *IEEE Trans. Intell. Transp. Syst.* **2018**, *19*, 4043–4048. [CrossRef]
31. Dewangan, D.K.; Sahu, S.P. Driving Behavior Analysis of Intelligent Vehicle System for Lane Detection Using Vision-Sensor. *IEEE Sens. J.* **2021**, *21*, 6367–6375. [CrossRef]
32. Wang, Q.; Han, T.; Qin, Z.; Gao, J.; Li, X. Multitask Attention Network for Lane Detection and Fitting. *IEEE Trans. Neural Netw. Learn. Syst.* **2022**, *33*, 1066–1078. [CrossRef]
33. Wu, C.-B.; Wang, L.-H.; Wang, K.-C. Ultra-Low Complexity Block-Based Lane Detection and Departure Warning System. *IEEE Trans. Circuits Syst. Video Technol.* **2019**, *29*, 582–593. [CrossRef]
34. Sivaraman, S.; Trivedi, M.M. Integrated Lane and Vehicle Detection, Localization, and Tracking: A Synergistic Approach. *IEEE Trans. Intell. Transp. Syst.* **2013**, *14*, 906–917. [CrossRef]
35. Zhang, W. Combination of SIFT, Canny Edge Detection for Registration Between SAR and Optical Images. *IEEE Geosci. Remote Sens. Lett.* **2022**, *19*, 4007205. [CrossRef]
36. Ding, Y.; Sun, Y.; Yu, X.; Cheng, D.; Lin, X.; Xu, X. Bezier-Based Hough Transforms for Doppler Localization of Human Targets. *IEEE Antennas Wirel. Propag. Lett.* **2020**, *19*, 173–177. [CrossRef]
37. Yang, W.; Luo, H.; Tse, K.-W.; Hu, H.; Liu, K.; Li, B.; Wen, C.-Y. Autonomous—Targetless Extrinsic Calibration of Thermal, RGB, and LiDAR Sensors. *IEEE Trans. Instrum. Meas.* **2024**, *73*, 4510011. [CrossRef]
38. Talpes, E.; Sarma, D.D.; Venkataramanan, G.; Bannon, P.; McGee, B.; Floering, B.; Jalote, A.; Hsiong, C.; Arora, S.; Gorti, A.; et al. Compute Solution for Tesla's Full Self-Driving Computer. *IEEE Micro* **2020**, *40*, 25–35. [CrossRef]
39. Ettinger, S.; Cheng, S.; Caine, B.; Liu, C.; Zhao, H.; Pradhan, S.; Chai, Y.; Sapp, B.; Qi, C.; Zhou, Y.; et al. Large Scale Interactive Motion Forecasting for Autonomous Driving: The Waymo Open Motion Dataset. In Proceedings of the IEEE/CVF International Conference on Computer Vision (ICCV), Montreal, QC, Canada, 10–17 October 2021; pp. 9690–9699.

40. Shyam, P.; Yoon, K.-J.; Kim, K.-S. Weakly Supervised Approach for Joint Object and Lane Marking Detection. In Proceedings of the IEEE/CVF International Conference on Computer Vision Workshops (ICCVW), Montreal, BC, Canada, 11–17 October 2021; pp. 2885–2895.
41. Tensor Flow Playground. Available online: https://playground.tensorflow.org (accessed on 3 July 2024).

technologies

MDPI

Article

Advanced Autonomous System for Monitoring Soil Parameters

Băjenaru Valentina-Daniela [1,*], Istrițeanu Simona-Elena [2] and Paul-Nicolae Ancuța [3]

[1] Intelligent Thermo-Technical Measurements Department, National Institute of Research and Development in Mechatronics and Measurement Technique, 021631 Bucharest, Romania
[2] Environmental Engineering and Renewable Energy Systems Department, National Institute of Research and Development in Mechatronics and Measurement Technique, 021631 Bucharest, Romania; simona.istriteanu@incdmtm.ro
[3] Complex Automation and Control Systems Department, National Institute of Research and Development in Mechatronics and Measurement Technique, 021631 Bucharest, Romania; paul.ancuta@incdmtm.ro
* Correspondence: valentina.bajenaru@incdmtm.ro

Abstract: Context: This research investigates the advantages of real-time monitoring of soil quality for various land management practices. It also highlights the significance of spatio-temporal soil modeling and mapping in providing a clear and visual understanding of how aridity changes over time and across different locations. **Aims**: This paper aims to provide a comprehensive guide to the key processes required for the development of a laboratory-based soil quality monitoring system. **Methods**: The applied methodologies involved the processes of sensor deployment, data acquisition infrastructure establishment, and sensor calibration. These procedures culminated in the development of a soil quality assessment model that was subsequently subjected to two months of laboratory testing using three distinct soil types. The analysis yielded a strong positive linear correlation between the measured and predicted soil quality values. **Key Results**: As expected, the assimilation of prior soil quality estimates within the modeling framework demonstrated a significant enhancement in the accuracy of real-time soil quality estimations. **Conclusions**: This research promotes the importance of iterative improvements of the soil quality monitoring system. The need for a long-term perspective and a plan for maintenance and continuous improvement of such systems in the ecosystem is important to improve the ease of making predictions to avoid soil aridization. The results of this research will be useful for researchers and practitioners involved in the design and implementation of soil monitoring systems.

Keywords: digital soil mapping; soil moisture sensing; soil monitoring

1. Introduction

Accurate monitoring of key soil parameters, including temperature, moisture, pH, electrical conductivity (EC), and nutrient levels (NPK), is crucial for predicting soil health and developing a comprehensive real-time understanding of soil conditions across any given area. This necessitates the adoption of advanced technological systems.

This shift towards advanced technology is a concerted effort to simultaneously conserve natural resources and enhance profitability by streamlining production processes and minimizing resource consumption. As regions grapple with dwindling water supplies and the increasing threat of drought, technology assumes a critical role in enabling accurate predictions and proactive mitigation strategies to avert water scarcity and its associated consequences.

Soil nutrients are critical for agricultural productivity, directly influencing plant growth and yield. Concurrently, soil moisture significantly impacts soil erosion processes as well as water and sediment transport within the soil profile [1]. These macronutrients, including nitrogen (N), phosphorus (P), and potassium (K), are essential for various biochemical processes within plants. Notably, nitrogen and phosphorus are crucial for plant growth and play a pivotal role in the soil–plant system [2]. While nitrogen and phosphorus are primarily found within the soil, their concentrations exhibit significant variability influenced by factors such as soil type, geographic location, and prevailing environmental conditions [3]. Soil factors such as temperature, moisture content, water table depth, and electrical conductivity are critical determinants of crop quality and yield. Precision agriculture can be defined as the strategic application of modern information technologies to acquire, process, analyze, and optimize the management of agricultural resources [4]. This directly involves the collection and analysis of site-specific data to enable informed and individualized management decisions that mitigate soil aridization and, crucially, prevent desertification.

2. Literature Review

This research commenced in 2023 with the initiation of the PN 23 43 05 02 "IoT-SOL" project at INCDMTM-Bucharest, spanning a four-year duration. The development of this manuscript was facilitated by the invaluable contributions of colleagues from the Departments of Environmental Engineering and Renewable Energy Systems, Intelligent Thermo-technical Measurements, and Complex Automation and Control Systems. The author declares no conflicts of interest regarding this research, which focuses on "advanced autonomous system for monitoring soil parameters." This work addresses the development of technological solutions by applying principles from natural sciences and carefully selecting appropriate materials. The reviewed literature, as cited, explores different aspects compared to the present study, such as:

Padmavathi et al. [3] present an IoT framework for agriculture, focusing on pest detection, automated irrigation, and alert systems. This framework necessitates the deployment of various sensors and IoT devices. In contrast, our research specifically focuses on measuring key soil quality parameters—temperature, moisture, electrical conductivity (EC), and nutrient levels (NPK)—at varying soil depths.

Rudi et al. [5] present the design and implementation of a portable IoT-based system for real-time monitoring of soil nutrients (nitrogen, phosphorus, and potassium) using field-based sensors. This system aims to enhance precision farming by enabling on-site soil analysis and providing tailored fertilization and management recommendations. In contrast, this study focuses on analyzing soil nutrient levels at various depths (up to 80 cm) to generate data for predicting and mitigating soil aridization.

We investigate the key processes involved in developing an operational on-farm system for high-resolution daily soil moisture mapping, capturing temporal, spatial, and vertical variations. The paper emphasizes the importance of iterative improvements, particularly in sensor recalibration and spatio-temporal modeling. In contrast, this study focuses on analyzing soil properties at various depths (up to 80 cm) to generate data for predicting and mitigating the risk of soil aridization.

Currently, this research is in the laboratory phase, where various data acquisition, transmission, storage, and display technologies are being evaluated. The objective is to identify the most suitable combination of technologies for the specific conditions of in-situ equipment installation. The acquired data will be stored and visualized on an Ecosystem IoT platform developed specifically for this project.

The proposed multisensory soil monitoring system is designed for easy integration into various substrates and soils through a compact probe design, enabling rapid assessments and optimization of cultivation practices. Moreover, this system facilitates the creation of geo-temporal maps of soil conditions across different regions, providing crucial data for informed decision making to mitigate soil aridization. The proposed autonomous, multisensory system will enhance the precision of digital soil mapping by providing a sustainable and renewable means of geographically characterizing the aridization status of various regions, ultimately supporting sustainable soil management practices.

The primary objective of this work is to develop a laboratory system capable of simultaneously acquiring data from three distinct soil types to enable comprehensive monitoring of soil characteristics and mitigate the risk of soil aridization.

The advantages of IoT-based soil monitoring, as illustrated in Figure 1, extend beyond immediate crop management. By collecting and analyzing historical soil data, it becomes possible to identify patterns and trends, leading to a deeper understanding of soil behavior and properties. This knowledge can then be leveraged to develop long-term soil management plans that prioritize soil health, nutrient cycling, and water conservation.

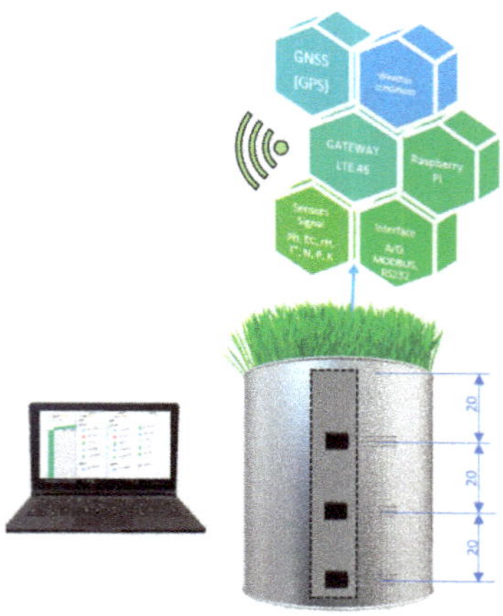

Figure 1. Virtual model of the soil parameter monitoring system on three sampling depths.

3. Materials and Methods

3.1. Overview

Soil quality assessment plays a crucial role in maintaining soil health, particularly in mitigating the risks of aridization and desertification. Prior to establishing any crop, thorough soil testing is essential. This practice enables farmers to determine the suitability of the soil for specific crops and to develop appropriate fertilization plans. Ideally, soil testing should be conducted at least once every four years to ensure ongoing soil health management [6].

One of the primary functions of soil is to produce phytomass, the raw material for food, clothing, fuel, and other essential products. This function is crucial for human sustenance and economic development. Enhancing soil health through practices like reducing energy consumption and adopting electric tractors is essential for optimizing this vital function [7].

For optimal plant growth, soil provides a diverse array of chemical elements essential for vegetation development and crop production. Among these elements, fourteen are recognized as essential nutrients for plants. Based on the quantities required by plants and their specific physiological and biochemical functions, these nutrients are categorized into two groups: macronutrients and micronutrients [6]. Macronutrients are further categorized into primary macronutrients (nitrogen (N), phosphorus (P), and potassium (K)) and secondary macronutrients (sulfur (S), calcium (Ca), and magnesium (Mg)) [8].

Nitrogen (N) is a significant component for plant growth, as it stimulates root growth and plant development as well as the absorption of other nutrients. A crop with a nitrogen deficiency will have reduced vegetative growth, discolored leaves, and poor yields, strictly correlated with the strength (or lack thereof) of the plants in the crop that have a nitrogen deficiency.

Phosphorus (P) is primarily a valuable source of energy; it is a valuable constituent of ATP (adenosine triphosphate), the molecule that provides the energy needed for a fairly large number of metabolisms. It is also a constituent of cell membranes and DNA molecules. This central role makes phosphorus an essential nutrient for plant structure and growth.

Potassium (K) plays an essential role in plants, participating in essential processes such as photosynthesis, cellular respiration, opening and closing of stomata, water absorption, protein metabolism, nutrient absorption and utilization, cell wall strengthening, and enzyme activation. As a result, this mineral is an essential nutrient for proper plant growth and development and must be controlled in any type of crop to ensure the most efficient agricultural production.

The group of micronutrients includes: Iron (Fe), Manganese (Mn), Cobalt (Co), Copper (Cu), Zinc (Zn), Boron (B), Molybdenum (Mo), and Chlorine (Cl) [9,10]. To accurately determines the macro- and micronutrient requirements of soils, it is essential to assess their nutrient content. This assessment is typically conducted as part of agrochemical mapping activities. The process generally involves three distinct phases:

(1) Field sampling, including the identification and sampling of target areas;
(2) Laboratory analysis, which involves time-consuming and often costly procedures;
(3) Data processing and decision making, which occur in an office setting.

Soil analysis is crucial for:

- Determining soil type: Identifying the specific soil type is fundamental for understanding its characteristics and limitations.
- Selecting appropriate crops: Determining the suitability of a particular soil for specific crops ensures optimal growth and yield.
- Optimizing fertilization programs: Soil analysis helps determine the precise amount of fertilizer required for each crop, maximizing nutrient utilization and minimizing nutrient losses.
- Assessing and mitigating risks: Soil analysis helps assess the risk of nutrient deficiencies or excesses as well as the potential for soil degradation, including aridization and desertification.
- Determining key soil properties: Soil analysis provides vital information on soil pH and other essential indicators, such as organic matter content, which are crucial for understanding overall soil health.

Soil sampling should be conducted under dry conditions to avoid inaccuracies in nitrogen level estimations. Ideal soil texture for sampling is friable, allowing it to be easily crushed in the hand without sticking. Before sampling, it is crucial to remove surface organic debris to a depth of 2–3 cm.

By deploying smart sensors at various depths (e.g., 20 cm, 40 cm, 60 cm, 80 cm), we can continuously monitor soil conditions and weather parameters in real-time, eliminating the need for frequent manual sampling. This approach offers significant advantages in terms of efficiency, cost-effectiveness, and data accuracy.

Following the framework outlined by Brendan et al. [11] and considering the importance of technological innovation in system design [12], a soil monitoring system can be established through the following key steps:

1. Define measurement parameters: Select the specific soil characteristics to be monitored based on the project's objectives (e.g., temperature, pH, moisture, macronutrients like NPK).
2. Choose sensor technology: Select appropriate smart sensors for the chosen parameters considering factors like accuracy, precision, cost, power consumption, and data logging capabilities.
3. Implement data acquisition and transmission: Develop a reliable system for collecting sensor data at regular intervals. This might involve wireless transmission protocols for efficient data transfer.
4. Establish data storage and processing: Set up a system for securely storing and processing the collected data. This might involve cloud-based storage solutions and data analysis tools.
5. Sensor deployment and calibration:
    a. Install smart sensors at various depths (e.g., 20 cm increments up to the desired depth) following proper installation procedures.
    b. Integrate the system to manage sensor calibration and recalibration processes, ensuring accurate and reliable data acquisition.
6. Monitor sensor performance:
    a. Regularly monitor the health and functionality of the deployed sensors in the field.
    b. Monitor and analyze the collected data to identify potential issues and ensure data integrity.

The current research primarily focuses on the initial stages of establishing a soil monitoring system, encompassing steps 1–4 outlined previously. These steps involve defining measurement parameters, selecting appropriate sensors, developing data acquisition and transmission systems, and establishing data storage and processing infrastructure.

Steps 5–6, which encompass sensor deployment, calibration, and ongoing monitoring, represent the practical implementation phase of the soil monitoring system. These aspects will be thoroughly investigated and analyzed as the research project progresses, providing valuable insights into the long-term operation and maintenance of the system.

LoRaWAN networks are known for their long-range communication capabilities, with outdoor coverage often exceeding 15 km in ideal conditions (line of sight, minimal interference) [13]. The soil sensors can use a battery with a solar panel, meaning they can be deployed over several hundred acres, providing a good indication of soil quality monitoring, or used for smart irrigation applications. Despite the benefits and extended coverage of LoRaWAN, this does not solve the problem of relaying data to a cloud platform or central system [14].

Soil quality is determined by using a soil sensor system that involves the integration of smart sensors to monitor a variety of characteristics, such as:

- Soil temperature;
- Soil moisture;
- Soil conductivity;
- Oxygen levels in the soil;
- Soil water potential;
- NPK sensors.

Buried electrode probes offer a reliable method for monitoring soil moisture content [15]. Soil moisture content is a cornerstone of hydrology, soil science, and agriculture. It significantly influences soil chemistry, plant growth, and groundwater recharge [16]:

- Adequate soil moisture is essential for plant growth. It allows plants to absorb nutrients and water, which are crucial for photosynthesis and overall health.
- Soil moisture content affects the movement and availability of nutrients within the soil. It influences chemical reactions and the leaching of nutrients
- Soil acts as a natural filter, allowing water to percolate into the ground and replenish groundwater reserves. Soil moisture content directly impacts this process.

By understanding and monitoring soil moisture content, we can optimize agricultural practices, manage water resources effectively, and protect our environment.

3.2. Method

Smart soil monitoring sensors offer a comprehensive approach to soil analysis. These advanced devices can simultaneously measure multiple critical parameters, including temperature, moisture, nitrogen (N), phosphorus (P), potassium (K), volumetric water content, water potential, pH, and soil oxygen levels. The collected data are wirelessly transmitted to a central hub (or cloud platform) for real-time visualization and in-depth trend analysis. This enables farmers and researchers to accurately assess the degree of soil aridity, as illustrated in Figure 2, and make informed decisions regarding irrigation, fertilization, and other crucial agricultural practices.

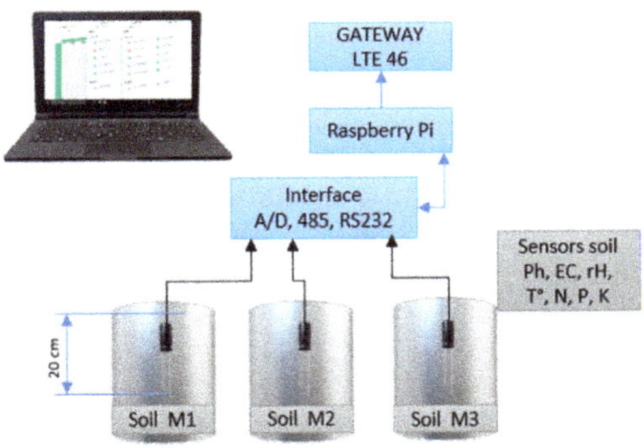

where:
Soil M1, M2, M3—The three types of soils sampled from three different geographical areas;
pH—The soil acidity or basicity of aqueous solutions
EC—Soil electric conductivity
rH—Soil moisture
T°—Soil temperature
N—Nitrogen
P—Phosphorus
K—Potassium

Figure 2. IoT system local architecture.

The final research on soil quality monitoring will provide a comprehensive solution for collecting soil data and transmitting it through the local network to a computer for processing. Sampling depths will be determined according to current standards, considering the specific crops present.

Leveraging these data allows for optimizing farming operations, identifying trends, and making subtle adjustments to maximize both yield and soil quality. This integration of smart sensors into agriculture is known as Smart Agriculture (or Smart Farming) [17]. Within Smart Agriculture, the Internet of Things (IoT) plays a central role as a precision component by enabling real-time signal reception, transmission, and analysis to support informed decision making.

This research focuses on simultaneously receiving data from sensors and processing them to validate and calibrate the sensors using known soil samples.

The tests were carried out on three types of known soils as is presented in Table 1:

- M1-Floralis soil: A commercial potting mix designed for flowering plants, typically containing a blend of peat moss, perlite, and other organic matter.

- M2-Soil for aromatic plants: A specialized soil blend formulated to support the growth of herbs and other aromatic plants, often enriched with nutrients and well-draining components.
- M3-Planting soil: A general-purpose potting mix suitable for a wide range of plants, commonly containing a mix of peat moss, compost, and other organic and inorganic materials.

Table 1. Technical parameters for the soil.

Parameters Soils to Analyze the Results	M1 *	M2 **	M3 **
pH (in water)	6.5	7.5	6.77
Electric conductivity (EC)	500 μS/m	340 μS/m	310 μS/m
Dry apparent density	250 kg/m^3	133 mg/kg	0
N	99 mg/kg	63 mg/kg	237 mg/kg
P	242 mg/kg	260 mg/kg	97 mg/kg
K	130 mg/kg	0	393 mg/kg

* Producer: ORVITAR, Italy. ** Producer: Green Project SRL, Iasi, Romania.

To conduct laboratory research, a portion of the architecture was implemented to acquire and display sensor data, as reproduced in Figure 3.

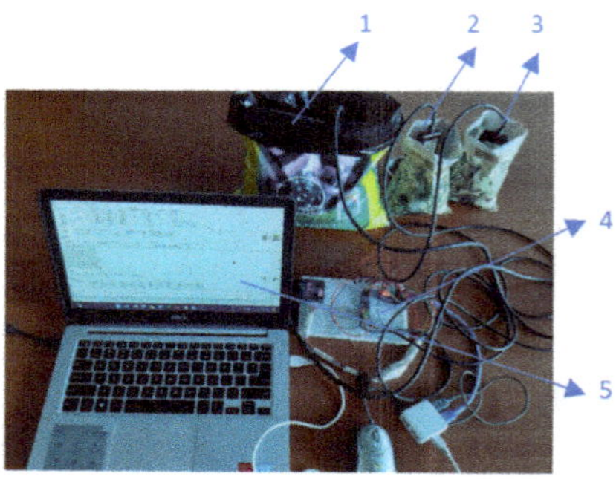

where:
1, 2, 3—The three types of soils within the Smart Sensor's 8 in 1
4—Raspberry Pi5
5—Notebook with dedicated software for receiving data from sensors

Figure 3. Laboratory pilot system for testing soil. Smart Sensor's 8 in 1—https://www.niubol.com/Agricultural-sensor/8-in-1-Soil-Integrated-Sensor.html (accessed on 10 April 2024).

3.3. Interface

Analog interfaces are employed for sensors that generate analog outputs, including temperature, pressure, electrochemical sensors, light and IR detectors, thermocouples, touch controllers, and others [18]. To interface these sensors with microcontrollers, an analog-to-digital converter (ADC) is necessary to convert the analog signal into a digital format for easier processing by microcontrollers and other digital devices [19].

The RS485 interface is a differential serial communication standard designed for long-distance data transmission. It is widely used in industrial applications where numerous devices require interconnection within a system. A broad range of sensors, including those for ground or air applications, utilize the Modbus protocol over the RS485 interface.

RS485 is a communication standard known for its robustness, especially in noisy environments. It achieves this by transmitting data differentially, meaning the signal is encoded in the voltage difference between two wires [20]. This differential signaling helps to cancel out common-mode noise, which is noise that affects both wires equally.

This standard was designed with the aim of expanding and improving the communication possibilities on a serial line. Among the improvements considered, the following can be mentioned:

- Increasing the maximum communication distance (approx. 1 km);
- Increasing immunity to noise;
- The possibility of multipoint communication (network communication);
- The use of a cheap communication medium.

Characteristics of the RS485 bus:

- A section of twisted bifilar cable is used, which has terminators (resistant) at both ends; both lines are used for transmission, there being no ground wire.
- Coding of binary data is done by positive and negative differential voltages measured on the two lines of the section; the minimum differential voltage considered valid is +/−200 mV.
- The emission circuits connected on the same section have tri-state outputs to allow several types of equipment to access the same communication section—access is multiplexed in time.

The RS485 standard allows the connection of up to 32 terminals (emission + reception). The RS485 standard does not specify the structure of the transmitted data, data flow control mechanisms, or error detection mechanisms. These can be taken from other serial communication standards (for example, RS232 or SDLC/HDLC) or can be defined by the user. This protocol is used as support for a series of protocols for industrial networks (for example, CAN, ModBUS, Profibus).

3.4. Smart Sensors

In this research, the smart sensors used (as illustrated in Figure 4) are sensors purchased from the ComWinTop company with the following technical parameters according to Table 2 [21].

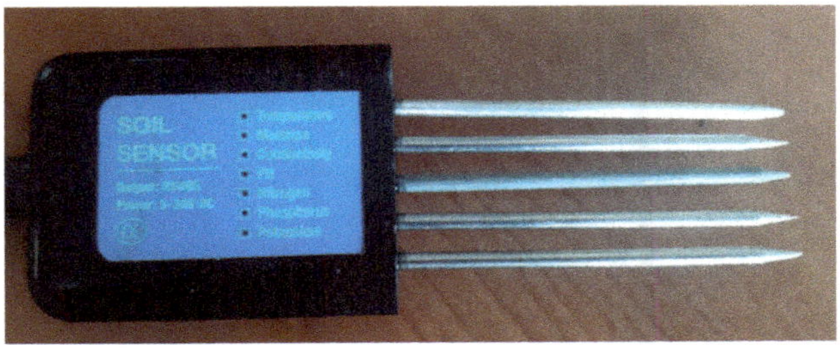

Figure 4. Smart sensor (own source).

Table 2. Technical parameters of smart sensor.

Characteristics	Accuracy
Temperature accuracy	±0.5 °C
Moisture accuracy	±3%
Conductivity accuracy	±10%
Accuracy of NPK	±2%
Salt accuracy	±10%
Measurement frequency range	50 Hz to 3 kHz
Nominal resistance	1000 Ω at 0 °C
Measuring current	0.3 mA
Connection	Pt/Ni wires, Ø 0.2 mm

The smart sensors utilized in this research were tested and calibrated at the Pressure Calibration Laboratory, accredited by RENAR within INCDMTM-Bucuresti. These sensors are a conductive type, exhibiting characteristics such as fast response time, resistance to chemical agents, excellent long-term stability, and an integrated RTD for temperature measurement and compensation.

3.5. Communication

Communication between the MASTER mode and the slave modules, responsible for data acquisition, is facilitated by the Modbus RTU protocol. This protocol defines a standardized message structure that controllers can readily recognize and utilize, regardless of the specific network type they are communicating with.

A communication protocol dictates how a controller requests access to another device, responds to requests from other devices, and handles error detection and reporting. It establishes a standardized format for message structure and content. The electronic data measurement and transmission equipment operates in two modes, remote and local, as illustrated in Figure 5.

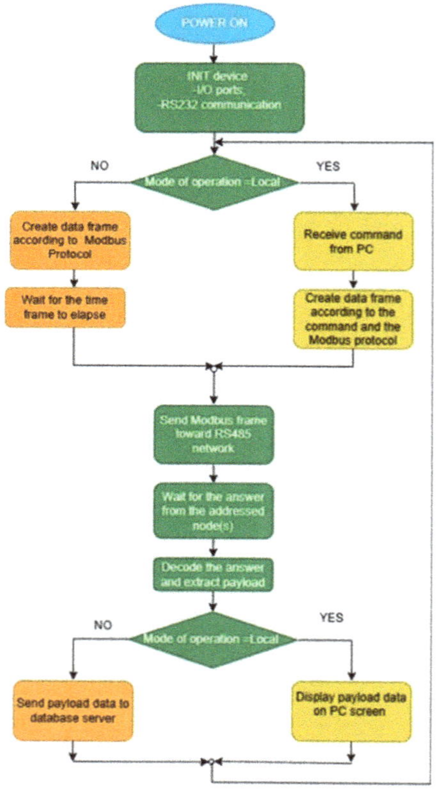

Figure 5. Logic diagram for data collection and processing via Modbus.

Upon power up, the microcontroller firmware determines the operational mode: REMOTE or LOCAL. The default mode is LOCAL. In LOCAL mode, data acquisition is initiated by issuing a command from a PC terminal.

Preliminary sensor operation tests are conducted by directly connecting the sensors to a PC via an RS485-USB interface:

(1) The MASTER module is connected to a PC using an RS232-USB interface adapter.

(2) The operator enters ASCII commands in the Terminal.exe program. These commands are sent to the MASTER module. Alternatively, a macro-command can be created within the Terminal.exe v1.93b - 20141030beta - by Br@y++ application and executed by pressing a software button.
(3) If the sent command is valid, the master module executes the program code associated with the command, as illustrated in Figure 5.

The flow chart, as illustrated in Figure 5, illustrates the workflow of a device interacting with other systems using the Modbus protocol. It operates in two modes: "Local" for autonomous data collection and processing and "Remote" for external control and data retrieval.

4. Calibration

Conductivity is a measure of the concentration of ions in an aqueous solution, such as moisture. It can be used to assess the quality and quantity of nutrients, salts, or impurities present in the solution [22,23]. The integrated temperature sensor enables both temperature measurement and compensation (if necessary). It can be strategically placed within the measurement area to enhance the accuracy of the acquired data [24].

Electrical conductivity in an aqueous solution is influenced by two key temperature-dependent factors [25]:

- Ion concentration: As the temperature increases, the kinetic energy of molecules and ions increases, leading to increased molecular motion and potentially greater dissociation of salts into ions. This generally results in a higher concentration of ions in the solution.
- Ion mobility: Higher temperatures typically increase the mobility of ions. As the temperature rises, the viscosity of the solution usually decreases, allowing ions to move more freely and conduct electricity more effectively.

When an electric voltage is applied between two electrodes immersed in an electrolyte (a solution containing ions), an electric current flows [26]. The voltage drop across an electrolyte is inversely related to its conductivity, which is significantly influenced by temperature. As the temperature increases, the conductivity of the electrolyte generally rises [27].

During the research, sensor testing and calibration software was obtained from the ComWinTop Store manufacturer. The calibration process involved determining the numerical coefficients A and B through curve fitting, specifically using a right-sided interpolation method.

$$Y = AX + B \tag{1}$$

where:

X is the raw measured value, and Y is the final measured value that is applied to the NPK sensors.

Sensor calibration was performed exclusively on the M1 soil type, as illustrated in Table 3. The calibration procedure consisted of two steps:

I. Initial calibration: Calibration was conducted using a solution of 200 mL distilled water with 2 g of NPK fertilizer.
II. Soil calibration: Subsequent measurements were taken on 1 kg of M1 soil moistened with 100 mL of water

Table 3. Calibration values—I.

I	T [°C]	M [%rH]	pH	N [mg/kg]	P [mg/kg]	K [mg/kg]	CE [uS/cm]	TDS
	21.0	18.0	6.4	38.2	42.1	13.0	201.0	195.2
	21.1	18.0	6.5	38.4	42.3	13.3	201.3	195.6
	21.3	18.0	6.4	38.3	42.2	13.4	201.0	195.6
	21.1	18.0	6.5	38.1	42.1	13.2	200.0	195.3

T—soil temperature; pH—degree of acidity of the soil; M—degree of soil moisture; N—nitrogen; P—potassium; K—phosphorus; CE—the electrical conductivity level of water in soil; TDS—total dissolved solids in soil.

5. Results

This research involved conducting tests and measurements on all three soil types using the calibrated smart sensors.

Each sensor generates daily readings at eight-hour intervals. The working architecture, illustrated in Figure 5, processes these readings in conjunction with the initial calibration data. By applying a manufacturer-provided equation, the system estimates soil parameters, as outlined in Table 4.

Table 4. Values measured on soils types.

	T [°C]	M [%rH]	pH	N [mg/kg]	P [mg/kg]	K [mg/kg]	CE [uS/cm]	TDS
M1	19.9	18.2	6.5	101.0	280.0	275.0	369.0	335.0
	19.8	18.4	6.4	96.0	268.0	262.0	354.0	322.0
	19.9	18.4	6.4	93.0	263.0	257.0	348.0	317.0
	19.8	18.3	6.4	98.0	274.0	368.0	361.0	329.0
M2	19.0	18.7	5.5	238.0	232.0	321.0	292.0	584.0
	19.0	19.6	5.5	238.0	232.0	319.0	290.0	581.5
	19.0	19.9	5.5	236.0	230.0	318.0	289.0	579.0
	18.9	18.1	5.4	240.0	234.0	322.0	293.0	587.0
M3	21.3	21.7	6.7	230.0	98.0	390.0	310.0	423.0
	21.4	21.6	6.8	231.0	97.0	393.0	308.0	420.0
	21.4	19.7	6.8	230.0	96.0	391.0	309.0	420.0
	21.4	20.5	6.8	229.0	97.0	390.0	310.0	421.0

The soil moisture sensor primarily responds to the clay content within the soil, which means that we expect similar values at various depths. Importantly, the calibration process does not significantly alter the observed pattern of soil moisture variation with depth. Recalibration does not affect the data model, resulting in soil wetting varying with the measurement depth in the soil profile in response to the contribution of meteorological conditions (amount of rain and high temperatures).

In this research, the correlation between the values obtained for the three soil types was determined using Pearson's correlation coefficient. The following generic formula was employed to calculate the correlation coefficient between two variables, x and y:

$$r_{xy} = \frac{\sum_i (x_i - \overline{x}) \cdot (y_i - \overline{y})}{\sqrt{\sum_i (x_i - \overline{x})^2 \cdot \sum_i (y_i - \overline{y})^2}} \quad (2)$$

n—sample size

x—individual values of the variable x

y—individual values of the variable y

$\overline{x}$—arithmetic mean of all x values
$\overline{y}$—arithmetic mean of all y values

Applying Colton's rules (stated in 1974):

*—A correlation coefficient from 0.25 to 0.50 (or from −0.25 to −0.50) means a weak correlation (acceptable degree of association).
**—A correlation coefficient from 0.50 to 0.75 (or from −0.50 to −0.75) means a moderate to good correlation.
***—A correlation coefficient greater than 0.75 (or less than −0.75) means a strong correlation (very good degree of association).

Limits of the Pearson coefficient:

$$-1 < r_{xy} < +1 \quad (3)$$

Thus, as the value of the Pearson correlation coefficient approaches 1 (in absolute value), the "intensity" of the linear relationship between the two variables will be higher.

The experimental results demonstrated a strong correlation between NPK values and soil moisture. This relationship is evident in Figure 6, which depicts a clear positive linear correlation between moisture levels and key soil nutrients. Notably, soil type M3 exhibited a particularly strong positive linear correlation between these parameters.

Table 5. Correlation of values for soil M1.

	T [°C]	M [%rH]	pH	N [mg/kg]	P [mg/kg]	K [mg/kg]	CE [uS/cm]	TDS
T [°C]	1							
M [%rH]	−0.938 ***	1						
pH	0.256 **	−0.429 **	1					
N [mg/kg]	−0.989 ***	0.916 ***	−0.222 *	1				
P [mg/kg]	−0.990 ***	0.927 ***	−0.238 *	0.999 ***	1			
K [mg/kg]	−0.972 ***	0.893 ***	−0.279 **	0.977 ***	0.977 ***	1		
CE [uS/cm]	−0.988 ***	0.915 ***	−0.000	0.999 ***	0.999 ***	0.978 ***	1	
TDS	−0.988 ***	0.914 ***	−0.221 *	0.999 ***	0.999 ***	0.978 ***	0.999 ***	1

*—A weak correlation; **—A good correlation; ***—A strong correlation.

Table 6. Correlation of values for soil M2.

	T [°C]	M [%rH]	pH	N [mg/kg]	P [mg/kg]	K [mg/kg]	CE [uS/cm]	TDS
T [°C]	1							
M [%rH]	−0.711 **	1						
pH	0.993 ***	−0.691 **	1					
N [mg/kg]	−0.997 ***	0.722 **	−0.996 ***	1				
P [mg/kg]	−0.997 ***	0.722 **	−0.996 ***	0.999 ***	1			
K [mg/kg]	−0.997 ***	0.723 **	−0.996 ***	0.999 ***	0.999 ***	1		
CE [uS/cm]	−0.997 ***	0.711 **	−0.996 ***	0.999 ***	0.999 ***	0.999 ***	1	
TDS	−0.997 ***	0.721 **	−0.996 ***	0.999 ***	0.999 ***	0.999 ***	0.999 ***	1

—A good correlation; *—A strong correlation.

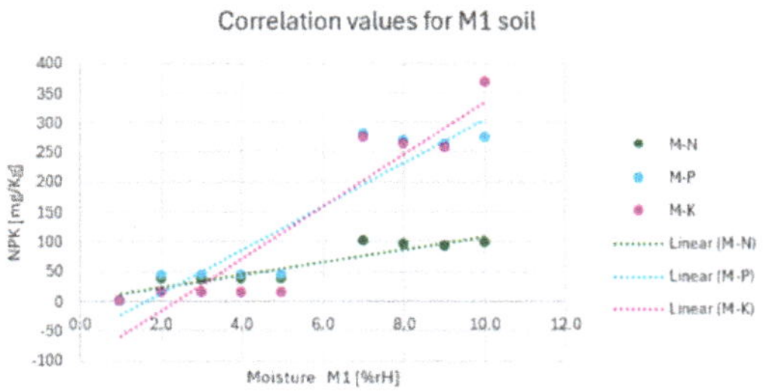

(a)

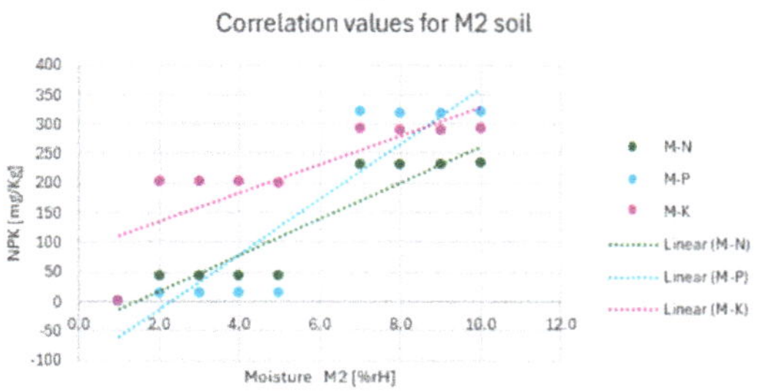

(b)

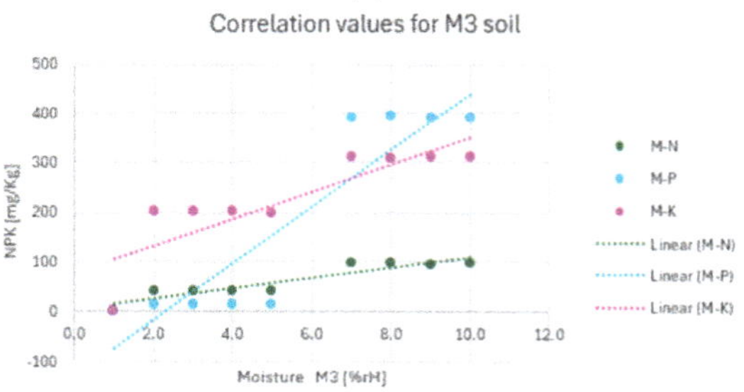

(c)

Figure 6. (**a**) M1 soil correlation values according Table 5, (**b**) M2 soil correlation values according Table 6, (**c**) M3 soil correlation values according Table 7.

Table 7. Correlation of values for soil M3.

	T [°C]	M [%rH]	pH	N [mg/kg]	P [mg/kg]	K [mg/kg]	CE [uS/cm]	TDS
T [°C]	1							
M [%rH]	0.728 **	1						
pH	0.813 ***	0.851 ***	1					
N [mg/kg]	0.833 ***	0.927 ***	0.961 ***	1				
P [mg/kg]	0.832 ***	0.932 ***	0.958 ***	0.999 ***	1			
K [mg/kg]	0.834 ***	0.927 ***	0.961 ***	0.999 ***	0.999 ***	1		
CE [uS/cm]	0.832 ***	0.926 ***	0.959 ***	0.999 ***	0.999 ***	0.999 ***	1	
TDS	0.832 ***	0.928 ***	0.959 ***	0.999 ***	0.999 ***	0.999 ***	0.999 ***	1

—A good correlation; *—A strong correlation.

The correlation values for M1, M2, and M3 soils are presented in Tables 5–7.

There is a general trend for macronutrients (N, P, K) to increase in concentration with increasing soil moisture, as is illustrated in Figure 6. In other words, the wetter the soil, the higher the nutrient concentration tends to be.

Strength of correlation:

N–M: The correlation between nitrogen and moisture appears to be moderate, with a linear increase in nitrogen concentration with increasing moisture.

P–M: The correlation between phosphorus and moisture is stronger than that between nitrogen and moisture, with a more pronounced increase in phosphorus concentration with increasing moisture.

K–M: The correlation between potassium and moisture is the strongest of the three, with an almost linear and consistent increase in potassium concentration with increasing moisture.

Data dispersion: The data for each nutrient show some dispersion around the trend line, indicating that factors other than moisture may influence the nutrient concentration in the soil.

Based on this graph, we can conclude that there is a positive relationship between M3 soil moisture content and NPK nutrient concentration. However, the strength of this relationship varies by nutrient, being strongest for potassium and weakest for nitrogen.

6. Discussion

This research has demonstrated the technology and processes required to enhance our understanding of soil quality through the implementation of a soil quality measurement network at various depths. Real-time monitoring of soil characteristics offers significant advantages in land management. By creating spatio-temporal maps based on data collected from a network of measurement points across different geographical areas, we can gain a clear and visual understanding of the evolving state of soil aridity and even the risk of desertification within these regions.

The future implementation of IoT-SOL technology for widespread soil quality monitoring across various geographical locations will enable more accurate predictions of areas exhibiting desertification tendencies.

This research will furnish critical insights into soil health, encompassing the identification of nutrient deficiencies and the presence of potentially harmful contaminants. It will facilitate the continuous monitoring of diurnal, weekly, monthly, and annual fluctuations in soil conditions. The compact design enables facile insertion into diverse substrates and soil types, permitting expeditious assessments. This, in turn, optimizes agricultural practices and empowers informed decision making to mitigate the risk of land desertification.

The resulting data can be leveraged to optimize agricultural operations, identify emerging trends, and even inform preliminary weather forecasts, ultimately maximizing yield and enhancing soil quality. The integration of IoT technologies within agriculture is widely recognized as Smart Agriculture or Precision Farming. Within this framework, the present advanced autonomous system for monitoring soil parameters emerges as a pivotal component for precision decision making.

By incorporating location-specific forecasts into desertification risk models, it becomes possible to generate more accurate predictions of future trends. These predictions can be further refined by incorporating seasonally adjusted forecasts of water availability and nutrient content within the soil profile.

7. Conclusions

This research has established foundational procedures for calibrating smart sensors and conducting valid soil quality measurements. The current system serves as a crucial initial step, representing a proof-of-concept laboratory model for the future development of an autonomous system IoT-SOL pilot station for in situ soil quality monitoring. As the first iterative system, this research focuses on the measurement and calibration of smart sensors.

Recalibration of sensors is conducted using a known soil type, emphasizing the importance of practical applicability within our research context. This necessitates rigorous testing on various known substrates. Future work will involve expanding these investigations to encompass different soil types and depths, ultimately enabling predictions of soil aridity levels.

Assessing soil quality is an evolving field intricately linked to the advancement of digital mapping and cartographic techniques, particularly in regions susceptible to desertification. Continued research in soil monitoring is crucial, necessitating the development of a long-term vision and a roadmap for technological advancements to ensure comprehensive data acquisition and analysis.

By deploying this technology across multiple geographical areas, it becomes possible to significantly enhance the efficiency of soil analysis. This enables the generation of comprehensive maps delineating regions at risk of desertification, facilitating early predictions, and enabling the implementation of targeted interventions to mitigate degradation. Ultimately, this approach contributes to expanding arable land and fostering sustainable soil management practices.

The advantages of an autonomous, multisensory soil monitoring system for assessing soil characteristics include:

Real-time data acquisition: Enables continuous and immediate monitoring of soil properties.

- Multi-channel measurement capability: Allows for simultaneous measurement of various soil parameters, providing a comprehensive understanding of soil conditions.
- Flexible data collection frequency: Permits adjustment of data collection intervals to optimize data acquisition while minimizing energy consumption.
- Wireless data transmission: Facilitates efficient and convenient data transfer through the local Wi-Fi network.
- Data export and reporting capabilities: Enables easy access, analysis, and dissemination of collected data.

This data-driven approach empowers informed decision making, optimizing the utilization of natural resources such as water and fertilizers. This, in turn, enhances crop productivity and sustainability while promoting environmentally sound agricultural practices. Crucially, this autonomous multi-sensor system for soil parameter monitoring serves as a valuable tool for identifying areas with a heightened risk of land degradation and desertification. The synergistic interplay of these advantages collectively contributes to environmental preservation.

Author Contributions: Conceptualization, B.V.-D.; methodology, I.S.-E.; software, P.-N.A.; validation, B.V.-D., I.S.-E. and P.-N.A.; formal analysis, I.S.-E.; investigation, B.V.-D.; resources, B.V.-D.; data curation, P.-N.A.; writing—original draft preparation, B.V.-D. and P.-N.A.; writing—review and editing, I.S.-E.; visualization, B.V.-D.; supervision, P.-N.A.; validated the obtained results and contributed in writing the final manuscript, B.V.-D. and P.-N.A.; implemented system and performed several real experiments, B.V.-D. and P.-N.A. All authors have read and agreed to the published version of the manuscript.

Funding: This research was funded by Ministry of Research, Innovation and Digitization, grant number PN 23 43 05 02 and The grant number PN 23 43 05 02, has funded the publication fees for this manuscript.

Institutional Review Board Statement: Not applicable.

Informed Consent Statement: Not applicable.

Data Availability Statement: No new data were created or analyzed in this study. Data sharing is not applicable to this article.

Conflicts of Interest: The authors declare no conflict of interest.

References

1. Popescu, D.; Stoican, F.; Stamatescu, G.; Ichim, L.; Dragana, C. Advanced UAV–WSN System for Intelligent Monitoring in Precision Agriculture. *Sensors* **2020**, *20*, 817. [CrossRef] [PubMed]
2. Singh, H.; Halder, N.; Singh, B.; Singh, J.; Sharma, S.; Shacham-Diamand, Y. Smart Farming Revolution: Portable and Real-Time Soil Nitrogen and Phosphorus Monitoring for Sustainable Agriculture. *Sensors* **2023**, *23*, 5914. [CrossRef] [PubMed]
3. Padmavathi, R.; Manikandan, M.; Sumithra, M.G.; Dhivyasri, G.; Inbanathan, F.P.N. Impact of Advanced Sensing Technologies in Agriculture with Soil, Crop, Climate and Farmland-Based Approaches Using Internet of Things. In *Computational Intelligence in Internet of Agricultural Things*; Studies in Computational Intelligence; Sumithra, M.G., Sathyamoorthy, M., Manikandan, M., Dhanaraj, R.K., Ouaissa, M., Eds.; Springer: Cham, Switzerland, 2024; Volume 1170. [CrossRef]
4. Coccia, M.; Roshani, S.; Mosleh, M. Scientific Developments and New Technological Trajectories in Sensor Research. *Sensors* **2021**, *21*, 7803. [CrossRef] [PubMed]
5. Hartono, R.; Yoeseph, N.M.; Purnomo, F.A.; Safi'Ie, M.A.; Bawono, S.A.T. Portable internet of things-based soil nutrients monitoring for precision and efficient smart farming. *Bull. Electr. Eng. Inform.* **2024**, *13*, 3326–3333. [CrossRef]
6. Diaconu, A.; Paraschiv, A.N.; Bîrsoghe, C.; Nanu, Ş.; Coteț, G.; Băjenaru, M.F. Quality characteristics of some cultivars of sweet potato grown on the sandy soils from the south of Oltenia. In Proceedings of the SHS Acta Horticulturae 1391: IX South-Eastern Europe Symposium on Vegetables and Potatoes, Bucharest, Romania, 9 September 2023. [CrossRef]
7. Tianyi, H.; Badea, F.; Maohua, X.; Shanhu, Z.; Badea, S.-I.; Badea, C.-R. Obstacle avoidance method for electric tractor based on improved dynamic window approach with priority of energy consumption. *INMATEH Agric. Eng.* **2023**, *70*, 309–319. [CrossRef]
8. Davidescu, D.; Davidescu, V.; Lacatusu, R. *Microelements in Agriculture*; Editura Academiei RSR: Bucharest, Romania, 1988.
9. Chiriță, A.P.; Baciu, I.M.; Cristescu, C.; Dumitrescu, L. Trends and solutions in mechanized soil sampling for mapping of agricultural land. In Proceedings of the International Symposium ISB-INMA-TEH, Agricultural and Mechanical Engineering, Bucharest, Romania, 31 October–1 November 2019; pp. 741–748.
10. Popescu, V.-S.; Popescu, I.-M. Impact of UV post processing on simple 3D printed parts using masked stereolithography. *Int. J. Mechatron. Appl. Mech.* **2024**, *18*, 86–92. [CrossRef]
11. Malone, B.; Glover, M.; Brown, S.; Searle, R.; Biggins, D.; Sharman, C. An experiential account with recommendations for the design, installation, operation and maintenance of a farm-scale soil moisture sensing and mapping system. *Soil Res.* **2024**, *62*, SR24004. [CrossRef]
12. Coccia, M. Sources of technological innovation: Radical and incremental innovation problem-driven to support competitive advantage of firms. *Technol. Anal. Strat. Manag.* **2016**, *29*, 1048–1061. [CrossRef]
13. Ribeiro, V.; Holanda, R.; Ramos, A.; Rodrigues, J.J.P.C. Enhancing Key Management in LoRaWAN with Permissioned Blockchain. *Sensors* **2020**, *20*, 3068. [CrossRef] [PubMed]
14. Coccia, M.; Roshani, S.; Mosleh, M. Evolution of Sensor Research for Clarifying the Dynamics and Properties of Future Directions. *Sensors* **2022**, *22*, 9419. [CrossRef] [PubMed] [PubMed Central]
15. Badea, S.I.; Constantin, A.; Badea, C.R.; Badea, F. Electronic air-operated apparatus for tighness measurement and detection used in automotive industry. *Int. J. Mechatron. Appl. Mech.* **2022**, *12*, 177–181. [CrossRef]
16. Stanislav, S. *PEDOLOGY (Soil Science: Genesis, Properties, Classification, Geography)*; Course of Lectures "Alecu Russo" State University of Bălti; Faculty of Natural Sciences and Agroecology: Bălți, Moldova, 2010.
17. Chetti, M.B.; Ashalatha, K.V.; Dolli, S.S. *Needs and Challenges of Smart Agriculture and Entrepreneurship Education—A Case Study by the University of Agricultural Sciences, Dharwad, Karnataka, India. Digital Transformation of Education and Learning—Past, Present and Future. OCCE 2021. Book IFIP Advances in Information and Communication Technology*; Springer: Cham, Switzerland, 2022; Volume 642. [CrossRef]
18. Udrea, I.; Petrache, S.; Ionascu, G.; Alionte, C.G.; Ionut Gheorghe, V.; Apostolescu, T.C.; Adrian Cartal, L. Optimizing the Placement of Indoor Thermal Climate Sensors of an Iot Solution. In Proceedings of the 12th International Conference on Electronics, Computers and Artificial Intelligence, ECAI 2020, Bucharest, Romania, 25–27 June 2020. [CrossRef]

19. Munteanu, I.S.; Ungureanu, L.M.; Caraiman, C.C.; Crisan, R.G.; Niculae, E.; Badea, S. Modelling and Simulation of Some Mechatronics Assembly Realized on Arduino Uno Board, Through the Tinkercad Application. In *International Conference on Reliable Systems Engineering;* Lecture Notes in Networks and Systems; Springer: Cham, Switzerland, 2023; Volume 762, pp. 374–384. [CrossRef]
20. Cioboata, D.; Abalaru, A.; Stanciu, D.; Logofatu, C.; Aiordachioaie, D. Advanced measurement systems for vibration signals. In Proceedings of the 5th International Symposium on Electrical and Electronics Engineering (ISEEE), Galati, Romania, 20–22 October 2017; pp. 1–6. [CrossRef]
21. Agricultural-Sensors. Available online: https://www.niubol.com/Agricultural-sensor/8-in-1-Soil-Integrated-Sensor.html (accessed on 10 April 2024).
22. Costache, A.; Băran, N.; Pătulea, A.S. A new solution for the oxygenation of stationary waters. *Environ. Eng. Manag. J.* **2017**, *16*, 25–30. [CrossRef]
23. Ovanisof, A.; Popa, C.; Costache, A.; Ion, G.C. Analysis of the dynamic interaction of an agricultural machine with the environment. *Int. Multidiscip. Sci. GeoConf. Surv. Geol. Min. Ecol. Manag. SGEM* **2018**, *18*, 57–64. [CrossRef]
24. Stanciu, D.; Popescu, V.; Logofătu, C. Design of an active thermal element for a solar thermal energy measurement system by simulating heat transfer processes using the finite element method. *Int. J. Mechatron. Appl. Mech.* **2023**, *13*, 119–127. [CrossRef]
25. Ni, W.; Wang, T.; Wu, Y.; Liu, X.; Li, Z.; Yang, R.; Zhang, K.; Yang, J.; Zeng, M.; Hu, N.; et al. Multi-task deep learning model for quantitative volatile organic compounds analysis by feature fusion of electronic nose sensing. *Sens. Actuators B Chem.* **2024**, *417*, 136206. [CrossRef]
26. Chu, T.; Zhou, Z.; Tian, P.; Yu, T.; Lian, C.; Zhang, B.; Xuan, F.-Z. Nanofluidic sensing inspired by the anomalous water dynamics in electrical angstrom-scale channels. *Nat. Commun.* **2024**, *15*, 7329. [CrossRef] [PubMed]
27. Zaini, M.F.M.; Hassan, M.K.; Saad, F.S.; Sudin, S.; Basah, S.N.; Basaruddin, K.S.; Safar, M.J. An IoT-Based System to Monitor Soil Parameter of Harumanis Tree. In *Intelligent Manufacturing and Mechatronics. SympoSIMM 2023. Lecture Notes in Mechanical Engineering;* Hamidon, R., Bahari, M.S., Sah, J.M., Zainal Abidin, Z., Eds.; Springer: Singapore, 2024. [CrossRef]

technologies

MDPI

Article

The Impact of Autonomous Vehicle Accidents on Public Sentiment: A Decadal Analysis of Twitter Discourse Using roBERTa

Romy Sauvayre [1,2,*], Jessica S. M. Gable [1], Adam Aalah [1], Melvin Fernandes Novo [2], Maxime Dehondt [2] and Cédric Chauvière [2,3]

1 Laboratoire de Psychologie Sociale et Cognitive, Université Clermont Auvergne, Centre National de la Recherche Scientifique, 63000 Clermont-Ferrand, France; jessica.gable@uca.fr (J.S.M.G.)
2 Clermont Auvergne INP, Centre National de la Recherche Scientifique, LAPSCO, Université Clermont Auvergne, 63000 Clermont-Ferrand, France; m.fnovo@outlook.fr (M.F.N.); maxime.dehondt@protonmail.com (M.D.); cedric.chauviere@uca.fr (C.C.)
3 Laboratoire de Mathématiques Blaise Pascal, Université Clermont Auvergne, Centre National de la Recherche Scientifique, 63000 Clermont-Ferrand, France
* Correspondence: romy.sauvayre@uca.fr

Abstract: In the field of autonomous vehicle (AV) acceptance and opinion studies, questionnaires are widely used. Additionally, AV experiments and driving simulations are utilized. However, few AV studies have investigated social media, and fewer studies have analyzed the impact of AV crashes on public opinion, often relying on limited social media datasets. This study aims to address this gap by exploring a comprehensive dataset of six million tweets posted over a decade (2012–2021), and neural networks, sentiment analysis and knowledge graphs are applied. The results reveal that tweets predominantly convey negative sentiment (40.86%) rather than positive (32.52%) or neutral (26.62%) sentiment. A binary segmentation algorithm was used to distinguish an initial positive sentiment period (January 2012–May 2016) followed by a negative period (June 2016–December 2021), which was initiated by a fatal Tesla accident and reinforced by a pedestrian killed by an Uber AV. The sentiment polarity exhibited in the posted tweets was statistically significant (U = 24,914,037,786; p value < 0.001). The timeline analysis revealed that the negative sentiment period was initiated by fatal accidents involving a Tesla AV driver and a pedestrian hit by an Uber AV, which was amplified by the mainstream media.

Keywords: autonomous vehicle; accident; Twitter; social media; acceptability; natural language processing; sentiment analysis; text mining

1. Introduction

Social media has become a major communication tool for widely sharing opinions [1] across countries, transforming the Web into a dynamic information exchange arena [2]. For example, platforms such as Twitter (now known as "X" since 23 July 2023) have facilitated unity around important social issues. The #MeToo movement is a well-recognized example [3]. However, this widespread dissemination has raised concerns regarding the infodemic problem of false information sharing [4].

Social media has opened a potentially valuable Pandora's box for the research community. Using deep learning and natural language processing, millions of tweets can be scrutinized and explained. For this particular task, sentiment analysis is widely employed in various research areas, such as research on vaccine hesitancy [5], monkeypox outbreaks [6], Asperger syndrome [7], and climate change [8].

In the field of autonomous vehicle (AV) acceptance and opinion studies, questionnaires are widely used methodologies, and include sociodemographic variables, which are used to define the level of AV acceptance across sex, income, and social class, for example [9–12]. Additionally, AV experiments [13,14] and driving simulations [15] have also been utilized. However, some rare AV studies have investigated social media platforms such as Twitter [1], TikTok [16], and YouTube [17]. Even fewer studies have analyzed the impact of AV crashes on public opinion [16,18,19], often relying on limited social media datasets. For example, Jefferson and McDonald [19] analyzed 11,164 tweets over a six-day period, whereas Jing et al. [16] scrutinized 16,635 comments extracted from TikTok and 9879 comments from Sina Weibo, a Chinese social media platform.

This study aims to address this gap by exploring a comprehensive dataset of six million tweets posted over a decade using sentiment and text content analysis tools. These datasets enable a thorough investigation of sentiment to comprehensively assess the impact of technological uncertainty, particularly when human lives are at risk.

2. Methods

The methodological stages of the study are summarized in Figure 1, and the corresponding explanations, from data collection to data analysis, are presented in the following subsections.

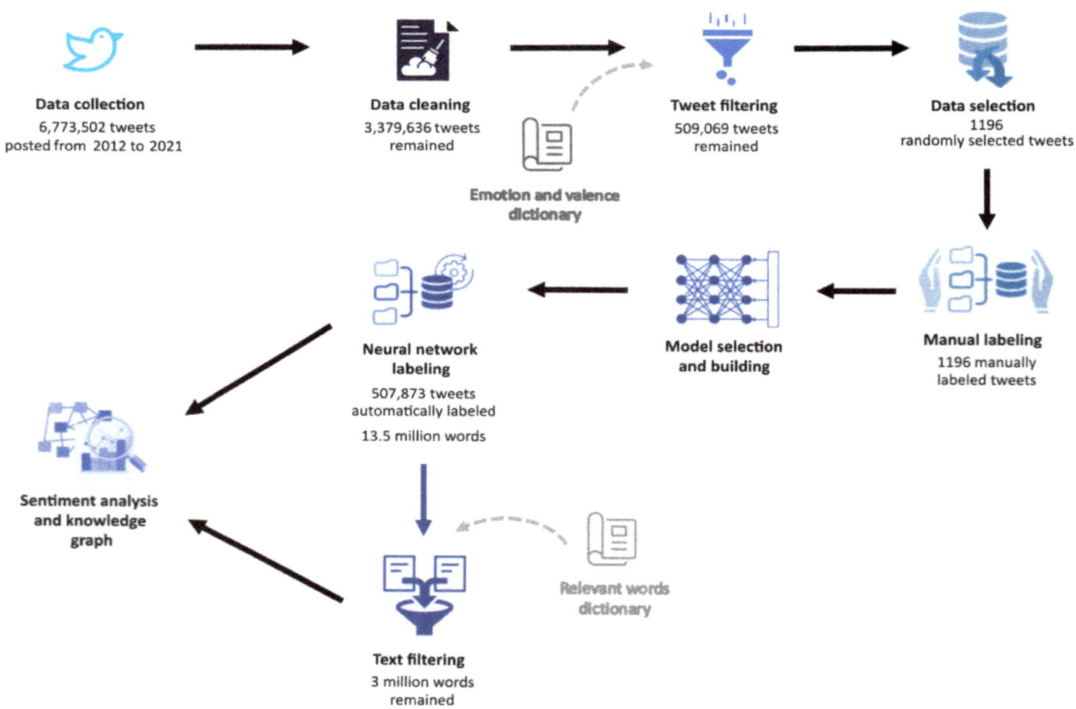

Figure 1. Flowchart of the methodological stages.

2.1. Data Collection

English messages posted on Twitter (tweets) discussing AVs between 1 January 2012 and 31 December 2021 were collected using API V2 Academic Research, utilizing pertinent keywords related to AVs (see Supplementary Material S1). A total of 6,773,504 tweets were subsequently extracted and saved in the MongoDB database.

2.2. Data Preprocessing

As the aim of this study is to analyze sentiment evolution on Twitter, the dataset was filtered using a specific emotion and valence dictionary (see Supplementary Material S2), and only tweets containing at least one emotional or valence word were retained. After removing duplicates, bot users and tweets with URLs, 3,379,636 messages were filtered to obtain a total of 509,069 tweets. A final cleaning was conducted to remove special characters (&gt, #, @, –, and |).

2.3. Data Labeling

Approximately 1200 tweets were randomly selected from the filtered final dataset and were assessed by two experienced individuals. Three labels were assigned to obtain a multiclass classification set (see Supplementary Material S3):

(0) "Negative" for tweets containing negative sentiments, such as distrust toward AVs or concerns about job losses;

(1) "Neutral" for tweets conveying neutral or informative content, such as commercial advertisements from car manufacturers, information about AV events, or informative statements without valency or an emotional perspective;

(2) "Positive" for tweets expressing favorable sentiments toward AVs, such as willingness to use them.

Notably, owing to the European General Data Protection Regulation (GDPR) [20], we are unable to provide examples of the tweets extracted from the dataset.

2.4. Artificial Neural Network Labeling

The pretrained "Twitter-roBERTa-base for Sentiment Analysis" model was selected and obtained from Huggingface [21] for training with multiclass labeling. This model was trained on approximately 58 million English tweets without URLs and fine-tuned specifically for sentiment analysis [22]. The manual labels were used for training, validation, and testing. The model achieved an accuracy of 0.69 and an F1-score of 0.69 for the test dataset. The 507,873 remaining unlabeled tweets were subsequently analyzed and automatically labeled using the trained RoBERTa model.

2.5. Data Analysis

Two types of analyses were conducted: (1) sentiment analysis with the automated labels obtained with the neural network model and (2) text mining analysis focusing on the content. To prepare the text, a dictionary of relevant words (see Supplementary Material S4), including misspellings, was compiled to filter the 13.53 million words (including 692,950 unique words). After rectifying misspellings and performing filtering, 3.04 million words (with 7699 unique words) were retained for text analysis and the construction of knowledge graphs. Note that mentions and hashtags were kept in the text as informative data for the purpose of the study. The knowledge graphs were created using Gephi 0.10 software. The two types of analyses were conducted using Jupyter Notebook and several Python libraries (Pandas, NumPy, Pyreadstat, Seaborn, Matplotlib, NLTK, re, Scikit-learn, Wordcloud, SpaCy, Stanza, SciPy, Ruptures, and NetworkX) for the text mining tasks (stemming, lemmatization, counting, vectorization, and text visualization), statistical analysis, text filtering, and graph construction.

3. Results

3.1. Tweet Count

The 507,873 analyzed tweets were posted by 299,468 unique users (i.e., tweeters) and contributed to 432,467 unique conversations. The most influential tweet received 45,927 likes and 8286 retweets. Over the studied decade (2012–2021), an average of 4232 tweets were posted per month, with a monthly range of 299 to 17,090 (Figure 2).

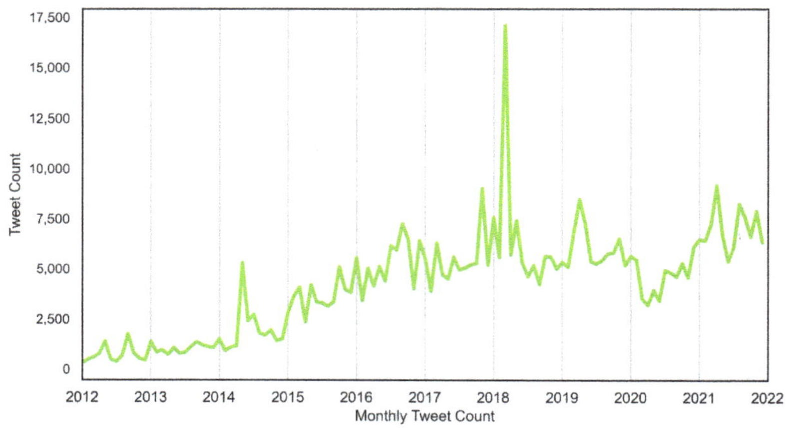

Figure 2. Monthly tweet counts from 1 January 2012 to 31 December 2021 (N = 507,873).

3.2. Sentiment Analysis

Most of the tweets from the studied decade were negative (40.86%) (Table 1). Negative tweets are associated with 'problem', 'kill', 'death', 'crash', 'technology', 'Tesla' or 'Google'. Conversely, positive tweets are associated with 'hope', 'wait', 'future', 'safe', 'love', 'great' and 'Tesla'.

Table 1. Sentiment of analyzed tweets.

Sentiment	Number of Tweets	%
Negative	207,508	40.86%
Positive	165,157	32.52%
Neutral	135,208	26.62%

A sentiment polarity analysis was conducted to evaluate the fluctuations in public sentiment toward AVs over time (Figure 3). The analysis employed a scale ranging from −1 for negative sentiment to +1 for positive sentiment. To identify significant shifts in public opinion, a binary segmentation algorithm was applied to the time-series data using the Ruptures Python library. The binary segmentation algorithm [23] is a multiple change point search method [24] that serves as an approximation with "an O (n log n) computational, where n is the number of data points" [25]. This algorithm operates by recursively partitioning the data into segments and identifying points where significant changes occur in the statistical properties of the data [24] (see Supplemental Material S5 for further methodological details). This methodological approach facilitated the detection of critical junctures in public sentiment regarding AV technology.

Two periods of sentiment are evident in the data: an initial positive period from 1 January 2012 to 22 June 2016, and a subsequent negative period from 23 June 2016 to 31 December 2021. Each period comprises two subperiods, labeled A and B, characterized by a decreasing average sentiment score (Figure 4).

During the first period, the monthly average sentiment polarity was positive (sentiment score = 0.046; N = 114,140 tweets). However, sentiment shifted toward a more negative trajectory during the second period, with the monthly average sentiment polarity decreasing to −0.121 (N = 393,733 tweets) (see Supplementary Material S6).

A Mann-Whitney U test indicated a statistically significant difference in sentiment polarity between the two periods (U = 24,914,037,786; p value < 0.001), and a Kruskal-Wallis H test indicated the same results for the four sentiment periods (H = 4755.07; p value < 0.001) (Figure 4).

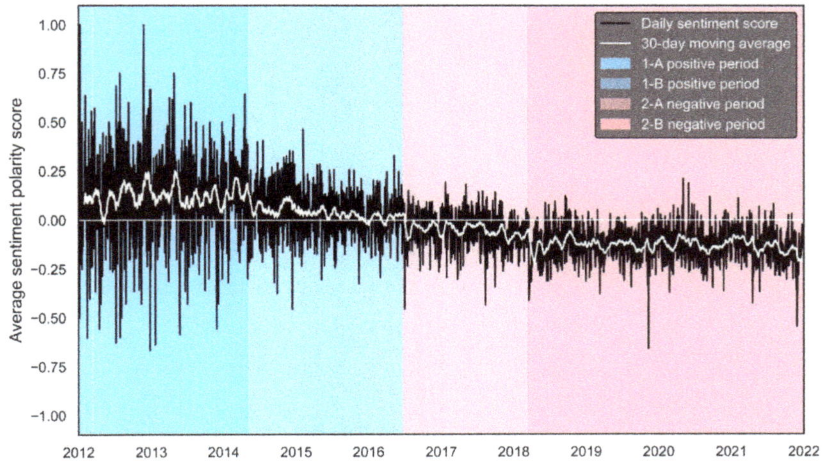

Figure 3. Daily average sentiment polarity score per tweet and monthly moving average from January 2012 to December 2021, with change point dates identified by the binary segmentation algorithm (binseg), with the l2-norm penalty model (model = "l2").

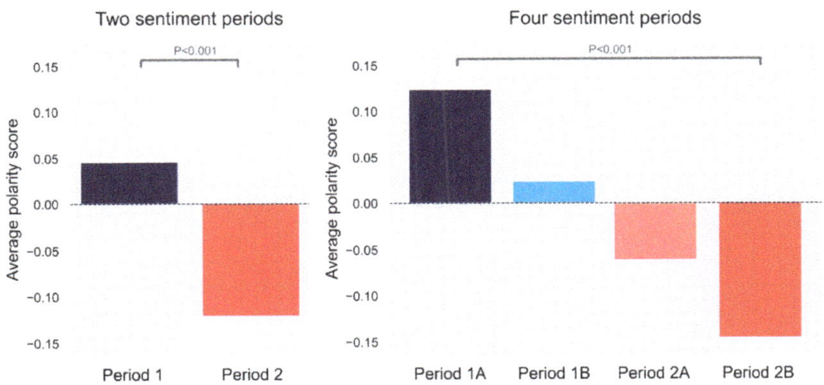

Figure 4. Average polarity scores and p values as a function of the sentiment period.

3.3. Text Mining

To better understand the content exchanged and discussions among tweeters, a text mining analysis of the relevant selected words was conducted. The term frequency-inverse document frequency (TF-IDF) score of the most important terms in the filtered dataset indicated that different terms were predominant in the two periods (Figure 5). 'Google' was more likely to be mentioned in the first period than in the second period. Conversely, 'Tesla' was most cited in the second period (see Supplementary Material S7 and S8). The term 'kill' was the first negative word in the top 20 most popular terms in the second period.

Some words were common in both periods, such as 'technology', 'traffic', 'life', 'accident', 'Uber', and 'Google'. Others were specific to the first period, such as 'love', 'hope', 'today', and 'interesting'. In contrast, the second period had new words such as 'Tesla', 'Tesla autopilot', 'artificial intelligence', 'kill', and 'robot'. This TF-IDF analysis identifies the main words used during conversation about AVs and provides insight into how negative terms influence period 2. Tesla, prominent in the second period, records a polarity score of −0.18, whereas Google, also prominent in the first period, achieves a positive score of 0.02 (see Supplementary Material S6). Common terms across both periods, such as 'technology', are mentioned in positive tweets during the first period (0.07) and in negative tweets during the second period (−0.09).

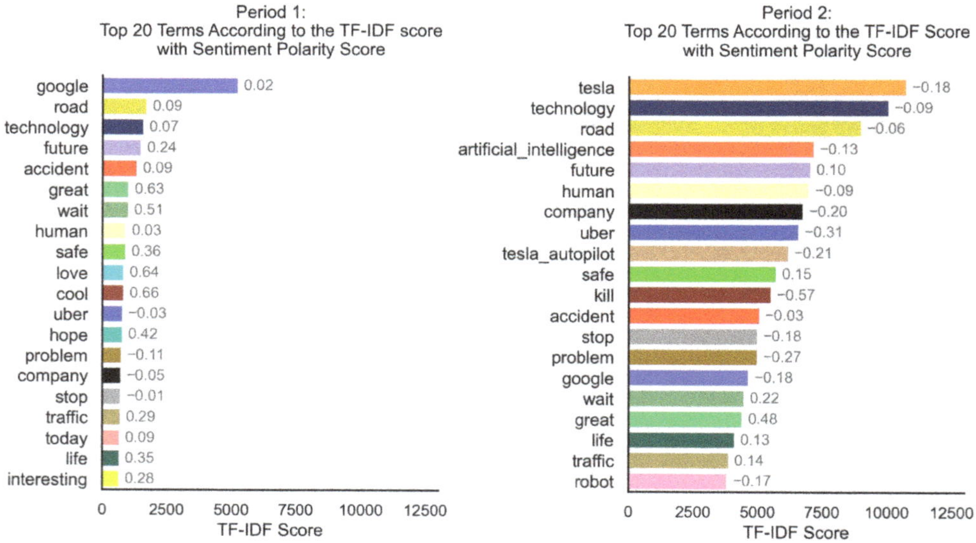

Figure 5. Top 20 terms according to the TF-IDF score and sentiment polarity score by period (period 1: positive—2012–2016; period 2: negative—2016–2021).

3.4. Knowledge Graphs

To deeply explore the connections between these words, knowledge graphs [26] were constructed. The knowledge graph facilitates this objective by employing nodes, representing words, and edges, which denote the relationships between them, to effectively capture semantic associations. Tweets were tokenized into individual words, and edges were established between the words within each tweet. Figure 6 shows that the content varied across the two sentiment periods.

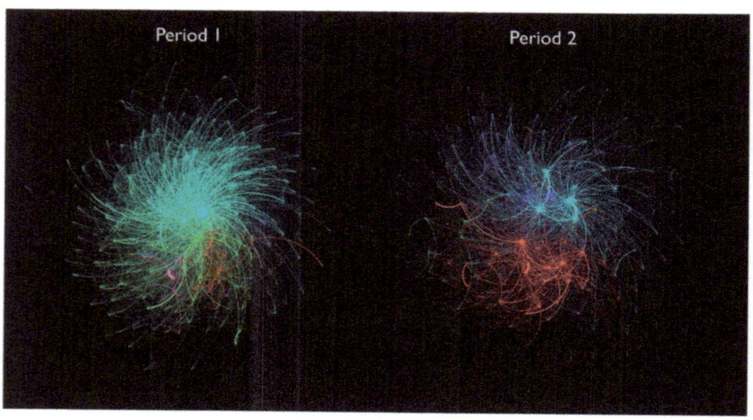

Figure 6. Knowledge graphs for sentiment periods (period 1: positive—2012–2016; period 2: negative—2016–2021). Visualization in Gephi using the Force Atlas 2 algorithm; the node size corresponds to the degree of weighting.

During the first positive period, the conversations revolved around the Google company, accompanied by optimism stemming from advancements in smart AV technology (turquoise class). AVs were anticipated to enhance road safety, facilitate smooth traffic flow (green class), and reduce accidents caused by human drivers (red class), ultimately saving lives (pink class).

In contrast, the second negative period was characterized by discussions focused on companies such as Tesla and Uber, as well as artificial intelligence embedded in AV technology (turquoise class). However, this optimism was overshadowed by concerns surrounding pedestrian and driver fatalities involving Tesla and Uber AVs (red class). Additionally, apprehensions regarding job losses resulting from the automation of human tasks were highlighted, as indicated in the smaller orange segment of the graph.

3.5. Turning Point Events

The discussion about AVs on Twitter initially began with a high level of positive sentiment reflecting hope regarding preserving lives on the road and smart technology development led by Google (Figure 7).

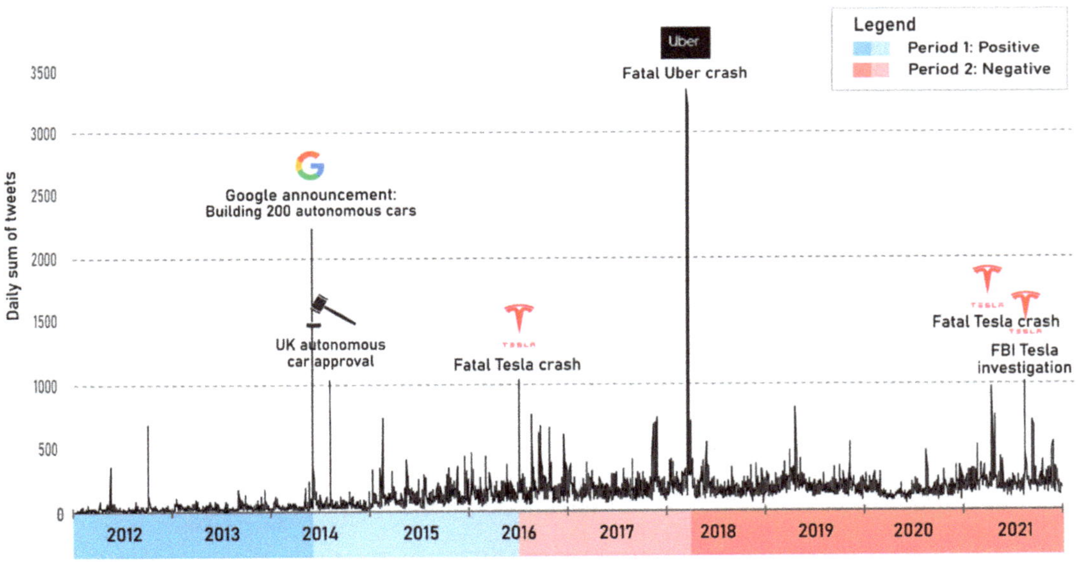

Figure 7. Daily AV tweet timelines per sentiment period, annotated with events corresponding to the days with the most tweets.

The first notable increase in tweet activity coincided with the approval of AV laws in Nevada and California in 2012, which occurred in February and September, respectively. A second wave of tweeting occurred in May 2014 when Google announced its plan to launch 200 AVs on the roads. Following this announcement, the average sentiment polarity decreased by approximately 80.65% (from 0.124 to 0.024). However, the most significant impact occurred after the first fatal accident involving the driver of a Tesla car equipped with an autopilot function in the United States on 7 May 2016. The decline in emotional polarity then reached 358.33% (from 0.024 to −0.062) during this first part of the negative period, which spans from 2016 to 2018. Finally, an accident involving a pedestrian killed by an Uber AV on 18 March 2018 generated a large surge of tweets, marking the onset of the most negative sentiment period of the decade regarding Twitter users' opinions about AVs. The sentiment polarity reached −0.147, representing a decrease of 137.10% (from −0.062 to −0.147).

4. Discussion

This study explores the sentiment content of tweets related to AVs over the past decade (2012–2021). The findings reveal that tweets predominantly convey negative sentiment (40.86%) rather than positive (32.52%) or neutral sentiment (26.62%), which is consistent with previous research [18,27]. Sentiment polarity analysis was used to differentiate two sentiment periods: an initial positive period from January 2012 to May 2016 and a subsequent negative period from June 2016 to December 2021. The sentiment polarity exhibited in the posted tweets is statistically significant (U = 24,914,037,786; p value < 0.001).

A timeline analysis of events revealed that the negative sentiment subperiods were initiated by fatal accidents involving a Tesla AV driver and a pedestrian hit by an Uber AV. The sentiment analysis revealed that these specific fatal accidents had an impact on the opinions of Twitter users. However, previous AV accidents did not have such an effect on opinion. For example, 11 minor accidents in November 2015, the first Tesla accident in China in January 2016, and a Google car hitting a bus in February 2016, received less attention. When fatal American accidents were widely covered in the mainstream media, including *The Guardian* [28,29] or *The New York Times* [30,31], a wave of negative sentiment was evident in the Twitter dataset.

This study demonstrates that public opinion changes over time. Initially, when AV technology was perceived as a promising life-saving innovation bridging the gap between fiction and reality, sentiment polarity was positive. Conversely, when AVs began sharing the road with humans and were involved in rare accidents, the perceived risk erased hope, concerns about safety arose, and sentiment polarity shifted to negative. While Wicki's study [32] investigating the effects of AV accidents on families indicates that the negative impact is transient, our study of social media suggests that the effect appears to be persistent and progressively negative over time.

The main result of this sentiment analysis is that negative publicity spread across mainstream media and social platforms can generate fear and reluctance toward technology, as history has shown [33,34]. As technology is increasingly released to the market before full development, some innovations may be slowed or halted due to malfunctions, particularly if they could cause fatalities.

5. Limitations

While our analysis considers various factors influencing sentiment, the dynamic nature of social media discourse may introduce biases that could impact the interpretation of sentiment trends. Furthermore, the variability in user engagement and the shifting landscape of public discourse surrounding autonomous vehicles may constrain the generalizability of our findings beyond the specific time frames examined.

Given that autonomous vehicle (AV) tweets contain a substantial amount of informative and promotional content, the textual data were filtered using emotion and valency dictionaries. Consequently, the analyzed content is not representative of all discussions, but rather focuses solely on the emotional aspects of the discourse. This limitation constrains the scope and generalizability of the conclusions drawn. Tweet sentiment analysis presents significant challenges due to the brevity of textual data (with a mean of 160 characters per tweet). This constraint may account for the F1 score of 0.69 achieved with the RoBERTa pretrained model. Despite these limitations, the model's performance is comparable to or surpasses that of other studies in tweet sentiment analysis employing manual labeling and the RoBERTa model. For example, Trivyza [27] reported an F1 score of 0.46, whereas Benítez-Andrades et al. [35] reported an F1 score of 0.74. These comparable results across various studies underscore the persistent challenges in Twitter sentiment analysis, suggesting that the current model's performance falls within an acceptable range for this specific domain. Nevertheless, the reliability of the conclusions warrants scrutiny. The analysis of a filtered large volume of data (509,069 tweets), coupled with binary segmentation and rigorous statistical analysis, facilitates the identification of reliable patterns and mitigates the impact of potential misclassifications. This approach suggests that false labeling may be considered mere noise in the dataset rather than a significant confounding factor.

6. Conclusions

The present study represents a significant advancement in understanding public acceptance and rejection of autonomous vehicle (AV) technology. Through the analysis of an extensive dataset comprising tweets posted over a decade (2012–2021), the results reveal a predominance of negative sentiments over positive or neutral expressions. However, the timeline analysis, conducted using binary segmentation techniques, indicates that public opinion initially leaned positive, highlighting the anticipated benefits of AV innovation. From 2016 onward, sentiment shifted toward negativity following the Tesla AV accidents reported by mainstream media. The perception of AV technology then transitioned from highly positive to predominantly negative as public concerns increasingly aligned with the technical challenges reported by the media. This trend also illustrates how traditional media can amplify legitimate public concerns and shape online sentiment toward AVs.

To further elucidate the impact of technological failures on public acceptance, additional research will explore the relationship between AV performance and individuals' perceptions of reliability using qualitative interview data.

Supplementary Materials: The following supporting information can be downloaded at: https://www.mdpi.com/article/10.3390/technologies12120270/s1, S1: Twitter API Queries; S2: Emotion and Valency Dictionary; S3: Sample of 1196 Manually Labeled Tweets Sorted By Label Type; S4: Relevant Word Dictionary; S5: Binary Segmentation Methodology; S6: Sentiment Score and Number of Tweets for the Two Defined Periods; S7: Term Frequency-Inverse Document Frequency (TF-IDF) Scores and Polarity Sentiment Scores for the Top 20 Words in the Two Defined Periods; S8: Trends in Sentiment and Tweet Volume for Mentions of Google and Tesla. Ref. [36] is cited in Supplementary Materials.

Author Contributions: R.S.: writing of the main manuscript and Supplementary Material, data collection, data labeling, data analysis, figure preparation, research design, and project management; J.S.M.G.: data labeling, dictionary building, and data analysis; A.A.: model coding and data analysis; M.F.N.: model coding; M.D.: model coding; C.C.: model coding and project management. All authors have read and agreed to the published version of the manuscript.

Funding: This research was funded by Engineering School Polytech Clermont and the Délégation à la Sécurité Routière (n°2201.305.286).

Institutional Review Board Statement: Not applicable.

Informed Consent Statement: Not applicable.

Data Availability Statement: All data are provided in the main article and the Supplementary Materials. Owing to the European General Data Protection Regulation (GDPR) [20], the original tweets cannott be shared.

Conflicts of Interest: The authors declare that they have no conflicts of interest. The funders had no role in the design of the study, in the collection, analyses, or interpretation of data; in the writing of the manuscript, or in the decision to publish the results.

References

1. Ding, Y.; Korolov, R.; Wallace, W.A.; Wang, X.C. How are sentiments on autonomous vehicles influenced? An analysis using Twitter feeds. *Transp. Res. Part C Emerg. Technol.* **2021**, *131*, 103356. [CrossRef]
2. Giachanou, A.; Crestani, F. Like It or Not: A Survey of Twitter Sentiment Analysis Methods. *ACM Comput. Surv.* **2016**, *49*, 1–41. [CrossRef]
3. Modrek, S.; Chakalov, B. The #MeToo Movement in the United States: Text Analysis of Early Twitter Conversations. *J. Med. Internet Res.* **2019**, *21*, e13837. [CrossRef] [PubMed]
4. Zarocostas, J. How to fight an infodemic. *Lancet* **2020**, *395*, 676. [CrossRef] [PubMed]
5. Gable, J.S.M.; Sauvayre, R.; Chauvière, C. Fight Against the Mandatory COVID-19 Immunity Passport on Twitter: Natural Language Processing Study. *J. Med. Internet Res.* **2023**, *25*, e49435. [CrossRef] [PubMed]

6. Bengesi, S.; Oladunni, T.; Olusegun, R.; Audu, H. A Machine Learning-Sentiment Analysis on Monkeypox Outbreak: An Extensive Dataset to Show the Polarity of Public Opinion From Twitter Tweets. *IEEE Access* **2023**, *11*, 11811–11826. [CrossRef]
7. Gabarron, E.; Dechsling, A.; Skafle, I.; Nordahl-Hansen, A. Discussions of Asperger Syndrome on Social Media: Content and Sentiment Analysis on Twitter. *JMIR Form. Res.* **2022**, *6*, e32752. [CrossRef]
8. Mohamad Sham, N.; Mohamed, A. Climate Change Sentiment Analysis Using Lexicon, Machine Learning and Hybrid Approaches. *Sustainability* **2022**, *14*, 4723. [CrossRef]
9. Zhang, Q.; Zhang, T.; Ma, L. Human acceptance of autonomous vehicles: Research status and prospects. *Int. J. Ind. Ergon.* **2023**, *95*, 103458. [CrossRef]
10. Bala, H.; Anowar, S.; Chng, S.; Cheah, L. Review of studies on public acceptability and acceptance of shared autonomous mobility services: Past, present and future. *Transp. Rev.* **2023**, *43*, 970–996. [CrossRef]
11. Golbabaei, F.; Yigitcanlar, T.; Paz, A.; Bunker, J. Individual Predictors of Autonomous Vehicle Public Acceptance and Intention to Use: A Systematic Review of the Literature. *J. Open Innov. Technol. Mark. Complex.* **2020**, *6*, 106. [CrossRef]
12. Hegner, S.M.; Beldad, A.D.; Brunswick, G.J. In Automatic We Trust: Investigating the Impact of Trust, Control, Personality Characteristics, and Extrinsic and Intrinsic Motivations on the Acceptance of Autonomous Vehicles. *Int. J. Hum. Comput. Interact.* **2019**, *35*, 1769–1780. [CrossRef]
13. Xu, Z.; Zhang, K.; Min, H.; Wang, Z.; Zhao, X.; Liu, P. What drives people to accept automated vehicles? Findings from a field experiment. *Transp. Res. Part. C Emerg. Technol.* **2018**, *95*, 320–334. [CrossRef]
14. Chaufrein, M.; Forte, C.; Colom, M.; Delage, L.; Ouafi, H.; Saran, R.; Sidane, Y.; Vieira, R.L.; Milanes, V.; Salomon, S. Tornado_Attentes et Acceptabilité Utilisateurs de VAC Expérimentaux. France. 2021. Available online: https://eexposit.perso.univ-pau.fr/tornado/downloads/L8%20Tornado%20Analyse%20d'acceptabilite%20et%20rapport%20final%20lot%208%20et%20lot%207.pdf (accessed on 9 January 2022).
15. Zou, X.; O'Hern, S.; Ens, B.; Coxon, S.; Mater, P.; Chow, R.; Neylan, M.; Vu, H.L. On-road virtual reality autonomous vehicle (VRAV) simulator: An empirical study on user experience. *Transp. Res. Part C Emerg. Technol.* **2021**, *126*, 103090. [CrossRef]
16. Jing, P.; Wang, B.; Cai, Y.; Wang, B.; Huang, J.; Yang, C.; Jiang, C. What is the public really concerned about the AV crash? Insights from a combined analysis of social media and questionnaire survey. *Technol. Forecast. Soc. Social Change* **2023**, *189*, 122371. [CrossRef]
17. Das, S.; Dutta, A.; Lindheimer, T.; Jalayer, M.; Elgart, Z. YouTube as a Source of Information in Understanding Autonomous Vehicle Consumers: Natural Language Processing Study. *Transp. Res. Rec.* **2019**, *2673*, 242–253. [CrossRef]
18. Othman, K. Public attitude towards autonomous vehicles before and after crashes: A detailed analysis based on the demographic characteristics. *Cogent Eng.* **2023**, *10*, 2156063. [CrossRef]
19. Jefferson, J.; McDonald, A.D. The autonomous vehicle social network: Analyzing tweets after a recent Tesla autopilot crash. *Proc. Human Factors Ergon. Soc. Annu. Meet.* **2019**, *63*, 2071–2075. [CrossRef]
20. GDPR Twitter. Twitter Controller-to-Controller (Outbound) Data Protection Addendum. Available online: https://gdpr.twitter.com/en/controller-to-controller-transfers.html (accessed on 25 April 2022).
21. Hugging Face. Twitter-roBERTa-Base for Sentiment Analysis. Available online: https://huggingface.co/cardiffnlp/twitter-roberta-base-sentiment (accessed on 25 September 2023).
22. Barbieri, F.; Camacho-Collados, J.; Espinosa Anke, L.; Neves, L. TweetEval: Unified Benchmark and Comparative Evaluation for Tweet Classification. In *Findings of the Association for Computational Linguistics: EMNLP 2020*; Cohn, T., He, Y., Liu, Y., Eds.; Association for Computational Linguistics: Stroudsburg, PA, USA, 2020; pp. 1644–1650. [CrossRef]
23. Scott, A.J.; Knott, M. A Cluster Analysis Method for Grouping Means in the Analysis of Variance. *Biometrics* **1974**, *30*, 507–512. [CrossRef]
24. Fryzlewicz, P. Wild Binary Segmentation for Multiple Change-Point Detection. *Ann. Stat.* **2014**, *42*, 2243–2281. [CrossRef]
25. Killick, R.; Fearnhead, P.; Eckley, I.A. Optimal Detection of Changepoints with a Linear Computational Cost. *J. Am. Stat. Assoc.* **2012**, *107*, 1590–1598. [CrossRef]
26. Wang, Q.; Mao, Z.; Wang, B.; Guo, L. Knowledge Graph Embedding: A Survey of Approaches and Applications. *IEEE Trans. Knowl. Data Eng.* **2017**, *29*, 2724–2743. [CrossRef]
27. Trivyza, M.-F. Autonomous Vehicles: Multi-Class Twitter Sentiment Analysis. Ph.D. Dissertation, National Technical University of Athens, Athens, Greece, 2021. Available online: https://dspace.lib.ntua.gr/xmlui/handle/123456789/54013?locale-attribute=en (accessed on 8 December 2023).
28. Levin, S.; Woolf, N.; The Guardian. Tesla Driver Killed While Using Autopilot was Watching Harry Potter, Witness Says. 2016. Available online: https://www.theguardian.com/technology/2016/jul/01/tesla-driver-killed-autopilot-self-driving-car-harry-potter (accessed on 20 April 2024).
29. Levin, S.; The Guardian. "Uber Should Be Shut Down": Friends of Self-Driving Car Crash Victim Seek Justice. 2018. Available online: https://www.theguardian.com/technology/2018/mar/20/uber-self-driving-car-crash-death-arizona-elaine-herzberg (accessed on 20 April 2024).
30. Vlasic, B.; Boudette, N.E.; The New York Times. Self-Driving Tesla Was Involved in Fatal Crash, U.S. Says. 2016. Available online: https://www.nytimes.com/2016/07/01/business/self-driving-tesla-fatal-crash-investigation.html (accessed on 20 April 2024).
31. Griggs, T.; Wakabayashi, D.; The New York Times. How a Self-Driving Uber Killed a Pedestrian in Arizona. 2018. Available online: https://www.nytimes.com/interactive/2018/03/20/us/self-driving-uber-pedestrian-killed.html (accessed on 20 April 2024).

32. Wicki, M. How do familiarity and fatal accidents affect acceptance of self-driving vehicles? *Transp. Res. Part F Traffic Psychol. Behav.* **2021**, *83*, 401–423. [CrossRef]
33. Rogers, E.M. *Diffusion of Innovations*, 5th ed.; Free Press: New York, NY, USA, 2003.
34. Juma, C. *Innovation and Its Enemies: Why People Resist New Technologies*; Oxford University Press: New York, NY, USA, 2016.
35. Benítez-Andrades, J.A.; Alija-Pérez, J.-M.; Vidal, M.-E.; Pastor-Vargas, R.; García-Ordás, M.T. Traditional Machine Learning Models and Bidirectional Encoder Representations from Transformer (BERT)–Based Automatic Classification of Tweets About Eating Disorders: Algorithm Development and Validation Study. *JMIR Med. Inform.* **2022**, *10*, e34492. [CrossRef]
36. Hastie, T.; Tibshirani, R.; Friedman, J. *The Elements of Statistical Learning*; Springer: New York, NY, USA, 2009. [CrossRef]

technologies

Article

EEG-Based Mobile Robot Control Using Deep Learning and ROS Integration

Bianca Ghinoiu [1], Victor Vlădăreanu [1,*], Ana-Maria Travediu [1,*], Luige Vlădăreanu [1], Abigail Pop [1], Yongfei Feng [2] and Andreea Zamfirescu [3]

1 Robotics and Mechatronics Department, Institute of Solid Mechanics of the Romanian Academy, 010141 Bucharest, Romania; bianca.ghinoiu@imsar.ro (B.G.); luige.vladareanu@vipro.edu.ro (L.V.); abigail.pop@imsar.ro (A.P.)
2 Faculty of Mechanical Engineering and Mechanics, Ningbo University, Ningbo 315211, China; fengyongfei@nbu.edu.cn
3 Faculty of medicine, University of Medicine and Pharmacy "Carol Davila", 050474 Bucharest, Romania; andreea.zamfirescu@umfcd.ro
* Correspondence: victor.vladareanu@imsar.ro (V.V.); ana.travediu@imsar.ro (A.-M.T.)

Abstract: Efficient BCIs (Brain-Computer Interfaces) harnessing EEG (Electroencephalography) have shown potential in controlling mobile robots, also presenting new possibilities for assistive technologies. This study explores the integration of advanced deep learning models—ASTGCN, EEGNetv4, and a combined CNN-LSTM architecture—with ROS (Robot Operating System) to control a two-wheeled mobile robot. The models were trained using a published EEG dataset, which includes signals from subjects performing thought-based tasks. Each model was evaluated based on its accuracy, F1-score, and latency. The CNN-LSTM architecture model exhibited the best performance on the cross-subject strategy with an accuracy of 88.5%, demonstrating significant potential for real-time applications. Integration with ROS was facilitated through a custom middleware, enabling seamless translation of neural commands into robot movements. The findings indicate that the CNN-LSTM model not only outperforms existing EEG-based systems in terms of accuracy but also underscores the practical feasibility of implementing such systems in real-world scenarios. Considering its efficacy, CNN-LSTM shows a great potential for assistive technology in the future. This research contributes to the development of a more intuitive and accessible robotic control system, potentially enhancing the quality of life for individuals with mobility impairments.

Keywords: BCI (Brain-Computer Interface); EEG (Electroencephalogram); MI (Motor Imagery); CNN (Convolutional Neural Network); LSTM (Long Short-Term Memory) networks; mobile robot; control; ROS (Robot Operating System)

1. Introduction

BCIs (Brain Computer Interfaces) represent a promising tool that facilitates the direct communication between the human brain and external devices [1], offering more and more innovative solutions in the realm of assistive technologies [2]. EEG-based (Electroencephalography-based) BCIs, especially, have gained traction due to the possibility of using non-invasive techniques providing the ability to capture neural activity. These captions can be translated into control commands for various devices including mobile robots. On a deeper level, such technology has the potential to significantly improve the quality of life for individuals with mobility impairments by allowing them to control robotic systems using only their thoughts. Considering the recent advancements in DL (Deep Learning) techniques and the flexibility of ROS (Robot Operating System), a great deal of opportunities has emerged to enhance the efficiency and accuracy of EEG-based control systems. This paper explores the integration of state-of-the-art DL models with

ROS to develop a robust BCI for controlling mobile robots, and discusses the feasibility of these technologies in real-world assistive applications.

The paper refers only to the non-invasive EEG technology which captures the electrical activity of the brain. The approach used to translate neural signals into actionable commands utilizes an endogenous BCI system. Unlike exogenous BCIs, which depend on external cues or stimuli to elicit brain responses, the endogenous approach involves that the control signals are generated by the user's voluntary mental activity. As discussed in [3], endogenous systems can rely on thoughts, MI (motor imagery), or cognitive tasks, offering greater autonomy to users by eliminating the need for external triggers. The system presented in this paper uses a MI-based control strategy, requiring users to imagine specific motor movements—such as moving a hand or foot—to generate control signals. When an individual imagines moving a limb, the same brain areas activate as when they are physically moving that limb. This design aligns with the core principles of non-invasive, user-driven interaction, making the system more intuitive and versatile for real-world applications. However, endogenous systems also present some challenges in terms of noise and variability [4], making robust DL models essential for accurate interpretation of the brain's spontaneous activity.

The advent of deep learning has proven to be a reliable solution to deal with these challenges leading to improved BCIs with complex algorithms capable of extracting relevant features from EEG signals [5]. Schirrmeister et al. [6] explores how CNNs can decode EEG signals, including MI data, and provide insights into how the visualization of learned features can help to understand the brain activity related to MI tasks. Their findings indicate that recent advancements in machine learning have significantly enhanced the performance of deep ConvNets (convolutional networks) in decoding MI EEG data. These improvements have led to decoding accuracies that match or surpass the widely adopted FBCSP (filter bank common spatial patterns) algorithm, with mean accuracies of 84.0% for deep ConvNets compared to 82.1% for FBCSP. Several CNN architectures have been specifically designed for EEG data classification, each with distinct features. EEGNet is a compact and efficient model that uses separable convolutions to capture spatial and temporal EEG patterns [7]. Shallow ConvNet focuses on low-level feature extraction, while Deep ConvNet utilizes multiple layers to capture complex signal patterns [8]. The Multi-Branch 3D CNN processes EEG data in a 3D format, learning from both spatial and temporal dimensions [9]. The Temporal-Spatial Deep ConvNet emphasizes capturing both temporal changes and spatial relationships across EEG channels [10]. EEG-Inception, inspired by the Inception model, applies parallel convolutions with different kernel sizes for multi-scale feature extraction [11]. However, the efficiency of training these deep models heavily relies on the optimization algorithms used. The Adam optimizer [12] is commonly employed due to its adaptive learning rate mechanism, which benefits from combining the strengths of AdaGrad and RMSProp. Despite its popularity, Adam can exhibit high variance in learning rate adaptation. To overcome this, the RAdam (Rectified Adam) optimizer introduces a warm-up mechanism that stabilizes training, leading to faster and more consistent convergence. This makes RAdam particularly effective for CNN like models [13,14].

ASTGCNs (Adaptive Spatiotemporal Graph Convolutional Networks) have been used in BCI applications to effectively capture the spatial relationships between different EEG channels. Sun et al. [15] propose an ASTGCN framework for MI-EEG classification, aiming to address the challenges faced by conventional GNN (graph neural network) models. While traditional GNN approaches have shown promise in various fields, their application to MI-EEG classification remains limited and often results in suboptimal performance [16,17]. The ASTGCN framework developed in [15] overcomes these limitations by capturing the spatiotemporal structure of multichannel EEG signals more effectively. Unlike traditional GNNs, which treat neighbour nodes with equal importance, ASTGCN adaptively determines the relevance of each neighbour node while simultaneously extracting temporal features. This approach enhances classification accuracy and robustness in real BCI applications. The proposed ASTGCN model demonstrated improved performance, achieving an average accuracy of 90.6% in the classification of two MI classes across 25 subjects. This result outperforms baseline methods, such as CNN-SAE [18] and EEGNet, which achieved average accuracies of 74.9% and 84.9%, respectively, highlighting ASTGCN's potential for advancing MI-EEG classification tasks.

CNNs (Convolutional Neural Networks) have shown promise in spatial feature extraction, while LSTM (Long Short-Term Memory) networks excel at capturing temporal dependencies in time-series data [19–21]. By combining these two architectures, hybrid CNN-LSTM models can leverage both spatial and temporal patterns, offering superior performance in EEG-based tasks. CNN-LSTM models proved to be more efficient compared to simple LSTM architectures [22,23]. Liu et al. [24] present a CNN-LSTM network with weight-sharing techniques for recognizing MI-EEG. The CNN extracts spatial features from EEG signals, while the LSTM captures time-domain dependencies, making it suitable for decoding MI tasks with high accuracy (highest accuracy rate of 82.3%), especially in multi-class scenarios.

In parallel, ROS provides a flexible middleware that facilitates the control and programming of robots. Integrating EEG-based BCIs with ROS allows for efficient translation of neural commands into robotic movements, offering an accessible and scalable solution for thought-controlled mobile robots. Previous studies have explored such integrations, though challenges related to system robustness and real-time control remained [25]. ROS-Neuro was introduced as an extension of ROS to address the lack of standardized platforms for integrating neural interfaces with robotics [26]. Despite the benefits of using ROS-Neuro, real-time control remains a complex challenge. The inherent delay in EEG signal processing and the potential noise from brain signals can affect the accuracy and reliability of robotic movements. Gloria Beraldo et al. [27] proposed a technique of shared control navigation, where the BCI provides high-level commands (e.g., turning directions), and ROS handles low-level control such as obstacle avoidance and path planning.

Despite these advancements, many EEG-based BCI systems still face limitations in terms of accuracy, latency, and scalability, particularly when deployed in real-world scenarios. This research seeks to address these challenges by developing a novel hybrid CNN-LSTM model that enhances both spatial and temporal EEG signal interpretation, integrated with ROS for real-time control of a mobile robot.

This paper presents a comprehensive evaluation of several deep learning models, including ASTGCN, EEGNetv4, and a CNN-LSTM hybrid architecture, for controlling a two-wheeled mobile robot using EEG data. The primary contributions of this work are: (1) the development of a high-performance CNN-LSTM model, (2) seamless integration with ROS for real-time control, and (3) a comparative analysis of model performance in terms of accuracy, latency, and robustness. The findings can further be used in assistive technology applications, particularly for individuals with mobility impairments. The need for "eHealth" in geriatric rehabilitation has been growing fast lately according to [28], showing the growth of the aging population, which supports the need for advanced technology dedicated to rehabilitation. Blanco-Diaz et al. [29] use EEGs to estimate lower-limb movements during pedalling tasks. They use an LSTM model to decode kinematic parameters for ankle and knee joint angles. They discuss the idea of using these systems for personalized rehabilitation therapies, enhancing motor recovery for individuals with neurological conditions like stroke. Camargo-Vargas et al. [30] review the use of EEG-based BCIs in rehabilitation of lower and upper limbs. The review includes details about preprocessing techniques like filtering, feature extraction (e.g., Common Spatial Patterns and wavelet transforms), and classification methods such as Support Vector Machines and Linear Discriminant Analysis to interpret motor intentions. The review also presents how these processed signals enable applications such as motor imagery training, neurofeedback, and controlling assistive devices like robotic limbs and exoskeletons.

The remainder of this paper is organized as follows: Section 2 details the methodology, including data pre-processing, model architecture, and ROS integration. Section 3 provides a comprehensive discussion on the experimental results, challenges encountered, and the implications of the proposed models for real-world mobile robot applications. Section 4 provides insights, while Section 5 presents the conclusions and potential future directions.

2. Materials and Methods

This section outlines the methodologies employed in developing a robust BCI system for controlling a mobile robot using MI data. It describes the process of acquiring EEG signals, the deep learning models developed for decoding these signals, and the integration of these models with ROS to enable real-time control. Additionally, it details the setup of the system, including hardware specifications, data pre-processing techniques, model training strategies, and the evaluation criteria used to assess the system's performance.

2.1. System Setup

The overall system configuration for this EEG-based BCI comprises a combination of hardware and software components that work in harmony to achieve real-time robotic control. As shown in Figure 1, the core hardware and software components of the system include:

1. EEG Acquisition Device: an OpenBCI EEG cap with 19 electrodes;
2. Computer System: equipped with an NVIDIA GEFORCE RTX 3060 Laptop GPU;
3. Mobile Robot: a two-wheeled mobile robot;
4. ROS (Robot Operating System) Noetic;
5. Deep Learning Framework;
6. Operating System: Ubuntu 20.04.

For the inference phase of the study, an OpenBCI EEG cap with 19 electrodes was employed [31], of which 16 electrodes (Fp1, Fp2, F4, Fz, F3, T3, C3, Cz, C4, T4, P4, Pz, P3, O1, O2, REF) were actively used to capture brain signals. The electrodes were placed following the international 10–20 system to ensure optimal coverage of the motor cortex. As described in [32] the system was connected to a computer using a Bluetooth dongle and a Cython Daisy module, enabling wireless transmission of EEG data in real-time. Additionally, the OpenBCI GUI (Graphical User Interface) was used for visualizing and recording the EEG signals [33]. OpenBCI GUI provides real-time feedback, including data visualization tools and customizable settings, which allows monitoring signal quality and electrode impedance during the setup. The OpenBCI hardware and GUI were selected due to their compatibility with open-source environments and their ability to provide accurate, non-invasive brainwave measurements necessary for real-time control tasks.

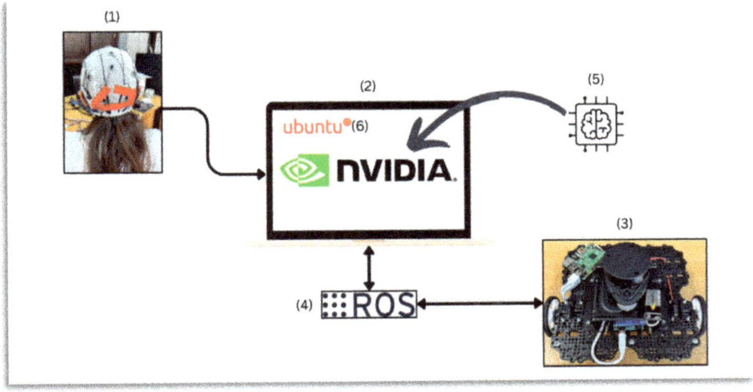

Figure 1. Overall system Architecture.

The mobile robot used in this project, derived from a customized version of a TurtleBot3-like platform [34], is equipped with a Raspberry Pi 2B and various sensors. The robot's primary function is to navigate autonomously in an environment using a differential drive mechanism, where each wheel is controlled independently to enable smooth turns and movement in all directions. The Raspberry Pi serves as the central processing unit, running ROS, which manages the data exchange between different components and coordinates the robot's actions.

Connection Setup and Commands Transmission

The integration between the Raspberry Pi and the other robotic components, such as the motor driver and sensors, is managed through ROS nodes that handle data flow. ROS nodes are created for different functionalities like motor control and command reception from the EEG classification system. To set up the communication, the Raspberry Pi is connected via an Arduino device to the motor driver L298N [35] through the GPIO pins, enabling direct control over the motors' speed and direction.

The Raspberry Pi is networked with a workstation ((2) from Figure 1) via a local Wi-Fi network, enabling remote access and debugging through SSH (Secure Shell) and ROS topics. This configuration allows for the real-time transfer of commands, ensuring that the robot can be monitored and controlled from a distance without the need for constant physical adjustments.

Once the EEG classification identifies the intended motor imagery movement as part of a class, an associated command such as moving forward or turning left or right is transmitted to the motors via Raspberry Pi. The classification system, which runs on the dedicated machine, publishes these commands to a predefined ROS topic, /cmd_vel. This topic is subscribed to by a ROS node on the Raspberry Pi, which then translates these high-level commands into motor control signals for the driver L298N. Details can be found in Section 2.4.

2.2. EEG Data Collection

2.2.1. Public Dataset for Model Training

The deep learning models used in this study were trained on a publicly available EEG dataset from an OpenBCI competition [36]. This dataset consists of EEG recordings from 9 subjects, each performing MI tasks involving 4 distinct movements: the imagination of movement of the left hand (class 1), right hand (class 2), both feet (class 3), and tongue (class 4). The data were collected in two sessions per subject, with each session comprising 6 runs. Each run contained 48 trials, evenly distributed across the four motor imagery tasks, resulting in 288 trials per session per subject. During each trial (6 s), subjects were instructed to imagine the requested movement according to the following sequence: in the beginning a short acoustic warning signal was played in parallel with a cross displayed on the screen (the cross remains on the screen for the entire trial); after 2 s an arrow is displayed for 1.25 s, "pointing either to the left, right, down or up (corresponding to one of the four classes left hand, right hand, foot or tongue)" [36], prompting the subjects to focus on the desired body part; in the end (after 6 s), a short break is signalized using a black screen; repeat.

The EEG signals were recorded using 22 Ag/AgCl electrodes, with electrode placement following a standard montage. The data were sampled at 250 Hz, and a band pass filter (0.5 Hz to 100 Hz) was applied to remove unwanted frequency components. A 50 Hz notch filter was also employed to mitigate line noise. The amplifier was set to a sensitivity of 100 μV to ensure high-quality signal capture. These pre-processing steps and signal acquisition settings were consistent across all subjects, ensuring high-quality recordings suitable for training the deep learning models. The dataset was subsequently labelled according to the motor imagery tasks. The labeling process came after a rigorous inspection carried out by an expert that marked the trials containing artifacts, providing a reliable foundation for the model training phase.

2.2.2. Data Acquisition and Pre-Processing

For real-time inference, the EEGs were recorded in a way that ensures the compatibility with the DL models trained on the public dataset described in Section 2.2.1. Thus, the subject was instructed to think of one of the specified movements for at least 6 s. In this way, the model could receive relevant data to classify later.

EEG signals were acquired at a sampling rate of 250 Hz using the OpenBCI system, which features 19 electrodes, with 16 actively used during the experiment. Furthermore, to improve the quality of the signals, pre-processing steps were applied. The raw EEG data was first filtered using a band pass filter between 0.5 Hz and 50 Hz to eliminate low-frequency drifts and high-frequency noise. A notch filter at 50 Hz was applied to mitigate power line interference. The cleaned data was segmented into 6-s segments, aligning with the motor imagery tasks performed in Section 2.2.1.

Lastly, the pre-processed signals were subsequently passed to the trained DL models for real-time prediction of motor imagery tasks, which involved the imagination of movements such as the left hand, right hand, both feet, or tongue. This setup ensured consistency between the training data from the public dataset [36] and the real-time inference system.

2.3. *Deep Learning Model*

2.3.1. Initial Models: EEGNetv4 and ASTGCN

The initial phase of the model experimentation involved the training and evaluation of two state-of-the-art models: EEGNetv4 and ASTGCN. EEGNetv4, a lightweight deep learning architecture specifically designed for EEG classification tasks, was chosen for its compact design and ability to extract both spatial and temporal features from EEG data. This model utilizes depth-wise and separable convolutions to reduce computational complexity while maintaining high classification accuracy in BCI applications [7].

Simultaneously, ASTGCN was explored to capture the spatial relationships between different EEG electrodes, as well as the temporal dynamics of EEG signals. ASTGCN leverages graph convolutional networks to model the connectivity between EEG channels and temporal convolutions to capture the progression of brain activity over time [15]. These approaches provided promising results during initial experimentation but faced challenges in generalizing to the MI tasks under study, particularly in multi-class scenarios.

2.3.2. Transition to CNN-LSTM Architecture

After evaluating the performance of EEGNetv4 and ASTGCN, a hybrid CNN-LSTM architecture was developed and tested to better capture the complex spatial-temporal patterns present in EEG signals during motor imagery. The CNN-LSTM model was designed to leverage the strengths of both convolutional layers for spatial feature extraction and LSTM layers for temporal sequence modelling. The same parameters were applied across all three architectures, with details about EEGNetv4 and ASTGCN provided in the Results section. The following paragraphs and Section 2.3.3 present the methodology used for the CNN-LSTM architecture, shown in Figure 2.

The CNN section included a single convolutional layer with 40 filters, a kernel size of 20, and a stride of 4, effectively reducing the dimensionality of the input data and extracting spatial features. The ReLU activation function was applied to introduce non-linearity, enabling the model to capture complex patterns. The ReLU function is defined as:

$$ReLU(x) = \max(0, x), \quad (1)$$

where x represents the input to the activation function. This function outputs the input directly if it is positive, otherwise, it outputs zero, which helps the model learn non-linear relationships. To prevent overfitting, a dropout layer with a rate of 0.5 was added, followed by batch normalization to stabilize and accelerate training. A max-pooling layer with a pool size of 4 and stride of 4 further reduced the spatial dimensions.

Following the CNN layer, the LSTM section comprised 2 LSTM layers with 30 units each, configured to return sequences. This configuration allowed the model to capture the temporal dynamics and long-term dependencies of the EEG signals. Dropout layers with a rate of 0.5 were again applied between LSTM layers, along with batch normalization, to enhance model robustness and generalization. A final dense layer with a softmax activation function was used to classify the EEG signals into their respective motor imagery classes.

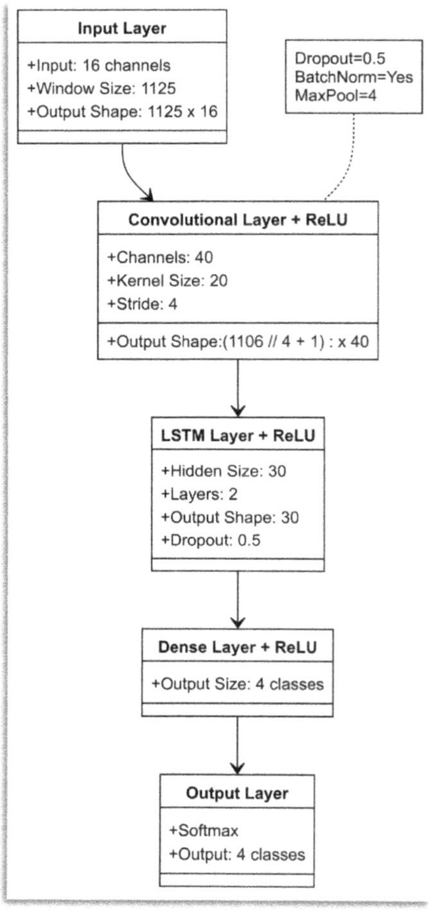

Figure 2. Model architecture for CNN-LSTM.

2.3.3. Training—Validation—Testing

The CNN-LSTM model was trained on the public EEG dataset [36], which includes motor imagery tasks involving four different movements (left hand, right hand, both feet, tongue). For training and validation, data from 8 subjects was used, with an 80/20 split within each subject's data for training and validation sets, respectively. The remaining 9th subject's data was reserved for testing, allowing for an evaluation of the model's ability to generalize to unseen participants. Two training strategies were employed: a within-subject approach, and a cross-subject approach. The within-subject strategy involves the dividing of the dataset into subsets, one for each subject, then the models being trained and validated on the same subject's data. The cross-subject approach means training the models on data from multiple subjects by combining data from all subjects into one large training/validation set.

The models were trained using two different optimizers. Initially, the Adam optimizer was applied, followed by the Radam optimizer, both paired with the categorical cross-entropy loss function to measure performance.

The Adam optimizer updates the model parameters by computing adaptive learning rates for each parameter using estimates of the first moment (mean) and the second moment (uncentered variance) of the gradients. The parameter update rule is given by:

$$\theta_{t+1} = \theta_t - \eta \frac{\hat{m}_t}{\sqrt{\hat{v}_t} + \varepsilon}, \tag{2}$$

where $\hat{m}_t$ and $\hat{v}_t$ are bias-corrected estimates of the first and second moments, respectively, η is the learning rate, and ϵ is a small constant for numerical stability.

RAdam extends Adam by introducing a variance rectification term, which helps to stabilize the training process, especially in the early stages. The rectified update is defined as:

$$\theta_{t+1} = \theta_t - \eta \cdot r_t \cdot \frac{\hat{m}_t}{\sqrt{\hat{v}_t} - \epsilon}, \tag{3}$$

where r_t is a rectification term that adjusts the variance based on the current training step, making the optimization process more stable.

For the loss function, the categorical cross-entropy was used to measure the difference between the predicted class probabilities and the true labels. It is defined as:

$$L(y, \hat{y}) = -\sum_{i=1}^{C} y_i \log(\hat{y}_i), \tag{4}$$

where y_i represents the true label for class i, $\hat{y}_i$ is the predicted probability of class i, and C is the total number of classes. This loss function helps the model adjust its predictions to minimize the difference between predicted probabilities and the actual class distribution, guiding the optimization process effectively.

To further refine the training process, the LRScheduler provided by the Skorch library [37] was used to dynamically adjust the learning rate during training. Specifically, the CosineAnnealingLR policy was applied, which gradually reduces the learning rate according to a cosine annealing schedule. In this approach, η_{max} is set to the initial learning rate, and T_{cur} represents the number of epochs since the last restart, as part of the SGDR (Stochastic Gradient Descent with Warm Restarts) mechanism [38]:

$$\eta_t = \eta_{min} + \frac{1}{2}(\eta_{max} - \eta_{min})\left(1 + \cos\left(\frac{T_{cur}}{T_{max}}\pi\right)\right), \tag{5}$$

The NeuralNetClassifier [39] from the Skorch library is used in this setup to streamline the process of training the deep learning models for classification. With NeuralNetClassifier, the training process is simplified: it automatically manages tasks like splitting the data into training and validation sets, adjusting learning rates during training, and saving the best-performing version of the model. A total of 300 training iterations (epochs) were conducted multiple times. The model was trained on an NVIDIA GEFORCE RTX 3060 Laptop GPU using CUDA 11.6 and the PyTorch 2.0.1 deep learning framework [40].

During the training phase, the model's performance was evaluated on the validation set to optimize hyperparameters and monitor overfitting. Metrics such as accuracy/loss and F1-score were calculated for each motor imagery class. After the validation phase, the model that achieved the highest performance was tested on an independent test set, which included unseen data from the 9th subject to evaluate the model's ability to generalise.

The CNN-LSTM model ultimately outperformed both EEGNetv4 and ASTGCN in terms of classification accuracy and robustness, achieving a testing accuracy of 88.5% for the cross-subject scenario. This model's ability to effectively decode motor imagery tasks with high accuracy made it the best candidate for real-time EEG-based robot control.

2.4. ROS Integration

The DL model was integrated with the ROS to enable real-time control of a two-wheeled mobile robot based on EEG signals. ROS was chosen due to its modular and flexible architecture, which allows seamless communication between the different components of the BCI system. The integration involved developing custom ROS nodes responsible for receiving, processing, and translating the neural commands predicted by the CNN-LSTM model into corresponding robot movement commands.

2.4.1. Architecture of ROS Integration

The overall ROS architecture consisted of three main modules:

- EEG Signal Acquisition Node
- Neural Command Processing Node
- Robot Control Node

EEG Signal Acquisition node handled the real-time data acquisition from the EEG device during the inference phase. The EEG signals were pre-processed, following the steps detailed in Section 2.2.2, and transmitted to the DL model for motor imagery classification. The EEG data was streamed in real-time to the ROS system using Bluetooth communication.

The processed EEG data was then fed into the pre-trained CNN-LSTM model, which was embedded within the Neural Command Processing node using a custom wrapper. This node utilized ROS messages to transmit predictions from the model to other system components. The predictions corresponded to motor imagery classes (e.g., left hand, right hand, both feet, tongue), which were mapped to specific control commands for the robot.

The output from the CNN-LSTM model was transformed into low-level robot control commands (e.g., turn left, turn right, forward, stop). These commands were sent to the robot's motor controllers through ROS's communication system. The Robot Control node responsible for robot control used a predefined action library to execute the commands based on the motor imagery classification results.

2.4.2. Real-Time Control and Feedback

To maintain real-time control of the robot, the system employed ROS Topics to publish and subscribe to different data streams efficiently. The neural commands predicted by the CNN-LSTM model were published to a specific ROS topic, which the robot's control node subscribed to. This modular architecture ensured low-latency communication between components, allowing the robot to respond to EEG-based commands in near real-time.

The tasks performed by the robot were designed to evaluate the system's ability to accurately interpret motor imagery commands and translate them into robot movements. The control tasks included directional movement. The robot was instructed to turn left, turn right, move forward by 0.5 m or stop based on the user's motor imagery of moving left hand, right hand, both feet or tongue, respectively. These tasks were designed to simulate real-world scenarios in which a user with mobility impairments could navigate a robotic assistant or wheelchair.

2.5. Performance Metrics and Statistical Analysis

The performance of the system was evaluated based on several key metrics. The primary metric for model performance was classification accuracy, which measured the ability of the deep learning models (CNN-LSTM, EEGNetv4, ASTGCNN) to correctly predict motor imagery tasks. The CNN-LSTM model achieved the highest accuracy at 88.5% during testing, outperforming the other models.

Response time was a critical metric in evaluating the system's real-time performance. This metric measured the time delay between when the EEG signals were acquired and when the corresponding robotic action was executed. The minimum latency achieved in real-time control averaged a response time of 200 ms.

The robustness of the system was evaluated based on its ability to maintain accurate control in varying conditions, such as noisy environments or variability in user EEG signals. The dropout layers in the CNN-LSTM model helped enhance the system's robustness. Tests conducted across multiple sessions demonstrated consistent performance for the same subject, but the process proved to be challenging for untrained users.

The cross-subject training strategy aimed to evaluate the model's ability to generalize across different users. The CNN-LSTM model showed improved generalization compared to EEGNetv4 and ASTGCNN, highlighting its adaptability in multi-subject scenarios.

To further validate the differences in performance between the models, McNemar's test was employed as a statistical tool to assess the significance of their classification discrepancies. McNemar's test is particularly useful in scenarios where models are compared on the same set of test data, focusing on the instances where their predictions differ. It evaluates whether the difference in the misclassification rates between two models is statistically significant, providing a deeper understanding of their comparative effectiveness.

In this study, McNemar's test was applied to evaluate the prediction discrepancies between the CNN-LSTM model and EEGNetv4, having the best accuracy rates. The outcomes of each model on the same test instances were categorized into four groups: (1) both models correctly predicted the outcome, (2) CNN-LSTM was correct while the other model was incorrect, (3) EEGNetv4 or ASTGCN was correct while CNN-LSTM was incorrect, and (4) both models made incorrect predictions. McNemar's test then focused on the second and third groups—instances where one model succeeded while the other failed—to determine whether these differences were statistically meaningful.

The test statistic for McNemar's test is derived from the formula:

$$\chi^2 = \frac{(B - C)^2}{B + C} \tag{6}$$

where B represents the number of cases where the CNN-LSTM model was correct but the compared model (e.g., EEGNetv4) was incorrect, and C represents cases where the opposite was true. The test follows a χ^2 distribution with one degree of freedom. A significant result (e.g., $p < 0.05$) indicates that the observed differences in prediction accuracy between the models are not due to random chance but reflect a genuine performance advantage of one model over the other.

By incorporating McNemar's test, this study ensures a rigorous statistical validation of the performance differences between the models. This approach proves the claim that the CNN-LSTM model not only achieves higher accuracy but also offers a statistically significant improvement over its counterparts in EEG-based motor imagery classification presented in this paper.

3. Results

This section presents the performance of the evaluated deep learning models—EEGNetv4, ASTGCN, and CNN-LSTM—in classifying motor imagery tasks and the integration of the CNN-LSTM model with ROS for real-time robotic control. The models were evaluated based on classification accuracy, F1-score, response time, robustness, and generalization ability.

The CNN-LSTM model outperformed both EEGNetv4 and ASTGCN, achieving the highest classification accuracy of 88.5% and an F1-score of 0.87 for cross-subject strategy. This suggests that the CNN-LSTM's ability to combine spatial feature extraction through convolutional layers with temporal sequence modelling via LSTM layers made it particularly effective for motor imagery classification tasks. The higher F1-score indicates a balanced precision and recall, making the CNN-LSTM model more reliable in distinguishing between different motor imagery classes.

In contrast, EEGNetv4 achieved a classification accuracy of 83.9% with an F1-score of 0.81, reflecting its effectiveness as a compact model, tailored for EEG signal classification in the case of the cross-subject strategy. While it did not achieve the same level of accuracy as the CNN-LSTM model, its relatively high performance demonstrates its utility in scenarios where a lightweight architecture is advantageous.

The ASTGCN model, despite its advanced graph-based approach for modelling the spatial relationships between EEG channels, achieved the lowest accuracy at 78.6% and an F1-score of 0.75 for cross-subject scenario. This lower performance may be attributed to the challenges of adapting graph-based models to the highly variable nature of EEG data, which may require more tuning or additional data for optimal results.

Overall, the results indicate that while all three models are capable of decoding motor imagery signals, the CNN-LSTM model's accuracy and robustness make it the most suitable candidate for real-time applications, particularly in the context of controlling mobile robots through the ROS framework. The results on within-subject strategy are also discussed in the next sections.

3.1. Classification Performance

This section provides an in-depth comparison of the three deep learning models—EEGNetv4, ASTGCN, and CNN-LSTM—evaluated for their ability to classify MI tasks using EEG data. Table 1 summarizes the best overall results for each model in both within-subject and cross-subject scenarios. In the case of within-subject strategy the best model was chosen as follows: a new model was trained with data from each new subject resulting in a set of 8 accuracy percentages; the best model was considered the model corresponding to the best accuracy percentage from the set.

Table 1. Best performance metrics of the evaluated models in within-subject and cross-subject evaluations.

Model	Accuracy (Cross-Subject)	Accuracy (Within-Subject)	F1-Score (Cross-Subject)	F1-Score (Within-Subject)
EEGNetv4	83.9%	93.5%	0.81	0.85
ASTGCN	78.6%	84.2%	0.75	0.80
CNN-LSTM	88.5%	98.7%	0.87	0.89

3.1.1. Within-Subject Evaluation

In the within-subject evaluation, each model was trained and tested using data from the same subject, allowing the models to learn the unique neural patterns associated with each individual. As shown in Table 1, the CNN-LSTM model achieved the highest accuracy of 98.7% and an F1-score of 0.89, outperforming EEGNetv4 and ASTGCN. This suggests that the hybrid architecture of CNN-LSTM, which combines convolutional layers for spatial feature extraction and LSTM layers for temporal pattern recognition, is particularly effective at capturing the intricacies of motor imagery signals. All three models obtained the best results for the same subject, pointing out how much of an influence the quality of data has.

The EEGNetv4 model performed well in this scenario, achieving an accuracy of 93.5% and an F1-score of 0.85. Despite its simpler architecture, EEGNetv4's ability to focus on the most relevant spatial and temporal features contributed to its strong performance. However, its lightweight nature resulted in a slightly lower performance compared to CNN-LSTM, indicating that more complex patterns may require deeper modelling.

The ASTGCN model, while leveraging graph-based representations to capture spatial relationships between EEG channels, achieved an accuracy of 84.2% and an F1-score of 0.80. Although it performed adequately, the model faced challenges in fully utilizing the spatial relationships. This suggests that the graph-based approach might require further tuning to better adapt to the motor imagery domain.

3.1.2. Cross-Subject Evaluation

The cross-subject evaluation provides a more challenging test of a model's generalization capability, as it involves training on data from multiple subjects and testing on an unseen participant. As shown in Table 1, the CNN-LSTM model again achieved the highest accuracy of 88.5% and an F1-score of 0.87%, demonstrating its ability to generalize well to new users.

In comparison, EEGNetv4 achieved a cross-subject accuracy of 83.9% with an F1-score of 0.81, showing a moderate decrease in performance compared to the within-subject scenario. This decrease is expected due to the inherent variability between subjects' neural patterns. However, EEGNetv4's relatively consistent performance suggests that it can be a viable option when a lightweight model with reasonable generalization capabilities is needed.

The ASTGCN model experienced a notable drop in performance in the cross-subject evaluation, achieving an accuracy of 78.6% and an F1-score of 0.75. This decline highlights the model's struggle with the variability in EEG patterns between different subjects, which is a common challenge in BCI applications. The reliance of ASTGCN on predefined graph structures to capture spatial relationships between EEG channels may have limited its ability to generalize across subjects with different neural patterns.

Figure 3 illustrates the confusion matrix for the ASTGCN model in this scenario, revealing that the model faced some difficulties in distinguishing between certain motor imagery classes (0—left hand, 1—right hand, 2—feet, 3—tongue). The model shows a good performance in predicting "tongue". It also performs well for "feet", having some misclassifications with "left hand" and "tongue". The performance for "left hand" raises some concerns, considering the notable confusions with "feet" and "tongue". The most difficult class for the model to distinguish seems to be "right hand", a particularly high number of misclassifications occurring between it and "feet" or "tongue" classes. This performance suggests that the model could not effectively differentiate finer motor tasks when faced with cross-subject variability. This points to a need for further optimization or more robust training strategies to improve the model's ability to generalize across users.

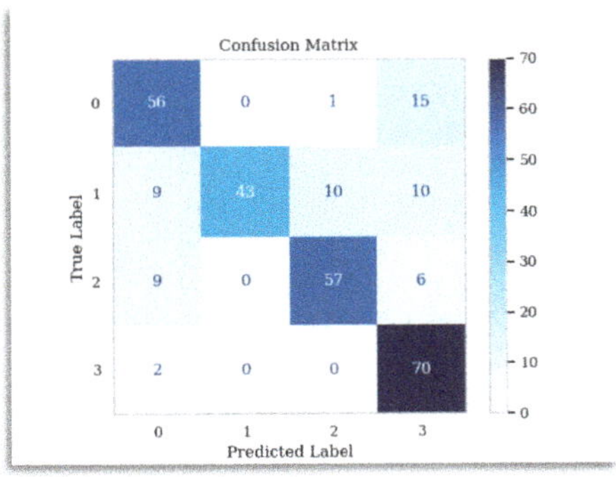

Figure 3. Confusion matrix for ASTGCN in the cross-subject evaluation.

3.1.3. Accuracy Trends During Training

Figure 4a shows the training accuracy trends of the three models—ASTGCN, EEGNetv4, and CNN-LSTM—over 100 epochs during cross-subject training. Figure 4b extends this analysis over 300 epochs but focuses on CNN-LSTM and EEGNetv4, as ASTGCN reached a performance plateau after the initial 100 epochs.

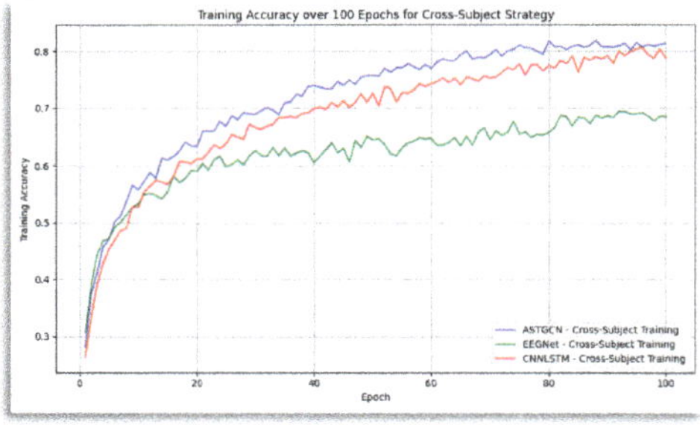

(**a**)

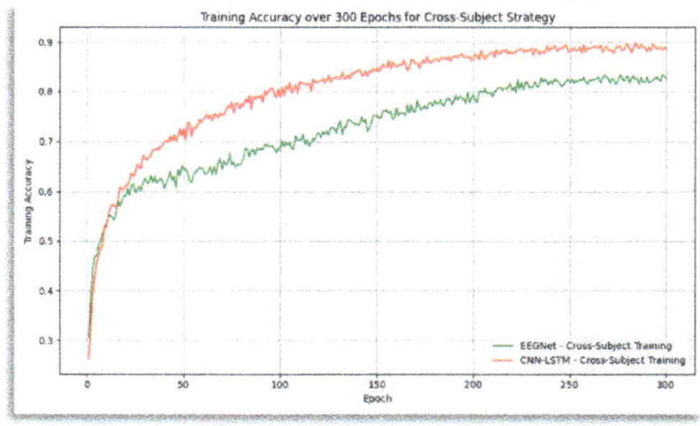

(**b**)

Figure 4. Training accuracy for Cross-Subject Strategy: (**a**) EEGNetv4, ASTGCN, and CNNLSTM (100 epochs); (**b**) EEGNetv4, and CNNLSTM (300 epochs).

Figure 4a shows that during the first 30 epochs, all models exhibit rapid learning, with ASTGCN showing a slight advantage in early-stage accuracy. This suggests that the ASTGCN model was initially more effective at capturing spatial-temporal relationships within the EEG data. However, after the 80th epoch, its learning curve began to plateau, indicating a limitation in the model's ability to further adapt to the nuances of cross-subject variability.

In contrast, the CNN-LSTM model demonstrated a more consistent improvement over the entire 100-epoch period. It reached ASTGCN's performance by the end of this phase. This smoother progression implies that the CNN-LSTM model could better capture both spatial and temporal features of the motor imagery data, maintaining a stable learning trajectory. This robustness is further observable in Figure 4b, where CNN-LSTM continued to increase in accuracy up to around 300 epochs. This consistency indicates that the model effectively generalized across different subjects without overfitting to specific patterns in the data.

EEGNetv4, while initially trailing behind ASTGCN in early epochs, exhibited a steady upward trend throughout the 100 epochs. The model managed to achieve a competitive accuracy, albeit with more pronounced fluctuations compared to CNN-LSTM. This variability could be attributed to EEGNetv4's simpler architecture, which may require more adjustments to fully capture the complex patterns in EEG data. In the longer training phase, EEGNetv4 continued to improve gradually, though its accuracy remained lower than CNN-LSTM. Regardless, it still managed to achieve a reasonable level of convergence.

The significant fluctuations in all models' accuracy suggest sensitivity to parameter adjustments and potential overfitting, highlighting the sensitivity to the diverse nature of cross-subject EEG data.

3.2. *Impact of Hyperparameter Tuning on Model Performance*

In this study, several critical hyper-parameters were fine-tuned to optimize the performance of the deep learning models—CNN-LSTM, EEGNetv4, and ASTGCN—on the motor imagery EEG data. Among these, the learning rate and choice of optimizer played pivotal roles in determining the models' convergence speed, stability, and final accuracy. The learning rate controls how much the model weights are adjusted with each update, while the choice of optimizer influences how these adjustments are made, impacting the efficiency of gradient descent.

3.2.1. Learning Rate Selection

Various learning rates were tested during the training phase, ranging from 0.0001 to 0.01. Through empirical experimentation, a learning rate of 0.001 was initially found to provide a balance between speed and stability for all three models CNN-LSTM, EEGNetv4 and ASTGCN. However, further analysis revealed that a lower learning rate of 0.0005 was particularly effective for the CNN-LSTM model. While this learning rate resulted in slower convergence during the initial training epochs, it ultimately led to a more stable and robust learning process. The slower convergence allowed the model to better adapt to the intricacies of the motor imagery EEG data, reducing overfitting and improving its generalization across subjects. This made the compromise of slower convergence worthwhile, as it contributed to higher final accuracy and a smoother training curve. For all models, a cosine annealing learning rate schedule was applied, gradually reducing the learning rate during training to fine-tune the models as they approached convergence, ensuring that the learning process did not stagnate.

3.2.2. Optimizer Comparison: Adam vs. RAdam

The choice of optimizer significantly impacted the training dynamics of the models. Initially, the Adam optimizer was used due to its adaptive learning rate capabilities and ease of implementation. Adam demonstrated effective convergence during the initial training stages, especially for CNN-LSTM, leading to faster accuracy gains in the first 50 epochs. However, as training progressed, the model's performance plateaued, indicating that a more stable optimization method might be beneficial.

Subsequently, the RAdam optimizer was tested. RAdam introduces a variance rectification term, which helps to stabilize the early stages of training by adjusting the learning rate more dynamically. This led to smoother convergence in all three models, reducing fluctuations in accuracy and improving overall generalization. While Adam performed well for initial training, RAdam's stability resulted in slightly higher accuracy and lower variance during cross-subject evaluation, making it the preferred choice for the final model training.

3.2.3. Final Model Selection Based on Parameter Tuning

Based on the results of the hyper-parameter tuning process, the CNN-LSTM model with a learning rate of 0.001 and the RAdam optimizer emerged as the best-performing configuration. This combination provided a balance between rapid initial learning and stable long-term convergence, ultimately achieving the highest accuracy and F1-score in cross-subject evaluations. The use of RAdam ensured smoother training curves and better generalization across diverse EEG patterns compared to Adam. These characteristics made the CNN-LSTM model particularly suitable for the complex nature of motor imagery classification, justifying its selection as the final model for real-time BCI applications.

Figure 5 presents a comparison of the training accuracy across 300 epochs for the CNN-LSTM model using the Adam and RAdam optimizers. As illustrated, the RAdam optimizer provided smoother convergence, with fewer fluctuations in accuracy beyond the 50th epoch.

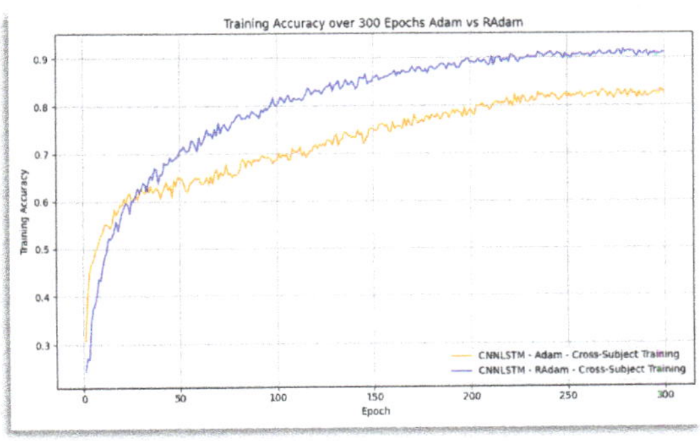

Figure 5. Comparison between Adam and RAdam.

3.3. Latency and Real-Time Response Analysis

The latency and real-time response of the system are critical factors in evaluating its suitability for practical applications, especially in scenarios where a user needs to control a mobile robot using MI. In this study, latency refers to the total time taken from the moment the subject begins imagining a movement to the point where the system classifies the movement and sends a corresponding command to the robot. A key aspect of this process is the 6-s window during which the subject imagines a specific movement, such as moving one hand, the feet or the tongue.

After this 6-s imagination period, the system processes the EEG data, classifies the imagined movement using the trained CNN-LSTM model, and translates the prediction into a control command for the robot. The time taken for this classification and command transmission is critical for ensuring a smooth and responsive interaction between the user and the robot. The experiments showed that the average time for processing and classification after the 6-s imagination window was approximately 200 milliseconds for the CNN-LSTM model. This included the time required for data pre-processing, feature extraction, and model inference.

The total response time, therefore, consisted of the 6-s period of motor imagery, followed by this 200 ms processing time. While the initial 6-s duration is necessary for the subject to focus and generate clear motor imagery signals, the rapid processing time of the CNN-LSTM model ensured that the system could provide timely feedback to the user.

3.4. Statistical Significance Analysis Using McNemar's Test

To evaluate whether the differences in classification performance between the CNN-LSTM model and EEGNetv4 are statistically significant, a McNemar's test was conducted. The test compares the models' performance on the same test dataset, focusing on instances where the models disagree on their predictions.

For the comparison, the test categorized outcomes into four groups:

1. instances where both models were correct,
2. instances where CNN-LSTM was correct but EEGNetv4 was incorrect,
3. instances where EEGNetv4 was correct but CNN-LSTM was incorrect, and
4. instances where both models were incorrect.

The McNemar's test resulted in a χ^2 value of 6.35 with a p-value of 0.01, indicating that the difference in performance between the two models is statistically significant at the 0.05 level. This suggests that the superior accuracy observed for the CNN-LSTM model over EEGNetv4 is not due to random chance but reflects a genuine improvement in model performance.

4. Discussion

The results of this study highlight the potential of using deep learning models, specifically the CNN-LSTM architecture, for EEG-based mobile robot control in a real-time BCI system. The CNN-LSTM model achieved the highest classification accuracy of 88.5% in the cross-subject evaluation, outperforming the other models, EEGNetv4 and ASTGCN. This finding is particularly important for practical applications, as the cross-subject setting represents a more realistic use case where the system must adapt to varying neural patterns from different users. The superior performance of CNN-LSTM can be attributed to its ability to effectively capture both the spatial features of EEG signals through convolutional layers and the temporal dependencies using LSTM layers. This makes it better suited for the dynamic and complex nature of motor imagery tasks compared to the more lightweight EEGNetv4 and the graph-based approach of ASTGCN.

Despite its success, the CNN-LSTM model also faced challenges, particularly related to training time and computational resources. This is due to the large number of parameters used to integrate a CNN for spatial feature and LSTMs for temporal sequences. The significant computational resources and memory needed are evident during training, especially when using a learning rate of 0.0005. Though beneficial for stability, this scenario shows slower convergence and requires more epochs to achieve optimal accuracy, extending the training time. This trade-off between convergence speed and model stability is crucial when designing real-time BCI systems, as the goal is to achieve both high accuracy and timely response. The use of the RAdam optimizer played a significant role in maintaining smooth training curves, ensuring that the model did not overfit to specific training data patterns while still adapting well to new subjects.

In response to these issues, several strategies can be adopted. Optimizing the model architecture by implementing techniques such as pruning, normalization or transfer learning, can be considered. These methods help by removing redundant weights at the cost of lowering precision, aiming for a smaller, more efficient model.

The latency analysis further supports the viability of the CNN-LSTM model for real-time control applications. The system's average response time of 200 milliseconds after a 6-s motor imagery period is competitive, providing a balance between the time required for signal acquisition and the need for quick robotic responses. This rapid processing time is crucial in real-world scenarios, such as controlling assistive devices for individuals with mobility impairments, where any delays can impact user experience and the system's usability. When scaling the application to more complex tasks, usually the data resolutions are also higher, resulting in challenges for the model. Inefficiencies can interfere during the data acquisition step leading to an inconsistent pre-processing phase, resulting in possible bottlenecks during the physical implementation. A possible solution for such challenges could be represented by a change in the length of the EEG data window necessary for classification. Shorter motor imagery windows can be used for classification (e.g., 4 s). The downside of this kind of a solution is the fact that the entire training process should be repeated from the beginning.

Moreover, the application of McNemar's test provided statistical validation for the differences in performance between the models. The test revealed that the observed improvement in the CNN-LSTM model's accuracy over EEGNetv4 was statistically significant ($p < 0.05$). This result underscores the robustness of the CNN-LSTM model in decoding motor imagery tasks compared to the other architectures, providing evidence that its performance is not merely a result of random variation in the dataset but a genuine improvement in prediction accuracy.

The study also highlighted the limitations of the ASTGCN model. Although ASTGCN initially exhibited better accuracy in early training epochs, it reached a performance plateau after 100 epochs, failing to match the long-term learning capability of CNN-LSTM. This plateau may be due to the model's reliance on predefined graph structures, which could limit its ability to adapt to diverse EEG patterns across different subjects. As a result, while ASTGCN's graph-based approach holds promise for capturing spatial relationships, it may require further tuning or more sophisticated strategies to fully leverage its potential in cross-subject BCI applications.

5. Conclusions

Although the application presented in this paper has shown promising results, there are some disadvantages that need to be addressed. EEG data is usually noisy and considerably dependent on the subject, which make them challenging. Even though the CNN-LSTM model performed well in cross-subject evaluations, extensive finetuning may be required, if it is to be applied to a broader population. If so, the computational resources needs will increase.

With the scaling of the application, another downside can be involved, namely the number of electrodes necessary for data acquisition. Numerous electrodes mean time consuming procedures, to prepare the subject, which can lead to a less user-friendly setup.

From a computational point of view, the CNN-LSTM model needs a lot of processing power, especially for training and running in real time. It depends on advanced GPUs, which might not be available to all users or organizations with limited resources. In addition, the 6-s time frame needed to collect motor imagery data can cause delays in situations where quick decisions are important. Even though the 200-millisecond processing time is quite fast, the total response time might still feel slow for tasks that need immediate feedback.

In terms of system integration, the study successfully demonstrated the feasibility of using ROS as a middleware to translate EEG-based commands into robotic actions. The custom ROS nodes for data acquisition, neural command processing, and robot control allowed for seamless communication between the CNN-LSTM model and the mobile robot, enabling precise control of the robot's movements. This setup proves to be a scalable solution that can be adapted to various robotic platforms, highlighting the versatility of combining ROS with deep learning models for BCI systems. One obvious advantage of this fact is the hands-free control provided which can allow, in a future version of the application, individuals with mobility impairments to interact with the environment intuitively.

Overall, this study offers a comprehensive evaluation of different deep learning architectures for EEG-based motor imagery classification and their integration into real-time control of a mobile robot. The results suggest that hybrid models like CNN-LSTM hold great promise for practical BCI applications, particularly in assistive technologies where adaptability and reliability are paramount. The low latency of CNN-LSTM architecture represents another advantage, enabling timely responses in real-time implementation.

Author Contributions: Conceptualization, B.G. and V.V.; methodology, L.V. and A.-M.T.; software, B.G. and A.P.; validation, A.Z., L.V. and V.V.; formal analysis, B.G. and A.-M.T.; investigation, B.G.; resources, L.V.; data curation, B.G., A.Z. and A.P.; writing—original draft preparation, B.G.; writing—review and editing, A.-M.T. and Y.F.; visualization, B.G.; supervision, V.V.; project administration, L.V. and Y.F.; funding acquisition, L.V. and Y.F. All authors have read and agreed to the published version of the manuscript.

Funding: The paper was funded by the European Commission Marie Skłodowska-Curie iMARS project, Intelligent Multi Agent Robotic Systems, HORIZON-MSCA-2023-SE-01-01-MSCA Staff Exchanges 2023, Grant agreement ID: 101182996; JESH 2023 (Joint Excellence in Science and Humanities) project Pose Estimation for Rehabilitation Robots (V. Vlădăreanu); Research on key technologies of intelligent multi-posture lower limb rehabilitation robot project, Ningbo Municipal International Science and Technology Cooperation; and Ningbo International Cooperation Project under Grant 2023H014.

Institutional Review Board Statement: Not applicable.

Informed Consent Statement: Informed consent was obtained from the author who was the only subject involved in the study.

Data Availability Statement: Restrictions apply to the availability of these data. Data were obtained from the Institute for Knowledge Discovery (Laboratory of Brain-Computer Interfaces) at Graz University of Technology and are available at https://www.bbci.de/competition/iv/ (accessed on 13 December 2024) with the permission of Clemens Brunner, Robert Leeb, Gernot Müller-Putz, Alois Schlögl, and Gert Pfurtscheller. The dataset includes EEG recordings of 4-class motor imagery (left hand, right hand, feet, tongue) with 22 EEG channels (0.5–100 Hz, notch filtered), 3 EOG channels, sampled at 250 Hz, covering 4 motor imagery classes across 9 subjects.

Acknowledgments: The authors gratefully acknowledge the support of the Robotics and Mechatronics Department of the Institute of Solid Mechanics of the Romanian Academy, and Zhejiang Youren Intelligent Robotics Co., Ltd., Ningbo University, and Ningbo Polytechnic by the "Research on Key Technologies of Multi-Posture Lower Limb Rehabilitation Robot" Project, Grant 2023H014.

Conflicts of Interest: The authors declare no conflicts of interest. The funders had no role in the design of the study; in the collection, analyses, or interpretation of data; in the writing of the manuscript; or in the decision to publish the results.

References

1. Vărbu, K.; Muhammad, N.; Muhammad, Y. Past, present, and future of EEG-based BCI applications. *Sensors* **2022**, *22*, 3331. [CrossRef]
2. Lazcano-Herrera, A.G.; Fuentes-Aguilar, R.Q.; Chairez, I.; Alonso-Valerdi, L.M.; Gonzalez-Mendoza, M.; Alfaro-Ponce, M. Review on BCI virtual rehabilitation and remote technology based on EEG for assistive devices. *Appl. Sci.* **2022**, *12*, 12253. [CrossRef]

3. Padfield, N.; Camilleri, K.; Camilleri, T.; Fabri, S.; Bugeja, M. A comprehensive review of endogenous EEG-based BCIs for dynamic device control. *Sensors* **2022**, *22*, 5802. [CrossRef] [PubMed]
4. Indurani, P.; Firdaus, B.B. A detailed analysis of EEG signal processing in E-healthcare applications and challenges. *Int. J. Innov. Res. Sci. Eng. Technol.* **2021**, *10*, 635–642.
5. AltahAltaheri, H.; Muhammad, G.; Alsulaiman, M.; Amin, S.U.; Altuwaijri, G.A.; Abdul, W.; Bencherif, M.A.; Faisal, M. Deep learning techniques for classification of electroencephalogram (EEG) motor imagery (MI) signals: A review. *Neural Comput. Appl.* **2023**, *35*, 14681–14722. [CrossRef]
6. Schirrmeister, R.T.; Springenberg, J.T.; Fiederer, L.D.J.; Glasstetter, M.; Eggensperger, K.; Tangermann, M.; Hutter, F.; Burgard, W.; Ball, T. Deep learning with convolutional neural networks for EEG decoding and visualization. *Hum. Brain Mapp.* **2017**, *38*, 5391–5420. [CrossRef] [PubMed]
7. Lawhern, V.J.; Solon, A.J.; Waytowich, N.R.; Gordon, S.M.; Hung, C.P.; Lance, B.J. EEGNet: A compact convolutional neural network for EEG-based brain–computer interfaces. *J. Neural Eng.* **2018**, *15*, 056013. [CrossRef]
8. Han, C.H.; Choi, G.Y.; Hwang, H.J. Deep convolutional neural network based eye states classification using ear-EEG. *Expert Syst. Appl.* **2022**, *192*, 116443. [CrossRef]
9. Zhao, X.; Zhang, H.; Zhu, G.; You, F.; Kuang, S.; Sun, L. A multi-branch 3D convolutional neural network for EEG-based motor imagery classification. *IEEE Trans. Neural Syst. Rehabil. Eng.* **2019**, *27*, 2164–2177. [CrossRef] [PubMed]
10. Mirzabagherian, H.; Menhaj, M.B.; Suratgar, A.A.; Talebi, N.; Sardari MR, A.; Sajedin, A. Temporal-spatial convolutional residual network for decoding attempted movement related EEG signals of subjects with spinal cord injury. *Comput. Biol. Med.* **2023**, *164*, 107159. [CrossRef]
11. Santamaria-Vazquez, E.; Martinez-Cagigal, V.; Vaquerizo-Villar, F.; Hornero, R. EEG-inception: A novel deep convolutional neural network for assistive ERP-based brain-computer interfaces. *IEEE Trans. Neural Syst. Rehabil. Eng.* **2020**, *28*, 2773–2782. [CrossRef]
12. Kingma, D.P.; Ba, J. Adam: A Method for Stochastic Optimization. In Proceedings of the 3rd International Conference on Learning Representations (ICLR), San Diego, CA, USA, 7–9 May 2015.
13. Melinte, D.O.; Vlădăreanu, L. Facial expressions recognition for human–robot interaction using deep convolutional neural networks with rectified adam optimizer. *Sensors* **2020**, *20*, 2393. [CrossRef] [PubMed]
14. Liu, L.; Jian, D.; He, T.; Chen, W.; Li, X. On the Variance of the Adaptive Learning Rate and Beyond. *arXiv* **2019**, arXiv:1908.03265.
15. Sun, B.; Zhang, H.; Wu, Z.; Zhang, Y.; Li, T. Adaptive spatiotemporal graph convolutional networks for motor imagery classification. *IEEE Signal Process. Lett.* **2021**, *28*, 219–223. [CrossRef]
16. Kipf, T.N.; Welling, M. Semi-supervised classification with graph convolutional networks. *arXiv* **2016**, arXiv:1609.02907.
17. Diao, Z.; Wang, X.; Zhang, D.; Liu, Y.; Xie, K.; He, S. Dynamic spatial-temporal graph convolutional neural networks for traffic forecasting. *Proc. AAAI Conf. Artif. Intell.* **2019**, *33*, 890–897. [CrossRef]
18. Tabar, Y.R.; Halici, U. A novel deep learning approach for classification of EEG motor imagery signals. *J. Neural Eng.* **2016**, *14*, 016003. [CrossRef] [PubMed]
19. Hochreiter, S. Long Short-term Memory. *Neural Comput.* **1997**, *9*, 1735–1780. [CrossRef] [PubMed]
20. Graves, A. Generating sequences with recurrent neural networks. *arXiv* **2013**, arXiv:1308.0850.
21. Gers, F.A.; Schmidhuber, J.; Cummins, F. Learning to forget: Continual prediction with LSTM. *Neural Comput.* **2000**, *12*, 2451–2471. [CrossRef]
22. Xu, G.; Ren, T.; Chen, Y.; Che, W. A one-dimensional CNN-LSTM model for epileptic seizure recognition using EEG signal analysis. *Front. Neurosci.* **2020**, *14*, 578126. [CrossRef]
23. Wang, X.; Wang, Y.; Liu, D.; Wang, Y.; Wang, Z. Automated recognition of epilepsy from EEG signals using a combining space–time algorithm of CNN-LSTM. *Sci. Rep.* **2023**, *13*, 14876. [CrossRef] [PubMed]
24. Liu, Y.; Zhao, B.; Zhang, S.; Xiao, W. Motor Imagery EEG Recognition Based on Weight-Sharing CNN-LSTM Network. In Proceedings of the 2022 34th Chinese Control and Decision Conference (CCDC), Hefei, China, 15–17 August 2022; IEEE: Piscataway, NJ, USA, 2022; pp. 1382–1386.
25. Li, H.; Li, X.; Millán, J.D.R. Noninvasive EEG-Based Intelligent Mobile Robots: A Systematic Review. In *IEEE Transactions on Automation Science and Engineering*; IEEE: Piscataway, NJ, USA, 2024.
26. Tonin, L.; Beraldo, G.; Tortora, S.; Menegatti, E. ROS-Neuro: An open-source platform for neurorobotics. *Front. Neurorobot.* **2022**, *16*, 886050. [CrossRef]
27. Beraldo, G.; Antonello, M.; Cimolato, A.; Menegatti, E.; Tonin, L. Brain-Computer Interface meets ROS: A robotic approach to mentally drive telepresence robots. In Proceedings of the 2018 IEEE International Conference on Robotics and Automation (ICRA), Brisbane, QLD, Australia, 21–25 May 2018; IEEE: Piscataway, NJ, USA, 2018; pp. 4459–4464.
28. Kraaijkamp, J.J.; Persoon, A.; Aurelian, S.; Bachmann, S.; Cameron, I.D.; Choukou, M.A.; Dockery, F.; Eruslanova, K.; Gordon, A.L.; Grund, S.; et al. eHealth in geriatric rehabilitation: An international survey of the experiences and needs of healthcare professionals. *J. Clin. Med.* **2023**, *12*, 4504. [CrossRef]
29. Blanco-Diaz, C.F.; Guerrero-Mendez, C.D.; de Andrade, R.M.; Badue, C.; De Souza, A.F.; Delisle-Rodriguez, D.; Bastos-Filho, T. Decoding lower-limb kinematic parameters during pedaling tasks using deep learning approaches and EEG. *Med. Biol. Eng. Comput.* **2024**, *62*, 3763–3779. [CrossRef]
30. Camargo-Vargas, D.; Callejas-Cuervo, M.; Mazzoleni, S. Brain-Computer Interfaces Systems for Upper and Lower Limb Rehabilitation: A Systematic Review. *Sensors* **2021**, *21*, 4312. [CrossRef]

31. EEG Electrode Cap Kit Website. Available online: https://shop.openbci.com/products/openbci-eeg-electrocap?srsltid=AfmBOooVHF6ZbmUqNRAamTVDu0Ij6Pz5WRE7juBK9nh71mJi7CgGi-X7 (accessed on 3 October 2024).
32. Gel Electrode Cap Guide Website. Available online: https://docs.openbci.com/AddOns/Headwear/ElectrodeCap/?_gl=1*l1hxj1*_gcl_au*MTg2MjU1MzgyNy4xNzI1OTU5NTIy*_ga*ODczMTAxNzk3LjE2ODY2NTMzODc.*_ga_HVMLC0ZWWS*MTcyOTY3MTQxOC42LjEuMTcyOTY3MTUxMS4zMS4wLjA (accessed on 3 October 2024).
33. The OpenBCI GUI Website. Available online: https://docs.openbci.com/Software/OpenBCISoftware/GUIDocs/?_gl=1*dypsg2*_gcl_au*MTg2MjU1MzgyNy4xNzI1OTU5NTIy*_ga*ODczMTxNzk3LjE2ODY2NTMzODc.*_ga_HVMLC0ZWWS*MTcyOTY3MTQxOC42LjEuMTcyOTY3MTQ3Ni4yLjAuMA (accessed on 3 October 2024).
34. TurtleBot3 Website. Available online: https://emanual.robotis.com/docs/en/platform/turtlebot3/features/ (accessed on 9 October 2024).
35. Interface L298N DC Motor Driver Module with Arduino Website. Available online: https://lastminuteengineers.com/l298n-dc-stepper-driver-arduino-tutorial/ (accessed on 9 October 2024).
36. Brunner, C.; Leeb, R.; Müller-Putz, G.; Schlögl, A.; Pfurtscheller, G. BCI Competition 2008–Graz data set A. *Inst. Knowl. Discov. (Lab. Brain-Comput. Interfaces) Graz Univ. Technol.* **2008**, *16*, 1–6.
37. Yan, B.; Root, A.J.; Gale, T.; Broman, D.; Kjolstad, F. Scorch: A Library for Sparse Deep Learning. *arXiv* **2024**, arXiv:2405.16883.
38. Xu, G.; Cao, H.; Dong, Y.; Yue, C.; Zou, Y. Stochastic gradient descent with step cosine warm restarts for pathological lymph node image classification via PET/CT images. In Proceedings of the 2020 IEEE 5th International Conference on Signal and Image Processing (ICSIP), Nanjing, China, 23–25 October 2020; IEEE: Piscataway, NJ, USA, 2020; pp. 490–493.
39. NeuralNet Subclasses for Classification Tasks Website. Available online: https://skorch.readthedocs.io/en/stable/classifier.html (accessed on 9 October 2024).
40. Install PyTorch Website. Available online: https://pytorch.org/ (accessed on 9 October 2024).

technologies

MDPI

Article

The Low-Cost Mechanism of a Defined Path Guide Slot-Based Passive Solar Tracker Intended for Developing Countries

José Luis Pérez-Gudiño [1], Marco Antonio Gómez-Guzmán [2], Chayanne García-Valdez [1], Roberto Valentín Carrillo-Serrano [1], Gerardo Israel Pérez-Soto [1] and Juvenal Rodríguez-Reséndiz [1,*]

1 Facultad de Ingeniería, Universidad Autónoma de Querétaro, Cerro de las Campanas s/n, Querétaro C.P. 76010, Mexico; jluis.perez.gudinho@gmail.com (J L.P.-G.); chayanne.garcia.valdez@gmail.com (C.G.-V.); roberto.carrillo@uaq.mx (R.V.C.-S.); israel.perez@uaq.mx (G.I.P.-S.)

2 Facultad de Ingeniería, Arquitectura y Diseño, Universidad Autónoma de Baja California, Carretera Transpeninsular Ensenada-Tijuana No. 3917, Ensenada C.P. 22860, Mexico; marco.guzman60@uabc.edu.mx

* Correspondence: juvenal@uaq.mx; Tel.: +52-442-170-2643

Abstract: Solar trackers represent a significant advancement in enhancing the efficiency of solar energy collection. This study describes the development and implementation of a passive solar tracker featuring a single horizontal axis of rotation and an innovative guide slot mechanism. The tracker is designed to be used with solar radiation-capturing devices. The guide slot mechanism is specifically engineered for a designated date, location, and period to follow the solar trajectory accurately. A contact follower moves along the guide slot, which drives a tracker disk to rotate by the solar trajectory. The mechanism is activated by the movement of a liquid container attached to a spring, thereby storing potential energy. The container releases the liquid through a mechanical valve that regulates the container's movement, while the guide slot mechanism converts this movement into controlled rotational motion, which is transferred to a mobile structure mounting the solar panel. Notably, the majority of materials utilized in this construction are recycled. Furthermore, the solar tracker proposed in this work is designed to be operable by individuals with limited prior knowledge on the topic, emphasizing the primary contribution of this study: its potential to revolutionize energy collection in developing countries and marginalized urban areas. No similar systems are found upon comparison with existing models in the literature. Experiments conducted with a static solar panel and the same panel integrated into the passive solar tracker revealed a 30.87% improvement in energy collection efficiency over static solar panels.

Keywords: solar energy; solar tracker; solar panel; low-cost technology; single-axis; guide slot

1. Introduction

The increasing demand for energy is leading to higher carbon emissions, which in turn accelerates concerns related to climate change. To address this issue, the deployment of renewable energy (RE) is on the rise, facilitating a global transition to sustainable energy sources [1]. As a clean energy option with minimal adverse environmental effects, regenerative energy presents a viable alternative to reduce dependence on fossil fuels [2,3]. Continuous innovation in industrial science is evolving to meet the urgent need for practical solutions within the energy and mechanical engineering sectors. Recent advancements in technology, mechanics, and materials have significantly enhanced sustainable energy production. Among these renewable sources, solar energy plays a crucial role, and scientific research is focused on increasing its efficiency and output [4,5]. Solar energy is one of the most abundant and essential renewable sources today due to its declining costs and increased accessibility [6,7]. It can be harnessed almost anywhere [8–10]. Solar cells are the primary source used to convert solar energy into electricity [11,12]. Most people rely on solar cells, a widely adopted technology integrated into compact devices, to generate photovoltaic (PV) energy. Solar cells convert solar radiation into electricity as expected [2,10,13]. To achieve optimal efficiency in this conversion, sunlight must hit the surface of the solar panel at a 90° angle [14]. Photovoltaic systems are now extensively used worldwide, connected to the power transmission grid and functioning as photovoltaic installations [15]. Photovoltaic technology is one of the most promising options for the future due to its simplicity, scalability, and lower costs associated with manufacturing, operation, and maintenance [16].

In recent years, solar PV, wind, and geothermal energy development has advanced significantly [13]. However, the amount of power generated by photovoltaic systems depends on several factors, including their efficiency, sunlight reaching the modules, and the technology employed [17]. Conventional PV panels need to be more robust in terms of efficiency. They typically generate only 12–18% of electricity and 82–88% of heat from solar radiation [18]. Therefore, improving conversion efficiency by reducing the operating temperature of PV systems is critical. Ongoing research aims to enhance energy production, address the challenges the photovoltaic sector faces, and achieve better results. The use of solar power systems has advantages and disadvantages, as outlined in Table 1 [3]:

Table 1. Advantages and disadvantages of employing PV systems.

Advantages	Disadvantages
Source of free energy.	Very costly to begin with.
Deliver eco-friendly power.	Setup requires ample space.
No detrimental greenhouse gases are released into the atmosphere when energy is generated.	Extreme reliance on technological progress.
Do not harm the environment in any way; eco-friendly.	Reliance on natural environments.
They generate power silently, making them ideal for use in urban and residential settings.	Solar panels still fall short, while other renewable energy sources are more efficient overall.
Minimal ongoing expenditures for upkeep compared to other renewable energy options.	

Research and development efforts are focused on maximizing energy collection in photovoltaic systems by studying and developing new technologies, as the power generated by these systems is directly influenced by the amount of solar radiation received [19,20]. The literature reports various techniques for increasing the efficiency of photovoltaic energy systems [3,21]. The main methods for improving power generation include cooling, cleaning, solar trackers, floating PV systems, and maximum power point tracking (MPPT) controllers [3].

One notable technique to optimize the efficiency of solar photovoltaic systems is the solar tracker [5,11,22–24]. A solar tracker is a mechanical device that adjusts the angle of solar panels to maximize sunlight absorption [5,11,23,25–27]. This alignment allows PV panels to maintain a right angle to the solar rays, enhancing energy production. The peak energy output occurs at a specific position called the maximum power position (MPP), which can change constantly based on variations in solar radiation and temperature. Monitoring MPPs is essential to maintain a consistently high level of energy generation [5,28,29]. Figure 1 shows the classification of solar tracker systems [3,30].

According to Figure 1 and based on their orientation mechanism, solar trackers can be divided into active and passive systems [6,22,30,31]. Passive tracking systems use stationary solar panels with minimal susceptibility to wind forces. These panels are positioned by exposing the solar cells to sunlight and aligning them towards the sun when its rays are most intense [12]. The cost-effective nature of this system can lead to an increase in collection efficiency of up to 23% [22,31]. Active tracking systems employ rotary or linear actuators, making their implementation more complex and costly [6].

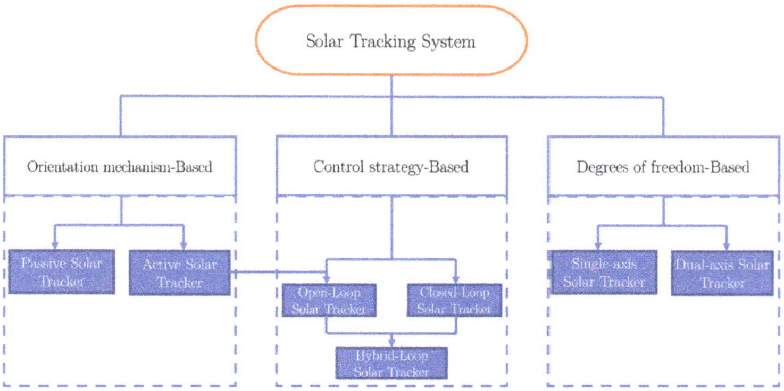

Figure 1. Solar tracker system classification.

Depending on the rotational movement of the axis, single-axis or dual-axis active tracking systems are available [29]. By tracking the path of the Sun along a single axis, such as horizontal, vertical, polar, or inclined [25,29,32], single-axis systems have the potential to improve their collection efficiency by 12–25% [16,22]. The efficiency of these trackers depends on factors such as climate, location, season, and system design [27,33,34]. Active dual-axis solar trackers have been reported to enhance collection efficiency by 17.1–31.1% [16,22]. Sun tracking systems with two axes generally revolve around either azimuthal and elevation axes or the polar and solar declination axes [25,29,31,32]. To achieve this design, pedestals or central support structures incorporating linear actuators for polar tracking and a slew motor for azimuthal monitoring can mount ring-rail-type structures designed to support extensive PV systems subject to high gusts. Dual-axis solar trackers are more effective than single-axis solar trackers because they can capture light from both the horizontal and vertical planes despite the higher production cost [24,33,35]. Studies [36] have confirmed the benefits of using solar trackers. Findings suggest that using a tracker to move a solar panel around might significantly improve its power output.

In recent work, talking about passive solar trackers [15], an innovative concept for a solar tracker was presented that would maximize the collection of solar energy by using intelligent materials. This technique features a passive solar tracker that employs a shape-memory alloy thermomechanical actuator to modify the inclination angle of the solar panels, allowing them to follow the Sun effectively.

In addition, in [37], a mechanical solar concentrating system was also introduced. This system includes a single-axis tracking mechanism that requires no energy, electronics, or specialized materials. It harnesses nocturnal wind energy to propel itself. A functional three-dimensional model with low-cost components was designed, constructed, and evaluated. In [38], a passive solar tracker based on bimetallic band deflectors was developed to operate independently of night temperatures. Field trials were conducted with both the proposed tracker and a fixed system. Energy harvesting, power density, and output were performance metrics. The suggested tracker produced 1081.7 Wh daily, compared to 716.7 Wh from a stationary system. The energy harvesting system suggested was 24.86% more effective than the fixed system.

In other examples, active solar trackers, such as single-axis solar tracker prototypes, have been proposed. For example, in [33], a solar tracking system with a single axis was developed and deployed using an Arduino Uno microcontroller to optimize daily energy production. This work proposed an automated system that tracks the Sun using a single axis and operates in a closed-loop configuration. A similar methodology was presented in [23,24]. Their Sun tracking system employed a mechanical frame, linear actuator, microprocessor, and azimuth positioning sensors. They obtained an efficiency of around 30.3% and 57.4%, respectively. Similarly, ref. [12] presented a fully autonomous single-axis closed-loop Sun tracking system using Arduino as a control device. They achieved 10–23% efficiency in the proposed system. Another example that did not use Arduino was proposed in [11], which implemented a system that drives a DC motor in response to inputs from light sensors, allowing the PV panel to move in sync with the system.

Following the aforementioned methodologies, in [27], a method was presented for sizing and designing a single-axis solar tracker using MATLAB R2020b as software simulation and Arduino for control actions.

Another type of solar tracker is the dual-axis tracker. For instance, using a closed-loop method [39], a dual-axes solar tracker based on Arduino and servomotors was proposed. The system was developed, built, and tested under various conditions to assess its efficiency, which was found to be 45%. In [10], a low-cost two-axis solar tracker was described, where researchers created a linear system to model the dynamics of a sun tracker using real-time data. This linear model was incorporated into the sun-tracking algorithms, leading to a reported 32% improvement in energy efficiency. For sensorless solar trackers, [7] suggested a low-cost solar tracking device to optimize PV panel solar energy collection in tropical regions. This design featured a mechanically operated ball-joint mechanism to achieve the objectives. The study focused on meticulously designing, manufacturing, and assembling three essential components: the tracking mechanism, collapsible solar panels, and the circuitry. The primary tracking mechanism involved a ball–joint system with four actuation motors, ensuring efficient operation. This solar tracking device outperformed conventional static panels by 37%. More recent methodologies, such as that in [40], introduced a genetic method to enable a solar tracker robot to evolve and accurately follow the movement of the Sun. The robotic system was constructed using an Arduino microcontroller and servomotors, demonstrating its ability to track the Sun's position effectively. Additionally, in [1], an autonomous solar tracking system that operates without sensors was presented. The system can monitor the movement of the Sun in horizontal and vertical axes. A unique solar tracking approach was developed using a robust sampling-based particle filter (PF) algorithm.

In another innovative robotic approach, [41] introduced a solar tracking technique using a collapsible solar gathering system designed for an amphibious robot. This system featured four servomotors that sequentially retracted four foldable small solar panels, allowing the robot to adjust the panel orientation for maximum power efficiency based on its location and time. This solar tracker proved effective, increasing solar energy collection efficiency by 62.4%. Furthermore, electronic monitoring systems for MPPT, along with solar tracking, have been integrated into dual-axis solar trackers to improve their accuracy and performance, as noted in [21].

Recent state-of-the-art reviews, such as those in [3,28], indicate that various methods have employed different control mechanisms, including sensor-based tracking algorithms and methodologies, astronomical equations, fuzzy logic [13], neural networks, time-based tracking systems, solar position calculation algorithms [34], Internet of Things methods (IoT) [8,30,42], and Petri networks [22].

This study makes several contributions related to solar tracking:

- The first contribution is the introduction of a new mechanism for passive solar trackers called the guide slot mechanism. This innovative design uses potential energy to imitate the solar trajectory, improving the ability of solar panels to track the Sun. A key feature of this mechanism is the guide slot, which regulates the rotation angle of the panel, enhancing its solar trajectory tracking accuracy.
- The second contribution highlights the efficiency observed in tests conducted. This study demonstrates an increase in solar radiation collection with the proposed solar tracker design compared to a static solar panel positioned parallel to the ground. The efficiency achieved with the new solar tracker design surpasses results from previous works on both passive and active solar trackers, as illustrated in Figure 17.
- The third contribution emphasizes the practicality and accessibility of this work. The solar tracker can be built and operated by individuals without technical expertise in solar tracking. Most materials used in the design are recycled, which showcases its

versatility and cost-effectiveness. This makes the design particularly suitable for use in developing countries, marginalized urban areas, and urban settings. Additionally, it can be integrated into high school curricula, enabling students to participate in the fight against climate change.

- The fourth contribution provides a method for creating the primary component of the solar tracker with the guide slot mechanism. It outlines the main variables needed to create the guide slot's trajectory and explains how to construct it using wood and simple tools. The disk with the guide slot is a key component. Ultimately, this work aims to present a functional solar tracker design that can be applied in various contexts to address environmental challenges, including thermal applications.

The organization of this paper is as follows. Section 2 outlines the methodology proposed for the single-axis solar tracker, along with details on the design and components. It also discusses the operational mechanism of the prototype. Section 3 presents the findings and limitations of the study. Finally, the conclusions of this study are summarized in Section 4.

2. Materials and Methods

This section outlines the components of the solar tracker test bench equipped with a guide slot and explains the function of each element. It also details the design of the guide slot for a specific location and date. Additionally, this section presents an example of a problem encountered when designing a guide slot and compares the trajectories of the guide slots needed to follow the solar path in June and December, specifically on the 15th day, at the same location. Finally, it discusses the design of a guide slot suitable for application in other regions.

2.1. The Proposed Solar Tracking System

The test bench utilized for this experimentation features a 3D prototype with components, as illustrated in Figure 2. Most of the materials used in this work are recycled, and their characteristics were chosen based on experimental evaluations. The prototype consists of a vertical support (1) that holds a piece of wood (2) securely at a specific height. Attached to one end of this piece of wood (2) is a spring (3), while the other end connects to a container (4) intended for storing liquid. When the container fills with water, the spring (3) is stretched, storing potential energy until the fluid is released from the container (4). Container (4) is fitted with a hose (6) and a valve (7) that permits controlled discharge of water. At the base of the container (5), a mechanical link (8) connects the vertical movement of the container (4) to a mechanism that converts this vertical motion into rotational movement, which is governed by the guide slot (10a) on the guide slot plate (10). The support (11) secures the guide slot plate (10) to a wooden base (14) with the aid of an angle support (13) and an inclined support (12). A follower disk (15) is linked to the shaft (17) through a mechanical connector (16). The guide slot plate (10) and the follower disk (15) are aligned centrally via a bushing, allowing for the free rotation of the follower disk (15). The shaft (17) is mounted on vertical supports (18) and (31), which are anchored to the wooden base (14) using angular supports (32) and (19). A structure for mounting the solar panel (30) attaches to the shaft (17) and comprises both aluminum parts (21, 24, 25, 28) and plastic components (22, 23, 26, 27). Consequently, as the follower disk (15) rotates, the solar panel (30) rotates in unison.

When container (4) is filled with liquid, spring (3) stretches, and container (4) moves downward. The solar tracker is initiated by manually opening valve (7) at a predetermined time, allowing a specific flow rate, which generates the process water discharge from the container over a period of time as shown in Figure 4a. A specific volume of liquid is discharged from a container (4), generating an upward vertical movement. This upward motion is transmitted through the link (8) to the follower disk (15) via a contact follower (9) attached to the link (8). The contact follower (9) tracks the trajectory of the guide slot (10a), generating rotational movement of the follower disk (15) as it is pushed by the contact follower (9) traversing the slot (15a). Thus, the rotational motion of the follower disk (15) is conveyed to the solar panel (30), enabling it to track the Sun's path on the specified date for which the guide slot (10a) was designed. As illustrated in Figure 3, the tracking disk is shown transparently to clarify the mechanical connection among the contact follower (9), slot (15a), and guide slot (10a).

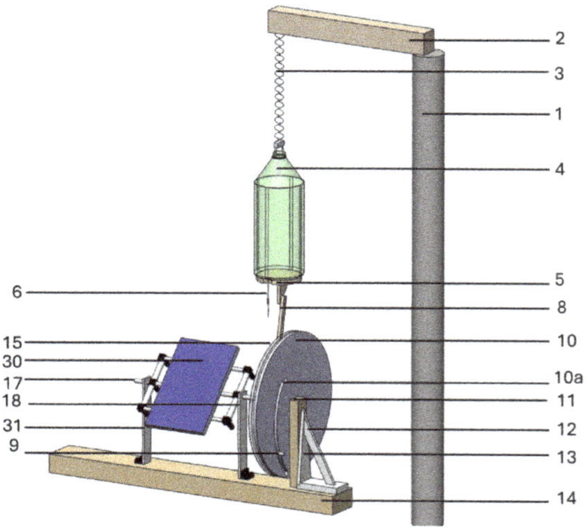

Figure 2. Three-dimensional design with enumerated elements of solar tracker test bench with guide slot, each number represents a part in the solar tracker design and a number with a letter represents a significant feature of a part.

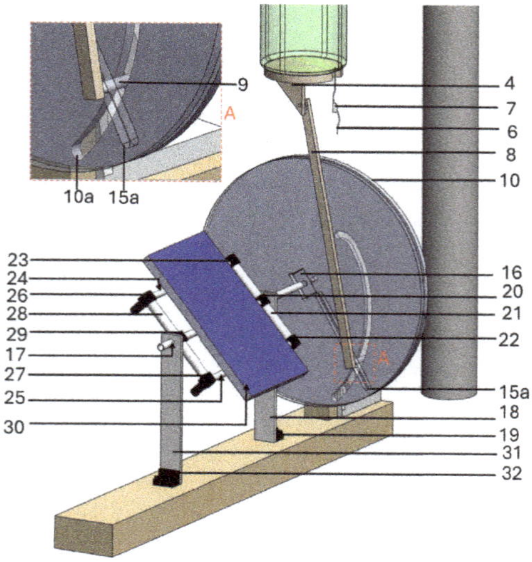

Figure 3. Three-dimensional design with enumerated elements of solar tracker test bench with guide slot and transparent follower disk (15), each number represents a part in the solar tracker design and a number with a letter represents a significant feature of a part.

2.2. Guide Slot Design

In the design of the guide slot, the container's vertical upward movement was first characterized. Experiment results are displayed in Figure 4a, which shows the initial discharge of water from the container at a rate of 48 mL over 2.5 min. After 10 h, 1.876 L of water remained out of a total of 9 L. The vertical upward movement of container M generated a trajectory of 30.5 cm over the 10 h, as shown in Figure 4b.

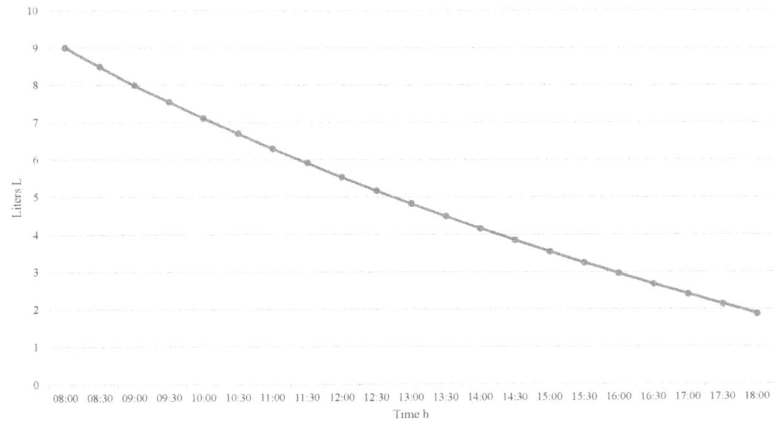

(**a**)

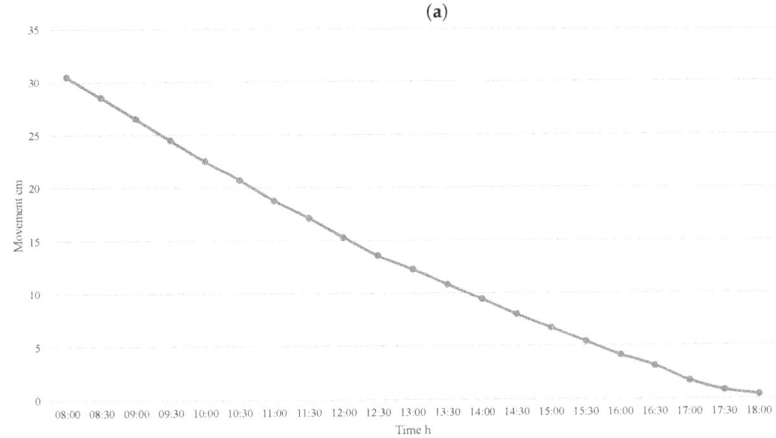

(**b**)

Figure 4. Results of the characterization. (**a**) Discharge of water from the container. (**b**) Vertical upward movement of the container over a 10 h period.

For the guide slot design, specific data were utilized. The first variable is the characterization of the vertical upward movement of the container, as illustrated in Figure 4b, represented by M_0 M_1 M_2 $\cdots$ M_{10}. In Figure 5, M_0 indicates the lowest point of the container when filled with a specified amount of water and serves as the starting point for solar tracking. The interval between M_0 and M_1 represents the vertically upward distance the container moved when discharging water through the manual valve over 1 h. M_{10} represents the total distance the container moved during the proposed 10 h period tracking the solar trajectory, from 8:00 a.m. to 6:00 p.m., moving from east (E) to west (W). The second variable consists of the angles needed to follow the solar trajectory along a single horizontal axis on a given date, represented by θ_0 θ_1 θ_2 $\cdots$ θ_{10}. Here, θ_0 is the angle pointing directly at the Sun at 8:00 a.m. Each θ corresponds to the angle required to point towards the Sun at specific times and locations throughout the day.

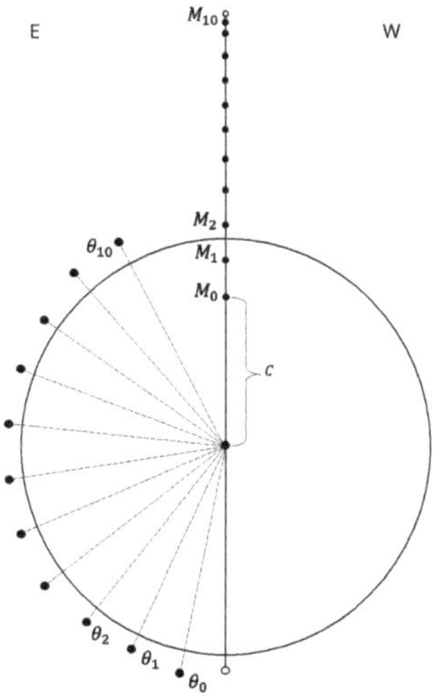

Figure 5. Variables for guide slot construction.

The proposed variable C represents the distance between the container and the guide slot mechanism's S-link relative to the follower disk's rotation axis. The length of the S-link was determined, with one end connected to point M_0 and the other connected to θ_0, as shown in Figure 6a at point P_1. Each M and corresponding θ were connected to form a shape represented in Figure 6b, and the points were joined with a curved line to create GS, the guide slot designed to follow the solar trajectory on a given date, as illustrated in Figure 6c. Consequently, the guide slot plate (10) is proportional to the movement of container M.

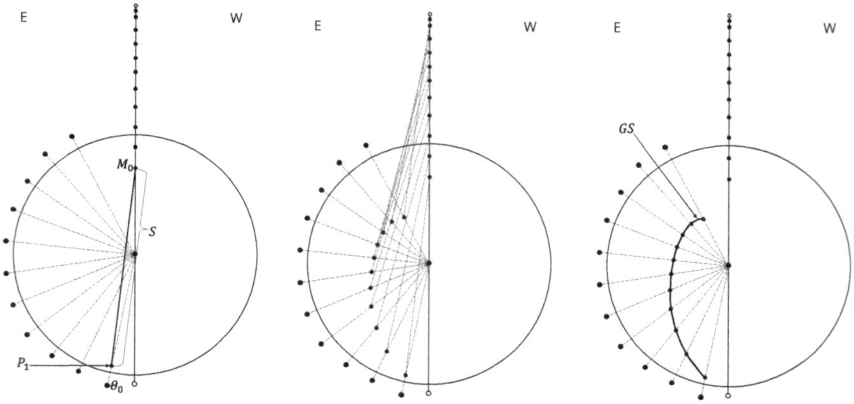

(a) (b) (c)

Figure 6. Guide slot design sequence. (**a**) S-link of the guide slot mechanism. (**b**) Marking the junction points. (**c**) Joining the points with a curved line to form GS.

In the design depicted in Figure 6a, links S and C were set at 38 cm and 16.5 cm, respectively. These dimensions were selected to ensure a smooth curve GS, preventing the mechanism from locking and ensuring the contact follower does not get stuck while crossing the guide slot. Figure 7 displays different GS with S-link measurements of 37.9 cm, 38 cm, and 38.1 cm. Significant length variations of S could cause the previously mentioned locking issue. Therefore, it is crucial to determine an appropriate length for the S-link to design a guide slot trajectory with a smooth curve using the proposed method.

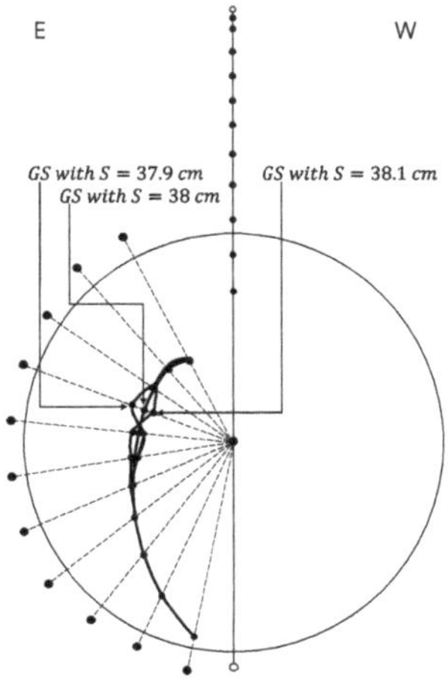

Figure 7. Different GS with $S = 37.9$, $S = 38$, and $S = 38.1$.

It is important to note that the guide slot is designed for a specific date. While a guide slot can function over several days, its accuracy in solar tracking diminishes over time. This article aims to address that concern. Additionally, the distance of the S must be considered. As shown in Figure 8, there are two guide slots for June 2023 and December 2023. The size and shape of the guide slots are noticeably different. The most significant point is that the June link needs to be more suitable for the December guide slot, which requires a link of a different length.

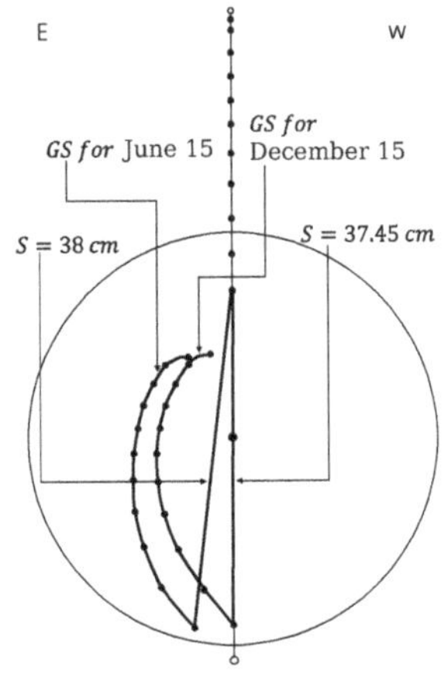

Figure 8. Different GS for the months of June and December.

2.3. Application of the Design in Other Regions

The proposed solar tracker design is not limited to a specific region but is adaptable to various locations. The development of the guide slots for these regions is shown in Figure 9a,b for Winnipeg, Canada, and Santa Cruz, Argentina, respectively. The only variables modified from the proposed design were the angles required to follow the solar trajectory concerning the proposed locations and S, with a length of 37.13 cm for Canada and 37.62 cm for Argentina. Both *GS* designs were developed on 15 March 2023, from 8:00 a.m. to 7:45 p.m. for Canada and from 9:00 a.m. to 7:00 p.m. for Argentina.

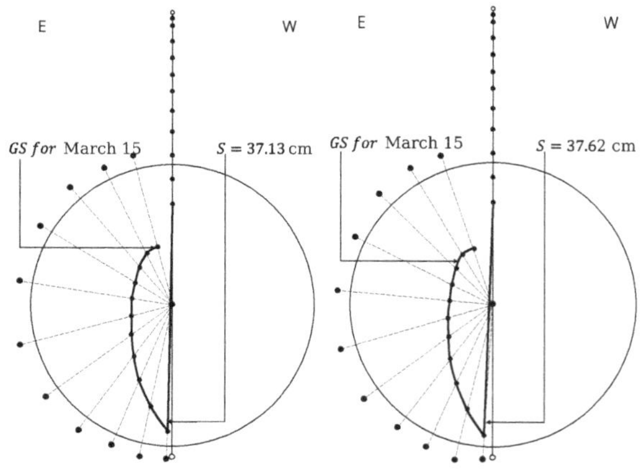

Figure 9. Guide slot in other regions. (**a**) Guide slot for Canada. (**b**) Guide slot for Argentina.

2.4. Construction of the Guide Slot

The construction of the guide slot is a detailed process that involves several steps. A vertical line V is drawn to create the guide slot, and a reference point C_0 is taken to draw the θ angles that follow the solar trajectory at a specific location and date, as shown in Figure 10a. Secondly, the P points were marked as shown in Figure 10b. By knowing the distances of S and C, the length between C_0 and P_1 is determined. The third step is to make circles of the diameter of the contact following the points marked previously, as shown in Figure 10c.

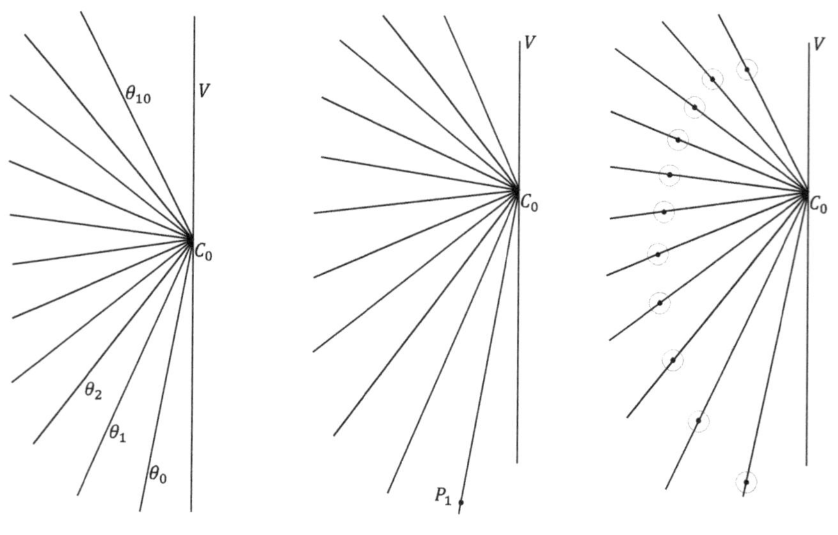

Figure 10. Guide slot construction sequence. (**a**) Making the angles that follow the solar trajectory. (**b**) Marking the points P. (**c**) Making circles of the diameter of the probe.

In the fourth step, the circles are joined by outlining a circular piece of proposed diameter to generate a smooth curve. The fifth step is to glue the drawing of the guide slot on the wooden disk in a centered way, as shown in Figure 11a,b.

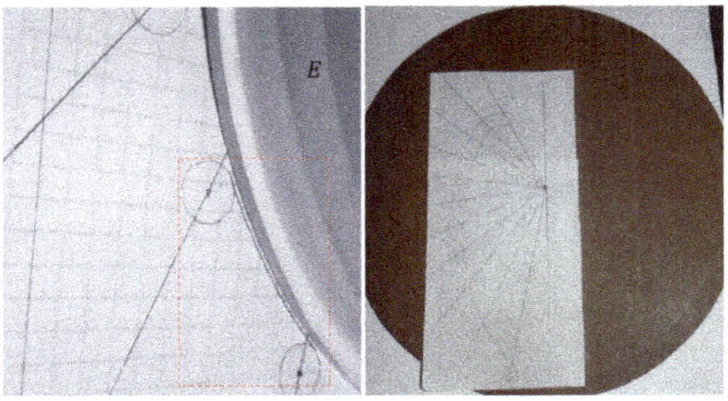

(a) (b)

Figure 11. (**a**) Joining the circles by means of a proposed circular piece. (**b**) Glueing the drawing of the guide groove to the wooden disk.

The sixth step consists of drilling holes large enough to allow the use of a woodcutter. The seventh step consists of filing the guide channel to the desired shape, as shown in Figure 12a,b.

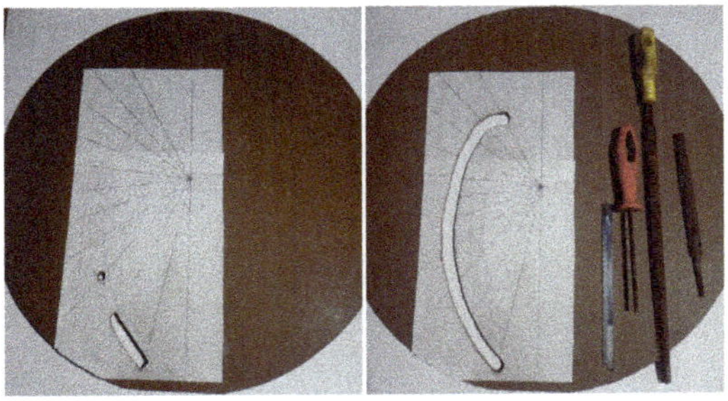

(a) (b)

Figure 12. (**a**) Drilling holes and cutting the wooden disk. (**b**) Filing the wood to form the guide slot.

3. Results and Discussion

Tests for radiation collection by a panel mounted on a solar tracker with a guide slot mechanism compared to a static panel were carried out on 14 June 2023 and 15 June 2023 from 8:00 a.m. to 6:00 p.m. at Cadereyta de Montes, Querétaro, Mexico. This location was chosen due to its high altitude of 2024 m above sea level and an atmospheric pressure of 1015 hPa, which provides a unique atmospheric condition for solar energy collection. The area is a semi-desert with a high temperature and arid environment and experiences moderate and heavy rainfall, making it an ideal test site for solar technology. In the location in the months of June, July, and May, less azimuthal movement of the solar panel is required to follow the trajectory of the sun, so the tests were performed in June, allowing the static panel to be placed parallel to the ground, which allows a comparison with the panel mounted on the solar tracker since it cannot perform the azimuthal movement. A similar test was also carried out on 12 November 2024; on this date, a wide azimuthal movement is required to be compared to the one required in June. The requirement of a higher azimuthal movement disfavors the solar radiation capture capacity of both panels, but the one which is more affected is the static solar panel. The project included a solar tracker of a single horizontal axis of rotation with a slot guide mechanism. A solar panel of 32 cm × 20.5 cm and 10 *W* (ECO-WORTHY PV-HS8303) was mounted, and a static solar panel of the same characteristics was positioned parallel to the ground (because of the location and date; the parallel position is a good choice for static panels). A spring of 32 cm was used at rest, as well as a container of 9 L, a guide slot mechanism, a mobile structure, a structure, a hose, and a manual valve, as shown in Figure 13a–c, and the panel rotated from east (E) to west (W).

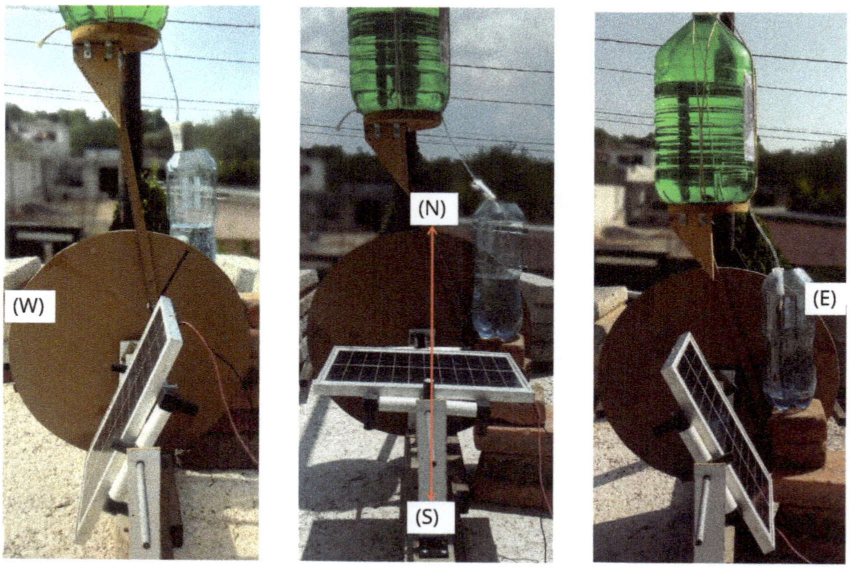

(**a**) (**b**) (**c**)

Figure 13. Single-axis solar tracker system proposed in this work completed a rotation of 152° from east (E) to west (W) over a 10 h period. (**a**) Evening position. (**b**) Noon position. (**c**) Morning position.

In order to ensure the correct execution of the system, the operator must perform two tasks:

- The first is to activate the valve at the indicated time.
- The second is to fill the container with the required amount of water. Marks should be placed on the container to verify the water required.

When the container was filled with 9 L of water (this process required no more than 10 min to complete), potential energy was stored in the spring, and the spring was stretched to 30.5 cm, giving a total length of 62.5 cm. The container descended vertically 30.5 cm, and the spring was stretched. The mobile structure was mechanically connected to the guide slot mechanism through the follower disk of the guide slot mechanism, which was pivotally connected to the lower part of the container. The mobile structure was used to mount the solar panel, while the container was employed to install the pipe and manual valve. We waited until 8:00 a.m. to activate the valve, considering an initial water discharge from the container of 48 mL in 2.5 min.

$$\eta = \frac{ST - SP}{SP}. \tag{1}$$

With the discharge flow mentioned, the container had a controlled vertical upward movement of 30.5 cm over 10 h. The panel completed a rotation of 152° from east (E) to west (W) and through Equation (1) [23], where the energy generated by a panel mounted on a solar tracker with a guide slot mechanism represented with ST and the energy generated by a static panel represented with SP, the results of the tests on 14 June 2023 and 15 June 2023 were 30.87 % and 30.17 % more energy captured by the solar panel mounted to the solar tracker of the single horizontal axis of rotation with guide slot mechanism. The results of the test on 12 November 2024 show an efficiency of 41.7% higher for the panel mounted to the solar tracker, but as previously mentioned, this is because in November a higher azimuthal movement is required to follow the solar trajectory than in June. Furthermore, in the test conducted in June, the conditions are more favorable for comparing the efficiency of the panel mounted to the tracker and the static panel parallel to the ground since less azimuthal movement is required. The prototype is shown in Figure 11a. Compared to the static solar panel horizontal to the ground, Tables 2–4 show the test data, and Figures 14–16 represent the collected data, further emphasizing the impact of this research. Additionally, the container was filled manually. The filling process must be conducted daily, and a manually activated valve was used to initiate the control of the fluid discharge from the container. A test was conducted using 9 L of water at the solar tracker location over 72 h to quantify water loss due to evaporation. After this period, the remaining water was measured with an electronic scale, yielding a result of 8.963 L. It was concluded that short-term evaporation does not significantly impact efficiency. Furthermore, a resistance test of the structure revealed that it can support 3.98 kg. However, it has already exhibited difficulty rotating the mobile structure. The increased weight necessitates greater effort from the spring to operate the mechanism. The panel utilized weighs 0.739 kg, thus allowing for the installation of at least five panels of the same dimensions in the proposed design. However, this would require modifications to the spring and increased water volume within the container to accommodate the augmented moving mass.

Table 2. Test power in W with data of a solar panel placed on a single-axis solar tracker using stored potential energy compared to a static solar panel. The experiments were conducted on 14 June 2023, from 8:00 a.m. to 6:00 p.m.

Number	Hour	Single-Axis Power	Static Panel Power
1	08:00	8.9182	4.0128
2	08:20	9.4299	5.2540
3	08:40	9.8056	5.7728
4	09:00	9.8551	6.6120
5	09:20	9.9123	7.1968
6	09:40	9.9258	7.7970
7	10:00	10.0100	8.4668
8	10:20	9.6162	9.0174
9	10:40	10.2065	9.4116
10	11:00	9.9900	9.3547
11	11:20	9.7755	9.5616
12	11:40	9.9750	9.6798
13	12:00	9.8700	9.7088
14	12:20	9.975	9.975
15	12:40	9.966	9.966
16	13:00	9.7148	9.7148
17	13:20	10.2145	10.1990
18	13:40	9.5756	9.2736
19	14:00	9.6052	9.2378
20	14:20	9.834	8.883
21	14:40	9.855	8.6716
22	15:00	9.9383	8.184
23	15:20	10.3581	7.9373
24	15:40	10.412	7.4703
25	16:00	10.3435	6.968
26	16:20	10.4643	6.2100
27	16:40	10.3853	5.392
28	17:00	9.6883	4.2752
29	17:20	9.504	3.8247
30	17:40	8.4609	2.3345
31	18:00	6.4701	1.6775

Table 3. Test power in W with data of a solar panel mounted on a single-axis solar tracker using stored potential energy compared to a stationary solar panel. The experiments were conducted on 15 June 2023, from 8:00 a.m. to 6:00 p.m.

Number	Hour	Single-Axis Power	Static Panel Power
1	08:00	8.8938	4.0774
2	08:20	9.4380	4.8008
3	08:40	9.6480	6.2567
4	09:00	9.8256	6.7803
5	09:20	9.7856	7.3564
6	09:40	9.6883	7.8546
7	10:00	9.7713	8.4501
8	10:20	9.7955	8.636
9	10:40	9.5810	8.7912
10	11:00	9.7585	9.2598
11	11:20	9.6425	9.4952
12	11:40	9.7608	9.6944
13	12:00	9.5192	9.5046
14	12:20	9.5922	9.5922
15	12:40	9.4685	9.4685
16	13:00	9.5991	9.5991
17	13:20	9.8603	9.7148
18	13:40	9.9207	9.5484
19	14:00	9.9256	9.3600
20	14:20	9.9207	8.8155
21	14:40	9.9056	8.437
22	15:00	10.1133	8.0848
23	15:20	9.9811	7.475
24	15:40	9.9012	6.888
25	16:00	10.1171	6.3456
26	16:20	10.0640	5.8080
27	16:40	10.0989	5.0236
28	17:00	9.0480	3.6465
29	17:20	9.4604	2.9841
30	17:40	8.9000	2.6052
31	18:00	4.9000	1.7290

Table 4. Test power in W with data of a solar panel placed on a single-axis solar tracker using stored potential energy compared to a static solar panel. The experiments were conducted on 12 November 2024, from 8:00 a.m. to 5:00 p.m. The solar trajectory could not be followed until 6:00 p.m. because of the mountains near the experimental area.

Number	Hour	Single-Axis Power	Static Panel Power
1	08:00	9.0248	2.229
2	08:20	9.7536	3.1777
3	08:40	9.6125	4.3616
4	09:00	10.108	5.236
5	09:20	10.0902	6.1752
6	09:40	10.0366	6.9285
7	10:00	10.1106	7.7376
8	10:20	10.1748	7.9488
9	10:40	10.1053	8.4132
10	11:00	10.0147	9.1512
11	11:20	9.9552	9.7944
12	11:40	9.6691	9.6154
13	12:00	9.516	9.6416
14	12:20	9.504	9.568
15	12:40	9.4189	9.4582

Table 4. *Cont.*

Number	Hour	Single-Axis Power	Static Panel Power
16	13:00	9.666	9.1977
17	13:20	9.7335	8.9298
18	13:40	9.6078	8.7596
19	14:00	9.5494	7.909
20	14:20	9.7512	7.776
21	14:40	9.576	7.3134
22	15:00	9.451	6.552
23	15:20	9.4428	5.736
24	15:40	9.2202	4.189
25	16:00	8.6258	3.894
26	16:20	8.1984	2.73
27	16:40	7.7698	2.0708
28	17:00	6.2866	1.7862

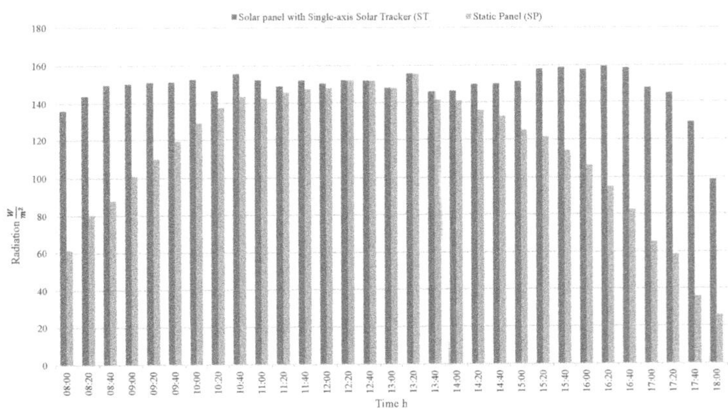

(a)

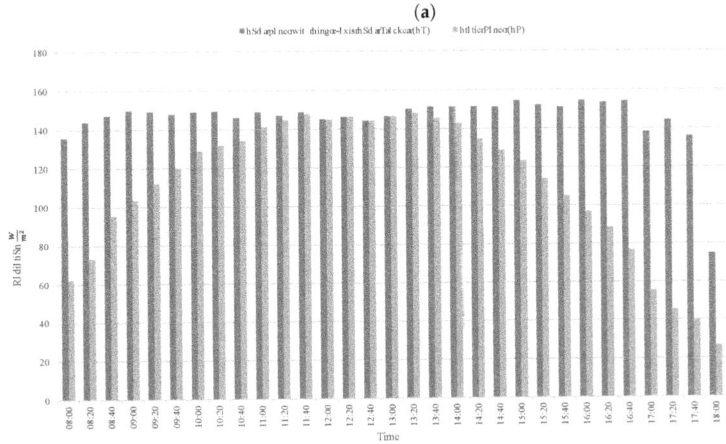

(b)

Figure 14. Solar radiation of the solar panel with a single-axis solar tracker and static panel during the period from 8:00 a.m. to 6:00 p.m. (**a**) On 14 June 2023. (**b**) On 15 June 2023.

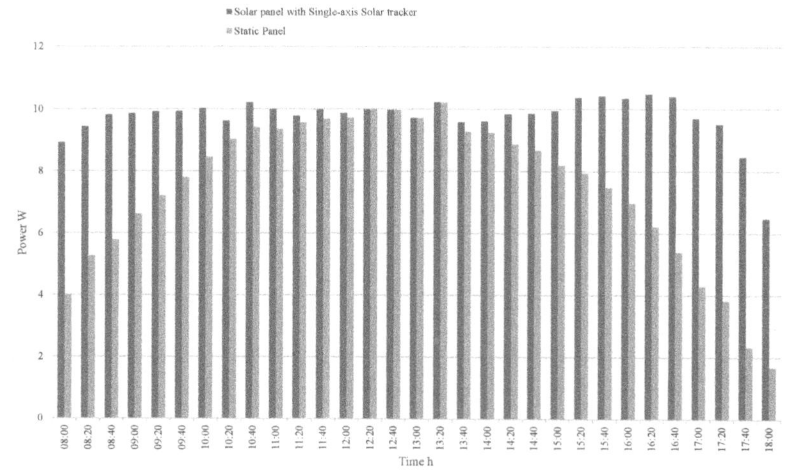

(a)

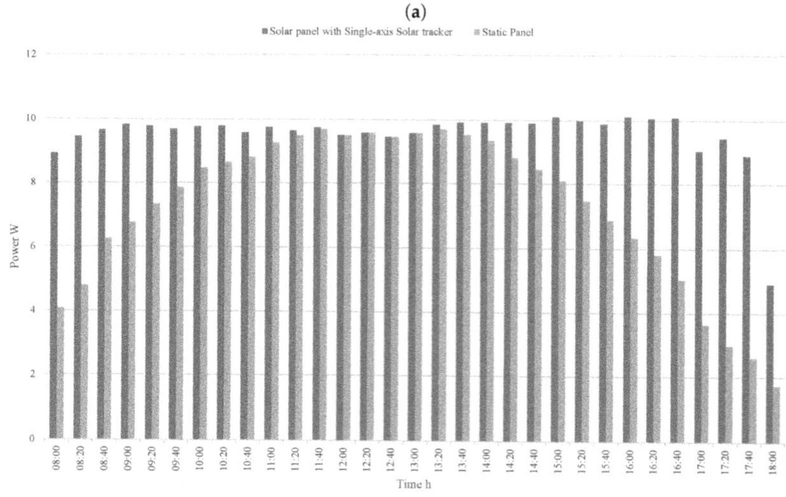

(b)

Figure 15. Power area graph of the solar panel with a single-axis solar tracker and static panel during the period from 8:00 a.m. to 6:00 p.m. (**a**) On 14 June 2023. (**b**) On 15 June 2023.

3.1. Comparison to Contemporary Related Work

Table 5 displays a comparative analysis between this research and previously published studies. The efficiency achieved in this study is comparable to prior efforts using microcontrollers and surpasses similar work with one-axis passive solar trackers. While previous studies using microcontroller methods have achieved better efficiency, it is essential to note that the production costs in those studies are significantly higher than those of the passive single-axis (horizontal) guide slot solar tracker.

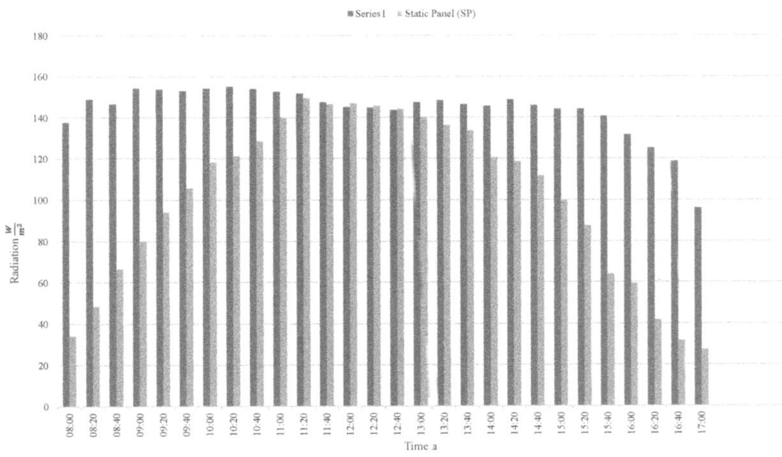

(a)

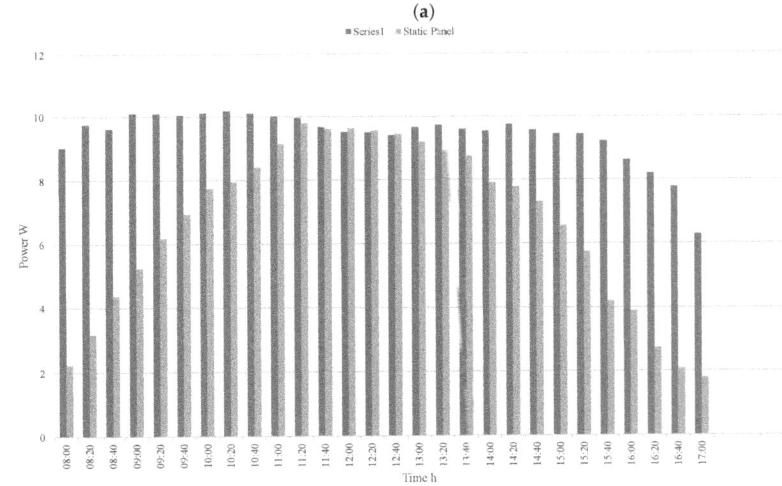

(b)

Figure 16. (**a**) Solar radiation and (**b**) power area graph of the solar panel with a single-axis solar tracker and static panel during the period from 8:00 a.m. to 5:00 p.m. on 12 November 2024.

Table 5. Comparison with related work.

Reference	Solar Tracking System	Energy Efficiency
[10]	Two-axis solar tracker	32%
[12]	Arduino based single-axis (horizontal)	10–23%
[23]	Microcontroller based single-axis solar tracker	30.3%
[31]	Solar Tracker with Active Orientation	30%
[33]	Arduino based single-axis solar tracking system	–
[38]	Passive solar tracker with a bimetallic band deflector	24.86%
This work	Passive single-axis (horizontal) with guide slot	30.87% and 30.17%

Additionally, as shown in Figure 17, the passive solar tracker design based on a defined guide slot path performs better than some active types of trackers utilizing microcontrollers and outperforms other passive solar tracker designs.

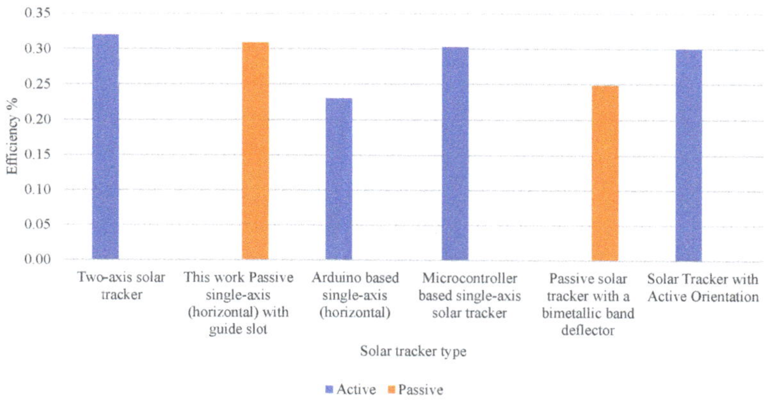

Figure 17. Comparison of the efficiency of active and passive solar trackers.

3.2. Limitations of the Study

One limitation of this study is the requirement for an appropriate climate, as energy production depends heavily on a predominantly sunny environment. Using a guide slot for this prototype is another limitation, as different guide slots would need to be manufactured depending on the geographical area. However, the design is scalable. Furthermore, this solar tracker can be adapted for other applications, such as thermal energy storage or dual-axis tracking systems, although changes in materials would be necessary based on operating conditions. For instance, a robust structure is essential in environments with strong winds, and durable materials such as metals or polymers must be used to prevent deterioration over time.

4. Conclusions

This paper introduces a passive solar tracking technology featuring a guide slot mechanism. The newly designed solar tracker harnesses stored potential energy to propel the guide slot mechanism, enabling the solar panel's movement and thereby improving solar energy harvesting efficiency. The solar tracker allows the solar cells to follow the sun's trajectory by adjusting the tilt angle. This device can encourage the use of solar energy, especially in developing countries, because of its low construction cost, use of everyday materials, ease of operation, and compatibility for use by non-technical individuals. The previous sections presented a model comprised of several components where the only purchased material for constructing the solar tracker test bench with a guide slot mechanism was wood, used to build the follower disk and the disk with the guide slot; all other materials were recycled from previous applications. In this design, solar tracking was achieved using energy manually stored in a spring.

Additionally, the mechanical valve limiting the movement of the container was manually operated, and the guide slot disk was manually adjustable. The solar tracker demonstrated significantly enhanced solar radiation collection compared to other trackers reported in the literature. Another notable aspect is its versatility, which is applicable in urban and rural settings.

Below is a summary of the contributions of this work.

- A new mechanism for passive solar trackers improves the ability to follow the solar trajectory.
- The efficiency achieved with the proposed solar tracker design surpasses previous works on passive and active solar trackers, as shown in Figure 17.
- The design is particularly well-suited for implementation in developing countries and marginalized urban areas, but it is also feasible for urban settings and could be taught to high school students.

- The method for creating the main component of the solar tracker with a guide slot mechanism is clearly illustrated, highlighting the critical variables involved in generating the guide slot trajectory.

The findings revealed a consistent upward vertical displacement of 30.5 cm over 10 h. During this period, the solar panel completed a rotation of 152° from east to west. In two separate tests, the solar panel mounted on the 1-axis solar tracker with a guide slot mechanism captured 30.87% and 30.17% more energy output than the stationary solar panel placed horizontally on the ground.

Author Contributions: Methodology, J.L.P.-G. and M.A.G.-G.; validation, J.R.-R.; investigation, C.G.-V. and G.I.P.-S.; resources, R.V.C.-S. All authors have read and agreed to the published version of the manuscript.

Funding: This research received no external funding.

Institutional Review Board Statement: Not applicable.

Informed Consent Statement: Not applicable.

Data Availability Statement: The original contributions presented in the study are included in the article, further inquiries can be directed to the corresponding author/s.

Acknowledgments: I would like to thank my family for supporting me throughout my professional career and allowing me to test the solar tracker at their home. I would like to take this opportunity to mention that the project is currently under application for intellectual property protection at the Mexican Institute of Industrial Property (IMPI) under application number MX-002394.

Conflicts of Interest: The authors declare no conflicts of interest.

References

1. Pirayawaraporn, A.; Sappaniran, S.; Nooraksa, S.; Prommai, C.; Chindakham, N.; Jamroen, C. Innovative sensorless dual-axis solar tracking system using particle filter. *Appl. Energy* **2023**, *338*, 120946. [CrossRef]
2. Dehshiri, S.S.H.; Firoozabadi, B. Comparison, evaluation and prioritization of solar photovoltaic tracking systems using multi criteria decision making methods. *Sustain. Energy Technol. Assess.* **2023**, *55*, 102989.
3. El Hammoumi, A.; Chtita, S.; Motahhir, S.; El Ghzizal, A. Solar PV energy: From material to use, and the most commonly used techniques to maximize the power output of PV systems: A focus on solar trackers and floating solar panels. *Energy Rep.* **2022**, *8*, 11992–12010. [CrossRef]
4. Poojitha, K.; Ashwini, L.; Anjali, B.; Ramprabhakar, J. Solar tracker using maximum power point tracking algorithm. In Proceedings of the 2019 International Conference on Intelligent Computing and Control Systems (ICCS), Madurai, India, 15–17 May 2019; pp. 1528–1531.
5. Klimek, K.; Kapłan, M.; Halchak, V.; Korobka, S.; Syrotyuk, S.; Konieczny, R.; Filipczak, G.; Dybek, B.; Wałowski, G. Orientation and Exposure Efficiency of a Solar Tracking Surface in Clear Sky. *Appl. Sci.* **2022**, *12*, 9118. [CrossRef]
6. Alexandru, C. Optimization of the bi-axial tracking system for a photovoltaic platform. *Energies* **2021**, *14*, 535. [CrossRef]
7. Ramful, R.; Sowaruth, N. Low-cost solar tracker to maximize the capture of solar energy in tropical countries. *Energy Rep.* **2022**, *8*, 295–302. [CrossRef]
8. Sritoklin, A.; Malee, W.; Prugsanantanatorn, A.; Sapaklom, T.; Ayudhya, P.N.N.; Mujjalinvimut, E.; Kunthong, J. A Low Cost, Open-source IoT based 2-axis Active Solar Tracker for Smart Communities. In Proceedings of the 2018 International Conference and Utility Exhibition on Green Energy for Sustainable Development (ICUE), Phuket, Thailand, 24–26 October 2018; pp. 1–4.
9. Ma, W.; Zhang, W.; Zhang, X.; Chen, W.; Tan, Q. Experimental investigations on the wind load interference effects of single-axis solar tracker arrays. *Renew. Energy* **2023**, *202*, 566–580. [CrossRef]
10. Vargas, A.N.; Francisco, G.R.; Montezuma, M.A.; Sampaio, L.P.; Acho, L. Low-cost dual-axis solar tracker with photovoltaic energy processing for education. *Sustain. Energy Technol. Assess.* **2022**, *53*, 102542. [CrossRef]
11. Mehdi, G.; Ali, N.; Hussain, S.; Zaidi, A.A.; Shah, A.H.; Azeem, M.M. Design and fabrication of automatic single axis solar tracker for solar panel. In Proceedings of the 2019 2nd International Conference on Computing, Mathematics and Engineering Technologies (iCoMET), Sukkur, Pakistan, 30–31 January 2019; pp. 1–4.
12. Haris, O.; Darmawan, A.; Juliansyah, A. Efficiency Analysis of Using Solar Panel System Tracker to Static Solar Panel. In Proceedings of the 2021 IEEE 7th International Conference on Computing, Engineering and Design (ICCED), Sukabumi, Indonesia, 5–6 August 2021; pp. 1–6.
13. Kumar, P.; Shrivastava, A. Maximum power tracking from solar PV system by using fuzzy-logic and incremental conductance techniques. *Mater. Today Proc.* **2022**, *79*, 267–277. [CrossRef]
14. Engin, M. Controller Design for Parallel Mechanism Solar Tracker. *Machines* **2023**, *11*, 372. [CrossRef]

15. Riad, A.; Zohra, M.B.; Alhamany, A.; Mansouri, M. Bio-sun tracker engineering self-driven by thermo-mechanical actuator for photovoltaic solar systems. *Case Stud. Therm. Eng.* **2020**, *21*, 100709. [CrossRef]
16. Gómez-Uceda, F.J.; Moreno-Garcia, I.M.; Jiménez-Martínez, J.M.; López-Luque, R.; Fernández-Ahumada, L.M. Analysis of the influence of terrain orientation on the design of pv facilities with single-axis trackers. *Appl. Sci.* **2020**, *10*, 8531. [CrossRef]
17. Al Garni, H.Z. The Impact of Soiling on PV Module Performance in Saudi Arabia. *Energies* **2022**, *15*, 8033. [CrossRef]
18. Rezk, H.; Fathy, A. Stochastic Fractal Search Optimization Algorithm Based Global MPPT for Triple-Junction Photovoltaic Solar System. *Energies* **2020**, *13*, 4971. [CrossRef]
19. da Rocha Queiroz, J.; da Silva Souza, A.; Gussoli, M.K.; de Oliveira, J.C.D.; Andrade, C.M.G. Construction and automation of a microcontrolled solar tracker. *Processes* **2020**, *8*, 1309. [CrossRef]
20. Piotrowski, L.J.; Farret, F.A. Feasibility of solar tracking and fixed topologies considering the estimated degradation and performance of photovoltaic panels. *Sol. Energy Mater. Sol. Cells* **2022**, *244*, 111834. [CrossRef]
21. Kumar, M.; Sharma, S.; Verma, N.; Jain, A.; Sharma, A.K. Design of a GPS Enabled Maximum Power Point Solar Tracker for Mobile Platform. In Proceedings of the 2021 6th International Conference on Communication and Electronics Systems (ICCES), Coimbatore, India, 8–10 July 2021; pp. 834–839.
22. Ruelas, J.; Muñoz, F.; Lucero, B.; Palomares, J. PV tracking design methodology based on an orientation efficiency chart. *Appl. Sci.* **2019**, *9*, 894. [CrossRef]
23. Ngo, X.C.; Nguyen, T.H.; Do, N.Y.; Nguyen, D.M.; Vo, D.V.N.; Lam, S.S.; Heo, D.; Shokouhimehr, M.; Nguyen, V.H.; Varma, R.S.; et al. Grid-connected photovoltaic systems with single-axis sun tracker: Case study for Central Vietnam. *Energies* **2020**, *13*, 1457. [CrossRef]
24. Kuttybay, N.; Saymbetov, A.; Mekhilef, S.; Nurgaliyev, M.; Tukymbekov, D.; Dosymbetova, G.; Meiirkhanov, A.; Svanbayev, Y. Optimized single-axis schedule solar tracker in different weather conditions. *Energies* **2020**, *13*, 5226. [CrossRef]
25. Gómez-Uceda, F.J.; Moreno-Garcia, I.M.; Perez-Castañeda, Á.; Fernández-Ahumada, L.M. Study of the dependence of solar radiation regarding design variables in photovoltaic solar installations with optimal dual-axis tracking. *Appl. Sci.* **2021**, *11*, 3917. [CrossRef]
26. Hailu, A. Manual tracking for solar parabolic concentrator–For the case of solar injera baking, Ethiopia. *Heliyon* **2023**, *9*, e12884. [CrossRef]
27. Baouche, F.Z.; Abderezzak, B.; Ladmi, A.; Arbaoui, K.; Suciu, G.; Mihaltan, T.C.; Raboaca, M.S.; Hudișteanu, S.V.; Țurcanu, F.E. Design and Simulation of a Solar Tracking System for PV. *Appl. Sci.* **2022**, *12*, 9682. [CrossRef]
28. Katche, M.L.; Makokha, A.B.; Zachary, S.O.; Adaramola, M.S. A Comprehensive Review of Maximum Power Point Tracking (MPPT) Techniques Used in Solar PV Systems. *Energies* **2023**, *16*, 2206. [CrossRef]
29. Musa, A.; Alozie, E.; Suleiman, S.A.; Ojo, J.A.; Imoize, A.L. A Review of Time-Based Solar Photovoltaic Tracking Systems. *Information* **2023**, *14*, 211. [CrossRef]
30. Gutierrez, S.; Rodrigo, P.M.; Alvarez, J.; Acero, A.; Montoya, A. Development and testing of a single-axis photovoltaic sun tracker through the Internet of Things. *Energies* **2020**, *13*, 2547. [CrossRef]
31. Petrusev, A.; Rulevskiy, V.; Sarsikeyev, Y.Z.; Lyapunov, D.Y. Solar tracker with active orientation. In Proceedings of the 2016 2nd International Conference on Industrial Engineering, Applications and Manufacturing (ICIEAM), Chelyabinsk, Russia, 19–20 May 2016; pp. 1–4.
32. Sawant, A.; Bondre, D.; Joshi, A.; Tambavekar, P.; Deshmukh, A. Design and analysis of automated dual axis solar tracker based on light sensors. In Proceedings of the 2018 2nd International Conference on I-SMAC (IoT in Social, Mobile, Analytics and Cloud)(I-SMAC) I-SMAC (IoT in Social, Mobile, Analytics and Cloud)(I-SMAC), Palladam, India, 30–31 August 2018; pp. 454–459.
33. Rani, P.; Singh, O.; Pandey, S. An analysis on Arduino based single axis solar tracker. In Proceedings of the 2018 5th IEEE Uttar Pradesh Section International Conference on Electrical, Electronics and Computer Engineering (UPCON), Gorakhpur, India, 2–4 November 2018; pp. 1–5.
34. Melo, K.B.d.; Moreira, H.S.; Villalva, M.G. Influence of Solar Position Calculation Methods Applied to Horizontal Single-Axis Solar Trackers on Energy Generation. *Energies* **2020**, *13*, 3826. [CrossRef]
35. Mubaarak, S.; Zhang, D.; Chen, Y.; Liu, J.; Wang, L.; Yuan, R.; Wu, J.; Zhang, Y.; Li, M. Techno-economic analysis of grid-connected pv and fuel cell hybrid system using different pv tracking techniques. *Appl. Sci.* **2020**, *10*, 8515. [CrossRef]
36. Manjhi, S.K.; Rohan, R.; Kumar, D. Comparison of Static and Single Axis Solar Tracker. In Proceedings of the 2022 IEEE 2nd International Symposium on Sustainable Energy, Signal Processing and Cyber Security (iSSSC), Gunupur, Odisha, India, 15–17 December 2022; pp. 1–5.
37. Elsayed, A.A.; Khalil, E.E.; Kassem, M.A.; Huzzayin, O.A. A novel mechanical solar tracking mechanism with single axis of tracking for developing countries. *Renew. Energy* **2021**, *170*, 1129–1142. [CrossRef]
38. Alemayehu, M.; Admasu, B.T. Passive solar tracker using a bimetallic strip activator with an integrated night return mechanism. *Heliyon* **2023**, *9*, e18174. [CrossRef]
39. Sahu, S.; Tiwari, S.; Patel, R. Analysis and Testing of Dual Axis Solar Tracker for a Standalone PV System. In Proceedings of the 2020 First International Conference on Power, Control and Computing Technologies (ICPC2T), Raipur, India, 3–5 January 2020; pp. 96–101.

40. Szabo, R.; Ricman, R.S. A Genetic Algorithm-Controlled Solar Tracker Robot with Increased Precision Due to Evolution. *Machines* **2023**, *11*, 430. [CrossRef]
41. Liu, C.; Sun, Z.; Huang, C.; Wang, S.; Xing, H.; Guo, S.; Liu, W.; Li, H. A Novel Solar Tracker with a Foldable Solar Harvesting Mechanism for an Amphibious Robot. In Proceedings of the 2022 IEEE International Conference on Mechatronics and Automation (ICMA), Guilin, China, 7–10 August 2022; pp. 1257–1262.
42. Williams, K.; Qouneh, A. Internet of Things: Solar array tracker. In Proceedings of the 2017 IEEE 60th International Midwest Symposium on Circuits and Systems (MWSCAS), Boston, MA, USA, 6–9 August 2017; pp. 1057–1060.

technologies

MDPI

Article

IoT-Enhanced Decision Support System for Real-Time Greenhouse Microclimate Monitoring and Control

Dragoș-Ioan Săcăleanu [1,*], Mihai-Gabriel Matache [2], Ștefan-George Roșu [1], Bogdan-Cristian Florea [1], Irina-Petra Manciu [1] and Lucian-Andrei Perișoară [1]

[1] Faculty of Electronics, Telecommunication and Information Technology, National University of Science and Technology Politehnica Bucharest, 060042 Bucharest, Romania; stefan.rosu@upb.ro (Ș.-G.R.); bogdan.florea@upb.ro (B.-C.F.); irina_petra.toma@upb.ro (I.-P.M.); lucian.perisoara@upb.ro (L.-A.P.)

[2] Testing Department, The National Institute of Research—Development for Machines and Installations Designed for Agriculture and Food Industry, 013813 Bucharest, Romania; matache@inma.ro

* Correspondence: dragos.sacaleanu@upb.ro

Abstract: Greenhouses have taken on a fundamental role in agriculture. The Internet of Things (IoT) is a key concept used in greenhouse-based precision agriculture (PA) to enhance vegetable quality and quantity while improving resource efficiency. Integrating wireless sensor networks (WSNs) into greenhouses to monitor environmental parameters represents a critical first step in developing a complete IoT solution. For further optimization of the results, including actuator nodes to control the microclimate is necessary. The greenhouse must also be remotely monitored and controlled via an internet-based platform. This paper proposes an IoT-based architecture as a decision support system for farmers. A web platform has been developed to acquire data from custom-developed wireless sensor nodes and send commands to custom-developed wireless actuator nodes in a greenhouse environment. The wireless sensor and actuator nodes (WSANs) utilize LoRaWAN, one of the most prominent Low-Power Wide-Area Network (LPWAN) technologies, known for its long data transmission range. A real-time end-to-end deployment of a remotely managed WSAN was conducted. The power consumption of the wireless sensor nodes and the recharge efficiency of installed solar panels were analyzed under worst-case scenarios with continuously active nodes and minimal intervals between data transmissions. Datasets were acquired from multiple sensor nodes over a month, demonstrating the system's functionality and feasibility.

Keywords: IoT; wireless sensor networks; wireless actuator nodes; LoRaWAN; precision agriculture; greenhouse; automation

1. Introduction

Agriculture has been one of the primary domains targeted by sensing technology since its inception. The reliable and continuous observation of environmental and plant-related data is essential to producing results that can positively impact crop quality. The IoT, big data, cloud computing, and advanced analytics, as key elements of the Industry 4.0 paradigm (with Agriculture 4.0 as a subset), empower precision agriculture (PA) to leverage the collection, processing, and analysis of data. These technologies are integrated into management systems, enabling informed decision making for optimized farming outcomes [1,2]. The decision support systems (DSSs) concept applied in agriculture (Agri-DSSs) have advanced with the integration of sensor networks and artificial intelligence (AI) technologies, enabling process automation [3]. These systems compile intricate agricultural data to achieve a unified objective: enhancing the quantity and quality of agricultural production. To deliver optimal solutions, specific components of Agri-DSSs must be tailored to environmental characteristics.

Since the 1990s, the demand for Agri-DSSs has significantly increased globally for various reasons [4]. Until recently, DSSs' focus was mainly on data analysis in that it was a next-process step after the initial data acquisition step. The output was missing real-time changing capabilities and was not instantly applied to enhance farm operations. The automatic control of environmental parameters was lacking due to the disproportionate development of electronic, communication, and information processing components. However, designing the right IoT architecture for a farm requires the careful consideration of factors such as sensing elements, communication protocols, the farm's data processing capacity, and time performance. A systematic architecture design approach is needed to meet the specific functional and quality requirements of a farm [5,6].

In 1994, PA was defined as a management strategy that uses information technology to improve agricultural quality and production [7]. As part of the transition to a new level of PA, and as an effective management approach for increasing agricultural yield via the more efficient utilization of resources, DSSs help farmers make well-informed decisions about their crops. With recent advancements, IoT-based architectures are increasingly being used in decision support systems for farmers. These architectures typically include several common elements, such as a WSN for data collection, IoT devices (smart sensors, actuators, and controllers), and user interfaces (such as mobile apps or web portals with information and recommendations). For more accurate results and timely responses, information can be processed with decision support algorithms and models [8].

With limited resources, small farmers are more prone to being affected by the ever-changing environmental conditions that severely impact agriculture. The challenges and opportunities offered to small-scale farmers by the latest technological advancements are reviewed in [9]. The need for affordable technological solutions to support them in enhancing productivity and sustainability now represents a primary direction of the research into monitoring and controlling solutions for greenhouses [10].

Greenhouses represent the ideal environment for modeling and testing PA solutions. Greenhouse technologies have been transformed from niche systems for specialty crops into the cornerstone of intensive agriculture. On the technology side, the expansion is driven by the need to meet rising consumer demands for consistently high-quality products available year-round. The impact of environmental factors and field management practices on the quality of harvested products is often underestimated, and decision support systems are in high demand once their importance is acknowledged. Sensing, monitoring, and controlling commonly imply a network of various sensors and actuators in devices that influence environmental parameters for improved output. The best candidates for those tasks are WSNs and the extended concept of Wireless Sensor and Actuator Networks (WSANs), which have the characteristics of low energy consumption, a low cost, and deployment versatility.

2. Related Work

In the 2000s, the principles of wireless technology applied to monitoring and control—networks of wireless sensors and actuators—were extensively described by works such as [11–18]. The characteristics of wireless communication positioned it to be a technology well suited for application in greenhouse environmental management.

Wireless technologies are already used as a common infrastructure for communication patterns in diverse scenarios [19]. A WSN solution for PA in an orchard is presented in Ref. [20]. The characteristics that WSNs must fulfill to be applicable in agriculture were also analyzed. The applications of WSNs in open-space agriculture are for both process monitoring and control. Influencing the growing environment is, in this case, more difficult due to the significant number of parameters in this context. In Ref. [21], typical applications of the IoT for agriculture were analyzed, with the problems encountered both from the implementation and development perspectives finally being highlighted. Examples of the hardware, sensors, and platforms used for the IoT in agriculture are described in Ref. [22]. The paper presents a broad view of WSNs in agriculture, focusing on the potential of IoT technologies, and emphasizing their increasing adoption and value for farmers. Additionally, the paper highlights the importance of standardizing IoT core technologies to ensure seamless operation across various platforms and operating systems. In Ref. [23], the authors provide a comprehensive review of emerging technologies for IoT-based smart agriculture, including wireless technologies, unmanned aerial vehicles, open-source IoT platforms, Software Defined Networking and Network Function Virtualization technologies, cloud/fog computing, and middleware platforms, while Ref. [24] presents a specific example of an in-field data acquisition sensor prototype.

To ensure the best possible plant evolution in greenhouses, solutions for parameter monitoring such as temperature, humidity, light intensity, soil moisture, and composition were designed using traditional methods before wireless technology was available. Initially, greenhouse operators relied on manual monitoring methods, which involved physically checking environmental parameters and using analog instruments like thermometers and soil moisture probes [25,26]. With the advancement of automation, analog control systems employing mechanical or pneumatic devices were introduced to regulate environmental conditions. In early greenhouses, automation featured wired sensor networks for real-time monitoring and control, transmitting data to a central control unit. During this period, greenhouse operators frequently used data logging techniques to track environmental data over time. This process involved using either simple handheld loggers or more advanced systems connected to computers, which collected and stored sensor measurements at regular intervals for later analysis. While these traditional methods required more manual effort and were less efficient than modern wireless monitoring systems, they laid the groundwork for greenhouse management practices and were essential for optimizing plant growth prior to the wireless technology era [27].

When addressing smaller-sized surfaces, greenhouse farming can be seen as a comprehensive system strategy for optimizing the production of agricultural crops in a controlled environment. In this context, greenhouses are often considered an ideal environment for pioneering the implementation of new agricultural technologies. Ref. [28] provides an in-depth review of wireless sensor networks for greenhouses, starting from the layout of crops, technologies used for sensor communication (such as ZigBee, GPRS, LoRa, Wi-Fi, and Bluetooth), and transmission techniques. Ref. [29] reviews the greenhouse environment from design to monitoring and control. Ref. [30] proposed a mobile and dynamic monitoring system based on autonomous quadruped vehicles connected with wireless sensors for a flower-cultivation greenhouse. The mobility of the system's elements facilitates monitoring capabilities without any control features being implemented.

The authors in Ref. [31] presented a real-time end-to-end deployment of a LoRaWAN-based sensor network in a greenhouse. They found that temperature and humidity had a larger impact on the sensor readings inside the greenhouse than initially expected. Their paper demonstrates the feasibility of leveraging LoRaWAN technology for PA applications in greenhouse environments, highlighting the importance of proper sensor enclosure design to obtain reliable data.

In Ref. [32], a low-power wireless sensor network was designed using commercial components and free or open-source software libraries, based on LoRaWAN protocol, with a focus on low-cost IoT applications for greenhouse monitoring. The whole system was implemented to demonstrate the feasibility of building a modular system with low-cost off-the-shelf components, including sensors, but with no actuation functions.

Another application of low-power communication technology for intelligent agricultural greenhouses is described in Ref. [33], where a wireless network detection and control system uses NB-IoT technology to facilitate remote monitoring and control of greenhouse conditions. In Ref. [34], the authors built a WSN employing low-cost, low-power sensor nodes that use solar power to operate independently. The sensor nodes were designed for low energy consumption, enabling them to be powered by small solar units. Additionally, a greenhouse controller was developed to interface with the WSN and provide IoT connectivity. The authors from Ref. [35] presented four types of sensing nodes: two powered by batteries and two more complex nodes that relied on renewable technology, designed for scenarios where monitoring is necessary during the daytime. Several power options were analyzed considering that the communication protocol used, namely Wi-Fi, has a high energy-demanding rate. Many IoT-based greenhouse solutions primarily involve the monitoring aspect [36–40]. Solutions also include a control part that usually uses low-cost and low-reliability relays [41,42], and it has only been implemented in experimental scenarios, with no plans for development into a commercial product.

This paper presents an IoT-based Agri-DSS utilizing a wireless sensor network designed to monitor and control environmental parameters in a greenhouse. This is used for an end-to-end application that includes various types of devices for a remote monitoring and controlling solution, providing flexibility in terms of the number of devices, types of sensors, communication protocols, and number of users. For testing, the environmental parameters of interest for greenhouse management, such as air temperature and humidity, air pressure, light intensity, UVA, UVB, CO_2, soil temperature, soil humidity at different depths, and soil tension, are monitored. Additionally, soil moisture is regulated through irrigation, and air temperature and humidity are controlled through airflow.

The system's architectural design, along with a description and the testing of its components, is provided. This is followed by an evaluation of the system's performance and the results obtained from its implementation in a greenhouse environment.

3. System Design and Implementation

The system developed and utilized in this paper is flexible, making it suitable for different greenhouse scenarios. The hardware used in this system includes wireless sensor nodes (WSns), wireless actuator nodes (WAns), and a gateway. In a general scenario (see Figure 1), the data flow begins with the WSn. The acquired parameters are then transmitted via a LoRa radio to a gateway, which sends the data over Wi-Fi to a web platform over the internet. There, the data are processed, displayed, and stored. Based on this, the user can send commands from the web platform through the gateway to the WAn. The system uses the LoRaWAN network architecture with a star topology both for sensors and actuator nodes, where the gateway exchanges messages between the nodes and the central network server.

Figure 1. The architecture of the proposed Agri-DSS.

Depending on the amount of area that needs to be monitored and on the systems that need to be controlled, the number of sensor or actuator nodes is scalable as the solution can be implemented from small-scale to large-scale greenhouses. Furthermore, multiple greenhouses in a certain area can be monitored and controlled due to the data communication range. The WSn and WAn architectures were developed to be compatible with the Arduino MKR developing boards family. For the presented scenario, the Arduino MKR WAN 1310 developing board was used with LoRa communication, but a series of other communication protocol options can be implemented, like Wi-Fi (Arduino MKR1000 WIFI), GSM (Arduino MKR GSM 1400), SigFox (Arduino MKR FOX 1200), or NarrowBand (Arduino MKR NB 1500).

3.1. Wireless Sensor Node

3.1.1. WSn Design

Wireless sensor nodes are responsible for acquiring data from sensors, processing them, and transmitting the information to the gateway. The proposed block diagram of the node, shown in Figure 2, highlights the various types of sensors that could be utilized, including analog sensors, I2C sensors, and one-wire sensors.

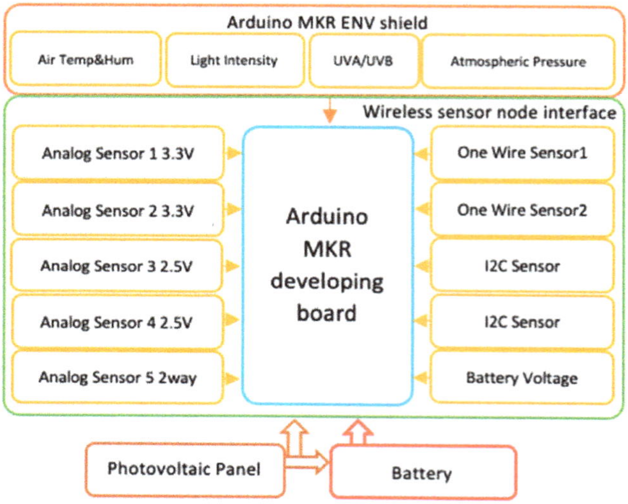

Figure 2. Wireless sensor node block diagram.

A flexible node interface was developed to support a variety of attached sensors and communication protocols. The central component of the node is the microcontroller-based development board from the Arduino MKR family. The advantages of using this off-the-shelf core include the low-power SAMD21 Cortex®-M0 + 32 bit ARM MCU, integration with a variety of wireless communication protocols used for WSN, the integration of the ATECC508 security chip, and support for power supply from Li-ion or Li-Po rechargeable batteries and an integrated recharge circuit. Additional advantages include management of the power consumption, personalized shield with environmental sensors, and a microSD card slot (Arduino MKR ENV Shield). For this experiment, the Arduino MKR WAN 1310 equipped with the Murata CMWX1ZZABZ LoRa® module was selected to utilize LoRaWAN communication.

3.1.2. WSn Development

Based on the parameters of interest tested in this paper, a set of sensors compatible with the WSn block diagram was selected. Table 1 presents the acquired parameters and the sensors used. The Arduino MKR ENV Shield was attached to the Arduino MKR WAN 1310 board. Each parameter was represented using two bytes, resulting in a total of 28 bytes, considering the battery voltage in addition to the 13 acquired parameters.

Table 1. The wireless sensor node's acquired parameters and sensors.

No	Parameter	Sensor	Type	Connector
1	Light Intensity	VISHAY TEMT6000	Analog	Arduino MKR ENV shield; two-row, 14-position header
2	Air Pressure	ST LPS22HB	SPI	
3	Node Temperature	ST HTS221		
4	Node Humidity			
5	UVA	VISHAY VEML6075	I2C	
6	UVB			
7	Air Temperature	Sensirion SHT31	I2C	4-terminal wire-to-board connector
8	Air Humidity			
9	Soil Temperature	DS18B20	One wire	3-terminal wire-to-board connector
10	CO_2	Sensirion SCD41	I2C	two-row, 4-position header
11	Soil Tension	Watermark Sensor	Analog	2-terminal wire-to-board connector
12	Soil Humidity depth1	Capacitive Sensor		3-terminal wire-to-board connector
13	Soil Humidity depth2			

For sensor connection and signal conditioning, an electrical schematic of the interface was designed and is shown in Figure 3.

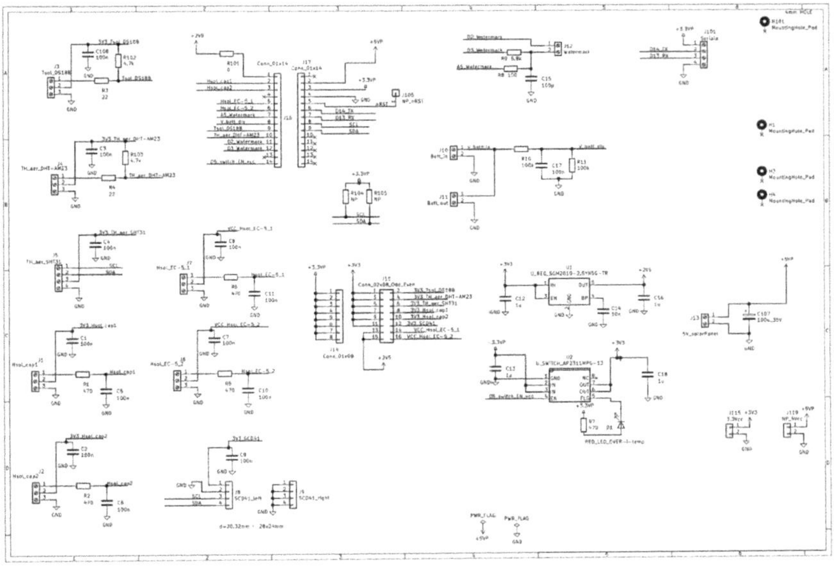

Figure 3. WSn electrical schematic.

The signal conditioning interface was designed as a two-layer PCB with dimensions of 85 × 66.5 mm. Figure 4 shows the top layer of the PBC (a), the PCB bottom layer (b), and the 3D model of the interface (c). The interface was equipped with a two-row, 14-pin header connector for the Arduino MKR developing board; eight wire-to-board terminal blocks for sensors; a two-row, four-position header connector for the CO_2 sensor; one-wire to-board terminal block for USART communication; and three wire-to-board terminal blocks for power supply (one for the rechargeable battery, one for the Arduino developing board, and one for the solar panel). To improve power efficiency, each sensor can be connected to the 3.3 V power supply directly or through a digital switch by using a jumper. The battery voltage level is acquired through an analog pin, passed previously through a

½ voltage divider. An additional 2.5 V power supply was included for two sensors with these requirements. The interface is compatible with analog sensors, I2C sensors, and one-wire sensors.

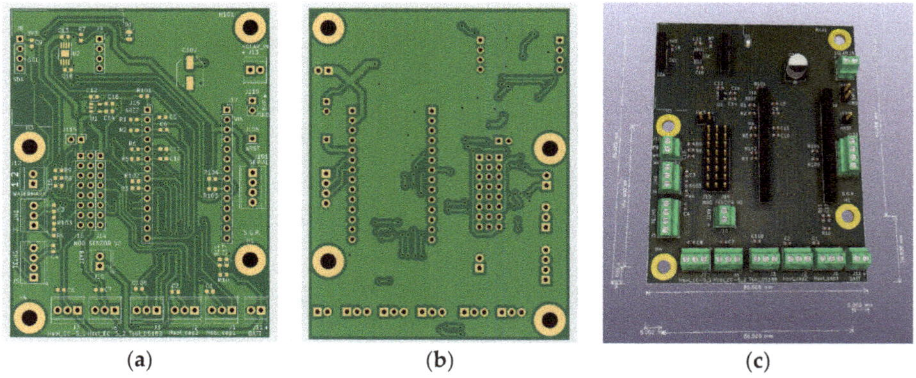

Figure 4. PCB of wireless sensor node signal conditioning interface: (**a**) top layer; (**b**) bottom layer; and (**c**) 3D model.

Figure 5 shows the manufactured signal conditioning interface with all the connected devices. Two Li-ion 18650 rechargeable batteries of 5000 mAh were used for power supply, and an 11 × 13.5 cm photovoltaic panel of 2 W was used for battery charging.

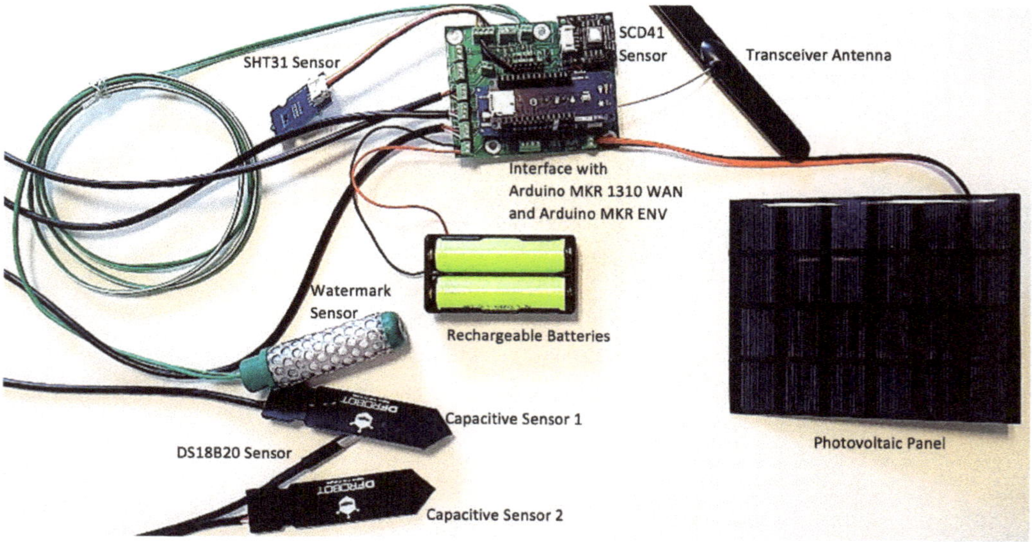

Figure 5. The wireless sensor node with attached components.

A custom covered case was developed using a 3D printer to protect the circuits (see Figure 6). The cover is provided with fixing pads for the interface, a custom pad for the SHT31 sensor, a special designed opening for the CO_2 sensor, a slit for the light, and UVA and UVB sensors.

Figure 7 shows the final version of the wireless sensor node.

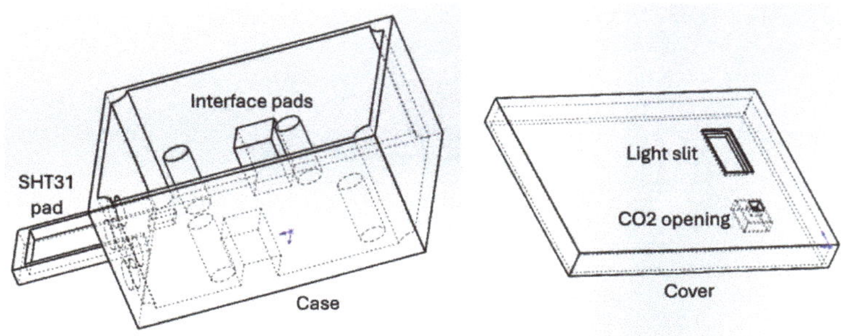

Figure 6. Wireless sensor node case 3D model and cover.

Figure 7. The final wireless sensor node installed in the greenhouse.

The WSn had a basic data processing software routine. After the initial setup for the microcontroller, transceiver, and individual sensors, the node acquired data from the sensors, processed them, stored them on the microSD card, and sent them to the gateway. Finally, the sensor's power was shut down, and the transceiver and the microcontroller entered sleep mode. The sleep time could be adjusted considering the application, but due to the LoRaWAN protocol, at least 2 min must past between two consecutive transmissions. When waking up, the WSn continued acquiring a new set of data.

3.1.3. WSn Laboratory Tests

The WSn was tested and evaluated in the laboratory to assess its functionality and viability time. Current consumption was measured to implement suitable power management solutions. The drain current from the rechargeable batteries was monitored during both data processing and the node's deep sleep mode.

Figure 8 depicts the waveform of the current consumption during o loop acquisition, with node data acquisition, transmission, and the deep sleep mode. During data acquisition, higher power consumption was recorded when collecting data from the CO_2 sensor. Data acquisition takes approximately 6 s, while the data transmission time varies depending on the parameters set for the LoRa protocol. The goal was to ensure reliable data reception at the gateway while considering range and power consumption.

Current consumption tests were conducted by changing LoRa parameters, including the Spread Factor (7–12), Power Level (0–20), Coding Rate (5–8), and Bandwidth (500–7.8 kHz). Figure 9 presents the results obtained by keeping three out of four parameters constant to ensure data transmission at the greatest distance while varying the fourth parameter. When the Power Level was changing, the average current consumption was measured. For the other parameters, focus was placed on tracking the data transmission time, with the average current consumption remaining constant.

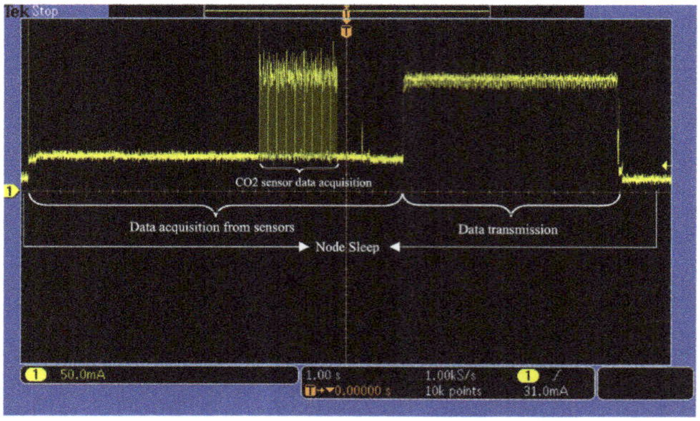

Figure 8. The current drain waveform during an acquisition loop.

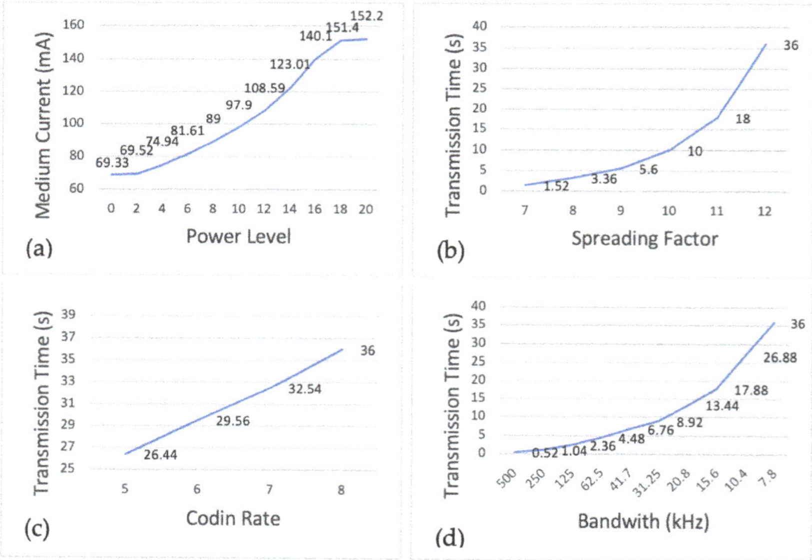

Figure 9. Tests conducted for different values of LoRa parameters: (**a**) medium current consumption regarding Power Level; (**b**) transmission time regarding Spread Factor; (**c**) transmission time regarding Coding Rate; (**d**) transmission time regarding Bandwidth.

To evaluate the node's battery life, the charge (i.e., current consumption in time mAh) was automatically measured using an oscilloscope with capabilities of integrating the current waveform during the studied event. Figure 10 shows the current consumption in transmission (red graph), when all parameters are set to transmit data at the longest distance. Thus, the 28 bytes are transmitted in 35.80 s with an average consumption of 152.5 mA.

In this case, the current consumption was the highest, and the duration of data transmission was very long. If it were to transmit data continuously, for a total battery capacity of 10 Ah (2 × 5000 mAh), the battery life would be up to 2 h.

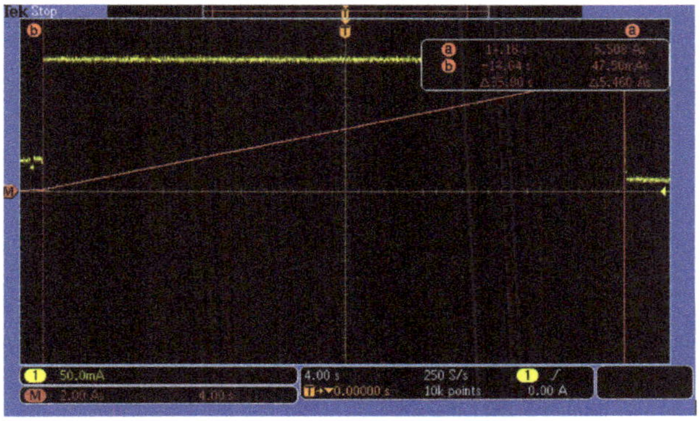

Figure 10. The charge during transmission with all LoRa parameters set to a maximum range.

For the application described in this paper, data acquisition is suited for longer time intervals (at least 10 min), when the node enters into a deep sleep state, consuming an average current of about 3 mA (see Figure 11). In this case, a lifespan of over 100 days can be achieved, not including battery charging from photovoltaic panels.

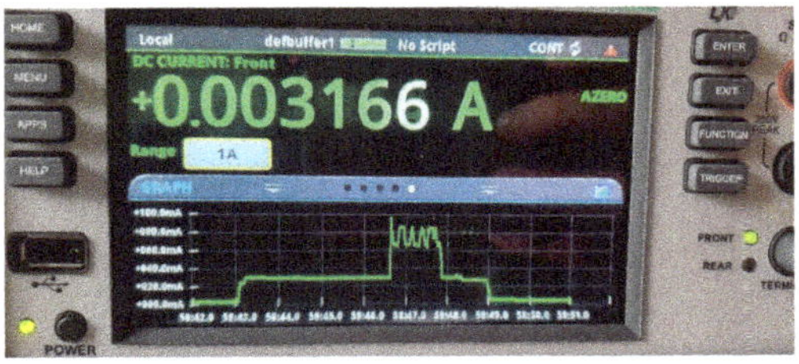

Figure 11. Node's current consumption in deep sleep mode.

The acquisition, storage, and transmission of data were also verified. Figure 12 depicts the raw data acquired and stored in a file on the node's memory card.

VOLTAGE	ILLUMINANCE	PRESSURE	NODE TEMP	NODE HUM	UVA	UVB	AIR TEMP	AIR HUM	SOIL TEMP	CO2	SOIL TENSION	SOIL HUM1	SOIL HUM2
1938,44	173,55	103,2	21,87	50,04	16,9	18,62	20,86	48,95	19,56	1342	3287,62	2547,02	2582,44
1932	167,1	103,2	21,91	50,56	15,9	18,62	20,9	49,64	19,56	1321	3287,62	2543,8	2582,44
1935,22	169,68	103,2	22,17	50,6	15,57	16,88	20,99	49,66	19,62	1807	3284,4	2543,8	2585,66
1935,22	144,52	103,2	22,1	50,5	15,12	17,57	21,02	48,78	19,69	1570	3287,62	2547,02	2582,44
1932	155,48	103,2	22,11	50,21	15,12	18,57	21,04	51,39	19,75	1448	3287,62	2547,02	2585,66
1928,78	172,26	103,2	22,15	50,41	15,57	18,88	21,04	49,13	19,75	1588	3287,62	2547,02	2585,66
1932	170,97	103,21	22,17	49,81	15,9	18,62	21,07	48,64	19,75	1439	3281,18	2547,02	2585,66
1932	171,61	103,2	22,06	49,63	15,57	17,88	21,06	[illegible]	19,75	1371	3287,62	2547,02	2582,44
1935,22	170,97	103,2	22,1	49,44	15,57	16,88	21,07	[illegible]	19,69	1294	3284,4	2547,02	2582,44
1932	171,61	103,21	22,04	49,34	16,35	16,93	21,07	[illegible]	19,75	1262	3287,62	2543,8	2582,44
1932	172,26	103,2	22,02	49,35	16,35	17,93	21,06	48,46	19,75	1276	3287,62	2547,02	2585,66
1935,22	172,9	103,2	22	49,81	16,35	17,93	21,07	48,79	19,75	1222	3287,62	2547,02	2582,44
1932	103,23	103,2	22	50,43	13,67	16,26	21,04	49,02	19,75	1399	3284,4	2547,02	2582,44
1935,22	109,68	103,2	22	50,89	13,67	16,26	21,07	49,64	19,69	1685	3287,62	2547,02	2582,44
1932	160	103,2	22,02	50,39	15,35	16,93	21,04	49,08	19,81	1706	3287,62	2543,8	2585,66
1935,22	171,61	103,2	22,04	50,42	16,35	17,93	21,1	48,95	19,75	1683	3284,4	2550,24	2582,44
1932	172,26	103,2	22,02	50,62	15,35	16,93	21,08	48,95	19,81	1729	3284,4	2547,02	2582,44

Figure 12. The raw data stored on the node's microSD card.

3.2. Wireless Actuator Node

3.2.1. WAn Design

The wireless actuator nodes control the activation and deactiviation of the control equipment for the microclimatic factors in a greenhouse based on commands received from users through the web platform via the gateway. Figure 13 presents the proposed block diagram for the wireless actuator node.

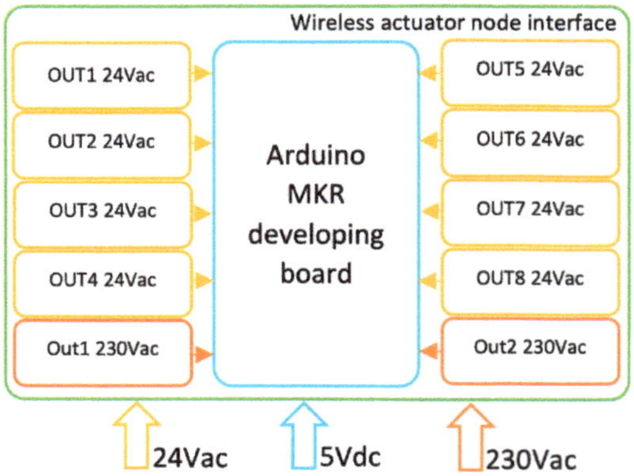

Figure 13. Wireless actuator node block diagram.

Common equipment in a greenhouse is powered by 24 Vac (e.g., solenoid valves for irrigation) and 230 Vac (e.g., fans and motors to control air temperature and humidity, CO_2, and light intensity). The WAn was developed by considering eight channels to control 24 Vac, max. 0.5 A devices and two channels to control 230 Vac, max. 4 A devices. Based on the greenhouse scenario, multiple nodes can be implemented. The Arduino MKR WAN 1310 was also used for the WAn with a 5 Vdc power supply.

3.2.2. WAn Development

The electrical schematic of the WAn is presented in Figure 14.

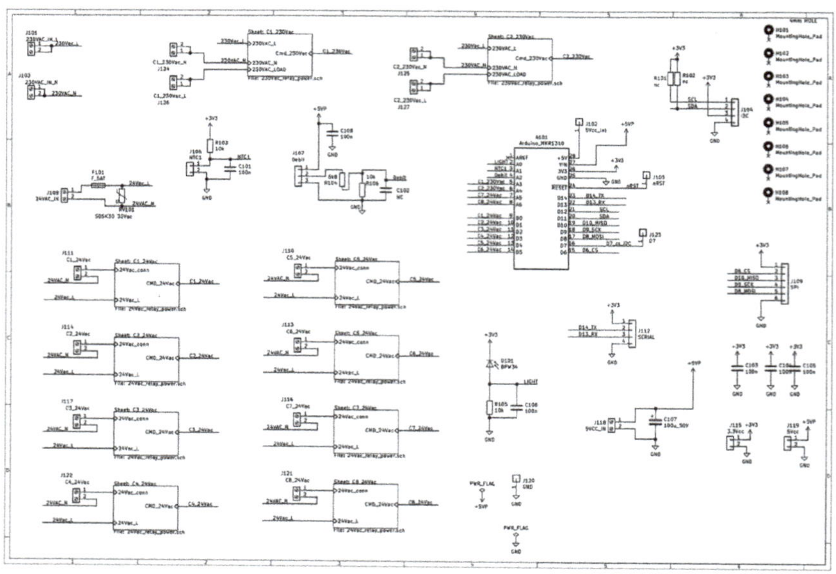

Figure 14. WAn electrical schematic.

The designed WAn signal conditioning interface has a two-layer PCB with dimensions of 217 × 131 mm. Figure 15 presents the PCB top layer (a) and the 3D model of the interface (b).

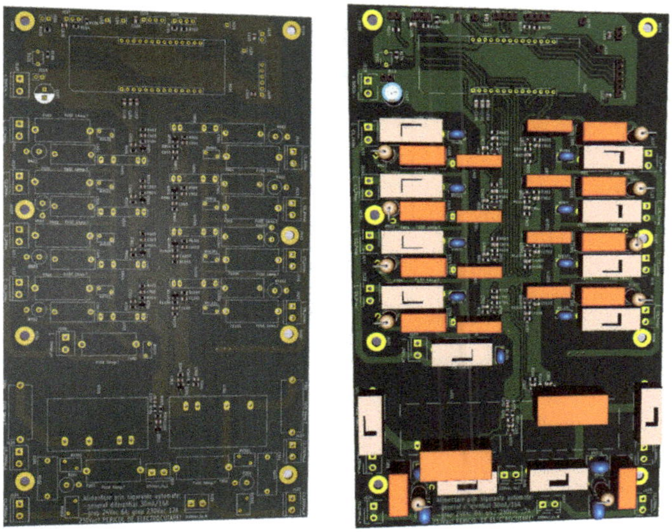

(**a**) (**b**)

Figure 15. PCB of wireless actuator node: (**a**) top layer; (**b**) 3D model.

Size and power consumption were not requirements for the WAn since these nodes are installed in fixed points in the greenhouse and are permanently connected to the power supply and main grid. The CPC1966Y IXYS Solid State Relay (SSR) is used for the 24 Vac channels, while the PF240D25 SSR is used for the 230 Vac channels. We chose SSRs because they have more advantages compared to mechanical relays despite the high cost. Due to the humid environment in the greenhouse, the absence of moving parts and contacts in SSRs extends the lifetime of the node. Also, the voltage zero-crossing turn-on capability of SSR reduces the generated switching noise of AC loads by minimizing the generation of transients.

For each SSR, a 47 nF and 100 Ω RC snubber was added to assure protection for inductive loads. Metal Oxide Varistors (MOVs) suppress high-voltage transients and offer protection against cable disconnection while under an inductive load. A 1 A fuse was introduced for the 24 Vac channels, and a 5 A fuse was added for the 230 Vac channels for protection. Indicator LEDs were installed for each channel. The final assembled PCB is presented in Figure 16.

A residual current circuit breaker with overcurrent protection (RCBO) ensures protection of the main supply and safeguards users against residual fault currents in the humid environment. A classical transformer was used for the 24 Vac power supply, and an AC-DC converter was used for the 5 Vcc power supply. All of these were encapsulated in a nearby IP65 electrical panel box. The setup for the WAn is presented in Figure 17.

The WAn was programmed to send an uplink packet to the gateway every 2 min, the minimum LoRaWAN communication interval. If a command from the web platform is received by the gateway, it is sent to the WAn. The WAn then extracts the information and sets each channel accordingly for a certain period. The data packet includes four bytes: the first byte is for the 24 Vac channels' activation (1 bit for each channel), the second byte is for the 230 Vac channels' activations (2 bits used for the two channels), and the last two bytes are for the activation time. A bit set to 0 means the channel is turned off, and a bit set to 1 means the channel is turned on. The node is always in the listening state with no sleep periods.

Figure 16. The wireless actuator node with all attached components.

(a) (b)

Figure 17. The wireless actuator node (**a**) and the power supply's transformers (**b**).

3.2.3. WAn Laboratory Tests

The WAn was tested in the laboratory regarding the functionality of the 24 Vac and 230 Vac outputs using a TA042 100:1 differential voltage probe and a TA167 current probe. For the 24 Vac channels, a 12 Ω/2.2 mH RL load (see Figure 18a) and a 45 Ω resistive load (see Figure 18b) were tested. The tests confirmed the correct operation of the SSRs for both loads triggered by the signal received from the microcontroller; there were no generated switching noises or high-voltage transients observed.

A 40 W incandescent light bulb was used as a test load for the 230 Vac channels. For higher power loads, SSRs can be used to drive a high-current contactor. Figure 19 plots the current (green) and voltage (blue) waveforms triggered by the digital command (pink) from the microcontroller. The large initial value of the current is due to the light bulb.

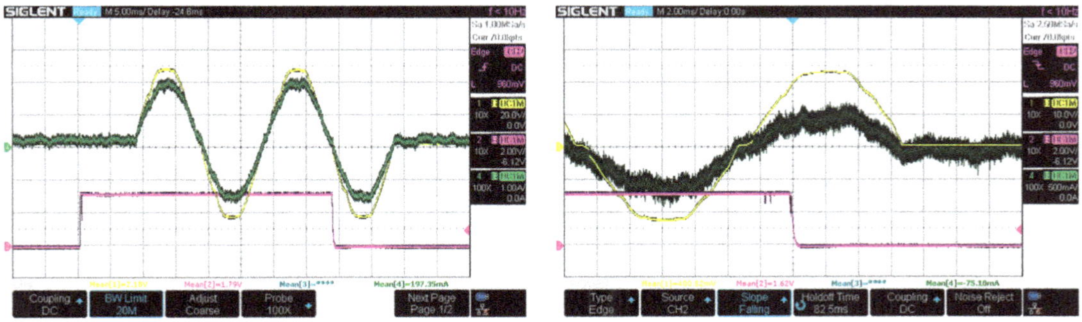

(a) (b)

Figure 18. 24 Vac channel testing (**a**) with a 12 Ω/2.2 mH RL load and (**b**) with a 45 Ω load.

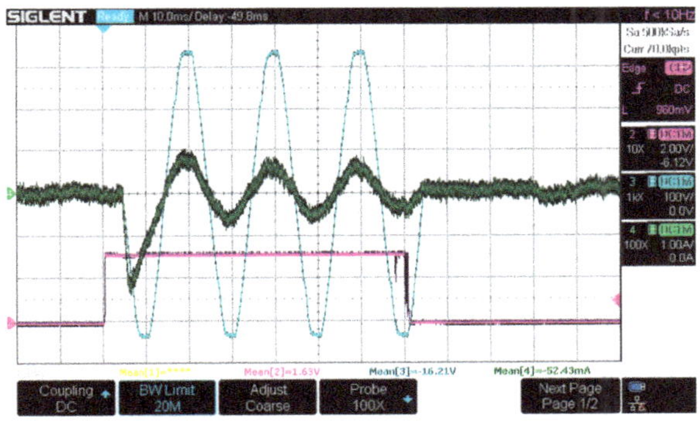

Figure 19. Testing 230 Vac channels with a 40 W incandescent light bulb as the load.

3.3. LoRaWAN Gateway

3.3.1. Gateway Design

The gateway is responsible for collecting data from wireless sensor nodes and transmitting them to the web platform. Additionally, it receives commands from the web platform to operate the microclimate control equipment within the greenhouse and transmits them to the wireless actuator nodes. The data transmission range of the LoRaWAN communication protocol allows the gateway to be located at significant distances, ranging from hundreds of meters to even kilometers from the greenhouse. The proposed block diagram of the gateway is presented in Figure 20.

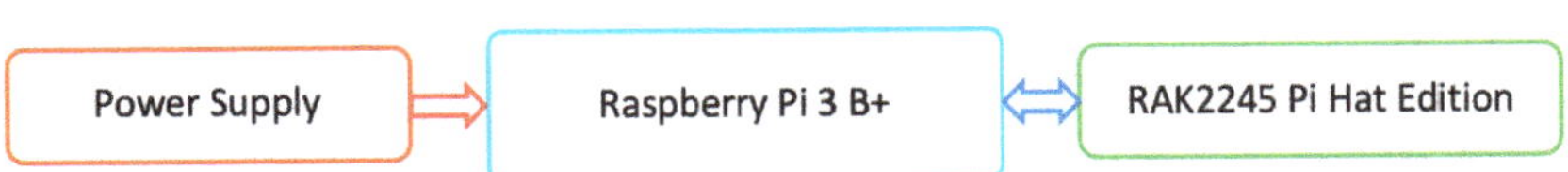

Figure 20. The gateway block diagram.

3.3.2. Gateway Development

The gateway was based on the Raspberry Pi 3 B+ developing board with the LoRaWAN concentrator RAK2245 Pi Hat Edition. This transceiver used the Semtech SX1301 base band processor for LoRa, emulating 49 LoRa demodulators with 10 parallel demodulation paths, supporting eight uplink channels and one down-link channel. The RAK2245 board was also equipped with a GPS module.

The gateway was embedded in a case equipped with a fan to maintain the optimal temperature for its operation. Figure 21 shows the assembled gateway with the box cover removed. A double 5 V power supply with USB Type A connectors was used for powering the Raspberry board and the fan.

The gateway had to be configured and registered on the ChirpStack platform to work with LoRaWAN (see Figure 22). To connect to the internet, the Wi-Fi interface for Raspberry Pi 3 B+ had to be configured. Additionally, on the ChirpStark platform, server address for data storage and the web platform was configured.

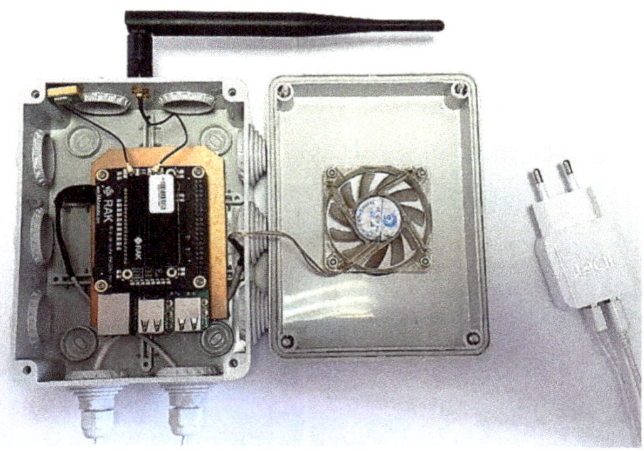

Figure 21. The final version of the gateway.

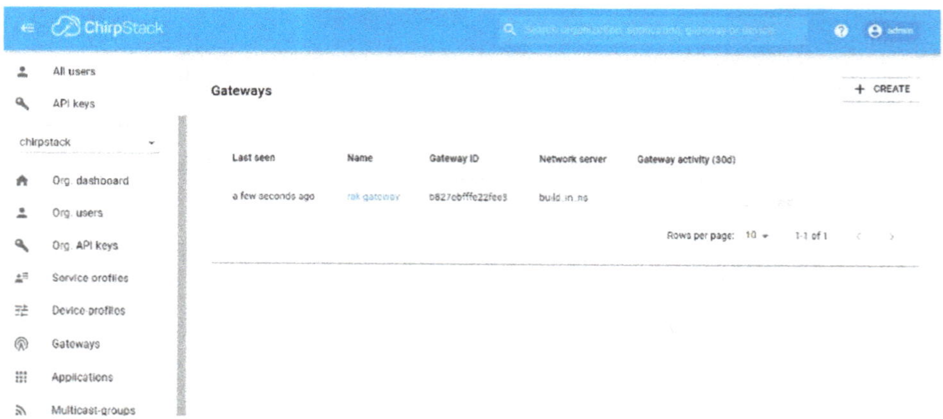

Figure 22. The gateway registered to the ChirpStark platform.

3.3.3. Gateway Laboratory Tests

To test the gateway and its connection with the WSn and WAn, three Arduino MKR WAN 1310 boards were integrated in the system, on the ChirpStark platform, using their Extended Unique Identifiers (EUIs): two as WSns and one as a WAn (see Figure 23). Data communication with these nodes was verified. Figure 23 also shows the test for the frames transmitted and the frames received by the gateway.

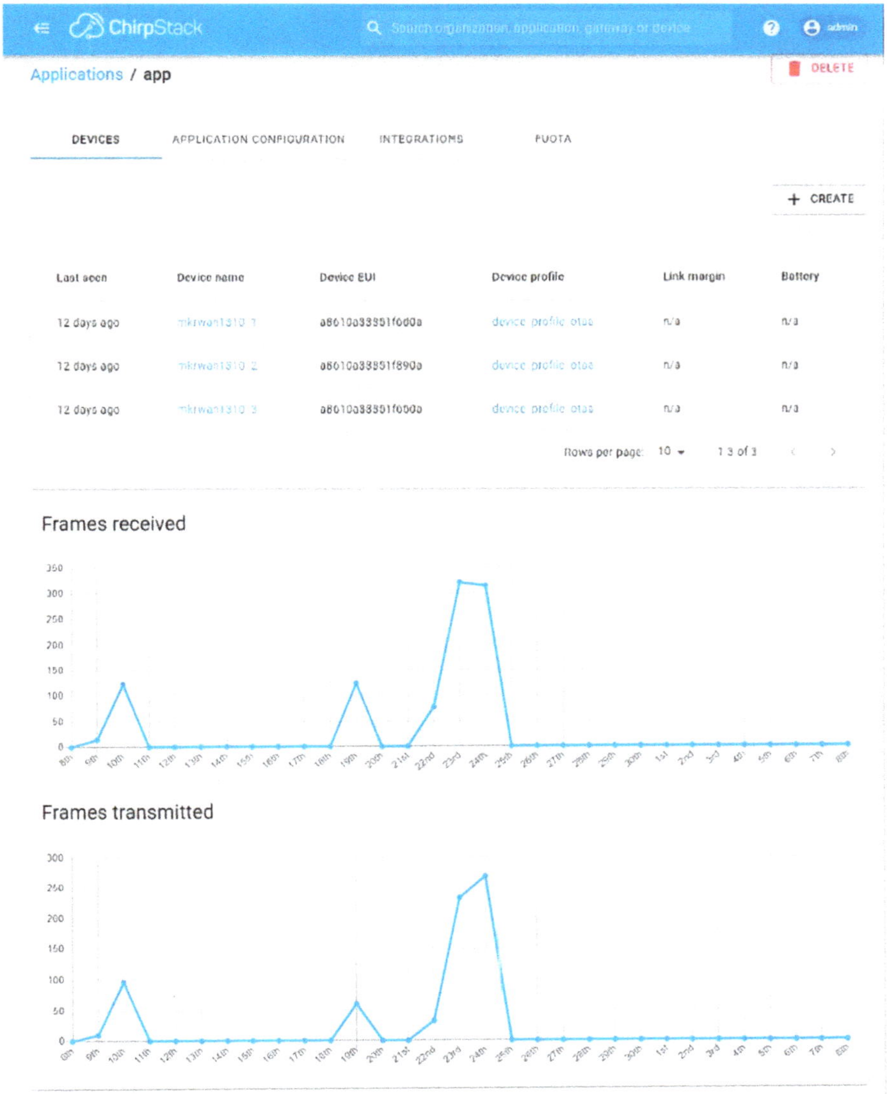

Figure 23. Nodes assigned and communication frames on the ChirpStark platform.

3.4. Web Platform

The role of the web platform was to acquire data from the WSn through the gateway; process, store, and display it to the user; and transmit user commands to the WAn, also via the gateway. This web platform was developed using PHP language and the Laravel framework integrated with a MySQL/MariaDB relational database. The application was developed using the MVC (Model–View–Controller) principle, which allows for the separation of the application logic (Controller) from the data (Model) and from the user interface (View). The platform allows users to create accounts and assign roles, such as user and administrator. The administrator manages the sensor and the actuator nodes with the ability to add, edit, or delete nodes and associate them with application users. The associated nodes can then be managed by users, who can remotely monitor and control greenhouse parameters. The database structure was designed to support these functionalities, ensuring communication between the gateway and the web server.

Communication was carried out as a string of bytes (28 bytes), allowing the web application to receive data from the registered nodes through an API interface. The API stores the IP address of the node from which the information is received and updates it every time it changes so that bidirectional communication is possible. The raw data extracted from the byte string are processed so that the actual value of the measured parameter is calculated and stored for each sensor attached to the node. The calculation formula and parameter identification in the byte string are defined in the node configuration page. The byte values are extracted from the byte string and substituted into the stored formula, with the calculation being performed dynamically based on the received values. For example, in Figure 24, byte 3 (B3) and byte 4 (B4) are used for the light intensity parameter. In this way, new sensors can be added to a node, as well as the definition of action that will be transmitted to the actuator nodes.

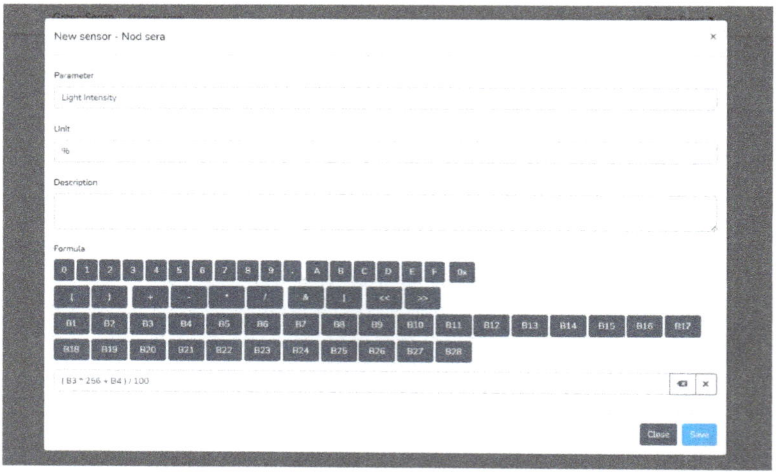

Figure 24. New parameters assigned to the node from the web platform.

The data could be displayed by selecting any parameter from any node and the interest period. The platform offers the possibility to export the data in .png or .cvs formats.

4. System Test and Evaluation

4.1. Tested Scenario

To evaluate the functionality and effectiveness of the IoT-based decision support system for greenhouse microclimate management, a structured experimental scheme was implemented. The greenhouse was divided into three distinct zones, with each being assigned one WSn and using a WAn for the entire greenhouse. The placement and operation of these nodes were carefully designed to maintain optimal environmental conditions. This configuration enabled real-time data collection on parameters such as air and soil temperature, air humidity, and soil moisture. The data were transmitted via a LoRaWAN gateway to a web platform, where it was processed and displayed, allowing users to monitor conditions and activate irrigation or ventilation as needed. The experimental scheme flowchart is presented in Figure 25.

To test the system in real conditions, a greenhouse from the National Institute of Research—Development for Machines and Installations Designed for Agriculture and Food Industry—INMA Bucharest was used. The gateway was installed in a building approximately 100 m away, with one concrete wall between it and the WSn and WAn.

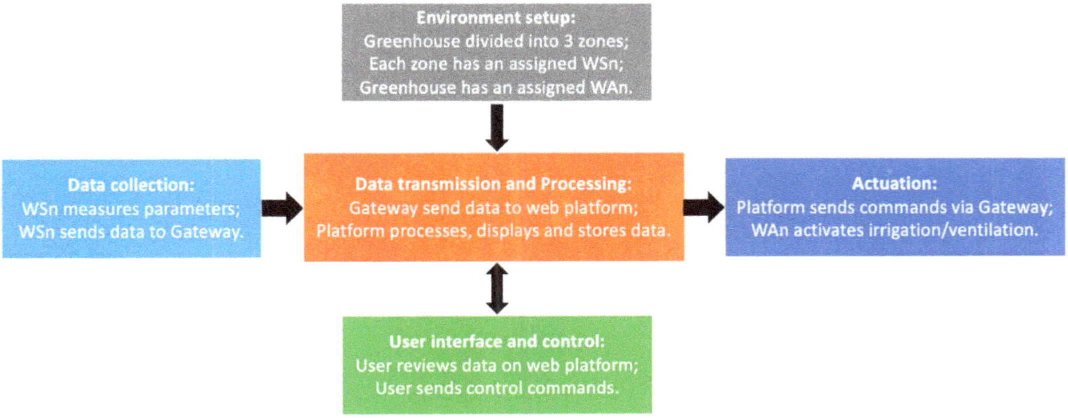

Figure 25. Experimental scheme flowchart for greenhouse microclimate management.

At the top of Figure 26, the greenhouse and the location of the gateway installation are shown using Google Maps. At the bottom, a screenshot from the Chipstark platform is displayed with details for the gateway (the blue pin represents the gateway).

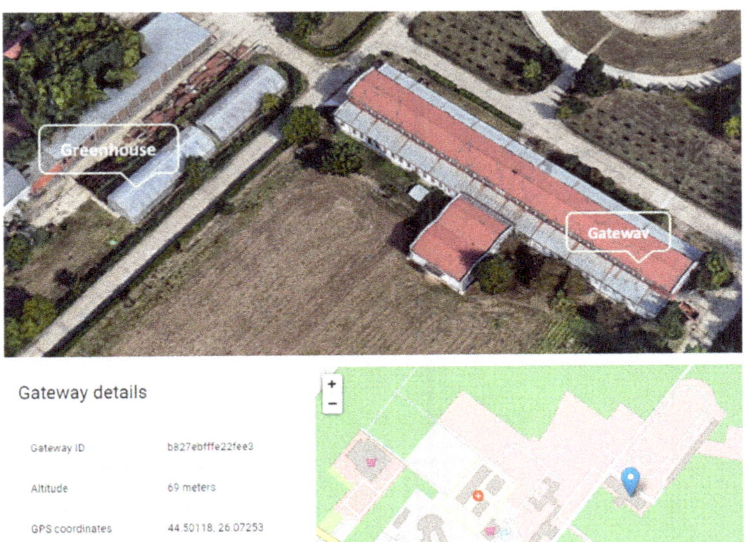

Figure 26. Positioning of greenhouse and gateway details.

Although the solution is suited for much larger-scale greenhouses, for functional testing, a scenario with three WSns and one WAn was considered for the chosen greenhouse. An example of a WSn and the WAn installation are presented in Figure 27.

The greenhouse was divided into three areas to enable targeted monitoring and control, as shown in Figure 28. Each area was monitored by a WSn, and an independent dripping irrigation system, controlled by a vane connected to the Wan, was assigned to each area. Additionally, a fan was connected to the WAn.

(**a**) (**b**)

Figure 27. WSn (**a**) and WAn (**b**) in greenhouse.

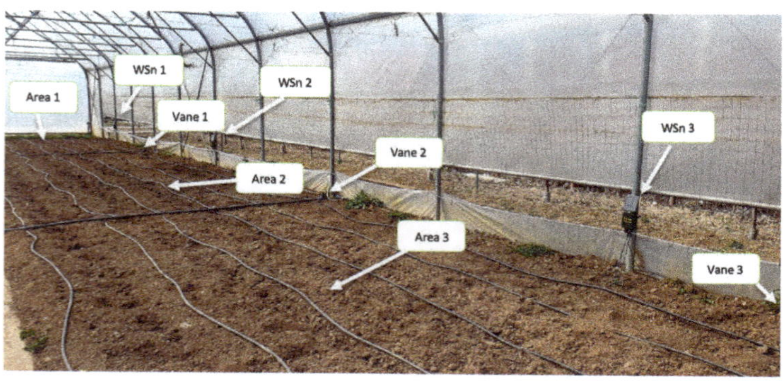

Figure 28. Scenario with three independent monitoring and irrigation areas in greenhouse.

4.2. Data Acquisition and Control

In the web platform, four Arduino MKR developing boards were assigned to the user: three represent the core of the three WSns, and one is the core for the WAn (Figure 29).

The user had the possibility to select a node and to see the data acquired (selected dates with blue in Figure 30), considering the interest parameters and period (see Figure 30).

For the commands, each channel could be modified through a dedicated page for the WAn using on/off buttons. Figure 31 presents an example where channel 1 and channel 4 of the 24 Vac outputs and channel 1 of the 230 Vac were activated for mkrwan1310_4 WAn. Additionally, a switch button was added for further developments of the system, where plans include integrating an autonomous activation system based on the microclimatic parameters acquired by the WSn.

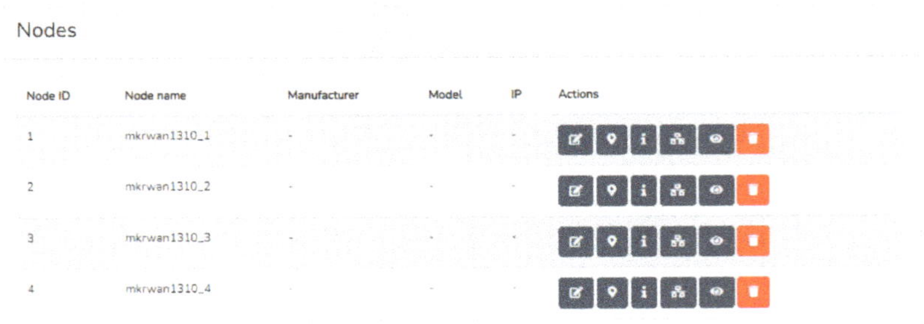

Figure 29. The nodes used in the described scenario (WSn: mkrwan1310_1, mkrwan1310_2, and mkrwan1310_3; WAn: mkrwan1310_4).

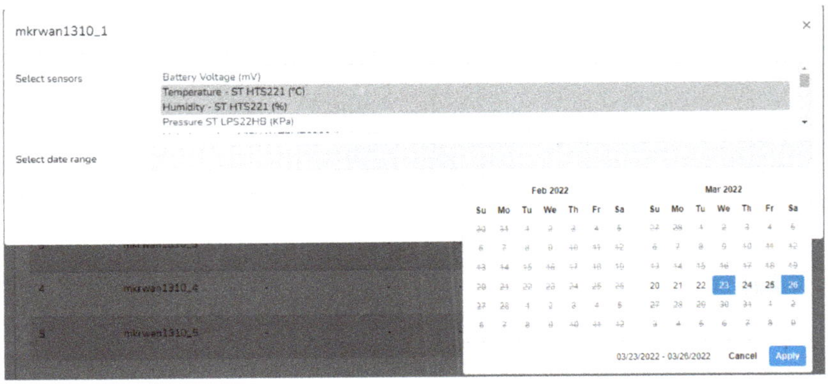

Figure 30. The selection of interest parameters and period for a WSn.

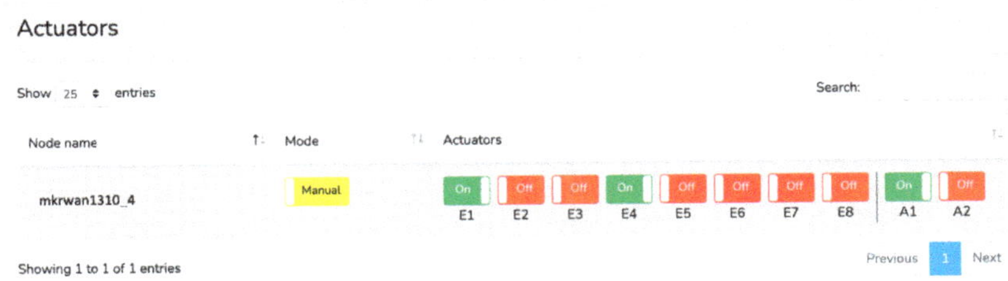

Figure 31. WAn channel activation from the web platform.

From the ChirpStark platform, the data packet sent from the WSn or the command sent to Wan can be viewed. Figure 32 shows a screenshot of the data from a WSn. Each parameter is coded on 2 bytes, and the web platform processes these data into values based on characteristic equations. For example, in the shown case, the first two bytes represent the voltage of the rechargeable battery. The value 0x025A represents the number 602 in decimals and, with a ½ voltage divider for the voltage, a 10-bit ADC resolution, and a 3.3 V reference voltage, results in approximately 3.88 V for the supply. Figure 32 shows the LoRa parameters, like the Bandwidth (125 kHz), Spread Factor (12), and Coding Rate (4/5). Together with a maximum Power Level (20), they were selected to ensure the maximum range was achieved for data communication.

Figure 32. The WSn data packet received by the gateway.

4.3. Results

To test the system in maximum data acquisition conditions, the minimum acquisition interval of two and a half minutes was programmed for the WSn. Under normal conditions, the environmental parameters from a greenhouse do not have very high dynamics, so the acquisition interval can be increased. The user can display the parameters of interest and, based on these, make decisions about which microclimate parameters need to be adjusted.

To demonstrate how the data were displayed on the web platform, a few parameters were extracted. The first example can be seen in the web platform screenshot in Figure 33, where the light intensity and soil temperature are shown. As daylight increases, the air temperature rises quickly, while the soil temperature follows with a delay due to the soil's higher specific heat capacity and slower heat absorption. Similarly, at night, the air cools faster, but the soil retains heat longer, causing a delay in cooling.

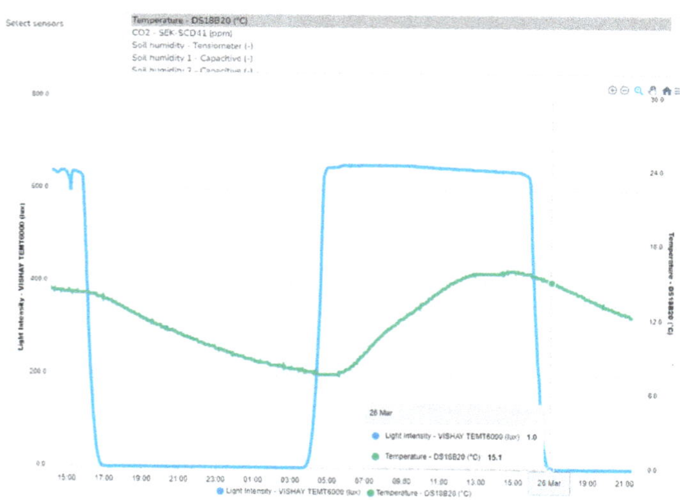

Figure 33. Web platform screenshot with WSn data on light intensity and soil temperature.

Figure 34 provides another example of data acquisition, demonstrating the activation of one channel of the WAn. The soil temperature and soil humidity at two depths are displayed, with increased soil humidity values appearing after the activation of irrigation.

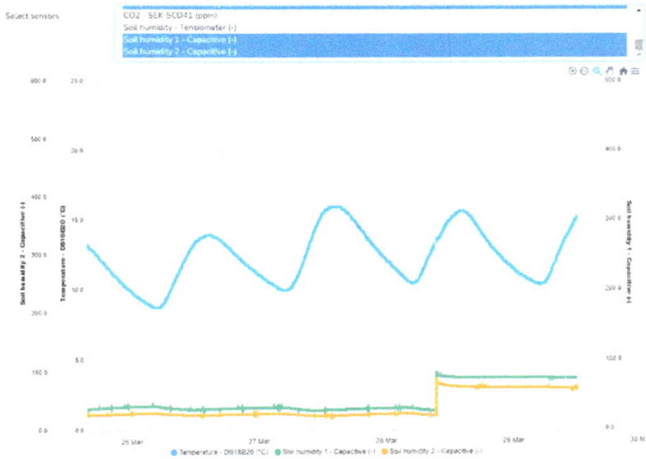

Figure 34. Web platform screenshot with soil temperature and humidity at two depths.

Another test was performed to verify the viability of the node's lifespan. The node was programmed for the worst case scenario, with no sleep time and data acquisition at the minimum interval. Additionally, the LoRa transceiver was set up with parameters that ensured the longest range and maximum energy consumption: a Spread Factor of 12, a Power Level of 20, a 4/5 Coding Rate, and a 125 kHz bandwidth. The battery voltage acquisition for two nodes is displayed in Figure 35. The light intensity was also introduced to highlight the correlation between daylight and the battery charging period. At the beginning of the chart, a continuous drain of energy can be observed. For about a week, the photovoltaic panel was disconnected to see WSn lifetime without charging. After the panel was reconnected, daily recharges were observed. On the days with less sunlight, the power drain was higher. Over a period of about a month, it can be seen that the photovoltaic panel efficiently charges the batteries during the day, even though the WSn is located in the greenhouse. The graph is exported directly from the web platform as an additional option for the user.

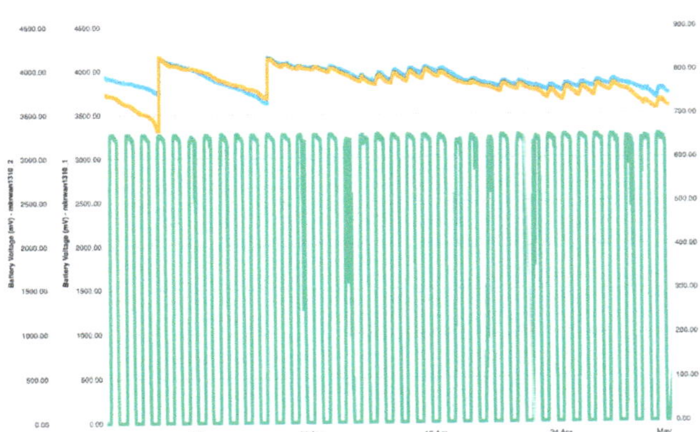

Figure 35. Battery voltage monitoring for nodes 1 and 2, corelated with light intensity.

The data could also be exported in a .cvs file. Figure 36 shows the temperature values acquired by the three WSns, plotted from an exported .csv file. Although the values of the parameter are slightly different due to the different positions occupied in the greenhouse, the evolution of the values follows the same path. Over 5 days, at a 2.5 min interval, more than 2800 samples are acquired by a single WSn.

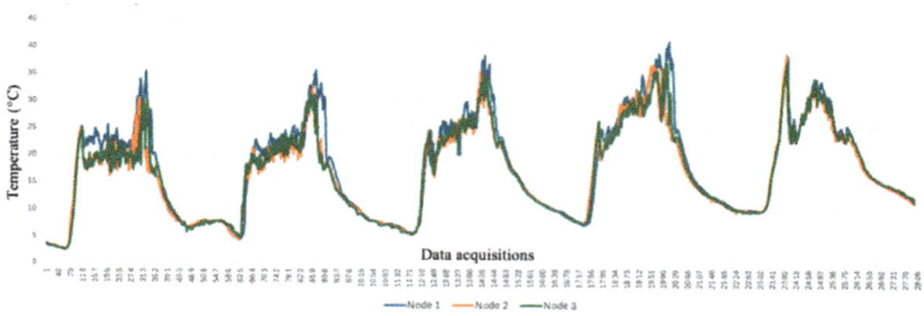

Figure 36. Air temperature values from three nodes over five days.

5. Conclusions

In recent years, digitalization has become a key focus in agriculture, particularly in the implementation of decision support systems, farm management, PA, and other related functions. The goal is to increase production efficiency, reduce losses, improve profitability, and promote sustainability. IoT plays an important role in decision-making processes, especially in agriculture crop monitoring and controlling systems.

This paper presents a demonstrator model of an IoT system with a wireless sensor network, designed for monitoring and controlling the microclimate within a greenhouse. The system allows for the automation of processes such as irrigation, ventilation, temperature and humidity control, and shading. The system is flexible and can be used to monitor and control a wide range of parameters depending on the specific needs of the greenhouse. Each sensor and/or actuator node can function independently, contributing to the automation of processes in vegetable greenhouses. Furthermore, the monitoring platform supports the integration of other types of sensor nodes that operate using the LoRaWAN protocol, and the system can also be utilized as a data display service.

For each independent part of the system, multiple tests were performed. For the WSn, tests focused on evaluating functionality and long-term viability. The node's lifespan was analyzed by measuring current consumption under different data transmission parameters. The acquisition, storage, and transmission of data were also tested. For the WAn, functionality was tested with 24 Vac and 230 Vac outputs with different loads. The gateway was tested for connectivity with both the WSn and WAn as well as the exchange of messages between them. The web platform was tested for data acquisition, storage and display, and command transmission. Finally, the entire system was tested in a real in-field scenario of a greenhouse.

The generated impact is both economic and social. Economically, the system reduces input costs, such as electricity, water for irrigation, and fertilizers, while increasing productivity by controlling the interest parameters in real time. Socially, the impact is represented by the streamlining of vegetable crop maintenance operations in greenhouses by shifting the role of the human operator from executing the functions to monitoring them.

Current and future work involves fully automating the greenhouse and enabling the system to make its own decisions based on machine learning algorithms applied on the acquired data. Additionally, the goal is to develop the system into a commercial solution through technology transfer to an economic operator.

Author Contributions: Conceptualization, D.-I.S., M.-G.M., Ş.-G.R., B.-C.F. and I.-P.M.; methodology, D.-I.S. and M.-G.M.; software, D.-I.S. and B.-C.F.; validation, D.-I.S., M.-G.M. and I.-P.M.; formal analysis, D.-I.S. and M.-G.M.; investigation, D.-I.S., M.-G.M., Ş.-G.R., B.-C.F. and I.-P.M.; resources,

D.-I.S. and I.-P.M.; data curation, D.-I.S.; writing—original draft preparation, D.-I.S. and I.-P.M.; writing—review and editing, M.-G.M. and L.-A.P.; visualization, D.-I.S. and L.-A.P.; supervision, D.-I.S., M.-G.M. and L.-A.P.; project administration, D.-I.S.; funding acquisition, D.-I.S. All authors have read and agreed to the published version of the manuscript.

Funding: This work was supported by a grant from the National Program for Research of the National Association of Technical Universities—GNAC ARUT 2023, contract no. 180/4 December 2023.

Data Availability Statement: Dataset available on request from the authors.

Conflicts of Interest: The authors declare no conflicts of interest.

References

1. Oztemel, E.; Gursev, S. Literature Review of Industry 4.0 and Related Technologies. *J. Intell. Manuf.* **2020**, *31*, 127–182. [CrossRef]
2. Majid, M.; Habib, S.; Javed, A.R.; Rizwan, M.; Srivastava, G.; Gadekallu, T.R.; Lin, J.C.-W. Applications of Wireless Sensor Networks and Internet of Things Frameworks in the Industry Revolution 4.0: A Systematic Literature Review. *Sensors* **2022**, *22*, 2087. [CrossRef] [PubMed]
3. Zhai, Z.; Martínez, J.F.; Beltran, V.; Martínez, N.L. Decision Support Systems for Agriculture 4.0: Survey and Challenges. *Comput. Electron. Agric.* **2020**, *170*, 105256. [CrossRef]
4. Ara, I.; Turner, L.; Harrison, M.T.; Monjardino, M.; deVoil, P.; Rodriguez, D. Application, Adoption and Opportunities for Improving Decision Support Systems in Irrigated Agriculture: A Review. *Agric. Water Manag.* **2021**, *257*, 107161. [CrossRef]
5. Köksal, Ö.; Tekinerdogan, B. Architecture Design Approach for IoT-Based Farm Management Information Systems. *Precis. Agric.* **2019**, *20*, 926–958. [CrossRef]
6. Mishra, A.; Alzoubi, Y.I.; Gavrilovic, N. Quality Attributes of Software Architecture in IoT-Based Agricultural Systems. *Smart Agric. Technol.* **2024**, *8*, 100523. [CrossRef]
7. Blackmore, S. Precision Farming: An Introduction. *Outlook Agric.* **1994**, *23*, 275–280. [CrossRef]
8. Verdouw, C.; Sundmaeker, H.; Tekinerdogan, B.; Conzon, D.; Montanaro, T. Architecture Framework of IoT-Based Food and Farm Systems: A Multiple Case Study. *Comput. Electron. Agric.* **2019**, *165*, 104939. [CrossRef]
9. Dhillon, R.; Moncur, Q. Small-Scale Farming: A Review of Challenges and Potential Opportunities Offered by Technological Advancements. *Sustainability* **2023**, *15*, 15478. [CrossRef]
10. Ding, J.; Chandra, R. Towards Low Cost Soil Sensing Using Wi-Fi. In Proceedings of the 25th Annual International Conference on Mobile Computing and Networking, Los Cabos, Mexico, 21–25 October 2019; Association for Computing Machinery: New York, NY, USA, 2019; pp. 1–16.
11. Heinzelman, W.R.; Kulik, J.; Balakrishnan, H. Adaptive Protocols for Information Dissemination in Wireless Sensor Networks. In Proceedings of the 5th Annual ACM/IEEE International Conference on Mobile Computing and Networking, Seattle, WA, USA, 15–20 August 1999; ACM: Seattle, WA, USA, 1999; pp. 174–185.
12. Shen, C.-C.; Srisathapornphat, C.; Jaikaeo, C. Sensor Information Networking Architecture and Applications. *IEEE Pers. Commun.* **2001**, *8*, 52–59. [CrossRef]
13. Akyildiz, I.F.; Su, W.; Sankarasubramaniam, Y.; Cayirci, E. A Survey on Sensor Networks. *IEEE Commun. Mag.* **2002**, *40*, 102–114. [CrossRef]
14. Akyildiz, I.F.; Kasimoglu, I.H. Wireless Sensor and Actor Networks: Research Challenges. *Ad Hoc Netw.* **2004**, *2*, 351–367. [CrossRef]
15. Deshpande, A.; Guestrin, C.; Hellerstein, J.M.; Madden, S.R.; Hong, W. Model-Driven Data Acquisition in Sensor Networks. In Proceedings of the Thirtieth International Conference on Very Large Data Bases, VLDB Endowment, Toronto, OT, Canada, 31 August–3 September 2004; Volume 30, pp. 588–599.
16. Rezgui, A.; Eltoweissy, M. Service-Oriented Sensor–Actuator Networks: Promises, Challenges, and the Road Ahead. *Comput. Commun.* **2007**, *30*, 2627–2648. [CrossRef]
17. Xia, F.; Tian, Y.-C.; Li, Y.; Sung, Y. Wireless Sensor/Actuator Network Design for Mobile Control Applications. *Sensors* **2007**, *7*, 2157–2173. [CrossRef]
18. Yick, J.; Mukherjee, B.; Ghosal, D. Wireless Sensor Network Survey. *Comput. Netw.* **2008**, *52*, 2292–2330. [CrossRef]
19. Singh, R.; Aernouts, M.; De Meyer, M.; Weyn, M.; Berkvens, R. Leveraging LoRaWAN Technology for Precision Agriculture in Greenhouses. *Sensors* **2020**, *20*, 1827. [CrossRef]
20. Tagarakis, A.C.; Kateris, D.; Berruto, R.; Bochtis, D. Low-Cost Wireless Sensing System for Precision Agriculture Applications in Orchards. *Appl. Sci.* **2021**, *11*, 5858. [CrossRef]
21. Xu, J.; Gu, B.; Tian, G. Review of Agricultural IoT Technology. *Artif. Intell. Agric.* **2022**, *6*, 10–22. [CrossRef]
22. Tzounis, A.; Katsoulas, N.; Bartzanas, T.; Kittas, C. Internet of Things in Agriculture, Recent Advances and Future Challenges. *Biosyst. Eng.* **2017**, *164*, 31–48. [CrossRef]
23. Friha, O.; Ferrag, M.A.; Shu, L.; Maglaras, L.; Wang, X. Internet of Things for the Future of Smart Agriculture: A Comprehensive Survey of Emerging Technologies. *IEEE/CAA J. Autom. Sin.* **2021**, *8*, 718–752. [CrossRef]

24. Săcăleanu, D.-I.; Manciu, I.-P.; Roşu, Ş.-G.; Perişoară, L.-A.; Tannouche, A.; Cretu, L.-E.S. GSM Wireless Sensor Node Prototype for Infield Environmental Parameters Acquisition. In Proceedings of the 2023 15th International Conference on Electronics, Computers and Artificial Intelligence (ECAI), Bucharest, Romania, 29–30 June 2023; pp. 1–6.
25. Bakker, J.C. Greenhouse ClimateControl: Constraints and Limitattions. *Acta Hortic.* **1995**, *399*, 25–36. [CrossRef]
26. Hanan, J.J. *Greenhouses: Advanced Technology for Protected Horticulture*, 1st ed.; Hanan, J.J., Ed.; CRC Press: Boca Raton, FL, USA, 2017; ISBN 9780203719824.
27. Stanghellini, C.; Kempkes, F.L.K.; Knies, P. Enhancing Environmental Quality in Agricultural Systems. *Acta Hortic.* **2003**, *609*, 277–283. [CrossRef]
28. Kochhar, A.; Kumar, N. Wireless Sensor Networks for Greenhouses: An End-to-End Review. *Comput. Electron. Agric.* **2019**, *163*, 104877. [CrossRef]
29. Badji, A.; Benseddik, A.; Bensaha, H.; Boukhelifa, A.; Hasrane, I. Design, Technology, and Management of Greenhouse: A Review. *J. Clean. Prod.* **2022**, *373*, 133753. [CrossRef]
30. Rosero-Montalvo, P.D.; Erazo-Chamorro, V.C.; López-Batista, V.F.; Moreno-García, M.N.; Peluffo-Ordóñez, D.H. Environment Monitoring of Rose Crops Greenhouse Based on Autonomous Vehicles with a WSN and Data Analysis. *Sensors* **2020**, *20*, 5905. [CrossRef]
31. Kumar, A.; Singh, V.; Kumar, S.; Jaiswal, S.P.; Bhadoria, V.S. IoT Enabled System to Monitor and Control Greenhouse. *Mater. Today Proc.* **2022**, *49*, 3137–3141. [CrossRef]
32. Placidi, P.; Morbidelli, R.; Fortunati, D.; Papini, N.; Gobbi, F.; Scorzoni, A. Monitoring Soil and Ambient Parameters in the IoT Precision Agriculture Scenario: An Original Modeling Approach Dedicated to Low-Cost Soil Water Content Sensors. *Sensors* **2021**, *21*, 5110. [CrossRef]
33. Ye, H.; Yang, Y.; Zhu, L. A Wireless Network Detection and Control System for Intelligent Agricultural Greenhouses Based on NB-IOT Technology. *J. Phys. Conf. Ser.* **2021**, *1738*, 012058. [CrossRef]
34. Van, T.L.; Thi, P.N.; Minh, P.V.; Thi, L.D.; Cong, H.L.; Phuong, T.N.T. Design and Implementation of a Wireless Sensor Network for Smart Greenhouse Controller. *CommIT (Commun. Inf. Technol.) J.* **2022**, *16*, 1–8. [CrossRef]
35. Hotei, Ş.-A.; Marghescu, C.I.; Negroiu, R.C.; Drumea, A. Towards Sustainable Subsistence Agriculture in Romania with Low-Cost IoT Modules and Solutions—Proof of Concept. *Inmateh* **2023**, *71*, 647–656. [CrossRef]
36. Codeluppi, G.; Cilfone, A.; Davoli, L.; Ferrari, G. LoRaFarM: A LoRaWAN-Based Smart Farming Modular IoT Architecture. *Sensors* **2020**, *20*, 2028. [CrossRef] [PubMed]
37. Erazo-Rodas, M.; Sandoval-Moreno, M.; Muñoz-Romero, S.; Huerta, M.; Rivas-Lalaleo, D.; Naranjo, C.; Rojo-Álvarez, J.L. Multiparametric Monitoring in Equatorian Tomato Greenhouses (I): Wireless Sensor Network Benchmarking. *Sensors* **2018**, *18*, 2555. [CrossRef] [PubMed]
38. Rezvani, S.M.-E.; Abyaneh, H.Z.; Shamshiri, R.R.; Balasundram, S.K.; Dworak, V.; Goodarzi, M.; Sultan, M.; Mahns, B. IoT-Based Sensor Data Fusion for Determining Optimality Degrees of Microclimate Parameters in Commercial Greenhouse Production of Tomato. *Sensors* **2020**, *20*, 6474. [CrossRef]
39. Singh, R.K.; Rahmani, M.H.; Weyn, M.; Berkvens, R. Joint Communication and Sensing: A Proof of Concept and Datasets for Greenhouse Monitoring Using LoRaWAN. *Sensors* **2022**, *22*, 1326. [CrossRef]
40. Sofwan, A.; Sumardi, S.; Ahmada, A.I.; Ibrahim, I.; Budiraharjo, K.; Karno, K. Smart Greetthings: Smart Greenhouse Based on Internet of Things for Environmental Engineering. In Proceedings of the 2020 International Conference on Smart Technology and Applications (ICoSTA), Surabaya, Indonesia, 20 February 2020; pp. 1–5. [CrossRef]
41. Tatas, K.; Al-Zoubi, A.; Christofides, N.; Zannettis, C.; Chrysostomou, M.; Panteli, S.; Antoniou, A. Reliable IoT-Based Monitoring and Control of Hydroponic Systems. *Technologies* **2022**, *10*, 26. [CrossRef]
42. Kirci, P.; Ozturk, E.; Celik, Y. A Novel Approach for Monitoring of Smart Greenhouse and Flowerpot Parameters and Detection of Plant Growth with Sensors. *Agriculture* **2022**, *12*, 1705. [CrossRef]

technologies

MDPI

Review

Enhancing Solar Plant Efficiency: A Review of Vision-Based Monitoring and Fault Detection Techniques

Ioannis Polymeropoulos, Stavros Bezyrgiannidis, Eleni Vrochidou and George A. Papakostas *

MLV Research Group, Department of Informatics, Democritus University of Thrace, 65404 Kavala, Greece; ioannis.k.polymeropoulos@gmail.com (I.P.); sbez@myip.gr (S.B.); evrochid@cs.duth.gr (E.V.)
* Correspondence: gpapak@cs.duth.gr; Tel.: +30-2510462321

Abstract

Over the last decades, environmental awareness has provoked scientific interest in green energy, produced, among others, from solar sources. However, for the efficient operation and longevity of green solar plants, regular inspection and maintenance are required. This work aims to review vision-based monitoring techniques for the fault detection of photovoltaic (PV) plants, i.e., solar panels. Practical implications of such systems include timely fault identification based on data-driven insights and problem resolution, resulting in enhanced energy outputs, extended lifetime spans for PV panels, cost savings, as well as safe and scalable inspections. Details regarding the main components of PV systems, operation principles and key non-destructive fault detection technologies are included. Advancements in unmanned aerial vehicles (UAVs), as well as in artificial intelligence (AI), machine learning (ML) and deep learning (DL) methods, offering enhanced monitoring opportunities, are in focus. A comparative analysis and an overall evaluation of state-of-the-art vision-based methods for detecting specific types of defects on PVs is conducted. The current performance and failures of vision-based algorithms for solar panel fault detection are identified, raising their capabilities, limitations and research gaps, towards effectively guiding future research. The results indicate that shading anomalies significantly impact the performance of PV units, while the top five fault detection methodologies, according to preset evaluation criteria, involve deep learning methods, such as CNNs and YOLO variations.

Keywords: renewable energy; fault detection; sustainability; photovoltaics; solar panel monitoring; deep learning; computer vision; artificial intelligence

1. Introduction

Solar energy is an inexhaustible clean power source that is increasingly significant in both technological advancements and environmental sustainability. As climate changes and the depletion of traditional energy resources pose serious threats to our future, photovoltaic (PV) systems emerge as a pioneering solution. These systems harness the photovoltaic effect to convert solar radiation into electrical energy, providing a clean and limitless power source [1].

The journey of PV technology began in 1839 when French physicist Edmond Becquerel discovered the photovoltaic effect. Since then, research and technological advancements have led to the development of the first PV cells, which now offer impressive performance and applications across various needs [2].

PV systems are not just technical innovations; they are ecological necessities. Each kilowatt-hour of electricity produced by photovoltaic systems reduces carbon dioxide emissions, making them vital for environmental protection. Additionally, solar energy provides economic benefits, especially in sunny regions where investing in photovoltaics can result in significant savings and profits [3]. Therefore, it is essential that PV plants remain reliable and function effectively, referring to excellent installation, frequent maintenance, and high-quality inspections for faults. Faults may occur while manufacturing, transporting, assembling and operating PV panels. Faults need to be detected on time, so as to be repaired and prevent safety issues and energy losses.

Currently, fault detection methods have been in research focus, especially those that are not intrusive and can also provide details on the location of faults. Vision-based inspection has prevailed over other methods, due to the continuous advancements of camera technologies and graphics processing unit (GPU) architectures, as well as the progress of artificial intelligence (AI) and computer vision (CV) algorithms. The latter combination has the potential to detect, classify and localize faults, with low costs, and high reliability.

Contemporary challenges in vision-based PV fault detection systems include data overload issues due to the vast amount of produced data from various integrated sensors, creating barriers to the need for real-time fault detection. High-resolution images are needed to accurately detect faults; yet, their processing requires significant time and resources. Contemporary challenges also include the need for the improvement of fault detection accuracies by developing more advanced detection algorithms. The investigation of common faults, resulting mainly due to external environmental conditions, need to be identified so as to focus research on their effective detection.

To this end, this work aims to provide a review on AI vision-based solar panel inspection techniques, focusing on dealing with contemporary challenges. Many reviews have been recently published on the subject [1,3–7]. Yet, most of these review works focus on specific monitoring techniques and are not meant to be generic so as to cover multiple aspects of PV systems. These approaches aim to holistically summarize the key detection technologies, as well as machine learning and deep learning methodologies. The primary gaps we identified in these review works, and eventually aim to address in the proposed work, are the following:

- The lack of study on faults in relation to the performance of photovoltaic modules.
- The lack of evaluation of the proposed methodologies.

To this end, the contributions of this work that are not addressed cumulatively in other papers are summarized as follows:

1. Presentation of PV systems' fundamentals.
2. Evolution of computer vision algorithms for PV fault detection within the decade.
3. Summarization of all key monitoring techniques for PV fault detection, along with individual and comparative assessment of their capabilities and limitations.
4. A focus on PV fault detection using AI-based computer vision, including machine learning and other pattern recognition methods, image processing techniques, and deep learning methods.
5. Common faults detectable by CV algorithms in PV systems and how they affect the systems' performance.
6. Review of CV-based fault detection methodologies, cumulative performance tables and guidelines to select the appropriate one based on proposed criteria.

The rest of the paper is structured as follows. Section 2 presents the research methodology. Section 3 summarizes the fundamentals of PV systems. Section 4 presents the evolution of CV algorithms in PVs over the last decade. Capabilities and limitations of basic detection technologies are included in Section 5, focusing on fault detection using AI-based CV algorithms. Section 6 summarizes CV detected PV faults and related PV system performance. Section 7 provides an overview of CV-based PV fault detection methodologies and their evaluation. Finally, Sections 8 and 9 discuss the research findings and conclude the paper, respectively.

2. Research Methodology

To provide a comprehensive review that manages to effectively address the identified gaps, we pose the following four research questions (RQ):

- RQ1: How have CV algorithms evolved in the context of fault detection in photovoltaic systems over the past decade?
- RQ2: What are the capabilities and limitations of key CV-based detection technologies concerning faults in photovoltaic systems?
- RQ3: What are the common faults that can be detected with CV in photovoltaic systems, and which of these significantly affect system performance?
- RQ4: What CV-based fault detection methodologies are identified in the literature, and how can the appropriate method be selected?

Figure 1 outlines the followed roadmap for addressing these four research questions. Research questions in this work are answered through a comprehensive review of identified articles relevant to the subject of interest. Figure 1 aims to illustrate the RQs and define the connection between them, as well as to indicate the exact order in which the questions are answered in the subsections entitled with the same name as each RQ, i.e., to align the RQs with specific subsections towards guiding the reader through the content logically.

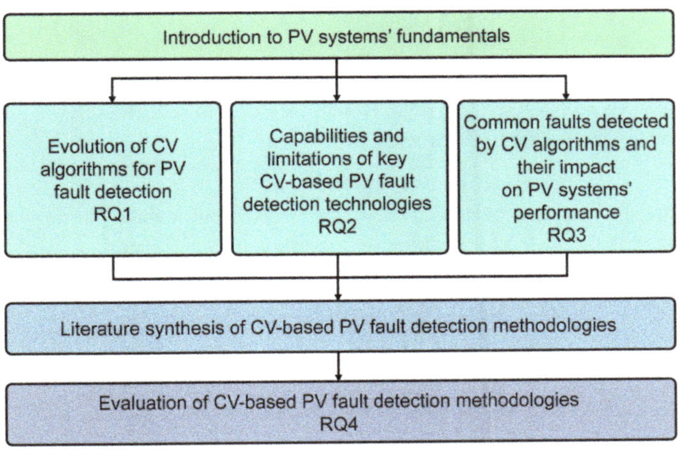

Figure 1. The followed roadmap. Connection of RQs and corresponding subjections where RQs are addressed.

The research of relevant articles in this work was conducted in the Scopus database within Article title, Abstract and Keywords, by using the query: "computer vision" AND "PV" AND "faults detection" OR "defects" OR "anomalies". The search returned 52 articles ranging from 2014–2024.

To further refine the research results, the following eligibility criteria were applied:

- Language was limited to English.
- Subject area was limited to Engineering and Computer Science.

- Document types were limited to Conference papers and Articles.

By applying these limitations, 38 related documents were identified and used as sources in the following.

3. Fundamentals of PV Systems

In this section, the fundamentals of PV systems are summarized, including the main components of a PV system and PV operating principles.

3.1. Components

A PV system comprises the following main components, as illustrated in Figure 2:

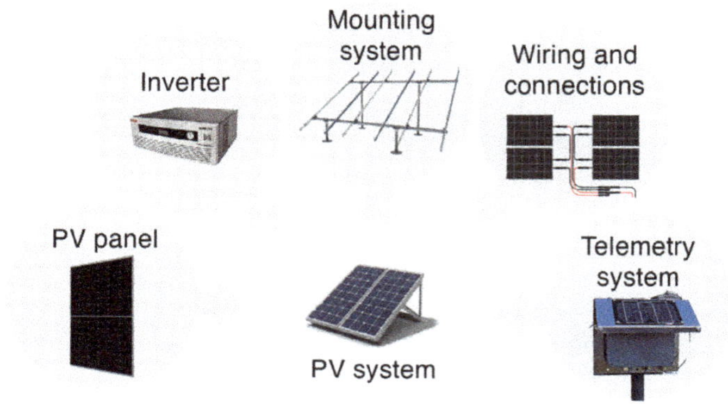

Figure 2. PV system main components.

- Photovoltaic Panels (PV Modules):
  a. Made up of photovoltaic cells that convert sunlight into electrical energy.
  b. Panels can be monocrystalline, polycrystalline or thin-film, each with unique performance characteristics and costs.
- Inverter:
  a. Converts the direct current (DC) produced by the photovoltaic panels into alternating current (AC) for use by electrical appliances or the grid.
  b. Different types of inverters, such as half-bridge and full-bridge, have various applications and features.
- Mounting System:
  a. Includes the supports and structures that hold the photovoltaic panels, either fixed or adjustable for solar tracking systems.
- Wiring and Connections:
  a. Essential for connecting the photovoltaic panels to the inverter and the power grid.
  b. Includes DC and AC cables, as well as grounding and lightning protection systems.
- Telemetry System:
  a. Ensures the monitoring and control of the photovoltaic system's performance.
  b. May include wireless or wired connections for data transmission.

3.2. Operating Principles

The photovoltaic effect relies on semiconductor materials that convert solar radiation into electrical energy. When photons (packets of energy from sunlight) hit the photovoltaic cells, they excite the electrons in the semiconductor materials, causing an electric current to flow. This current is then collected and converted into usable electrical energy by the inverter.

The efficiency of a photovoltaic system depends on several factors, including the quality of materials, the intensity of solar radiation, and environmental conditions. Despite its limitations, photovoltaic technology continues to advance, offering more efficient and cost-effective solutions for generating clean energy.

In summary, photovoltaic systems represent an innovative and sustainable response to modern energy challenges, providing an environmentally friendly and economically viable solution. Continuous research and development in this field promise a bright future for solar energy and its role in creating a sustainable and clean environment.

4. Evolution of Computer Vision Algorithms in PVs over the Last Decade

This section provides a comprehensive overview of how computer vision algorithms have evolved in photovoltaic fault detection over the last decade (RQ1). Using Scopus, we explored over 60 relevant studies. Table 1 includes the findings we have traced regarding the advancements and shifts in focus in this scientific field. More specifically, for each distinct period within the decade, the focus of research, the current state-of-the-art technologies and algorithms, as well as the key developments and limitations of each period are identified and summarized in the table.

Table 1. Evolution of computer vision algorithms in FV fault detection over the last decade.

Period	Focus	Technologies/ Algorithms	Key Developments	Limitations
Early 2010s	Traditional Image Processing	Edge Detection, Segmentation [8]	Rule-based techniques, manual parameter tuning	Manual feature extraction, accuracy of fault detection
Mid 2010s	Introduction of Machine Learning	SVM [9], Random Forests [10]	Use of handcrafted features, initial use of feature classifiers	Feature engineering, scalability, complexity of faults, generalization
Late 2010s	Shift to Deep Learning	CNNs [11]	Automated feature learning, significant accuracy improvements	Benchmark datasets, training time, computational resources
Early 2020s	Integration of Multiple Modalities	CNNs with IR, Visible, and EL Imaging [12–14]	Enhanced fault detection under various conditions	Data overload, synchronization, fusion, computational burden, interpretability
Current Trend	Real-Time Detection and Adaptability	CNNs, YOLO, On-Site Processing [15]	Real-time processing, adaptability to environmental changes	Cost and scalability
Future Direction	Scalability and Economic Viability	Scalable DL models and Economic Analysis [16]	Scalable deep learning models incorporating economic analysis	Cybersecurity

In the early 2010s, traditional image processing techniques like edge detection and segmentation dominated the field [8]. These methods relied heavily on rule-based techniques and manual parameter adjustments. The latter posed limitations, since manual feature extraction can be time-consuming and may fail to capture the inherent characteristics of faults, leading to poor detection accuracies especially for complex faults. As the decade progressed, machine learning started to make its mark. Algorithms such as Support Vector Machine (SVM) [9] and Random Forest (RF) [10] appeared, employing handcrafted features and initial feature classifiers to improve detection accuracy. The limitation of feature engineering, feature extraction and selection, was still evident, while problem complexities could not efficiently be handled. Moreover, generalization issues were reported due to the varying environmental conditions and different PV systems, making algorithms difficult to generalize well. By the late 2010s, the field experienced a significant shift with the advent of deep learning, particularly Convolutional Neural Networks (CNNs) [11]. These models enabled automated feature learning, leading to substantial improvements in detection accuracy and efficiency. However, data requirements were excessive. Large benchmark datasets with annotated data were needed, while the training time of algorithms and the needs for computational resources began to augment. In the early 2020s, the focus shifted towards integrating multiple modalities, using CNNs in combination with infrared (IR), visible and electroluminescence (EL) imaging [12–14]. This integration resulted in enhanced fault detection capabilities under various conditions. Multiple data modalities posed many challenges, such as data overload, and data synchronization. Moreover, the need for sophisticated fusion techniques emerged. The processing of multiple data streams increased system complexity and computational burden. At the same time, the need for explainable deep learning algorithms started to show, revealing the research gap of interpretability of multimodal deep models. Currently, the trend is moving towards real-time detection and adaptability [17]. Advanced models like CNNs and YOLO are being employed for on-site processing, enabling real-time detection and adaptability to varying environmental conditions [15]. Interpretable AI algorithms, adaptability to new faults, and robustness to environmental changes were, therefore, in focus. Limitations included costs and scalability, since the size of PV installations tend to increase, producing vast amount of data and needing significant computational power.

Looking ahead, the future direction of research in this field is expected to focus on scalability and economic viability. Researchers are working on developing scalable deep learning models that can be economically viable and provide comprehensive fault detection solutions. A foreseen challenge is that of cybersecurity, since AI systems may be vulnerable to cyber and adversarial attacks, requiring robust AI models and secure communication protocols and encryption techniques to protect algorithms and data integrity.

Subsequently, by analyzing the content of the studied papers, and by using the functionalities of Scopus, Figure 3 was derived. Figure 3 depicts the key developments and research efforts, in terms of published works, over the past decade regarding the use of computer vision algorithms for detecting faults, defects and anomalies in PV systems, along with the key technological developments that marked the decade. The research was conducted within Article title, Abstract and Keywords, by using the query: "computer vision" AND "PV" AND "faults detection" OR "defects" OR "anomalies". The search returned 52 articles ranging from 2014–2024. It is clear that the introduction of CNNs in PV fault detection in the late 2010s has brought a significant increase in the number of related documents, resulting an upward trend in the following years.

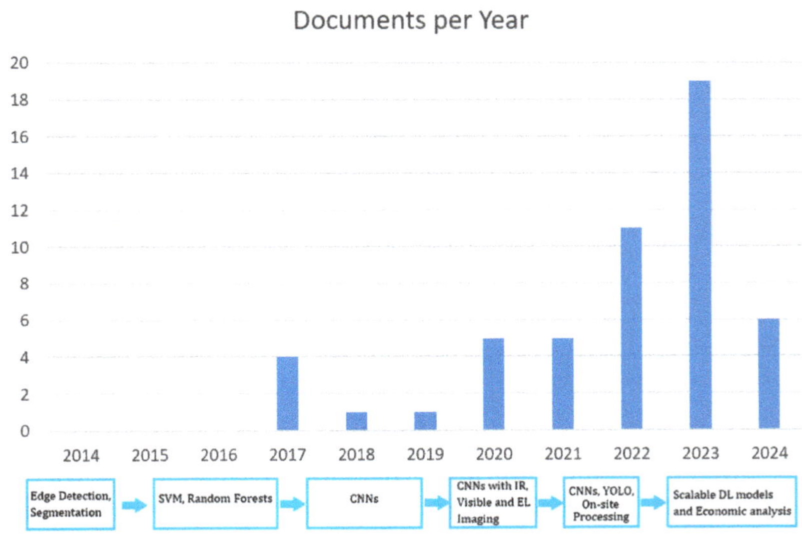

Figure 3. Evolution of trends and the corresponding number of papers on computer vision algorithms for PV fault detection according to Scopus, on the same reference timeline from 2014 to 2024.

5. Capabilities and Limitations of Basic Detection Technologies

Faults and failures in PV modules can be detected with many methods, including UAV-based or visual inspections, I-V curve and electromagnetic induction measurements, infrared thermography, electroluminescence and photoluminescence imaging, ultraviolet fluorescence methods, and spectroscopy. In what follows, the key fault detection technologies for PV systems are reviewed, reporting their capabilities and limitations. Moreover, extended research in CV based fault detection technologies is conducted (RQ2).

5.1. Key Fault Detection Technologies for PV Systems

5.1.1. UAV-Based Inspection

The effectiveness of basic detection technologies has been tested in several preliminary laboratory experiments. These promising results have encouraged researchers to explore using these inspection techniques for large photovoltaic installations. The solution identified by field experts, which has become a standard in recent years, involves using specialized unmanned aerial vehicles (UAVs), such as drones, equipped with cameras for fault detection [18]. This method has two main advantages: (1) it is suitable for inspecting large photovoltaic fields as the entire installation can be surveyed in a few flights (depending on the size of the installation and the UAV's battery life), and (2) it significantly reduces the cost and time required for analysis compared to traditional inspection techniques. The suitability of this solution has been evaluated through qualitative analysis in real photovoltaic fields to verify which anomalies are visible with moving cameras and to determine the impact of flight parameters on detection capabilities, thus testing the reliability of specialized UAVs [19–24].

Specifically, two types of architectures for anomaly detection can be identified: (1) real-time image analysis of photovoltaic modules during the UAV flight, and (2) offline image analysis, examining the video recorded during the inspection. Naturally, the first solution is faster and allows the operator to verify in real-time whether the photovoltaic modules have been inspected correctly; yet it requires careful software design to accelerate the image processing algorithm. Moreover, for real-time inspection, UAVs need to operate at certain heights and at specific time in the day so as to clearly capture details without sun reflections and facilitate processing. Moreover, note that UAVs can detect only visible external defects, while internal defects are not considered, e.g., non-functional diodes.

UAVs typically carry thermal cameras, visible light RGB cameras and photoluminescence cameras. Thermal cameras are used for thermographic analysis, while visible light cameras can store color images related to potential anomalies identified by the image processing algorithm. The idea is that images of defective photovoltaic modules, accompanied by geographical coordinates measured by the GPS sensor, can serve as a powerful and effective tool for automatic photovoltaic inspection [20]. However, the current accuracy of GPS sensors is in the order of several meters, whereas the required accuracy for the geographical placement of photovoltaic panels should be within a few centimeters. Therefore, with the current state of technology, computer vision algorithms cannot utilize the geographical coordinates calculated by GPS sensors to recognize and identify each photovoltaic panel but must provide a mechanism for tracking each unit and detecting potential anomalies in the image. The latter is a challenge being addressed by several techniques, as reviewed in the following.

5.1.2. Visual Inspection

Visual inspection refers to the process of examining the PV panels visually to identify signs of damage, wear, or malfunction and it is considered the fastest and most efficient way especially when conducted by experts. However, it is not suitable for modules exposed to weather conditions and it must be conducted before and after the exposure of modules to stress, either electrical, mechanical, or environmental. Common stress testing methods to evaluate modules indoor include moisture cooling or thermal cycles, liquid heat testing, ultraviolet (UV) radiation testing, mechanical loads, application of thermal stress, etc. [25]. International Electrotechnical Commission (IEC) standards 61646 [26] and 61215 [27] require illumination of more than 1000 lux to conduct visual tests towards for considering defects visible to the naked eye. Such defects include: delamination, yellowing, and blistering on the front of the module; cracks, broken parts, and discoloration of the reflective coating on the cells; burning and oxidation of metallization; bending, breaking, scratches, and poor alignment of the module frame; delamination, yellowing, scratches, burning, and more, as referenced in [4,28].

Specifically, visible defects such as yellowing of the encapsulant have been identified as major causes of power loss [29,30]. In order to identify defects visually and assess their impact, the modules are compared with a reference similar and intact module [29]. Such approaches can be found in the literature; Bouaichi et al. in their study [29] identified discoloration on panels exposed to hot climate for a period of two years, associated to power loss of modules. The same conclusion was made by Kahoul et al. [30] who also associated power loss to modules being exposed to severe environmental conditions for more than a decade, same as in [31]. In addition to power loss, several defects have been detected in all cases, such as cell cracking, corrosion, glass breakage, discoloration and more kinds of visible degradations. It should be noted that discoloration is commonly observed to panels that operate in extreme hot conditions, such as in deserts [32].

5.1.3. I-V Curve Measurements

The current-voltage (I-V) curve measurement for PC fault detection involves the analysis of I-V characteristics of a panel towards identifying potential faults or abnormalities [33], and it is considered as the most comprehensive among all detection method [34].

Measurements can be conducted in either indoor or outdoor conditions, under artificial lighting sources or the sunlight, respectively. In both cases, measurements are first converted to standard test conditions (STC) towards being compared with the reference measurements set by the manufacturers. From the conducted comparison between the I-V reference and measured curves, any observed variations are associated to modules' degradation. If the variations between the I-V curves are small, referring to minor failures on the panels, these may fail to be identified [35]. Moreover, it should be noted that the study of the I-V curve characteristics does not provide any information of the exact defects' location [36]. An alternative measurement to identify faults involves electromagnetic methods [37]. Electromagnetic methods use electromagnetic waves to detect faults in PV modules through the analysis of their electrical or magnetic properties, such as electrical conductivity, electromagnetic inference (EMI), frequency responses, partial discharges, induced currents, and more. Regarding the electrical properties of PV modules, DC testings analyze and evaluate electrical parameters, such as insulation resistance, continuity and electrical output, directly related to the PV modules' performance, [38] while in AC testing, alternating current is used to test systems that operate on AC, focusing more on parameters related to AC power quality and performance [39].

Other methods to identify electrical and morphological failures in PV modules include electron beam-induced current (EBIC) and scanning acoustic microscopy (SAM) [40–42]. EBIC is performed by using a scanning electron microscope, which scans the solar cells with an electron beam aiming to generate electron-hole pairs towards measuring current properties [43]. SAM methods use sound waves to map the internal structure of the materials of panels, revealing cracks, voids and delamination; thus, it is more appropriate to detect morphological failures. The combination of both methods can provide a more comprehensive understanding of both electrical and structural integrity of PV modules, allowing for more accurate fault detection assessments [44,45].

One more method that belongs in this category is the differential current analysis, which involves the comparison of the current flow entering and leaving different sections of the modules [25], by using current sensors placed in the PV system. Thus, the difference between measured input and output currents at different points is calculated, indicating potential defects if significant differences in the currents are measured. A major advantage of this method is that it can indicate the exact location of the fault, which makes it useful to accurately detect and locate faults for timely maintenance of modules.

5.1.4. Infrared Thermography

Infrared thermography (IR) involves measuring the surface heat of PV modules. By capturing and analyzing the temperature patterns emitted by the components of the system, possible defects can be detected. Studies have shown that there's a correlation between cell power output and temperature variations in IR images [46].

In such cases, IR cameras are used, that can detect infrared variation, referring to the heat emitted by the system. All components of the PV system may emit heat, in varying levels, which may alter in case of defects. Therefore, the IR camera can capture the temperature variations across the entire system, indicating anomalies such as hot spots. Note that hot spots are known to reduce the overall efficiency of PV modules, therefore early detection can prevent significant damages and deterioration of its efficiency [47].

Based on the source of thermal excitation, thermographic measurements can be: (1) Passive or under steady conditions, when the module is scanned during its operation in outdoor environments and is not heated by external sources [48] (Figure 4a); it can also be performed in doors by detaching the module and take in-lab measurements [47] (Figure 4b). Setups for indoor and outdoor thermography can also be found in [49]. (2) Active or lock-in thermography when the module is heated periodically by an external source. This technique has less thermal impact on cells and can be performed in dark or illuminated conditions [50–55]; (3) Flash or pulse thermography when flashes of light are used to heat the surface of PV modules. The surface temperature rises uniformly, and a high-resolution thermal camera captures images to detect defects like bubbles and electrical connection anomalies. Various defects visible in IR images are provided in Figure 5 [56].

Several aspects need to be considered during IR imaging [57] regarding emissivity setup, shading effect, and more, as well as regarding the setup of thermal camera such as its distance from the PV module since glass reflections can provoke measurement errors. Adjusting the camera angle can help reduce reflection issues [57]. As already mentioned, severe environmental conditions can impact defects. Modules in hot climates with detected hot spots tend to display greater degradation under IR thermography compared to those located in less hot regions [58].

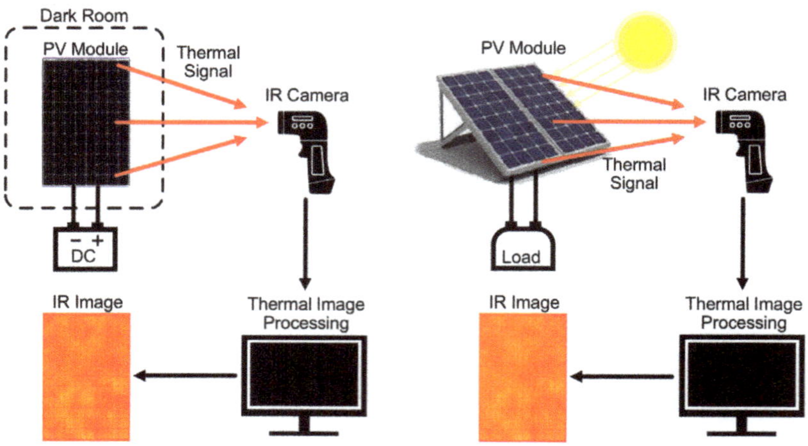

(a) (b)

Figure 4. (**a**) Indoor and (**b**) outdoor thermography setups [49].

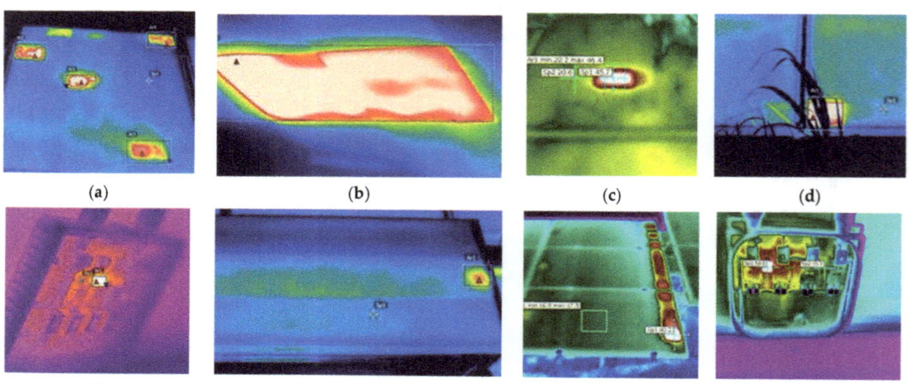

(a) (b) (c) (d) (e) (f) (g) (h)

Figure 5. Defects in IR Imaging: (**a**) breakage of front glass; (**b**) overheated cell due to internal cell problems; (**c**) hot spot; (**d**) overheating due to external shading; (**e**) open junction box and overheated diode; (**f**) overheated junction box; (**g**) overheating due to shading by neighboring PV module row; (**h**) overheated bypass diode [56]. Colors from green to red indicate cold to heat-up (defected) areas. Images serve as indicative depictions of the specified defects in IR imaging, and the letterings within them are of no significance.

5.1.5. Electroluminescence Imaging

Electroluminescence (EL) imaging involves capturing images of the luminescent effect that is produced when an electric current comparable to the module's short-circuit current (ISC) passes through the solar cells, causing them to emit EL radiation [59,60]. EL radiation is commonly detected by charge-coupled device (CCD) cameras that are more affordable, by indium gallium arsenide sensors that typically are more expensive, as well as by modified RGB cameras [61]. EL imaging is conducted in dark settings, with defects captured as dark areas/lines on grayscale images, and have been employed in several studies towards defects detection [62]. A reported disadvantage is due to the challenges related to the detection of faults in outdoor EL imaging due to casual dark regions and spots on the images [63] that may obstruct the process. However, it could be advantageous, i.e., quick and accurate, for indoor defects detection. An EL imaging experimental setup is illustrated in Figure 6, while typical defects in EL images can be visualized in Figure 7 [56].

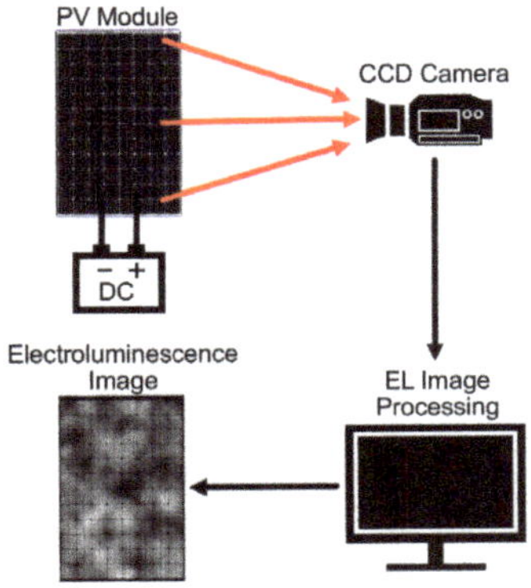

Figure 6. EL imaging setup [11].

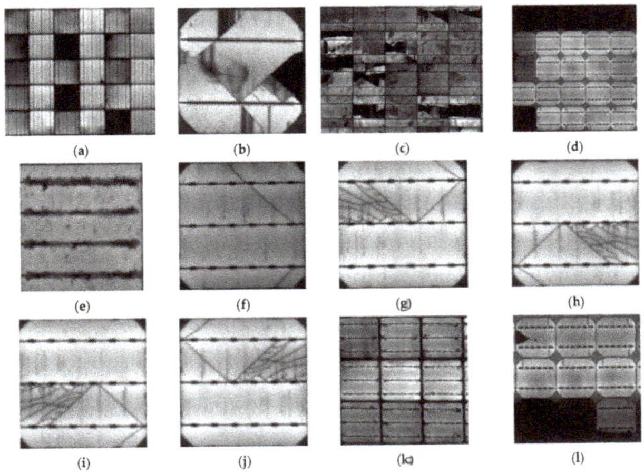

Figure 7. Different types of defects in EL imaging [56]: (**a**) PID-s affected module; (**b**) crack pattern due to impacts; (**c**) polycrystalline PV module with cracked cells; (**d**) monocrystalline PV module with potential induced degradation; (**e**) busbar corrosion in cell; (**f**) cracked cell; (**g**) cracked cell of original orientation; (**h**) cracked cell of different orientation, rotated 180°; (**i**) cracked cell of different orientation, flipped about x-axis; (**j**) cracked cell of different orientation, flipped about y-axis; (**k**) module having undergone damp-heat exposure; (**l**) monocrystalline PV module with induced degradation.

The average pixel intensity of a cell in an EL image is strongly associated to the module's maximum power output [62]. The latter helps to determine the degree of the module's degradation. Moreover, EL emissions' intensity is correlated to the degree of applied voltage, thus, defective regions can be identified by comparing EL images under different polarizations [64].

5.1.6. Photoluminescence Imaging

Photoluminescence (PL) imaging is another effective approach for PV modules' defects detection, by capturing images of the luminescent effect which occurs when the PV materials absorb photons and retransmit them as light. More specifically, the PV absorbs energy that causes electrons to jump to a higher energy level triggering them to emit light when they return to their original state. Specialized camera sensors are able to capture the emitted light, which is analyzed to detect variations of the luminescence across the PV module [65]. A typical PL imaging setup is shown in Figure 8.

Additionally, PL imaging can be performed by using optical filters and current modulation. Optical filtering is employed to allow the selective passing of specific wavelengths of light, so as to isolate it from environmental noises. Thus, PL images are clearer and thus easier to detect underlying anomalies. Current modulation aims to improve the signal-to-noise ratio, by modulating the luminescence signal to separate it from background noises. The latter process allows for more accurate and high-quality PL imaging towards easily detecting defects in PV systems. The obtained PL images are then compared with the EL images towards identifying cracks, high-disorder areas, and poorly performing cells [66]. This enhanced PL imaging setup, and the resulting image are shown in Figure 9.

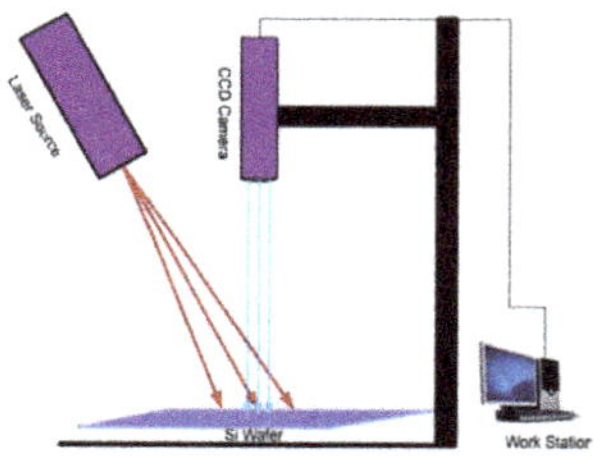

Figure 8. Typical PL imaging setup [65].

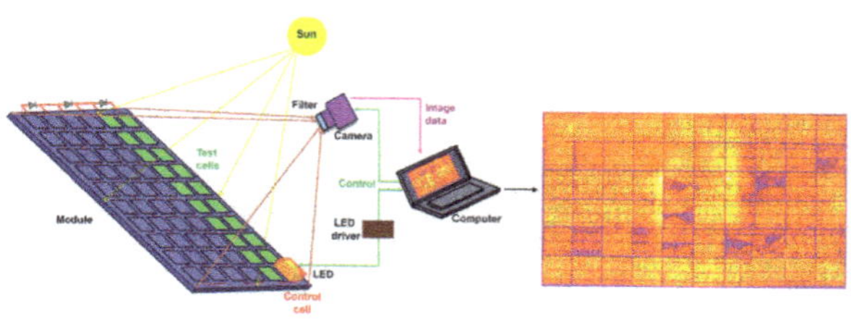

Figure 9. Enhanced PL imaging setup using optical filtering and current modulation [66].

The combination of spectral and spatially resolved PL imaging can be used to obtain a more comprehensive understanding of the condition of materials in a PV system. The type and location of defects can be identified, providing valuable feedback for timely maintenance and quality control of modules [67].

5.1.7. Ultraviolet Fluorescence Method

Ultraviolet fluorescence (UVF) was first exploited to detect discoloration issues such as yellowing effect in PV modules [28]. Later, dark lines in a UVF were associated with cracks in the panel.

UV-based detection is based on fluorescence effect of the material in PV modules namely polymeric lamination. Fluorescence refers to the emitted light by a material like the encapsulant that is active due to absorption of light [68]. A camera with UV-pass filter can capture the fluorescence, which is being interrupted by defects on solar cells. Thus, a variety of fluorescence patterns can be formed, providing information about the type of defect, their age and severity [69,70]. UVF experiments are conducted in darkness to eliminate inferences from ambient light, therefore, to capture a clearer fluorescent image. By exposing the PV module to sunlight prior imaging, helps to charge the materials within the module, resulting to more intense luminescence and high-quality images. Typically a 30-s exposure time is recommended [71]. An experimental UV fluorescence imaging setup is shown in Figure 10, including a PV module, a CCD camera, a highpass filter and a UV light source.

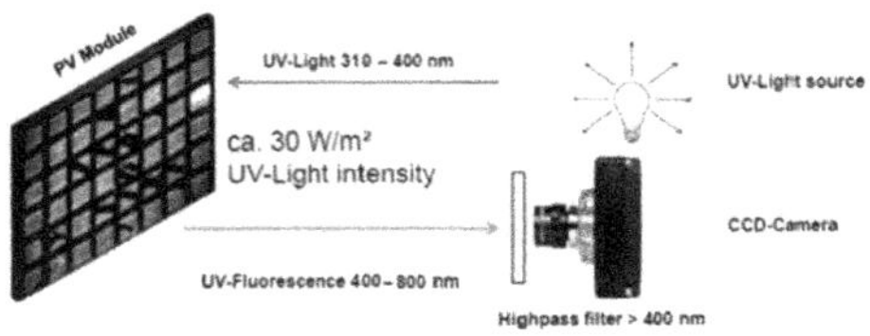

Figure 10. UV-F imaging setup for cells in outdoor and laboratory conditions [4].

The emitted fluorescent falls within the visible region of the electromagnetic spectrum, thus it can be captured by a digital camera. To ensure accurate imaging, filters are typically employed to block out any remaining UV rays to prevent them from interfering with the captured images. Both UVF and EL imaging provide valuable information about PV modules defects resulting in similar visual representations of the condition of modules, where defective areas are highlighted with darker color [72]. However, UVF imaging uses external UV light while EL imaging applies electric current to the module, to excite its materials. Therefore, UVF can be implemented outdoors during the module's operation while EL imaging requires controlled environment. Both methods can be used complementary towards providing a more comprehensive analysis of a PV module's status [70].

5.1.8. Spectroscopy

Spectroscopy is a powerful technique that is used to analyze the interaction of matter with electromagnetic radiation. When spectroscopy is applied to PV fault detection, refers to the measurements of the produced spectra by using spectrometers when the PV module is exposed to different light wavelengths. Several types of spectroscopies are available, such as photoluminescence, Raman, electroluminescence, impedance, Fourier transform infrared, and fluorescence spectroscopy.

Raman spectroscopy is capable of identifying stress, stain and several other defects on PV modules by using inelastic scattering of photons that provides information about the molecular and structural composition of materials. When laser light interacts with the molecules in the material's structure, mainly it scatters elastically, while a small part scatters inelastically, namely the Raman scattering light. The latter results in a shift in the light's energy which is analogous to the vibrational modes of the molecules, thus, it can characterize the material's composition. The Raman scattering light is collected and analyzed using a spectrometer. A hyper Raman head measure is employed to measure the spectrometry maps and detect defects PV modules [73]. To map snail trails, point measurements are taken using Raman spectroscopy, and then converted into Raman maps, which visually represent the spatial distribution of different materials and defects across the PV module. At this step, florescence images can also be produced to provide complementary information to Raman maps. To enhance the quality of maps, Gaussian fiters can be employed to smooth the image and reduce noise effects. Such a measurement setup is shown in Figure 11 [73]. Raman spectroscopy also measures thermomechanical stresses in PV modules during manufacturing [74]. A confocal Raman spectrometer is used to measure stress in solar cells, caused by metallization, lamination, etc., during manufacturing, by detecting shifts in the Raman peaks, associated to changes in the vibrational modes of materials [74].

Fluorescence spectroscopy is used in [71] to study modules exposed to ageing. The module is illuminated by a light source, that excites the electrons in the material of the PV modules, making them move to higher energy states. Returning to their initial state causes them to emit light of different wavelengths, i.e., fluorescence. Fluorescence light is detected and measured using a spectrometer. The properties of the detected light such as the intensity and wavelength can provide insight regarding the properties of the module.

Fourier transform infrared spectroscopy (FTIR) is used to acquire and analyze the molecular structure of PV materials [71]. The interaction between mid-infrared radiation and the material can excite molecular vibrations corresponding to specific absorption wavelengths which appear in the infrared spectra, revealing detailed information about the molecular structure of the material.

Figure 11. Measurement setup using a Raman spectrometer and Raman superhead [73].

5.1.9. Electromagnetic Induction-Based Measurements

Electromagnetic (EM) radiation induction for PV fault detection uses electromagnetic waves to identify faults in the modules. Usually, it is combined with IR thermography and EL to provide more comprehensive assessments since they provide complementary type of information; EM analyzes changes in the electrical properties of a PV module exposed to electromagnetic waves and can detect electrical faults, thermography measures the thermal profile of modules with an IR camera and can detect thermal anomalies, while EL measures emitted light by the modules when electric current is applied and can detect structural defects.

The combination of IR thermography with EM induction can effectively detect defects in PV modules. An electromagnetic wave is applied to the PV module to heat the electrical resistant materials, inducing currents within the module. The induced currents heat the defected areas that disrupt the flow of current, revealing impurities. An IR camera captures the thermal properties of the module, aiming to indicate faults in the module. Figure 12a illustrates an active electromagnetic induction infrared thermography system for PV cells from the literature [75].

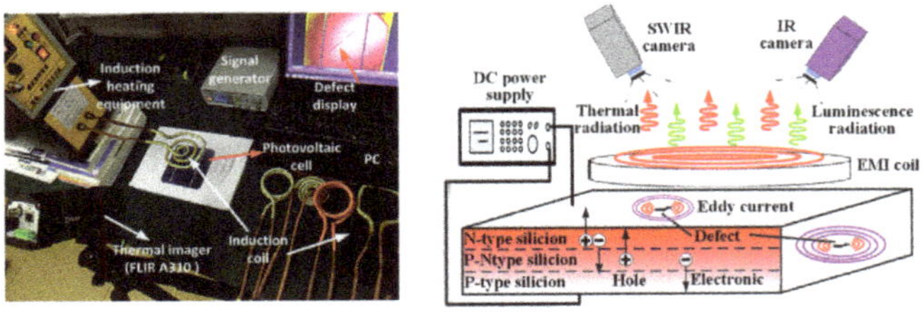

(a) (b)

Figure 12. (**a**) Experimental setup of an EIIT thermography system for PV cells [75]; (**b**) thermography and EL imaging setup based on electromagnetic induction [76].

Similarly, the combination of EL imaging with EM induction can provide the accuracy of PV fault detection. First, EM induction is employed, while applied electric current causes electroluminescence captured by an IR camera that provides the EL image with highlighted the defected areas.

In general, the combination of different techniques can provide a more complete picture of the module's health status. Towards this direction, Yang et al. [76] in their work compare the fusion results of a set of techniques, evaluating PV performance based on well-known metrics. The used EM induction-based thermography and EL imaging setup of Yang et al. is shown in Figure 12b.

5.1.10. Capabilities and Limitations

After reviewing the key detection technologies individually, this section aims to identify their capabilities and limitations by examining fault detection technologies in combination, aiming to answer RQ2. To achieve this, we utilize two comprehensive tables (Tables 2 and 3) that detail the strengths and limitations of the different basic detection technologies and ultimately how they relate to various faults in photovoltaic systems, based on an extensive literature analysis.

Table 2. Cumulative table of limitations and capabilities of basic PV fault detection technologies. CV based fault detection technologies are marked in bold.

Technology	Description	Capabilities	Limitations
UAV-based inspection	Specialized UAVs equipped with cameras for fault detection fly over PV farms.	Suitable for inspecting large photovoltaic fields Reduces the cost and time required for analysis com-pared to traditional inspection techniques	Limited accuracy of GPS sensors Need to track each unit Only defects visible from distance can be detected Not suitable for real-time detection
Visual Inspection	Defects detected with naked eye, such as delamination, browning, yellowing, corrosion, bending, bubbling and degradation of the anti-reflective coating.	Quick and efficient No instrumentation required	Cannot detect non-visible defects Not feasible for large-scale outdoor applications
I-V Curve Analysis	A primary approach for characterizing silicon cells. Typically combined with other methods for detailed information. Changes in the I-V curve lead to identification of PV module degradation.	Low-cost methodology Easy measurements Can be used for quantitative calculations	Cannot pinpoint the exact location of defects May be ineffective with minor variations Contact method requiring instruments
TG/IR Imaging	A method that measures the surface temperature of PV modules. Infrared rays emitted by the modules are captured by thermal cameras. Various types suitable for different applications.	Suitable for large-scale outdoor applications Easily detects hot spots Provides quantitative measurements High-resolution images Non-destructive Can detect areas of internal short circuits	Difficult to precisely locate the defect Expensive thermal cameras Long measurement time with lock-in IR method Thermal blur issues Indoor IR requires external power source Micro-crack damage is not fully represented
EL Imaging	Captures electroluminescence radiation emitted by cells due to electron-hole recombination. This radiation is in the near-infrared spectrum.	Primarily for detecting micro-cracks and edge interruptions Fast, efficient and accurate for indoor use Non-destructive Can be performed with a modified digital camera	Random dark spots/lines/areas in the background due to crystallographic defects Requires more experience and expertise Requires external power source Mainly for indoor use Induction heating issues blur interior areas
PL Imaging	The sample is stimulated with light radiation/laser source and luminescence radiation is emitted near-infrared region.	Fast Non-destructive High spatial resolution Can detect cracks	Requires an excitation source Branched areas appear quite blurred

Table 2. *Cont.*

Technology	Description	Capabilities	Limitations
Spectroscopy	Measuring and studying spectra produced by the interaction with radiation.	Highly sensitive Can differentiate between different fault types	Costly equipment Complexity of spectral data Affected by external conditions
UV-F Imaging	Uses an ultraviolet light source to stimulate the luminescent pigments in the encapsulating material. This stimulation leads to the emission of fluorescence luminescence The emitted rays are then imaged by a camera.	Easy detection of snail trails Easy detection of discolorations Can detect cracks Fluorescent light is in the visible range, so a digital camera can be used Non-destructive	Requires long exposure time for good fluorescence image Requires light source for stimulation Fluorescence effect develops in modules after prolonged outdoor use Cannot detect PID Shorted or open bypass diode is not detectable
EM induction	Identifies variations in electrical properties caused by faults	Scalability for large systems monitoring Fast scanning	Complex interpretations Environmental interference

Table 3. Comparative table of limitations and capabilities of basic CV-based PV fault detection technologies.

Ref.	Technologies	Findings
[77]	Indoor vs. Outdoor TG/IR	External IR thermography results show relatively fewer or no defects in PV modules. Conversely, internal IR thermography images depict defects more clearly. Possible reasons for differences include absorption of radiation by other parts such as the backsheet, high heat dissipation rate, abrupt environmental changes causing thermal instability and minor defects of negligible impact.
[78]	UV-F vs. EL	Cracks in EL images clearly correlate with dark areas in UV-F images. However, due to darkness around cell edges, cracks along the edges are not detectable in UV-F images. The marble pattern in EL images caused by crystallographic defects in polycrystalline silicon makes crack detection in EL images harder compared to UV-F. UV-F better illustrates areas typically hotter during operation.
[79–83]	TG/IR Imaging vs. EL Imaging	EL Imaging / IR Imaging: Advantages EL Imaging: High resolution Direct measurement (non-contact) recognizable defects: defective laser cut, shorted bypass circuits, disconnected cell areas, short circuits broken cells and layer defects IR Imaging: Recognizable defects: different thermal behavior, short circuits, hot spots, moisture, shading, incompatibilities, installation failures, etc. Disadvantages EL Imaging: Origin of defect not recognizable Hard to determine defect impact on cell/module performance Normal-looking EL images can reveal high-temperature areas in IR images because both techniques capture different physical properties IR Imaging: Not all defects cause temperature rise High-temperature areas are not always defect sources Difficult to pinpoint exact defect location in numerous small spots Requires electrical interface Cannot distinguish between weak and high series resistance
[84–86]	Visual Inspection vs. TG/IR vs. UV-F	Hot-spots easily detectable with IR, but EL and UV-F do not clearly detect them Hot-spots above 120 °C easily visible with visual inspection, appearing as dark black or brown area in RGB images Cell cracks not clearly detected with IR thermography but evident in EL images. UV-F shows similar crack patterns, but formation can take weeks Snail trails are easily detected with UV-F and EL Potential Induced Degradation (PID) faults are detected with IR thermography, EL images, but not with UV-F Shorted/opened bypass diodes detectable by all methods except UV-F and partially by visual inspection Common visible faults include discoloration, broken glass and backsheet tearing

Besides the individual application of each basic detection technology, various studies examine the comparative application of multiple CV-based technologies on PV modules. The findings of these comparative applications are summarized in Table 3.

5.2. Fault Detection Using AI-Based Computer Vision

Computer vision is rapidly gaining traction as a groundbreaking technology aiming to replace conventional monitoring systems in the PV sector, satisfying escalating global energy demands driven by the exponential growth of population. The integration of AI into PV energy systems is becoming a topic of interest, since AI is foreseen to play a pivotal role in addressing future energy requirements.

Computer vision systems in the PV sector comprise high-resolution camera, sophisticated imaging devices, such as RGB, EL, IR cameras or Light Detection and Ranging (LiDARs) devices, drones for aerial inspections, edge computing devices for on-site processing, and corresponding machine/deep learning algorithms to analyze the captured images and identify underlying issues. Thus, computer vision systems aim to make the latter components work together, to endow devices with adequate intelligence, so as to enhance the real-time monitoring, maintenance, and efficiency of PV systems based on image data analysis. The extracted information is then used by control systems for efficient decision making, leading to automated alerts, predictive maintenance and optimization actions, performance reports, and more, to ensure high efficiency and extended lifespan of PV systems. The computer vision-based inspection process is implemented similarly as experienced human workers perform visual inspections, yet they enhance the process with their energy and labor savings, risk reduction, speed, accuracy, and advanced analytical capabilities.

Essentially, the monitoring and fault detection in PV systems are automated through machine learning and deep learning algorithms and image processing techniques, as extensively acknowledged in the literature. Deep learning, in particular, has demonstrated exceptional performance in this domain. For instance, automated image classification and detection systems can replace EL image analysis of PV cells or modules, while automatic edge detection in IR imaging, defects detection and localization in RGB imaging, quality assessment of silicon wafer in PL images, and cracks segmentation tasks in EL imaging are also notable examples.

In these examples, computers or machines exhibit human intelligence, referred to as automated or AI-based methods, regardless the used data [87], and are utilized for several tasks, including predictions, modeling, and predictive maintenance analyses [88–90]. Specific types of algorithms are selected depending on the task; SVMs, ANNs, CNNs, etc., for both classification and regression. Regarding the most commonly used image processing techniques, Canny edge detection, color quantification, filtering, morphological operations, and data augmentation are reported. Moreover, in classification tasks, a preprocessing step includes usually features extraction and features selection methodologies. At present, AI-based methods are minimally utilized in PV monitoring. Yet, rising energy demands and the ongoing establishment of large PV farms, foretell the indispensable adoption of automated methods.

5.2.1. Machine Learning and Other Pattern Recognition Methods

Automatic classification of PV images as either normal or defective, is implemented by using machine learning algorithms. Demant et al. [91] classified cracked and normal photoluminescence images using the SVM algorithm. In [92], crack patterns were defined using the gradient location and orientation histogram (GLOH). A limitation of the method is that it is sensitive to region errors, which can be corrected, but will result in a very time-consuming algorithm implementation.

In order to classify a module as defective or not, image feature extraction methods can be employed, along with a classifier to assess the panels' status. In [93], Kato extracted features, using HOG [94] and SURF [95] algorithms, from PV image sequences resulting from a captured video, and employed an SVM classifier to assess faults resulted by the collision of PV cells with metal conductors in varying forces.

Pattern recognition methods can also be used. Demant et al. [96] in their work used an SVM classifier with radial basis function kernel to automatically detect cracks in photoluminescence and IR images, by utilizing pattern recognition methods based on the extraction of local descriptors.

Other approaches, such as the one presented in [63], use Fourier image reconstruction techniques towards detecting defects on PV panels. In the latter approach, faults were visible in images like bar or line-shaped objects, and the authors concluded in an effective approach, yet with some limitations; faults with more complex shapes could not be detected, and the implementation was relatively slow, reporting inference of 0.29 s for testing one cell.

Pre-processing tasks are also reported in the literature, such as filtering, towards extracting crack saliency maps [97]. In [97], crack saliency maps were created by employing evidence filtering in EL images. The map was then processed with a local threshold process to detect cracks based on segmentation. Then, the minimum spanning tree connected crack fragments, and finally, cracks were detected by skeleton extraction. A drawback of the method was that the segmented crack may miss a part when morphological operations were applied to remove non-crack pixels, affecting the performance of the detection algorithm especially when curvilinear crystal grains were in the background.

Another reported technique included independent component analysis (ICA) [98]. ICA reconstruction procedure was initiated by selecting a normal image for training after being preprocessed to be centered and whitened. Then the ICA algorithm was used to compute the independent components, that were sorted in downward order and rearranged so as to select a number of them, and the unmixing matrix, that was reshaped. Thus, the image was reconstructed and binarized. As a reported disadvantage of this method, was the fact that finger interruptions in cells were handled identically to small and deep cracks.

In general, the limitations of machine learning algorithms, as already mentioned in Section 4, are due to the need for representative features for each fault type. The latter process can be time-consuming and could prove insufficient to capture the characteristics of each fault. Traditional machine learning methods fail to generalize well in case of new unseen data, which is a limitation in case of PV faults, where input images can be under various and different environmental conditions. Moreover, large datasets and high-resolution images are hard to feasibly handle and process in real-time.

Referenced methods of this section are further comparatively evaluated in Section 7, based on preset performance criteria.

5.2.2. Image Processing Techniques

Several image processing methods are also utilized for PV defects detection, based on the literature [99]. Alsafasfeh et al. [100] captured IR images of a PV farm using a drone. The captured images were subjected to grayscale conversion and segmentation, and morphological operations were applied, along with Canny edge detection. A reported disadvantage of the proposed approach was the appearance of shadowing in images, seriously obstructing hot spots detection.

Li et al. [101], aiming to detect visible faults like snake trails and dust, implemented other image processing techniques to the captured RGB images of PV systems from a drone. Image conversion to single-channel model (red, green, blue) was first implemented to make the processing more efficient and reduce complex computations, followed by image filtering by using the first derivative of the Gaussian function (FODG) towards noise reduction. Finally, to determine the faults, an edge detection algorithm was used. A disadvantage of this approach was the limitation of the drone's flight height, restricted sun-angles and flights conducted only in ideal weather conditions, so as to provide efficient results.

Canny edge detection method was used as a preprocessing step for segmentation tasks towards the identification of hot spots in IR images [102,103]. Both works reported as limitation the fact that Canny edge, in case of any specular object present in the background, caused grey-level variations that were false assumed as hot spots. Segmentation is also used to detect defects in infrared module images [104], yet was not efficiently performing in case of whole modules with several defects. Dotenco et al. [105] employed statistical methods and other image processing methodologies to evaluate PV faults from UAV IR images. In [106], the authors used a combination of segmentation and morphological methods to detect hot spots in PV panels. However, the proposed method could not detect other types of faults.

Segmentation was also combined with filtering operations for PV fault detection [99,107]. In [47], preprocessing included filtering, color quantization, and Canny edge detection towards faults detection of different severities (normal, slight defected, severe defected) in IR images.

Finally, the vesselness-based algorithm for segmentation can also be used for the automatic fault detection scheme. This method was used in [108] for EL images. It has some limitations, such as only considering cracks longer than 20 mm, and disregarding other defect types and cracks shorter than 20 mm.

Same as in traditional machine learning algorithms for PV fault detection, the limitations of image processing methods, as already mentioned in Section 4, are due to the need for exhausting manual feature extraction. Such methods are sensitive to noise and environmental variations, leading to poor adaptability, requiring fine-tuning for each specific case, and subsequently resulting in poor detection performances. Scalability for covering large PV farms, and complexity of large datasets, are also evident.

Referenced methods of this section are further comparatively evaluated in Section 7, based on preset performance criteria.

5.2.3. Deep Learning Methods

Deep learning methods are also used for PV defects detection, as reported in the literature [109–112]. For example, Demant et al. [113] engaged a CNNs in the production of solar cells, to perform quality control and monitor the process. Their method, however, was constrained by the used low-resolution camera.

Mehta and Azad, in [114], used a Mask FCNN model to predict defects and localize them in PV modules, also aiming to predict power losses. All methodologies mentioned refer to the detection of visible faults. Yet, there are also works that use deep learning methods to both EL and IR images. In [114], the authors utilize EL images, features extraction methods including KAZE, SIFT, HOG, and SURF, and an SVM model.

It should be noted that optimal performances were reported by utilizing CNNs and transfer learning. In both works [115,116], the researchers proposed CNN architectures, and an open EL image dataset of PV cells, and applied transfer learning utilizing the VGG model. Evaluation results indicated deterioration in the detection performance due to labelling errors, particularly at the edges of cracks.

Akram et al. [11] used a lightweight CNN model and generalization approaches to detect faults in EL images of various defects. Data augmentation was employed to balance the dataset and deal with limited original image data. The authors reported efficient performance by utilizing simple hardware; however, all results were from in-lab testing.

In another work, the same authors Akram et al. [49], employ standalone deep learning and transfer learning, to detect faults in IR imaging. Regarding standalone learning, the authors utilized a lightweight CNN trained from scratch. Regarding transfer learning, the authors utilized a base pre-trained model on another EL image dataset. The second approach with transfer learning returned better performance results, while classification errors were mainly noticed for defects with small number of images in the dataset.

Greco et al. [117] employed a YOLO model to detect hot spots in IR images. The proposed method conducted features fusion using bypass connections, and image segmentation for hot spots detection. Results implied a robust method with high efficiency, that could run in real-time without vast resources.

In [118,119], the authors use VGG and MobileNet models towards faults detection and classification from IR imaging. The captured images were subjected to feature extraction, by using SIFT and dense SIFT algorithm, and were classified with an SVM model as normal and defective. Both polynomial and radial basis function kernels were tested for the SVM, with the first one reporting optimal performance. Reported disadvantages include model complexities, and computational burden, that need to be further considered.

Wei et al. [12] employed a Faster R-CNN towards detecting hot spots in thermal IR images. For the latter implementation, the weights of the pre-trained model were adjusted based on the used dataset. Moreover, preprocessing steps included Hough line transform and Canny edge detection. The used deep model reported efficient results, yet with high computational demands, posing a challenge for UAV-based implementations considering their limited capabilities in memory and GPU for processing. Transfer learning was also used by Buratti et al. [120]. The authors conducted features extraction from EL images and classification of faults, reaching 96% of accuracy. The used dataset comprised monocrystalline silicon cell EL images (busbar-free, with 3 busbars, and with 5 busbars), and their matching I-V parameters.

These methods and applications highlight the potential of deep learning in detecting and classifying defects in PV systems, emphasizing their effectiveness and significance in the field.

In general, the limitations of deep learning algorithms, as already mentioned in Section 4, are due to the need for large amounts of labeled and diverse input data. Data acquisition and annotation could be exhausting. Moreover, deep models require powerful GPUs especially for real-time applications. Explainability of deep models is an additional challenge, closely related to the trust on their outputs, especially for stakeholders who want to invest in this technology.

Referenced methods of this section are further comparatively evaluated in Section 7, based on preset performance criteria.

6. CV Detectable Faults and Related Performance of PV Systems

Photovoltaic modules (PVMs) can experience various types of failures, often covered by the system's warranty if they happen under normal operating conditions [93]. When these systems fail, it can lead to safety risks, reduced efficiency, decreased power availability and compromised system reliability. Common issues found in PVMs include discoloration, cracks, snail trails, damage to the reflective coating, bubbles, pollution, oxidation of distribution bars, corrosion and breakdown of encapsulation on cells and interconnections. Additionally, problems like loss of adhesion of the back sheet are also noted [28,121–128].

There are various strategies to detect these failures, focusing on issues like encapsulation, unit corrosion, cell cracks and problems with the photovoltaic inverter [128]. Failures in PVMs are generally categorized into two types: permanent and temporary. Permanent issues include delamination, bubbles, yellowing, scratches and burned cells, typically requiring the replacement of the defective modules. Temporary problems, like partial shading, dust accumulation, dirt and snow on the PVM, can usually be resolved by the users without needing to replace the modules. Failures can arise from both external and internal causes, both of which can decrease the system's output power, efficiency and reliability.

The main types of failures that can occur in a PVM are summarized in Table 4. Moreover, their effects on the systems' performance are also included in the table, along with the affected elements and the causes, based on the examined literature (RQ3). More details regarding failures and their relation to performance can be found in the following subsections.

Table 4. Summary of fault types, effected elements, causes and effects on system performance.

Ref.	Fault Type	Affected Element	Causes		Effects
			External	Internal	
[36,125,129–133]	Hot Spot Faults (HSF)	PV Cells, PV Modules	• Covered by: Dust, Snow, Shadow • Different classes of PV Modules or technology	• Fragmentation of cells • Current mismatch between cells • High-resistance or "cold" solder points • Aging and degradation of solar cells	• Destruction of PV panels • Open circuits • Reduced efficiency • Reliability issues
[93,134–136]	Diode Faults (DF)	Bypass Diode (BpD), Blocking Diode (BkD)	• Partially shaded cells • Overheating	-	• Destruction of diodes • Short circuited diode • Open circuited or Isolated diode
[137,138]	Junction Box Faults (JB)	Junction Box	-	• Wear • Corrosion • Loosen connections • Oxidation	• Destruction of PV cells • Fire hazard • Reduce efficiency • Reliability issues
[4,28,123,139]	PV module faults (PVMF), PV array fault (PVAF)	PV Modules	• Glass breakage of PV Modules frameless caused by the clamps • Connector failure • Ground Isolation • Encapsulation • Installation wiring mistake	• Corrosion of solar cells • Manufacturing defects • Delaminated • Bubbles effect • Yellowing • Scratches • Burnt solar cells	• Isolated modules • Short circuit between modules • Current leakage • Destruction PV modules • Reduce efficiency • Reliability issues • Reduced output power
[140–143]	Ground Faults (GF)	PV Array, PV String	-	• Insulation failure of cables • Wire ground fault • Ground fault inside solar panel cable insulation during installation • Ground fault inside solar panel from bad sealing • Insulation destruction of cables • Short circuit inside the solar panel junction box	• Fire hazard

Table 4. *Cont.*

Ref.	Fault Type	Affected Element	Causes		Effects
			External	Internal	
[144,145]	Arc Faults (AF)	PV Modules	-	• Wire short break • Two wires with potencies different are place near one other • Bad soldering connection • Leakage inside to solar panel from mechanical damage • Wildlife junction box • Loosening of screws	• Destruction of PV panels • Fire hazard
[146]	Line to line faults (LLF)	PV Array	-	• Low resistance between two points with potencies different • Insulation failure of cables • Short circuit between wires • Insulation failure between string connectors • Mechanical stress	• Destruction of PV panels • Wires damage • Fire hazard

6.1. Hot Spot Faults

Hot spot (HS) faults can happen when some cells in a photovoltaic (PV) panel have differing current–voltage (I–V) characteristics [125]. This typically occurs due to inconsistencies in manufacturing, which lead to high-resistance points or poor solder joints [125]. Dust and dirt buildup on the panels [129,130,147,148] (Figure 13b), aging of the cells, incomplete insulation at the edges with transparent materials, manufacturing tolerances and uneven sunlight exposure can also contribute to these issues. Partial shading of the panels (Figure 13a) is a common example of such imbalances. HS issues (Figure 13c) arise when the bypass diodes of shaded cells fail or become isolated. This results in a drop in current and a negative voltage, causing the shaded cells to consume energy from the non-shaded cells instead of generating it. If this condition persists, it can damage the affected solar cells [133] (Figure 13d). Detection methods for HS faults are discussed in [36], with many quick detection techniques relying on infrared measurements to identify the problematic areas.

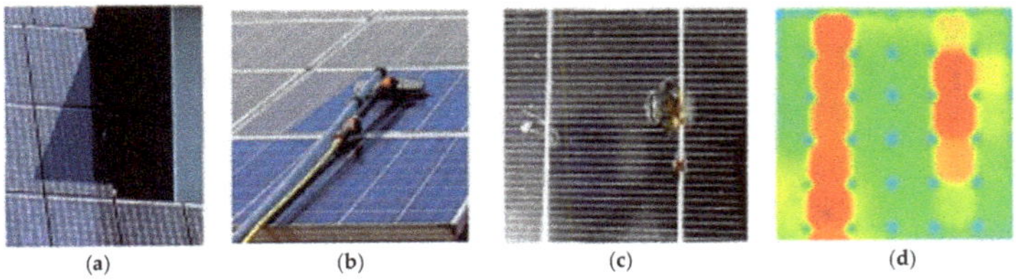

Figure 13. HS faults: (**a**) shading; (**b**) soiling and dust accumulation; (**c**) HS damaged on solar cells; (**d**) detected HS phenomena on a PVM using infrared equipment [87].

6.2. Diode Faults

Bypass and blocking diodes are vital components in PV systems, ensuring their efficient and safe operation. Bypass diodes (BpD) help protect the system from reverse voltage while blocking diodes (BkD) prevent reverse current. Common issues with these diodes include short circuits and open circuits, which can occur if a PV string is partially shaded for long periods [134]. The bypass diode is critical for the system's safe operation [93], but the blocking diode, which is connected in series with the PV module, can sometimes interfere with the proper functioning of Overcurrent Protection Devices (OCPD) [136]. If the reverse current drops below a certain level, known as the Negative Loading Point (LLF), the blocking diode will cut off the current, causing the system to fail. To avoid these types of faults, it is important to carefully choose and thoroughly test both bypass and blocking diodes.

6.3. Junction Box Faults

The junction box (JB) is a critical component for the reliability of photovoltaic (PV) panels during their operation in the field [137]. Corrosion over time can cause the resistance in the JB to increase rapidly [138]. This can lead to electrical arcing between connections, resulting in overheating and melting of the junction box. Such incidents can damage the PV modules and the entire string, leading to significant energy production losses for the system owner. To avoid these issues, several actions and recommendations have been proposed. Regular inspections and maintenance can help detect early signs of wear and corrosion. Ensuring proper installation and using high-quality materials can also reduce the risk of faults. Implementing these strategies can significantly enhance the reliability and lifespan of the junction box, thereby improving the overall performance of the PV system [137].

6.4. PV Module Faults

PV module faults can happen for a variety of reasons, such as corrosion, aging components, internal current leaks, or manufacturing defects. These issues can cause disconnections or internal short circuits within the modules [28,123,124]. When such faults occur, they can pose serious risks like electric shocks or fires. For example, Figure 14 shows various types of defects in PV modules; Figure 14a illustrates a broken glass panel, Figure 14b–d show common problems like oxidation, delamination and bubbles, respectively. These kinds of defects are often seen in PV modules and can affect both the safety and performance of the system. To prevent these issues from escalating, regular inspections and maintenance are crucial. Identifying and addressing these problems early can help maintain the system's efficiency and longevity.

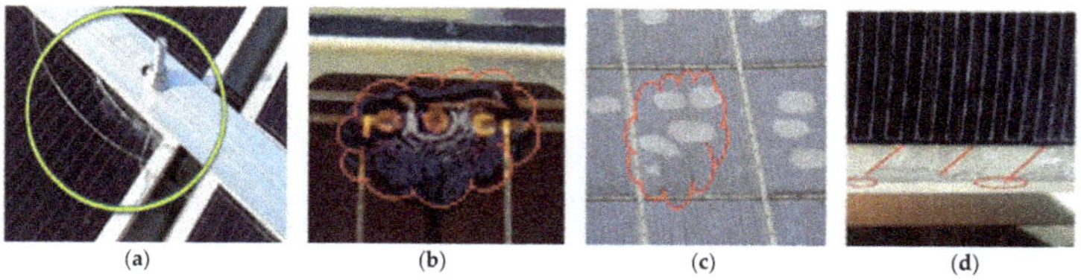

Figure 14. Module defects: (**a**) broken glass; (**b**) oxidation and discoloration; (**c**) delamination; (**d**) bubbles [87].

6.5. Ground Faults

Ground faults in photovoltaic systems (PVSs) happen when there's an unintended electrical short circuit between the ground and one or more of the system's energized wires [141]. These faults are a major safety concern because they can create DC electrical arcs at the fault location, which, if left unaddressed, can lead to fires [140]. Detecting ground faults is especially challenging in ungrounded PV systems, as these faults don't produce enough fault current to be easily detected during normal operations [142]. Ground faults are the most common type of fault in PVSs and can arise from various causes. These include accidental short circuits between wires and the ground, insulation failure of cables and internal ground faults within PV modules (PVMs). A common outcome of ground faults is Potential Induced Degradation (PID), which happens when there's a significant voltage difference between the cells and the ground. These faults not only pose a fire risk but also affect the overall performance of the system. To mitigate these risks, it's recommended to use Ground Fault Detectors to monitor insulation in both residential and large-scale PV systems, enhancing safety and reliability [143]. Regular maintenance and timely detection are key to preventing ground faults and ensuring the longevity of PV systems.

6.6. Arc Faults

An arc fault happens when electricity jumps across a gap through the air or another insulating material. These faults come in two main types: (1) Series Arc Faults (AFa), when there is a break or gap in a single electrical wire, and (2) Parallel Arc Faults (AFa), between two wires with potential difference [144]. It is essential for every electrical system to have an Arc Fault Detector to identify these faults.

There are two primary methods for detection [145]:

- DC Method: This method involves monitoring the DC in a wire. By adding a small resistance in series with the circuit, the voltage across the resistor can be measured to detect any anomalies.
- AC Method: this method uses the AC flowing through a wire, with a current transformer acting as a sensor to detect changes caused by an arc fault.

To prevent fires and protect the photovoltaic system (PVS), these detectors need to activate safety circuits when an arc fault is detected. Arc faults pose a significant fire hazard, so detecting and preventing them is critical for the safety and reliability of PV systems. By implementing these detection methods, we can ensure that the system runs safely and efficiently.

6.7. Line-to-Line Faults

Line-to-line faults (LLFs) happen when there is an unintended low-resistance connection between two points with potential different in an electrical system. In PV system, this usually means a short circuit between the cables of different PVMs or arrays with different voltages [146]. These faults in PV arrays can be caused by:

- Cable Insulation Failure: when the insulation around cables deteriorates or fails, it can lead to accidental short circuits between wires.
- Poor Insulation and Mechanical Stress: if the insulation between string connectors is inadequate or if the cables are subjected to mechanical stress, it can result in LLFs.

To prevent these faults, many companies have developed specialized protective devices. These devices detect and mitigate LLFs, ensuring the system remains safe and functional. Along with using these protective devices, regular maintenance and careful installation are key to prevent LLFs and ensure the reliability and safety of photovoltaic systems.

6.8. Relationship of Faults-Performance of PV Systems

The study [149] explores how different environmental factors impact the performance of PV systems. It specifically looks at four factors: (1) dust accumulation, (2) water droplets, (3) bird droppings and (4) partial shading. The key findings from the study are:

- Dust, Shading and Bird Droppings: these factors significantly reduce the current and voltage in PV systems, leading to lower energy production.
- Shading: This has the most significant impact on PV efficiency. When shading covers a quarter, half and three-quarters of the panel surface, the power output drops by 33.7%, 45.1% and 92.6%, respectively.
- Water Droplets: inlike the other factors, water droplets can actually help by cooling the panels, which increases the voltage difference and boosts power output by at least 5.6%.
- Dust: accumulation of dust on panels reduces power output by 8.80% and efficiency by 11.86%.
- Bird Droppings: these decrease system performance by about 7.4%.

These findings emphasize the need for regular cleaning and maintenance of PV panels to ensure they perform at their best. By keeping the panels clean, we can minimize the negative effects of environmental factors and maintain optimal energy production.

In general, environmental factors such as extreme weather conditions, can also severely impact the effectiveness of PV fault detection technologies. Extreme heat can affect thermal cameras to misinterpret overheated areas, while extreme cold may reduce the operational time of drones and cameras by affecting their battery. Rain and humidity can cause obstructions and blur to camera lenses, posing obstacles for accurate faults detection. Strong wind conditions can cause blurry images due to stabilization issues of cameras, while drones could not be able to operate in case of strong winds. Snow and ice may cover the panels, obstructing detection or ever damaging drones and cameras. Finally, direct sunlight may also affect the quality of images due to sun glaring.

7. Evaluation of CV-Based PV Fault Detection Methodologies

Having outlined the fundamental detection and imaging technologies concerning key faults in photovoltaic systems, we now aim to evaluate the effectiveness of the detection methodologies identified in the literature, as imposed by RQ4. For this purpose, a comprehensive table, Table 5, has been structured, linking all the primary automated detection technologies with the use of computational intelligence algorithms, for detecting each specific set of anomalies in PV systems in the literature. The table records the performance of each methodology achieved in each study, in relation to (1) the ability to identify photovoltaic panels and (2), the performance of each methodology in detecting a corresponding set of anomalies.

However, since Table 5 is extensive and conclusions cannot easily draw, a color-coded evaluation table (Table 6) was also created. More specifically, the information from the cumulative Table 5 which connects the performance of each identified technique with the corresponding faults, has been coded by using four color levels: red for performances 0–30%, yellow for 30–70%, green for 70–100%, gray when no numerical performance is reported. UAV-based applications were also considered. Next, three evaluation criteria were selected:

1. The total number of green indicators, showing the range of faults that the methodology effectively addressed (degree of satisfactory for anomaly coverage).
2. Whether it satisfactorily detects shading anomalies (dust, snail trails, bird droppings and snow deposits), which significantly affect cell performance, as already discussed.
3. The degree of automation provided by the methodology, consisting of two sub-questions:
    a. Does the methodology in this study detected photovoltaic units? (Column: "Panel Detection")
    b. Was the automated image acquisition in this study via UAV technology? (Column: "UAV Inspection")

By applying these criteria to each row of Table 6, we rank the top five optimal methods from our literature findings in the final column. The latter approach aims to identify and evaluate the best performing approaches of the literature according to preset criteria.

It should be noted that cost-effectiveness and economic viability of each proposed PV fault detection method is crucial, especially towards their large-scale adaption in the solar industry. Yet, the comparison of the various methods could not include such cost information since the latter was not reported within the articles and therefore was not available. Moreover, the cost-effectiveness of camera-based PV panel inspection systems is not easily comparable since the viability of each method depends on several factors, such as the type of the used cameras, and the size of the solar installation that will be applied to. Low cost RGB cameras can be used, however hotspots and other defects can be better detected by thermal cameras which are most cost effective. For cameras mounted on drones, high resolution is essential, which are more pricey. Combined systems integrating both thermal and high-resolution cameras are more advanced and expensive options that may offer enhanced detection capabilities. Yet costs are closely related to the size of the solar installation. Ground based inspection systems can be more affordable, yet they are not feasible solutions for large scale PV farms. Drone-based systems on the contrary, can be affordable for large scale PV installations regardless costly mounted high-resolution cameras and thermal imaging equipment, while the latter would not be economically beneficial to use it in small PV installations. Therefore, in order to compare and choose the most cost-effective method, all the above aspects should be carefully considered according to each application case.

Table 5. Evaluation summary of PV fault detection methodologies.

Ref.	Technology	Input Data	Panel Detection Methodology	Fault Detection Methodology	Panel Detection Evaluation (%)	Anomalies Detection Evaluation
[109]	Multispectral imaging	15,330 PV cell images without defects 5915 images with defective cells Training 80% Testing 20%	-	Multispectral (MSI) CNN	-	Accuracy: Thick Line: 76.4% Broken gate: 80.4% Scratches: 48.6% Paste Spot: 82.1% Color diff.: 100% Dirty Cells: 87.2% No Anomalies: 98.1%
[105]	IR Thermography	37 images with 1544 PV cells (Images from UAV)	Creation of background temperature map, automatic thresholding to segment panels from background, removal of unwanted background, estimation of PV panel row orientation, panel dimension correction, preparation for panel analysis	Grid Cell Medians: Division of the panel into a 9 × 10 cell grid and calculation of the median temperature from the individual temperatures in each grid cell.	F1-score: 92.8%	Hot Spots, Hot Substring, Hot Panel (overheat) Average F1-score: 93.9%
[114]	RGB Imaging	Original dataset: 45,754 images Training set: 27,537 Validation set: 18,217	-	Detection Model (ImpactNet), Localization Technique (Mask FCNN) to predict power loss and soiling localization, localization enhancement through BiDIAF, soiling type categorization with WebNN	-	Dust, Snow, Bird Poop, Crack Overall Accuracy: 84.5%
[100]	Visible light camera (CCD) & IR Thermography	- (Images from UAV)	Morphological transformation and Canny Edge algorithm	Thermal imaging and CCD video processing, Hot Pixel-based hot spot detection	-	Hot Spots Cracks & Wear, Delamination Connection Faults
[150]	IR Thermography	A series of flights on a test site (Images from UAV)	Template matching	Template matching	Accuracy: 81%	Hot Spots, Bypass Diodes, Mechanically damaged cells, Fault Contact points Mean Accuracy: 85%

Table 5. *Cont.*

Ref.	Technology	Input Data	Panel Detection Methodology	Fault Detection Methodology	Panel Detection Evaluation (%)	Anomalies Detection Evaluation
[151]	Visible light camera (RGB) & IR Thermography	15 videos manually annotated for local and general thermal anomalies by three thermal cameras resolutions (Images from UAV)	Image preprocessing to remove noise from the image, Canny algorithm to detect PV edges, Line Separation using Hough Transform, Line Segmentation and Processing, Panel Model Application	Local Hot Spot Detection to detect thermal anomalies within the area of each photovoltaic panel, Global Hot Spot Detection, tracking algorithm to identify and follow the same panels across different frames as the UAV flies over the photovoltaic park	Overall Accuracy: 83%	Local hot spot Accuracy: 73% Global hot spot Accuracy: 85%
[152]	IR Thermography	4.3 million IR images of 107,842 pv panels Panel detection: Training 90%, Testing 10% Anomaly detection: Training 70%, Testing 20%, Validation 10% (Images from UAV)	Panel segmentation through Mask R-CNN	ResNet-50 classifier	Overall Accuracy: 90.01%	Accuracy: Healthy panel: 95.35 ± 0.21% Connection interruption–panel: 98.83 ± 0.42% Short circuit: 66.67 ± 47.14% Connection interruption-string: 100 ± 0% Short circuit string: 83.80 ± 0.76% PID panel: 86.69 ± 1.75% Multiple hot cells: 33.33 ± 23.57% Single hot cell: 57.41 ± 6.93% Hot cells: 80.39 ± 0.26% Diode overheating: 90.06 ± 0.55% Hot spost: 7.07 ± 7.04%
[153]	EL Imaging	148 images of PV cells for the U-net Training: 108 (73%) Testing: 30 (20%) Validation: 10 (7%)	-	Encoder VGG-16 to extract features, Semantic Segmentation with U-net to predict the presence and type of defects	-	Recall: Cracks: 84% Offline areas: 69% Faults in the panel's conductor lines: 53%
[108]	EL Imaging	47 images of PV panels: 7 healthy panel 40 panels with cracks of different lengths	-	Enhanced Crack Segmentation (eCS)	-	Cracks from 20 mm up to the entire length of the panel AUC: 91.14%

Table 5. *Cont.*

Ref.	Technology	Input Data	Panel Detection Methodology	Fault Detection Methodology	Panel Detection Evaluation (%)	Anomalies Detection Evaluation
[154]	IR & RGB Imaging	2038 thermal images (LWIR) for hotspot detection: Training: 1426 (70%) Testing: 306 (15%) Validation: 306 (15%) 1500 low-res visible spectrum digital images (VIS-LR): Training: 1050 (70%) Testing: 225 (15%) Validation: 225 (15%) (Images from UAV)	Canny Algorithm to detect edges of PV modules, Line Separation using Hough Transform, Image rotation optimal detection	YOLOv3	Accuracy: 98%	Accuracy: hotspot: 80.30% hotspot on junction box accuracy: 90.27% puddle accuracy: 82.48% bird dropping accuracy: 81.97% raised panel: 84.00% delamination: 93.61% strong soiling: 73.75% soiling accuracy: 90.00%
[155]	RGB Imaging	126 images of multiple defects on PV panels: Training 66.6% Testing 33.3% (Images from UAV)	-	Detecting anomalies with the Kirsh Operator image segmentation technique, the trained CNN extracts feature vectors of anomalies, the resulting anomaly vectors are inserted into a Multi Class-SVM which classifies 5 final anomalies	-	Accuracy: Dust shading: 97.63% Encapsulant delamination: 98.59% Glass breakage: 98.42% Gridline Corrosion: 95.84% Snail trails: 95.03% Yellowing: 97.76%
[156]	EL Imaging	Dataset 19,228 EL images 640 × 512 For YOLO model 1025 images used: Training: 762 (74.5%) Testing: 134 (12.5%) Validation: 134 (13.0%)	Automatic Perspective Transform, Automatic Cell Segmentation to identify cell boundaries, UNet to extract panel features, OpenCV for Line and Corner Detection.	Object Detection with YOLOv3 Model, Image Classification with ResNet18, ResNet50 and ResNet152 models to classify cells into 4 types of anomalies (cracks, intra-cell defects, oxygen induced defects and solder disconnections)	Accuracy: 98.6%	Average F1-score: YOLO: 78% ResNet18: 83%
[157]	EL Imaging	PV Multi-Defect dataset: 305 images 5800 × 3504 of 5 types of anomalies. After preprocessing, 1108 anomaly images: 80% for Training 20% for Testing and Validation	-	Ghost convolution with BottleneckCSP YOLOv5 (GBH-YOLOv5)	-	mAP: Broken Glass: 99.5 ± 0.01 Hot Spot: 97.5 ± 0.02% Black_Border: 97.2 ± 0.02% Scrath: 97.4 ± 0.02% No_Electricity: 98.0 ± 0.02%
[117]	IR Thermography	18 videos, of which: 13 (72%) for Training 5 (28%) for Testing (Images from UAV)	YOLOv2 and YOLOv3: Image Inclusion, Image Division, Bounding Box Predictions	-	YOLOv2: Accuracy 89% YOLOv3: Accuracy 91%	-

Table 5. *Cont.*

Ref.	Technology	Input Data	Panel Detection Methodology	Fault Detection Methodology	Panel Detection Evaluation (%)	Anomalies Detection Evaluation
[158]	RGB Imaging	3150 images with 6 anomaly classes (Images from UAV)	-	AlexNet for Feature Extraction, J48 decision tree for Feature Selection, Classification with k-nearest neighbors (kNN): Locally weighted learning (LWL) and K-star are compared	-	Accuracy: Delamination: 99.61% Burn marks: 97.90% Discoloration: 98.85% Snail Trail: 99.61% Glass Breakage: 99.61% Good Panel: 98.09%
[159]	EL Imaging	UCF EL Defect Dataset inluding 17,064 EL images: 80–20 ratio for training and testing/validation	-	Semantic Segmentation with DeepLabv3 and ResNet-50 as backbone	-	Accuracy: No Defect: 98% Crack: 81% Contact: 66% Interconnection Interruption: 26% Corrosion: 69%
[160]	EL Imaging	6264 images: 5011 images (80%) for training, 1253 images (20%) for testing	-	Unsupervised ML–Principal Component Analysis—PCA to reduce the dimensionality of image data, Hierarchical Clustering to group images based on features similarity, Feature Extraction–Haralick Feature, Supervised ML–CNN and SVM classification	-	Defects: Cracks, Busbar corrosion, Dark spots, Clear or in good condition Mean accuracy of Models: SVM: 98.95% CNN: 98.24%
[161]	IR Thermography	Infrared Solar Modules dataset: 20,000 IR images: 10,000 with no anomalies 10,000 with 11 categories of anomalies: For feature extraction the model Efficientb0 used was pre-trained. (Images from UAV) For classification in SVM, 80% was used for Training/20% for Testing	-	The Efficientb0 model for feature extraction, Network Component Analysis (NCA) method to select most significant features, Classification with SVM classifier	-	F1-scores: Hot-Spot: 88.05% Multiple Cells Hot-spot: 84.27% Cracks: 91.40% Active bypass diode: 97.51% Diodes: 95.04% Thin film hot-spot: 84.45% Multiple film hot-spots: 85.89% Offline module: 90.93% Shadowing: 91.01% Soiling: 82.17% Vegetation: 89.30% No anomaly: 97.85%

Table 5. *Cont.*

Ref.	Technology	Input Data	Panel Detection Methodology	Fault Detection Methodology	Panel Detection Evaluation (%)	Anomalies Detection Evaluation
[162]	EL Imaging	3629 images, 2129 defective and 1500 non-defective: Training: 847 defective images and 452 non-defective images	-	Bidirectional Attention Feature Pyramid Network (BAFPN), Multi-head Cosine Non-local Attention Module, Embedding of BAFPN into Region Proposal Network (RPN) in Faster RCNN+FPN	-	Classification: F-score: 98.70% Detection: mAP: 88.7%
[163]	IR Thermography and RGB Imaging	240 panel images: 80% for Training, 20% for Testing	Region proposal by Maximally Stable Extremal Regions (MSER) + filtering by size	Segmentation by binary thresholding	-	Accuracy: Hot spot: 97%
[164]	IR Thermography	1171 panel images with hot spots (Images from UAV)	Edge extraction by Hough transform + postprocessing	Segmentation by binary thresholding	F-score: 69%	Hot Spot F-score: 59.0%
[23]	IR Thermography and RGB Imaging	34 visual and 34 IR images (Images from UAV)	From visual images, module recognition, mosaicking, numbering and counting	From IR images, image filtering and elaboration, defect identification	-	-
[165]	IR Thermography	panel images with one anomaly class (Images from UAV)	Template matching	Template matching	F-score: 83.0%	Hot Spot F-score: 75.0%
[166]	IR Thermography	100 thermal images: Training 80%, Testing 20% (Images from UAV)	Rectangle extraction by adaptive thresholding + SVM classifier on texture features	-	F-score: 98.9%	-
[167]	IR Thermography	798 panel images, with 398 images of 4 class anomalies and 400 non-defective images: Training 80%, Testing 20%	-	Defect classification: SIFT feature extraction + RF classifier, VGG16 and MobileNet	-	Accuracy: Feature-based: up to 91.2% DL models: up to 89.5%
[168]	IR Thermography	235 panel images: Training 92%, Testing 8% (Images from UAV)	DL semantic segmentation (ResNet-34+U-Net)	-	F-score: 97.11%	-
[169]	IR Thermography	Dataset of frames of videos recorded in grayscale (Images from UAV)	-	Segmentation by VGG-16 based DL model	-	Hot spot, disconnections (strings and substrings)
[170]	IR Thermography	3336 thermal images, with 811 of damaged and 2525 of normal PV cells: 80% Training, 20% Testing (Images from UAV)	-	DCNN (training by VGG-16) of entire video frame	-	2 classes: defective (e.g., hot spot), normal mean F1-score: up to 69.0%

Table 5. *Cont.*

Ref.	Technology	Input Data	Panel Detection Methodology	Fault Detection Methodology	Panel Detection Evaluation (%)	Anomalies Detection Evaluation
[171]	Near-infrared EL image	PVEL-AD-2021 benchmark dataset	-	Partial Convolution and Switchable Atrous Convolution YOLOv7	-	Precision: 88.3%
[172]	RGB imaging	Solar panel soiling image dataset of 45,469 images	-	Vision transformer (ViT)	-	Accuracy: 97%
[173]	EL imaging	Training with 2018 images of bright and 101,376 of non-bright hot spots patches	-	Feature extraction and generative adversarial networks (GANs)	-	F1-score: 93%
[174]	RGB imaging	4500 PV defect datasets including cracks, broken grids, black cores, thick lines and hot spot	-	Faster-RCNN and YOLOv5	-	mAP: Faster-RCNN: 92.6% YOLOv5q 91.4%
[175]	EL imaging	PVEL-AD dataset	-	YOLOv4 with an improved Convolutional Block Attention Module (YOLO-iCBAM)	-	F1-score: 71.6% mAP: 74.8%
[176]	EL imaging	593 cell images, 80,000 images	-	C2f module in YOLOv8 to replace the C3 module in the backbone network	-	mAP: 67.5%
[177]	IR Thermography	Thermal camera mounted on a UAV (Images from UAV)	-	Image processing: contour defining, color/pixel selection	-	Accuracy: 75%
[178]	RGB imaging	2624 grayscale images of solar cells of two classes	-	Decision Tree, SVM, KNN, Ensemble and Discriminant	-	Accuracy: up to 98.34% with Ensemble
[179]	EL imaging	Global public dataset of EL images of Hebei and Beijing University (80–20 split)	-	YOLOv8	-	Average precision: 90.5%
[180]	IR Thermography	Database from a solar power plant of 42,048 modules (Images from UAV)	-	Mask R-CNN	-	mAP: 72.1%
[181]	EL imaging	584 of normal (300 × 300) and 197 images of abnormal solar cells		GAN and auto-encoder (AE)		Accuracy: 90%

Table 6. Evaluation summary of PV fault detection methodologies (Performance color code: red for performances 0–30%, yellow for 30–70%, green for 70–100%, gray for no numerical performance reported). Shading anomalies are marked in blue font.

Ref.	Hot spots	Cracks	Glass Breakage	Scratches	Delamination	Discoloration	Corrosion	Connection Faults	Short Circuit	PID Ground Faults	Diode Faults	Burn Marks	Inactive Cells	Dust	Snail Trails	Bird Poop	Snow	Pamel Detection	UAV Inspection	Rank
[109]		X	X		X		X		X	X		X	X		X	X	X	X	X	5
[105]		X	X	X	X	X	X	X	X	X	X	X	X	X	X	X	X		✓	
[114]	X		X	X	X	X	X	X	X	X	X	X	X		X			X	X	
[100]			X	X		X	X		X	X	X	X	X	X	X	X	X	X	✓	
[150]		X	X	X	X	X	X	X	X	X		X		X	X	X	X		✓	
[151]		X	X	X	X	X	X	X	X	X	X	X	X	X	X	X	X		✓	
[152]		X	X	X	X	X	X					X		X	X	X	X		✓	1
[153]	X		X	X	X	X	X		X	X	X	X		X	X	X	X	X	X	
[108]	X		X	X	X	X	X	X	X	X	X	X	X	X	X	X	X	X	X	
[154]		X	X	X		X	X		X	X	X	X	X		X		X		✓	3
[155]	X	X		X				X	X	X	X	X	X			X	X	X	✓	2
[156]	X		X	X	X	X		X	X	X	X	X		X	X	X	X		X	
[157]		X			X	X	X		X	X	X	X		X	X	X	X	X	X	
[117]	X	X	X	X	X	X	X	X	X	X	X	X	X	X	X	X	X		✓	
[158]	X	X		X			X	X	X	X	X		X	X		X	X	X	✓	4
[159]	X		X	X	X	X			X	X	X	X		X	X	X	X	X	X	
[160]	X		X	X	X	X		X	X	X	X		X	X	X	X	X	X	X	
[161]			X	X	X	X	X	X	X	X		X		X	X	X	X	X	✓	
[162]			X	X		X	X	X	X	X	X	X	X	X	X	X	X	X	X	
[163]		X	X	X	X	X	X	X	X	X	X	X	X	X	X	X	X	X	X	
[164]		X	X	X	X	X	X	X	X	X	X	X	X	X	X	X	X		✓	
[23]			X	X	X	X		X	X	X	X	X	X	X		X	X		✓	
[165]		X	X	X	X	X	X	X	X	X	X	X	X	X	X	X	X		✓	
[166]	X	X	X	X	X	X	X	X	X	X	X	X	X	X	X	X	X		✓	
[168]	X	X	X	X	X	X	X	X	X	X	X	X	X	X	X	X	X		✓	
[169]		X	X	X	X	X	X		X	X	X	X	X	X	X	X	X	X	✓	
[170]		X	X	X	X	X	X	X	X	X	X	X	X	X	X	X	X	X	✓	
[171]			X	X		X	X	X	X	X	X	X	X	X	X	X	X	X	X	
[172]		X	X	X	X	X	X	X	X	X	X	X	X		X			X	X	
[173]		X	X	X	X	X	X	X	X	X	X	X	X	X	X	X	X	X	X	
[174]				X		X	X	X	X	X	X		X	X	X	X	X	X	X	
[175]			X	X		X	X	X	X	X	X	X	X	X	X	X	X	X	X	
[176]			X	X	X	X	X	X	X	X	X	X	X	X	X	X	X	X	X	
[177]	X		X	X	X	X	X			X		X	X		X	X	X	X	✓	

Table 6. *Cont.*

Ref.	Hot spots	Cracks	Glass Breakage	Scratches	Delamination	Discoloration	Corrosion	Connection Faults	Short Circuit	PID Ground Faults	Diode Faults	Burn Marks	Inactive Cells	Dust	Snail Trails	Bird Poop	Snow	Pamel Detection	UAV Inspection	Rank
[178]	X		X	X	X	X	X	X	X	X	X	X	X	X	X	X	X	X	X	
[179]	X		X	X			X	X		X	X		X	X	X	X	X	X	X	
[180]		X	X	X	X	X	X			X	X	X		X	X	X	X	X	✓	
[181]			X	X	X	X	X		X	X	X	X	X	X	X	X	X	X	X	

8. Discussion

In this holistic literature review, we analyzed existing methodologies for fault detection in photovoltaic systems using computer vision, machine learning and deep learning techniques. The main observations and conclusions of the study are summarized as follows:

- Evolution of Detection Technologies: The advancement of computer vision algorithms in recent years has significantly improved the accuracy and effectiveness of fault detection. In particular, DL techniques, especially CNNs, have proven to be highly efficient in detecting anomalies in photovoltaic units.
- Shading Anomalies: Fault detection and regular maintenance of photovoltaic panels are critical for maintaining optimal performance. Environmental factors that increase panel shading, such as various types of dust and bird droppings, can significantly impact system performance, making continuous monitoring and cleaning essential.
- Methodology Evaluation: From the evaluation of various methodologies, the CNN variant Resnet 50 shows a very promising future among the other literature findings. It is also evident that DL techniques, such as YOLO variants and combinations of CNN with SVM classifiers, provide high detection accuracy and cover a wide range of faults. However, traditional methods, such as thresholding techniques, while satisfactory in some cases, have limitations in covering different types of anomalies.

To further improve fault detection in photovoltaic systems and develop more efficient and economically viable solutions, the following directions are proposed:

- Scalability and Economic Viability: The development of scalable deep learning models that can incorporate economic analyses will be important. This will enable the application of these technologies on a large scale and ensure the viability of solutions in large photovoltaic parks.
- Real-Time Detection: Adapting and improving real-time detection techniques is crucial. Developing algorithms that can operate effectively under various environmental conditions and provide immediate feedback will enhance maintenance efficiency and the performance of photovoltaic systems.
- Integration of Multiple Technologies: Integrating technologies such as infrared imaging, electroluminescence imaging and RGB imaging, combined with deep learning algorithms, will allow for better fault detection and diagnosis. Hybrid models that could combine different AI techniques could also be investigated to improve the accuracy of PV fault detection, as well as the integration of IoT and edge computing devices for continuous real-time data collection. All the above could lead to more comprehensive and reliable detection solutions.
- Data augmentation and synthetic data generation: data collection can be also enhanced through augmentation techniques and the generation of synthetic data, towards creating balanced benchmark datasets of all kinds of faults to effectively train AI models.

With ongoing research and development in these areas, fault detection in photovoltaic systems is expected to improve significantly, offering higher performance and longer lifespan for photovoltaic systems. Therefore, practical implications of vision-based PV systems that could be translated into actionable insights for PV industry stakeholders, include the following:

- Cost management due to the early detection of faults, preventing minor faults to expand and ruin the entire system, therefore reducing repairing and replacement costs for PV farms. Data analysis could also aim towards preventing faults before occurring through the identification of patterns, resulting in PV installations performance optimization. In general, data-based insights can overall improve predictive maintenance strategies of PV installations, due to the ability to prevent, plan and act.

- Efficiency of operations for large PV installations, since automated monitoring solutions can reduce inspection time, as well as both human labor and human error.
- By reducing human involvement, safety is provided for PV installation personnel, since inspections in the field involve hazards due to the nature of the PV structures that require the worker to climb ladders or high places in order to properly inspect, as well as their exposure to potentially adverse environmental conditions.
- Safety is also a requirement for PV system operations. Fault detection aims towards compliance with regulations, i.e., standards and requirements for PV installations, to ensure their operation safety as predefined by corresponding guidelines.
- Computer-vision PV fault detection strategies may lead to more consistent, reliable and efficient PV inspection, making PV installations that adapt such technologies more competitive in the market.

More analytically, regarding the color-coded evaluation of Table 6, we observe that the detection methodology from the study [152] ranks first. This methodology was based on infrared thermography with UAVs, using Mask FCNNs for detecting photovoltaic units, and employed the DL network Resnet 50 to detect and classify seven out of the total seventeen anomalies. Of these, six were detected with satisfactory accuracy and one with average (less than 70%) accuracy.

The second highest performance according to our criteria, goes to the methodology presented in [155], which utilizes RGB imaging via UAVs, CNN for feature extraction and SVM for anomaly classification. This method also satisfactorily covers six out of seventeen faults. However, it lacks an integrated algorithm for detecting photovoltaic units, which reduces its level of automation compared to the top-ranked method. It is worth noting that of the six faults detected with satisfactory accuracy, two are shading anomalies (dust accumulation and snail trails). Given our observations on our second research finding—shading anomalies significantly impact the performance and output of PV units—this could potentially place the methodology in the first rank depending on the priorities of each specific implementation (e.g., resource allocation relative to desired PV unit performance). Accordingly, we could continue to rank all other methodologies based on the overall degree of satisfactory anomaly coverage, anomaly detection capability and the level of automation included in each specific study.

Another significant observation from the evaluation results is that the top five methodologies all involve DL techniques, with the top three including CNNs or their variations and two using YOLO variations. In contrast, segmentation methodologies with thresholding, while providing satisfactory accuracy, are able to detect a narrow range of different anomaly types. It is also noteworthy that the SVM classifier was found in the second position. This shows that even when combined with a CNN for feature extraction, SVM remains a highly competitive ML method for effective anomaly detection in photovoltaic units, despite the current trend towards using DL algorithms in computer vision tasks.

Practical applications and real-world implementations of vision-based PV fault detection can be found solely for large scale PV installations. The most well-known PV power station is that of Kamuthi in Tamil Nadu region in India. The latter is the largest PV farm, spreading across an area of 10 km^2. The farm employes drones equipped with high-resolution cameras and thermal sensors to overall monitor the status of all PV modules. Drones fly over the PV farm to collect images, and data analysis is performed afterwards to detect anomalies and various types of faults. Challenges in real-world implementations include as already mentioned in Section 6.8, mainly the effects of environmental conditions that influence the accuracy of cameras, and the demanding processing of the vast number of generated data

9. Conclusions

In this work, a comprehensive review was conducted focusing on vision-based monitoring techniques for fault detection of PV systems. The research was guided by four research questions, aiming to identify (1) the evolution of computer vision algorithms for PV fault detection within the decade, (2) to present all key monitoring techniques for PV fault detection, along with an individual and comparative assessment of their capabilities and limitations, focusing on AI-based machine vision techniques, (3) to identify the common faults in PV system and how they affect the systems' performance and finally (4) to conclude to the most efficient CV-based methodologies through the review of the literature. Results indicated that among seventeen identified faults, shading anomalies are those that significantly impact the performance of PV units, while the top five CV-based PV fault detection methodologies, according to preset evaluation criteria, involve deep learning methods, such as CNNs and YOLO variations.

Key findings reveal that advancements of computer vision algorithms in recent years have significantly improved the accuracy of PV fault detection, indicating CNNs as highly efficient performing models for PV fault detection. Moreover, DL techniques, such as YOLO variants and combinations of CNN with SVM classifiers, can provide high detection accuracies and cover a wide range of different faults. Research concluded that fault detection and regular maintenance of photovoltaic panels are critical for maintaining optimal performance, while environmental factors are those to mainly affect the systems' performance.

It is evident from the literature that research on PV fault detection is ongoing, and it is expected that future technological developments, such as powerful processors to run AI-powered CV algorithms in real-time on UAVs, will further enhance this area of research, offering higher efficiency and longer lifetime for PV systems. Future research direction stemming from this work suggest the development of cutting-edge CV algorithms that could combine different sensing modalities, such as thermography and electroluminescence, towards more efficient PV fault detection. Hybrid models that could combine different AI techniques could also be investigated to improve the accuracy of PV fault detection. Real-time monitoring is a requirement in fault detection; therefore, efforts could focus on the integration of IoT and edge computing devices for continuous real-time data collection. Data collection can be also enhanced through the generation of synthetic data, towards creating balanced benchmark datasets of all kinds of faults to train AI models.

Author Contributions: Conceptualization, G.A.P.; methodology, G.A.P., I.P. and S.B.; investigation, I.P. and S.B.; resources, I.P. and S.B.; writing—original draft preparation, I.P., S.B. and E.V.; writing—review and editing, I.P., S.B., E.V. and G.A.P.; visualization, G.A.P.; supervision, G.A.P. All authors have read and agreed to the published version of the manuscript.

Funding: This research received no external funding.

Informed Consent Statement: Not applicable.

Data Availability Statement: Not applicable.

Acknowledgments: This work was supported by the MPhil program "Advanced Technologies in Informatics and Computers", which was hosted by the Department of Informatics, Democritus University of Thrace, Kavala, Greece.

Conflicts of Interest: The authors declare no conflicts of interest.

References

1. Meribout, M.; Kumar Tiwari, V.; Pablo Peña Herrera, J.; Najeeb Mahfoudh Awadh Baobaid, A. Solar Panel Inspection Techniques and Prospects. *Measurement* **2023**, *209*, 112466. [CrossRef]

2. Prabhakaran, S.; Annie Uthra, R.; Preetharoselyn, J. Deep Learning-Based Model for Defect Detection and Localization on Photovoltaic Panels. *Comput. Syst. Sci. Eng.* **2023**, *44*, 2683–2700. [CrossRef]
3. Miquela, A.; Bagul, D.; Ezzat, A.A. Defect Detection in Solar Photovoltaic Systems Using Unmanned Aerial Vehicles and Machine Learning. In Proceedings of the International Conference on Industrial Engineering and Operations Management, Houston, TX, USA, 13–16 June 2023; IEOM Society International: Southfield, MI, USA, 2023.
4. Waqar Akram, M.; Li, G.; Jin, Y.; Chen, X. Failures of Photovoltaic Modules and Their Detection: A Review. *Appl. Energy* **2022**, *313*, 118822. [CrossRef]
5. Hussain, T.; Hussain, M.; Al-Aqrabi, H.; Alsboui, T.; Hill, R. A Review on Defect Detection of Electroluminescence-Based Photovoltaic Cell Surface Images Using Computer Vision. *Energies* **2023**, *16*, 4012. [CrossRef]
6. Hijjawi, U.; Lakshminarayana, S.; Xu, T.; Piero Malfense Fierro, G.; Rahman, M. A Review of Automated Solar Photovoltaic Defect Detection Systems: Approaches, Challenges, and Future Orientations. *Sol. Energy* **2023**, *266*, 112186. [CrossRef]
7. Tang, W.; Yang, Q.; Dai, Z.; Yan, W. Module Defect Detection and Diagnosis for Intelligent Maintenance of Solar Photovoltaic Plants: Techniques, Systems and Perspectives. *Energy* **2024**, *297*, 131222. [CrossRef]
8. Chao, K.-H.; Ho, S.-H.; Wang, M.-H. Modeling and Fault Diagnosis of a Photovoltaic System. *Electr. Power Syst. Res.* **2008**, *78*, 97–105. [CrossRef]
9. Yi, Z.; Etemadi, A.H. A Novel Detection Algorithm for Line-to-Line Faults in Photovoltaic (PV) Arrays Based on Support Vector Machine (SVM). In Proceedings of the 2016 IEEE Power and Energy Society General Meeting (PESGM), Boston, MA, USA, 17–21 July 2016; IEEE: New York, NY, USA, 2016; pp. 1–4.
10. Malof, J.M.; Bradbury, K.; Collins, L.M.; Newell, R.G.; Serrano, A.; Wu, H.; Keene, S. Image Features for Pixel-Wise Detection of Solar Photovoltaic Arrays in Aerial Imagery Using a Random Forest Classifier. In Proceedings of the 2016 IEEE International Conference on Renewable Energy Research and Applications (ICRERA), Birmingham, UK, 20–23 November 2016; IEEE: New York, NY, USA, 2016; pp. 799–803.
11. Akram, M.W.; Li, G.; Jin, Y.; Chen, X.; Zhu, C.; Zhao, X.; Khaliq, A.; Faheem, M.; Ahmad, A. CNN Based Automatic Detection of Photovoltaic Cell Defects in Electroluminescence Images. *Energy* **2019**, *189*, 116319. [CrossRef]
12. Wei, S.; Li, X.; Ding, S.; Yang, Q.; Yan, W. Hotspots Infrared Detection of Photovoltaic Modules Based on Hough Line Transformation and Faster-RCNN Approach. In Proceedings of the 2019 6th International Conference on Control, Decision and Information Technologies (CoDIT), Paris, France, 23–26 April 2019; IEEE: New York, NY, USA, 2019; pp. 1266–1271.
13. Su, Y.; Tao, F.; Jin, J.; Zhang, C. Automated Overheated Region Object Detection of Photovoltaic Module with Thermography Image. *IEEE J. Photovoltaics* **2021**, *11*, 535–544. [CrossRef]
14. Shen, Y.; Fan, T.; Lai, G.; Na, Z.; Liu, H.; Wang, Z.; Wang, Y.; Jiao, Y.; Chen, X.; Lou, Z.; et al. Modified U-Net Based Photovoltaic Array Extraction from Complex Scene in Aerial Infrared Thermal Imagery. *Sol. Energy* **2022**, *240*, 90–103. [CrossRef]
15. Yin, W.; Lingxin, S.; Maohuan, L.; Qianlai, S.; Xiaosong, L. PV-YOLO: Lightweight YOLO for Photovoltaic Panel Fault Detection. *IEEE Access* **2023**, *11*, 10966–10976. [CrossRef]
16. Jalal, M.; Khalil, I.U.; Haq, A. ul Deep Learning Approaches for Visual Faults Diagnosis of Photovoltaic Systems: State-of-the-Art Review. *Results Eng.* **2024**, *23*, 102622. [CrossRef]
17. Iqbal, M.S.; Niazi, Y.A.K.; Amir Khan, U.; Lee, B.-W. Real-Time Fault Detection System for Large Scale Grid Integrated Solar Photovoltaic Power Plants. *Int. J. Electr. Power Energy Syst.* **2021**, *130*, 106902. [CrossRef]
18. Aghaei, M.; Grimaccia, F.; Leva, S.; Mussetta, M. Unmanned Aerial Vehicles in Photovoltaic Systems Monitoring Applications. In Proceedings of the 29th European Photovoltaic Solar Energy Conference and Exhibition, Amsterdam, The Netherlands, 22–26 September 2014; pp. 2734–2739.
19. Grimaccia, F.; Leva, S.; Dolara, A.; Aghaei, M. Survey on PV Modules' Common Faults After an O&M Flight Extensive Campaign Over Different Plants in Italy. *IEEE J. Photovolt.* **2017**, *7*, 810–816. [CrossRef]
20. Tsanakas, J.A.; Ha, L.D.; Al Shakarchi, F. Advanced Inspection of Photovoltaic Installations by Aerial Triangulation and Terrestrial Georeferencing of Thermal/Visual Imagery. *Renew. Energy* **2017**, *102*, 224–233. [CrossRef]
21. Leva, S.; Aghaei, M.; Grimaccia, F. PV Power Plant Inspection by UAS: Correlation between Altitude and Detection of Defects on PV Modules. In Proceedings of the 2015 IEEE 15th International Conference on Environment and Electrical Engineering (EEEIC), Rome, Italy, 10–13 June 2015; IEEE: New York, NY, USA, 2015; pp. 1921–1926.
22. Aghaei, M.; Dolara, A.; Leva, S.; Grimaccia, F. Image Resolution and Defects Detection in PV Inspection by Unmanned Technologies. In Proceedings of the 2016 IEEE Power and Energy Society General Meeting (PESGM), Boston, MA, USA, 17–21 July 2016; IEEE: New York, NY, USA, 2016; pp. 1–5.
23. Grimaccia, F.; Leva, S.; Niccolai, A. PV Plant Digital Mapping for Modules' Defects Detection by Unmanned Aerial Vehicles. *IET Renew. Power Gener.* **2017**, *11*, 1221–1228. [CrossRef]
24. Quater, P.B.; Grimaccia, F.; Leva, S.; Mussetta, M.; Aghaei, M. Light Unmanned Aerial Vehicles (UAVs) for Cooperative Inspection of PV Plants. *IEEE J. Photovolt.* **2014**, *4*, 1107–1113. [CrossRef]

25. Sinha, A.; Sastry, O.S.; Gupta, R. Nondestructive Characterization of Encapsulant Discoloration Effects in Crystalline-Silicon PV Modules. *Sol. Energy Mater. Sol. Cells* **2016**, *155*, 234–242. [CrossRef]
26. International Electrotechnical Commision (IEC). *IEC 61646 Ed2.0-Thin-Film Terrestrial Photovoltaic (PV) Modules-Design Qualification and Type Approval*; International Electrotechnical Commision (IEC): Geneva, Switzerland, 2008.
27. International Electrotechnical Commision (IEC). *IEC 61215-2: Crystalline Silicon Terrestrial Photovoltaic (PV) Modules—Design Qualification and Type Approval*; International Electrotechnical Commision (IEC): Geneva, Switzerland, 2016.
28. Köntges, M.; Kurtz, S.; Packard, C.E.; Jahn, U.; Berger, K.; Kato, K.; Friesen, T.; Liu, H.; Van Iseghem, M. *Review of Failures of Photovoltaic Modules*; International Energy Agency: Putrajaya, Malaysia, 2014; ISBN 9783906042169.
29. Bouaichi, A.; Merrouni, A.A.; El Hassani, A.; Naimi, Z.; Ikken, B.; Ghennioui, A.; Benazzouz, A.; El Amrani, A.; Messaoudi, C. Experimental Evaluation of the Discoloration Effect on PV-Modules Performance Drop. *Energy Procedia* **2017**, *119*, 818–827. [CrossRef]
30. Kahoul, N.; Chenni, R.; Cheghib, H.; Mekhilef, S. Evaluating the Reliability of Crystalline Silicon Photovoltaic Modules in Harsh Environment. *Renew. Energy* **2017**, *109*, 66–72. [CrossRef]
31. Bouraiou, A.; Hamouda, M.; Chaker, A.; Lachtar, S.; Neçaibia, A.; Boutasseta, N.; Mostefaoui, M. Experimental Evaluation of the Performance and Degradation of Single Crystalline Silicon Photovoltaic Modules in the Saharan Environment. *Energy* **2017**, *132*, 22–30. [CrossRef]
32. Bouraiou, A.; Hamouda, M.; Chaker, A.; Neçaibia, A.; Mostefaoui, M.; Boutasseta, N.; Ziane, A.; Dabou, R.; Sahouane, N.; Lachtar, S. Experimental Investigation of Observed Defects in Crystalline Silicon PV Modules under Outdoor Hot Dry Climatic Conditions in Algeria. *Sol. Energy* **2018**, *159*, 475–487. [CrossRef]
33. Tománek, P.; Škarvada, P.; Macků, R.; Grmela, L. Detection and Localization of Defects in Monocrystalline Silicon Solar Cell. *Adv. Opt. Technol.* **2010**, *2010*, 1–5. [CrossRef]
34. Gallardo-Saavedra, S.; Hernández-Callejo, L.; Alonso-García, M.d.C.; Santos, J.D.; Morales-Aragonés, J.I.; Alonso-Gómez, V.; Moretón-Fernández, Á.; González-Rebollo, M.Á.; Martínez-Sacristán, O. Nondestructive Characterization of Solar PV Cells Defects by Means of Electroluminescence, Infrared Thermography, I–V Curves and Visual Tests: Experimental Study and Comparison. *Energy* **2020**, *205*, 117930. [CrossRef]
35. Osawa, S.; Nakano, T.; Matsumoto, S.; Katayama, N.; Saka, Y.; Sato, H. Fault Diagnosis of Photovoltaic Modules Using AC Impedance Spectroscopy. In Proceedings of the 2016 IEEE International Conference on Renewable Energy Research and Applications (ICRERA), Birmingham, UK, 20–23 November 2016; IEEE: New York, NY, USA, 2016; pp. 210–215.
36. Simon, M.; Meyer, E.L. Detection and Analysis of Hot-Spot Formation in Solar Cells. *Sol. Energy Mater. Sol. Cells* **2010**, *94*, 106–113. [CrossRef]
37. Du, B.; Yang, R.; He, Y.; Wang, F.; Huang, S. Nondestructive Inspection, Testing and Evaluation for Si-Based, Thin Film and Multi-Junction Solar Cells: An Overview. *Renew. Sustain. Energy Rev.* **2017**, *78*, 1117–1151. [CrossRef]
38. Cotfas, D.T.; Cotfas, P.A.; Kaplanis, S. Methods to Determine the Dc Parameters of Solar Cells: A Critical Review. *Renew. Sustain. Energy Rev.* **2013**, *28*, 588–596. [CrossRef]
39. Cotfas, D.T.; Cotfas, P.A.; Kaplanis, S. Methods and Techniques to Determine the Dynamic Parameters of Solar Cells: Review. *Renew. Sustain. Energy Rev.* **2016**, *61*, 213–221. [CrossRef]
40. Yu, J.; Song, L.; Chen, F.; Fan, P.; Sun, L.; Zhong, M.; Yang, J. Preparation of Polymer Foams with a Gradient of Cell Size: Further Exploring the Nucleation Effect of Porous Inorganic Materials in Polymer Foaming. *Mater. Today Commun.* **2016**, *9*, 1–6. [CrossRef]
41. Meng, L.; Nagalingam, D.; Bhatia, C.S.; Street, A.G.; Phang, J.C.H. SEAM and EBIC Studies of Morphological and Electrical Defects in Polycrystalline Silicon Solar Cells. In Proceedings of the 2010 IEEE International Reliability Physics Symposium, Anaheim, CA, USA, 2–6 May 2010; IEEE: New York, NY, USA, 2010; pp. 503–507.
42. Topolovec, S.; Krenn, H.; Würschum, R. Electrochemical Cell for in Situ Electrodeposition of Magnetic Thin Films in a Superconducting Quantum Interference Device Magnetometer. *Rev. Sci. Instrum.* **2015**, *86*, 063903. [CrossRef]
43. de Andrade, M.C.; de Escobar, A.L.; Taylor, B.J.; Berggren, S.; Higa, B.; Dinh, S.; Fagaly, R.L.; Talvacchio, J.; Nechay, B.; Przybysz, J. Detection of Far-Field Radio-Frequency Signals by Niobium Superconducting Quantum Interference Device Arrays. *IEEE Trans. Appl. Supercond.* **2015**, *25*, 1–5. [CrossRef]
44. Nakatani, Y.; Hayashi, T.; Itozaki, H. Observation of Polycrystalline Solar Cell Using a Laser-SQUID Microscope. *IEEE Trans. Appl. Supercond.* **2011**, *21*, 416–419. [CrossRef]
45. Nakatani, Y.; Hayashi, T.; Miyato, Y.; Itozaki, H. SQUID Microscopy of Magnetic Field Induced in Solar Cell by Laser Spot Irradiation. *Phys. Procedia* **2012**, *27*, 340–343. [CrossRef]
46. Takyi, G. Correlation of Infrared Thermal Imaging Results with Visual Inspection and Current-Voltage Data of PV Modules Installed in Kumasi, a Hot, Humid Region of Sub-Saharan Africa. *Technologies* **2017**, *5*, 67. [CrossRef]
47. Waqar Akram, M.; Li, G.; Jin, Y.; Chen, X.; Zhu, C.; Zhao, X.; Aleem, M.; Ahmad, A. Improved Outdoor Thermography and Processing of Infrared Images for Defect Detection in PV Modules. *Sol. Energy* **2019**, *190*, 549–560. [CrossRef]

48. Rajput, P.; Tiwari, G.N.; Sastry, O.S.; Bora, B.; Sharma, V. Degradation of Mono-Crystalline Photovoltaic Modules after 22 Years of Outdoor Exposure in the Composite Climate of India. *Sol. Energy* **2016**, *135*, 786–795. [CrossRef]
49. Akram, M.W.; Li, G.; Jin, Y.; Chen, X.; Zhu, C.; Ahmad, A. Automatic Detection of Photovoltaic Module Defects in Infrared Images with Isolated and Develop-Model Transfer Deep Learning. *Sol. Energy* **2020**, *198*, 175–186. [CrossRef]
50. Chung, T.; Wang, C.-H.; Chang, K.-J.; Chen, S.-Y.; Hsieh, H.-H.; Huang, C.-P.; Arthur Cheng, C.-H. Evaluation of the Spatial Distribution of Series and Shunt Resistance of a Solar Cell Using Dark Lock-in Thermography. *J. Appl. Phys.* **2014**, *115*, 034901. [CrossRef]
51. Isenberg, J.; Warta, W. Spatially Resolved Evaluation of Power Losses in Industrial Solar Cells by Illuminated Lock-in Thermography. *Prog. Photovoltaics Res. Appl.* **2004**, *12*, 339–353. [CrossRef]
52. Kasemann, M.; Schubert, M.C.; The, M.; Köber, M.; Hermle, M.; Warta, W. Comparison of Luminescence Imaging and Illuminated Lock-in Thermography on Silicon Solar Cells. *Appl. Phys. Lett.* **2006**, *89*, 224102. [CrossRef]
53. Netzelmann, U.; Walle, G.; Lugin, S.; Ehlen, A.; Bessert, S.; Valeske, B. Induction Thermography: Principle, Applications and First Steps towards Standardisation. *Quant. Infrared Thermogr. J.* **2016**, *13*, 170–181. [CrossRef]
54. Vinod, P.N.; Joseph, S.; John, R. The Detection and Quantification of the Defects in Adhesive Bonded Joints of the Piezoelectric Sensors by Infrared Thermographic Nondestructive Testing. *Nondestruct. Test. Eval.* **2017**, *32*, 185–199. [CrossRef]
55. Wang, Y.; Ke, H.; Shi, J.; Gao, B.; Tian, G. Impact Damage Detection and Characterization Using Eddy Current Pulsed Thermography. In Proceedings of the 2016 IEEE Far East NDT New Technology & Application Forum (FENDT), Nanchang, China, 22–24 June 2016; IEEE: New York, NY, USA, 2016; pp. 223–226.
56. Glavas, H.; Vukobratovic, M.; Primorac, M.; Mustran, D. Infrared Thermography in Inspection of Photovoltaic Panels. In Proceedings of the 2017 International Conference on Smart Systems and Technologies (SST), Osijek, Croatia, 18–20 October 2017; IEEE: New York, NY, USA, 2017; pp. 63–68.
57. Chattopadhyay, S.; Dubey, R.; Bhaduri, S.; Zachariah, S.; Singh, H.K.; Solanki, C.S.; Kottantharayil, A.; Shiradkar, N.; Arora, B.M.; Narasimhan, K.L.; et al. Correlating Infrared Thermography with Electrical Degradation of PV Modules Inspected in All-India Survey of Photovoltaic Module Reliability 2016. *IEEE J. Photovolt.* **2018**, *8*, 1800–1808. [CrossRef]
58. Buerhop, C.; Wirsching, S.; Bemm, A.; Pickel, T.; Hohmann, P.; Nieß, M.; Vodermayer, C.; Huber, A.; Glück, B.; Mergheim, J.; et al. Evolution of Cell Cracks in PV-modules under Field and Laboratory Conditions. *Prog. Photovoltaics Res. Appl.* **2018**, *26*, 261–272. [CrossRef]
59. Kirchartz, T.; Helbig, A.; Reetz, W.; Reuter, M.; Werner, J.H.; Rau, U. Reciprocity between electroluminescence and quantum efficiency used for the characterization of silicon solar cells. *Prog. Photovolt. Res. Appl.* **2009**, *17*, 394–402. [CrossRef]
60. Frazão, M.; Silva, J.A.; Lobato, K.; Serra, J.M. Electroluminescence of Silicon Solar Cells Using a Consumer Grade Digital Camera. *Measurement* **2017**, *99*, 7–12. [CrossRef]
61. Ramspeck, K.; Bothe, K.; Hinken, D.; Fischer, B.; Schmidt, J.; Brendel, R. Recombination Current and Series Resistance Imaging of Solar Cells by Combined Luminescence and Lock-in Thermography. *Appl. Phys. Lett.* **2007**, *90*, 153502. [CrossRef]
62. Islam, M.A.; Hasanuzzaman, M.; Rahim, N.A. Investigation of the Potential Induced Degradation of On-Site Aged Polycrystalline PV Modules Operating in Malaysia. *Measurement* **2018**, *119*, 283–294. [CrossRef]
63. Tsai, D.-M.; Wu, S.-C.; Li, W.-C. Defect Detection of Solar Cells in Electroluminescence Images Using Fourier Image Reconstruction. *Sol. Energy Mater. Sol. Cells* **2012**, *99*, 250–262. [CrossRef]
64. Crozier, J.L.; van Dyk, E.E.; Vorster, F.J. Identifying Voltage Dependant Features in Photovoltaic Modules Using Electroluminescence Imaging. In Proceedings of the 29th EU-PVSEC, Amsterdam, The Netherlands, 22–26 September 2014; pp. 22–26.
65. Haunschild, J.; Reis, I.E.; Chipei, T.; Demant, M.; Thaidigsmann, B.; Linse, M.; Rein, S. Rating and Sorting of Mc-Si as-Cut Wafers in Solar Cell Production Using PL Imaging. *Sol. Energy Mater. Sol. Cells* **2012**, *106*, 71–75. [CrossRef]
66. Bhoopathy, R.; Kunz, O.; Juhl, M.; Trupke, T.; Hameiri, Z. Outdoor Photoluminescence Imaging of Photovoltaic Modules with Sunlight Excitation. *Prog. Photovoltaics Res. Appl.* **2018**, *26*, 69–73. [CrossRef]
67. Olsen, E.; Flø, A.S. Spectral and Spatially Resolved Imaging of Photoluminescence in Multicrystalline Silicon Wafers. *Appl. Phys. Lett.* **2011**, *99*, 011903. [CrossRef]
68. Kontges, M.; Morlier, A.; Eder, G.; Fleis, E.; Kubicek, B.; Lin, J. Review: Ultraviolet Fluorescence as Assessment Tool for Photovoltaic Modules. *IEEE J. Photovolt.* **2020**, *10*, 616–633. [CrossRef]
69. Eder, G.C.; Voronko, Y.; Hirschl, C.; Ebner, R.; Újvári, G.; Mühleisen, W. Non-Destructive Failure Detection and Visualization of Artificially and Naturally Aged PV Modules. *Energies* **2018**, *11*, 1053. [CrossRef]
70. Eder, G.C.; Voronko, Y.; Dimitriadis, S.; Knöbl, K.; Újvári, G.; Berger, K.A.; Halwachs, M.; Neumaier, L.; Hirschl, C. Climate Specific Accelerated Ageing Tests and Evaluation of Ageing Induced Electrical, Physical, and Chemical Changes. *Prog. Photovolt. Res. Appl.* **2019**, *27*, 934–949. [CrossRef]
71. Morlier, A.; Siebert, M.; Kunze, I.; Mathiak, G.; Kontges, M. Detecting Photovoltaic Module Failures in the Field during Daytime with Ultraviolet Fluorescence Module Inspection. *IEEE J. Photovolt.* **2017**, *7*, 1710–1716. [CrossRef]

72. Muehleisen, W.; Eder, G.C.; Voronko, Y.; Spielberger, M.; Sonnleitner, H.; Knoebl, K.; Ebner, R.; Ujvari, G.; Hirschl, C. Outdoor Detection and Visualization of Hailstorm Damages of Photovoltaic Plants. *Renew. Energy* **2018**, *118*, 138–145. [CrossRef]
73. de Biasio, M.; Leitner, R.; Hirschl, C. Detection of Snail Tracks on Photovoltaic Modules Using a Combination of Raman and Fluorescence Spectroscopy. In Proceedings of the 2013 Seventh International Conference on Sensing Technology (ICST), Wellington, New Zealand, 3–5 December 2013; IEEE: New York, NY, USA, 2013; pp. 334–337.
74. Beinert, A.J.; Romer, P.; Büchler, A.; Haueisen, V.; Aktaa, J.; Eitner, U. Thermomechanical Stress Analysis of PV Module Production Processes by Raman Spectroscopy and FEM Simulation. *Energy Procedia* **2017**, *124*, 464–469. [CrossRef]
75. He, Y.; Du, B.; Huang, S. Noncontact Electromagnetic Induction Excited Infrared Thermography for Photovoltaic Cells and Modules Inspection. *IEEE Trans. Ind. Inform.* **2018**, *14*, 5585–5593. [CrossRef]
76. Yang, R.; Du, B.; Duan, P.; He, Y.; Wang, H.; He, Y.; Zhang, K. Electromagnetic Induction Heating and Image Fusion of Silicon Photovoltaic Cell Electrothermography and Electroluminescence. *IEEE Trans. Ind. Inform.* **2020**, *16*, 4413–4422. [CrossRef]
77. Kropp, T.; Berner, M.; Stoicescu, L.; Werner, J.H. Self-Sourced Daylight Electroluminescence from Photovoltaic Modules. *IEEE J. Photovolt.* **2017**, *7*, 1184–1189. [CrossRef]
78. Köntges, M.; Kajari-Schröder, S.; Kunze, I. Cell Cracks Measured by UV Fluorescence in the Field. In Proceedings of the 27th European Photovoltaic Solar Energy Conference and Exhibition, Frankfurt, Germany, 24–28 September 2012; pp. 3033–3040.
79. Breitenstein, O.; Bauer, J.; Bothe, K.; Hinken, D.; Mueller, J.; Kwapil, W.; Schubert, M.; Warta, W. Luminescence Imaging versus Lock-in Thermography on Solar Cells and Wafers. In Proceedings of the 26th European Photovoltaic Solar Energy Conference and Exhibition, Hamburg, Germany, 5–6 September 2011; pp. 1031–1038.
80. Ebner, R.; Kubicek, B.; Újvári, G.; Novalin, S.; Rennhofer, M.; Halwachs, M. Optical Characterization of Different Thin Film Module Technologies. *Int. J. Photoenergy* **2015**, *2015*, 159458. [CrossRef]
81. Breitenstein, O.; Bauer, J.; Hinken, D.; Bothe, K. The Reliability of Thermography- and Luminescence-Based Series Resistance and Saturation Current Density Imaging. *Sol. Energy Mater. Sol. Cells* **2015**, *137*, 50–60. [CrossRef]
82. Berardone, I.; Lopez Garcia, J.; Paggi, M. Analysis of Electroluminescence and Infrared Thermal Images of Monocrystalline Silicon Photovoltaic Modules after 20 Years of Outdoor Use in a Solar Vehicle. *Sol. Energy* **2018**, *173*, 478–486. [CrossRef]
83. Hoyer, U.; Buerhop, C.; Jahn, U. Electroluminescence and Infrared Imaging for Quality Improvements of PV Modules. In Proceedings of the 23rd EU-PVSEC, Valencia, Spain, 1–5 September 2008; pp. 2913–2916.
84. Mühleisen, W.; Hirschl, C.; Brantegger, G.; Neumaier, L.; Spielberger, M.; Sonnleitner, H.; Kubicek, B.; Ujvari, G.; Ebner, R.; Schwark, M.; et al. Scientific and Economic Comparison of Outdoor Characterisation Methods for Photovoltaic Power Plants. *Renew. Energy* **2019**, *134*, 321–329. [CrossRef]
85. Sulas, D.B.; Johnston, S.; Jordan, D.C. Comparison of Photovoltaic Module Luminescence Imaging Techniques: Assessing the Influence of Lateral Currents in High-Efficiency Device Structures. *Sol. Energy Mater. Sol. Cells* **2019**, *192*, 81–87. [CrossRef]
86. van Mölken, J.I.; Yusufoğlu, U.A.; Safiei, A.; Windgassen, H.; Khandelwal, R.; Pletzer, T.M.; Kurz, H. Impact of Micro-Cracks on the Degradation of Solar Cell Performance Based on Two-Diode Model Parameters. *Energy Procedia* **2012**, *27*, 167–172. [CrossRef]
87. Mellit, A.; Tina, G.M.; Kalogirou, S.A. Fault Detection and Diagnosis Methods for Photovoltaic Systems: A Review. *Renew. Sustain. Energy Rev.* **2018**, *91*, 1–17. [CrossRef]
88. Wu, Y.; Lan, Q.; Sun, Y. Application of BP Neural Network Fault Diagnosis in Solar Photovoltaic System. In Proceedings of the 2009 International Conference on Mechatronics and Automation, Changchun, China, 9–12 August 2009; IEEE: New York, NY, USA, 2009; pp. 2581–2585.
89. Lu, X.; Lin, P.; Cheng, S.; Lin, Y.; Chen, Z.; Wu, L.; Zheng, Q. Fault Diagnosis for Photovoltaic Array Based on Convolutional Neural Network and Electrical Time Series Graph. *Energy Convers. Manag.* **2019**, *196*, 950–965. [CrossRef]
90. Mellit, A.; Kalogirou, S.A. Artificial Intelligence Techniques for Photovoltaic Applications: A Review. *Prog. Energy Combust. Sci.* **2008**, *34*, 574–632. [CrossRef]
91. Demant, M.; Oswald, M.; Welschehold, T.; Nold, S.; Bartsch, S.; Schoenfelder, S.; Rein, S. Micro-Cracks in Silicon Wafers and Solar Cells: Detection and Rating of Mechanical Strength and Electrical Quality. In Proceedings of the 29th European PV Solar Energy Conference and Exhibition, Amsterdam, The Netherlands, 22–26 September 2014. [CrossRef]
92. Mikolajczyk, K.; Schmid, C. A Performance Evaluation of Local Descriptors. *IEEE Trans. Pattern Anal. Mach. Intell.* **2005**, *27*, 1615–1630. [CrossRef] [PubMed]
93. Kato, K. PV Module Failures Observed in the Field-Solder Bond and Bypass Diode Failures. In Proceedings of the 27th EUPVSEC, Frankfurt, Germany, 24–28 September 2012.
94. Dalal, N.; Triggs, B. Histograms of Oriented Gradients for Human Detection. In Proceedings of the 2005 IEEE Computer Society Conference on Computer Vision and Pattern Recognition (CVPR'05), San Diego, CA, USA, 20–25 June 2005; IEEE: New York, NY, USA, 2005; Volume 1, pp. 886–893.
95. Bay, H.; Ess, A.; Tuytelaars, T.; Van Gool, L. Speeded-Up Robust Features (SURF). *Comput. Vis. Image Underst.* **2008**, *110*, 346–359. [CrossRef]

96. Demant, M.; Welschehold, T.; Oswald, M.; Bartsch, S.; Brox, T.; Schoenfelder, S.; Rein, S. Microcracks in Silicon Wafers I: Inline Detection and Implications of Crack Morphology on Wafer Strength. *IEEE J. Photovolt.* **2016**, *6*, 126–135. [CrossRef]
97. Chen, H.; Zhao, H.; Han, D.; Liu, K. Accurate and Robust Crack Detection Using Steerable Evidence Filtering in Electroluminescence Images of Solar Cells. *Opt. Lasers Eng.* **2019**, *118*, 22–33. [CrossRef]
98. Tsai, D.-M.; Wu, S.-C.; Chiu, W.-Y. Defect Detection in Solar Modules Using ICA Basis Images. *IEEE Trans. Ind. Inform.* **2013**, *9*, 122–131. [CrossRef]
99. Vergura, S.; Marino, F.; Carpentieri, M. Processing Infrared Image of PV Modules for Defects Classification. In Proceedings of the 2015 International Conference on Renewable Energy Research and Applications (ICRERA), Palermo, Italy, 22–25 November 2015; IEEE: New York, NY, USA, 2015; pp. 1337–1341.
100. Alsafasfeh, M.; Abdel-Qader, I.; Bazuin, B.; Alsafasfeh, Q.; Su, W. Unsupervised Fault Detection and Analysis for Large Photovoltaic Systems Using Drones and Machine Vision. *Energies* **2018**, *11*, 2252. [CrossRef]
101. Li, X.; Yang, Q.; Chen, Z.; Luo, X.; Yan, W. Visible Defects Detection Based on UAV-based Inspection in Large-scale Photovoltaic Systems. *IET Renew. Power Gener.* **2017**, *11*, 1234–1244. [CrossRef]
102. Tsanakas, J.A.; Chrysostomou, D.; Botsaris, P.N.; Gasteratos, A. Fault Diagnosis of Photovoltaic Modules through Image Processing and Canny Edge Detection on Field Thermographic Measurements. *Int. J. Sustain. Energy* **2015**, *34*, 351–372. [CrossRef]
103. Tsanakas, J.A.; Vannier, G.; Plissonnier, A.; Ha, D.L.; Barruel, F. Fault Diagnosis and Classification of Large-Scale Photovoltaic Plants through Aerial Orthophoto Thermal Mapping. In Proceedings of the 31st European Photovoltaic Solar Energy Conference and Exhibition, Hamburg, Germany, 14–18 September 2015; pp. 1783–1788.
104. Hepp, J.; Machui, F.; Egelhaaf, H.; Brabec, C.J.; Vetter, A. Automatized Analysis of IR-images of Photovoltaic Modules and Its Use for Quality Control of Solar Cells. *Energy Sci. Eng.* **2016**, *4*, 363–371. [CrossRef]
105. Dotenco, S.; Dalsass, M.; Winkler, L.; Wurzner, T.; Brabec, C.; Maier, A.; Gallwitz, F. Automatic Detection and Analysis of Photovoltaic Modules in Aerial Infrared Imagery. In Proceedings of the 2016 IEEE Winter Conference on Applications of Computer Vision (WACV), Lake Placid, NY, USA, 7–10 March 2016; IEEE: New York, NY, USA, 2016; pp. 1–9.
106. Aghaei, M.; Gandelli, A.; Grimaccia, F.; Leva, S.; Zich, R.E. IR Real-Time Analyses for PV System Monitoring by Digital Image Processing Techniques. In Proceedings of the 2015 International Conference on Event-based Control, Communication, and Signal Processing (EBCCSP), Krakow, Poland, 17–19 June 2015; IEEE: New York, NY, USA, 2015; pp. 1–6.
107. Petrosyan, A.; Hovhannisyan, A. Infrared Image Processing for Solar Cell Defect Detection. In Proceedings of the International Conference Computer Science and Information Technologies, Lviv, Ukraine, 21–23 August 2017.
108. Stromer, D.; Vetter, A.; Oezkan, H.C.; Probst, C.; Maier, A. Enhanced Crack Segmentation (ECS): A Reference Algorithm for Segmenting Cracks in Multicrystalline Silicon Solar Cells. *IEEE J. Photovolt.* **2019**, *9*, 752–758. [CrossRef]
109. Chen, H.; Pang, Y.; Hu, Q.; Liu, K. Solar Cell Surface Defect Inspection Based on Multispectral Convolutional Neural Network. *J. Intell. Manuf.* **2020**, *31*, 453–468. [CrossRef]
110. Ding, S.; Yang, Q.; Li, X.; Yan, W.; Ruan, W. Transfer Learning Based Photovoltaic Module Defect Diagnosis Using Aerial Images. In Proceedings of the 2018 International Conference on Power System Technology (POWERCON), Guangzhou, China, 6–8 November 2018; IEEE: New York, NY, USA, 2018; pp. 4245–4250.
111. Li, X.; Yang, Q.; Lou, Z.; Yan, W. Deep Learning Based Module Defect Analysis for Large-Scale Photovoltaic Farms. *IEEE Trans. Energy Convers.* **2019**, *34*, 520–529. [CrossRef]
112. Li, X.; Yang, Q.; Wang, J.; Chen, Z.; Yan, W. Intelligent Fault Pattern Recognition of Aerial Photovoltaic Module Images Based on Deep Learning Technique. In Proceedings of the IMCIC 2018-9th International Multi-Conference on Complexity, Informatics and Cybernetics, Proceedings, Orlando, FL, USA, 13–16 March 2018; pp. 1287–1289.
113. Demant, M.; Virtue, P.; Kovvali, A.S.; Yu, S.X.; Rein, S. Deep Learning Approach to Inline Quality Rating and Mapping of Multi-Crystalline Si-Wafers. In Proceedings of the 35th European Photovoltaic Solar Energy Conference and Exhibition, Brussels, Belgium, 24–28 September 2018; pp. 814–818.
114. Mehta, S.; Azad, A.P.; Chemmengath, S.A.; Raykar, V.; Kalyanaraman, S. DeepSolarEye: Power Loss Prediction and Weakly Supervised Soiling Localization via Fully Convolutional Networks for Solar Panels. In Proceedings of the 2018 IEEE Winter Conference on Applications of Computer Vision (WACV), Lake Tahoe, NV, USA, 12–15 March 2018; IEEE: New York, NY, USA, 2018; pp. 333–342.
115. Buerhop-Lutz, C.; Brabec, C.J.; Camus, C.; Hauch, J.; Doll, B.; Berger, S.; Gallwitz, F.; Maier, A.; Deitsch, S. A Benchmark for Visual Identification of Defective Solar Cells in Electroluminescence Imagery. In Proceedings of the 35th European Photovoltaic Solar Energy Conference and Exhibition, Brussels, Belgium, 24–28 September 2018; pp. 1287–1289.
116. Deitsch, S.; Buerhop-Lutz, C.; Sovetkin, E.; Steland, A.; Maier, A.; Gallwitz, F.; Riess, C. Segmentation of Photovoltaic Module Cells in Uncalibrated Electroluminescence Images. *arXiv* **2018**. [CrossRef]
117. Greco, A.; Pironti, C.; Saggese, A.; Vento, M.; Vigilante, V. A Deep Learning Based Approach for Detecting Panels in Photovoltaic Plants. In Proceedings of the Proceedings of the 3rd International Conference on Applications of Intelligent Systems, Las Palmas de Gran Canaria, Spain, 7–12 January 2020; ACM: New York, NY, USA, 2020; pp. 1–7.

118. Mahmud, A.; Shishir, M.S.R.; Hasan, R.; Rahman, M. A Comprehensive Study for Solar Panel Fault Detection Using VGG16 and VGG19 Convolutional Neural Networks. In Proceedings of the 2023 26th International Conference on Computer and Information Technology (ICCIT), Cox's Bazar, Bangladesh, 13–15 December 2023; IEEE: New York, NY, USA, 2023; pp. 1–6.
119. Tang, C.; Ren, H.; Xia, J.; Wang, F.; Lu, J. Automatic Defect Identification of PV Panels with IR Images through Unmanned Aircraft. *IET Renew. Power Gener.* **2023**, *17*, 3108–3119. [CrossRef]
120. Buratti, Y.; Sowmya, A.; Evans, R.; Trupke, T.; Hameiri, Z. Half and Full Solar Cell Efficiency Binning by Deep Learning on Electroluminescence Images. *Prog. Photovoltaics Res. Appl.* **2022**, *30*, 276–287. [CrossRef]
121. Colli, A. Failure Mode and Effect Analysis for Photovoltaic Systems. *Renew. Sustain. Energy Rev.* **2015**, *50*, 804–809. [CrossRef]
122. Djordjevic, S.; Parlevliet, D.; Jennings, P. Detectable Faults on Recently Installed Solar Modules in Western Australia. *Renew. Energy* **2014**, *67*, 215–221. [CrossRef]
123. Munoz, M.A.; Alonso-García, M.C.; Vela, N.; Chenlo, F. Early Degradation of Silicon PV Modules and Guaranty Conditions. *Sol. Energy* **2011**, *85*, 2264–2274. [CrossRef]
124. Forman, S.E. Performance of Experimental Terrestrial Photovoltaic Modules. *IEEE Trans. Reliab.* **1982**, *31*, 235–245. [CrossRef]
125. Massi Pavan, A.; Mellit, A.; De Pieri, D.; Lughi, V. A Study on the Mismatch Effect Due to the Use of Different Photovoltaic Modules Classes in Large-scale Solar Parks. *Prog. Photovolt. Res. Appl.* **2014**, *22*, 332–345. [CrossRef]
126. Massi Pavan, A.; Tessarolo, A.; Barbini, N.; Mellit, A.; Lughi, V. The Effect of Manufacturing Mismatch on Energy Production for Large-Scale Photovoltaic Plants. *Sol. Energy* **2015**, *117*, 282–289. [CrossRef]
127. Massi Pavan, A.; Mellit, A.; De Pieri, D.; Kalogirou, S.A. A Comparison between BNN and Regression Polynomial Methods for the Evaluation of the Effect of Soiling in Large Scale Photovoltaic Plants. *Appl. Energy* **2013**, *108*, 392–401. [CrossRef]
128. Cristaldi, L.; Faifer, M.; Lazzaroni, M.; Khalil, M.M.A.F.; Catelani, M.; Ciani, L. Diagnostic Architecture: A Procedure Based on the Analysis of the Failure Causes Applied to Photovoltaic Plants. *Measurement* **2015**, *67*, 99–107. [CrossRef]
129. Massi Pavan, A.; Mellit, A.; De Pieri, D. The Effect of Soiling on Energy Production for Large-Scale Photovoltaic Plants. *Sol. Energy* **2011**, *85*, 1128–1136. [CrossRef]
130. Adinoyi, M.J.; Said, S.A.M. Effect of Dust Accumulation on the Power Outputs of Solar Photovoltaic Modules. *Renew. Energy* **2013**, *60*, 633–636. [CrossRef]
131. Ndiaye, A.; Charki, A.; Kobi, A.; Kébé, C.M.F.; Ndiaye, P.A.; Sambou, V. Degradations of Silicon Photovoltaic Modules: A Literature Review. *Sol. Energy* **2013**, *96*, 140–151. [CrossRef]
132. Hu, Y.; Cao, W.; Ma, J.; Finney, S.J.; Li, D. Identifying PV Module Mismatch Faults by a Thermography-Based Temperature Distribution Analysis. *IEEE Trans. Device Mater. Reliab.* **2014**, *14*, 951–960. [CrossRef]
133. Yang, H.; Xu, W.; Wang, H.; Narayanan, M. Investigation of Reverse Current for Crystalline Silicon Solar Cells—New Concept for a Test Standard about the Reverse Current. In Proceedings of the 2010 35th IEEE Photovoltaic Specialists Conference, Honolulu, HI, USA, 20–25 June 2010; IEEE: New York, NY, USA, 2010; pp. 002806–002810.
134. Winter, C.J.; Sizmann, R.L.; Vant-Hull, L.L. Solar Power Plants: Fundamentals, Technology, Systems, Economics. *Choice Rev. Online* **1992**, *29*, 29–3922. [CrossRef]
135. Rezgui, W.; Mouss, N.K.; Mouss, L.-H.; Mouss, M.D.; Amirat, Y.; Benbouzid, M. Faults Modeling of the Impedance and Reversed Polarity Types within the PV Generator Operation. In Proceedings of the 3rd International Symposium on Environmental Friendly Energies and Applications (EFEA), Paris, France, 19-21 November 2014; IEEE: New York, NY, USA, 2014; pp. 1–6.
136. Zhao, Y.; Lehman, B.; de Palma, J.-F.; Mosesian, J.; Lyons, R. Challenges to Overcurrent Protection Devices under Line-Line Faults in Solar Photovoltaic Arrays. In Proceedings of the 2011 IEEE Energy Conversion Congress and Exposition, Phoenix, AZ, USA, 17–22 September 2011; IEEE: New York, NY, USA, 2011; pp. 20–27.
137. Maoyi, C.; Chienyu, C.; Hsueh, C.H.; Hsieh, W.J.; Yen, E.; Ho, K.L.; Chuang, H.P.; Lee, C.Y.; Chen, H.M. The Reliability Investigation of PV Junction Box Based on 1GW Worldwide Field Database. In Proceedings of the 2015 IEEE 42nd Photovoltaic Specialist Conference (PVSC), New Orleans, LA, USA, 14–19 June 2015; IEEE: New York, NY, USA, 2015; pp. 1–4.
138. Jakobi, K.-M.; Nasse, W.; Parterna, M.; Ansorge, F.; Baar, C.; Ring, K. Faults of Contacts in PV Module Junction Boxes Due to Fretting Corrosion. In Proceedings of the 29th EUPVSEC, Amsterdam, the Netherlands; 2014; pp. 2505–2510.
139. Stellbogen, D. Use of PV Circuit Simulation for Fault Detection in PV Array Fields. In Proceedings of the Conference Record of the Twenty Third IEEE Photovoltaic Specialists Conference-1993 (Cat. No.93CH3283-9), Louisville, KY, USA, 10–14 May 1993; IEEE: New York, NY, USA, 1993; pp. 1302–1307.
140. Falvo, M.C.; Capparella, S. Safety Issues in PV Systems: Design Choices for a Secure Fault Detection and for Preventing Fire Risk. *Case Stud. Fire Saf.* **2015**, *3*, 1–16. [CrossRef]
141. Zhao, Y.; Lehman, B.; de Palma, J.-F.; Mosesian, J.; Lyons, R. Fault Analysis in Solar PV Arrays under: Low Irradiance Conditions and Reverse Connections. In Proceedings of the 2011 37th IEEE Photovoltaic Specialists Conference, Seattle, WA, USA, 19–24 June 2011; IEEE: New York, NY, USA, 2011; pp. 002000–002005.
142. Karmacharya, I.M.; Gokaraju, R. Fault Location in Ungrounded Photovoltaic System Using Wavelets and ANN. *IEEE Trans. Power Deliv.* **2018**, *33*, 549–559. [CrossRef]

143. Flicker, J.; Johnson, J.; Albers, M.; Ball, G. Recommendations for Isolation Monitor Ground Fault Detectors on Residential and Utility-Scale PV Systems. In Proceedings of the 2015 IEEE 42nd Photovoltaic Specialist Conference (PVSC), New Orleans, LA, USA, 14–19 June 2015; IEEE: New York, NY, USA, 2015; pp. 1–6.
144. Johnson, J.; Montoya, M.; McCalmont, S.; Katzir, G.; Fuks, F.; Earle, J.; Fresquez, A.; Gonzalez, S.; Granata, J. Differentiating Series and Parallel Photovoltaic Arc-Faults. In Proceedings of the 2012 38th IEEE Photovoltaic Specialists Conference, Austin, TX, USA, 3–8 June 2012; IEEE: New York, NY, USA, 2012; pp. 000720–000726.
145. McCalmonit, S. Low Cost Arc Fault Detection and Protection for PV Systems. *Contract* **2013**, *303*, 275–300.
146. Zhao, Y.; Ball, R.; Mosesian, J.; de Palma, J.-F.; Lehman, B. Graph-Based Semi-Supervised Learning for Fault Detection and Classification in Solar Photovoltaic Arrays. *IEEE Trans. Power Electron.* **2015**, *30*, 2848–2858. [CrossRef]
147. Lorenzo, E.; Moretón, R.; Luque, I. Dust Effects on PV Array Performance: In-field Observations with Non-uniform Patterns. *Prog. Photovoltaics Res. Appl.* **2014**, *22*, 666–670. [CrossRef]
148. Kalogirou, S.A.; Agathokleous, R.; Panayiotou, G. On-Site PV Characterization and the Effect of Soiling on Their Performance. *Energy* **2013**, *51*, 439–446. [CrossRef]
149. Mustafa, R.J.; Gomaa, M.R.; Al-Dhaifallah, M.; Rezk, H. Environmental Impacts on the Performance of Solar Photovoltaic Systems. *Sustainability* **2020**, *12*, 608. [CrossRef]
150. Addabbo, P.; Angrisano, A.; Bernardi, M.L.; Gagliarde, G.; Mennella, A.; Nisi, M.; Ullo, S. A UAV Infrared Measurement Approach for Defect Detection in Photovoltaic Plants. In Proceedings of the 2017 IEEE International Workshop on Metrology for AeroSpace (MetroAeroSpace), Padua, Italy, 21–23 June 2017; IEEE: New York, NY, USA, 2017; pp. 345–350.
151. Carletti, V.; Greco, A.; Saggese, A.; Vento, M. An Intelligent Flying System for Automatic Detection of Faults in Photovoltaic Plants. *J. Ambient. Intell. Humaniz. Comput.* **2020**, *11*, 2027–2040. [CrossRef]
152. Bommes, L.; Pickel, T.; Buerhop-Lutz, C.; Hauch, J.; Brabec, C.; Peters, I.M. Computer Vision Tool for Detection, Mapping, and Fault Classification of Photovoltaics Modules in Aerial IR Videos. *Prog. Photovolt. Res. Appl.* **2021**, *29*, 1236–1251. [CrossRef]
153. Pratt, L.; Govender, D.; Klein, R. Defect Detection and Quantification in Electroluminescence Images of Solar PV Modules Using U-Net Semantic Segmentation. *Renew. Energy* **2021**, *178*, 1211–1222. [CrossRef]
154. Di Tommaso, A.; Betti, A.; Fontanelli, G.; Michelozzi, B. A Multi-Stage Model Based on YOLOv3 for Defect Detection in PV Panels Based on IR and Visible Imaging by Unmanned Aerial Vehicle. *Renew. Energy* **2022**, *193*, 941–962. [CrossRef]
155. Li, X.; Li, W.; Yang, Q.; Yan, W.; Zomaya, A.Y. An Unmanned Inspection System for Multiple Defects Detection in Photovoltaic Plants. *IEEE J. Photovolt.* **2020**, *10*, 568–576. [CrossRef]
156. Chen, X.; Karin, T.; Jain, A. Automated Defect Identification in Electroluminescence Images of Solar Modules. *Sol. Energy* **2022**, *242*, 20–29. [CrossRef]
157. Li, L.; Wang, Z.; Zhang, T. GBH-YOLOv5: Ghost Convolution with BottleneckCSP and Tiny Target Prediction Head Incorporating YOLOv5 for PV Panel Defect Detection. *Electronics* **2023**, *12*, 561. [CrossRef]
158. Naveen Venkatesh, S.; Sugumaran, V. Machine Vision Based Fault Diagnosis of Photovoltaic Modules Using Lazy Learning Approach. *Measurement* **2022**, *191*, 110786. [CrossRef]
159. Fioresi, J.; Colvin, D.J.; Frota, R.; Gupta, R.; Li, M.; Seigneur, H.P.; Vyas, S.; Oliveira, S.; Shah, M.; Davis, K.O. Automated Defect Detection and Localization in Photovoltaic Cells Using Semantic Segmentation of Electroluminescence Images. *IEEE J. Photovolt.* **2022**, *12*, 53–61. [CrossRef]
160. Karimi, A.M.; Fada, J.S.; Liu, J.; Braid, J.L.; Koyuturk, M.; French, R.H. Feature Extraction, Supervised and Unsupervised Machine Learning Classification of PV Cell Electroluminescence Images. In Proceedings of the 2018 IEEE 7th World Conference on Photovoltaic Energy Conversion (WCPEC) (A Joint Conference of 45th IEEE PVSC, 28th PVSEC & 34th EU PVSEC), Waikoloa, HI, USA, 10–15 June 2018; IEEE: New York, NY, USA, 2018; pp. 0418–0424.
161. Duranay, Z.B. Fault Detection in Solar Energy Systems: A Deep Learning Approach. *Electronics* **2023**, *12*, 4397. [CrossRef]
162. Su, B.; Chen, H.; Zhou, Z. BAF-Detector: An Efficient CNN-Based Detector for Photovoltaic Cell Defect Detection. *IEEE Trans. Ind. Electron.* **2022**, *69*, 3161–3171. [CrossRef]
163. Jeong, H.; Kwon, G.-R.; Lee, S.-W. Deterioration Diagnosis of Solar Module Using Thermal and Visible Image Processing. *Energies* **2020**, *13*, 2856. [CrossRef]
164. Arenella, A.; Greco, A.; Saggese, A.; Vento, M. Real Time Fault Detection in Photovoltaic Cells by Cameras on Drones. In *Lecture Notes in Computer Science (Including Subseries Lecture Notes in Artificial Intelligence and Lecture Notes in Bioinformatics)*; Springer: Berlin/Heidelberg, Germany, 2017; pp. 617–625. ISBN 9783319598758.
165. Addabbo, P.; Angrisano, A.; Bernardi, M.L.; Gagliarde, G.; Mennella, A.; Nisi, M.; Ullo, S.L. UAV System for Photovoltaic Plant Inspection. *IEEE Aerosp. Electron. Syst. Mag.* **2018**, *33*, 58–67. [CrossRef]
166. Vega Díaz, J.J.; Vlaminck, M.; Lefkaditis, D.; Orjuela Vargas, S.A.; Luong, H. Solar Panel Detection within Complex Backgrounds Using Thermal Images Acquired by UAVs. *Sensors* **2020**, *20*, 6219. [CrossRef]
167. Dunderdale, C.; Brettenny, W.; Clohessy, C.; van Dyk, E.E. Photovoltaic Defect Classification through Thermal Infrared Imaging Using a Machine Learning Approach. *Prog. Photovolt. Res. Appl.* **2020**, *28*, 177–188. [CrossRef]

168. Zhang, H.; Hong, X.; Zhou, S.; Wang, Q. Infrared Image Segmentation for Photovoltaic Panels Based on Res-UNet. In *Lecture Notes in Computer Science (Including Subseries Lecture Notes in Artificial Intelligence and Lecture Notes in Bioinformatics)*; Springer: Berlin/Heidelberg, Germany, 2019; pp. 611–622. ISBN 9783030316532.
169. de Oliveira, A.V.; Aghaei, M.; Rüther, R. Automatic Fault Detection of Photovoltaic Array by Convolutional Neural Networks during Aerial Infrared Thermography. In Proceedings of the 36th European Photovoltaic Solar Energy Conference and Exhibition, Marseille, France, 9–13 September 2019; pp. 9–13.
170. Pierdicca, R.; Malinverni, E.S.; Piccinini, F.; Paolanti, M.; Felicetti, A.; Zingaretti, P. Deep Convolutional Neural Network for Automatic Detection of Damaged Photovoltaic Cells. *Int. Arch. Photogramm. Remote Sens. Spat. Inf. Sci.* **2018**, *2*, 893–900. [CrossRef]
171. Zhang, J.; Yang, W.; Chen, Y.; Ding, M.; Huang, H.; Wang, B.; Gao, K.; Chen, S.; Du, R. Fast Object Detection of Anomaly Photovoltaic (PV) Cells Using Deep Neural Networks. *Appl. Energy* **2024**, *372*, 123759. [CrossRef]
172. Dwivedi, D.; Babu, K.V.S.M.; Yemula, P.K.; Chakraborty, P.; Pal, M. Identification of Surface Defects on Solar PV Panels and Wind Turbine Blades Using Attention Based Deep Learning Model. *Eng. Appl. Artif. Intell.* **2024**, *131*, 107836. [CrossRef]
173. Thirwani, A.; Nair, R.; Kulkarni, K. A Generative Adversarial Network Based Approach for Accurate Detection of Bright Spots in Photovoltaic Panels. In Proceedings of the 2024 11th International Conference on Signal Processing and Integrated Networks (SPIN), Noida, India, 21–22 March 2024; IEEE: New York, NY, USA, 2024; pp. 349–354.
174. Wang, Y.; Zhang, Z.; Zhang, J.; Han, J.; Lian, J.; Qi, Y.; Liu, X.; Guo, J.; Yin, X. Research on Surface Defect Detection Method of Photovoltaic Power Generation Panels——Comparative Analysis of Detecting Model Accuracy. *EAI Endorsed Trans. Energy Web* **2024**, *11*. [CrossRef]
175. Bao, J.; Yuan, X. YOLO-ICBAM: An Improved YOLOv4 Based on CBAM for Defect Detection. In Proceedings of the Fifteenth International Conference on Signal Processing Systems (ICSPS 2023), Xi'an, China, 17–19 November 2023; Zhang, Z., Li, C., Eds.; SPIE: Bellingham, WA, USA, 2024; p. 58.
176. Wang, Z.; Geng, Y.; Wu, Z. An Approach to PV Fault Defect Detection Based on Computer Vision. In Proceedings of the Proceedings of the 2023 7th International Conference on Deep Learning Technologies, Dalian, China, 27–29 July 2023; ACM: New York, NY, USA, 2023; pp. 45–50.
177. Nitturkar, K.; Vitole, S.; Jadhav, M.; Sridhar, V.G. Solar Panel Fault Detection Using Machine Vision and Image Processing Technique. In Proceedings of the 2023 International Conference on Next Generation Electronics (NEleX), Vellore, India, 14–16 December 2023; IEEE: New York, NY, USA, 2023; pp. 1–4.
178. Faniar, A.A.; Şeker, C. Detection of Faulty Solar Panels Using Artificial Intelligence and Machine Learning Methods. In Proceedings of the 2023 IEEE 3rd Mysore Sub Section International Conference (MysuruCon), Hassan, India, 1–2 December 2023; IEEE: New York, NY, USA, 2023; pp. 1–4.
179. Nadia, D.; Fathia, C. Automatic Detection of Solar Cell Surface Defects in Electroluminescence Images Based on YOLOv8 Algorithm. *Indones. J. Electr. Eng. Comput. Sci.* **2023**, *32*, 1392. [CrossRef]
180. Rocha, D.; Lopes, M.; Teixeira, J.P.; Fernandes, P.A.; Morais, M.; Salome, P.M.P. A Deep Learning Approach for PV Failure Mode Detection in Infrared Images: First Insights. In Proceedings of the 2022 IEEE 49th Photovoltaics Specialists Conference (PVSC), Philadelphia, PA, USA, 5–10 June 2022; IEEE: New York, NY, USA, 2022; pp. 0630–0632.
181. Shou, C.; Hong, L.; Ding, W.; Shen, Q.; Zhou, W.; Jiang, Y.; Zhao, C. Defect Detection with Generative Adversarial Networks for Electroluminescence Images of Solar Cells. In Proceedings of the 2020 35th Youth Academic Annual Conference of Chinese Association of Automation (YAC), Zhanjiang, China, 16–18 October 2020; IEEE: New York, NY, USA, 2020; pp. 312–317.

technologies

MDPI

Article

Improving Diabetes Education and Metabolic Control in Children Using Social Robots: A Randomized Trial

Tareq Alhmiedat [1,2,*], Laila A. AlBishi [3], Fady Alnajjar [4], Mohammed Alotaibi [1], Ashraf M. Marei [1] and Rakan Shalayl [1]

1 Faculty of Computers & Information Technology, University of Tabuk, Tabuk 71491, Saudi Arabia; mmalotaibi@ut.edu.sa (M.A.); aemam@ut.edu.sa (A.M.M.); shlaayl@gmail.com (R.S.)
2 Artificial Intelligence & Sensing Technologies (AIST) Research Center, University of Tabuk, Tabuk 71491, Saudi Arabia
3 Faculty of Medicine, University of Tabuk, Tabuk 71491, Saudi Arabia; lalbishi@ut.edu.sa
4 College of Information Technology (CIT), United Arab Emirates University (UAEU), Al Ain 15551, United Arab Emirates; fady.alnajjar@uaeu.ac.ae
* Correspondence: t.alhmiedat@ut.edu.sa

Abstract: Robot engagement in healthcare has the potential to alleviate medical personnel workload while improving efficiency in managing various health conditions. This study evaluates the impact of robot-assisted education on knowledge acquisition and metabolic control in children with Type 1 Diabetes Mellitus (T1DM) compared to traditional education methods. A randomized controlled trial was conducted at the pediatric diabetes clinic of the University of Tabuk Medical Center, Saudi Arabia. Thirty children aged 5–15 years with T1DM were randomly divided into two groups: the robot education (intervention) group and the control education group. Both groups participated in six weekly one-hour educational sessions, with the intervention group interacting with a Pepper robot assistant and the control group receiving education from a qualified diabetes educator nurse. Knowledge was assessed using a 12-item questionnaire before and after the intervention, while metabolic control was evaluated through weekly mean home blood glucose measurements and HbA1c levels before and three months post intervention. The intervention group demonstrated a significantly greater improvement in knowledge scores compared to the control group ($p < 0.05$). Weekly mean blood glucose levels were consistently lower in the intervention group throughout the study period ($p < 0.05$ for all samples). Both groups showed a reduction in HbA1c levels after three months, with the intervention group exhibiting a greater mean decrease. The engagement of the Pepper robot in T1DM education for children resulted in improved knowledge acquisition and better metabolic control compared to traditional education methods. This approach may establish a foundation for "learning by interacting with robots" in long-term diabetes management. Further research with larger sample sizes and longer follow-up periods is warranted to confirm these findings and explore the long-term benefits of robot-assisted education in pediatric diabetes care.

Keywords: type 1 diabetes mellitus (T1DM); robot-assisted education; pediatric diabetes management; Pepper robot; knowledge acquisitions; metabolic control

1. Introduction

Type 1 Diabetes Mellitus (T1DM) is a chronic condition affecting approximately 0.2 million children and adolescents worldwide [1]. Managing T1DM in children presents unique challenges, requiring consistent education and support to maintain optimal glycemic control and prevent complications. The complexity of diabetes management, coupled with factors such as short attention spans, potential feelings of isolation, and the challenge of maintaining consistent motivation for self-care tasks, can make traditional education methods less engaging and effective for children with T1DM.

The management of T1DM extends beyond clinical settings, with home-based care playing a crucial role in long-term health outcomes. Home rehabilitation and continuous education are essential components of effective diabetes management, particularly for children [2]. The COVID-19 pandemic has further emphasized the importance of robust home-based care systems [3]. In this context, innovative solutions that can provide consistent support and education in the home environment are increasingly valuable. Social robots offer a promising avenue for enhancing home rehabilitation and education for children with T1DM, potentially improving adherence to treatment regimens and overall disease management.

Recent advancements in Artificial Intelligence (AI) and robotics have opened new avenues for healthcare management, particularly in chronic conditions like T1DM [4] or asthma [5]. Social robots, a subset of AI technology, have shown promise in various healthcare applications, including patient education and disease management [6–8]. These robots offer an innovative approach to diabetes education and management, potentially improving knowledge retention and treatment adherence [9].

However, while several studies have explored the use of robots in healthcare, their specific application in T1DM education and management for children remains understudied. There is a need for comprehensive research that evaluates the impact of advanced robot-assisted interventions on both knowledge acquisition and metabolic control in pediatric T1DM patients.

This paper aims to evaluate the impact of robot engagement, specifically using the Pepper robot platform, on knowledge acquisition and metabolic control in children with T1DM. Our study contributes to the field through the following:

1. Developing a reliable robot interaction system for T1DM education in children.
2. Investigating the acceptability of the Pepper robot platform among children with T1DM.
3. Validating the efficiency of the developed social robot system compared to traditional education methods through a controlled study.

By addressing these objectives, we seek to fill the gap in understanding how robot-assisted education can enhance T1DM management in pediatric populations, both in clinical settings and as part of home-based care. The findings of this study have the potential to inform future developments in pediatric diabetes care, particularly in the context of home rehabilitation and long-term disease management.

The rest of this paper is organized as follows: Section 2 discusses the recently developed robot-based diabetes management and education systems. In Section 3, the experiment setup is presented, including the design of this study, the participants, and the robot platform. The results obtained from this study are presented and discussed in Section 4, whereas Section 5 summarizes the key findings, interprets the obtained results, and compares the obtained results with recently developed systems. Finally, Section 6 concludes the work presented in this paper and presents several issues that need to be considered in future studies.

2. Related Works

Recent research on social robots in diabetes management for children can be categorized into two main areas: diabetes management systems and diabetes education systems. This section critically examines the existing literature, highlighting the key findings, methodologies, and gaps in the current knowledge.

First, the diabetes management systems are considered: The majority of studies have focused on using robots for diabetes management. Al-Taee et al. [10] investigated the use of NAO robots with 22 participants, reporting the high acceptability of the robot solution. This was further corroborated by another study [11] with a larger sample size of 37, which found an overall acceptability of 86.7%. These studies suggest that children are generally receptive to robot-assisted diabetes management.

Alhmiedat and Alotaibi [12] explored a different platform, the SARA robot, with a small sample of five participants. Despite the limited sample size, they reported a reasonable acceptance rate of 82.2%, indicating that various simple robot platforms may be suitable for this purpose.

Several studies utilized the NAO robot platform for different aspects of diabetes management. Blanson Henkemans et al. [13] reported an increase in diabetes knowledge among 27 participants. Van Der Drift et al. [14] found that children shared more personal experiences in their diaries when interacting with the NAO robot, albeit with a small sample size of six. These studies suggest that robot interaction may enhance engagement and knowledge retention.

Cañamero and Lewis [15] and Kruijff-Korbayová et al. [16] both used NAO robots with sample sizes of 17 and 20, respectively, reporting positive outcomes in terms of social interaction and children's interest in engaging with the robot. This indicates that robots can serve as effective companions in diabetes management.

Robinson et al. [17] conducted a small-scale study with four participants, demonstrating that the NAO robot could help children minimize high-energy food intake and increase their confidence and motivation. Sinoo et al. [18] found that children felt stronger friendship towards the NAO robot in a study with 21 participants.

Second, the diabetes education systems are considered: Fewer studies have focused specifically on robot-assisted diabetes education. Looije et al. [19] used an NAO robot for educational purposes with 17 participants, reporting that children had very positive experiences. Henkemans et al. [20] assessed the effects of personalized robot behaviors on health education using NAO, noting an increment in knowledge among five participants.

While these studies collectively suggest positive outcomes for robot-assisted diabetes management and education, several limitations are evident:

1. The majority of studies used the NAO robot platform, with limited exploration of other robot types.
2. Most research focused on acceptability and engagement, with fewer studies examining concrete health outcomes or long-term impacts.
3. There is a notable lack of controlled studies comparing robot-assisted interventions with traditional methods.
4. The distinction between management and education is often blurred, with many studies incorporating elements of both.

Despite the promising results, there remains a significant gap in understanding how robot-assisted interventions compare to traditional methods in terms of both knowledge acquisition and metabolic control. Most studies have focused on either management or education, but few have combined both aspects in a controlled study with a significant sample size and measurable health outcomes.

Table 1 encapsulates the current landscape of robot-assisted interventions for children with diabetes. While these studies collectively suggest promising outcomes, they also highlight the need for larger-scale, controlled studies that combine both management and education aspects and explore diverse robot platforms. Our study aims to address these gaps through the following:

1. Utilizing the Pepper robot, expanding beyond the commonly used NAO platform. The Pepper robot may be more effective than NAO for interacting with children with T1DM due to its taller, more humanoid design, touch screen interface, advanced sensors, expressive gestures, and superior speech capabilities. These features create stronger emotional connections, personalized interactions, and enhanced engagement, improving educational outcomes for T1DM management [21].
2. Conducting a controlled study comparing robot-assisted education with traditional methods.
3. Measuring both knowledge acquisition and metabolic control outcomes.
4. Including a larger sample size to enhance the reliability and generalizability of findings.

Table 1. A comparison study among the recently developed robot systems for diabetic issues.

Research Study	Target Function	Robot Platform	Sample Size	Obtained Results
[10]	Diabetes management	NAO	22	High acceptability of NAO robot solution
[11]	Diabetes management	NAO	37	Overall acceptability of 86.7%
[12]	Diabetes management	SARA	5	Reasonable acceptance rate of 82.2%
[13]	Diabetes management	ALIZ-E	9	Children could benefit from social robots motivation
[14]	Diabetes management	NAO	6	Children shared more personal experiences in diary and their relationship with the NAO robot
[15]	Diabetes management	NAO	17	An engaging social interaction partner
[16]	Diabetes management	NAO	20	A high interest in children in engaging with the robot
[17]	Diabetes management	NAO	4	The robot could help diabetic children to minimize their high-energy food and drink intake and increase their confidence and motivation
[18]	Diabetes management	NAO	21	Children felt stronger friendship towards the NAO robot
[19]	Educational	NAO	17	Children had very positive experience
[20]	Diabetes management	NAO	27	An increase in diabetes knowledge

By addressing these aspects, our research seeks to provide a more comprehensive understanding of the potential of social robots in T1DM management and education for children.

3. Methods

3.1. Study Design

This study employed a randomized controlled trial design to evaluate the impact of robot-assisted education on knowledge acquisition and metabolic control in children with Type 1 Diabetes Mellitus (T1DM). This study was conducted at the pediatric diabetes clinic of the Medical Center, University of Tabuk, Saudi Arabia, between 1 September 2023 and 31 November 2023. The experimental setup for the control group is presented in Figure 1A, whereas Figure 1B depicts the experimental setup for the robot group. Both areas consist of a diabetic child, a parent (mother, father, or both), and an observer. However, the control testbed area includes a nurse educator, whereas the intervention testbed area includes a Pepper robot platform.

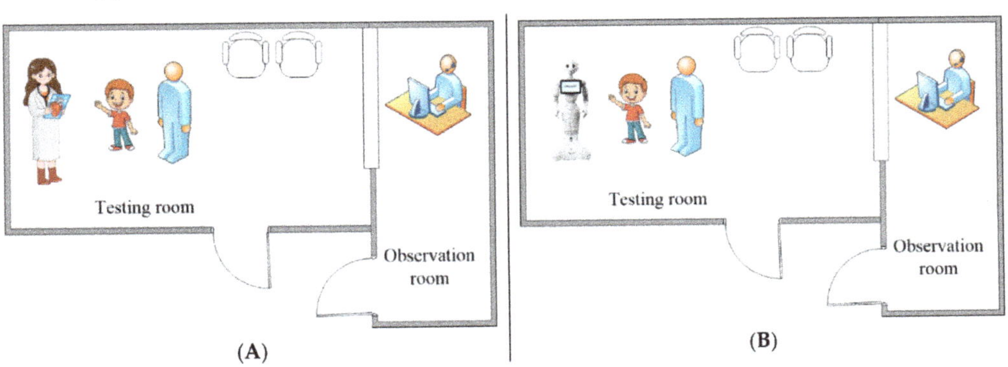

Figure 1. Setup for the testbed area: (**A**) the control testbed area and (**B**) the robot testbed area.

3.2. Participants

Children aged 5–15 years with T1DM were eligible for inclusion. The inclusion criteria were as follows: confirmed diagnosis of T1DM, disease duration within the first year after diagnosis, Saudi nationality, and having educated, cooperative parents. The exclusion criteria included the following: non-Saudi participants, Type 2 diabetes or other types of diabetes, diabetes with other associated autoimmune or chronic disorders, and those with incomplete data.

A total of 30 participants were recruited and randomly assigned to either the robot education (intervention) group (n = 15) or the control education group (n = 15). The adopted methodology for this study is presented in Figure 2, starting from the enrolment stage, then collecting the last HBA1C and knowledge assessment test which is presented in Appendix A, starting the education stage, and finally performing the knowledge test and HBA1C test. The questions of the knowledge assessment test have been obtained from [22].

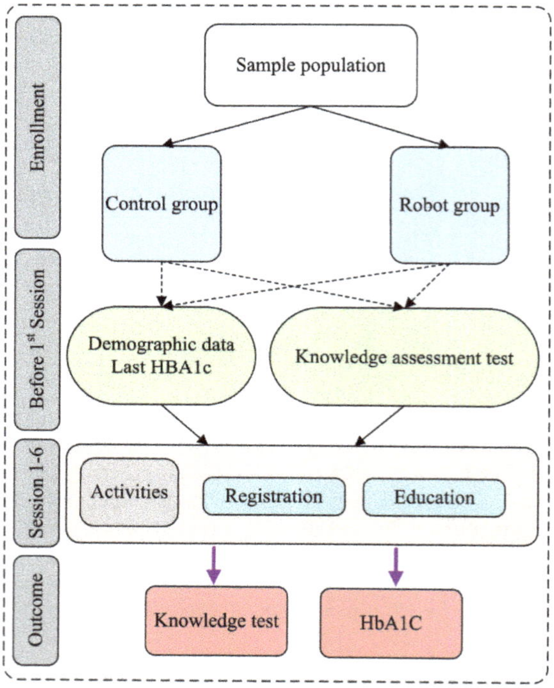

Figure 2. The adopted study methodology.

The age distributions for the two groups are presented in Figure 3, where the average age of the children in the control group was equal to 8 years old, and the average age of the children in the intervention (robot) group was equal to 9 years old. On the other hand, participants were categorized based on the time since their initial T1DM diagnosis, as depicted in Figure 4. Four categories were established: 1–3 months, 3–6 months, 6–9 months, and 9–12 months post diagnosis. This categorization allows for the analysis of how the duration of T1DM might influence the effectiveness of the educational intervention. The figure illustrates the distribution of participants across these categories for both the intervention and control groups.

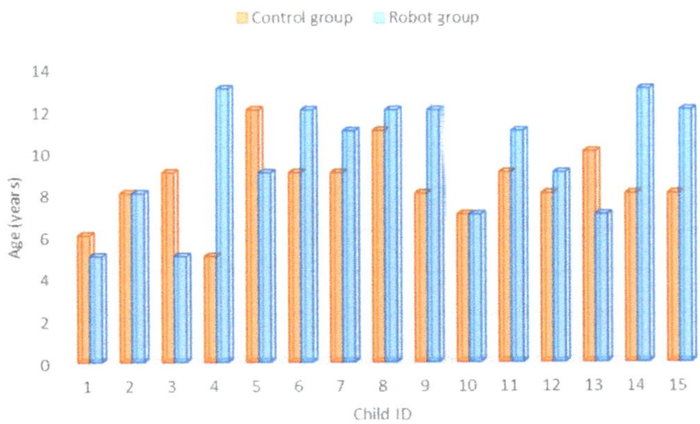

Figure 3. The age distribution of children who were involved in this study.

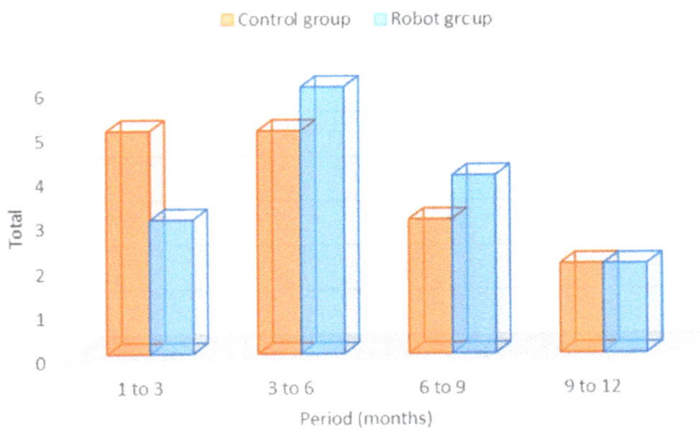

Figure 4. Distribution of time since T1DM diagnosis among participants.

3.3. Robot Platform and Intervention Group

The intervention group received education from a Pepper robot platform, chosen for its high acceptability rate among children [23]. Pepper is a 120 cm tall humanoid robot designed for human interaction, capable of perceiving its environment using touch, distance, vision, and voice sensors, Figure 5. The Pepper robot was located in the medical center at the University of Tabuk.

A robot application for the Pepper platform was developed for the purpose of allowing the robot to interact with diabetic children, where we employed the Python SDK and NAOQi OS 2.8.7 to accomplish this task. The robot platform was implemented using the Choregraphe development environment. Choregraphe is a development environment for Pepper and NAO robots, and it offers a reliable method for developing a robot application that contains services, dialogs, and robot behaviors.

The developed robot platform relied on Python 2.7 to obtain data from Pepper's sensors, process the received data, and control the Pepper robot accordingly. In addition, JavaScript language was employed to develop an application for the Pepper robot's tablet. Both Python and JavaScript environments were combined in a single robot application to provide a reliable interaction system for the Pepper robot.

For the purpose of developing an effective human–robot interaction approach, a set of packages and tools were adopted, and a number of functions were developed. These functions enabled Pepper to interact dynamically with the children during educational sessions, as shown in Figure 6. The developed robot education system for children with T1DM integrated several packages and tools, as follows:

- NAOqi motion: this package allows the Pepper robot to move and perform animations through a communication link with the physical actuators (head, arms, and legs).
- NAOqi audio: using this package, the developed application can access Pepper's loudspeaker and microphones.
- NAOqi vision: this package allows for communication with the physical RGB and RGB-D cameras in order to process and analyze the received captured frames.
- NAOqi people detection: this is used to analyze the emotional aspects of people facing the robot.
- NAOqi sensors: this package is mainly employed to access onboard sensors including obstacle avoidance, infrared, touch, and sonar.

Figure 5. Pepper robot platform in the clinic.

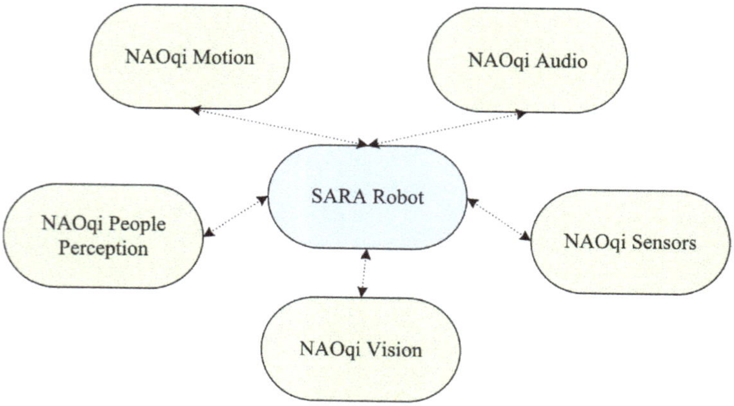

Figure 6. The main developed functions for the education robot system.

The robot was programmed to perform various interactive functions, including greeting the child, asking about their name and status, shaking hands, dancing, hugging, and mimicking animals. Figure 7 presents the Pepper robot interacting with a diabetic child and her mother.

Figure 7. A diabetic child with her mother interacting with the Pepper robot.

A Python SDK is available to communicate with the Pepper robot's sensors and actuators. Therefore, we developed several Python-based functions to communicate with sensors through the adoption of Pepper's sensor API to obtain data from microphones and cameras and the distance to objects surrounding the Pepper robot.

Moreover, several functions were implemented to control the Pepper robot's actuators (animation and movement) through communication with actuators using the actuator API. In addition, a GUI was implemented to allow the child to interact with the robot and to display several productive pictures; this GUI application was implemented using JavaScript and initiated using Python SDK. The Pepper JavaScript SDK allows for the Pepper robot's animation and speech to be shown. Figure 8 presents the software architecture for the developed Pepper robot application.

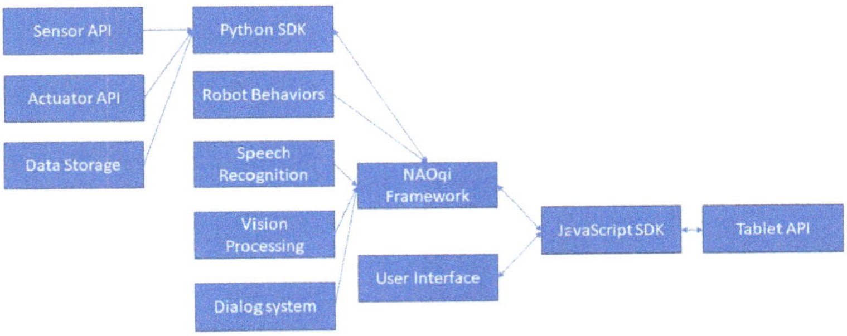

Figure 8. The developed application for the Pepper robot.

3.4. Control Group

The control group received traditional education from a qualified diabetes educator nurse, following the same session structure and content as the intervention group, Figure 1A. For both groups, the robot platform and the educator nurse were required to deliver educational content through a series of six weekly one-hour sessions. Each session included the following:

- Five minutes for registering mean blood glucose data from the previous week.
- Five minutes of entertainment and games.
- In total, 30–40 min of diabetes education presentation.

All interactions were conducted in Arabic, the first language of all participants.

3.5. Data Collection

Data were collected at baseline and after the six-week intervention period. Measures included the following:

1. Demographic and control data.
2. Knowledge assessment: a 12-item multiple-choice questionnaire developed by diabetes educators and reviewed by consultants.
3. Metabolic control: weekly mean home blood glucose measurements and HbA1c levels.
4. Parent and child perceptions: questionnaires on the acceptability and perceived effectiveness of the education program.

The nature of our intervention, which compared robot-assisted education to traditional human-led education, made full participant blinding unfeasible. However, to minimize potential bias, outcome assessors evaluating the knowledge questionnaires and analyzing HbA1c results were blinded to group allocation. We acknowledge this limitation and address strategies to mitigate it in our discussion of future research directions.

3.6. Data Analysis

Data were analyzed using SPSS version 22.0. Descriptive statistics were used for demographic data. Comparisons between groups were made using t-tests for continuous variables and chi-square tests for categorical variables. Repeated-measures ANOVA was used to assess changes in knowledge scores and metabolic control over time. A p-value < 0.05 was considered statistically significant.

4. Results

This study assessed the impact of robot engagement on knowledge acquisition and metabolic control in children with T1DM. We present findings from our analysis of demographic characteristics, knowledge test scores, weekly mean home blood glucose measurements, and HbA1C percentages between the control and intervention groups.

4.1. Participant Characteristics

Table 2 provides a comparative analysis of the demographic variables between the control and intervention groups. Both groups showed similar age distributions across all categories (≤5 years, 6–10 years, >10 years). The control group comprised 40% males and 60% females, while the intervention group had 26.7% males and 73.3% females, with no significant difference in gender distribution between groups. The T1DM duration categories (≤3 months, 3–6 months, 6–12 months, and >12 months) were comparable between groups. No significant differences were observed in the occurrence of symptomatic hypo- or hyperglycemic events or in the frequency of Diabetic Ketoacidosis (DKA) admissions between groups (all $p > 0.05$).

Table 2. Demographic characteristics of participants in the control and intervention groups.

Variable	Control Group (N = 15)	Intervention Group (N = 15)	p-Value
	Age (years)		
≤5	3 (20%)	3 (20%)	

Table 2. *Cont.*

Variable	Control Group (N = 15)	Intervention Group (N = 15)	p-Value
6–10	7 (46.7%)	7 (46.7%)	
≥10	5 (33.3%)	5 (33.3%)	
	Gender		
Male	6 (40%)	4 (26.7%)	
Female	9 (60%)	11 (73.3%)	
	DM duration (months)		
≤3 months	4 (26.7%)	2 (13.3%)	
3–6 months	2(13.3%)	3(20%)	
6–12 months	5 (33.3%)	5 (33.3%)	>0.05
>12 months	4(26.7%)	5 (33.3%)	
	Asymptomatic hypoglycemic events		
0	5 (33.3%)	7 (46.7%)	
1	5 (33.3%)	4 (26.7%)	
2	5 (33.3%)	4 (26.7%)	
	Symptomatic hypoglycemic events		
0	15 (100%)	14 (93.3%)	
1	0 (0%)	1 (6.7%)	
	Admission due to DKA		
0	12 (80%)	14 (93.3%)	
1	3 (20%)	1 (6.7%)	

4.2. Knowledge Acquisition

Knowledge test scores for both groups before and after the intervention are presented in Table 3. The control group's scores ranged from 6 to 10 before this study and 8 to 11 after. The intervention group's scores ranged from 6 to 11 before and 10 to 12 after this study. The percentage changes in scores for the control group ranged from 0.0% to 57.1%, while the intervention group showed changes from 9.1% to 83.3%. Paired *t*-tests showed significant improvements within both groups ($p < 0.05$). An independent *t*-test comparing both groups showed a significant difference ($p < 0.05$), indicating that the overall improvement in test scores differed significantly between the two groups.

Table 3. Knowledge test scores before and after the intervention for control and intervention groups.

Sample No.	Control Group		Percentage Difference	Intervention Group		Percentage Difference	p-Value
	Before	After		Before	After		
1	8	9	12.5%	8	11	37.5%	
2	9	9	0.0%	10	12	20.0%	
3	10	11	10.0%	6	10	66.7%	
4	9	10	11.1%	6	11	83.3%	
5	8	8	0.0%	9	10	11.1%	
6	10	10	0.0%	10	11	10.0%	
7	7	11	57.1%	10	12	20.0%	
8	9	10	11.1%	11	12	9.1%	<0.05 *
9	9	10	11.1%	11	12	9.1%	
10	8	9	12.5%	10	11	10.0%	
11	6	8	33.3%	9	11	22.2%	
12	8	10	25.0%	8	11	37.5%	
13	9	9	0.0%	7	10	42.9%	
14	8	10	25.0%	10	12	20.0%	
15	7	9	28.6%	10	12	20.0%	

* Paired *t*-test *p*-values for both groups are less than 0.05.

To provide a more comprehensive analysis of the knowledge test scores, we calculated summary statistics and conducted statistical tests based on the individual scores presented in Table 4, where this table presents a summary of these findings.

Table 4. Summary of knowledge test scores.

Group	Pre Intervention (Mean ± SD)	Post Intervention (Mean ± SD)	*p*-Value (Within Group)
Control	8.33 ± 1.11	9.53 ± 0.99	<0.05 *
Intervention	9.00 ± 1.69	11.27 ± 0.80	<0.05 *

* Paired *t*-test *p*-values for both groups are less than 0.05.

As shown in Table 4, both groups demonstrated significant improvements in their knowledge scores following the intervention. The control group's mean score increased from 8.33 ± 1.11 to 9.53 ± 0.99 ($p < 0.05$, paired *t*-test). The intervention group showed improvement as well, with mean scores increasing from 9.00 ± 1.69 to 11.27 ± 0.80 ($p < 0.05$, paired *t*-test).

To compare the effectiveness of the two educational approaches, an independent *t*-test was conducted to analyze the difference in the improvement between the groups. This test revealed a significant difference ($p < 0.05$), indicating that the overall improvement in test scores differed significantly between the two groups.

4.3. Metabolic Control

4.3.1. Weekly Mean Blood Glucose Levels

Table 5 presents the weekly mean home blood glucose measurements for both groups. In most cases, the average blood glucose levels were lower in the intervention group compared to the control group. All comparisons between groups showed statistically significant differences ($p < 0.05$), with some *p*-values as low as 0.0005.

Table 5. Weekly mean home blood glucose measurements (mg/dL) for control and intervention groups.

Sample	Control Group	Intervention Group	*p*-Value
1	195	178	0.003
2	173	166	0.007
3	204	142	0.002
4	161	134	0.015
5	219	129	0.001
6	185	155	0.020
7	178	111	0.005
8	236	123	0.0005
9	190	137	0.006
10	157	131	0.018
11	212	145	0.004
12	182	130	0.008
13	199	126	0.002
14	169	102	0.005
15	225	170	0.007

To provide a clearer comparison between the two groups, Figure 9 presents the mean weekly blood glucose levels for the control and intervention groups, along with their respective standard deviations. As illustrated, the intervention group demonstrated a substantially lower mean blood glucose level (138.60 ± 21.17 mg/dL) compared to the control group (192.33 ± 24.78 mg/dL). This visual representation underscores the significant difference in glycemic control achieved by the two groups over the study period.

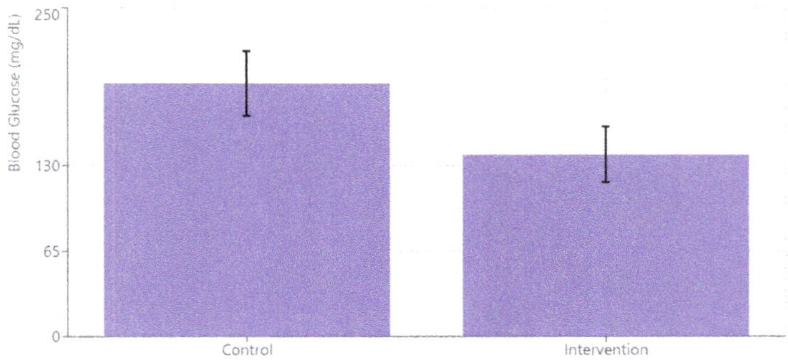

Figure 9. Mean weekly blood glucose levels (mg/dL) for control and intervention groups. Error bars represent standard deviation.

4.3.2. HbA1C Levels

Both groups showed a reduction in HbA1C percentages three months post intervention, as illustrated in Table 6. The control group's mean HbA1C decreased from 9.00 ± 0.50 to 8.25 ± 0.75 (p = 0.04). The intervention group's mean HbA1C decreased from 8.75 ± 0.25 to 7.75 ± 0.25 (p = 0.03). An independent t-test comparing the changes between groups showed a significant difference (p = 0.0330).

Table 6. HbA1C percentages before and three months after the intervention for control and intervention groups.

Time	Control Group (Mean ± SD)	Intervention Group (Mean ± SD)
Before	9.00 ± 0.50	8.75 ± 0.25
Three months after	8.25 ± 0.75 * p-value 0.04	7.75 ± 0.25 *,† p-value 0.03

* Significant reductions within both groups; † greater reduction in intervention group.

To visually represent the changes in HbA1c levels, Figure 10 presents the mean HbA1c percentages before and three months after the intervention for both the control and intervention groups.

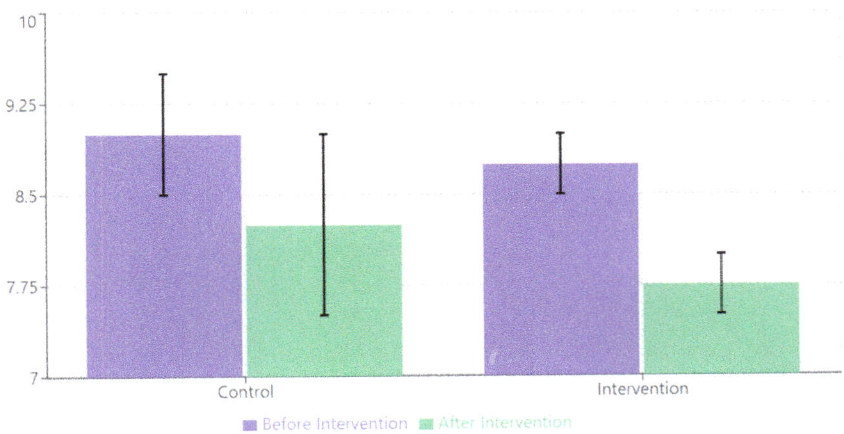

Figure 10. Changes in mean HbA1c levels before and after intervention. Error bars represent standard deviation.

4.4. Participant Engagement

During the intervention, observers noted that children in the robot-assisted group showed higher levels of engagement compared to the control group. Children interacted enthusiastically with the Pepper robot, responding positively to its introductions, handshakes, and playful activities such as dancing and animal mimicry. In contrast, children in the control group typically maintained interest for only the first 3–6 min of each session before showing signs of disengagement.

5. Discussion

5.1. Summary of Key Findings

This study evaluated the impact of robot-assisted education on knowledge acquisition and metabolic control in children with T1DM. Our results demonstrated significant improvements in both the knowledge scores and metabolic control measures in the robot-assisted group compared to the traditional education group.

5.2. Interpretation of Results

As presented earlier in Table 3, the robot-assisted group showed a significantly higher mean increase in the knowledge scores compared to the control group. This greater improvement suggests that robot engagement offers a superior method for educating children with T1DM. The interactive nature of the Pepper robot, including its ability to introduce itself, shake hands, and engage in playful activities, likely contributed to this enhanced learning. This aligns with previous findings that interactive, technology-based interventions can improve health education outcomes [24,25].

The intervention group demonstrated consistently lower weekly mean blood glucose levels compared to the control group, with differences ranging from 7 mg/dL to 113 mg/dL (all $p < 0.05$). Moreover, the intervention group showed a greater reduction in HbA1c (1.00% vs. 0.75% in the control group, $p = 0.0330$). These improvements in both short-term and long-term glycemic control indicators suggest that enhanced knowledge translates to better disease management. This connection between education and clinical outcomes is crucial, as it demonstrates the potential real-world impact of robot-assisted education on T1DM management [26,27].

Observational data indicated that children in the robot-assisted group maintained engagement throughout the 30–40-min sessions, contrasting with the control group where interest waned after 3–6 min. This sustained engagement is particularly noteworthy given the wide age range of participants (5–15 years) and varied disease durations ($\leq$3 months to >12 months). The ability of the robot to capture and maintain attention across these diverse groups suggests its potential adaptability to different developmental stages and experience levels with T1DM [28,29].

5.3. Comparison with Existing Literature

While previous studies have shown the potential of robots in improving the understanding of health conditions [24], our study uniquely demonstrates both educational and clinical benefits in T1DM management. The magnitude of the improvement in HbA1c (1.00%) in our robot-assisted group over just six weeks is particularly noteworthy, comparing favorably with a 6-month telehealth intervention that achieved a 0.5% reduction [30]. This suggests that robot-assisted education may offer accelerated benefits compared to other technology-based interventions.

5.4. Limitations and Future Directions

We believe that several factors may contribute to the observed outcomes. The novelty of interacting with an AI-powered robot, the "Pepper robot", could have increased the initial engagement, though long-term studies are needed to assess if this effect persists. The robot's ability to provide consistent information delivery may have reduced the variability in education quality [31]. Additionally, children might have felt more comfortable asking questions to a robot than a human educator, potentially leading to better understanding.

Our findings suggest that integrating robot-assisted education into T1DM management could significantly enhance care for children. The practical implications include supplementing traditional education, where robots could provide reinforcement between clinic visits. Robot interactions could be tailored based on age, disease duration, and individual learning needs, allowing for personalized interventions. Furthermore, robots could handle routine education tasks, potentially optimizing resources by allowing healthcare providers to focus on more complex aspects of care.

Several limitations should be considered when interpreting our results. Our relatively small sample size (N = 30; 15 per group) and six-week study period limit the generalizability of findings and preclude the assessment of the long-term effects or potential waning of novelty associated with robot interaction. As a single-center study conducted at one clinic in Saudi Arabia, cultural and healthcare system specifics may limit the broader applicability of our results. Furthermore, due to the nature of the intervention, blinding participants to their group assignment was impossible, potentially introducing bias. Lastly, the frequency and style of interactions differed between robot and human educators, which could have influenced the results beyond the simple robot/human distinction.

To address these limitations and expand upon our findings, future research should conduct larger, multi-center, longer-term studies to validate and generalize the results. Incorporating adaptive and personalized robot behaviors to explore sustained engagement over extended periods is crucial, building on the existing literature that suggests engagement levels can vary based on robot interaction personalization [32–34]. Additionally, comparing different robot platforms could identify features that most effectively enhance educational and therapeutic outcomes, as existing studies indicate that variations in robot design can significantly impact user engagement and effectiveness [35].

Future studies should also investigate the specific aspects of robot-assisted education contributing to improved outcomes and explore personalized interventions based on individual patient characteristics. To address the limitation of participant blinding, we propose implementing a crossover design where participants experience both educational approaches (robot-assisted and traditional) in a randomized order, with a washout period between interventions. This design would allow for within-subject comparisons, potentially mitigating biases associated with a lack of blinding and providing insights into individual preferences and responses to different educational approaches.

These strategies will help address the current limitations and advance our understanding of robot-assisted education in pediatric diabetes management, paving the way for more effective and personalized interventions in the future.

6. Conclusions

This study provides promising evidence for the effectiveness of robot-assisted education in improving both knowledge acquisition and metabolic control in children with Type 1 Diabetes Mellitus (T1DM). The intervention group, which interacted with the Pepper robot, showed significant improvements in diabetes knowledge and glycemic control compared to the traditional education group. These findings suggest that robot-assisted education can offer a more engaging and effective approach for managing T1DM in children.

This study makes several novel contributions to the field of robot-assisted diabetes education. It is the first to utilize the advanced features of the Pepper robot specifically for T1DM education in children, combining both educational and clinical outcome measures. Our research uniquely demonstrates the effectiveness of robot-assisted education across a wide age range and in the cultural context of Saudi Arabia. By successfully integrating robot-assisted education into standard care protocols, we provide a practical model for implementing this innovative approach in clinical settings. These findings not only advance our understanding of how social robots can enhance diabetes management in children but also pave the way for more personalized and engaging educational interventions in pediatric chronic disease management.

The cultural context of Saudi Arabia, where interactions with robots are less common, may also have contributed to a novelty effect, enhancing engagement. Therefore, it is essential to conduct similar studies in diverse settings to assess the generalizability of these results. In regions like Japan, where children are more familiar with robots, the outcomes may differ.

Looking forward, advancements in Large Language Models (LLMs) present exciting possibilities for even more personalized and interactive robot-assisted education. Future robots equipped with advanced LLMs could provide more nuanced, adaptive, and culturally sensitive interactions, further enhancing the effectiveness of this approach.

While our study has limitations, including a small sample size and a short study duration, it contributes valuable insights into the potential of robotic systems in pediatric diabetes education. Integrating sophisticated robot-assisted education into existing diabetes care frameworks represents a promising avenue for improving management and long-term health outcomes for children with T1DM. Future research should focus on larger, multi-center studies with longer follow-up periods to validate these findings and explore the long-term benefits of robot-assisted education.

Author Contributions: M.A. and A.M.M. surveyed the recently developed social robot systems for managing type 1 diabetes among children. T.A. and R.S. developed the robot application using Choregraph and Python development environments. L.A.A. and T.A. performed the clinical experiments, whereas F.A. wrote and reviewed this manuscript. All authors have read and agreed to the published version of the manuscript.

Funding: The authors extend their appreciation to the Deputyship for Research & Innovation, Ministry of Education in Saudi Arabia, for funding this research work through project number (0049-1442-S).

Institutional Review Board Statement: An ethical approval for this study was granted by the Ethics Committee of Tabuk University, at Tabuk city Saudi Arabia (No. UT-316-156-2023). The approval included the research protocol data, collection of informed consent forms from participants, and the final report submitted at the end of this study.

Informed Consent Statement: During the routine clinic visits, participants were informed about the study objectives, methodology, risks, and benefits, and if they were willing to be enrolled in this study, they signed the consent form before starting this study. Participants were first requested to give their consent to participate in this study before enrollment. The data of the study participants were kept confidential and coded to preserve the participants' anonymity. They were informed about the study objectives, methodology, risks, and benefits. The investigators were responsible for keeping the participants' privacy and security of the data. Personal information (e.g., name, contact info) was not included in the study data entry software to conserve the participants' privacy. Each subject was assigned a unique identifier code.

Data Availability Statement: In accordance with ethical guidelines and privacy regulations, the data presented in this article are not available for public.

Conflicts of Interest: The authors declare no conflicts of interest.

Appendix A

This appendix includes the list of questions related to demographic and diabetes data.
Demographic and Diabetes Data
What is your age?
Gender?

- Male
- Female

Diabetes duration in year?
Last HbA1c

Insulin treatment

- twice a day injection
- Multiple doses
- Continuous perfusion pump

Mild hypoglycemia (per week)

- None
- Once
- More than once

Severe hypoglycemia that needs hospitalization (past one year)

- None
- Once
- More than once

Admission due to hyperglycemia (past one year)

- None
- Once
- More than once

Parent education, mothers

- Less than high school graduate
- High school graduate
- Bachelor and above Parent education, fathers
- Less than high school graduate
- High school graduate
- Bachelor and above

Knowledge questionnaire
Q1: what is the ideal glucose level range for type 1 diabetes you look for?

a) 60–80 mg/dL
b) 80–120 mg/dL
c) 180–300 mg/dL
d) Not sure

Q2: what is the ideal HbA1C level that should be targeted for to diabetes complication

a) Less than 7.5
b) 7–9
c) 9–10
d) Not sure

Q3: what is about Type 1 diabetes is a disease?

a) Is always life threatening when first diagnosed
b) Could be cured by healthy lifestyle
c) Can be treated by insulin
d) Not sure

Q4: which one of the following is true about type1 diabetes and diet?

a) A diabetic diet should be low in fat, high in fiber, low in added sugar
b) It is ok to eat fried take away food 3 times a week
c) The diet should be free of sugar
d) Not sure

Q5: Why is doing exercise regularly or being physically active good for type 1 diabetes?

a) It can help to control blood sugar
b) It cures type 1 diabetes

c) Not sure

Q6: what should you do if your child gets ill?

a) Check the blood sugar more frequent every 2–4 h
b) Stop giving insulin
c) eat lots of foods
d) Unsure

Q7: Children with type 1 diabetes need to check their eyes, kidney function,

a) Every 6 month
b) Every year
c) 2–3 year
d) Unsure

Q8: which of the following medications is true?

a) If the blood sugar is normal for 2 month stop the insulin because the diabetes is cured
b) Regular medical advice is necessary to adjust the dose and type of insulin
c) No need to worry about your diet if you are taking the insulin
d) Unsure

Q9: If your child has hypoglycemia, you should

a) Immediately take some insulin
b) Rest and wait until she is better
c) Immediately get some sugary foods
d) Unsure

Q10: why do we need to test the blood sugar regularly?

a) To be alert about the patterns of blood sugar level
b) To help making decisions in certain situations such as exercise, illness etc
c) It can make me confident about my child diabetes
d) Unsure

Q11: How often should your child do exercise

a) Once a month for one hour
b) Once a week for one hour
c) Most days for 30 min
d) Unsure

Q12: what you will do if you invited for a party?

a) Feel confident to join while observe my blood sugar and getting my insulin
b) Go to the party, join the food without checking my glucose level
c) Go to the party, join the food without my insulin
d) Do not go

References

1. Gong, B.; Yang, W.; Xing, Y.; Lai, Y.; Shan, Z. Global, regional, and national burden of type 1 diabetes in adolescents and young adults. *Pediatr. Res.* **2024**, 1–9. [CrossRef] [PubMed]
2. Abedi, A.; Colella, T.J.; Pakosh, M.; Khan, S.S. Artificial intelligence-driven virtual rehabilitation for people living in the community: A scoping review. *NPJ Digit. Med.* **2024**, *7*, 25. [CrossRef] [PubMed]
3. Boeijen, J.A.; van de Pol, A.C.; van Uum, R.T.; Venekamp, R.P.; Smit, K.; Kaasjager, K.A.; van den Broek, R.; Zwart, D.L.; Schoonhoven, L.; Rutten, F.H.; et al. Home-based management of hypoxaemic COVID-19 patients: Design of the Therapy@ Home pilot study. *BMJ Open* **2024**, *14*, e079778. [CrossRef] [PubMed]
4. Atlas, D. International diabetes federation. In *IDF Diabetes Atlas*, 7th ed.; International Diabetes Federation: Brussels, Belgium, 2015.
5. Alotaibi, M.; Alnajjar, F.; Alsayed, B.A.; Alhmiedat, T.; Marei, A.M.; Bushnag, A.; Ali, L. An Observational Pilot Study of a Tailored Environmental Monitoring and Alert System for Improved Management of Chronic Respiratory Diseases. *J. Multidiscip. Healthc.* **2023**, *16*, 3799–3811. [CrossRef]

6. Rosner, B.; Roman-Urrestarazu, A. Health-related quality of life in paediatric patients with Type 1 diabetes mellitus using insulin infusion systems. A systematic review and meta-analysis. *PLoS ONE* **2019**, *14*, e0217655. [CrossRef]
7. González-González, C.S.; Violant-Holz, V.; Gil-Iranzo, R.M. Social robots in hospitals: A systematic review. *Appl. Sci.* **2021**, *11*, 5976. [CrossRef]
8. Alhmiedat, T.; Alotaibi, M. Design and evaluation of a personal Robot playing a self-management for Children with obesity. *Electronics* **2022**, *11*, 4000. [CrossRef]
9. Cifuentes, C.A.; Pinto, M.J.; Céspedes, N.; Múnera, M. Social robots in therapy and care. *Curr. Robot. Rep.* **2020**, *1*, 59–74. [CrossRef]
10. Al-Taee, M.A.; Al-Nuaimy, W.; Muhsin, Z.J.; Al-Ataby, A. Robot assistant in management of diabetes in children based on the internet of things. *IEEE Internet Things J.* **2016**, *4*, 437–445. [CrossRef]
11. Al-Taee, M.A.; Kapoor, R.; Garrett, C.; Choudhary, P. Acceptability of robot assistant in management of type 1 diabetes in children. *Diabetes Technol. Ther.* **2016**, *18*, 551–554. [CrossRef]
12. Alhmiedat, T.; Alotaibi, M. Employing Social Robots for Managing Diabetes Among Children: SARA. *Wirel. Pers. Commun.* **2023**, *130*, 449–468. [CrossRef]
13. Blanson Henkemans, O.A.; Hoondert, V.; Schrama-Groot, F.; Looije, R.; Alpay, L.L.; Neerincx, M.A. "I just have diabetes": Children's need for diabetes self-management support and how a social robot can accommodate their needs. *Patient Intell.* **2012**, *4*, 51–61. [CrossRef]
14. Van Der Drift, E.J.; Beun, R.J.; Looije, R.; Blanson Henkemans, O.A., Neerincx, M.A. A remote social robot to motivate and support diabetic children in keeping a diary. In Proceedings of the 2014 ACM/IEEE International Conference on Human-Robot Interaction, Bielefeld, Germany, 3–6 March 2014; pp. 463–470.
15. Cañamero, L.; Lewis, M. Making new "New AI" friends: Designing a social robot for diabetic children from an embodied AI perspective. *Int. J. Soc. Robot.* **2016**, *8*, 523–537. [CrossRef]
16. Kruijff-Korbayová, I.; Oleari, E.; Baroni, I.; Kiefer, B.; Zelati, M.C.; Pozzi, C.; Sanna, A. Effects of off-activity talk in human-robot interaction with diabetic children. In Proceedings of the 23rd IEEE International Symposium on Robot and Human Interactive Communication, Edinburgh, UK, 25–29 August 2014; IEEE: Piscataway, NJ, USA, 2014; pp. 649–654.
17. Robinson, N.L.; Connolly, J.; Hides, L.; Kavanagh, D.J. A social robot to deliver an 8-week intervention for diabetes management: Initial test of feasibility in a hospital clinic. In *International Conference on Social Robotics*; Springer International Publishing: Cham, Switzerland, 2020; pp. 628–639.
18. Sinoo, C.; van Der Pal, S.; Henkemans, O.A.B.; Keizer, A.; Bierman, B.P.; Looije, R.; Neerincx, M.A. Friendship with a robot: Children's perception of similarity between a robot's physical and virtual embodiment that supports diabetes self-management. *Patient Educ. Couns.* **2018**, *101*, 1248–1255. [CrossRef] [PubMed]
19. Looije, R.; Neerincx, M.A.; Peters, J.K.; Henkemans, O.A.B. Integrating robot support functions into varied activities at returning hospital visits: Supporting child's self-management of diabetes. *Int. J. Soc. Robot.* **2016**, *8*, 483–497. [CrossRef]
20. Henkemans, O.A.B.; Bierman, B.P.; Janssen, J.; Looije, R.; Neerincx, M.A.; van Dooren, M.M.; de Vries, J.L.; van der Burg, G.J.; Huisman, S.D. Design and evaluation of a personal robot playing a self-management education game with children with diabetes type 1. *Int. J. Hum.-Comput. Stud.* **2017**, *106*, 63–76. [CrossRef]
21. Pirborj, L.M.; Alnajjar, F.; Mathew, S.; Damseh, R.; Nadimuthu, M.K. A Set of Serious Games Scenarios Based on Pepper Robots as Rehab Standing Frames for Children with Cerebral Palsy. In *International Conference on Social Robotics*; Springer Nature Singapore: Singapore, 2023; pp. 104–119.
22. International Diabetes Federation. *International Standards for Diabetes Education*, 3rd ed.; IDF: Brussels, Belgium, 2009.
23. Castellano, G.; De Carolis, B.; D'Errico, F.; Macchiarulo, N.; Rossano, V. PeppeRecycle: Improving children's attitude toward recycling by playing with a social robot. *Int. J. Soc. Robot.* **2021**, *13*, 97–111. [CrossRef]
24. Beran, T.N.; Ramirez-Serrano, A.; Kuzyk, R.; Fior, M.; Nugent, S. Understanding how children understand robots: Perceived animism in child–robot interaction. *Int. J. Hum.-Comput. Stud.* **2013**, *71*, 699–704. [CrossRef]
25. Li, J.; Cai, Z.; Kennedy, J. Enhancing child-robot interaction with verbal and non-verbal social behaviors. *Int. J. Soc. Robot.* **2019**, *11*, 241–250.
26. Perez-Cruz, P.; Shim, J.K.; Wallin, P. Robots as educators and care coordinators for chronic disease management: A systematic review. *J. Diabetes Sci. Technol.* **2020**, *14*, 221–229.
27. Cardenas, I.; Liu, Y.; Scoglio, C. Impact of social robots on chronic disease management and outcomes: A systematic review and meta-analysis. *Healthcare* **2021**, *9*, 1515.
28. Lee, S.; Simmons, R. Pediatric diabetes demographics: A comprehensive review. *J. Pediatr. Endocrinol. Metab.* **2017**, *24*, 67–82.
29. Johnson, A.; Smith, L. Age distribution in pediatric diabetes and implications for treatment. *Diabetes Res. Clin. Pract.* **2019**, *31*, 128–141.
30. Dhediya, R.; Chadha, M.; Bhattacharya, A.D.; Godbole, S.; Godbole, S. Role of Telemedicine in Diabetes Management. *J. Diabetes Sci. Technol.* **2023**, *17*, 775–781. [CrossRef] [PubMed]
31. Alhmiedat, T. Enhancing autonomy in social robots through a real-time teleoperation system. *Auton. Intell.* **2024**, *7*. [CrossRef]
32. Rakhymbayeva, N.; Amirova, A.; Sandygulova, A. A long-term engagement with a social robot for autism therapy. *Front. Robot. AI* **2021**, *8*, 669972. [CrossRef]

33. Laban, G.; Kappas, A.; Morrison, V.; Cross, E.S. Building long-term human–robot relationships: Examining disclosure, perception and well-being across time. *Int. J. Soc. Robot.* **2024**, *16*, 1–27. [CrossRef]
34. van Otterdijk, M.T.; de Korte, M.W.; van den Berk-Smeekens, I.; Hendrix, J.; van Dongen-Boomsma, M.; Den Boer, J.C.; Buitelaar, J.K.; Lourens, T.; Glennon, J.C.; Barakova, E.I. The effects of long-term child–robot interaction on the attention and the engagement of children with autism. *Robotics* **2020**, *9*, 79. [CrossRef]
35. Ragno, L.; Borboni, A.; Vannetti, F.; Amici, C.; Cusano, N. Application of social robots in healthcare: Review on characteristics, requirements, technical solutions. *Sensors* **2023**, *23*, 6820. [CrossRef]

technologies

MDPI

Article

Virtual Teleoperation System for Mobile Manipulator Robots Focused on Object Transport and Manipulation

Fernando J. Pantusin [1,*], Christian P. Carvajal [2,3], Jessica S. Ortiz [1,*] and Víctor H. Andaluz [1]

[1] Departamento de Eléctrica y Electrónica, Universidad de las Fuerzas Armadas-ESPE, Sangolquí 171103, Ecuador; vhandaluz1@espe.edu.ec
[2] Instituto de Automática (INAUT), Universidad Nacional de San Juan-CONICET, Av. San Martín (Oeste) 1109, San Juan 5402, Argentina; cpcarvajal@inaut.unsj.edu.ar
[3] Centro de Investigación en Ciencias Humanas y de la Educación (CICHE), Facultad de Ingenierías, Ingeniería Industrial, Universidad Tecnológica Indoamérica, Ambato 180103, Ecuador
* Correspondence: fjpantusin@espe.edu.ec (F.J.P.); jsortiz4@espe.edu.ec (J.S.O.)

Abstract: This work describes the development of a tool for the teleoperation of robots. The tool is developed in a virtual environment using the Unity graphics engine. For the development of the application, a kinematic model and a dynamic model of a mobile manipulator are used. The mobile manipulator robot consists of an omnidirectional platform and an anthropomorphic robotic arm with 4 degrees of freedom (4DOF). The model is essential to emulate the movements of the robot and to facilitate the immersion in the virtual environment. In addition, the control algorithms are established and developed in MATLAB 2020 software, which improves the acquisition of knowledge to teleoperate robots and execute tasks of manipulation and transport of objects. This methodology offers a cheaper and safer alternative to real physical systems, as it reduces both the costs and risks associated with using a real robot for training.

Keywords: teleoperation; virtual environment; mobile manipulator; kinematic model; dynamic model

1. Introduction

Service robotics focuses on the development of robotic systems capable of performing a wide range of beneficial tasks in non-industrial environments, including industrial automation applications, with a special focus on interacting with humans to improve their quality of life [1]. With the most recent technological advances, attention has turned not only to meeting human needs, but also to improving comfort and human interaction in various areas of daily life, from the home to hospitals and public spaces [2,3]. Service robotics comprises two main groups, professional and personal use according to the IFR [4]. Among these groups are a number of approaches such as: (i) Transport and logistics:Service robots for logistics fulfil areas of transport, handling, packaging, sorting and delivery of goods in offices, airports, post offices, among others [5]; (ii) Cleaning: where robotic systems are developed for the cleaning of large or crowded areas, most of the commercially available home service robots have been developed with respect to requirements posed exclusively by a specific domestic task such as floor cleaning [2]; (iii) Medicine: providing assistance in surgeries, rehabilitation and patient monitoring, as well as patient transport and orientation tasks, which represents up to 46% of hospital expenses. In addition, virtual AI-based psychotherapeutic devices are used in the field of mental health and for the treatment of diseases that require prolonged observation of the patient that can be managed through online monitoring [6,7]; (iv) Hospitality: focused on entertainment and improving the quality of the human experience; several hotels are even using robots to communicate with guests or perform hotel operations [8]; finally, (v) Agriculture: robotic systems are being developed for outdoor cultivation, improving productivity and reducing farmers' working hours [9]. Resulting in the need to develop more complex robotic systems.

Due to the complexity of the applications and environments in which service robots must be deployed, the need has arisen to create systems with diverse morphologies and the combination of multiple robots to address a variety of tasks [10,11]. However, the acquisition of highly complex systems entails considerable investment, either for their implementation or study. This is further complicated when considering the need to train individuals in the handling of these robots, in addition to requiring the presence of trained supervisors to ensure their correct use and learning by the users. Currently, the most recent technological advances have opened new alternatives in the field of service robotics, facilitating the learning process through innovative approaches, such as virtual environments, programming with LEGO kits and pedagogical systems, with a STEM educational approach focused on service and educational robotics [12], such educational systems allow me to give a hint in the operation of robotics and programming, but their acquisition cost is quite considerable, in addition to its operation in the presence of people or other objects not considered, can become damaged or cause damage. Another disadvantage is that these educational systems cannot handle large weight loads or perform precision tasks, which generate great limitations [13,14].

To facilitate the learning process in situations that seek to replicate reality, various technological tools are available, with simulators being one of the most prominent in virtual robotics education [15,16]. Within this broad set of tools, virtual environments stand out, allowing the creation of immersive environments that simulate real situations [17,18]. These environments benefit from the use of devices such as helmets, gloves, sensors and controls, which are now widely available at the simulation level [19]. This technology has made it possible to develop virtual reality experiences within these environments, which, in addition to reducing costs compared to the use of real equipment and associated resources, provides a level of fail-safety in the learning process that cannot be achieved in a real physical environment [17].

In this context, the present work proposes the development of a teaching-learning system based on virtual environments in the Unity 3D graphics engine using an omnidirectional robot with an anthropomorphic arm controlled by means of MATLAB 2020 software of MathWorks through a communication channel. In order to facilitate the understanding of the various applications of service robotics and the complexity of robot morphologies. This is achieved by considering the mathematical modeling of the robot in question and a haptic device that allows to train users to perform autonomous and teleoperated tasks in an accessible way in an immersive virtual environment which presents different challenges for user understanding [20].

Finally, this article is organized in sections to address these aspects in a structured way. Section 2 presents the methodology needed to carry out this process, with a focus on educational robotics. Section 3 focuses on the mathematical basis required for the modeling and control of the robot. Section 4 is devoted to the development of the virtual environment. Section 5 presents the results obtained, and Section 6 contains the conclusions derived from this study.

2. Methodology and Process Conceptualisation

The challenge in service robotics lies in operating in unstructured environments, which are highly unpredictable and difficult to manage. Creating a completely unstructured system is complicated by the nature of these environments. Therefore, it is essential to have a thorough understanding of the real world so that the assumed foundations are sufficiently flexible and adaptable to the variability of the environment. Although the current development of robotic systems has advanced, it is still far from achieving effective operation in completely unstructured environments with fully autonomous control, therefore, a semi-autonomous control is established through the use of teleoperation of robotic systems, in this context, it is proposed the following work methodology to address this issue.

As can be seen in the scheme above (Figure 1), It starts from service robotics present in the real world and contextualize it using knowledge gained through experience and theoretical background. This allows us to develop a mental model that describes the operation of an omnidirectional robot and provides an understanding of its behavior. Subsequently, we build a formal model based on physical and geometrical principles, resulting in the mathematical model of the mobile manipulator robot contemplated by the mobile platform and the robotic arm, therefore, the model of each of these robots is considered. In addition, depending on the control objective, the independent model of each robot can be used, or a unified model can be established to control the end-effector of the whole robot. In response to the demands of the environment, a robotic process is created that combines the two previously defined systems for the purpose of evaluating the behavior, limitations and constraints of the robotic system.

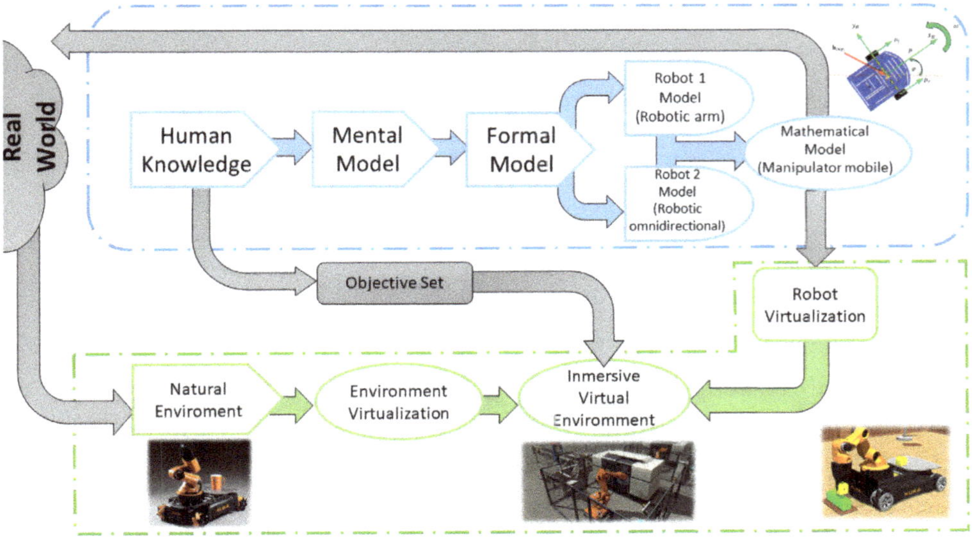

Figure 1. Methodology of the work proposal.

Simultaneously, it creates an environment that adapts to real-world demands and leverages contextualized human knowledge. This environment is designed to host multiple tasks or objectives that require system intervention. Subsequently, we carry out the virtualization of this defined environment through the use of CAD software and graphics engines, with the purpose of familiarizing the user and facilitating clarity in the learning process. A schematic of the conceptualisation process involved is presented in the Figure 2.

Therefore, the virtual system designed in the Unity graphic engine includes a mobile manipulator robot, previously modelled in CAD software, with an environment composed of two predefined scenes, based on external resources of the real robot and for the simulation scenarios. The CAD software used is Solid Works 2019.Through a formal mathematical model, which incorporates the kinematics and dynamics of the robotic system, the animations of the robot's movements are generated by means of scripts integrated in the graphic engine. In addition, control algorithms are developed in MATLAB, which allow the execution of the necessary actions to accomplish the tasks desired by the user. These actions are commanded through the Novint Falcon haptic device, which is connected to the control software. The communication between the control software and the graphics engine is done through a Dynamic-Link Libraries (DLL). Where, MATLAB software sends the control actions to Unity and receives the information from the robot. On the other hand, control actions can also be transmitted to a real robot, using a TCP/IP wireless communication protocol, which allows virtual tasks to be replicated in a physical environment, making it possible to evaluate the controller to remotely control the robot experimentally and also design an autonomous controller for the robot to perform a defined task.

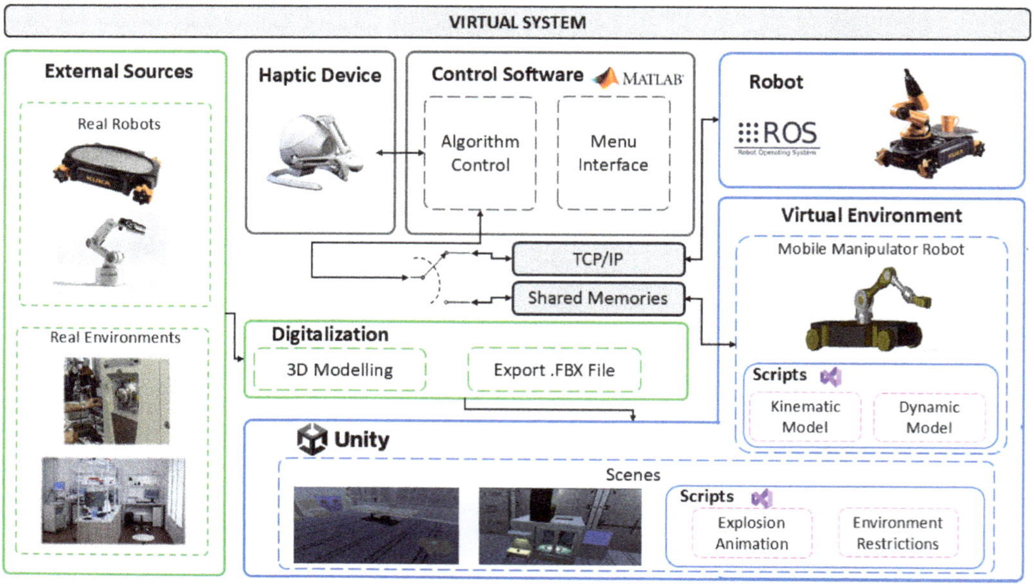

Figure 2. Diagram of the conceptualisation process.

In this way, a virtual environment is created with predefined goals to be achieved by the robotic system driven by a human operator. It can also be used to evaluate autonomous control algorithms for the execution of defined tasks.

3. Modeling and Control

A mobile manipulator robot refers to robots that consist of a robotic arm (also known as a manipulator) mounted on a mobile platform or vehicle. These robots enable tasks to be carried out that require the capability to navigate and manipulate. These systems are characterized by high redundancy.

3.1. Kinematic Model

The kinematics determines the characteristics of motion in the plane or in space of a robot, the kinematics of robots are described here.

3.1.1. Omnidirectional Mobile Robot

The position of the mobile robot is defined in the fixed reference space defined by $\eta(t) = \left[\eta_x(t), \eta_y(t), \psi(t)\right]^T$. The kinematic configuration of the omnidirectional robot can be observed in Figure 3.

Now, it is necessary to obtain the model of the mobile robot as a function of its manoeuvrability velocities. The differential kinematics of the omnidirectional robot is represented by:

$$\begin{aligned} \dot{\eta}_x &= u_l \cos(\psi) - u_m \sin(\psi) \\ \dot{\eta}_y &= u_l \sin(\psi) + u_m \cos(\psi) \\ \dot{\eta}_\psi &= \omega \end{aligned} \quad (1)$$

written in matrix form (1) results:

$$\dot{\eta}(t) = \mathbf{J_P}(\psi)\mathbf{u}(t) \quad (2)$$

with $\dot{\eta}(t) = \left[\dot{\eta}_x, \dot{\eta}_y, \dot{\psi}\right]^T$ which represents the velocity vector of the point of interest with respect to the inertial reference system $\{R\}$; $\mathbf{J_P}(\psi) \in \Re^{3\times3}$ is the Jacobian matrix that represents the motion characteristics of the omnidirectional robot; and $\mathbf{u}(t) \in \Re^3$ is the manoeuvrability vector of the omnidirectional robot with respect to $\{R_P\}$ [21].

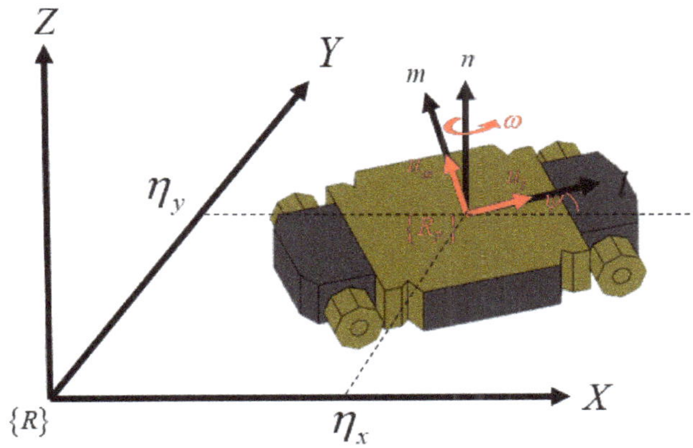

Figure 3. Omnidirectional Robot Kinematic.

3.1.2. Robotic Arm

The position of the robotic arm in the fixed workspace $\{R_B\}$ is defined in terms of its independent articulations, so that it $\mathbf{h}(t) = f(\mathbf{q_a})$, where the vector of independent coordinates is $\mathbf{q_a}(t) = \begin{bmatrix} q_{a1} & q_{a2} & \ldots & q_{an_a} \end{bmatrix}$. The configuration of the robotic arm can be observed in Figure 4.

Now, taking the fixed reference system $\{R_B\}$; and the number of independent arm joints is four, i.e., a 4DOF anthropomorphic robotic arm, (see Figure 4). The position and orientation of the robotic arm is determined:

$$\mathbf{h}(t) = \begin{cases} h_r(t) = l_2 S_{q2} C_{q1} + l_3 S_{q2q3} C_{q1} + l_4 S_{q2q3q4} C_{q1} \\ h_s(t) = l_2 S_{q2} S_{q1} + l_3 S_{q2q3} S_{q1} + l_4 S_{q2q3q4} S_{q1} \\ h_t(t) = l_1 + l_2 C_{q2} + l_3 C_{q2q3} + l_4 C_{q2q3q4} \end{cases} \tag{3}$$

where, the expressions in (3) represent: $S_a = \sin(a)$; $C_a = \cos(a)$; $S_{ab..n} = \sin(a + b + \ldots + n)$; and $C_{ab..n} = \cos(a + b + \ldots + n)$.

Now, the model of the arm as a function of its velocities is obtained through the partial derivative of $f(\mathbf{q_a})$ in relation to $\mathbf{q_a}$, where is obtained the differential kinematics of the robot described in matrix form as:

$$\dot{\mathbf{h}}(t) = \mathbf{J_a}(\mathbf{q_a}(t))\dot{\mathbf{q}}_\mathbf{a}(t) \tag{4}$$

where, $\dot{\mathbf{q}}_\mathbf{a}$ is the joint velocity vector of the robotic arm joints; $\dot{\mathbf{h}}(t) = \left[\dot{h}_x(t), \dot{h}_y(t), \dot{h}_z(t)\right]^T$ is the vector of arm end-effector velocities in workspace; and $\mathbf{J_a}(\mathbf{q_a}) \in \Re^{3\times4}$ is the Jacobian of the robotic arm that transforms the manoeuvring velocities of the arm to the velocities of the end-effector.

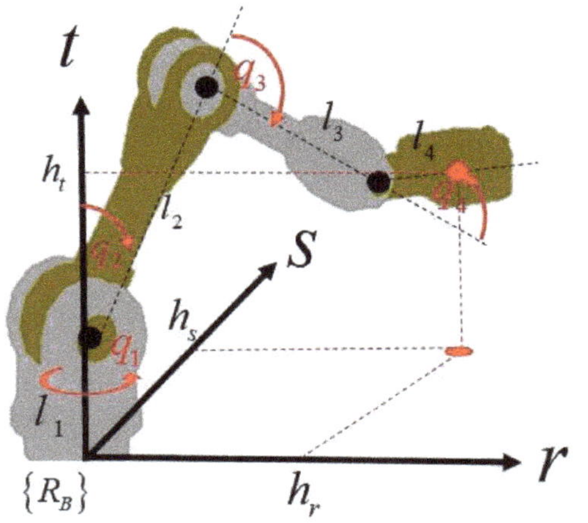

Figure 4. Kinematic of Robotic Arm.

3.1.3. Omnidirectional Mobile Manipulator

The mobile manipulator robot considered in this work consists of a robotic arm located on a mobile robot with omnidirectional traction. The configuration of the mobile manipulator robot is known when the position and orientation of all its points with respect to an inertial reference system is known $R(X,Y,Z)$. The kinematic configuration of the robot can be seen in Figure 5.

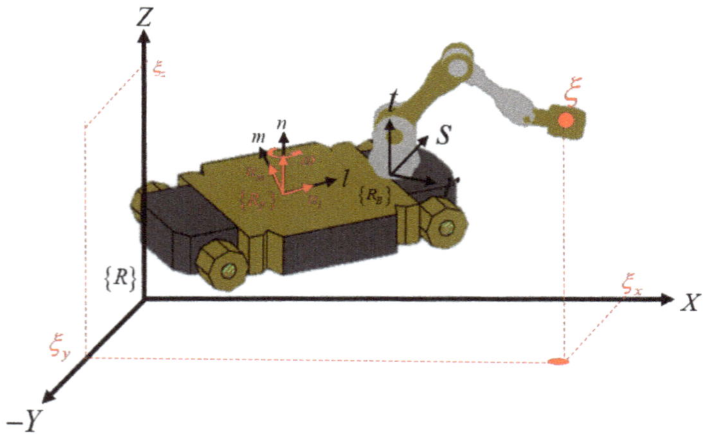

Figure 5. Mobile Robot Kinematic.

The direct kinematics of the mobile manipulator robot defines the position and location of the end-effector. $\xi(t)$ as a function of the configuration of the robotic arm and the mobile robot with omnidirectional traction $\xi(t) = f(\mathbf{q_p}, \mathbf{q_a})$;

$$\xi(t) = \eta(t) + R_z(\psi)\begin{bmatrix} a \\ b \\ 0 \end{bmatrix} + \mathbf{h_a}(\mathbf{q_a}, \psi) \tag{5}$$

where, $\eta(t) = [\eta_x(t), \eta_y(t), \eta_P(t)]^T$ represents the position of the omnirectional robot relative to the inertial reference frame $R(X,Y,Z)$; $\eta_x(t)$ y $\eta_y(t)$ are the positions on the axes X, Y, while η_P represents the height of the mobile robot with respect to Z; a y b represent the distance of the robotic arm location from the moving reference system located at the center of gravity of the omnidirectional robot $\{R_P\}$; $R_z(\psi)$ represents the rotation matrix with respect to the Z-axis of the reference system $R(X, Y, Z)$; and $\mathbf{h}(\mathbf{q}, \psi)$ considers the position of the robotic arm with respect to the position and orientation of the omnidirectional robot, i.e.,

$$\mathbf{h_a}(\mathbf{q_a}, \psi) = \begin{bmatrix} C_{q1\psi}(l_2 S_{q2} + l_3 S_{q2q3} + l_4 S_{q2q3q4}) \\ S_{q1\psi}(l_2 S_q 2 + l_3 S_{q2q3} + l_4 S_{q2q3q4}) \\ \eta_P + l_1 + l_2 C_{q2} + l_3 C_{q2q3} + l_4 C_{q2q3q4} \end{bmatrix} \quad (6)$$

Considering Equations (6) and the position of the mobile robot in (5), the direct kinematics of the mobile manipulator robot can be represented as:

$$\xi(t) = \begin{cases} \xi_x(t) = \eta_x + aC_\psi - bS_\psi + C_{q1\psi}(l_2 S_{q2} + l_3 S_{q2q3} + l_4 S_{q2q3q4}) \\ \xi_y(t) = \eta_y + aS_\psi + bC_\psi + S_{q1\psi}(l_2 S_{q2} + l_3 S_{q2q3} + l_4 S_{q2q3q4}) \\ \xi_z(t) = \eta_P + l_1 + l_2 C_{q2} + l_3 C_{q2q3} + l_4 C_{q2q3q4} \end{cases} \quad (7)$$

Finally, the differential kinematic model of the mobile manipulator robot establishes the derivative of the end-effector location as a function of the derivative of the configuration of the robotic arm and the omnidirectional robot, i.e., $\dot{\xi}(t) = \frac{d}{dt}\xi(t)$. As a result, it follows that:

$$\dot{\xi}(t) = \begin{cases} \dot{\xi}_x = u_l C_\psi - u_m S_\psi - aS_\psi - bC_\psi - (l_2 S_{q1\psi} C_{q2} + l_3 S_{q1\psi} C_{q2q3} + l_4 S_{q1\psi} C_{q2q3q4})\dot{q}_1 + \dots \\ (l_2 C_{q1\psi} S_{q2} + l_3 C_{q1\psi} S_{q2q3} + l_4 C_{q1} S_{q2q3q4})\dot{q}_2 + (l_4 C_{q1\psi} S_{q2q3q4})\dot{q}_4 + \dots \\ (l_3 C_{q1\psi} S_{q2q3} + l_4 C_{q1\psi} S_{q2q3q4})\dot{q}_3 \\ \dot{\xi}_y = u_l S_\psi + u_m C_\psi + aC_\psi - bS_\psi - (l_2 C_{q1\psi} C_{q2} + l_3 C_{q1\psi} C_{q2q3} + l_4 C_{q1\psi} C_{q2q3q4})\dot{q}_1 + \dots \\ (l_2 S_{q1\psi} S_{q2} + l_3 S_{q1\psi} S_{q2q3} + l_4 S_{q1} S_{q2q3q4})\dot{q}_2 + + (l_4 S_{q1\psi} S_{q2q3q4})\dot{q}_4 + \dots \\ (l_3 S_{q1\psi} S_{q2q3} + l_4 S_{q1\psi} S_{q2q3q4})\dot{q}_3 \\ \dot{\xi}_z = (l_2 C_{q2} + l_3 C_{q2q3} + l_4 C_{2q3q4})\dot{q}_2 + (l_3 C_{q2q3} + l_4 C_{q2q3q4})\dot{q}_3 + (l_4 C_{q2q3q4})\dot{q}_4 \end{cases} \quad (8)$$

The differential kinematic model (8) of the robot is written in matrix form:

$$\dot{\xi}(t) = \mathbf{J}(\mathbf{q})\mathbf{v}(t) \quad (9)$$

where, $\mathbf{J}(\mathbf{q}) \in \Re^{3\times7}$ represents the Jacobin matrix of the mobile manipulator robot, which defines a linear mapping between the joint velocity vector defined by $\mathbf{v}(t) = [u_l, u_m, \omega, \dot{q}_1, \dot{q}_2, \dot{q}_3, \dot{q}_4] \in R^7$ and the end-effector velocity vector $\dot{\xi}(t) = [\dot{\xi}_x, \dot{\xi}_y, \dot{\xi}_z] \in \Re^3$. The Jacobian matrix $\mathbf{J}(\mathbf{q}) \in \Re^{3\times7}$ is a non-square matrix where the number of rows is less than the number of columns; therefore, the mobile manipulator robot is a redundant system.

3.2. Control

The teleoperation scheme allows to command any robot over long distances, i.e., it allows to operate the robot to perform a specific task by the human operator (Figure 6). The defined task usually consists of several operation processes, and these commonly include three stages: (i) approach; (ii) manipulation, and (iii) return process. When the mission is initiated, the human operator must move the mobile robot manipulator close to the object, the robotic arm should be considered to be within its working space. Once the mobile robot reaches the proximity of the target object, the human operator switches the locomotion mode to manipulation mode (control of the robotic arm). When the manipulation mission is completed, the human operator switches the manipulation mode back to locomotion mode and the mobile manipulator robot shall return to a safe area. To accomplish this task, the teleoperation scheme proposed for this work is presented in Figure 7.

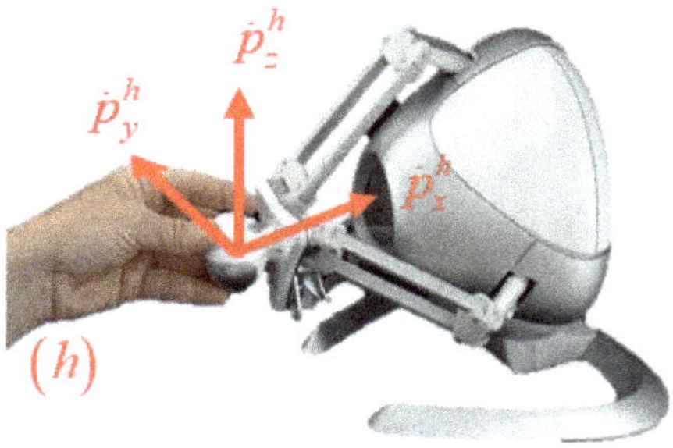

Figure 6. Human operator with haptic device.

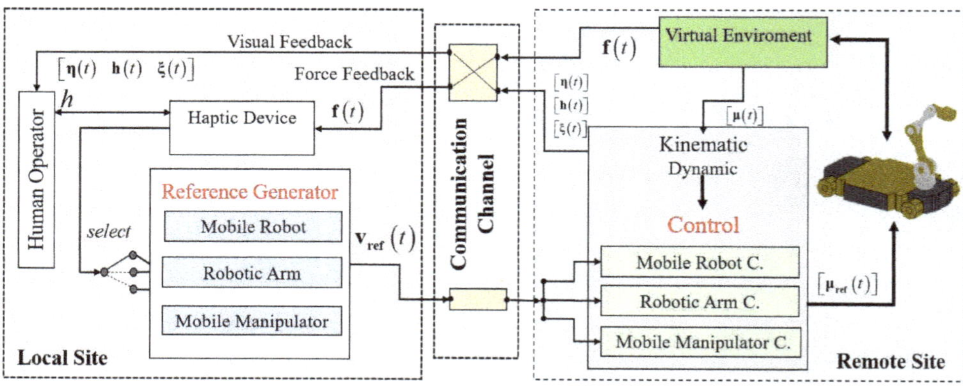

Figure 7. Teleoperation schematic for the mobile manipulator robot.

3.2.1. Local Site

The proposed scheme allows the generation of reference commands for each robot depending on the task selected by the human operator (h). The reference vectors generated by the human operator are $\dot{\eta}^h_{\text{ref}}(t)$, $\dot{\mathbf{h}}^h_{\text{ref}}(t)$ y $\dot{\xi}^h_{\text{ref}}(t)$; such that, each reference is dependent on the haptic device, i.e., $\left(\dot{\eta}^h_{\text{ref}}(t), \dot{\mathbf{h}}^h_{\text{ref}}(t), \dot{\xi}^h_{\text{ref}}(t)\right) = f\left(\dot{\mathbf{p}}^h_{\text{ref}}(t)\right)$, where $\dot{\mathbf{p}}^h_{\text{ref}}(t)$ is the direct reference that the haptic device generates at each instant (t) when excited by the human operator (h), and is defined by:

$$\dot{\mathbf{p}}^h_{\text{ref}}(t) = \begin{bmatrix} \dot{p}^h_x(t) \\ \dot{p}^h_y(t) \\ \dot{p}^h_z(t) \end{bmatrix} \tag{10}$$

3.2.2. Locomotion

The human operator can select: (i) to control only the omnidirectional mobile robot, (ii) to control the total mobile manipulator robot. For both locomotion cases the commands generated by the human operator through the haptic device shall correspond to velocity commands.

(i) Omnidirectional Robot (Reference Generation). This mode allows only the omnidirectional robot to be controlled. For this, the human operator (h) commands the point of interest of the omnidirectional robot by the haptic device. Therefore, the velocity reference for the robot is obtained through the differential kinematics of the mobile robot (2), such that:

$$\dot{\eta}^h_{\text{ref}} = \mathbf{J}_{\mathbf{P}}(\psi)\mathbf{u}^h_{\text{ref}}(t) \tag{11}$$

Remark 1. *In this case the reference $\dot{p}_z^h$ is not translated to linear velocity but to rotational velocity of the robot since the omnidirectional robot only moves in the XY-plane and rotates around the $\dot{p}_z^h$-axis of the fixed reference system.*

(ii) Mobile Manipulator Robot (Reference Generation). Now, in this mode the operator commands the entire mobile manipulator robot, i.e., he controls the end-effector by the haptic device. Considering the human operator's reference vector $\dot{\mathbf{p}}^h_{\mathbf{ref}}(t) \in R^3$, the reference generator considers the mapping of these velocities generated by the human operator as follows:

$$\dot{\xi}^h_{\mathbf{ref}}(t) = \mathbf{R}(\psi, q_1)\dot{\mathbf{p}}^h_{\mathbf{ref}}(t) \tag{12}$$

where, $\dot{\xi}^h_{\mathbf{ref}}(t) \in \Re^3$ is the reference velocity of the end-effector of the mobile manipulator robot; and $\mathbf{R}(\psi, q_1) : \dot{\mathbf{p}}^h_{\mathbf{ref}}(t) \rightarrow \dot{\xi}^h_{\mathbf{ref}}(t)$ is a matrix of that maps the velocities generated by (h) at the reference velocities of the operational point of the robot.

3.2.3. Manipulation

(i) Robotic Arm (Reference Generator). In this mode the human operator (h) controls only the robotic arm; for which, the commands generated by (h) through the haptic device $\dot{\mathbf{p}}^h_{\mathbf{ref}}(t)$ will correspond to position commands of the end-effector of the robotic arm. $\dot{\mathbf{h}}^h_{\mathbf{ref}}(t) \in \Re^3$. The same expression of (12) is considered, however, taking into account that for this the reference velocities generated by (h) are limited according to the manipulability of the robotic arm, so that:

$$\dot{\mathbf{h}}^h_{\mathbf{ref}}(t) = \mathbf{s_{at}}\dot{\mathbf{p}}^h_{\mathbf{ref}}(t) \quad \mathbf{s_{at}} = \begin{cases} \mathbf{0}_{3\times3} & w \leq \lambda \\ \mathbf{I}_{3\times3} & w > \lambda \end{cases} \tag{13}$$

where $w = \sqrt{\det\left(\mathbf{J_a}\mathbf{J_a}^T\right)}$, is the manipulability index [22]; and $\lambda \in \Re^+$ is a real value we define the minimum manipulability for the robotic arm such that $\lambda > 0$.

3.2.4. Remote Site

The remote station considers the implementation of control algorithms that consider the signals generated by the human operator (h), through the haptic device. $\dot{\mathbf{p}}^h_{\mathbf{ref}}(t)$, and convert them into signals for the mobile manipulator robot, according to the mode of operation selected by the operator (h). Therefore, each controller generates the vector of manoeuvrability velocities of the robot $\mathbf{v_{ref}}(t)$. It is defined by:

$$\mathbf{v_{ref}}(t) = \begin{bmatrix} \mathbf{u_{ref}}(t) \\ \mathbf{q_{a_{ref}}}(t) \end{bmatrix} = \begin{bmatrix} u_{l_{ref}} & u_{m_{ref}} & \omega_{ref} & \dot{q}_{1_{ref}} & \dot{q}_{2_{ref}} & \dot{q}_{3_{ref}} & \dot{q}_{4_{ref}} \end{bmatrix}^T \tag{14}$$

(i) Kinematic Control of Omnidirectional Mobile Robot. The kinematic model of Equation (2) is considered, therefore, the proposed control law for the omnidirectional robot is:

$$\mathbf{u_{ref}}(t) = \mathbf{J_P}^{-1}(\psi)\left(\dot{\eta}^h_{\mathbf{ref}}(t) + \mathbf{K_p}\tanh(\tilde{\dot{\eta}}(t))\right) \tag{15}$$

where, $\dot{\eta}^h_{\mathbf{ref}}(t)$ represents the desired velocity generated by the human operator (h) through the haptic device; $\mathbf{J_P}^{-1}(\psi)$ represents the Jacobian matrix of the behaviour of the omnidirectional robot; $\mathbf{K_p} \in \Re^{3\times3}$ is the gain matrix that weights the velocity errors of the local controller of the omnidirectional robot; and $\mathbf{u_{ref}}(t)$ represent the manoeuvrability velocities of the omnidirectional robot. The motion control error of the omnidirectional robot can be defined as the difference between the commands generated by human operator and the motion velocity of the omnidirectional robot, i.e:

$$\tilde{\dot{\eta}}(t) = \dot{\eta}^h_{\mathbf{ref}}(t) - \dot{\eta}(t) \tag{16}$$

As the operator generates commands only for the mobile robot, then the robotic arm should remain in a fixed position, therefore a control law is defined to keep the robotic arm static during the locomotion task. Let be the desired position of the arm end-effector with respect to the reference frame of the mobile robot $\mathbf{h_d}(t) = [h_{xd}, h_{xd}, h_{xd}]^T$. The controller that generates the reference velocities of the robotic arm joints is given by:

$$\dot{\mathbf{q}}_{\mathbf{a}_{\mathbf{ref}}}(t) = \mathbf{J_a}^{\#}\mathbf{K_a}\tanh(\tilde{\mathbf{h}}_{\mathbf{a}}(t)) + \left(\mathbf{I} - \mathbf{J_a}^{\#}\mathbf{J_a}\right)\mathbf{H}\tanh(\chi) \tag{17}$$

where, $\mathbf{K_a} \in \Re^{3\times3}$ is a positive diagonal matrix weighing the control error $\tilde{\mathbf{h}}_{\mathbf{a}}(t) = \mathbf{h_d}(t) - \mathbf{h_a}(t)$; $\mathbf{H} \in \Re^{4\times4}$ is a positive diagonal matrix weighing the error of the desired configuration of the robotic arm $\chi = [\tilde{q}_1, \tilde{q}_3, \tilde{q}_3, \tilde{q}_4]^T$. As the Jacobian of the arm has more columns than rows, the controller is based on secondary objectives as it has several degrees of freedom; and $\mathbf{J_a}^{\#}$ is the pseudo-inverse matrix of the robotic arm.

(ii) Robotic Arm Kinematic Control. The position control of the end-effector position of the robotic arm, the kinematic model defined in Equation (4) is considered; therefore, the proposed control law is:

$$\dot{\mathbf{q}}_{\mathbf{aref}}(t) = \mathbf{J}_{\mathbf{a}}^{\#}\left(\dot{\mathbf{h}}^h_{\mathbf{ref}} + \mathbf{K_a}\tanh(\tilde{\mathbf{h}}_{\mathbf{a}}(t))\right) + \left(\mathbf{I} - \mathbf{J}_{\mathbf{a}}^{\#}\mathbf{J_a}\right)\mathbf{H}\tanh(\chi) \tag{18}$$

where, $\mathbf{J}_{\mathbf{a}}^{\#}(\mathbf{q_a}) = \mathbf{J}_{\mathbf{a}}^{T}(\mathbf{J_a}\mathbf{J}_{\mathbf{a}}^{T})^{-1}$ is the pseudo-inverse matrix of the robotic arm; $\mathbf{h}^h_{\mathbf{ref}}(t) = \int_{t_0}^{t_f}\dot{\mathbf{h}}^h_{\mathbf{ref}}(\tau)$ represents the desired position of the end-effector of the robotic arm; $\dot{\mathbf{h}}^h_{\mathbf{ref}}(t)$ is the desired velocity generated by the operator (h); $\tilde{\mathbf{h}}_{\mathbf{a}}(t) = \mathbf{h}^h_{\mathbf{ref}}(t) - \mathbf{h_a}(t)$ represents the error vector of the position of the robotic arm; $\mathbf{h_a}(t)$ represents the actual position of the end-effector of the robotic arm. Finally, in this case, the omnidirectional mobile robot maintains its position, i.e., it does not make any movement $\dot{\eta}^h_{\mathbf{ref}}(t) = \mathbf{0}_3$, therefore, the reference velocity in this case is:

$$\mathbf{u}_{\mathbf{ref}}(t) = \begin{bmatrix} 0 & 0 & 0 \end{bmatrix}^T \tag{19}$$

(iii) Kinematic Control of the Mobile Manipulator Robot. Similarly, the kinematic model of Equation (9) is considered, therefore, the proposed control law is:

$$\mathbf{v}_{\mathbf{ref}}(t) = \mathbf{J}^{\#}\left(\dot{\xi}^h_{\mathbf{ref}}(t) + \mathbf{K_1}\tanh\left(\dot{\tilde{\xi}}(t)\right)\right) + \left(\mathbf{I}_{7\times7} - \mathbf{J}^{\#}\mathbf{J}\right)\mathbf{K_2}\tanh(\zeta) \tag{20}$$

where, $\mathbf{v}_{\mathbf{ref}}(t) \in \Re^7$ represent the manoeuvrability velocities of the mobile manipulator robot; $\dot{\xi}^h_{\mathbf{ref}}(t)$ represents the desired velocity of the end-effector of the mobile manipulator robot generated by the human operator (h) through the haptic device; $\mathbf{J}^{\#}(\psi, \mathbf{q}_a) = \mathbf{J}^T(\mathbf{J}\mathbf{J}^T)^{-1}$ is the pseudo-inverse matrix of the mobile manipulator robot; $\mathbf{K_1} \in \Re^3$; $\mathbf{K_2} \in \Re^{7\times7}$ are positive diagonal matrices weighing the robot end-effector position control error and the secondary target control vector errors respectively. The motion control error of the mobile manipulator robot is defined as the difference between the commands generated by the human operator and the motion velocity of the end-effector of the mobile manipulator robot, such that:

$$\dot{\tilde{\xi}}(t) = \dot{\xi}^h_{\mathbf{ref}}(t) - \xi(t) \tag{21}$$

For this work, the configuration of the robotic arm is considered as secondary objectives, therefore, the secondary objective vector is defined as:

$$\zeta(t) = \begin{bmatrix} 0 & 0 & 0 & q_{1d} - q_1 & q_{2d} - q_2 & q_{3d} - q_3 & q_{4d} - q_4 \end{bmatrix}^T \tag{22}$$

where, q_{id} con $i = 1, 2, 3, 4$ represents the desired position of each joint of the robotic arm; and q_i is the current position of each joint of the robotic arm.

3.3. Dynamic of the Robots

To emulate the behaviour of the robot with its dynamic characteristics. In this section the models of the omnidirectional robot and the robotic arm are defined. Therefore, the robot in the 3D virtual environment allows to replicate the real system behaviour as close to real as possible. With this we simulate in real time the physical performance of the robot. This methodology is a tool that provides a safe and ideal environment for the validation of control techniques in the development of prototypes and for educational purposes for handling robotic prototypes. Figure 8 shows the interpretation of the virtual robot.

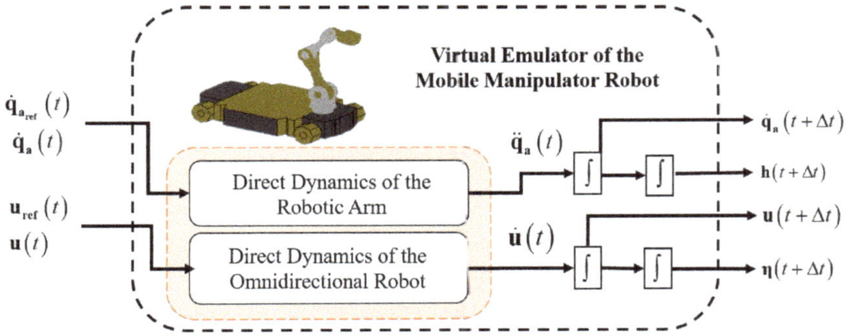

Figure 8. Virtual emulator of the mobile manipulator robot scheme.

3.3.1. Direct Dynamics of the Omnidirectional Robot

The dynamic model is a mathematical formulation that describes the dynamic behaviour of a system. It establishes the relationships between the robot's joint coordinates or coordinates of interest, velocities, accelerations, forces and torques applied at its joints and the robot's parameters, such as masses and moments of inertia. The model used in this work is a simplified [23] model, this model is represented in terms of reference velocities, because it is easier to apply velocities than torques, as in traditional robot models. Therefore, to emulate the dynamics of the robot, the direct dynamic model of the robot is used. For this purpose, the inverse dynamic model $\mathbf{u}^{\mathbf{d}}_{\mathbf{ref}}(t) = \mathbf{M}(\sigma)\dot{\mathbf{u}}(t) + \mathbf{C}(\sigma,\omega)\mathbf{u}(t)$ is used. Now, the direct dynamic model used in this work is defined by:

$$\dot{\mathbf{u}}(t) = \mathbf{A_P}(\sigma)\mathbf{u}_{\mathbf{ref}}(t) + \mathbf{B_P}(\sigma,\omega)\mathbf{u}(t) \tag{23}$$

where, $\mathbf{u}_{\mathbf{ref}}(t) \in \Re^3$ is the reference velocity vector of the omnidirectional robot; $\dot{\mathbf{u}}(t) = \begin{bmatrix} \dot{u}_l & \dot{u}_m & \dot{\omega} \end{bmatrix}^T \in \Re^3$ is the vector of accelerations of the omnidirectional robot obtained from the direct dynamics; $\mathbf{u}(t) \in \Re^3$ is the actual velocity vector of the robot; $\mathbf{A_P}(\sigma) = \mathbf{M}(\sigma)^{-1}$; $\mathbf{B_P}(\sigma,\omega) = -\mathbf{M}(\sigma)^{-1}\mathbf{C}(\sigma,\omega)$. The matrix $\mathbf{M}(\sigma) \in \Re^{3\times3}$ is the mass matrix of the robot, is square and positive definite; and $\mathbf{C}(\sigma,\omega) \in \Re^{3\times3}$ is a quadratic matrix representing the centripetal and coriolis forces of the robot. The matrices are given by:

$$\mathbf{M}(\sigma) = diag([\sigma_1,\sigma_2,\sigma_3]) \quad \mathbf{C}(\sigma,\omega) = \begin{bmatrix} \sigma_4 & -\omega\sigma_5 & 0 \\ \omega\sigma_6 & \sigma_7 & 0 \\ 0 & 0 & \sigma_8 \end{bmatrix} \tag{24}$$

where, $\sigma = [\sigma_1,\sigma_2,\ldots\delta_8]^T$ is the vector of the dynamic parameters of the omnidirectional robot.

3.3.2. Direct Dynamics of the Robotic Arm

Similar to the omnidirectional robot, the dynamic model used in this work is represented in terms of reference velocities and not in terms of forces and torques. That is to say, the structure of the dynamic model is given by $\dot{\mathbf{q}}_{\mathbf{a}_{ref}}(t) = \mathbf{M_a}(\delta)\ddot{\mathbf{q}}_{\mathbf{a}}(t) + \mathbf{C_a}(\delta, \dot{\mathbf{q}}_{\mathbf{a}})\dot{\mathbf{q}}_{\mathbf{a}}(t) + \mathbf{g}(\delta)$. Where, $\ddot{\mathbf{q}}_{\mathbf{a}}(t) = [\ddot{q}_1, \ddot{q}_2, \ddot{q}_3, \ddot{q}_4]^T$ is the vector of accelerations of the robotic arm; $\mathbf{M_a}(\delta) \in \Re^{4\times4}$ is the mass and inertia matrix of the robotic arm; $\mathbf{C_a}(\delta, \dot{\mathbf{q}}_{\mathbf{a}}) \in \Re^{4\times4}$ is the matrix of centripetal and coriolis forces; y $\mathbf{g_a}(\delta) \in \Re^4$ is the gravity vector.

$$\begin{array}{ll} \mathbf{M_a}(\delta) = \begin{bmatrix} m_{11}(\delta) & m_{12}(\delta) & m_{13}(\delta) & m_{14}(\delta) \\ m_{21}(\delta) & m_{22}(\delta) & m_{23}(\delta) & m_{24}(\delta) \\ m_{31}(\delta) & m_{32}(\delta) & m_{33}(\delta) & m_{34}(\delta) \\ m_{41}(\delta) & m_{42}(\delta) & m_{43}(\delta) & m_{44}(\delta) \end{bmatrix} & \mathbf{g_a}(\delta) = \begin{bmatrix} g_1(\delta) \\ g_2(\delta) \\ g_3(\delta) \\ g_4(\delta) \end{bmatrix} \\ \mathbf{C_a}(\delta, \dot{\mathbf{q}}_{\mathbf{a}}) = \begin{bmatrix} c_{11}(\delta, \dot{\mathbf{q}}_{\mathbf{a}}) & c_{12}(\delta, \dot{\mathbf{q}}_{\mathbf{a}}) & c_{13}(\delta, \dot{\mathbf{q}}_{\mathbf{a}}) & c_{14}(\delta, \dot{\mathbf{q}}_{\mathbf{a}}) \\ c_{21}(\delta, \dot{\mathbf{q}}_{\mathbf{a}}) & c_{22}(\delta, \dot{\mathbf{q}}_{\mathbf{a}}) & c_{23}(\delta, \dot{\mathbf{q}}_{\mathbf{a}}) & c_{24}(\delta, \dot{\mathbf{q}}_{\mathbf{a}}) \\ c_{31}(\delta, \dot{\mathbf{q}}_{\mathbf{a}}) & c_{32}(\delta, \dot{\mathbf{q}}_{\mathbf{a}}) & c_{33}(\delta, \dot{\mathbf{q}}_{\mathbf{a}}) & c_{34}(\delta, \dot{\mathbf{q}}_{\mathbf{a}}) \\ c_{41}(\delta, \dot{\mathbf{q}}_{\mathbf{a}}) & c_{42}(\delta, \dot{\mathbf{q}}_{\mathbf{a}}) & c_{43}(\delta, \dot{\mathbf{q}}_{\mathbf{a}}) & c_{44}(\delta, \dot{\mathbf{q}}_{\mathbf{a}}) \end{bmatrix} & \end{array} \quad (25)$$

where, $\delta = [\delta_1, \delta_2, \ldots \delta_n]^T$ is the vector of dynamic parameters of the robotic arm. Finally, to emulate the robotic arm, the direct dynamics defined by:

$$\ddot{\mathbf{q}}_{\mathbf{a}}(t) = \mathbf{A_a}(\delta)\dot{\mathbf{q}}_{\mathbf{a}_{ref}}(t) + \mathbf{B_a}(\delta, \dot{\mathbf{q}}_{\mathbf{a}})\dot{\mathbf{q}}_{\mathbf{a}}(t) + \mathbf{C_a}(\delta) \quad (26)$$

where, $\mathbf{A_a}(\delta) = \mathbf{M_a}(\delta)^{-1}$; $\mathbf{B_a}(\delta, \dot{\mathbf{q}}_{\mathbf{a}}) = -\mathbf{M_a}(\delta)^{-1}\mathbf{C_a}(\delta, \dot{\mathbf{q}}_{\mathbf{a}})$; y $\mathbf{C_a}(\delta) = -\mathbf{M_a}(\delta)^{-1}\mathbf{g}(\delta)$.

4. Virtual Environment

This section presents the development of an immersive environment, a 3D virtual environment is developed in the Unity 3D graphics engine to simulate the teleoperation tasks of a mobile manipulator robot in two completely different scenes. The virtual environment is focused on teaching and learning in the area of robotics, so it allows interaction with different users. To do this, in the first instance, the virtualisation of the 4 DOF robotic arm and the omnidirectional robot is carried out, to subsequently place them in 2 environments where the tasks demanded by the user are carried out through a means of communication between the operator and the virtual environment.

4.1. Virtualization of the Mobile Manipulator Robot

In order to carry out the digitalization process of the mobile manipulator robot, it is necessary to take external resources as a reference. As shown in the diagram above (Figure 9), a 4 DOF robot arm is used for the manipulation of an object in question, while a KUKA omnidirectional robot is used as a reference for the movement of the robot [24]. Then, using CAD software, a 3D solid object is modelled for each of the robots, with the necessary physics for their respective movements and constraints in order to develop the required animation. Once the CAD design of the two robots has been completed, it is exported to Autodesk 3DS-Max 2024 software, which allows the design to be rendered, dimension and rotation changes to be made, and exported in the format required for the graphics engine. In addition, the rotation axes of each joint of the robotic arm are configured and the centre of the axis of the mobile robot is established during the animation phase. At this stage, the movement of each joint and of the platform is checked to ensure that it matches the axes of movement of the real robots. Each component of the robot can then be exported separately to the graphics engine, as each part has its own animation and movement, determined by the kinematic and dynamic model through script programming.

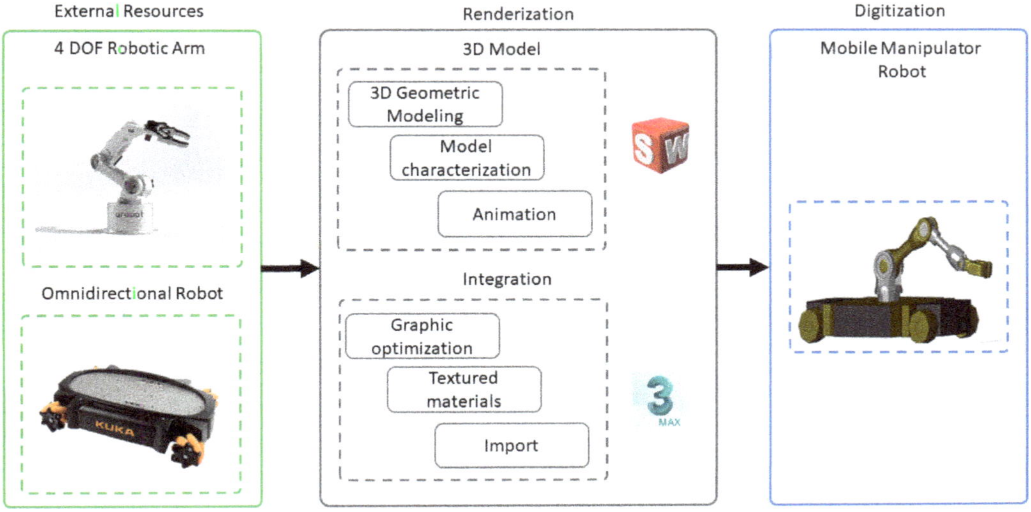

Figure 9. 4 DOF Robotic Arm and Omnidirectional Robot Virtualization.

4.2. Scenario Virtualization

For the development of each scenario, it is essential to identify the places that will be used for the creation of the environment. In this case, the project has focused on two scenes in which dangerous objects are handled. To do this, an exhaustive analysis of the objects that make up the scenarios in a real environment is carried out (view Figure 10).

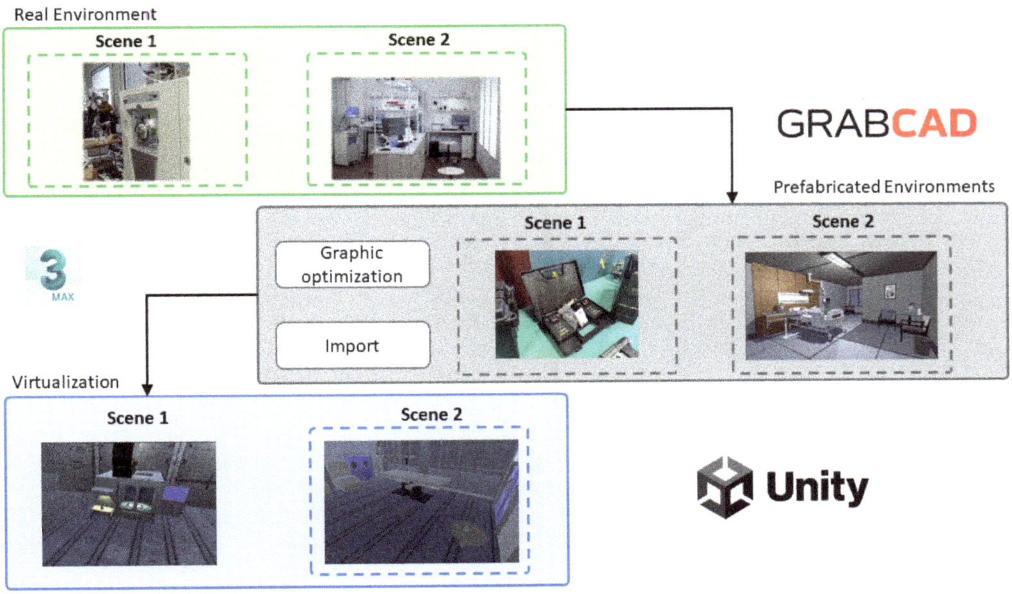

Figure 10. Virtual Environment Digization.

For the development of the virtual environment, The use of prefabricated scenarios that provide a high degree of realism in the objects present in the real environment. This approach facilitates the creation of the virtual scenes and allows for a more efficient development process. Since the main objective of the project is the teaching and learning of service robotics and robot morphology. The use of these prefabricated designs ensures an accurate and functional representation of the different scenarios.

Once the prefabricated scenarios and objects have been selected, we proceed to render the scenes, adjusting to the scale and dimensions of the robot as necessary. For this purpose, 3DS Max software is used, which acts as a link between the prefabricated design and the Unity graphics engine.

Once the export and rendering of the prefabricated scenarios in the Unity graphic engine is completed, we proceed to add the attributes, materials and physical properties to each of the elements present. In this project, two main scenarios have been developed. The first is an environment dedicated to the handling of explosives, where a grenade has been placed near a machine; in this case, the object of interest is the bomb. The second scenario represents a laboratory for handling chemicals, with a flask filled with an explosive liquid as the main object, as shown in the graphic above (Figure 11).

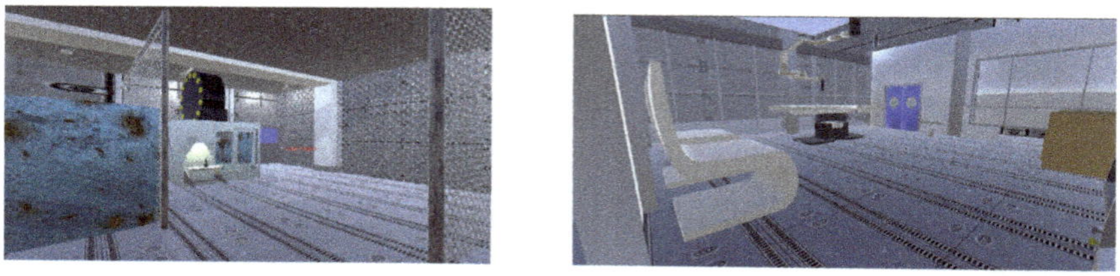

(**a**) Bomb scene. (**b**) Chemical scene.

Figure 11. Virtual Environment Scenes.

The objective in both scenarios is to move the object of interest to a safe place, away from the risk area, using exclusively the movements of the mobile omnidirectional manipulator robot.

To enable navigation through the environment by moving the mobile manipulator robot, a visual interface has been developed and is shown in the figure (Figure 12). This interface presents the virtual environment from the perspective of the manipulator robot as the main screen, providing an overview of the operating area. Additionally, three auxiliary cameras have been incorporated to provide different perspectives crucial to the task. One of these auxiliary cameras provides a detailed view of the operating end, which is essential for precise manipulations. The other two cameras focus on the objects of interest in each scene, allowing a clear visualization of the target elements to be manipulated. This multi-camera setup ensures that the user has a complete understanding of the environment in order to monitor and control the robot, thus improving efficiency and accuracy in task execution. According to the type of task to be performed, whether it is locomotion or object manipulation by the mobile manipulator robot, the control law is selected by means of the Novint Falcon device, as described in Section 3.2. Additionally, for the movement of the end-effector, there are different types of sensors that help this movement, such as force, optical or piezo-resistive sensors, but for this application, by means of the haptic device, an on/off switching of the gripper is generated, which grips the object as long as it is close to the target.

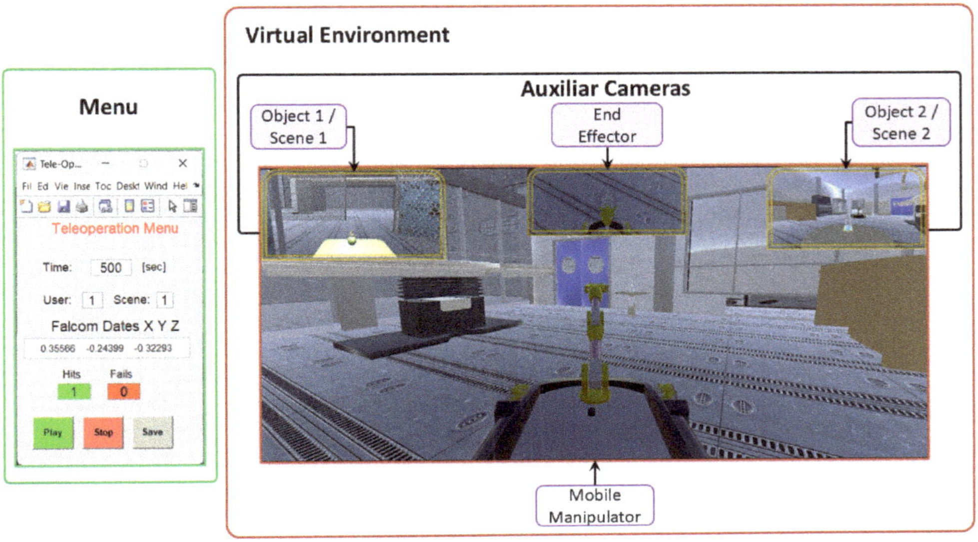

Figure 12. Teaching—learning tool environment.

Additionally, an interface developed in MATLAB software is used, which requests the necessary information to select the predetermined scene and set the duration of the simulation. This interface presents the following data:

- Execution Time
- User
- Scene.

This menu also displays the X, Y, Z coordinates obtained from the Falcon haptic device, as well as the hits and misses related to the manipulation of the objects of interest in the environment. Including Play, Stop, and Save buttons, in order to start or end the simulation.

As mentioned above, the goal of the teaching-learning system is to transport an object of interest to a safe location using the mobile manipulator robot. This safe place is located outside the two main scenes, and is where the dangerous object should be deposited. If the task is performed successfully, the menu increases the number of successes; otherwise, the number of failures is increased (view Figure 13). Otherwise, if the object of interest falls in an area outside the safe area or contacts any other part of the environment, such as walls, machines or other objects present in the scenes, the number of failures is increased.

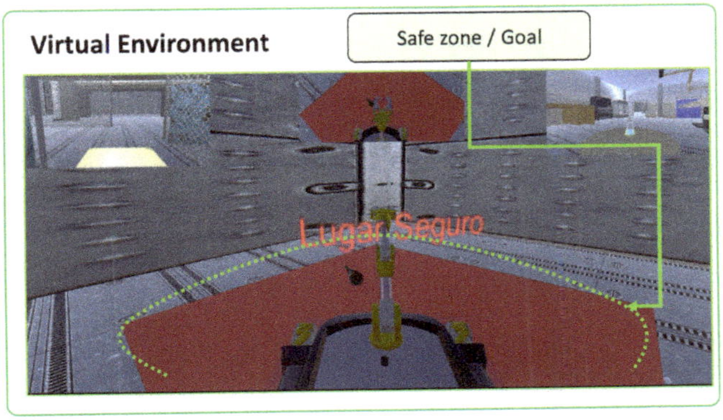

Figure 13. Safe Zone.

4.3. Communication Chanel

Finally, once the virtualization of the scenarios and objects in the graphics engine has been completed and the control algorithms have been established in MATLAB, a bilateral communication channel known as Shared Memories is used to facilitate the exchange of information between the virtual environment and the MATLAB mathematical software, using a Dynamic Link Library (DLL) that creates a shared memory in RAM (SM) for the exchange of data between different programs [25].Through the SM, the control actions calculated in the target controller are integrated into the mathematical model of the robotic system. This model calculates the position and velocity outputs, which are then sent to the mathematical software, thus closing the control loop by providing feedback on the robot's output states. The desired task can be selected by the haptic device, or in the case of using an autonomous control, the user can define the desired task to be performed, e.g., positioning, trajectory tracking or path following, where the computation of the control algorithms is performed by MATLAB mathematical software [21]. Subsequently, the references generated by the controllers are applied to the robot. The Figure 14 indicates the communication scheme used for bilateral communication.

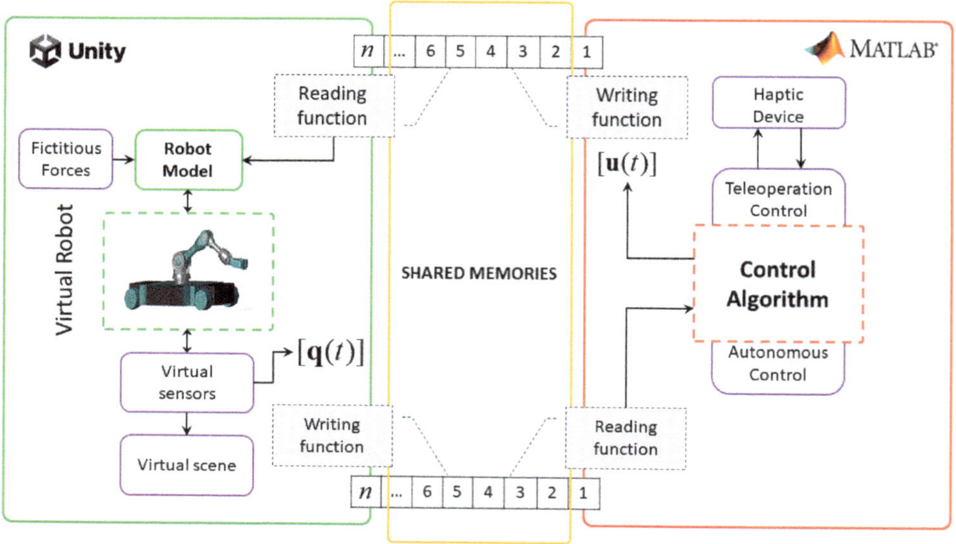

Figure 14. Communication channel scheme.

5. Experimental Results

This section presents the results of the use of the virtual environment as a teaching-learning development tool in the field of educational robotics. In addition, a brief usability analysis of the tool on a given number of students is presented. The hardware used for the simulation of the tool is described as follows: Intel i7-7700HQ processor, CPU 2.80 GHz × 8 (Intel, Santa Clara, CA, USA) and Ge-Force GTX 1050 graphics (Nvidia Corporation, Santa Clara, CA, USA). The characteristics of such hardware is not strictly related to the performance of the tool. Nevertheless, for better animation, it is strongly recommended to include specialized graphics hardware. The implemented system for the teleopraticon is shown in Figure 15. Here, you can see the human operator with the haptic device teleoperated to the robot in the developed virtual environment. In [26] you can watch a video showing the operation of the developed application, where the scenarios and tasks developed by the user are shown.

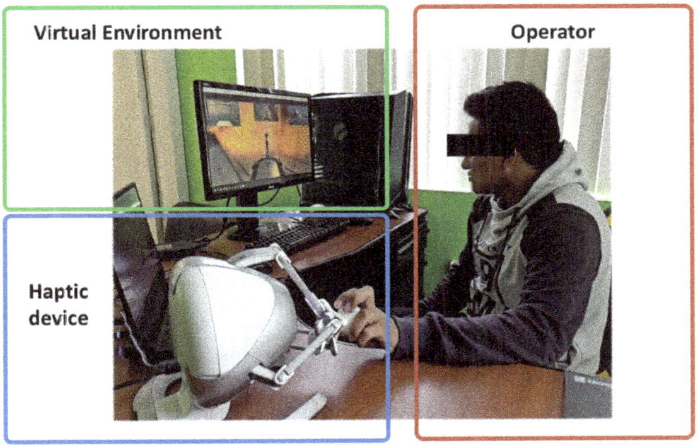

Figure 15. Experimental tests in the virtual environment for the teaching-learning of robotics through the human operator.

When the objective of the task is accomplished, with each of the limitations presented by the movements of the robot and the environment, the menu shows a success in bringing the object of interest, in this case an explosive, to the safe place. Figure 16 shows how the object is transported to the safe place by the robot commanded by the human operator.

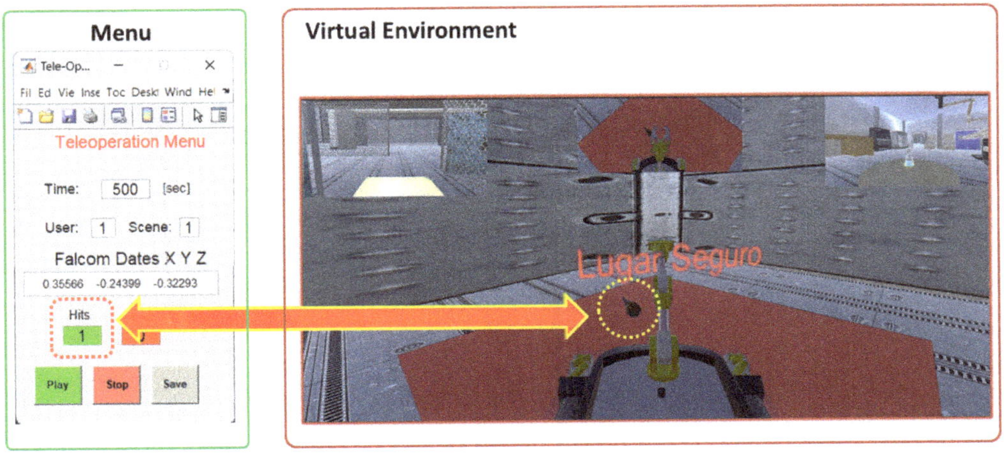

Figure 16. Object moved to safe place correctly.

Otherwise, if due to a wrong movement by the user when controlling the mobile manipulator robot, and the object falls somewhere other than the safe zone, the environment presents an explosion animation and the menu indicates an increase in the number of failures due to poor execution of the program, thus resetting the object in its initial position, as shown in the next graphic (Figure 17).

Figure 17. Error in the transport of the object.

Usability Evaluation

To identify the usability and relevance of the tool, a comprehensive evaluation of the didactic application of teaching and learning is performed. For this purpose, 20 students of the Electronics and Automation Engineering course of the University of the Armed Forces ESPE-L have been chosen to use the virtual environment. These students have basic knowledge in kinematic and dynamic modeling of robots, control systems and virtual reality, which allows them to correctly evaluate the tool. The survey consists of 10 questions focused on evaluating the functionality and intuitiveness of the developed tool. Student responses will be collected using a scale from 1 to 5, where 1 represents "Very difficult", 2 "Difficult", 3 "Intermediate", 4 "Easy" and 5 "Very easy". The list of questions proposed to the users is presented in Table 1.

Table 1. List of questions.

Ord.	Questions
1	How easy was it for you to learn how to use our virtual environment tool?
2	How useful have you found our tool in improving your understanding of service robotics?
3	Do you find the user interface of our tool intuitive and easy to use?
4	Do virtual environments offer an adequate variety of resources (videos, images, etc.) to facilitate your learning?
5	Are the instructions provided in the tool clear and easy to follow?
6	Do you consider that the tool is interactive and allows you to actively participate in the learning process about the cinematic model of the robot?
7	Are you satisfied with the functionality and accuracy of the robot's movements and rotations in the simulation?
8	Has the tool helped you better understand the concepts of movements and rotations of a mobile omnidirectional manipulator robot?
9	Do you consider that the virtual environment has provided you with a valuable educational experience compared to other learning methods?
10	Overall, would you recommend our simulation tool in Unity to other students or teachers interested in learning about robotics?

The results of the usability evaluation of the system are presented in the graphic above (Figure 18). For the first question, a mean of 3.25 with a standard deviation of 0.79 was obtained. The second question showed a mean of 3.35 with a deviation of 0.88. The third question registered a mean of 3.40 with a deviation of 0.68, while the fourth question reached a mean of 3.80 with a deviation of 0.52. The fifth question had a mean of 3.40 and a standard deviation of 0.88. For the sixth question, the mean was 3.30 with a deviation of 0.69, and for the seventh question, a mean of 3.30 with a deviation of 0.8 was obtained.

The eighth question recorded a mean of 3.65 with a standard deviation of 0.67. The ninth question obtained a mean of 3.35 with a deviation of 0.75, while the tenth question yielded a mean of 4.00 with a deviation of 0.85.

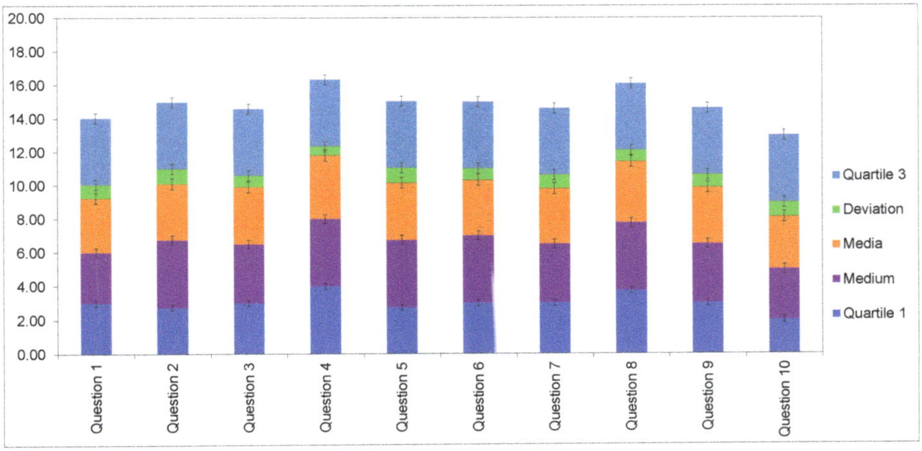

	Q.1	Q.2	Q.3	Q.4	Q.5	Q.6	Q.7	Q.8	Q.9	Q.10
Quartile 1	3.00	2.75	3.00	4.00	2.75	3.00	3.00	3.75	3.00	2.00
Medium	3.00	4.00	3.50	4.00	4.00	4.00	3.50	4.00	3.50	3.00
Media	3.25	3.35	3.40	3.80	3.40	3.30	3.30	3.65	3.35	3.10
Deviation	0.79	0.88	0.68	0.52	0.88	0.69	0.80	0.67	0.75	0.85
Quartile 3	4.00	4.00	4.00	4.00	4.00	4.00	4.00	4.00	4.00	4.00

Figure 18. Results of the list of questions to the students.

The usability evaluation data, illustrated in the figure above (Figure 18), provide detailed insight into how users perceive the teaching-learning tool. The error bars in the figure show the variability of responses among students, indicating the range within which the responses of the rest of the population fall.

Overall, the results suggest a positive evaluation of the virtual environment tool. The relatively small standard deviations reveal a favorable perception of the users regarding the usability of the system. Thus indicating an ease of use of the tool.

In addition, a traditional theoretical teaching method on kinematic and dynamic modeling of robots was chosen to be used with a different group of 20 additional students, but with similar characteristics to those who used the tool. Subsequently, a comparative evaluation of the knowledge acquired in both groups was carried out. The results indicated that the students who used the teaching-learning system demonstrated greater knowledge about motions, rotations, and the kinematic and dynamic modeling of robots, compared to the group that received conventional theoretical instruction.

6. Conclusions

The kinematic and dynamic modeling of the robot using virtual environments significantly increases the realism of the simulation tool. By replicating with greater precision the movements and behaviors of the robot in question, resulting in the simulation being remarkably close to the behavior of the real robot. This fidelity allows users to interact with the virtual environment in a way that almost identically mimics the operation of the robot in real situations. This results in a much more effective and realistic learning experience, providing users with a more accurate understanding of how the robot behaves in a real situation.

The implementation of virtual environments facilitates the development of new learning tools, offering several significant advantages. First of all, these environments allow a much more accessible and economical system acquisition, by considerably reducing costs compared to the purchase of real systems. In addition, they eliminate the risks associated with the use of physical equipment, such as possible damage and the need to operate with caution. This results in a safe and hazard-free learning experience. Similarly, virtual environments do not require the presence of expert operators for training, which simplifies the process and results in greater accessibility for users. In summary, virtual environments reduce costs, risks and also optimize the teaching-learning process, offering a practical and efficient solution compared to real systems.

The use of the Falcon haptic device in the development of the teaching-learning system proves to be an excellent tool to enhance interaction between the environment and the users. The ability to provide feedback allows students to experience increased realism, manipulation and control of robots, which significantly enriches the learning process. Overcoming the limitations inherent in traditional theoretical teaching methods. In short, the use of the haptic device in combination with virtual environments offers an innovative and highly effective approach to robotics education, benefiting both students and instructors.

The development of a teaching-learning system using virtual environments, presented in this work, facilitates the acquisition of new knowledge on robot modeling and control for users with basic or limited knowledge on the subject. This approach is more effective compared to theoretical, classical or conventional teaching methods, which present limitations for both the instructor and the students in the learning process.

Author Contributions: Conceptualization, F.J.P., C.P.C., J.S.O. and V.H.A.; methodology, F.J.P., C.P.C., J.S.O. and V.H.A.; software, F.J.P., C.P.C., J.S.O. and V.H.A.; validation, F.J.P., C.P.C., J.S.O. and V.H.A.; formal analysis, F.J.P., C.P.C., J.S.O. and V.H.A.; investigation, F.J.P., C.P.C., J.S.O. and V.H.A.; resources, F.J.P., C.P.C., J.S.O. and V.H.A.; data curation, F.J.P., C.P.C., J.S.O. and V.H.A.; writing—original draft preparation, F.J.P., C.P.C., J.S.O. and V.H.A.; writing—review and editing, F.J.P., C.P.C., J.S.O. and V.H.A.; visualization, F.J.P., C.P.C., J.S.O. and V.H.A.; supervision, F.J.P., C.P.C., J.S.O. and V.H.A.; project administration, F.J.P., C.P.C., J.S.O. and V.H.A.; funding acquisition V.H.A. and J.S.O. All authors have read and agreed to the published version of the manuscript.

Funding: This research received no external funding.

Institutional Review Board Statement: Not applicable.

Informed Consent Statement: Not applicable.

Data Availability Statement: If anyone wants to get the original data of this paper, please contact with Fernando J. Pantusin.

Acknowledgments: The authors would like to thank the Universidad de las Fuerzas Armadas ESPE for the support given to research, development, and innovation, through the "Autonomous Control of Aerial Manipulators Robots" research project in Ecuador; the ARSI research group; CICHE Research Center and SISAu Research Group. The results of this work also are part of the project "Tecnologías de la Industria 4.0 en Educación, Salud, Empresa e Industria" developed by Universidad Tecnológica Indoamérica; the German Academic Exchange Service, also known by its German acronym (DAAD) for Scholarship Award in third Country Programme Latin America; and the Instituto de Automática of the Universidad Nacional de San Juan and CONICET in Argentina.

Conflicts of Interest: The authors declare no conflict of interest.

References

1. Gonzalez-Aguirre, J.A.; Osorio-Oliveros, R.; Rodríguez-Hernández, K.L.; Lizárraga-Iturralde, J.; Morales Menendez, R.; Ramírez-Mendoza, R.A.; Ramírez-Moreno, M.A.; Lozoya-Santos, J.d.J. Service Robots: Trends and Technology. *Appl. Sci.* **2021**, *11*, 10702. [CrossRef]
2. Zachiotis, G.A.; Andrikopoulos, G.; Gornez, R.; Nakamura, K.; Nikolakopoulos, G. A Survey on the Application Trends of Home Service Robotics. In Proceedings of the 2018 IEEE International Conference on Robotics and Biomimetics (ROBIO), Kuala Lumpur, Malaysia, 12–15 December 2018; pp. 1999–2006. [CrossRef]
3. Jeon, J.; Jung, H.r.; Pico, N.; Luong, T.; Moon, H. Task-Motion Planning System for Socially Viable Service Robots Based on Object Manipulation. *Biomimetics* **2024**, *9*, 436. [CrossRef] [PubMed]
4. Zielinska, T.T. History of Service Robots and New Trends. In *Novel Design and Applications of Robotics Technologies*; IGI Global: Hershey, PA, USA, 2019; pp. 158–187. [CrossRef]
5. Karabegovi, I.; Karabegovi, E.; Mahmi, M.; Husak,E. The application of service robots for logistics in manufacturing processes. *Adv. Prod. Eng. Manag.* **2015**, *10*, 185–194. [CrossRef]
6. Dobrev, Y.; Vossiek, M.; Christmann, M.; Bilous, I.; Gulden, P. Steady Delivery: Wireless Local Positioning Systems for Tracking and Autonomous Navigation of Transport Vehicles and Mobile Robots. *IEEE Microw. Mag.* **2017**, *18*, 26–37. [CrossRef]
7. Abdel-Basset, M.; Chang, V.; Nabeeh, N.A. An intelligent framework using disruptive technologies for COVID-19 analysis. *Technol. Forecast. Soc. Change* **2021**, *163*, 120431. [CrossRef] [PubMed]
8. Leung, R. Smart hospitality: Taiwan hotel stakeholder perspectives. *Tour. Rev.* **2019**, *74*, 50–62. [CrossRef]
9. Ju, C.; Son, H.I. Modeling and Control of Heterogeneous Agricultural Field Robots Based on Ramadge–Wonham Theory. *IEEE Robot. Autom. Lett.* **2020**, *5*, 48–55. [CrossRef]
10. Pecka, M.; Zimmermann, K.; Reinstein, M.; Svoboda, T. Controlling Robot Morphology From Incomplete Measurements. *IEEE Trans. Ind. Electron.* **2017**, *64*, 1773–1782. [CrossRef]
11. Saltaren, R.; Aracil, R.; Alvarez, C.; Yime, E.; Sabater, J.M. Field and service applications-Exploring deep sea by teleoperated robot-An Underwater Parallel Robot with High Navigation Capabilities. *IEEE Robot. Autom. Mag.* **2007**, *14*, 65–75. [CrossRef]
12. Anwar, S.; Bascou, N.; Menekse, M.; Kardgar, A. A Systematic Review of Studies on Educational Robotics. *J. Pre-College. Eng. Educ. Res.* **2019**, *9*, 2. [CrossRef]
13. Guerrero-Osuna, H.A.; Nava-Pintor, J.A.; Olvera-Olvera, C.A.; Ibarra-Pérez, T.; Carrasco-Navarro, R.; Luque-Vega, L.F. Educational Mechatronics Training System Based on Computer Vision for Mobile Robots. *Sustainability* **2023**, *15*, 1386. [CrossRef]
14. Arshad, N.I.; Hashim, A.S.; Mohd Ariffin, M.; Mohd Aszemi, N.; Low, H.M.; Norman, A.A. Robots as Assistive Technology Tools to Enhance Cognitive Abilities and Foster Valuable Learning Experiences among Young Children With Autism Spectrum Disorder. *IEEE Access* **2020**, *8*, 116279–116291. [CrossRef]
15. Charão dos Santos, M.C.; Sangalli, V.A.; Pinho, M.S. Evaluating the Use of Virtual Reality on Professional Robotics Education. In Proceedings of the 2017 IEEE 41st Annual Computer Software and Applications Conference (COMPSAC), Torino, Italy, 4–8 July 2017; Volume 1, pp. 448–455. [CrossRef]
16. Safaric, R.; Sinjur, S.; Zalik, B.; Parkin, R. Control of robot arm with virtual environment via the Internet. *Proc. IEEE* **2003**, *91*, 422–429. [CrossRef]
17. Carvajal, C.P.; Méndez, M.G.; Torres, D.C.; Terán, C.; Arteaga, O.B.; Andaluz, V.H. Autonomous and Tele-Operated Navigation of Aerial Manipulator Robots in Digitalized Virtual Environments. In Proceedings of the 5th International Conference on Augmented Reality, Virtual Reality, and Computer Graphics, Otranto, Italy, 24–27 June 2018; De Paolis, L.T., Bourdot, P., Eds.; Springer: Cham, Switzerland, 2018; pp. 496–515. [CrossRef]
18. Pantusin, F.J.; Cordonez, J.W.; Quimbita, M.A.; Andaluz, V.H.; Vargas, A.D. Training System for the Tomato Paste Production Process Through Virtual Environments. In Proceedings of the Intelligent Systems and Applications, Barcelona, Spain, 13–17 March 2023; Arai, K., Ed.; Springer: Cham, Switzerland, 2024; pp. 46–55. [CrossRef]
19. Vera-Mora, G.; Sanz, C.V.; Coma-Roselló, T.; Baldassarri, S. Model for Designing Gamified Experiences Mediated by a Virtual Teaching and Learning Environment. *Educ. Sci.* **2024**, *14*, 907. [CrossRef]
20. Saunier, L.; Hoffmann, N.; Preda, M.; Fetita, C. Virtual Reality Interface Evaluation for Earthwork Teleoperation. *Electronics* **2023**, *12*, 4151. [CrossRef]
21. Andaluz, V.H.; Carvajal, C.P.; Arteaga, O.; Pérez, J.A.; Valencia, F.S.; Solís, L.A. Unified Dynamic Control of Omnidirectional Robots. In Proceedings of the Towards Autonomous Robotic Systems, Guildford, UK, 19–21 July 2017; Gao, Y., Fallah, S., Jin, Y., Lekakou, C., Eds.; Springer: Cham, Switzerland, 2017; pp. 673–685. [CrossRef]
22. Yoshikawa, T. Manipulability of Robotic Mechanisms. *Int. J. Robot. Res.* **1985**, *4*, 3–9. [CrossRef]
23. Falkenhahn, V.; Mahl, T.; Hildebrandt, A.; Neumann, R.; Sawodny, O. Dynamic Modeling of Bellows-Actuated Continuum Robots Using the Euler–Lagrange Formalism. *IEEE Trans. Robot.* **2015**, *31*, 1483–1496. [CrossRef]
24. Bischoff, R.; Huggenberger, U.; Prassler, E. KUKA youBot—A mobile manipulator for research and education. In Proceedings of the 2011 IEEE International Conference on Robotics and Automation, Shanghai, China, 9–13 May 2011; pp. 1–4. [CrossRef]

25. Gallardo, C.; Pogrebnoy, A.; Varela-Aldás, J. Development and Use of Dynamic Link Libraries Generated Under Various Calling Conventions. In *Information Technology and Systems: ICITS 2021*; Springer International Publishing: Cham, Switzerland, 2021; Volume 1, pp. 220–232. [CrossRef]
26. Carvajal, C.P.; Pantusin, F.J.; Ortiz, J.S.; Andaluz, V.H. Virtual Teleoperation System for Mobile Manipulator Robots Focused on Object Transport. 2024. Available online: https://youtu.be/76nzhxMp3SM (accessed on 24 July 2024).

technologies

MDPI

Article

Deep Learning-Based Vision Systems for Robot Semantic Navigation: An Experimental Study

Albandari Alotaibi [1], Hanan Alatawi [1], Aseel Binnouh [1], Lamaa Duwayriat [1], Tareq Alhmiedat [2,3,*] and Osama Moh'd Alia [1]

1 Computer Science Department, Faculty of Computers and Information Technology, University of Tabuk, Tabuk 47713, Saudi Arabia; 441000399@stu.ut.edu.sa (A.A.); 421010046@stu.ut.edu.sa (H.A.); 441000451@stu.ut.edu.sa (A.B.); 431010357@stu.ut.edu.sa (L.D.); oalia@ut.edu.sa (O.M.A.)

2 Information Technology Department, Faculty of Computers and Information Technology, University of Tabuk, Tabuk 47713, Saudi Arabia

3 Artificial Intelligence and Sensing Technologies (AIST) Reseach Center, University of Tabuk, Tabuk 71491, Saudi Arabia

* Correspondence: t.alhmiedat@ut.edu.sa

Abstract: Robot semantic navigation has received significant attention recently, as it aims to achieve reliable mapping and navigation accuracy. Object detection tasks are vital in this endeavor, as a mobile robot needs to detect and recognize the objects in the area of interest to build an effective semantic map. To achieve this goal, this paper classifies and discusses recently developed object detection approaches and then presents the available vision datasets that can be employed in robot semantic navigation applications. In addition, this paper discusses several experimental studies that have validated the efficiency of object detection algorithms, including Faster R-CNN, YOLO v5, and YOLO v8. These studies also utilized a vision dataset to design and develop efficient robot semantic navigation systems, which is also discussed. According to several experiments conducted in a Fablab area, the YOLO v8 object classification model achieved the best results in terms of classification accuracy and processing speed.

Keywords: robot semantic navigation; deep learning-based vision systems; vision datasets

1. Introduction

Autonomous robot navigation is considered one of the most challenging problems in robotics. It aims to provide a robot with the ability to inspect the area of interest, travel independently, avoid obstacles, and plan a path to the destination point. Autonomous robot navigation involves different functions, from examining the environment and planning paths to building a map of the area of interest [1].

To achieve these tasks, existing robot navigation systems can be separated into two main categories: geometric and semantic navigation systems. The former employs range-finder methods to build a geometry map. In contrast, the latter adopts complicated sensing units, including vision systems, to construct a semantic map with rich information about the area of interest [2].

Robot semantic navigation is complicated because it involves adopting computer vision and deep learning techniques for understanding and navigating the environment based on semantic information, where the goal is to go beyond basic obstacle avoidance and enable robots to recognize and interpret the meanings of objects and structures in their surroundings [3].

World representation is considered one of the most significant issues in the robotics literature. Its importance stems from the necessity of developing an intelligent robot system that can understand the environment to allow the robot to plan, reason, and execute tasks [4].

Recently, robot semantic navigation systems have received considerable attention. Researchers are driven to create a robot platform that understands the navigation environment and acts accordingly. Existing semantic navigation systems gather semantic information via two different systems: LiDAR-based approaches and vision-based systems [5].

The importance of employing a semantic navigation system stems from the requirement of employing mobile robots in complicated environments. Mainly, robot semantic navigation depends on vision systems for the purpose of performing object detection and classification. Therefore, it is important to review, analyze, and assess the efficiency of the recently developed object detection algorithms that have been employed in robot semantic navigation approaches.

Hence, this paper presents an investigation and analysis on the existing vision-based systems that can be employed in robot semantic navigation systems. In addition, it presents experimental studies using the COCO vision dataset to validate the efficiency of different object detection methods in robot semantic navigation applications. It offers reliable guidance for developing an efficient robot semantic navigation system. The main contributions of this paper lie in the following aspects:

1. It reviews object detection algorithms that have been employed in robot semantic navigation systems.
2. It discusses and analyzes existing vision datasets for indoor robot semantic navigation systems.
3. It validates the efficiency of several object detection algorithms along with an object detection dataset through several experiments conducted in indoor environments.

The remainder of this paper is organized as follows: Section 2 discusses recently developed object detection algorithms that have been employed for robot semantic navigation systems. Section 3 discusses different vision datasets, whereas Section 4 presents several experimental studies to assess the efficiency of three different object detection systems. Section 5 discusses the obtained results, and finally, Section 6 concludes the paper.

2. Object Detection Algorithms for Robot Semantic Navigation

In general, robot semantic navigation applications heavily rely on object detection. Object detection facilitates the semantic interpretation of visual data by precisely locating and identifying items in images and videos. Robots can then use this information to make decisions and successfully traverse their surroundings. Object detection is important for many different applications, such as the following:

1. Indoor Robot Navigation: Object detection allows robots to perceive and recognize obstacles, furniture, or specific objects within indoor environments. This capability lets them plan optimal paths, avoid collisions, and safely navigate complex spaces [6].
2. Manufacturing Quality Control: Object detection is essential in automated quality control systems within manufacturing settings. It helps identify defects, anomalies, or irregularities in products, ensuring consistent quality and minimizing errors during the production process [7].
3. Autonomous Driving: Object detection is a fundamental component of autonomous driving systems. By detecting and tracking vehicles, pedestrians, traffic signs, and other objects in real-time, object detection enables self-driving cars to perceive their surroundings, make informed decisions, and respond to dynamic traffic situations [8].

In this research, existing vision systems for robot semantic navigation were classified into three main categories, as presented in Figure 1: convolutional neural networks (CNNs), recurrent neural networks (RNNs), and deep reinforcement learning (DRL). The following subsections provide a brief introduction to these algorithms.

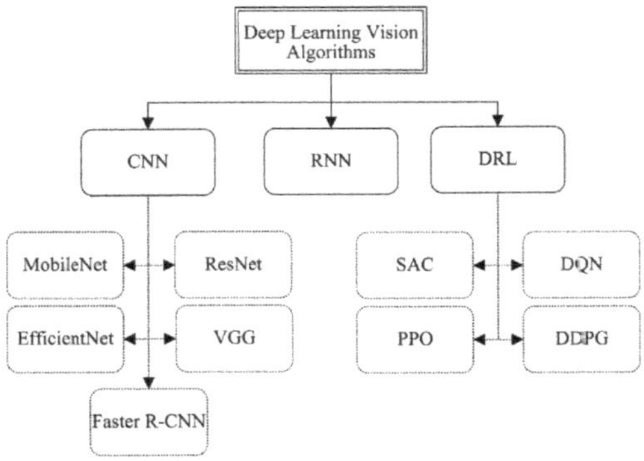

Figure 1. Deep learning vision algorithms for robot semantic navigation.

2.1. Convolutional Neural Network (CNN) Object Detection Algorithms

Convolutional neural networks (CNN) are one of the most representative models of deep learning. They continue to evolve, undergoing gradual advancements in terms of their architectural depth. The CNN trend highlights a significant shift toward constructing more complex and sophisticated neural network models, characterized by an increasing number of layers and hierarchical representations. The progressive deepening of a CNN enables it to effectively capture and understand intricate patterns, greatly enhancing its capabilities in various image recognition and analysis tasks [9].

CNNs have been employed widely within robot semantic navigation systems to enable the robots to interpret visual data and make informed decisions. CNN-based robot semantic navigation systems can be further classified into Residual Network (ResNet), Visual Geometry Group (VGG), MobileNet, EfficientNet, YOLO, and Faster R-CNN models.

2.1.1. Residual Network (ResNet)

ResNet is known for its deep architecture with residual blocks, which helps in training very deep networks. ResNet has been widely used for various computer vision tasks, including object detection and classification. The works presented in [10–12] involve employing the ResNet method to improve an image-matching algorithm based on feature points to enhance the robot's overall semantic navigation capability and ability to resist interference.

2.1.2. Visual Geometry Group (VGG)

Visual Geometry Group (VGG) is a multi-layered CNN architecture. The most popular models are VGG-16 and VGG-19, which consist of 16 and 19 convolutional layers, respectively [13]. The work presented in [14] involves a multi-scale fully convolutional network (FCN). The output is an image containing pixel-by-pixel predictions that can be used in different navigation strategies.

2.1.3. MobileNet

The MobileNet architecture was designed for portable and embedded vision applications. It is based on a simplified architecture that employs deeply separable convolutions to build light deep neural networks; it has low latency for mobile and embedded devices. The works presented in [15,16] involved the employment of MobileNet architecture to provide a practical approach for implementing autonomous indoor navigation systems based on semantic image segmentation using a state-of-the-art mobile performance model.

2.1.4. EfficientNet

EfficientNet is a CNN-based architecture and measurement method that scales all depth and width resolution dimensions uniformly using a composite coefficient. The authors of [17] proposed an efficient pixel-level terrain recognition network EfferDeepNet to achieve global perception of an outdoor environment.

2.1.5. YOLO

YOLO is a single-shot object detector that can recognize objects in an image in a single pass with no need for multiple stages. YOLO is one of the most popular single-shot object detectors [18]; it employs a single CNN to predict the class labels and bounding boxes of objects within an image.

Several robot semantic navigation approaches have employed the YOLO object detection algorithm to build a semantic map with rich semantic information. For instance, the work presented in [19] proposed a semantic framework to build an improved metric representation of the environment. In [20], the authors proposed a reliable approach to create an improved map of their environment with object-level information, where the developed framework adopted a YOLO object detection algorithm to identify, localize, and track different classes of objects in the area of interest.

A vision-based navigation system was proposed in [21], based on the employment of the YOLO algorithm to detect objects in the area of interest. On the other hand, the work presented in [22] developed a hybrid framework that consists of a metric map along with semantic information. In [23], the authors presented an enhanced version of ORB-SLAM3 through a combination with the YOLO v8 algorithm for real-time pose estimation and semantic segmentation.

The work presented in [24] involved the development of a semantic navigation system through the employment of ORB-SLAM2 and an object detection algorithm (YOLO v3). In [25], the authors proposed the employment of a novel dataset for semantic segmentation using the YOLO object detection algorithm. The works presented in [26–30] presented robot semantic navigation systems through the employment of a YOLO object detection algorithm. Moreover, the authors of [31–37] focused on developing robot semantic navigation systems through the employment of YOLO object detection algorithms.

2.1.6. Faster R-CNN

Faster R-CNN is an improvement on the Fast R-CNN object detection model. It utilizes a Region Proposal Network (RPN) with the CNN model. Faster R-CNN involves a two-stage object detection model, where it first identifies the region of interest and then passes these regions to a CNN model. Faster R-CNN achieves an efficient classification accuracy and has been employed in several applications, including robot semantic navigation systems. For instance, the works presented in [38–42] employed Faster R-CNN in the area of robot semantic navigation.

2.2. Recurrent Neural Network (RNN) Object Detection Algorithms

In general, a recurrent neural network (RNN) is a type of neural network that can be employed with sequences including text, videos, sounds, and much more. An RNN can understand sequences and time. Unlike CNNs, an RNN is used to deal with sequential data to represent time dependencies [43]. The integration of a CNN and RNN is useful for understanding actions in videos by analyzing multiple frames instead of only one. The works presented in [11,44–48] employed an RNN algorithm in robot semantic navigation systems.

2.3. Deep Reinforcement Learning (DRL) Object Detection Algorithms

DRL-based object detection models are designed to recognize and detect objects within an environment. These models aim to improve their detection accuracy over time by learning from their interactions and experiences [49]. DRL algorithms can be further classified into Deep Q-Network (DQN), Deep Deterministic Policy Gradient (DDPG), Soft Actor-Critic (SAC), and Proximal Policy Optimization (PPO) algorithms.

2.3.1. Deep Q-Network (DQN)

Deep Q-Network (DQN) is a deep reinforcement learning algorithm that has been applied to various tasks, including robot navigation. In robot semantic navigation, DQN learns a strategy to navigate through an environment by interacting with an agent, an environment, and a reward signal. The agent learns to perform actions in the environment to maximize cumulative rewards over time, such as reaching a goal or avoiding obstacles.

The work presented in [50] introduced a DQN-based approach for global path planning, enabling swift optimal path determination in dense settings for mobile robots. The DQN algorithm can be trained to make decisions based on the YOLO output, such as in autonomous driving scenarios. Through reinforcement learning, the DQN adjusts its policy based on the effectiveness of its decisions, improving its interaction with the environment [51].

Applying a DQN to semantic navigation involves training a deep neural network to approximate the Q-function, the expected cumulative reward for a given action in a given state, and using it to make navigation decisions in environments where understanding the semantic meaning of the environment is critical to successful navigation [52–55].

2.3.2. Deep Deterministic Policy Gradient (DDPG)

Deep Deterministic Policy Gradients (DDPG) is a model-free off-policy algorithm that learns continuous actions. DDPG integrates the concepts of Deterministic Policy Gradients (DPG) and DQN. The authors of [56] proposed a DDPG with an averaged state-action estimation (Averaged-DDPG) algorithm, to minimize the adverse effects of conflict. In [57], the authors reviewed DRL-based navigation frameworks, where the presented work involved a comparison and analysis of the relationship between four typical application scenarios: local obstacle avoidance, social navigation, indoor navigation, and multi-robot navigation.

2.3.3. Soft Actor-Critic (SAC)

Soft actor-critic (SAC) is a reinforcement learning (RL) algorithm that optimizes a stochastic policy in an off-policy manner, meaning that it learns the policy using information from past experiences that may have been generated by a different policy. This approach is particularly efficient in terms of sample usage (i.e., it can learn more effective policies with fewer interactions with the environment than other methods).

SAC is one of several state-of-the-art algorithms for RL, particularly in domains with high-dimensional states and action spaces. It is an active area of research and is frequently updated with improvements in efficiency and performance.

Xin Yu et al. [58] proposed an Autonomous Underwater Vehicle (AUV) system using Soft SAC. In [59], the authors presented a controller for a wheeled robot, enabling collision-free navigation in dynamic environments. In [60], the authors employed the SAC algorithm and a global planner to enhance exploration and reduce the training costs in semantic robot navigation.

2.3.4. Proximal Policy Optimization (PPO)

In [61], the authors presented a Proximal Policy Optimization (PPO) as one of the most efficient DRL algorithms, known for achieving state-of-the-art performances across a wide range of challenging tasks. The experiments involved testing the PPO on various benchmark tasks, including simulated robotic locomotion and Atari game playing. The obtained results demonstrated that the PPO model achieves better results than other online policy gradient methods; it also strikes a favorable balance between sample complexity, simplicity, and wall time.

As presented above, several object detection models have been employed recently to detect and recognize objects of interest in the navigation environment. Figure 2 shows the overall employment of object detection models among recently developed robot semantic navigation systems. For instance, the ResNet, MobileNet, and SAC object detection models have received little attention in robot semantic navigation systems. However, Faster

R-CNN, RNN, and DQN have been employed in several robot semantic navigation systems. Finally, the YOLO object detection model received the highest employment rate, used in almost 17 robot semantic navigation systems to detect and recognize objects of interest in the navigation area.

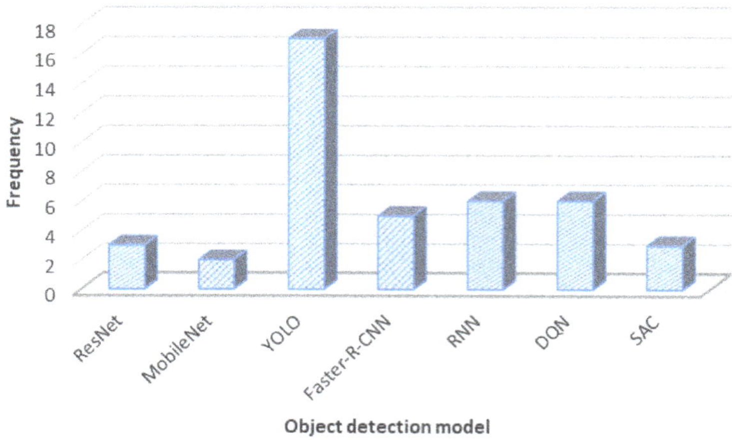

Figure 2. Frequency of object detection models in existing semantic navigation systems.

3. Vision Datasets for Robot Semantic Navigation

The employment of robot semantic navigation systems requires the adoption of an efficient object detection algorithm and a vision dataset to recognize objects of interest in the navigation area, and thus construct a semantic map with rich information. Recently, several vision datasets have been constructed to achieve this, with diverse application types, a range of objects, and classification accuracy. This section discusses the recently constructed vision datasets that can be employed with robot semantic navigation systems.

Vision datasets can be categorized into indoor, outdoor, and hybrid based on their employment environment. The indoor vision datasets include COCO and Matterport 3D, whereas the outdoor datasets include PASCAL VOC and KITTI. Finally, the hybrid vision dataset includes ADE20K.

3.1. *Microsoft Common Objects in Context Dataset (MS COCO)*

The Microsoft Common Objects in Context dataset (MS COCO) [62] is a large vision dataset that has been employed in several vision applications. The MS COCO dataset consists of 80 different classes, where 82,783 objects are assigned for training tasks, 40,504 for validation, and 80,000 for testing. Recently, the MS COCO dataset has been employed in diverse robot semantic navigation systems; for instance, the work presented in [11,37] employed the MS COCO dataset for object detection to identify multiple indoor locations. On the other hand, the study presented in [22] involved a DL-based end-to-end object detection method, achieving accurate results, including 35 fps on YOLO v3 and 55.3 mAP on the COCO dataset. Moreover, the authors of [20,30,63] focused on the detection of objects within indoor environments for robot semantic navigation systems using the COCO dataset.

3.2. *Matterport 3D Dataset (MP3D)*

The MP3D dataset, created by Stanford University, is a large-scale semantic navigation dataset that contains detailed 3D models of real-world indoor scenes along with fine-grained semantic annotations. The dataset is intended for training and evaluating algorithms for semantic navigation and understanding in the visual domain. In the context of MP3D examples, semantic annotations such as object categories, room labels, and other contextual information play a crucial role in guiding navigation [64–67].

3.3. Pascal VOC 2012 Dataset

The Pascal VOC [68] is a popular dataset that has been employed to accomplish various computer tasks, including object detection, segmentation, and classification. The VOC dataset consists of 20 classes with 2913 images split into two sets: 1464 images for the training task and 1449 for testing.

The Pascal dataset was employed in [25] to achieve semantic segmentation. This study employed the VOC2012 and CityScapes datasets, and their results showed that the CityScapes dataset was more useful for robot navigation, even though it was created for semantic segmentation.

3.4. KITTI Dataset

'KITTI' stands for the Karlsruhe Institute of Technology and the Toyota Technological Institute, and KITTI is a popular dataset used to train and test algorithms for autonomous driving. The KITTI dataset consists of various sensor data collected from a moving vehicle, including high-resolution images, LiDAR scans, GPS coordinates, and other relevant information, including the following 11 classes: sidewalks, bicycles, fences, poles, buildings, trees, sky, automobiles, signs, roads, and pedestrians [69]. The KITTI dataset is a car segmentation dataset that contains 3714 images for training, 144 images for validation, and 120 images for testing.

To perform semantic navigation with the KITTI dataset, an algorithm must process its sensor data and extract the semantic information [70]. This can be carried out using deep learning techniques, such as CNNs for image processing and point cloud algorithms for LiDAR data [71].

Using the semantic annotations in the KITTI dataset, autonomous vehicles can better understand their surroundings. This enables them to make informed decisions and navigate safely in urban environments, contributing to the development of self-driving cars and intelligent transportation systems [72]. Semantic navigation using the KITTI dataset has been extensively studied in the field of autonomous driving.

3.5. ADE20K Dataset

The ADE20K dataset [73] is a large-scale dataset designed for semantic segmentation tasks. It consists of over 20,000 images in the training set, 2000 images in the validation set, and 3000 images in the testing set. The dataset provides pixel-level annotations for semantic segmentation across 150 object categories. These categories encompass a wide range of semantic classes, including common elements such as sky, roads, and grass, as well as discrete objects like people, cars, and beds. The dataset's evaluation includes a total of 150 semantic categories for comprehensive analysis and benchmarking.

The authors of [74] employed the ADE20K dataset to reduce the gap between robot and animal perception by offering a novel approach to scene understanding that captures both geometric and semantic characteristics in an unknown environment. Table 1 provides a summary of the vision datasets discussed earlier in this section, highlighting the datasets commonly used in robot semantic navigation.

Table 1. A comparison between the existing vision datasets for robot semantic navigation.

Dataset	Application	Records	Classes	Size
COCO	Indoor	330,000	80	25 GB
Matterport	Indoor	10,800	40	176 GB
Cityscapes	Outdoor	5000	30	11 GB
PASCAL	Outdoor	11,530	20	2 GB
KITTI	Outdoor	3978	11	5.27 GB
ADE20K	Hybrid	20,210	150	4.38 GB

Various object detection datasets were presented above along with their diverse classification accuracy, size, and application. Figure 3 presents the employment frequency of each vision dataset in the literature. The COCO dataset has received high attention recently in the area of robot semantic navigation. This is due to its wide range of classes, which are beneficial for many robot semantic navigation applications.

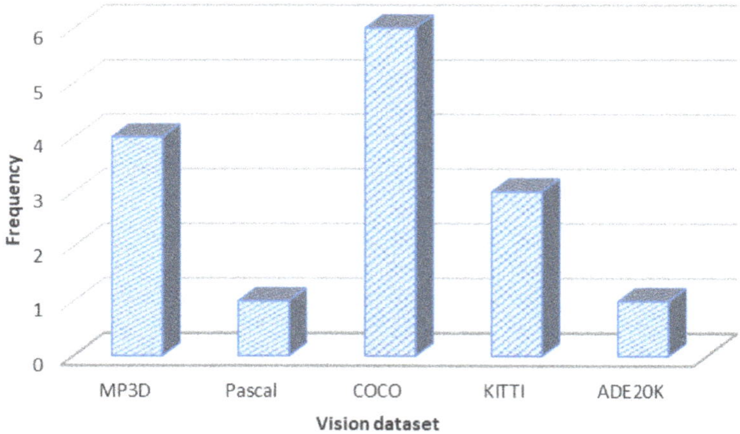

Figure 3. Frequency of vision datasets in existing semantic navigation systems.

4. Experimental Study

This section discusses the experimental studies that were conducted to assess the efficiency of various object detection algorithms in robot semantic navigation systems. In addition, it discusses the robot platform designed to validate the efficiency of three object detection algorithms in the experimental environment.

As outlined earlier in Section 2 (Object Detection Algorithms for Robot Semantic Navigation), recent developments in robot semantic navigation have predominantly emphasized CNN-based methodologies. This emphasis is often attributed to the ability of CNNs to effectively process spatial information, making them well suited for tasks such as scene understanding and environment perception in navigation scenarios.

While RNNs excel in capturing sequential dependencies and RL models in learning through interaction with environments, the specific demands of robot semantic navigation, which heavily rely on spatial data processing and real-time decision making, align more closely with the strengths of CNN architectures. This specialization allows for efficient feature extraction and mapping, crucial for successful navigation tasks.

Given these considerations and the current landscape of research in robot semantic navigation, we opted to concentrate on CNNs for our experimental evaluation to provide a focused and relevant analysis within the context of this study.

4.1. Environment Development

This subsection delves into the details of the robot platform and the experimental environment used in this study. To ensure the validity of our results, this research utilized a two-wheel drive robot platform as depicted in Figure 4. This platform was built using a Raspberry Pi 4 computer [75] and incorporates essential components for comprehensive environmental sensing and perception.

One crucial component is the RPLiDAR A1 unit [76], which plays a vital role in the robot's environmental sensing capabilities. The RPLiDAR A1 is a LiDAR sensor that utilizes laser technology to precisely measure distances and generate a detailed 2D point cloud map of the surroundings. This enables the robot to perceive its environment accurately and create a representation of nearby objects, obstacles, and the overall spatial layout.

Figure 4. The employed robot platform.

By leveraging the RPLiDAR A1's scanning capabilities, the developed robot platform can navigate and avoid obstacles in real time, ensuring safe and efficient operation. The generated point cloud data can be processed and analyzed to extract valuable information for various applications, such as mapping, localization, and object recognition.

In addition to the RPLiDAR A1, the proposed robot platform also incorporates a Logitech Webcam for visual perception [77], allowing for the capture of real-time video footage. These visual data, combined with the LiDAR-based point cloud information, enable a more comprehensive understanding of the robot's surroundings, facilitating tasks such as object detection, tracking, and scene understanding. To provide a comprehensive understanding of the robot's capabilities, its specifications are detailed in Table 2, outlining key parameters such as its dimensions, weight, power supply, and communication interfaces. Moreover, the robot architecture is presented in Figure 5, which involves the main units of the employed robot platform.

Table 2. The specifications of the developed mobile robot.

Specification	Value
Processor	Raspberry Pi 4—4 GB RAM
Driver control	O-drive
Ranger-finder	RPLiDAR A1
Vision unit	2MP Logitech Webcam
Robot dimension	55 × 45 cm
Robot speed	0.5 m/s

The experimental studies were conducted at the state-of-the-art Artificial Intelligence and Sensing Technologies (AIST) research center at the University of Tabuk. This facility provided an ideal setting for our research, equipped with a diverse range of components including a pepper robot, fish tank, 3D printer, whiteboards, computers, furniture, plants,

TV, and various other items. The center's environment, though challenging for robot navigation due to its crowded nature, offers a compact testing area of approximately 2000 ft^2, as depicted in Figure 6.

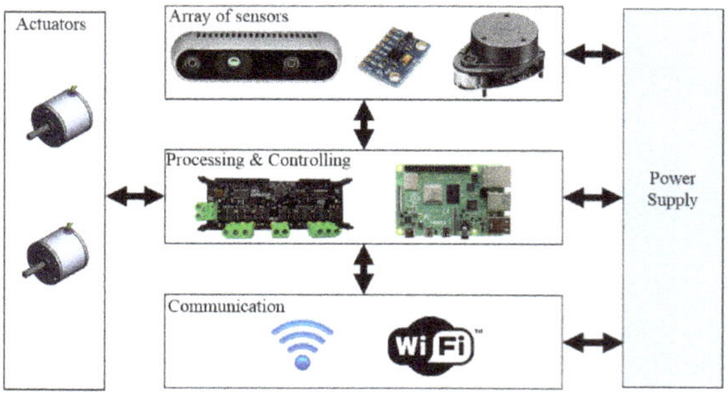

Figure 5. The robot architecture in terms of employed hardware units.

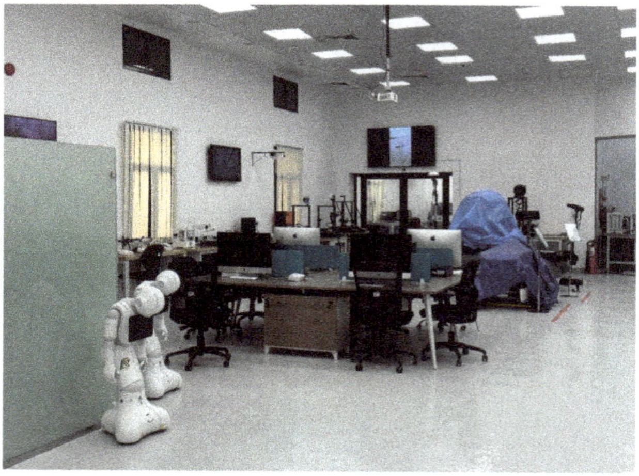

Figure 6. The Artificial Intelligence and Sensing Technologies (AIST) research center—experimental testbed.

For a comprehensive evaluation, this study meticulously assessed the efficiency and performance of three state-of-the-art object detection algorithms: YOLO v5, YOLO v8, and Faster R-CNN. These algorithms were selected based on their proven effectiveness and widespread use in a variety of robot applications, exemplifying their suitability for these evaluation objectives.

To ensure a robust evaluation, this research employed the widely recognized COCO dataset in its experimental studies. The COCO dataset is renowned for its extensive collection of annotated images, encompassing a diverse range of indoor objects. By leveraging this dataset, the researchers were able to evaluate the algorithms' capabilities in detecting and recognizing various objects commonly encountered in indoor environments.

In utilizing the COCO dataset, the proposed evaluation encompassed a wide array of object categories, ensuring a comprehensive analysis of the algorithms' performance. This dataset provided a solid foundation for assessing the algorithms' accuracy, generalization, and suitability for real-world robot applications.

Through a rigorous evaluation process, this study aimed to provide valuable insights into the strengths and limitations of the YOLO v5, YOLO v8, and Faster R-CNN algorithms, enabling informed decisions regarding their adoption and utilization in robotic systems.

4.2. Experimental Results

The obtained results are discussed in this subsection, where the employed object detection models are assessed by analyzing three different validation metrics, object detection rate, object detection accuracy, and processing time, which are defined as follows:

1. Object detection rate (ODR): This refers to the total number of objects that were successfully detected (true positive detections) using the employed object detection model, denoted as 'TP' in Equation (1), compared to the total number of existing objects in the environment, and referred to as '$TotalObjects$' in the following equation:

$$ODR = \frac{TP}{TotalObjects} \tag{1}$$

2. Object detection accuracy: This refers to the classification accuracy of the object detection model. In our study, we utilized the mean Average Precision (mAP) metric to evaluate the model's performance comprehensively. The mAP aggregates precision scores across classes. Here is how it can be mathematically described.
Let

    - AP_i represent the Average Precision value for class i;
    - N be the total number of classes.

    The mAP is calculated by averaging the AP across all classes, as follows:

$$mAP = \frac{1}{N} \sum_{i=1}^{N} AP_i \tag{2}$$

In this equation, the AP for each class is calculated individually, and then the mean of these values is calculated to obtain the mAP score. To get to this point, we have to calculate the AP_i for class i, as shown in the following equation:

$$AP_i = \sum_{r \in R} (P(r).\Delta r) \tag{3}$$

where $P(r)$ is the precision at recall level r, and Δr is the change in recall from the previous recall level.
The AP_i for a given class i is calculated by adding the precision values at various recall levels and weighting them by calculating the change in the recall. This technique aids in assessing how well the model detects objects of a certain class at varying confidence levels.
The following is how to calculate both $P(r)$ and Δr in the average precision:

    (a) Finding $P(r)$ at a Specific Recall Level r:

        - To calculate precision at a specific recall level r, we need to consider the precision value associated with the highest recall that is less than or equal to r, as follows:

$$P(r) = max_{Recall_i \leq r}(Precision_i) \tag{4}$$

        - The precision at a specific recall level is the maximum precision value for all detections with a recall greater than or equal to that recall level.

    (b) Determining Δr (change in the Recall):

        - Δr represents the change in recall from the previous recall level to the current recall level in the precision–recall curve, and it is calculated as follows:

$$\Delta r = Recall_i - Recall_{i-1} \tag{5}$$

        - For each recall level, Δr can be calculated as the difference between the current recall level and the previous recall level.

By computing precision at different recall levels and measuring the change in recall from one level to the next, we can effectively determine the precision–recall curve and subsequently calculate the AP for a specific class in object detection tasks.
Finally, to determine the recall and precision for each class, we used the following equations:
Precision:

$$Precision = \frac{TP}{TP + FP} \tag{6}$$

Recall:

$$Precision = \frac{TP}{TP + FN} \tag{7}$$

where

- True Positives (TP): Instances that the model correctly identifies as positive.
- False Positives (FP): Instances that the model wrongly classifies as positive.
- False Negatives (FN): Instances that the model wrongly classifies as negative but are positive.

3. Processing time for the object detection model: This refers to the total time required for the model to process the input frames obtained from the vision unit and perform the detection task. The processing time for the object detection model can be calculated as the difference between the end time and the start time of the processing task, formulated as follows:

$$ProcessingTime = EndTime - StartTime \tag{8}$$

In Figure 7, the object detection rate for the three object detection models is depicted. As presented, YOLO v5 and v8 achieved almost the same object detection rate of 60.91% and 57.47%, respectively. However, the Faster R-CNN model offers the lowest object detection rate across almost all the existing classes, with an average of 32.18%. The main reason for this is the complexity of the Faster R-CNN model, which leads to the slow processing of frames from the RGB camera.

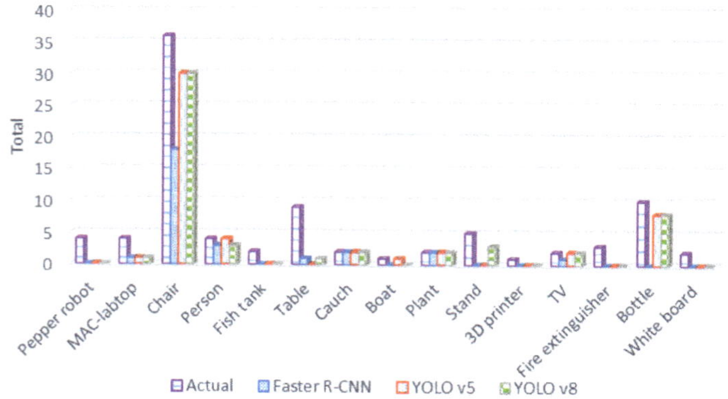

Figure 7. Object detection rate for 16 classes using three object detection models.

In addition, the object detection rate for all three models was almost zero for a few classes, including the pepper robot, fish tank, 3D printer, and whiteboards, even though the webcam was able to capture the whole scene reliably. However, the COCO dataset does not contain the aforementioned classes. Table 3 presents the object detection rate for each object in the experimental testbed, using the three object detection models.

Table 3. The object detection of each object in the experimental testbed.

Object	Total Exist	Faster R-CNN	YOLO v5	YOLO v8
Pepper robot	4	0	0	0
MAC-PC	4	1	1	1
Chair	36	18	30	30
Person	4	3	4	3
Fish tank	2	0	0	0
Table	9	1	0	1
Couch	2	2	2	2
Boat	1	0	1	0
Plant	2	2	2	2
Stand	5	0	0	3
3D printer	1	0	0	0
TV	2	1	2	2
Fire extinguisher	3	0	0	0
Bottle	10	0	8	8
Whiteboard	2	0	0	0

Figure 8 presents the average object detection accuracy for each class by vision detection system. For all the object detection models, the object classification accuracy was estimated. For instance, the average object classification accuracy for YOLO v5 and v8 is 53.90%, and 53.00%, respectively, whereas the Faster R-CNN model achieved the worst object classification accuracy with a percentage of 36.35%. Table 4 presents the classification accuracy for each object in the experiment testbed using the three object detection models.

In examining the experimental outcomes, the discrepancies in object detection performance among the models, as evidenced by Figure 8, underscore the nuanced impact of the model architecture and training data on detection capabilities. For instance, the failure of YOLOv5 to detect tables while successfully identifying a boat raises questions about the models' inherent design choices and the diversity of objects in the training data. This discrepancy prompts a deeper exploration into how the specific architectural features of each model influence their detection prowess in varied scenarios. Moreover, understanding the cases or environments wherein each model excels is crucial for optimizing their applicability. Given the nuances of the COCO dataset, which includes 'dining tables' but not explicitly 'tables', and features 'boat' objects, the detection capabilities of YOLOv5 can be further contextualized. The presence of 'dining tables' in the dataset, although slightly different from generic 'tables', may explain YOLOv5's failure to detect tables in our experimental setup. This discrepancy underscores the importance of precise object class definitions within the training data and their impact on model performance.

Conversely, the successful detection of boat instances by YOLOv5 aligns with the model's exposure to boat objects in the COCO dataset. The dataset's inclusion of boat annotations likely contributed to YOLOv5's ability to identify boat objects in our experiments accurately. This highlights the significance of training data composition in shaping a model's detection capabilities, emphasizing the need for datasets that encompass a diverse range of object classes relevant to the target application scenarios. Understanding these dataset-specific intricacies is essential in interpreting the performance variations observed among object detection models. By considering the subtleties of object class definitions and dataset contents, we can gain insights into how training data characteristics influence model behavior and detection outcomes in real-world environments. This underscores the importance of dataset curation and annotation precision in enhancing the effectiveness of object detection models like YOLOv5 across varied object categories and environmental conditions. Further investigation is warranted to discern the strengths and limitations of each model type, delineating their optimal use cases based on factors such as object complexity, scene clutter, and dataset diversity. By delving into these nuances, we can elucidate the interplay between model architectures, training data composition, and their respective performance in object detection tasks across different environmental contexts.

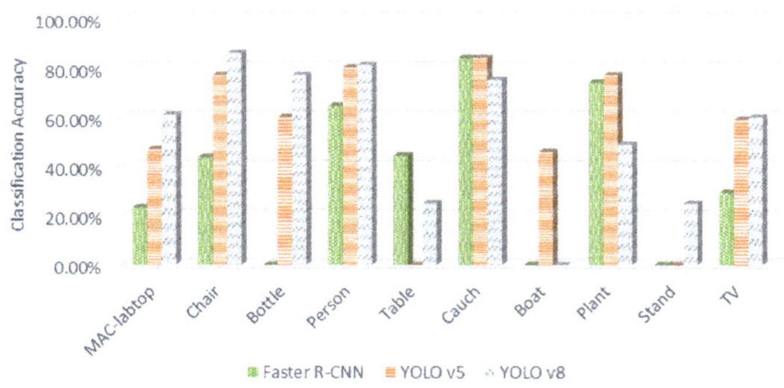

Figure 8. Object classification accuracy for three object detection models.

Table 4. The object classification accuracy for each object in the experimental testbed using three classifiers.

Object	Faster R-CNN	YOLO v5	YOLO v8
MAC-PC	23.25%	47%	61%
Chair	43.75%	77%	86%
Person	64.50%	80%	81%
Table	44.50%	0%	25%
Couch	84%	84%	75%
Boat	0%	46%	0%
Plant	74%	77%	49%
Stand	0%	0%	25%
TV	29.50%	59%	60%
Bottle	0%	60%	77%

The processing time for the object detection models is essential for real-time applications; therefore, it was important to investigate the processing time for each object detection algorithm. As presented in Figure 9, the YOLO v5 and YOLO v8 algorithms processed almost four to five frames per second using the Raspberry Pi 4 computer. However, the Faster R-CNN algorithm processed almost one frame every four seconds on average.

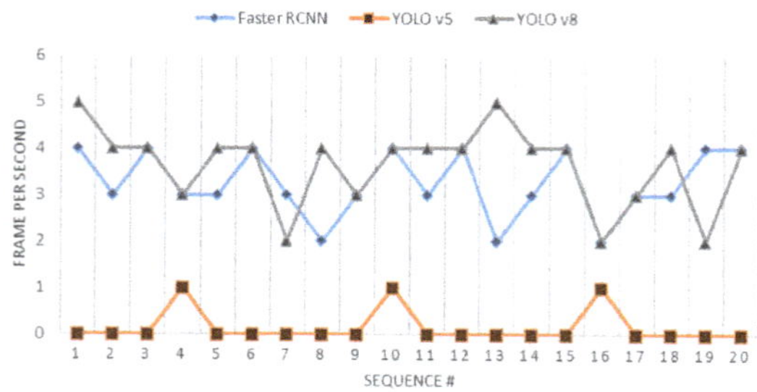

Figure 9. Processing time for the three object detection models.

Based on the evaluation results obtained, the YOLO v5 and YOLO v8 algorithms demonstrated superior performance in real-time object detection for robot systems compared to the Faster R-CNN algorithm.

5. Discussion

The importance of deep learning in semantic navigation stems from its capacity to provide robots with spatial awareness and contextual comprehension, where semantic navigation enables accurate navigation, object identification, and scene interpretation by determining the semantic properties of objects and situations. The deep learning approach is a cornerstone of semantic navigation, providing a thorough grasp of spatial contexts and object interactions. Its applications across varied datasets, together with continuous developments and prospects, highlight its critical role in defining the course of computer vision, autonomous systems, and human–machine interaction. As semantic navigation advances, the influence of deep learning will increase, ushering in a new era of intelligent and context-aware computers [1].

Based on the obtained results, it is evident that the Faster R-CNN model exhibits a slower processing speed compared to the YOLO models, making it unsuitable for real-time environments such as robot navigation systems. Furthermore, the Faster R-CNN model demonstrates inferior performance in terms of both detection and accuracy rates when compared to the YOLO models.

Both YOLO v5 and YOLO v8 are efficient object detection models that are capable of processing real-time images. However, YOLO v8 is a better choice for applications that necessitate real-time object detection.

As presented above, several object detection models have been employed in robot semantic navigation with diverse object detection accuracy, complexity, and processing time. However, according to the obtained results, the YOLO object detection model achieves the best object detection accuracy and offers minimum processing time.

The employment of the COCO dataset in robot semantic navigation supports the robot's exploration and understanding of various indoor and outdoor settings, allowing deep learning models to understand item interactions, spatial layouts, and contextual relationships. This capacity has applications in robotics, augmented reality, and human–computer interaction, among other areas. While the set of 80 classes in the COCO dataset proves suitable for numerous applications, these research experiments indicate the need to incorporate additional class groups to accommodate other common object types. Therefore, it is crucial to expand and enhance the COCO dataset to meet the requirements for developing deep learning applications based on these models.

Semantic navigation is poised for further improvement and development, with an emphasis on improving interpretability, generalization, and adaptation across varied situations. The combination of reinforcement learning, continuous learning, and multi-modal perception has the potential to improve the capabilities of semantic navigation systems, allowing them to traverse complicated, dynamic, and previously unexplored settings.

6. Conclusions

One of the most important aspects of robotics is semantic navigation, which emphasizes how important it is for robots to understand the semantics of their environment in order to make intelligent decisions. In this paper, common vision models for robot semantic navigation systems were examined, and the robot vision datasets that are currently available were investigated. This study clarified the relative performance of three different object detection models by means of an empirical analysis that sought to determine each model's effectiveness using the COCO vision dataset. The results show that, out of all the algorithms tested, the YOLO v8 object identification model performed the best in terms of classification rates, accuracy, and processing times, making it the best option for real-time robot semantic navigation systems. In the future, further research should be conducted to understand better the effects of using different object identification models in various case studies. This will help to develop a more thorough understanding of the models' applicability and performance subtleties in the context of robot semantic navigation. This extended analysis not only synthesizes the existing literature but also opens the door to improved approaches and future developments in robotic semantic navigation systems. Additionally, it is desirable to look into the robustness and adaptability of object detection models in a variety of dynamic environments, as it is crucial to evaluate these models' performance in a variety of lighting, weather, and cluttered scenarios to improve the dependability of semantic navigation systems.

Author Contributions: A.B., L.D., H.A. and A.A. surveyed and analyzed the recent developed robot semantic navigation systems that employed vision subsystems. T.A., A.A. and H.A. implemented three vision systems and performed several real experiments. O.M.A. validated the obtained results and contributed in writing the final manuscript. All authors have read and agreed to the published version of the manuscript.

Funding: This research received no external funding

Informed Consent Statement: Not applicable.

Data Availability Statement: This study employed the MS-COCO vision dataset to perform semantic classification, where MS-COCO dataset can be accessed through https://cocodataset.org/#home.

Conflicts of Interest: The authors declare no conflicts of interest.

References

1. Alenzi, Z.; Alenzi, E.; Alqasir, M.; Alruwaili, M.; Alhmiedat, T.; Alia, O.M. A semantic classification approach for indoor robot navigation. *Electronics* **2022**, *11*, 2063. [CrossRef]
2. Alhmiedat, T.; Marei, A.M.; Messoudi, W.; Albelwi, S.; Bushnag, A.; Bassfar, Z.; Alnajjar, F.; Elfaki, A.O. A SLAM-based localization and navigation system for social robots: The pepper robot case. *Machines* **2023**, *11*, 158. [CrossRef]
3. Bhatt, D.; Patel, C.; Talsania, H.; Patel, J.; Vaghela, R.; Pandya, S.; Modi, K.; Ghayvat, H. CNN Variants for Computer Vision: History, Architecture, Application, Challenges and Future Scope. *Electronics* **2021**, *10*, 2470. [CrossRef]
4. Alamri, S.; Alamri, H.; Alshehri, W.; Alshehri, S.; Alaklabi, A.; Alhmiedat, T. An autonomous maze-solving robotic system based on an enhanced wall-follower approach. *Machines* **2023**, *11*, 249. [CrossRef]
5. Alqobali, R.; Alshmrani, M.; Alnasser, R.; Rashidi, A.; Alhmiedat, T.; Alia, O.M. A Survey on Robot Semantic Navigation Systems for Indoor Environments. *Appl. Sci.* **2023**, *14*, 89. [CrossRef]
6. Uçar, A.; Demir, Y.; Güzeliş, C. Object recognition and detection with deep learning for autonomous driving applications. *Simulation* **2017**, *93*, 759–769. [CrossRef]
7. Hernández, A.C.; Gómez, C.; Crespo, J.; Barber, R. Object Detection Applied to Indoor Environments for Mobile Robot Navigation. *Sensors* **2016**, *16*, 1180. [CrossRef] [PubMed]
8. Krizhevsky, A.; Sutskever, I.; Hinton, G.E. Imagenet classification with deep convolutional neural networks. In Proceedings of the Advances in Neural Information Processing Systems 25, Lake Tahoe, NV, USA, 3–6 December 2012.
9. Li, Z.; Liu, F.; Yang, W.; Peng, S.; Zhou, J. A Survey of Convolutional Neural Networks: Analysis, Applications, and Prospects. *IEEE Trans. Neural Netw. Learn. Syst.* **2022**, *33*, 6999–7019. [CrossRef] [PubMed]
10. Ni, J.; Gong, T.; Gu, Y.; Zhu, J.; Fan, X. An improved deep residual network-based semantic simultaneous localization and mapping method for monocular vision robot. *Comput. Intell. Neurosci.* **2020**, *2020*, 7490840. [CrossRef]
11. Mousavian, A.; Toshev, A.; Fišer, M.; Košecká, J.; Wahid, A.; Davidson, J. Visual representations for semantic target driven navigation. In Proceedings of the 2019 International Conference on Robotics and Automation (ICRA), Montreal, QC, Canada, 20–24 May 2019; pp. 8846–8852.
12. Teso-Fz-Betoño, D.; Zulueta, E.; Sánchez-Chica, A.; Fernandez-Gamiz, U.; Saenz-Aguirre, A. Semantic segmentation to develop an indoor navigation system for an autonomous mobile robot. *Mathematics* **2020**, *8*, 855. [CrossRef]
13. Simonyan, K.; Zisserman, A. Very deep convolutional networks for large-scale image recognition. *arXiv* **2014**, arXiv:1409.1556.
14. Dang, T.V.; Bui, N.T. Multi-scale fully convolutional network-based semantic segmentation for mobile robot navigation. *Electronics* **2023**, *12*, 533. [CrossRef]
15. Kim, W.; Seok, J. Indoor semantic segmentation for robot navigating on mobile. In Proceedings of the 2018 Tenth International Conference on Ubiquitous and Future Networks (ICUFN), Prague, Czech Republic, 3–6 July 2018; pp. 22–25.
16. Dang, T.V.; Tran, D.M.C.; Tan, P.X. IRDC-Net: Lightweight Semantic Segmentation Network Based on Monocular Camera for Mobile Robot Navigation. *Sensors* **2023**, *23*, 6907. [CrossRef] [PubMed]
17. Wei, Y.; Wei, W.; Zhang, Y. EfferDeepNet: An Efficient Semantic Segmentation Method for Outdoor Terrain. *Machines* **2023**, *11*, 256. [CrossRef]
18. Liu, W.; Anguelov, D.; Erhan, D.; Szegedy, C.; Reed, S.; Fu, C.Y.; Berg, A.C., SSD: Single Shot MultiBox Detector. In *Lecture Notes in Computer Science*; Springer International Publishing: Berlin/Heidelberg, Germany, 2016; pp. 21–37. [CrossRef]
19. Bersan, D.; Martins, R.; Campos, M.; Nascimento, E.R. Semantic map augmentation for robot navigation: A learning approach based on visual and depth data. In Proceedings of the 2018 Latin American Robotic Symposium, 2018 Brazilian Symposium on Robotics (SBR) and 2018 Workshop on Robotics in Education (WRE), João Pessoa, Brazil, 6–10 November 2018; pp. 45–50.

20. Martins, R.; Bersan, D.; Campos, M.F.; Nascimento, E.R. Extending maps with semantic and contextual object information for robot navigation: A learning-based framework using visual and depth cues. *J. Intell. Robot. Syst.* **2020**, *99*, 555–569. [CrossRef]
21. Dos Reis, D.H.; Welfer, D.; De Souza Leite Cuadros, M.A.; Gamarra, D.F.T. Mobile robot navigation using an object recognition software with RGBD images and the YOLO algorithm. *Appl. Artif. Intell.* **2019**, *33*, 1290–1305. [CrossRef]
22. Wang, L.; Li, R.; Sun, J.; Zhao, L.; Shi, H.; Seah, H.S.; Tandianus, B. Object-Aware Hybrid Map for Indoor Robot Visual Semantic Navigation. In Proceedings of the 2019 IEEE International Conference on Robotics and Biomimetics (ROBIO), Dali, China, 6–8 December 2019; pp. 1166–1172.
23. Anebarassane, Y.; Kumar, D.; Chandru, A.; Adithya, P.; Sathiyamurthy, K. Enhancing ORB-SLAM3 with YOLO-based Semantic Segmentation in Robotic Navigation. In Proceedings of the 2023 IEEE World Conference on Applied Intelligence and Computing (AIC), Sonbhadra, India, 29–30 July 2023; pp. 874–879.
24. Mengcong, X.; Li, M. Object semantic annotation based on visual SLAM. In Proceedings of the 2021 Asia-Pacific Conference on Communications Technology and Computer Science (ACCTCS), Shenyang, China, 22–24 January 2021; pp. 197–201.
25. Miyamoto, R.; Adachi, M.; Nakamura, Y.; Nakajima, T.; Ishida, H.; Kobayashi, S. Accuracy improvement of semantic segmentation using appropriate datasets for robot navigation. In Proceedings of the 2019 6th International Conference on Control, Decision and Information Technologies (CoDIT), Paris, France, 23–26 April 2019; pp. 1610–1615.
26. Henke dos Reis, D.; Welfer, D.; de Souza Leite Cuadros, M.A.; Tello Gamarra, D.F. Object Recognition Software Using RGBD Kinect Images and the YOLO Algorithm for Mobile Robot Navigation. In *Intelligent Systems Design and Applications: 19th International Conference on Intelligent Systems Design and Applications (ISDA 2019) held December 3–5. 2019*; Springer: Berlin/Heidelberg, Germany, 2021; pp. 255–263.
27. Xia, X.; Zhang, P.; Sun, J. YOLO-Based Semantic Segmentation for Dynamic Removal in Visual-Inertial SLAM. In *Proceedings of the 2023 Chinese Intelligent Systems Conference*; Springer: Berlin/Heidelberg, Germany, 2023; pp. 377–389.
28. Truong, P.H.; You, S.; Ji, S. Object detection-based semantic map building for a semantic visual SLAM system. In Proceedings of the 2020 20th International Conference on Control, Automation and Systems (ICCAS), Busan, Republic of Korea, 13–16 October 2020; pp. 1198–1201.
29. Liu, X.; Muise, C. A Neural-Symbolic Approach for Object Navigation. In Proceedings of the 2nd Embodied AI Workshop (CVPR 2021), Virtual, 20 June 2021; pp. 19–25.
30. Chaves, D.; Ruiz-Sarmiento, J.R.; Petkov, N.; Gonzalez-Jimenez, J. Integration of CNN into a robotic architecture to build semantic maps of indoor environments. In *Advances in Computational Intelligence: 15th International Work-Conference on Artificial Neural Networks, IWANN 2019, Gran Canaria, Spain, June 12–14. 2019, Proceedings, Part II 15*; Springer: Berlin/Heidelberg, Germany, 2019; pp. 313–324.
31. Joo, S.H.; Manzoor, S.; Rocha, Y.G.; Bae, S.H.; Lee, K.H.; Kuc, T.Y.; Kim, M. Autonomous navigation framework for intelligent robots based on a semantic environment modeling. *Appl. Sci.* **2020**, *10*, 3219. [CrossRef]
32. Qiu, H.; Lin, Z.; Li, J. Semantic Map Construction via Multi-sensor Fusion. In Proceedings of the 2021 36th Youth Academic Annual Conference of Chinese Association of Automation (YAC), Nanchang, China, 28–30 May 2021; pp. 495–500.
33. Fernandes, J.C.d.C.S. Semantic Mapping with a Mobile Robot Using a RGB-D Camera. Master's Thesis, Laboratório de Robótica Móvel, Instituto de Sistemas e Robótica-Universidade de Coimbra, Coimbra, Portugal, 2019.
34. Xu, X.; Liu, L.i.; Xiong, R.; Jiang, L. Real-time instance-aware semantic mapping. *J. Phys. Conf. Ser.* **2020**, *1507*, 052013. [CrossRef]
35. Liu, X.; Wen, S.; Pan, Z.; Xu, C.; Hu, J.; Meng, H. Vision-IMU multi-sensor fusion semantic topological map based on RatSLAM. *Measurement* **2023**, *220*, 113335. [CrossRef]
36. Xie, Z.; Li, Z.; Zhang, Y.; Zhang, J.; Liu, F.; Chen, W. A multi-sensory guidance system for the visually impaired using YOLO and ORB-SLAM. *Information* **2022**, *13*, 343. [CrossRef]
37. Qi, X.; Wang, W.; Liao, Z.; Zhang, X.; Yang, D.; Wei, R. Object semantic grid mapping with 2D LiDAR and RGB-D camera for domestic robot navigation. *Appl. Sci.* **2020**, *10*, 5782. [CrossRef]
38. Sun, H.; Meng, Z.; Ang, M.H. Semantic mapping and semantics-boosted navigation with path creation on a mobile robot. In Proceedings of the 2017 IEEE International Conference on Cybernetics and Intelligent Systems (CIS) and IEEE Conference on Robotics, Automation and Mechatronics (RAM), Ningbo, China, 19–21 November 2017; pp. 207–212.
39. Shao, C.; Zhang, L.; Pan, W. Faster R-CNN learning-based semantic filter for geometry estimation and its application in vSLAM systems. *IEEE Trans. Intell. Transp. Syst.* **2021**, *23*, 5257–5266. [CrossRef]
40. Sevugan, A.; Karthikeyan, P.; Sarveshwaran, V.; Manoharan, R. Optimized navigation of mobile robots based on Faster R-CNN in wireless sensor network. *Int. J. Sens. Wirel. Commun. Control* **2022**, *12*, 440–448. [CrossRef]
41. Sun, Y.; Su, T.; Tu, Z. Faster R-CNN based autonomous navigation for vehicles in warehouse. In Proceedings of the 2017 IEEE International Conference on Advanced Intelligent Mechatronics (AIM), Munich, Germany, 3–7 July 2017; pp. 1639–1644.
42. Zhang, Z.; Zhang, J.; Tang, Q. Mask R-CNN based semantic RGB-D SLAM for dynamic scenes. In Proceedings of the 2019 IEEE/ASME International Conference on Advanced Intelligent Mechatronics (AIM), Hong Kong, China, 8–12 July 2019; pp. 1151–1156.
43. Sinha, R.K.; Pandey, R.; Pattnaik, R. Deep Learning For Computer Vision Tasks: A review. *arXiv* **2018**, arXiv:1804.03928
44. Cheng, J.; Sun, Y.; Meng, M.Q.H. A dense semantic mapping system based on CRF-RNN network. In Proceedings of the 2017 18th International Conference on Advanced Robotics (ICAR), Hong Kong, China, 10–12 July 2017; pp. 589–594.
45. Xiang, Y.; Fox, D. DA-RNN: Semantic mapping with data associated recurrent neural networks. *arXiv* **2017**, arXiv:1703.03098.

46. Zubair Irshad, M.; Chowdhury Mithun, N.; Seymour, Z.; Chiu, H.P.; Samarasekera, S.; Kumar, R. SASRA: Semantically-aware Spatio-temporal Reasoning Agent for Vision-and-Language Navigation in Continuous Environments. In Proceedings of the 2022 26th International Conference on Pattern Recognition (ICPR), Montreal, QC, Canada, 21–25 August 2022.
47. Zhang, Y.; Feng, Z. Crowd-Aware Mobile Robot Navigation Based on Improved Decentralized Structured RNN via Deep Reinforcement Learning. *Sensors* **2023**, *23*, 1810. [CrossRef]
48. Ondruska, P.; Dequaire, J.; Wang, D.Z.; Posner, I. End-to-end tracking and semantic segmentation using recurrent neural networks. *arXiv* **2016**, arXiv:1604.05091.
49. Le, N.; Rathour, V.S.; Yamazaki, K.; Luu, K.; Savvides, M. Deep Reinforcement Learning in Computer Vision: A Comprehensive Survey. *arXiv* **2021**, arXiv:2108.11510. [CrossRef]
50. Zhou, S.; Liu, X.; Xu, Y.; Guo, J. A deep Q-network (DQN) based path planning method for mobile robots. In Proceedings of the 2018 IEEE International Conference on Information and Automation (ICIA), Wuyishan, China, 11–13 August 2018; pp. 366–371.
51. Reddy, D.R.; Chella, C.; Teja, K.B.R.; Baby, H.R.; Kodali, P. Autonomous Vehicle Based on Deep Q-Learning and YOLOv3 with Data Augmentation. In Proceedings of the 2021 International Conference on Communication, Control and Information Sciences (ICCISc), Idukki, India, 16–18 June 2021; Volume 1, pp. 1–7.
52. Zeng, F.; Wang, C.; Ge, S.S. A survey on visual navigation for artificial agents with deep reinforcement learning. *IEEE Access* **2020**, *8*, 135426–135442. [CrossRef]
53. Dai, Y.; Yang, S.; Lee, K. Sensing and Navigation for Multiple Mobile Robots Based on Deep Q-Network. *Remote Sens.* **2023**, *15*, 4757. [CrossRef]
54. Vuong, T.A.T.; Takada, S. Semantic Analysis for Deep Q-Network in Android GUI Testing. In Proceedings of the SEKE, Lisbon, Portugal, 10–12 July 2019; pp. 123–170.
55. Kästner, L.; Marx, C.; Lambrecht, J. Deep-reinforcement-learning-based semantic navigation of mobile robots in dynamic environments. In Proceedings of the 2020 IEEE 16th International Conference on Automation Science and Engineering (CASE), Hong Kong, China, 20–21 August 2020; pp. 1110–1115.
56. Xu, J.; Zhang, H.; Qiu, J. A deep deterministic policy gradient algorithm based on averaged state-action estimation. *Comput. Electr. Eng.* **2022**, *101*, 108015. [CrossRef]
57. Zhu, K.; Zhang, T. Deep reinforcement learning based mobile robot navigation: A review. *Tsinghua Sci. Technol.* **2021**, *26*, 674–691. [CrossRef]
58. Haarnoja, T.; Zhou, A.; Hartikainen, K.; Tucker, G.; Ha, S.; Tan, J.; Kumar, V.; Zhu, H.; Gupta, A.; Abbeel, P.; et al. Soft actor-critic algorithms and applications. *arXiv* **2018**, arXiv:1812.05905.
59. Sharma, S. SAC-RL: Continuous Control of Wheeled Mobile Robot for Navigation in a Dynamic Environment. Ph.D. Thesis, Indian Institute of Technology Patna, Patna, India, 2020.
60. Wahid, A.; Stone, A.; Chen, K.; Ichter, B.; Toshev, A. Learning object-conditioned exploration using distributed soft actor critic. *Proc. Conf. Robot. Learn. PMLR* **2021**, *155*, 1684–1695.
61. Schulman, J.; Wolski, F.; Dhariwal, P.; Radford, A.; Klimov, O. Proximal Policy Optimization Algorithms. *arXiv* **2017**, arXiv:1707.06347.
62. Lin, T.Y.; Maire, M.; Belongie, S.; Bourdev, L.; Girshick, R.; Hays, J.; Perona, P.; Ramanan, D.; Zitnick, C.L.; Dollár, P. Microsoft COCO: Common Objects in Context. *arXiv* **2015**, arXiv:1405.0312.
63. Pereira, R.; Gonçalves, N.; Garrote, L.; Barros, T.; Lopes, A.; Nunes, U.J. Deep-learning based global and semantic feature fusion for indoor scene classification. In Proceedings of the 2020 IEEE International Conference on Autonomous Robot Systems and Competitions (ICARSC), Ponta Delgada, Portugal, 15–17 April 2020; pp. 67–73.
64. Georgakis, G.; Bucher, B.; Schmeckpeper, K.; Singh, S.; Daniilidis, K. Learning to map for active semantic goal navigation. *arXiv* **2021**, arXiv:2106.15648.
65. Yu, D.; Khatri, C.; Papangelis, A.; Namazifar, M.; Madotto, A.; Zheng, H.; Tur, G. Common sense and Semantic-Guided Navigation via Language in Embodied Environments. In Proceedings of the International Conference on Learning Representations ICLR 2020, Addis Ababa, Ethiopia, 30 April 2020.
66. Krantz, J. Semantic Embodied Navigation: Developing Agents That Navigate from Language and Vision. Ph.D. Thesis. Oregon State University, Corvallis, OR, USA, 2023.
67. Narasimhan, M.; Wijmans, E.; Chen, X.; Darrell, T.; Batra, D.; Parikh, D.; Singh, A. Seeing the un-scene: Learning amodal semantic maps for room navigation. In *Computer Vision—ECCV 2020: 16th European Conference, Glasgow, UK, August 23–28. 2020, Proceedings, Part XVIII 16*; Springer: Berlin/Heidelberg, Germany, 2020; pp. 513–529.
68. Vicente, S.; Carreira, J.; Agapito, L.; Batista, J. Reconstructing PASCAL VOC. In Proceedings of the IEEE Conference on Computer Vision and Pattern Recognition (CVPR), Columbus, OH, USA, 23–28 June 2014.
69. Geiger, A.; Lenz, P.; Stiller, C.; Urtasun, R. Vision meets robotics: The KITTI dataset. *Int. J. Robot. Res.* **2013**, *32*, 1231–1237. [CrossRef]
70. Behley, J.; Garbade, M.; Milioto, A.; Quenzel, J.; Behnke, S.; Stachniss, C.; Gall, J. Semantickitti: A dataset for semantic scene understanding of lidar sequences. In Proceedings of the IEEE/CVF International Conference on Computer Vision, Seoul, Republic of Korea, 27 October–2 November 2019; pp. 9297–9307.
71. Behley, J.; Garbade, M.; Milioto, A.; Quenzel, J.; Behnke, S.; Gall, J.; Stachniss, C. Towards 3D LiDAR-based semantic scene understanding of 3D point cloud sequences: The SemanticKITTI Dataset. *Int. J. Robot. Res.* **2021**, *40*, 959–967. [CrossRef]

72. Kostavelis, I.; Gasteratos, A. Semantic mapping for mobile robotics tasks: A survey. *Robot. Auton. Syst.* **2015**, *66*, 86–103. [CrossRef]
73. Zhou, B.; Zhao, H.; Puig, X.; Fidler, S.; Barriuso, A.; Torralba, A. Scene Parsing through ADE20K Dataset. In Proceedings of the 2017 IEEE Conference on Computer Vision and Pattern Recognition (CVPR), Honolulu, HI, USA, 21–26 July 2017; pp. 5122–5130. [CrossRef]
74. Zhang, C.; Yang, Z.; Xue, B.; Zhuo, H.; Liao, L.; Yang, X.; Zhu, Z. Perceiving like a Bat: Hierarchical 3D Geometric and ndash;Semantic Scene Understanding Inspired by a Biomimetic Mechanism. *Biomimetics* **2023**, *8*, 436. [CrossRef] [PubMed]
75. Raspberry Pi 4 2024. Available online: http://www.raspberrypi.com/products/raspberry-pi-4-model-b/ (accessed on 21 August 2024).
76. RPLiDAR A1 2024. Available online: http://www.slamtec.ai/product/slamtec-rplidar-a1/ (accessed on 21 August 2024).
77. Logitech Webcam 2024. Available online: https://www.logitech.com/en-sa/products/webcams/c920-pro-hd-webcam.960-001055.html (accessed on 21 August 2024).

technologies

MDPI

Article

Fast Detection of the Stick–Slip Phenomenon Associated with Wheel-to-Rail Sliding Using Acceleration Sensors: An Experimental Study

Gabriel Popa [1], Mihail Andrei [2], Emil Tudor [3,*], Ionuț Vasile [3] and George Ilie [4]

1. Rolling Stock Department, National University of Science and Technology POLITEHNICA Bucharest, 060042 Bucharest, Romania; gabriel.popa@upb.ro
2. Railway Safety Supervisory Department, Romanian Railway Safety Authority AGFR, 010719 Bucharest, Romania; mihai.andrei@agifer.ro
3. Renewable Sources and Energy Efficiency Department, National Institute for Research and Development in Electrical Engineering ICPE-CA, 030138 Bucharest, Romania; ionut.vasile@icpe-ca.ro
4. Technical Department, Romanian Railway Authority—AFER, 010719 Bucharest, Romania; george.ilie@sigurantaferoviara.ro

* Correspondence: emil.tudor@icpe-ca.ro

Abstract: The stick–slip phenomenon, the initial stage when the traction wheel starts sliding on the rail, is a critical operation that needs to be detected quickly to control the traction drive. In this study, we have developed an experimental model that uses acceleration sensors mounted on the wheel to evaluate the amplitude of the stick–slip phenomena. These sensors can alert the driver or assist the traction control unit when a stick–slip occurs. We propose a method to reduce the amplitude of the stick–slip phenomenon using special hydraulic dampers and viscous dampers mounted on the tractive axles of the locomotive to prevent slipping during acceleration. This practical solution, validated through numerical simulation, can be readily implemented in railway systems. The paper's findings can be used to select the necessary sensors and corresponding vibration dampers. By implementing these sliding reducers, a locomotive can significantly improve traction, apply more torque to the wheel, and increase the load of a carrier train, instilling confidence in the efficiency of the proposed solution.

Keywords: stick–slip; electronic sensors; sliding detection; vibration dampers

1. Introduction

Electric traction units for locomotives are prevalent in today's rail traffic because they can provide more power to the wheels. In [1], the authors extensively discussed the challenges related to the initial movement of electric vehicles.

A comparative analysis of the interaction conditions of locomotive wheels with rails under electric and diesel traction for open-pit railway transport [2] is provided. Conditions that promote the formation of welding bridges (setting) between microbridges of the contacting surfaces are described. Conclusions are drawn on the influence of the interaction modes of locomotive wheels with the rails on their traction ability.

The work [3] presents and discusses the effect of different tangential contact models on the vehicle's dynamic response.

The paper [4] investigates the effect of slip rate on the traction coefficient of the wheel/rail interface using a twin-disc machine under replicated tribological and locomotive operating conditions. The traction coefficient decreases with increasing slip rate.

The study [5] investigated wheel–rail contact, particularly the multifaceted aspects of wear phenomena in railway engineering, focusing on their significant implications for environmental costs and operational efficiency. Experimental trials were conducted using a high-performance bi-disc apparatus, evaluating various materials, contact pressures, and lubrication conditions.

The paper [6] presents the electric traction system of the main line of two-unit freight diesel locomotives. Modernising a combined diesel engine startup system and a power supply for consumers of an onboard network using a synchronous machine in starter/generator mode increases the efficiency of locomotive electrical equipment usage. There are ways to improve regular axle control to increase diesel locomotive traction and power characteristics. Suggested solutions enhance the traction and anti-slip locomotive characteristics by modernising the traction transmission system and electrical equipment microprocessor control algorithms. According to the tests and operations carried out, axle control allows individual control of the tangential tractive effort of each axis of the locomotive. The benefits of such methods are as follows: limiting the speed of excessive sliding of the wheelset (no more than 1–3 m/s) with loss of adhesion, reducing the wheelset wear by 16%, minimising sand consumption by 20%, and minimising the loss of tangential power during wheel slippage. Thus, electronic control of the axle during traction aims to increase the tangential tractive effort and, accordingly, the traction coefficient of the locomotive by 12–15%, resulting in a 15% increase in the tonnage rating of the transported goods.

Controlling traction is improved using dedicated methods, such as direct torque control applied for dual-star induction motors, to reduce harmonic currents, torque ripples, and steady-state torque error [7].

The stick–slip phenomenon, which commonly affects the starting of freight locomotives, is presented in [8] as an example of stick–slip and stick–slip-separation waves.

The study [9] discusses the implications of obstacle curvature, material orthotropy, and friction to the flutter and divergence instabilities of elastic media.

The presented work is focused on researching the dynamical effects of a rail vehicle while running on a railway track created in a commercial multibody model [10].

The paper [11] analyses the results of acceleration signal measurements obtained from the Rail Vehicle and Rail Track Monitoring System prototype. This prototype measures acceleration signals on designated elements of the electric multiple unit (EMU), which comprise components such as bogie frames, wheels, and bodies of railway vehicles.

The study [12] states that structural dynamics are essential for understanding and assessing any engineering product performance, and knowledge of dynamic structural response is fundamental to ensuring a sustainable and safe product's functioning. By using piezo sensors and FEM analysis, the authors aim to validate the dynamic finite elements model realised to certify the crashworthiness of locomotive design and to evaluate the body interaction with bogie and track to avoid locomotive structural resonance phenomena.

Bogie-hunting instability is one of the common faults in railway vehicles. It not only affects ride comfort but also threatens operational safety. Due to the lower operating speed of metro vehicles, their bogie-hunting stability is often overlooked. Acceleration and displacement sensors are installed on metro vehicles to collect data, which are processed in real-time in 2 s intervals [13].

Several works deal with the measured dynamical response of a vehicle (vertical acceleration of rails and noise emission of a car), which is analysed in the time and frequency domain [14,15].

Previous work [16] focused on compensating for the elimination of load transfer effects by using an algorithm to redistribute the traction effort between the tractive axles equipped with electric traction motors.

Conventional vibration monitoring systems relying on wired sensors present several limitations for continuous monitoring projects on many structures. In the work [17], an intelligent wireless monitoring system is developed for bridge modal identification to provide an alternative tool to wired sensors in this field. The main peculiarities of the designed wireless accelerometers are the low cost, the ease of installation on the structure, and the long-term autonomy granted by using energy harvesting techniques.

In the paper [18], several acceleration sensors for online measurement were installed on the lateral sides of the wheel axle of a test bogie. The accelerometers used are wireless three-axis sensors with a capacity of 60 g, and data were acquired at 6000 Hz.

The research presented in [19] examined how vibration signals could be used for real-time train and track control. Experiments are essential to validate these methods when studying vibration in transportation because it is essential to consider various nonlinear dynamic forces that can occur during travel.

The reviews [20] and [21] provide more information about the vibration sensors used in railway equipment.

Faced with these challenges, the authors propose a method to evaluate the stick–slip phenomenon using electronic acceleration sensors placed on the wheel. They also propose a new method for mitigating the effects of the stick–slip phenomenon during the locomotive's start by using a dampener on the wheelset. Simulations are used to prove that the dampener solution can improve the locomotive's behaviour.

2. Materials and Methods

2.1. Selecting the Acceleration Sensors (Material, Range)

To validate the mathematical model used in the simulations of the stick–slip phenomenon, we measured and recorded the phenomenon produced at the axles of the 5100 kW electric locomotive.

For the measurement, we used an accelerometer mounted on one of the axle wheels where the stick–slip movement was generated. The accelerometer was positioned to measure the wheel's tangential acceleration during stick–slip movement.

The data measured by this accelerometer were recorded on an SD card and subsequently transferred to a laptop for processing and analysis. It was impossible to connect directly to the computer and record the data in real time because the measurement and recording system rotated with the wheel on which it was mounted.

2.1.1. The Accelerometer

Selecting the acceleration sensor, we aim to use a low-weight device with low consumption and high accuracy.

Measuring range regarding acceleration is ± 10 to ± 20 g.

The accelerometer used to perform the measurements of stick–slip movement must meet the following conditions:

- smaller mass and dimensions;
- low power consumption to be able to power it from a small battery;
- measurement accuracy (not more than 0.5% measurement errors);
- immunity to electromagnetic disturbances;
- immunity to strong magnetic fields;
- be simple to connect with the recording installation.

The selected device was the MPU-6050 [22] accelerometer produced by InvenSense Inc. This device is a three-axis accelerometer combined with a three-axis gyroscope integrated into a single $4 \times 4 \times 0.9$ mm chip in MEMS technology.

The integrated MPU-6050 accelerometer can be purchased as a SparkFun development board [23]. The sensor is mounted on a printed circuit board with all the necessary peripheral components, as presented in Figure 1. It is easy to use by simply connecting to a microcontroller.

Figure 1. The MPU-6050 acceleration sensor mounted on a development board [23].

Characteristics of the integrated MPU-6050 accelerometer that are relevant for this application are as follows:

- Wiring plate dimensions: 27 × 15 × 4 mm;
- Supply voltage: 2.3–3.4 Vdc;
- Three–axes accelerometer measurement available scales: ±2 g, ±4 g, ±8 g or ±16 g;
- Built-in temperature sensor;
- Serial output data are transmitted using I2C protocol;
- Integrated 16-bit analog-to-digital converter;
- Current consumption: 500 μA;
- Shock resistance: 10,000 g;
- Operating temperature: −40 °C ÷ 85 °C;
- Temperature sensitivity variation: ±0.02 %/°C;
- Maximum sampling frequency: 1 kHz;
- Mass: 1.5 g.

2.1.2. The Microcontroller

The microcontroller uses a serial communication channel with the accelerometer and must receive the transmitted data, format them, and save them to the microSD card as text files.

In addition to managing the received data, the microcontroller uses a start–stop button that commands the start and stop of the recording, as well as two LEDs that provide the status signal of the microcontroller.

The visual information displayed on those two LEDs are:

- blinking red: state of sleep (waiting);
- blinking green: data recording;
- red flash blinking intermittently: write error on micro SD card (missing card, full card, or defective card);

We chose an Atmega32u4 microcontroller card equipped with a micro SD card slot for storing data. Adafruit built the card's commercial version, known as Adafruit Feather 32u4 Adalogger [24], as presented in Figure 2.

This microcontroller board has the following characteristics:

- Dimensions: 51 mm × 23 mm × 8 mm;
- Mass: 5.1 g;
- ATmega32u4 microcontroller @ 8 MHz with 3.3 V logic;
- Voltage regulator of 3.3 V and 500 mA;
- Micro USB connector for programming, troubleshooting, and communications;
- Hardware for serial communications, I2C, and SPI;
- Seven pins with PWM capabilities;

- Ten pins of analogue inputs and outputs.

Figure 2. Adalogger board using Atmega32u4 microcontroller (51 mm × 23 mm × 8 mm).

This microcontroller board was mounted on a printed wiring circuit board and placed alongside the other components (connectors, start–stop button, battery switch, etc.) in an aluminium box for mechanical protection and protection against electromagnetic interference.

2.2. The Hardware of the Experimental Model Is Based on an Acceleration Sensor

Although theoretically, the acceleration sensor could have been placed in the same case as the microcontroller, we opted to separate them to protect the sensor from the resonance frequencies and harmonics coming from the vibrations of the rest of the components.

The electrical diagram of the measuring system is provided in Figure 3.

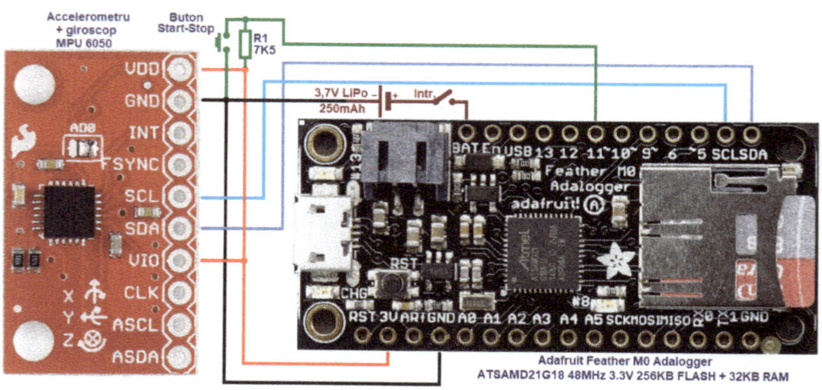

Figure 3. Electrical diagram of the measuring system.

Figure 4 shows the fully assembled measuring system, and Figure 5 shows the system attached to the wheel.

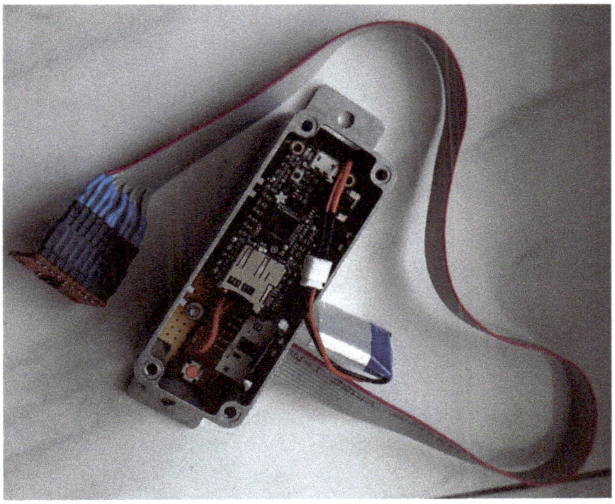

Figure 4. The experimental setup of the measuring system (105 mm × 30 mm × 12 mm).

Figure 5. The experimental setup and the on-wheel placement (wheel diameter 850 mm).

2.3. Mounting the Acceleration Sensors on the Wheel

The aluminium box, including the microcontroller, was also fixed to the wheel with solid magnets (made of Neodym).

A 10-wire ribbon cable with connectors at both ends connected the accelerometer and the microcontroller.

The experimental setup was mounted on the wheel's interior without any mechanical drills on the metal part of the wheel. Magnets were used to properly attach the components of the experimental model to the wheel, making them easy to disassemble at the end of the tests. The tests were performed on the powerful locomotive available [25] when trying to push another blocked locomotive, thus generating the stick–slip located at the tractive wheels.

2.4. Software Developed for the Experimental Model

The microcontroller's main task was to read the data transmitted serially by the acceleration sensor and write them to the microSD card.

Also, the microcontroller was required to display the status using two LEDs and to periodically read the status of the start–stop button.

Even though the acceleration sensor performed acceleration measurements at 1000 samples per second, the system's speed was much lower. The limiting factor was the low write speed on the micro SD card.

For this reason, the microcontroller's program had to be optimised to achieve an acceptable sampling speed. Mitigating the number of accesses to the micro SD card was necessary. Ultimately, we obtained a measured sampling speed of 304,135 Hz, which is enough for the intended purpose. This sampling speed allows for the recording of a spectrum of frequencies up to 152 Hz.

The microcontroller program was written in C++, compiled, and loaded into the microcontroller's memory with the Arduino development environment.

2.5. Hydraulic Shock Absorbers for the Experimental Model

Due to the adverse effects manifested during the stick–slip movements of the driving axles, including the accentuated wear of the wheels on the treads and oscillatory tensions in the mounted axle, we searched for a method that would eliminate this phenomenon. We proposed a system of damping stick–slip movement at the driving axles.

2.5.1. Solution for Reducing the Stick–Slip Phenomenon

The proposed technical solution uses a set of shock absorbers on the wheel discs and axle drive gear.

A shock absorber is a flywheel encapsulated in a metal housing filled with a viscous liquid (mineral oil). The flywheel can rotate freely from the housing. The play between the flywheel and the housing is small enough, and the relative movement of the flywheel to the housing produces significant viscous friction, which achieves energy dissipation and damping of oscillations.

This technical solution was identified in the flywheel used in the 12LDA28 diesel engine [26] with which 060DA electric diesel locomotives [27] are equipped, as presented in Figure 6. The two crankshafts at the free end are provided with viscous dumpers [28] used as shock absorbers to reduce the torsion vibrations to which these shafts are subjected during the motor's operation.

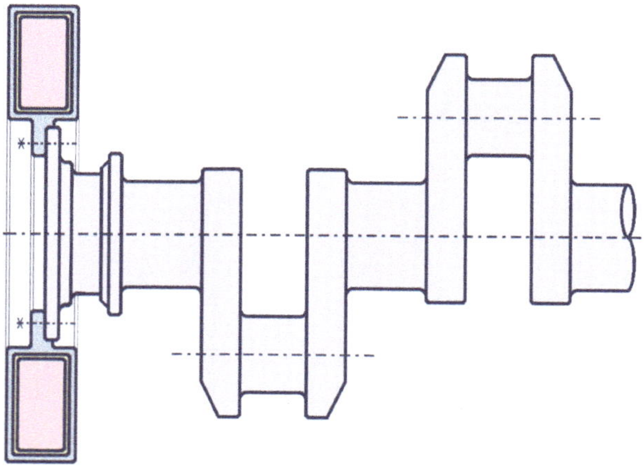

Figure 6. Mounting of the vibration damper (pink) on the crankshaft (grey) of the 12LDA28 motor.

The operation of such an oscillation damper is as follows: the damper housing tracks the movement of the shaft, which consists of a constant-speed component superimposed on an oscillating component. Due to the relatively high inertia, the flywheel tends toward uniform movement. The difference in gears between the flywheel and its housing generates viscous friction forces between the housing and the flywheel, and the torque of these forces dampens the shaft's oscillations.

To reduce the oscillations of the driving axle's stick–slips, we propose using vibration dampers, like the ones shown in Figure 7, on the locomotive axle.

Figure 7. Picture of a vibration damper for the tractive axle (diameter, 640 mm; width, 66 mm).

We identified two solutions for placing the dampers on the wheelset: one on the wheel's interior and the other inside the drive gear, as presented in Figure 8.

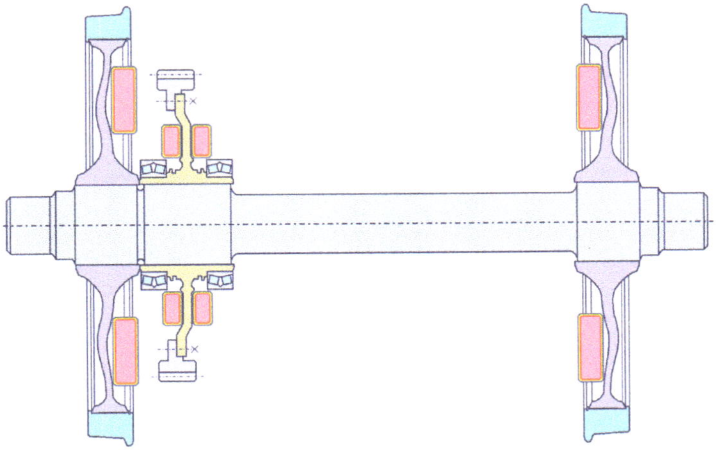

Figure 8. Possibilities of placing vibration shock absorbers on the elements of the mounted axle: one on the wheel's interior and the other inside the drive gear.

The presence of wheel-mounted brake discs limits the installation of shock absorbers on the axle wheels. The space available in the gear housing also affects the possibility of mounting the dampers on the axle drive gear.

2.5.2. The Mathematical Model Used for the Simulation

We studied the efficiency of such a damping system through simulations of the stick–slip behaviour of a driving axle fitted with two shock absorbers mounted on the discs of the two wheels, as presented in [29]. We have rewritten the system of differential equations used in previous simulations to model the stick–slip behaviour of such an axle provided with a damping system. To carry this out, we have completed the differential equations corresponding to the movement of the two wheels with terms expressing the resistance torque applied to the wheels by the two shock absorbers.

3. Results

3.1. The Presentation of the Rough Data Saved during the Tests

The microcontroller's data were saved in text format to be quickly examined immediately after the measurements were finished.

The data in text format were converted to Excel format for quick visualisation as charts. In this format, it was also possible to remove the data that were not of interest (areas before the start of the measurements and regions after the end of the measurements).

Writing software that graphically represents the acquired data was necessary to visualise them. The first recording was made with the immobilised wheel to record the noise of the acceleration signal. While recording, we checked the noise level of the recorded signal and the presence of the sound signal of some components resulting from electromagnetic disturbances in the railway environment (50 Hz components and their harmonics coming from electric traction installations or 75 Hz components from the signalling installations). The values are steady, and a $-1.85\ \text{m/s}^2$ offset was recorded; this background noise affects the measurement values by only 0.0457%. Also, checking the noise spectrum recorded using a scope, no dominant components with 50 Hz, 75 Hz, or multiples of these frequencies were found.

Tests were carried out with the active locomotive providing the tractive force, having the accelerometer mounted on the front wheel, and trying to move a blocked locomotive. This simulates the most significant effort during a train's launch: the initial movement when the brakes are closed and must be opened with the movement.

Figure 9 shows one of the recordings made when the wheel starts the stick–slip phenomenon. The amplitude of the acceleration rises to $78\ \text{m/s}^2$. The frequency can be measured on the graphic, with two successive peak values of 0.018 s, corresponding to a 55 Hz oscillation.

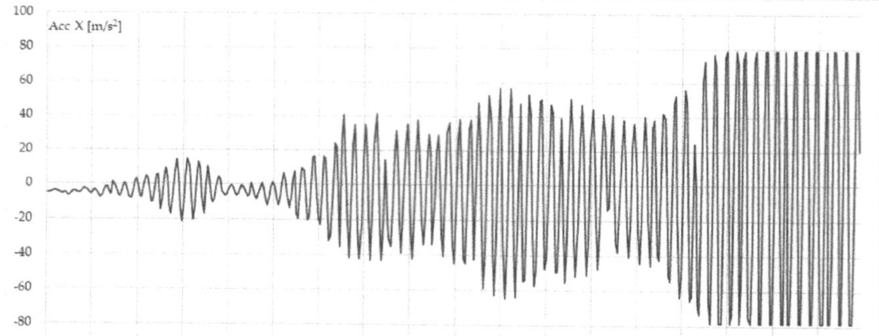

Figure 9. Data resulting from measuring wheel acceleration during start of a braked locomotive.

In Figures 9–12, the vibrations were so strong that, in some portions, they exceeded the sensor's maximum measuring range (8·g). The analysis of these datasets was carried out only on the portion where the level of the measured accelerations was within the transducer's measuring range.

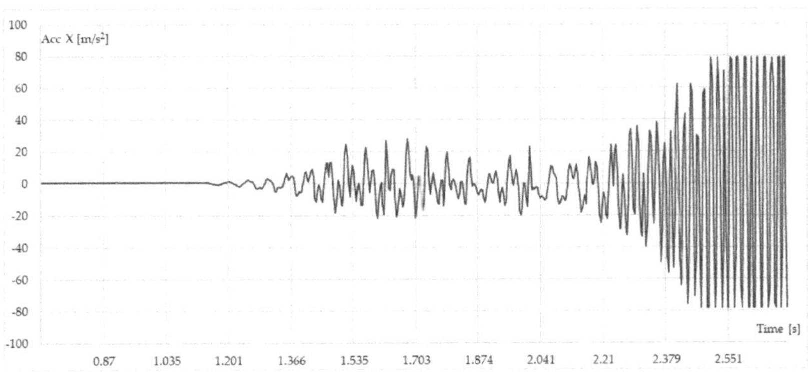

Figure 10. Data resulting from measurements; stick–slip occurred when the wheels rotates.

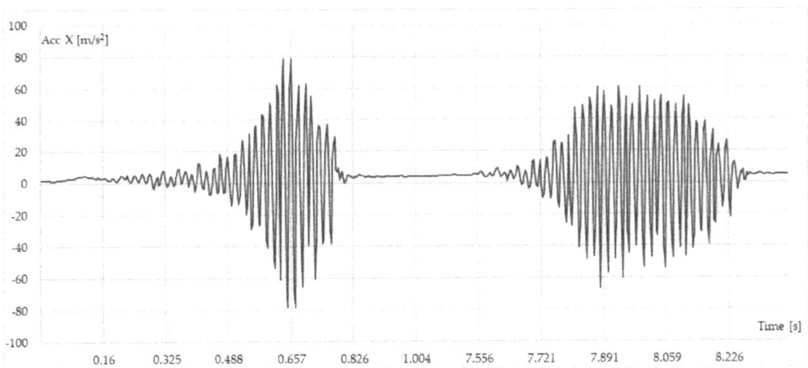

Figure 11. Data resulting from measurements; a small stick–slip occurred during restart.

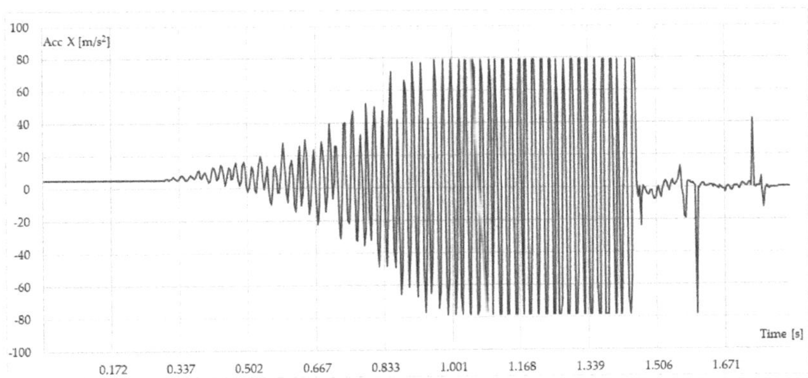

Figure 12. Data resulting from measurements, with a successful start of the train at moment 1.45 s.

Figures 9–11 show that after exceeding the adhesion limit, the amplitude of the oscillations increases then decreases a little, a situation that differs from the graphs resulting from the simulations. This decrease in amplitude is caused by a slight increase in the coefficient of friction between the wheel and the rail because, due to friction, the impurities existing on the surface of the wheel and rail are partially removed.

In Figure 10, the measuring system records some wheels sliding in the time intervals of 1.2–2.21 s until correct sanding of the rail-wheel surface increases the adherence, and the amplitude of the vibrations rises to central values after the 2.4 s point.

In Figure 11, it can be seen that the measuring system recorded the start of the tandem locomotives, with the initial stick–slip at low amplitude and duration (maximum 75 m/s^2 for 0.3 s), when the first locomotive has the pneumatical brake released, the bumpers compressed, and a new brake release with stick–slip with a maximum acceleration of 60 m/s^2 (for 0.5 s).

In Figure 12, it can be seen that the measuring system detached from the wheel surface at some point, causing the amplitude of the vibrations to drop sharply to zero.

The frequency spectra obtained from simulations and measurements are similar except for the noise in the spectrum of the measurement data. This noise is attributed to the sensors' offset and the irregularities on the wheel and rail surfaces.

The acceleration frequency is 55 Hz, which each measurement can detect. This value is essential for finding the proper shock absorbers.

3.2. *Presentations of the Effects of Hydraulic Shock Absorbers*

To highlight the two-wheeled shock absorbers' effect, we integrated the differential Equations (23)–(28) systems from [29], first without shock absorbers and then with shock absorbers. The two integrations were carried out strictly with the same parameters and starting from the same initial conditions, the difference being only the presence or absence of shock absorbers. The results of the two integrations (graphs of the angular speeds of the two wheels) were then compared.

The simulation was made with a program obtained by adapting the program used in stick–slip simulations, which achieves the parallel integration of the two systems of differential equations.

The two-wheeled shock absorbers were supposedly identical with the following parameters:

$$I_{A1} = I_{A2} = \frac{I_{R1}}{3} = 62\ \text{Kg}\cdot\text{m}^2 \quad (1)$$

$$\rho_{A1} = \rho_{A2} = 500\ \text{N}\cdot\text{m}\cdot\text{s}/\text{radian} \quad (2)$$

I_{A1} and I_{A2}—the moments of inertia of the two flywheels;
ρ_{A1} and ρ_{A2}—the damping introduced into the system by the two dampers.

Several simulations were carried out for different drive torques at the wheel cover, starting from the torque corresponding to the adhesion limit.

The first simulation was carried out at a wheel cover torque of 8720 N·m. At this torque value, the adhesion limit is slightly exceeded.

At these conditions, the skating of the axle begins, accompanied by a stick–slip (the blue line from Figure 13). In the absence of the damping system, the oscillation amplitude increases to infinity. In the presence of the damping system, the stick–slip phenomenon is triggered. Still, after a few oscillations, it pays off, restoring adhesion (the orange line from Figure 13). This behaviour is explained by the fact that at values close to the adhesion limit, the energy input in the oscillating system of the driving axle is small enough to be picked up and dissipated immediately by the damping system.

At higher torque (9040 Nm), the axle begins skating, and shock absorbers cannot avoid the wheel movement but affect the oscillation amplitude, as seen in Figure 14.

Simulations performed with higher torque show that the axle will begin skating and that the acceleration is proportional to the applied torque. Even in the presence of the shock absorbers, the wheels skate but do so with reduced oscillations. In Figure 15, we present the skating of the wheel, while using shock absorbers, at major torque of 9840 Nm and 9287 Nm. The simulations with increasing motor torque values were carried out to evaluate the conformity of the simulation, as the higher the torque applied, the higher the acceleration is.

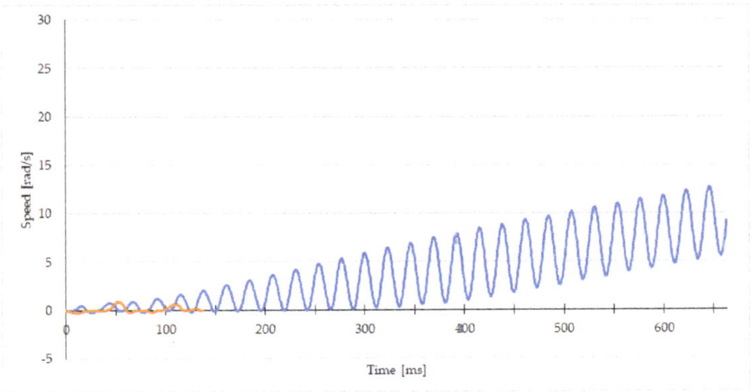

Figure 13. Comparison between the evolution of axle movement in stick–slip conditions without (blue line) and with shock absorbers (orange line) for 8720 N·m torque.

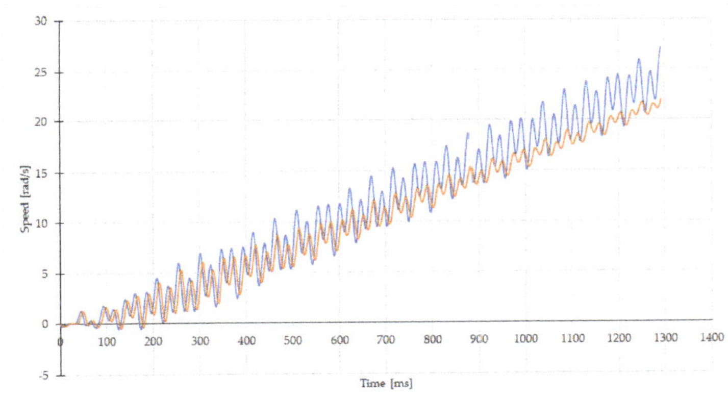

Figure 14. Comparison between the evolution of axle movement in stick–slip conditions without (blue line) and with shock absorbers (orange line) at a 9040 Nm torque.

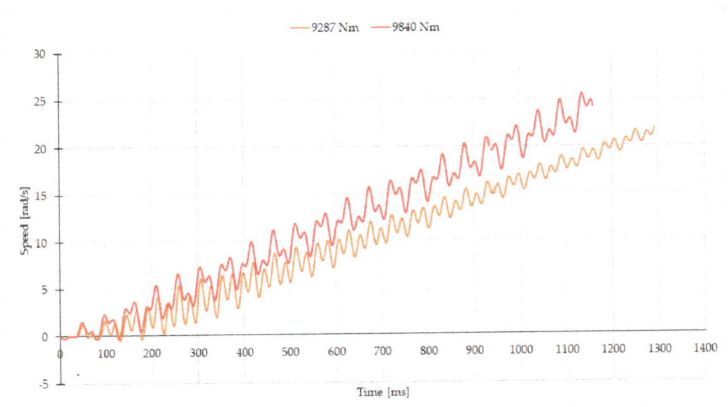

Figure 15. Comparison of axle movement evolution in stick–slip conditions with shock absorbers (orange line) at a 9280 Nm torque and with shock absorbers (red line) at 9840 Nm torque.

4. Discussion

The results are adjusted for a locomotive equipped with DC traction motors, which are known to have significant problems during startup. However, the solution can also be applied to locomotives powered by AC. Minimising the amplitude of the stick–slip phenomenon can enhance the available traction force and reduce wheel wear. It has been observed that the simulation data obtained using the proposed mathematical model sufficiently approximates the data obtained from measurements.

Variations in the coefficient of friction can cause differences in friction between the wheel and rail. These variations are caused by substances contaminating the surfaces of the wheel or rail, such as water, oil, dust, and metal powders, as well as the roughness and wear condition of the wheel surface and rail.

Based on the simulations, the damping system does not eliminate the stick–slip phenomenon. However, it does reduce the amplitude of the phenomenon and, to a lesser extent, the frequency of the oscillations produced, which is beneficial during operation. Additionally, the damping system improves the behaviour of the axle when the wheels lock during braking.

The simulations show that at higher torque values, the shock absorbers can no longer fully take over the energy introduced into the elastic system by wheel skating. This results in skating accompanied by stick–slips, and the amplitude of the oscillations increases towards infinity. However, the amplitude of stick–slip oscillations is reduced in the presence of shock absorbers, and the frequency of oscillations is significantly lower. This benefits the operation of the tread wear and the axle's fatigue stress.

The disadvantages of using the damping system include increasing the unsprung mass of the axle, which has adverse effects, especially at high speeds. Additionally, the limited space available in the area of the driving axles makes it challenging to mount shock absorbers, especially when the brake discs are mounted on wheels.

One can consider implementing systems for the elastic retention of the wheel or axle dampers to reduce unsprung mass. If brake discs are present, these shock absorbers can be situated between them and the wheels.

Freight trains running on steep inclines may experience a phenomenon called stick–slip over a prolonged period. This can cause the shock absorbers to generate significant heat, so cooling fins may be necessary to dissipate heat effectively.

Developments in the field of stick–slip detection are related to increasing the freight transportation payload and can include the use of electronic sensors powered by batteries, in a similar constriction as the pressure sensors used by cars, to help the automatic launch procedure performed by the traction control unit of the locomotive. Also, for old-fashioned locomotives using DC traction motors, the use of such shock absorbers as presented can reduce the effect of the stick–slip phenomena.

5. Conclusions

The developed measurement system for the wheel's centripetal acceleration can detect the critical accelerations involved during stick–slip phenomena at acceleration rates up to 200 m/s^2. As described in the article, the system was used to record data for estimating the amplitude and frequency of the stick–slip movement of the tractive wheels for a DC traction locomotive. The experimental setup can detect stick–slip phenomena, and can signalise to the driver when stick–slip phenomena is detected, for acceleration values starting with 1 g.

The system can be enhanced to provide signals to the control system and the driver. Based on the alarms generated during the detected stick–slip, the tractive force can be automatically or manually reduced. After extensive testing, the information obtained during slipping can be used to improve the train's starting.

The proposed method of reducing the amplitude of the stick–slip phenomenon using special hydraulic dampers and viscous dampers mounted on the locomotive's tractive axles prevents slipping during acceleration, as demonstrated using numerical simulation with two vibrations dampeners consisting of the flywheels used in the 12LDA28 diesel engine [26], with which the 060DA electric diesel locomotive is equipped, mounted on the wheels of a DC traction locomotive.

Installing shock absorbers to reduce the oscillation amplitude caused by stick–slip could be particularly effective in locomotives designed for pulling freight trains. Due to the significant forces, the stick–slip phenomenon occurs at high frequencies and lower traffic speeds, and the extra unsprung mass of the driving axle has no adverse effects.

Author Contributions: Conceptualization, G.P. and M.A.; methodology, G.P. and M.A.; software, M.A.; validation, G.P., E.T. and G.I.; formal analysis, E.T. and I.V.; investigation, M.A. and G.I.; resources, M.A.; data curation, E.T.; writing—original draft preparation, M.A.; writing—review and editing, E.T. and I.V.; visualisation, I.V.; supervision, G.I.; project administration, G.P.; funding acquisition, G.P. All authors have read and agreed to the published version of the manuscript.

Funding: This work was funded by National University of Science and Technology POLITEHNICA Bucharest through Project PubArt, and partially by the Ministry of Research, Innovation, and Digitalization, through Nucleus Program 42N/2023, project number PN23140102.

Institutional Review Board Statement: Not applicable.

Informed Consent Statement: Not applicable.

Data Availability Statement: All the data substantiating the conclusion of this study are included. Other primary datasets are available, upon reasonable request, from the author.

Conflicts of Interest: The authors declare no conflicts of interest. The funders had no role in the study's design, data collection, analysis, interpretation, or manuscript writing or in the decision to publish the results.

References

1. Popa, G.; Tudor, E. *Vehicule Feroviare de Tracțiune cu Motoare Asincrone (Traction Rail Vehicles with Asynchronous Motors)*, 3rd ed.; Editura MatrixRom: Bucharest, Romania, 2024; pp. 46–67.
2. Keropyan, A.M. Features of interaction of traction wheels of an electric locomotive and a diesel locomotive with rails in the conditions of open mountain works. *J. Frict. Wear* **2016**, *37*, 78–82. [CrossRef]
3. Millan, P.; Pagaimo, J.; Magalhães, H.; Ambrósio, J. Clearance joints and friction models for the modelling of friction damped railway freight vehicles. *Multibody Syst. Dyn.* **2022**, *58*, 21–45. [CrossRef]
4. Rahaman, M.L.; Bernal, E.; Spiryagin, M.; Bosomworth, C.; Sneath, B.; Wu, Q.; Cole, C.; McSweeney, T. An investigation into the effect of slip rate on the traction coefficient behaviour with a laboratory replication of a locomotive wheel rolling/sliding along a railway track. *Tribol. Int.* **2023**, *187*, 108773. [CrossRef]
5. Zani, N.; Mazzù, A.; Solazzi, L.; Petrogalli, C. Examining Wear Mechanisms in Railway Wheel Steels: Experimental Insights and Predictive Mapping. *Lubricants* **2024**, *12*, 93. [CrossRef]
6. Shamardina, V.N.; Anishchenko, M.V.; Lemeshko, S.M.; Kanunnikov, R.V. Functional efficiency enhancement of diesel-electric locomotive traction system. In Proceedings of the International Conference on Modern Electrical and Energy Systems (MEES), Kremenchuk, Ukraine, 15–17 November 2017; pp. 20–23. [CrossRef]
7. Guedida, S.; Tabbache, B.; Nounou, K.; Benbouzid, M. Direct torque control scheme for less harmonic currents and torque ripples for dual star induction motor. *Rev. Roum. Des Sci. Tech. Sér. Électrotech. Énergétique* **2023**, *68*, 331–338. [CrossRef]
8. Moirot, F.; Nguyen, Q.-S.; Oueslati, A. An example of stick–slip and stick–slip–separation waves. *Eur. J. Mech. A/Solids* **2003**, *22*, 107–118. [CrossRef]
9. Pinto da Costa, A.; Agwa, M.A. Frictional instabilities in orthotropic hollow cylinders. *Comput. Struct.* **2009**, *87*, 1275–1286. [CrossRef]
10. Dižo, J.; Blatnický, M.; Harušinec, J.; Suchánek, A. Assessment of Dynamics of a Rail Vehicle in Terms of Running Properties While Moving on a Real Track Model. *Symmetry* **2022**, *14*, 536. [CrossRef]
11. Kostrzewski, M. Analysis of selected acceleration signals measurements obtained during supervised service conditions—A study of hitherto approach. *J. Vibroengineering* **2018**, *20*, 1850–1866. [CrossRef]
12. Manea, I.; Sebesan, I.; Ghita, G.; Matache, M.-G.; Arsene, S. Experimental modal analysis of an electric locomotive body. *MATEC Web Conf.* **2017**, *112*, 07008. [CrossRef]
13. Zheng, B.; Wei, L.; Zeng, J.; Zhang, D. Experimental and Numerical Investigation of Bogie Hunting Instability for Railway Vehicles Based on Multiple Sensors. *Sensors* **2024**, *24*, 4027. [CrossRef] [PubMed]
14. Hába, A.; Zelenka, J.; Musil, M.; Vágner, J.; Kohout, M.; Havlíček, P. Diagnostics of railway vehicle based on dynamical response measurement. *Vibroeng. Procedia* **2014**, *3*, 272–277.
15. Zanelli, F.; Debattisti, N.; Mauri, M.; Argentino, A.; Belloli, M. Development and Field Validation of Wireless Sensors for Railway Bridge Modal Identification. *Appl. Sci.* **2023**, *13*, 3620. [CrossRef]

16. Andrei, M.; Popa, G.; Tudor, E.; Anghelița, P.; Matache, M.-G. The Electric Traction Motors Balancing for Load Transfer Effects Compensation. *INMATEH-Agric. Eng.* **2023**, *71*, 290–300. [CrossRef]
17. Gonzalo, A.-P.; Entezami, M.; Weston, P.; Roberts, C.; Garcia Marquez, F.-P. Railway Track and Vehicle Onboard Monitoring: A Review. *E3S Web Conf.* **2023**, *409*, 02014. [CrossRef]
18. Cho, H.; Park, J.; Park, K. Analysis of Axial Acceleration for the Detection of Rail Squats in High-Speed Railways. *CivilEng* **2023**, *4*, 1143–1156. [CrossRef]
19. Celiński, I.; Burdzik, R.; Młyńczak, J.; Kłaczyński, M. Research on the Applicability of Vibration Signals for Real-Time Train and Track Condition Monitoring. *Sensors* **2022**, *22*, 2368. [CrossRef] [PubMed]
20. Kostrzewski, M.; Melnik, R. Condition Monitoring of Rail Transport Systems: A Bibliometric Performance Analysis and Systematic Literature Review. *Sensors* **2021**, *21*, 4710. [CrossRef] [PubMed]
21. Bernal, E.; Spiryagin, M.; Cole, C. Onboard Condition Monitoring Sensors, Systems and Techniques for Freight Railway Vehicles: A Review. *IEEE Sens. J.* **2019**, *19*, 4–24. [CrossRef]
22. MPU-6050. Available online: https://invensense.tdk.com/products/motion-tracking/6-axis/mpu-6050/ (accessed on 11 July 2024).
23. MPU-6000A. Available online: https://cdn.sparkfun.com/datasheets/Components/General%20IC/PS-MPU-6000A.pdf (accessed on 11 July 2024).
24. Adalogger. Available online: https://www.adafruit.com/product/2795 (accessed on 11 July 2024).
25. 060-EA Locomotives. Available online: https://ro.dbcargo.com/rail-ro-en/db-cargo-romania-fleet/locomotives/5-100-kW-060-EA-type-locomotives (accessed on 11 July 2024).
26. 060-DA Locomotives. Available online: https://ro.dbcargo.com/rail-ro-en/db-cargo-romania-fleet/locomotives/060-DA-Diesel-locomotives (accessed on 11 July 2024).
27. Sulzer 12LDA28C Engine. Available online: https://www.derbysulzers.com/12LDA28C.html (accessed on 11 July 2024).
28. Viscous Damper. Available online: https://www.vibratechtvd.com/torsional-dampers#crankshaft (accessed on 11 July 2024).
29. Andrei, M.; Popa, G.; Ilie, G.; Tudor, E. Stick-Slip Movement in Driving Axles of Railway Vehicles equipped with Damping Devices. *Electroteh. Electron. Autom.* **2023**, *71*, 32–39. [CrossRef]

MDPI AG
Grosspeteranlage 5
4052 Basel
Switzerland
Tel.: +41 61 683 77 34

Technologies Editorial Office
E-mail: technologies@mdpi.com
www.mdpi.com/journal/technologies

www.ingramcontent.com/pod-product-compliance
Lightning Source LLC
Chambersburg PA
CBHW061556220926
51850CB00005B/354
9783725865901